THE ROUTLEDGE COMPANION
TO WORLD HISTORY SINCE 1914

The Routledge Companion to World History since 1914 is an outstanding compendium of facts and figures on world history. Fully up-to-date, reliable and clear, this volume is an indispensable source of information on a thorough range of topics such as:

- a chronology of events of the Arab–Israeli conflict
- anti-Semitism and the Holocaust
- the world's major famines and natural disasters since 1914
- whether key countries of the world have a king, president, prime minister or other governance
- GNP of the world's major states, year by year
- biographies of key figures
- civil rights movements
- the Vietnam War
- the rise of terrorism
- globalization

Thematically presented, the book covers topics relevant to history, politics and international relations, from the First World War to the Iraq War of 2003, from post-colonial Africa to conflicts and movements in south-east Asia. With maps, chronologies and full bibliography, this user-friendly reference work is the essential companion for students of history, politics and international relations, and for all those with an interest in world history.

Chris Cook is the former Head of the Modern Archives Unit at the London School of Economics and editor of the best-selling *Pears Cyclopaedia*.

John Stevenson is Reader in History at Worcester College, Oxford. He is the editor of *English Historical Documents, 1914–1957*.

Routledge Companions to History

Series Advisors: Chris Cook and John Stevenson

Routledge Companions to History offer perfect reference guides to key historical events and eras, providing everything that the student or general reader needs to know. These comprehensive guides include essential apparatus for navigating through specific topics in a clear and straightforward manner – including introductory articles, biographies and chronologies – to provide accessible and indispensable surveys crammed with vital information valuable for beginner and expert alike.

THE ROUTLEDGE COMPANION TO WORLD HISTORY SINCE 1914

Chris Cook and John Stevenson

Routledge
Taylor & Francis Group

LONDON AND NEW YORK

First published 2005 by Routledge
2 Park Square, Milton Park, Abingdon, Oxon OX14 4RN

Simultaneously published in the USA and Canada
by Routledge
270 Madison Ave, New York, NY 10016

Previously published by Longman 1991

Routledge is an imprint of the Taylor & Francis Group

© 2005 Chris Cook and John Stevenson

Typeset in Times by RefineCatch Ltd, Bungay, Suffolk
Printed and bound in Great Britain by
MPG Books, Bodmin, Cornwall

British Library Cataloguing in Publication Data
A catalogue record for this book is available from the British Library

Library of Congress Cataloging-in-Publication Data
Cook, Chris, 1945–
  The Routledge companion to world history since 1914 / Chris Cook and
John Stevenson.
    p. cm. – (Routledge companions to history)
  Prev. ed. published under the title: Longman handbook of world history
since 1914.
  Includes bibliographical references and index.
  ISBN 0–415–34584–7 (hardback : alk. paper) – ISBN 0–415–34585–5
(pbk.: alk. paper)
  1. History, Modern--20th century--Handbooks, manuals, etc. I.
Stevenson, John, 1946– II. Cook, Chris, 1945– Longman handbook of world
history since 1914. III. Title. IV. Series.
  D421.C64 2005
  909.82 – dc22   2005006118

ISBN 0–415–34584–7 (hbk)
ISBN 0–415–34585–5 (pbk)

CONTENTS

CONTENTS

MAPS

PREFACE AND ACKNOWLEDGEMENTS

This new Routledge Companion (the successor to the former *Longman Handbook of World History since 1914*) attempts to provide a convenient reference work for both teachers and students of the modern world from the outbreak of the First World War to the present day. It is a highly condensed work, bringing together chronological, statistical and tabular information which is not to be found elsewhere within a single volume. The Companion covers not only political and diplomatic events, but also the broader fields of social and economic history. It includes biographies of important individuals, a wealth of material on wars and conflicts, a wide-ranging topic bibliography and an extensive glossary.

No book of this type can be entirely comprehensive, nor is it intended as a substitute for textbooks and more specialist reading, but we have attempted to include those key facts and figures which we believe are most useful for understanding courses in the history of the world during the last hundred years. The coverage of the volume is designed to reflect the key themes now studied by modern historians – the two world wars, Nazism and communism, imperialism and decolonization, the rise of America to global hegemony, the emergence of China and the changed world since the fall of the Soviet Union. Its geographical coverage is worldwide, from the Asia-Pacific Rim to the Baltic, and from Latin America to the Middle East. The term *billion* is used to mean a thousand million.

The Companion also covers very recent events, from developments in the American war on terrorism after 11 September 2001 to the historic changes now taking place in the enlarged European Union. As courses in world history continue to change and as new research puts events in global history in a different perspective, both authors would welcome suggestions for additional material to be included in future editions of this Routledge Companion.

Chris Cook, London School of Economics
John Stevenson, Worcester College, Oxford

I
POLITICAL HISTORY

EUROPE

THE FIRST WORLD WAR

1914 June 28	Franz Ferdinand assassinated in Sarajevo.
July 28	Austria–Hungary declares war on Serbia.
Aug. 1	Germany declares war on Russia.
Aug. 2	Germany invades Luxembourg.
	British fleet mobilized.
Aug. 3	Germany declares war on France.
Aug. 4	Germany invades Belgium; Britain and Belgium declare war on Germany.
Aug. 5	Turkey closes Dardanelles.
Aug. 5–12	Germans seize Liège.
Aug. 6	Austria declares war on Russia.
Aug. 7	British troops arrive in France.
Aug. 10	Austrians invade Russian Poland.
Aug. 10–20	Austrian advance on Serbia halted at Battle of the Jadar.
Aug. 12	Britain and France declare war on Austria.
Aug. 14–24	French suffer defeats in Lorraine, the Ardennes and on the Sambre; British retreat from Mons.
Aug. 17–20	Russians invade East Prussia and Galicia.
Aug. 20	Germans occupy Brussels.
Aug. 22	Hindenburg becomes German Commander in East Prussia.
Aug. 26–8	Germans cross the Meuse.
Aug. 26–9	Russians defeated at Tannenberg.
Sept. 5–9	Battle of the Marne.
Sept. 5–11	Austrians defeated in the Battle of Rawa Ruska.
Sept. 8–16	Serbs halt second Austrian invasion.
Sept. 10–14	Russians forced to retreat from East Prussia following Battle of the Masurian Lakes.
Sept. 14	Falkenhayn replaces Moltke as German Commander-in-Chief.
Sept. 14–18	Allied offensive fails at first Battle of the Aisne.
Sept. 27	Russians invade Hungary.
Sept. 28–Nov. 1	Austro-German offensive in east checked, leading to withdrawal from Poland.
Sept.–Oct.	'Race for the Sea': series of outflanking manoeuvres towards the Channel fails.

Oct. 9   Germans take Antwerp.
Oct. 12–Nov. 11   First Battle of Ypres: Germans fail to reach Channel
                 ports; Allied counter-attack fails.
Oct. 16   'Race for the Sea' concluded by Battle of the Yser.
Nov. 1   Hindenburg becomes German Commander-in-Chief on
                 Eastern Front.
Nov. 2   Russians renew advance on East Prussia.
                 Britain declares North Sea a war-zone and begins blockade
                 of Germany.
Nov. 5–Dec. 15   Serbs repel third Austrian invasion.
Nov. 11–Nov. 24   Russians retreat after Battle of Lódź.
Nov. 14   Turkey proclaims Holy War.
Dec. 2   Austrians take Belgrade.

1915 Jan. 8–15   French attack halted by Germans at Battle of Soissons.
Jan. 23   German and Austrian armies launch offensive in Carpathians.
Feb. 7–21   Germans encircle Russian Tenth Army at Battle of Masuria;
                 Austrian attack in Carpathians collapses.
Feb. 11   British air-raid on Ostend and Zeebrugge.
Feb. 18   Germany commences submarine warfare against merchant
                 vessels.
Feb. 19–Mar. 18   British Navy fails to force the Dardanelles Straits.
Mar. 10–13   British advance checked at Battle of Neuve-Chapelle.
Mar. 14–15   Battle of Saint-Eloi.
Mar. 19–20   Germans mount raid on Yarmouth and King's Lynn.
Mar. 31   Zeppelin raids on southern English counties begin.
Apr. 22–May 25   Second Battle of Ypres: Germans employ poison-gas for
                 the first time.
Apr. 25   Allied forces land on Gallipoli Peninsula.
May 2–4   Russian line between Gorlice and Tarnow broken by
                 German–Austrian offensive, forcing Russians to retreat.
May 4   Italy leaves the Triple Alliance.
May 7   *Lusitania* sunk.
May 9–June 18   Second Battle of Artois.
May 15–25   Battle of Festubert.
May 23   Italy enters war on Allied side and declares war on Germany
                 and Austria.
June 1   German air-raid on London.
June 20–July 14   German offensive in the Argonne fails.
July 16–18   Russians defeated in Battle of Krasnotav.
Aug. 4–5   Germans enter Warsaw.
Aug. 6–21   Allied attacks in Dardanelles fail.
Sept. 18   Germany limits submarine attacks in view of American
                 hostility.

Sept. 25–Nov. 6   Allied offensives at Loos and in Champagne.

Sept. 28   British enter Kut el Amara after defeating Turks.

Oct. 5   Allied forces land in Salonika.

Oct. 7   Serbian army collapses in face of joint German–Austrian–Bulgarian offensive, and is evacuated to Corfu.

Dec. 3   Joffre becomes French Commander-in-Chief.

Dec. 7   Turkish forces lay siege to British at Kut el Amara.

Dec. 19   Haig replaces French as British Commander-in-Chief.

Dec. 20   Allied forces evacuated from Anzac and Suvla Bay in Dardanelles (completed 9 Jan. 1916).

1916 Feb. 21–Dec. 18   Battle of Verdun results in 550,000 French and 450,000 German casualties.

Mar. 15   Admiral von Tirpitz resigns.

Apr. 29   British surrender at Kut el Amara.

May 15–June 17   Austrians defeat Italians at Asiago but withdraw to strengthen Eastern front.

May 24   Britain introduces conscription.

May 31–June 1   Battle of Jutland.

June 4–Sept. 20   Massive Russian offensive south of Pripet Marshes results in heavy casualties on both sides.

June 5   Arab revolt against Turkish rule begins.

June 6   HMS *Hampshire* sunk: Lord Kitchener drowns.

June 10   Russians cross Dniester.

June 21   Turks begin offensive against Persia.

July 1–Nov. 18   Allied offensive at Battle of the Somme fails to achieve major breakthrough; results in 420,000 British, 195,000 French and 400,000 German casualties.

Aug. 26   Italy declares war on Germany.

Aug. 27   Romania enters war and commences invasion of Transylvania.

Aug. 29   Hindenburg becomes German Chief of General Staff.

Sept. 10–Nov. 19   Allied forces launch offensive in Salonika.

Sept. 15   British use tanks for first time during Battle of the Somme.

Oct. 24–Dec. 18   French launch successful counter-attacks at Verdun.

Dec. 3   Nivelle succeeds Joffre as French Commander-in-Chief.

Dec. 6   Bucharest captured; Russians and Romanians forced to retreat.

Dec. 7   Lloyd George forms coalition government in Britain.

Dec. 12   Central Powers make peace offer.

Dec. 13   British begin offensive in Mesopotamia.

Dec. 30   Allies reject peace offer made by Central Powers.

1917 Jan. 31   Germans announce resumption of unrestricted submarine warfare.

Feb. 23–Apr. 5   Expecting an Allied offensive, Germans withdraw to Hindenburg Line.

Feb. 25   British recapture Kut el Amara.

Mar. 11   British enter Baghdad.

Mar. 12   Revolution in Russia leads to abdication of Tsar Nicholas II.

Mar. 16–19   Germans take stand along Siegfried Line.

Mar. 26–7   British fail to capture Gaza.

Apr. 4   British launch offensive in Artois.

Apr. 6   USA declares war on Germany.

Apr. 9   French begin offensive in Champagne.

Apr. 9–May 3   Canadians take Vimy Ridge during Battle of Arras.

Apr. 16–May 9 French offensive fails at second Battle of the Aisne.

Apr. 17–19   British attack fails in second Battle of Gaza.

June 7–8   British capture Messines Ridge.

June 15   Pétain becomes French Commander-in-Chief.

June 20   Outbreak of mutinies in French Army.

June 25   US troops land in France.

July 31–Nov. 6 Third Battle of Ypres results in eventual capture of Passchendaele.

Sept. 20   British resume offensive near Ypres.

Oct. 24–Nov. 12 Italians forced to retreat after Battle of Caporetto.

Oct. 31–Nov. 7 Turks forced to withdraw following third Battle of Gaza.

Nov. 2   Germans retreat behind Aisne-Oise and Ailette Canals.

Nov. 4   British forces reach Italian front.

Nov. 6   British take Passchendaele.

Nov. 7   Bolshevik Revolution in Russia.

Nov. 17   Clemenceau becomes French Premier.

Nov. 20–Dec. 3 First mass use of tanks at Battle of Cambrai leads to temporary Allied breach of Hindenburg Line.

Dec. 2   Fighting ceases on Russian front.

Dec. 3   Austro-German campaign in Italy suspended.

Dec. 7   USA declares war on Austria–Hungary.

Dec. 9   Romania signs armistice.

                Allenby enters Jerusalem.

1918 Jan. 8   President Wilson issues his 'Fourteen Points' for ending the conflict.

Feb. 18   Fighting resumes between Russia and Germany.

Mar. 3   Bolsheviks accept German peace terms at Brest-Litovsk.

Mar. 21–Apr. 4 Germans launch offensive on the Somme.

Apr. 9–29   Germans launch offensive on the Lys.

Apr. 14   Foch becomes Supreme Commander of Allied forces in France.

Apr. 22–3   British raid on Zeebrugge.

May 7	Romania concludes Treaty of Bucharest with Central Powers.
May 27–June 6	Germans launch offensive on the Aisne.
June 9–13	Germans launch Noyon-Montidier offensive.
June 15–24	Italians repulse Austrian attack across the Piave.
July 13	Final Turkish offensive in Palestine.
July 15–17	Germans launch final (Champagne-Marne) offensive.
July 18–Aug. 6	Allied forces launch Aisne-Marne offensive, leading to reduction of Marne salient.
Aug. 8–Sept. 3	Amiens salient is reduced.
Sept. 3	German armies commence retreat to Hindenburg Line.
Sept. 14	Allied armies begin offensive against Bulgarians.
Sept. 19	Turkish army defeated in Battle of Megiddo.
Sept. 25	Bulgaria requests armistice.
Sept. 26	Foch launches final offensive, breaching Hindenburg Line on 27 Sept.
Sept. 29	Bulgaria concludes armistice.
Oct. 1	French forces take St Quentin. British forces enter Damascus.
Oct. 3	Prince Max of Baden becomes German Chancellor.
Oct. 9–10	British take Cambrai and Le Cateau.
Oct. 14	USA demands cessation of submarine warfare.
Oct. 17	British reach Ostend.
Oct. 20	Submarine warfare abandoned by Germany.
Oct. 24–Nov. 4	Italians defeat Austrians at Vittorio Veneto.
Oct. 31	Armistice with Turkey comes into force.
Nov. 3	Austria agrees to Allied peace terms. Mutiny in German High Seas fleet.
Nov. 4	Armistice concluded on Italian front. Germans withdraw to Antwerp–Meuse line.
Nov. 9	Revolution in Berlin leads to proclamation of Republic.
Nov. 10	William II flees to Holland; Emperor Charles of Austria abdicates.
Nov. 11	Armistice concluded on Western Front.
Nov. 21	German High Sees fleet surrenders to British.

MANPOWER AND CASUALTIES OF MAJOR COMBATANTS, 1914–18

	Standing armies and trained reserves	*Total mobilized*	*Killed or died of wounds*
Austria–Hungary	3,000,000	7,800,000	1,200,000
British Empire	975,000	8,904,000	908,000
France	4,017,000	8,410,000	1,363,000
Germany	4,500,000	11,000,000	1,774,000
Italy	1,251,000	5,615,000	460,000
Russia	5,971,000	12,000,000	1,700,000
Turkey	210,000	2,850,000	325,000
United States	309,208	3,200,000	50,300

PEACE TREATIES AFTER THE FIRST WORLD WAR

The Treaty of Versailles, 28 June 1919

1. Germany surrendered territory:

   (a) Alsace-Lorraine to France.
   (b) Eupen-Malmédy to Belgium (following plebiscite in 1920).
   (c) Northern Schleswig to Denmark (following plebiscite in 1920).
   (d) Pozania and West Prussia to Poland, Upper Silesia to Poland (following plebiscite in 1921).
   (e) Saar put under League of Nations control for 15 years and mining interests under French control (returned to Germany following 1935 plebiscite).
   (f) Danzig (Gdansk) put under League of Nations control.
   (g) Memel placed under Allied control, then transferred to Lithuania.
   (h) German colonies become mandated territories of the League of Nations: German East Africa (to Britain); German South-West Africa (to South Africa); Cameroons and Togoland (to Britain and France); German Samoa (to New Zealand); German New Guinea (to Australia); Marshall Islands and Pacific Islands north of the Equator (to Japan).

2. Germany lost concessions and trading rights in China, Egypt and Middle East.
3. Demilitarization of the Rhineland and Heligoland.
4. German army limited to 100,000 men, denied U-boats and airforce.
5. Army of occupation on west bank of the Rhine and bridgeheads at Cologne, Coblenz and Mainz from Jan. 1920.
6. Germany accepts 'war guilt' clause.
7. Germany agreed to pay reparations and accepted responsibility for war damage.
8. The Treaty of Brest-Litovsk declared void; Germany required to evacuate Baltic States and other occupied territory.
9. The Covenant of the League of Nations written into the Treaty.

The Treaty of Saint-Germain, 10 Sept. 1919

1. The Austro-Hungarian Empire was effectively dissolved:

   (a) Austria and Hungary to become separate states with total loss of control over other former parts of the Austro-Hungarian Empire.
   (b) New state of Czechoslovakia created.
   (c) New state of Yugoslavia set up.
   (d) Galicia ceded to Poland.
   (e) Transylvania ceded to Romania.
   (f) South Tyrol, Trentino and Istria ceded to Italy.
   (g) Plebiscite to define boundary with Austria in southern Carinthia.

2. Austria forbidden to unite with Germany without League of Nations approval.
3. Austrian army limited to 30,000 men.
4. Reparations required for war damage.
5. Covenant of League of Nations written into the Treaty.

The Treaty of the Trianon, 4 June 1920

1. Hungary accepted break-up of Austro-Hungarian Empire and surrender of territory to Romania, Czechoslovakia, Yugoslavia, Poland, Italy and the new Austrian republic.
2. Hungarian army limited to 35,000 men.
3. Hungary required to pay reparations.
4. Covenant of the League of Nations written into the Treaty.

The Treaty of Sèvres, 10 Aug. 1920 (never ratified by Turkey)

1. Turkish Empire lost territory:

   (a) Cyprus to Britain.
   (b) Rhodes, the Dodecanese, and Adalia ceded to Italy.
   (c) Part of European Turkey to Bulgaria.
   (d) Eastern Thrace to Greece; Greek claims to Chios and other islands recognized; Greece allowed to occupy Smyrna for five years until a plebiscite held.
   (e) Hejaz and Arabia become independent.
   (f) League of Nations mandates over Syria (to France); Palestine, Iraq and Transjordan (to Britain).

2. The Straits placed under international control.
3. Turkey occupied by British, French and Italian troops.
4. The Covenant of the League of Nations was written into the Treaty.

The Treaty of Neuilly, 27 Nov. 1919

1. Bulgaria lost territory:

   (a) Territory along Bulgaria's western boundary ceded to Yugoslavia.
   (b) Part of western Thrace ceded to Greece.

2. Bulgaria gained territory from European Turkey.
3. Bulgarian army limited to 20,000 men.
4. Bulgaria made liable for reparations.
5. The Covenant of the League of Nations written into the Treaty.

The Treaty of Lausanne, 24 July 1923

1. Turkey surrendered its claims to territories of the Ottoman Empire occupied by non-Turks, effectively surrendering the Arab lands.
2. The Turks retained Constantinople and Eastern Thrace in Europe; both sides of Greek–Turkish border demilitarized.
3. Turkey takes Smyrna from Greece but surrenders all the Aegean Islands except Imbros and Tenedos which return to Turkey.
4. Turkey recognizes the annexation of Cyprus by Britain and of the Dodecanese by Italy.
5. Turkey left free of foreign troops.
6. The Straits were declared to be demilitarized (in July 1936 by the Montreux Convention Turkey was allowed to refortify the Straits).
7. No restrictions were placed on Turkey's armed forces and no reparations required.

THE RUSSIAN REVOLUTION AND STALIN'S RUSSIA, 1914–41

1914	Aug. 1	Germany declares war on Russia.
	Aug. 26	Russia defeated at Battle of Tannenberg.
	Sept. 3–12	Russians force Austrians from Galicia.
	Sept. 5	Russia suffers severe losses at battle of the Masurian Lakes.
1915	May	Austro-German offensive in Galicia defeats Russians.
	July	Further Austro-German offensive leads to over a million Russian casualties by the autumn.
	Aug. 1	Duma meets to consider the way the war is being conducted.
	Aug. 22	Six parties in the Duma form the Progressive Bloc and demand a responsible ministry.
	Sep. 6	Tsar assumes supreme command of the armed forces.
	Sept. 8	Reform programme put before council of ministers by Progressive Bloc.
	Sept. 15	Tsar rejects offer of resignation by his ministers to make way for a more popular administration.
	Sept. 16	Tsar prorogues Duma.
1916	Feb. 15	Duma meets; Goremykin replaced as Prime Minister by Sturmer.
	June–Oct.	Brusilov offensive gains territory but fails to achieve decisive victory and costs over a million casualties.
	Sept.–Oct.	Wave of strikes in Russia; sporadic mutinies of soldiers at the front.
	Oct.	Survey of manpower resources reveals that after Feb. 1917 the Russian army would begin to decline in numbers.
1917	Feb. 27	Duma meets.
	Mar. 7	Tsar leaves Petrograd for army GHQ; beginnings of large-scale demonstrations in the capital.
	Mar. 8	Queues at bakeries and crowds continue to demonstrate against the regime.
	Mar. 9	Police fire on crowds.
	Mar. 10	Strikes break out and soldiers join with the people; the Tsar orders suppression of the trouble.
	Mar. 11	Police fire at demonstrators, but more soldiers join the protesters. Tsar prorogues Duma.
	Mar. 12	Formation of Committee of State Duma to replace Tsarist government. Formation of Petrograd Soviet of Workers' and Soldiers' Deputies.
	Mar. 13	Soviet news sheet *Izvestya* calls on people to take affairs into their own hands.
	Mar. 14	Appointment of ministers of the Provisional Government.

	'Army Order No. 1' issued by Petrograd Soviet puts armed forces under its authority and urges rank and file to elect representatives to the Soviet.
Mar. 15	Tsar abdicates in favour of his brother, Grand Duke Michael, at the same time confirming the new ministry and asking the country to support it. Duke Michael chose not to accept the throne unless he was bid to do so by the Assembly. The provisional government forbids the use of force against rioting peasants.
Mar. 16	Constituent Assembly meets; abdication of Grand Duke Michael.
Apr. 11	All-Russian Conference of Soviets overwhelmingly votes to continue war in spite of Bolshevik opposition.
Apr. 16	Lenin arrives back in Petrograd.
May 3–5	Bolshevik-organized demonstrations by garrison in Petrograd against the Ministers Guchkov and Milyukov. Kornilov resigns command of forces in Petrograd and Milyukov and Guchkov resign from the government.
May 18	Kerensky helps to reorganize provisional government.
June 18	Start of renewed offensive on southern front.
June 26	Soldiers at front refuse to obey orders. Kornilov insists on offensive being called off and is appointed Commander-in-Chief.
July 2	Start of northern offensive backed by Kerensky, Minister of War. Germans and Austrians drive Russians back after early successes.
July 12	Provisional government restores capital punishment and courts martial.
July 16–18	Bolsheviks organize demonstrations by sailors and Red Guards but the unrest is put down by loyal troops.
July 18	Fearing arrest, Lenin flees to Finland.
July 20	Lvov and Kadet ministers resign.
July 21	Formation of new government with Kerensky as Prime Minister.
Aug. 3	Kerensky resigns. Party leaders give him a free hand to form new government.
Aug. 25–8	Kerensky holds Moscow State Conference to settle differences with Kornilov, but fails to reach agreement.
Sept. 3	Riga falls to Germans.
Sept. 8	Troops begin to move against Petrograd and Kerensky denounces Kornilov 'plot' against the government. Collapse of movement, followed by arrest of Kornilov and fellow generals.
Sept. 19	Bolshevik majority in Moscow Soviet.

Oct. 6	Trotsky becomes Chairman of Petrograd Soviet.
Oct. 23	Decision by Bolshevik Central Committee to organize an armed rising.
Oct. 25	Formation of Military Revolutionary Committee by Bolsheviks.
Nov. 1	Provisional government tries to remove units from the Petrograd garrison, but Bolsheviks prevent this.
Nov. 2	Parliament refuses to give Kerensky powers to suppress the Bolsheviks.
Nov. 6	Bolsheviks organize headquarters in Peter and Paul fortress and move on strategic points. Lenin takes command.
Nov. 7	Bolsheviks seize power in Petrograd, taking key installations and services. The Winter Palace cut off and ministers of provisional government arrested. Kerensky flees. Lenin announces the transfer of power to the Military Revolutionary Committee and the victory of the socialist revolution.
Nov. 8	Lenin makes the Decree on Peace, an appeal for a just peace without annexations and indemnities, and the Decree on Land, affirming that all land is the property of the people. A Bolshevik government is formed.
Nov. 13	Counter-offensive by Kerensky against Petrograd fails.
Nov. 15	Bolsheviks establish power in Moscow.
Dec. 1	Left-wing social revolutionaries enter government after agreement with Bolsheviks.
Dec. 2	Escape of Kornilov and fellow generals from prison in Bykhov.
Dec. 3	Bolsheviks occupy Supreme Headquarters at Mogilev.
Dec. 17	Russia and Germany agree a ceasefire and start negotiations for a peace treaty in Brest-Litovsk (22nd).
Dec. 20	Establishment of the *Cheka*, the secret political police of post-revolutionary Russia.
1918 Jan. 18	Opening of Constituent Assembly.
Jan. 19	Constituent Assembly dispersed.
Feb. 1–14	Introduction of the Gregorian calendar.
Feb. 9	Central Council of the Ukraine concludes separate peace with Central Powers, having declared its independence.
Feb. 10	Brest-Litovsk negotiations broken off after German ultimatum.
Feb. 18	Germany resumes hostilities in the Ukraine.
Feb. 24	Soviet government decides to accept German peace ultimatum.
Mar. 2	Germans occupy Kiev.

Mar. 3	Russians sign Treaty of Brest-Litovsk, giving up large areas of pre-Revolutionary Russia (see p. 271). (see p. 271) German troops continue to advance into central Russia and the Crimea.
Mar. 12	Soviet government moves from Petrograd to Moscow.
Mar. 13	Trotsky appointed Peoples' Commissar of War.
Apr. 5	Allied ships and troops arrive in Murmansk.
Apr. 13	Kornilov killed fighting with anti-Bolshevik 'Volunteer army'. Bolsheviks mount drive against anarchists and other deviant elements. Germans take Odessa.
Apr. 14	Germans and Finns occupy Helsinki.
Apr. 29	Germans set up puppet Ukrainian government.
May	Georgia, Armenia, and Azerbaijan declare independence.
May 8	Germans occupy Rostov.
May 14	Czech Legion (ex-prisoners recruited into service against the Central Powers) clash with Soviets at Chelyabinsk on their way to Vladivostok.
May 25	Revolt of Czech Legion who seize eastern part of Trans-Siberian Railway.
May 29	Partial conscription introduced for Red Army.
June 23	Allied reinforcements arrive in Murmansk.
July 16	Execution of Imperial family at Ekaterinburg.
Aug. 2	Establishment of anti-Bolshevik Government at Archangel, followed by landing of more Allied troops.
Aug. 6	White forces take Kazan.
Aug. 14	Allied forces land at Baku. British, Japanese and American forces land at Vladivostok.
Sept. 10	Bolsheviks take Kazan.
Sept. 13	Allied forces leave Baku.
Sept. 23	'White' forces set up Directorate as All Russian Provisional Government.
Oct. 9	Directorate fixes capital at Omsk.
Nov. 13	Following armistice between Allies and Germany, the Soviet Government denounces the Brest-Litovsk Treaty.
Nov. 18	Directorate suppressed at Omsk. Kolchak assumes supreme power.
Dec. 14	Collapse of Skoropadsky regime in the Ukraine.
Dec. 17	French land in Odessa.
1919 Jan. 3	Red Army takes Riga and Kharkov.
Feb. 6	Red Army occupies Kiev.
Feb. 15	Denikin assumes supreme command of White forces in south-east Russia.

Mar. 2–7	First Congress of Communist International in Moscow. Creation of Politburo and Communist International.
Mar. 13	Spring offensive by Kolchak.
Mar. 21	Allies decide to withdraw forces from Russia.
Apr. 5	British and Indian troops leave Transcaspia.
Apr. 8	French evacuate Odessa.
Apr. 10	Soviet troops enter Crimea.
May 19	Denikin begins offensive against Bolsheviks.
June 4	Kolchak defeated in centre and south, but Denikin continues advance, capturing Kharkov by end of month.
July 15	Red Army takes Chelyabinsk.
Aug. 23	Denikin takes Odessa.
Aug. 31	Denikin occupies Kiev.
Sept. 19	Allies evacuate Archangel.
Sept. 28	Yudenich reaches suburbs of Petrograd.
Oct. 14–20	Denikin takes Orel, but is forced to retreat; general retreat of White armies.
Nov. 14	Defeat of Yudenich by Red Army and occupation of Omsk.
Dec. 12	Red Army occupies Kharkov.
Dec. 16	Red Army occupies Kiev.
1920 Jan. 4	Abdication of Kolchak as Supreme Ruler.
Jan. 8	Red Army takes Rostov.
Jan. 15	Czechs hand Kolchak over to revolutionaries in control of Irkutsk.
Feb. 7	Execution of Kolchak.
Feb 19	Northern government at Archangel collapses.
Apr. 4	Denikin succeeded by Wrangel.
Apr. 24	Outbreak of Russo-Polish War. Poles invade the Ukraine.
May 6	Polish forces take Kiev.
June 12	Red Army retakes Kiev.
July 11	Russian counter-attack takes Minsk and Vilna (14th).
July 20	Second Congress of Communist International.
Aug. 17	Russian forces almost reach Warsaw, but are beaten back by Polish counter-offensive.
Sept. 21	Start of Russo-Polish peace negotiations.
Oct. 12	Russo-Polish provisional peace treaty.
Oct. 25	Red Army offensive against Wrangel.
Nov. 2	Wrangel forced to retreat to the Crimea.
Nov. 11–14	Defeat and evacuation of Wrangel's forces in the Crimea.
1921 Feb.	Strikes in Petrograd. Red Army invades Georgia.
Mar. 1	Beginnings of revolt of Kronstadt sailors.
Mar. 5	Trotsky delivers ultimatum to sailors.

Mar. 16–17	Bombardment and assault of Kronstadt.
Mar. 18	Kronstadt Rising crushed. Treaty of Riga defines Russo-Polish frontier. 10th Party Congress; Lenin introduces New Economic Policy (NEP), allowing peasants to keep their surplus grain for disposal on the open market.
Apr.	Beginnings of famine in the Volga regions.
Aug.	Famine relief agreements signed with America and the Red Cross.
1922 Mar.–Apr.	11th Party Congress. Stalin becomes General Secretary. Lenin forced to convalesce after operation to remove two bullets, the result of Kaplan's attempted assassination in 1918.
Apr. 16	Treaty of Rapallo with Germany establishes close economic and military co-operation.
May 26	Lenin has stroke.
Oct. 2	Lenin returns to Moscow.
Dec.	Lenin's second stroke.
Dec. 23–6	Lenin dictates the *Letter to the Congress*.
Dec. 30	Formation of Union of Soviet Socialist Republics, federating Russia, the Ukraine, White Russia and Transcaucasia.
1923 Jan. 4	Lenin adds codicil to the *Letter*, warning of Stalin's ambitions.
Mar.	Lenin's third stroke.
Apr.	12th Party Congress.
July	Constitution of USSR published.
1924 Jan. 21	Death of Lenin.
Feb. 1	Great Britain recognizes Soviet Union.
Feb. 3	Rykov elected prime minister.
May 23	13th Party Conference opens. Zinoviev demands Trotsky's recantation of belief in 'Permanent Revolution'.
1925 Jan. 16	Trotsky dismissed as War Commissar.
Jan. 21	Japan recognizes Soviet Union.
April	14th Party Conference adopts 'socialism in one country'.
1926 Oct. 19	Trotsky and Kamenev expelled from Politburo.
1927 May 26	Britain temporarily severs relations with Soviet Union because of continued Bolshevik propaganda.
Nov.	Trotskyists organize political demonstrations and Trotsky expelled from Party.
Dec.	15th Party Conference condemns all deviations from party line and resolves upon the collectivization of agriculture. Stalin emerges as dominant voice.

17

1928	Jan.	Trotsky banished to provinces.
	Spring	Serious grain procurement crisis.
	Sept.	Bukharin publishes opposition articles in *Pravda* in support of peasants.
	Oct. 1	Beginning of First Five Year Plan, aimed at developing heavy industries.
	Nov.	Bukharin and Tomsky exiled to Turkey.
1929	Jan.	Trotsky exiled to Turkey.
	Autumn	Start of forced collectivization and dekulakization.
	Nov. 17	Bukharin and other 'rightists' expelled from Party.
1930	Jan.	Quickening of tempo of collectivization; resistance harshly dealt with by force and deportation.
		Widespread disorder and destruction in rural areas.
	Mar.	Stalin publishes *Dizzy with Success*, calling for slowing down of collectivization.
	Nov.–Dec.	Trial of so-called 'Industrial Party' for alleged conspiracy within the State Planning Commission, Gosplan.
1931	Mar.	Trial of Mensheviks.
	July	Harvest failure as a result of chaos of collectivization.
1932	Apr.	Central Committee resolves reform of literary and artistic organizations.
		Beginnings of famine in Ukraine and other parts of Russia.
	Dec.	Introduction of internal passport.
1933	Nov.	Second Five Year Plan inaugurated. USA recognizes the Soviet government.
1934	Jan.	17th Party Conference.
	July	GPU (former *Cheka*) reorganized as NKVD.
	Sept.	USSR joins League of Nations.
	Dec.	Assassination of leading Bolshevik Kirov by Nikolayev leads Central Executive Committee to issue a directive ordering summary trial and execution of 'terrorists' without appeal.
	Dec. 28–9	Nikolayev and 13 'accomplices' tried in secret and subsequently executed.
1935	Jan.	Zinoviev, Kamenev and 17 others tried in secret for 'moral responsibility' for Kirov's assassination and sentenced to imprisonment. Widespread arrests of 'oppositionists'.
	Feb.	Statute regulating collective farms promulgated. Commission appointed to draw up a new constitution.
	June	Draft constitution presented to Central Committee for approval.

Aug.	'Stakhanovite' programme launched to encourage industrial production.
Sept.	Reintroduction of ranks in Red Army.
Dec.	Central Committee declares that the purge is complete.

1936 Jan.	Renewed purge of party members.
Aug. 19–24	Trial and execution of Zinoviev, Kamenev and other members of the 'Trotskyite-Zinovievite Counter-Revolutionary Bloc' for alleged plotting against the leadership. Tomsky commits suicide following accusations made at their trial.
Sept. 25	Yagoda dismissed as head of NKVD and replaced by Yezhov.
Dec. 5	Eighth Congress of Soviets approves the new constitution.

1937 Jan.	Trial of Radek, Pyatakov and 15 others for alleged conspiracy with Trotsky and foreign powers to overthrow the Soviet system. 4 are imprisoned, the rest shot.
Mar.	Bukharin, Rykov and Yagoda expelled from the Party.
June	Tukhachevsky, Chief of the General Staff, and other senior officers tried in secret for plotting with Germany and executed. Widespread purge of the armed forces begins, removing over 400 senior officers.

1938 Mar. 2–13	Third Five Year Plan inaugurated. Trial of Bukharin, Rykov, Krestinsky, Rakovsky, Yagoda, and other leading party and NKVD members for terrorism, sabotage, treason and espionage.
Mar. 28	Stalin offers support to Czechoslovakia if attacked.
Mar. 29	Russia offers to assist Czechoslovakia if Romania and Poland will allow the passage of Russian troops across their territory; both refuse.
Dec.	Beria succeeds Yezhov as head of NKVD.

1939 Mar.	18th Party Congress.
Apr. 18	USSR proposes defence alliance with Great Britain and France. Offer not taken up by the western allies.
May 3	Molotov replaces Litvinov as commissar of foreign affairs in the USSR.
Aug. 12	Anglo-French mission to USSR begins talks in Moscow.
Aug. 18	Germany makes commercial agreement with USSR.
Aug. 22	Ribbentrop, German Foreign Minister, arrives in Moscow.
Aug. 23	Nazi–Soviet Pact signed. A non-aggression pact, it also contains secret clauses on the partition of Poland and allocation of Finland, Latvia, Estonia and Bessarabia to Soviet sphere of influence.
Aug. 31	Supreme Soviet ratifies German non-aggression pact.

Sept. 17	Red Army invades eastern Poland.
Sept. 22	Red Army occupies Lvov.
Sept. 28	Secret accord with Germany transfers Lithuania to Soviet sphere of influence.
Sept. 29–Oct. 10	Estonia, Latvia, and Lithuania conclude treaties with USSR allowing Soviet military bases in their territory.
Oct. 12	Talks in Moscow between Finland and USSR. Stalin presents his territorial demands.
Nov. 9	Finns reject Soviet demands.
Nov. 29	USSR breaks off diplomatic relations with Finland.
Nov. 30	Russians bomb Helsinki and Red Army crosses Finnish frontier.
Dec.	Finnish forces inflict heavy defeats on Russia in the south and east.

1940	Feb. 1–12	Major Russian offensive on Karelian isthmus.
	Mar. 12	Treaty of Moscow concludes war. Finns cede ten per cent of their territory, including the Karelian isthmus and territory in the north-east.
	June 15–17	Soviet troops occupy Lithuania, Latvia and Estonia.
	June 28	Soviet troops occupy Bessarabia and north-eastern Bukovina.
	July 21	Lithuania, Latvia and Estonia 'request' incorporation into USSR.
	Nov. 17	USSR demands control of Bulgaria and withdrawal of German troops from Finland before joining Tripartite Pact of Germany, Italy and Japan.
	Dec. 18	Hitler issues directive for Operation Barbarossa, the invasion of Russia.

1941	Apr. 13	Non-aggression Pact signed with Japan.
	June 22	Germany invades USSR.
	June 29	State Defence Committee formed.
	July 3	Stalin broadcasts to the people.
	July 12	Anglo-Soviet mutual assistance agreement signed.
	July 15	Fall of Smolensk.
	Aug. 7	Stalin becomes Supreme Commander of the Soviet Armed Forces.
	Sept. 8	Kiev captured.
	Oct. 2	German offensive against Moscow opens.
	Oct. 19	Declaration of state of siege in Moscow. Stalin remains in city, though thousands are evacuated or flee in panic.
	Nov. 27	German forces come within 20 miles of Moscow.
	Dec. 5	Russian counter-offensive in Moscow sector. Hitler abandons Moscow offensive for winter.

GERMANY 1918–39

1918	Jan. 8	President Wilson outlines his 'Fourteen Points'.
	Mar. 3	Treaty of Brest-Litovsk with Russia. Only Independent Socialists in the Reichstag vote against it.
	Mar. 21	Ludendorff begins 'St Michael' offensive on the Western Front.
	Mar. 26	After initial success, the first German offensive comes to a halt within 75 miles of Paris.
	Apr. 9	Renewed German offensive in Flanders.
	May 27	Germans reach the Marne.
	July 18	Allied counter-attack begins.
	Aug. 8	'The Black Day of the German Army' (Ludendorff) as German forces break under fresh allied offensive.
	Sept. 11	Allies break through the Hindenburg line.
	Sept. 28	Ludendorff concedes that military victory is impossible.
	Sept. 30	Chancellor von Herling resigns in the face of proposals to transform Germany into a democracy.
	Oct. 1	Ludendorff asks parliament to make peace.
	Oct. 3	Prince Max of Baden appointed Chancellor and asks the USA for an armistice on the basis of the 'Fourteen Points'.
	Oct. 12	Germany and Austria–Hungary agree to Wilson's terms that they withdraw from occupied territory, but hesitate over demands for a democratic, civilian government.
	Oct. 20	Germany suspends submarine warfare.
	Oct. 21	German sailors at Wilhelmshaven mutiny.
	Oct. 23	Wilson refuses to make peace with an autocratic regime in Germany.
	Oct. 26	Ludendorff is forced to resign. The Reichstag makes the Chancellor dependent on parliament and military appointments are to be countersigned by the Minister of War.
	Oct. 29	Kaiser leaves Berlin for army headquarters at Spa.
	Nov. 2	Scheidemann, one of the majority Socialist leaders, writes to Prince Max requesting the Kaiser's abdication.
	Nov. 3	German Grand Fleet mutinies at Kiel. Sailors set up their own workers' and sailors' councils, mainly for redress of grievances.
	Nov. 7	Bavaria is proclaimed a republic and a socialist government is set up in Munich. In Berlin, the majority Socialist Party executive threatens to withdraw support from the government unless the Kaiser abdicates.
	Nov. 9	General Strike in Berlin. The Kaiser flees to Holland. Prince Max resigns and hands office to Ebert. Scheidemann proclaims a Republic from the Reichstag building and Ebert

forms a socialist-dominated government. Ebert makes pact with Groener, with the army assuring its support in return for suppression of Bolshevism.

Nov. 11 German representatives sign armistice with Allies at Compiègne.

Nov. 22 Agreement reached for transitional government until a National Constituent Assembly meets.

Dec. 20 Workers' and soldiers' delegates in Berlin demand nationalization of major industries.

Dec. 30 German Communist Party (KPD) founded by Spartacists and other groups. They decide to boycott the elections for the National Constituent Assembly and stage a rising in Berlin.

1919 Jan. 5–11 Spartacist revolt in Berlin put down by Ebert-Noske government using 'Free Corps' (*Freikorps*) of ex-soldiers.

Jan. 15 Rosa Luxemburg and Karl Liebknecht, leaders of the Spartacists, are arrested and murdered by Free Corps.

Jan. 19 National Constituent Assembly elected on basis of proportional representation but fails to give any party an outright majority.

Feb. 8 National Constituent Assembly meets at Weimar.

Feb. 11 Ebert becomes President of Weimar Republic, following the formation of coalition of majority socialists and the centre and democratic parties under Scheidemann.

Feb. 13 Scheidemann forms a Cabinet.

Feb. 21 Assassination of the Premier of the Bavarian Republic, Kurt Eisner, by right-wingers.

Apr. Bavarian Republic overthrown by Federal German forces.

June 29 Treaty of Versailles signed (see p. 9).

1920 Mar. 13–17 Kapp Putsch. *Freikorps* officers attempt to make Wolfgang Kapp Chancellor of the Reich in pro-monarchist *coup d'état* in Berlin. Although troops refuse to fire on the *Freikorps* and the Government is forced to flee Berlin, a general strike frustrates the putsch.

Apr. Hitler's German Workers' Party changes its name to the National Socialist German Workers' Party (Nazis).

1921 Aug. 29 Assassination of Matthias Erzberger, leader of Centre Party, by right-wing officers.

1922 Apr. 16 Treaty of Rapallo provides for economic and military co-operation between Germany and Russia.

June 24 Assassination of Walter Rathenau, Foreign Secretary, by right-wing nationalists.

1923	Jan. 11	Non-payment of reparations leads to French and Belgian troops occupying the Ruhr. Germany adopts passive resistance to the occupation.
	Aug. 12	Stresemann becomes Chancellor.
	Sept.–Nov.	Massive inflation in Germany. Interest rates raised to 90% (15 Sept.) but by October German mark trading at rate of 10,000 million to the £.
	Sept. 26	Passive resistance in Ruhr ends. A state of military emergency is declared.
	Oct. 22	Bavarian troops take an oath of allegiance to right-wing regime in Bavaria. Communist revolt in Hamburg put down and left-wing governments deposed in Saxony and Thuringia.
	Nov. 8–9	Unsuccessful 'Beer Hall' putsch in Munich led by Hitler and Ludendorff. Hitler captured.
	Nov. 20	German currency stabilized by establishment of the *Rentenmark*, valued at one billion old marks.
	Nov. 23	Stresemann becomes foreign minister.
1924	Apr. 1	Hitler sentenced to five years' imprisonment for part in Munich putsch (but released in Dec.)
	Apr. 9	Dawes Plan provides a modified settlement of the reparations issue.
	May 4	In Reichstag elections, Nationalists and Communists gain many seats from the moderate parties.
	Dec. 7	In further elections, Nationalists and Communists lose seats to Socialists.
	Dec. 15	Beginning of Cabinet crisis in Germany.
1925	Jan. 15	Hans Luther, an Independent, succeeds Wilhelm Marx of the Centre as Chancellor, with Stresemann as Foreign Minister.
	Feb. 28	Death of President Ebert.
	Apr. 26	Hindenburg elected President.
	July 7	French troops begin to leave Rhineland.
	Oct. 16	Locarno Pact guarantees Franco-German and Belgian–German frontiers and the demilitarization of the Rhineland.
1926	May 17	Marx takes over from Luther as Chancellor.
	Sept. 8	Germany admitted to the League of Nations.
1927	May 13	'Black Friday' with collapse of economic system.
	Sept. 16	Hindenburg, while dedicating the Tannenburg memorial, repudiates Article 231 of the Versailles Treaty, the 'War Guilt' clause.

1928	May 20	Social Democrats win victory at elections, mainly at the expense of the Nationalists.
	June 28	Hermann Müller, a socialist, is appointed Chancellor, following resignation of Marx's ministry on the 13th.
1929	Feb. 6	Germany accepts Kellogg–Briand Pact, outlawing war and providing for the pacific settlements of disputes.
	June 7	Publication of Young Plan for rescheduling German reparation payments in the form of annuities over 59 years, amounting to a quarter of the sum demanded in 1921.
	July 9	Nationalists and Nazis form a National Committee to fight the Young Plan with Hugenberg as chairman and Hitler a leading member.
	Oct. 3	Death of Stresemann.
	Oct. 29	Wall Street crash and cessation of American loans to Europe.
	Dec. 29	National referendum accepts Young Plan, frustrating Nationalist hopes.
1930	Mar.	Young Plan approved by Reichstag and signed by Hindenburg.
	Mar. 17	Müller's socialist cabinet resigns in Germany.
	Mar. 30	Heinrich Bruning, of the Centre, forms a minority coalition of the Right.
	May 17	Young Plan reparations come into force.
	June 30	Last Allied troops leave Rhineland.
	July 16	Hindenburg authorizes German budget by decree, when Reichstag fails to pass it.
	Sept. 14	In Reichstag elections, Hitler and the Nazi Party emerge as a major party with 107 seats, second only to the Socialists with 143 seats.
	Oct.	Rohm becomes leader of SA or 'Brownshirts'.
1931	July	Worsening economic crisis in Germany. Unemployment reaches over 4.25 million. Bankruptcy of German Danatbank (13th) leads to closure of all banks until 5 Aug.
	Oct. 11	Hitler forms an alliance at Hartzburg with the Nationalists led by Hugenberg – the Hartzburg Front.
1932	Jan. 7	Bruning declares that Germany cannot and will not resume reparations payments.
	Mar. 13	In presidential elections Hindenburg receives 18 million votes against Hitler's 11 million, and a communist's 5 million. With failure to achieve an overall majority, a new election is called for 10 Apr.
	Apr. 10	Hindenburg re-elected President with an absolute majority of 19 million against Hitler's 13 million and communist 3 million.

Apr. 14	Bruning unsuccessfully attempts to disband the SA and SS (see pp. 484, 487).
Apr. 24	Nazis achieve successes in local elections.
May 30	When Hindenburg withdraws support for disbanding the SA and SS, Bruning resigns.
June 1	Franz von Papen forms a ministry, with von Schleicher as Minister of Defence and von Neurath as Foreign Minister.
June 16	Ban on SA and SS, in operation since Apr., is lifted.
July 31	In Reichstag elections Nazis win 230 seats and become largest party, producing a stalemate since neither they nor the Socialists (133 seats) will enter a coalition.
Aug. 13	Hindenburg asks Hitler to serve as Vice-Chancellor under Von Papen, but he refuses.
Sept. 12	Von Papen dissolves the Reichstag.
Sept. 14	Germany leaves League of Nations disarmament conference.
Nov. 6	New elections fail to resolve the stalemate, with the Communists only gaining a few seats from the Nazis.
Nov. 17	Von Papen forced to resign by Schleicher; Hitler rejects Chancellorship.
Dec. 2–4	Schleicher becomes Chancellor and forms a ministry, attempting to conciliate the centre and left.
1933 Jan. 28	Schleicher's ministry is unable to secure a majority in the Reichstag and resigns.
Jan. 30	Hindenburg accepts a Cabinet with Hitler as Chancellor, von Papen as Vice-Chancellor and Nationalists in other posts.
Feb. 27	Reichstag fire blamed on Communists and made pretext for suspension of civil liberties and freedom of press.
Mar. 5	The Nazis make gains in elections, winning 288 seats, but fail to secure overall majority.
Mar. 13	Goebbels becomes minister of propaganda and 'enlightenment'. Pope Pius XI praises Hitler's anti-communism.
Mar. 17	Schacht becomes President of the Reichsbank.
Mar. 23	Hitler obtains Enabling Law with the support of the Centre Party, granting him dictatorial powers for four years.
Mar. 30	German bishops withdraw opposition to Nazis.
Apr. 1	National boycott of all Jewish businesses and professions.
Apr. 7	Civil Service law permits removal of Jews and other opponents.
July 5	Centre Party disbands.
July 8	Concordat signed between Nazi Germany and Holy See.
July 14	The Nazi Party is formally declared the only political party in Germany: all others are suppressed.

July 20	Concordat ratified.
Sept.	Ludwig Müller, leader of minority 'German Christians', becomes 'Bishop of the Reich'.
1934 Mar. 21	'Battle for Work' begins.
May	German Protestants at Barmen synod express disapproval of close complicity of Müller and 'German Christians' with Nazis.
June 14	Hitler visits Mussolini in Italy.
June 20	Hindenburg demands dissolution of SA.
June 30	'Night of the Long Knives'. Nazis liquidate thousands of opponents within and outside the Party. Over 170 leading Nazis lose their lives including Röhm, leader of the SA, and Strasser, leader of Berlin Nazis. General von Schleicher also a victim.
Aug. 2	Death of President Hindenburg. Hitler assumes Presidency, but retains title *Der Führer*. Army swears oath of allegience. Schacht becomes Minister of Economics.
Oct. 24	German Labour Front founded, a Nazi organization to replace trade unions.
1935 Jan. 13	Saar plebiscite favours rejoining Germany.
Mar. 16	Germany repudiates disarmament clauses in Treaty of Versailles, restores conscription and announces expansion of the peacetime army to over half a million men.
June 18	By the Anglo-German Naval Agreement Germany agrees that its naval tonnage shall not exceed a third of that of the Royal Navy.
Sept. 15	Nuremberg laws prohibit marriage and sexual intercourse between Jews and German nationals.
1936 Mar. 7	German troops reoccupy the demilitarized Rhineland in violation of the Treaty of Versailles.
Aug.	Olympic Games in Berlin turned into an advertisement for Nazi Germany.
Aug. 24	Germany adopts 2-year compulsory military service.
Oct. 19	Hitler announces four-year plan under Goering as economic overlord.
Nov. 1	Rome–Berlin Axis proclaimed.
Nov. 18	Germany and Italy recognize the Franco government.
1937 Dec.	Schacht resigns as Minister of Economics. Leading members of the Protestant opposition arrested, including Pastor Niemoller.
1938 Feb. 4	Hitler appoints Joachim von Ribbentrop Foreign Minister. Fritsch is relieved of his duties as Commander-in-Chief of

26

		the army. Hitler takes over personal control of the armed forces. The War Ministry is abolished and the OKW (High Command of the Armed Forces) is set up.
	Mar. 11	The *Anschluss*: German troops enter Austria, which is declared part of the Reich (13th).
	Apr. 23	Germans in the Sudetenland (Czechoslovakia) demand autonomy.
	Aug. 18	Beck resigns as Chief of the Army General Staff.
	Aug. 21	Germany mobilizes over Czech crisis.
	Sept. 30	Munich agreement gives Sudetenland to Germany.
	Nov. 9–10	Anti-Jewish pogrom, the *Kristallnacht*.
1939	Jan. 21	Schacht dismissed from presidency of Reichsbank.
	Mar. 15	German troops occupy remaining part of Czechoslovakia.
	Aug. 23	Nazi–Soviet Pact signed.
	Sept. 1	Germany invades Poland.
	Sept. 3	Britain and France declare war on Germany.

FRANCE, 1918–44

1918 Jan. 14	Cailloux, former Premier, arrested for treason.
Mar. 21	German offensive brings them within 75 miles of Paris. Paris bombarded by long-range guns.
Mar. 26	Foch assumes united command of armies on Western Front.
Apr. 27	Renewed German offensive captures Rheims.
July 15–Aug. 4	Second battle of the Marne halts German offensive.
July 22	Allies cross the Marne.
Sept. 4	Germans retreat to Siegfried Line.
Oct. 30	Allies sign armistice with Turkey.
Nov. 1	Anglo-French forces occupy Constantinople.
Nov. 3	Allies sign armistice with Austria-Hungary.
Nov. 11	Allies sign armistice with Germany at Compiègne.
1919 June 28	Versailles Treaty signed.
Nov.	Victory of right-wing 'Bloc National' in elections to the Assembly.
1920 Jan. 17	Deschanel elected President of France. Resignation of Clemenceau; Millerand forms ministry.
May. 16	Joan of Arc canonized.
Sept. 7	Franco-Belgian military convention.
Dec. 23	Millerand becomes French President.
Dec. 29	French socialists at Tours agree to join Moscow International; formation of French Communist Party.
1921 Jan. 16	Briand becomes Prime Minister.
Jan. 24–29	Paris conference agrees reparations for France.
Feb. 19	Franco-Polish alliance.
1922 Jan. 15	Poincaré becomes Prime Minister and Foreign Minister.
Dec. 9–11	International conference in London considers Germany's request for a reparations moratorium.
1923 Jan. 11	Franco-Belgian occupation of the Ruhr in retaliation for non-payment of reparations; passive resistance by German workers.
1924 Apr. 16	Germany accepts Dawes Plan on reparations and agreement reached that France should withdraw from the Ruhr.
May	*Cartel des Gauches* wins victory at the elections.
June 10	Millerand resigns as President. Doumergue elected President (13th); Herriot becomes Prime Minister (15th).
1925 Apr. 10	Painlevé becomes French Prime Minister.
July 20	French begin evacuation of Ruhr.

Dec. 1	Locarno Treaties guaranteeing Franco-German and Belgian–German frontiers signed.
1926 Jan. 31	First part of the Rhineland evacuated.
May 26	Rebel Abd-el-Krim in Morocco submits to France.
July 15	Briand resigns over financial crisis; Poincaré becomes premier of French National Union ministry. Measures taken to stabilize the franc.
1927 Nov. 11	Treaty of friendship between France and Yugoslavia.
1928 Apr. 22–9	Left-wing parties win victory at elections.
June 24	Devaluation of the franc. Decision to build Maginot Line; military service reduced to one year.
Aug. 27	France and 64 other states sign the Kellogg–Briand Pact, outlawing war and providing for peaceful settlement of international disputes.
1929 July 27	Poincaré resigns as Prime Minister and is succeeded by Briand.
Sept. 5	Briand proposes a European federal union.
1930 May 17	Young Plan for reduced German reparations comes into force. Briand produces memorandum on united states of Europe.
June 30	Last section of Rhineland evacuated.
1931 Jan. 27	Laval becomes French Premier.
May 13	Doumer elected French President.
June 20	Hoover Plan for moratorium of one year for reparations and war debts in view of world economic crisis.
1932 Feb. 21	Tardieu ministry formed.
May 1	*Cartel des Gauches* successful in elections.
May 6	President Doumer assassinated; succeeded by Lebrun (10th).
June 4	Herriot ministry formed.
Dec. 18	Paul–Boncour ministry formed.
1933 Jan. 31	Daladier ministry formed (until Oct. 1933).
Dec.	Flight of Stavisky brings about scandal of financial corruption amongst politicians.
1934 Jan. 30	Daladier second ministry formed, after brief ministries by Sarraut and Chautemps.
Feb. 6–7	Rioting in Paris. Police kill 14 right-wing demonstrators.
Feb. 7	Daladier resigns and Doumergue forms National Union ministry of centre and moderate parties (8th).
Feb. 12	French CGT calls General Strike. Demonstrations in defence of the Republic.

Mar. 16	The French complete suppression of rebel Berber tribes in Morocco.
Oct. 9	Barthou, Foreign Minister, and King Alexander of Yugoslavia assassinated at Marseilles.
1935 Mar. 7	Saar basin restored to Germany following plebiscite (13 Jan.).
Apr. 11–14	Stresa Conference of Britain, France and Italy to discuss alliance.
May 2	Franco-Russian treaty of mutual assistance.
July 14	Mass demonstrations throughout France demanding democracy and the dissolution of right-wing Leagues.
July 27	French government granted emergency financial powers.
Nov. 3	Socialist groups merge as Socialist and Republican Union under Léon Blum; later forming with Radical Socialists and Communists a Popular Front.
1936 Jan.	Popular Front agrees common programme.
May 3	Popular Front wins major success in elections with 387 seats to 231 for other parties.
June 4	Blum forms Popular Front government.
June 17	Decrees 40-hour week, collective labour agreements, and paid holidays.
Sept.	Widespread strikes in French industry.
Oct. 2	Franc devalued.
Nov. 18	In spite of protests from the Left, Blum proposes non-intervention in the Spanish Civil War.
1937 Jan.	Blum slows down social reform programme.
Feb. 27	French Chamber passes defence plan; Schneider-Creusot factory nationalized and Maginot Line extended.
June 21	Chamber rejects Blum's programme of financial reforms. Blum resigns, replaced by the radical Chautemps.
1938 Mar. 13	Blum forms second Popular Front government, but Senate rejects financial reforms.
Apr. 10	Blum resigns, replaced by Daladier.
Sept. 29	France signs Munich agreement.
Nov. 9	France recognizes Italian conquest of Abyssinia.
1939 Feb. 27	France recognizes Franco's government in Spain; Pétain sent as first ambassador.
Mar. 17	Daladier granted powers to speed rearmament.
Mar. 31	France and Britain guarantee support for Poland.
Apr. 13	France and Britain guarantee independence of Romania and Greece.
Aug. 26–31	Negotiations by Daladier and Chamberlain with Hitler fail.

Sept. 3	Britain and France declare war on Germany.
Sept. 4	Franco-Polish agreement.
Sept. 26	Daladier dissolves French Communist Party.
Sept. 30	British Expeditionary Force sent to France.
Nov. 3	Roosevelt allows France to purchase US arms on 'cash and carry' basis, amending Neutrality Act of May 1937.
1940 Mar. 21	Reynaud succeeds Daladier as Premier.
May 10	German attack on Holland, Belgium and Luxembourg.
May 12	German panzer forces cross into France.
May 14	German forces cross the Meuse.
May 19	General Weygand takes command of the French army from General Gamelin.
May 20	German forces reach Channel, cutting off Allied armies in the north.
May 29	British begin evacuation from Dunkirk.
June 10	Italy declares war on France.
June 14	Germans enter Paris.
June 16	Reynaud resigns, replaced by Pétain.
June 18	De Gaulle, from London, calls for continued resistance.
June 22	French sign armistice with Germany at Compiègne.
June 23	British government supports London-based French National Committee, 'Free French', headed by De Gaulle and breaks off relations with Pétain government.
June 24	Armistice signed with Italy.
July 1	French government moves to Vichy.
July 3	British attack on French fleet at Mers-el-Kebir.
July 5	Vichy regime breaks off relations with Britain.
July 10	National Assembly votes full powers to Pétain as 'Head of the French State', ending Third Republic.
Oct. 22–4	Laval, followed by Pétain, holds discussions with Hitler at Montoire.
Dec. 13	Laval dismissed. Replaced by Darlan.
1941 Apr. 18	Vichy government withdraws from League of Nations.
May	Darlan offers French air bases in Syria to the Germans.
June 6	Allied invasion of Syria.
June 30	Vichy government breaks off relations with Russia.
1942 Apr. 18	Laval returns to head government.
Nov. 11	German troops occupy Vichy France.
Nov. 27	French fleet scuttled at Toulon.
1944 June 6	Allied landings in Normandy.
Aug. 25	Paris is liberated.
Oct. 23	De Gaulle's provisional government recognized by Allies.

SPAIN: THE CIVIL WAR AND ITS BACKGROUND, 1923–39

1923 Dec. 14	Primo de Rivera assumes Spanish dictatorship, supported by military and middle classes and with acquiescence of King, Alfonso XIII.
1930 Dec. 28	The King accepts the resignation of Primo de Rivera, following Spain's deteriorating economic condition and failure to achieve progress towards constitutional government.
1931 Apr. 14	King Alfonso XIII abdicates. Spain becomes a constitutional republic.
May 10	Left-wing Republican, Azaña, becomes Premier.
Oct. 20	'Protection of the Republic' Law passed in Spain.
Dec. 9	Spanish Republican Constitution introduced; Zamora elected President.
1933 Jan. 2–12	Rising of anarchists and syndicalists in Barcelona.
Nov. 19	Spanish right wins elections to the Cortes.
	Foundation of *Falango Española* by José Antonio Primo de Rivera (son of the dictator).
1934 Jan. 14	Catalan elections won by the Left.
Oct. 4	Right forms a Ministry; followed by socialist rising in Asturias and Catalan separatist revolt in Barcelona. Moroccan troops used to suppress risings with great ferocity.
1936 Feb. 16	Popular Front wins elections; Azaña elected President and re-establishes 1931 constitution. Amnesty granted to rebels of 1934; growing clashes between Left and Right with assassinations and attacks on church property.
Apr. 20	Cortes dismiss President Zamora.
May 10	Azaña elected Spanish President, although large numbers of voters boycott the elections.
July 17–18	Outbreak of Spanish Civil War with rising of the army in Morocco under General Franco; revolt spreads to mainland led by General Mola.
July 19	Rebels reject offer of a ceasefire and the formation of an all-party national government. Republican Giral government formed and orders arming of revolutionary organizations.
July 20–31	Republican forces seize the Montana barracks in Madrid and secure Catalonia, the Basque country and much of the south. The rebels, or Nationalists, overrun Morocco, parts of southern Spain and much of the north.
July 26	Léon Blum declares that France cannot intervene on behalf

of the Republic. Communist Comintern decides to raise international force of volunteers – the International Brigades – for service in Spain.

Hitler offers aircraft and supplies to the Nationalists, as does Mussolini.

Aug. 6	France and Britain submit draft 'non-intervention' agreement to the European powers.
Aug. 19	Britain imposes embargo on arms to Spain.
Aug. 21	Italy accepts non-intervention, but makes exceptions for 'volunteers' and financial support.
Aug. 23	Germany accepts non-intervention, as does the Soviet Union, although both continue to supply advisers and other support.
Sept. 4	Formation of Largo Caballero government in Madrid, composed of republicans, socialists and communists.
Sept. 27	Nationalists capture Toledo.
Oct. 1	Nationalists appoint Franco Generalissimo and head of state.
Oct. 22	Most of Spanish gold reserves shipped to the Soviet Union. Russian advisers supervise reorganization of Republican army and appoint political commissars.
Nov.	Nationalist forces advance on Madrid. Air-raids on Madrid and Republican forces by German Condor Legion. First International Brigades go into action and assist in repelling nationalist advance. Republican government moves to Valencia.
Nov. 18	Germany and Italy recognize Franco government.
Dec. 16	Protocol signed in London by major powers agreeing non-intervention in Spain.
1937 Feb. 8	Malaga falls to Nationalists.
Mar. 3–12	Republican government orders disarming of workers' and anarchist militias in Catalonia following clashes between them and the communists.
Mar. 20–3	Battle of Guadalajara. Republicans defeat Italian forces advancing on Madrid.
Apr. 19	Franco orders unification of the Nationalist movement, fusing the Falange and other political bodies into a single political body, and para-military groups into a militia responsible to the army.
Apr. 26	German Condor Legion destroys village of Guernica in Basque country.
Apr. 30–May 6	Street fighting in Barcelona between workers' militias and republican-communists.

May 15	Largo Caballero resigns in opposition to communist call for greater control and suppression of rival groups.
May 17	Negrin government formed with backing of Comintern to pursue victory by means of communist control of the republican forces.
June 18	Anarchist militia (POUM) dissolved and leaders arrested; anti-Stalinist leader, Nin, executed.
June 19	Nationalists capture Basque capital of Bilbao.
July 5–28	Failure of Republican offensive at Brunete to restore position in north.
Sept. 10–14	Following attacks on shipping by Italian submarines and aircraft, Nyon Conference of 9 European powers agrees to patrol the Mediterranean and sink submarines attacking non-Spanish ships. Italy and Germany do not attend, but sinkings cease.
Oct. 17	Largo Caballero denounces repressive policies of Negrin government.
Oct. 20–2	Franco's forces complete reduction of north-west with capture of Gijon and Oviedo.
Oct. 31	Republican government moves to Barcelona.
Dec. 15–26	Republican forces go over to the offensive at Teruel to avert threat to Madrid.
1938 Feb. 5–22	Nationalists launch counter-offensive at Teruel; recaptured (23rd). Nationalist offensive in Aragon.
Mar.	Nationalists begin advance from Aragon to the Mediterranean with aim of cutting Republican territory in half, and achieve rapid early success.
Apr. 15	Nationalist forces reach Mediterranean at Vinaroz, cutting off Catalonia from the rest of Republican Spain.
Apr.–May	Opening of French frontier permits some resupply of Republican forces. 200,000 new conscripts called up and organized on flanks of the Nationalist corridor.
July–Aug.	Last Republican offensive on the Ebro forces Franco to suspend attack on Valencia.
Aug.	Basque and Catalan separatist ministers resign from Negrin ministry.
Nov. 15	Last Republican forces driven out of Ebro bridgehead.
Dec.	Nationalists begin offensive against Catalonia.
1939 Jan. 26	Fall of Barcelona to Nationalist forces.
Feb. 7	President Azaña goes into exile in France (resigns on 24th).
Feb. 9	End of resistance in Catalonia by Republican forces; over 200,000 cross French frontier and are disarmed. Negrin

	makes last attempt to obtain a negotiated peace without reprisals.
Feb. 26	Negrin tries to organize last stand of Republic at Cartagena naval base.
Mar. 4	Negrin appoints communist military leaders to key defence positions.
Mar. 5–12	Military commander in Madrid, Casado, leads rebellion against Negrin government on account of its communist domination and sets up a National Defence Council. On Comintern instructions, communists attempt to defeat the rebellion, but are themselves defeated by non-communist elements. Negrin flees to France.
Mar. 23	Casado sends emissaries to Nationalist capital in Burgos to negotiate peace terms. Franco demands surrender of Republican Air Force by 25 Mar. and rest of armed forces by 27 Mar.
Mar. 25	Franco breaks off negotiations because his terms are not met.
Mar. 27	Last meeting of National Defence Council.
Mar. 28	Nationalist forces enter Madrid.
Apr. 1	General Franco announces end to the Civil War.

ITALY, 1919–45

1919 Mar. 23	Foundation of the first *Fascio di Combattimento* by Mussolini in Milan.
Aug. 25	Italian forces evacuate Fiume.
Sept. 2	Universal suffrage and proportional representation introduced.
Sept. 12	D'Annunzio, Italian nationalist and irredentist, seizes Fiume.
Nov. 11	The Pope lifts the prohibition against Catholics participating in political life.
Nov. 16	Socialists and Catholics receive strong support in the elections; fascists gain only a fraction of the vote.
1920 June 9	Giolitti takes over as Prime Minister from Nitti.
Aug. 31–Sept.	Widespread strikes and lockouts in engineering, metal and steel industries.
Nov. 12	Treaty of Rapallo settles disputes between Italy and Yugoslavia. Fiume to be an independent state.
Nov. 21	Fascists fire on crowd in Bologna during Mayor's inauguration.
Dec. 1	D'Annunzio declares war on Italy.
Dec. 24–5	Clashes between Italian troops and Fiuman troops. *Andrea Doria* shells the royal palace.
Dec. 31	D'Annunzio makes peace with Italy.
1921 Jan. 5	D'Annunzio leaves Fiume.
Feb. 27	Communists and Fascists clash in Florence.
May 15	Liberals and Democrats successful at the elections.
June 26	Giolitti cabinet falls, replaced by Bonomi.
1922 Feb. 9	Bonomi government resigns.
Feb. 25	Facta heads new government.
May	Fascist takeover in Bologna.
Aug. 3–4	Fascist takeover in Milan.
Oct. 24	Mussolini calls on Facta to resign and for the formation of a fascist cabinet. Facta refuses.
Oct. 28	Fascist 'March on Rome'.
Oct. 30	Mussolini arrives in Rome and organizes victory march.
Oct. 31	Mussolini forms cabinet.
Nov. 25	Mussolini is granted temporary dictatorial powers to institute reforms.
1923 Jan. 14	King Victor Emmanuel authorizes voluntary fascist militia.
July 21	Electoral law passed, guaranteeing two-thirds of the seats in the Chamber to the majority party.
1924 Jan. 27	Treaty with Yugoslavia recognizes Fiume as Italian, but cedes surrounding area to Yugoslavia.

Apr. 6	Fascists obtain almost two-thirds of votes in election amidst widespread use of violence and intimidation.
May 30	Matteotti launches attack on the Fascist government.
June 10	Matteotti is abducted and murdered. Non-fascists resign from Chambers and condemn violence.
July	Press censorship introduced.

1925 Oct. 2	Palazzo Vidoni pact between industrialists' association (Confindustria) and the fascist syndicates.
Dec. 24	Mussolini's dictatorial powers increased. Press censorship tightened, secret non-fascist organizations banned, and widespread arrests.

1926 Jan. 31	Government decrees given the power of law.
Apr. 3	Right to strike abolished: collective contracts reserved to the fascist syndicate.
Apr. 7	Mussolini wounded in assassination attempt.
Nov. 25	Law for defence of the state; creation of a special tribunal for political crimes; death penalty introduced for plotting against royal family or head of state.

1927 Dec. 21	Exchange rate fixed at 'quota 90' (92.45 lira to £1).

1929 Feb. 11	Lateran Treaties with Papacy creating the Vatican City as a sovereign independent state (see p. 472).

1933 Jan. 23	Creation of IRI, organization for Italian industry on corporatist lines.

1934 Jan. 17	Mussolini signs the Rome Protocols with Austria and Hungary.
June 14	Meeting of Hitler and Mussolini at Venice.
July	Mussolini sends troops to the Austrian frontier following Hitler's attempted coup.
Nov. 10	Council of Corporations inaugurated at Rome.

1935 Oct. 3	Italy begins invasion of Ethiopia (Abyssinia).

1936 May 5	Italian forces occupy Addis Ababa.
Oct. 24	Rome–Berlin Axis formed.

1938 July 14	Publication of *Manifesto della Razza* – first anti-Semitic measures.

1939 Jan. 19	Creation of the *Camera del Fascie delle Corporazioni*, replacing parliament.
Apr. 7	Italy invades Albania.
May 22	Pact of Steel signed between Hitler and Mussolini.

1940	June 10	Mussolini declares war and invades France. First air attacks on Malta.
	Aug. 3	Italy invades British Somaliland.
	Sept. 13	Italian forces invade Egypt.
	Oct. 28	Italy invades Greece.
	Nov. 11–12	Destruction of large part of Italian fleet at Taranto by British aircraft.
	Dec. 9	British offensive in North Africa routs the army of Graziani.
1941	Mar. 24	Italians defeated in British Somaliland.
	Mar. 27–8	Italian fleet defeated at Cape Matapan.
	Apr. 6	British enter Addis Ababa.
	May 16	Capitulation of Italian forces under the Duke of Aosta in Italian East Africa.
	Dec. 11	Italy declares war on United States.
1942	June	Allied convoys resupply Malta.
	Nov. 4	British break through Axis line at El Alamein.
1943	May	Surrender of Axis forces in North Africa.
	July 10	Allied invasion of Sicily.
	July 25	Grand Council of Fascism votes Mussolini out of power. Badoglio takes over the Italian government.
	Aug. 17	Sicily finally conquered by the Allies.
	Sept. 8	Italian surrender announced. Nazis take over power in Italy.
	Sept. 9	Salerno landing by US 5th Army.
	Sept. 12	Skorzeny rescues Mussolini.
	Sept. 23	Mussolini announces creation of fascist social republic of Salò.
1944	Jan. 22	Anzio landing by US 5th Army; German counter-attack stalls advance.
	Mar. 15	Allies bomb Monte Cassino.
	Mar. 17	Monte Cassino falls.
	June 4	Rome falls.
1945	Apr. 28	Mussolini executed by partisans at Dongo.

INTERNATIONAL BACKGROUND TO THE SECOND WORLD WAR

1933	Jan. 30	Hitler becomes Chancellor of Germany.
	Mar. 16	Britain's plan for disarmament fails as Germany insists on exclusion of the SA (paramilitary 'Brownshirts').
	Mar. 19	Mussolini proposes pact between Britain, France, Italy and Germany, signed as the Rome Pact.
	Mar. 27	Japan announces intention to leave League of Nations.
	July 15	Rome Pact binds Britain, France, Germany and Italy to the League Covenant, the Locarno Treaties, and the Kellogg–Briand Pact.
	Oct. 14	Germany leaves disarmament conference and League of Nations.
1934	June 14–15	Hitler meets Mussolini for the first time, in Venice.
	July 25	Austrian Chancellor Dollfuss murdered in Nazi coup.
	July 30	Kurt Schuschnigg becomes new Austrian Chancellor.
	Dec. 5	Italian and Ethiopian troops clash at Wal Wal inside Ethiopia.
1935	Feb. 1	Anglo-German conference on German rearmament; Italy sends troops to East Africa.
	Mar. 15	Hitler repudiates the military restrictions on Germany imposed by the Treaty of Versailles, restores conscription and announces that the peacetime army strength is to be raised to half a million men. Germany announces the existence of the Luftwaffe.
	Apr. 11–14	Britain, France and Italy confer at Stresa to establish a common front against Germany.
	May 2	France and the Soviet Union sign a treaty of five years' mutual assistance.
	May 16	Czechoslovakia and Soviet Union sign mutual assistance pact.
	May 19	Pro-Nazi Sudeten Party makes gains in Czechoslovak elections.
	June 18	Anglo-German Naval Agreement. Germany undertakes that its navy shall not exceed a third of the tonnage of the Royal Navy.
	June 27	League of Nations attempts to defuse the Wal Wal crisis shows strong support for the League.
	Sept. 3	League of Nations attempts to defuse the Wal Wal Oasis incident by stating that neither country was to blame as possession was unclear.
	Oct. 2	Italian forces invade Ethiopia.
	Oct. 7	League of Nations declares Italy the aggressor in Ethiopia and votes sanctions.

Oct. 19	League of Nations sanctions against Italy come into force.
Dec. 9	Hoare–Laval Pact, lenient to Italy, is met by hostile public reaction in Britain and France.
Dec. 13	Benes succeeds Masaryk as President of Czechoslovakia.
1936 Feb. 16	Popular Front wins a majority in the Spanish elections.
Mar. 3	Britain increases defence expenditure, principally on the air force.
Mar. 8	German troops reoccupy the demilitarized Rhineland in violation of the Treaty of Versailles.
May 5	Italians take Addis Ababa; Emperor Haile Selassie flees. Italy annexes Ethiopia (9th).
July 11	Austro-German convention acknowledges Austrian independence.
July 18	Spanish Army revolt under Emilio Mola and Francisco Franco begins Spanish Civil War.
Aug. 24	Germany introduces compulsory conscription.
Sept. 9	Conference held in London on non-intervention in Spanish Civil War.
Oct. 1	Franco appointed 'Chief of the Spanish State' by the nationalist rebels.
Oct. 14	Belgium renounces its military pact with France in order to ensure its liberty of action in the face of German reoccupation of the Rhineland.
Oct. 19	Germany begins 4-year economic plan to develop its economic base for war.
Nov. 1	Mussolini proclaims Rome–Berlin Axis.
Nov. 18	Germany and Italy recognize Franco's government.
Nov. 24	Germany and Japan sign Anti-Comintern Pact.
Dec. 16	Protocol signed in London for non-intervention in Spain.
1937 Jan. 2	Mussolini signs agreement with Britain ensuring the safety of shipping in the Mediterranean.
Jan. 15	Amnesty granted for Austrian Nazis.
Feb. 27	France extends Maginot Line.
Mar. 18	Defeat of Italian push on Madrid.
Apr. 27	Basque town of Guernica destroyed by German Condor Legion.
June 18	Spanish nationalist forces take Bilbao.
June 23	Germany and Italy withdraw from non-intervention committee.
July 7	'China incident'; outbreak of Sino-Japanese War (see pp. 299–300)

July 17	Naval agreements between Britain and Germany, and Britain and Soviet Union.
Sept. 10–14	At Nyon Conference, 9 nations adopt system of patrol in Mediterranean to protect shipping.
Oct. 13	Germany guarantees inviolability of Belgium.
Oct. 17	Riots in Sudeten area of Czechoslovakia.
Oct. 21	Franco's forces complete conquest of Basque country.
Nov. 5	Hitler informs his generals in the Hossbach memorandum that Austria and Czechoslovakia will be annexed as the first stage in *Lebensraum* for Germany.
Nov. 6	Italy joins Anti-Comintern Pact.
Nov. 8	Japanese take Shanghai.
Nov. 17–21	Lord Halifax (Lord President of the Council) accepts unofficial invitation to visit Germany, where he has inconclusive discussions with Hitler about a European settlement.
Nov. 29	Sudeten Germans secede from Czech Parliament following a ban on their meetings.
Dec. 11	Italy leaves the League of Nations.
Dec. 12	American patrol boat sunk on Yangste river in China by Japanese aircraft.
Dec. 13	Japanese take Nanking.
1938 Feb. 4	Von Ribbentrop becomes German Foreign Minister.
Feb. 12	At Berchtesgaden Hitler forces the Austrian Chancellor Schuschnigg to accept a Protocol promising the release of Nazis in Austria, accepting a pro-Nazi (Seyss-Inquart) as Minister of the Interior and virtually attaching the Austrian army to that of Germany, subject to the consent of Austrian President Miklas.
Feb. 16	Amnesty for Nazis proclaimed in Austria; Seyss-Inquart becomes Minister of the Interior.
Feb. 20	In a speech to the Reichstag Hitler proclaims the need to protect the ten million Germans on the frontiers of the Reich.
Mar. 6	President Miklas of Austria accepts Schuschnigg's proposal of a plebiscite on the future independence of Austria. Announced on 9 Mar., voting was to take place on the 13th.
Mar. 10	Hitler mobilizes for immediate invasion of Austria.
Mar. 11	Schuschnigg accepts Hitler's ultimatum demanding that the plebiscite not be held.
Mar. 12	German army marches into Austria.
Mar. 13	Austria is declared part of Hitler's Reich.
Mar. 28	Hitler encourages German minority in Czechoslovakia to make such demands as will break up the state.

Apr. 16	In Anglo-Italian pact Britain recognizes Italian sovereignty in Ethiopia in return for withdrawal of Italian troops from Spain.
Apr. 24	Germans in Sudetenland demand full autonomy.
Apr. 29	Britain reluctantly joins France in diplomatic action on behalf of the Czech government.
May 9	Russia promises to assist Czechoslovakia in the event of a German attack if Poland and Romania will permit the passage of Russian troops. Both, however, refuse.
May 18–21	German troop movements reported on Czech border; Czech government calls up reservists (20th); and partial mobilization (21st).
May 22	Britain warns Germany of dangers of military action, but makes it clear to France that it is not in favour of military action itself.
Aug. 3	Walter Runciman visits Prague on mediation mission between Czechs and Sudeten Germans.
Aug. 11	Under British and French pressure, the Czech Prime Minister Benes opens negotiations with the Sudeten Germans.
Aug. 12	Germany begins to mobilize.
Sept. 4	Henlein, leader of the Sudeten Germans, rejects Benes's offer of full autonomy and breaks off relations with the Czech government (7th).
Sept. 7	France calls up reservists.
Sept. 11	Poland and Romania again refuse to allow the passage of Russian troops to assist Czechoslovakia.
Sept. 12	Hitler demands that Czechs accept German claims.
Sept. 13	Unrest in Sudetenland put down by Czech troops.
Sept. 15	Chamberlain visits Hitler at Berchtesgaden. Hitler states his determination to annex the Sudetenland on the principle of self-determination.
Sept. 18	Britain and France decide to persuade the Czechs to hand over territory in areas where over half of the population is German.
Sept. 20–1	Germany completes invasion plans. The Czech government initially rejects the Anglo-French proposals, but accepts them on the 21st.
Sept. 22	Chamberlain meets Hitler at Godesberg. Hitler demands immediate occupation of the Sudetenland and announces 28 Sept. for the invasion. The Czech cabinet resigns.
Sept. 23	Czechoslovakia mobilizes; Russia promises to support France in the event of its aiding the Czechs.
Sept. 25	France and Britain threaten Hitler with force unless he negotiates.

Sept. 26	Partial mobilization in France.
Sept. 27	The Royal Navy is mobilized.
Sept. 28	Hitler delays invasion for 24 hours pending a four-power conference at Munich.
Sept. 29	At the Munich conference Chamberlain, Daladier, Hitler and Mussolini agree to transfer the Sudetenland to Germany, while guaranteeing the remaining Czech frontiers.
Sept. 30	Hitler and Chamberlain sign the 'peace in our time' communiqué.
Oct. 1	Czechs cede Teschen to Poland. Germany begins occupation of the Sudetenland.
Oct. 5	Benes resigns.
Oct. 6–8	Slovakia and Ruthenia are granted autonomy.
Oct. 25	Libya is declared to be part of Italy.
Dec. 1	British prepare for conscription.
Dec. 6	Franco-German pact on inviolability of existing frontiers.
Dec. 17	Italy denounces 1935 agreement with France.
Dec. 23	Franco begins final offensive against last Republican stronghold in Catalonia.
1939 Jan. 10	Chamberlain and Halifax visit Rome for discussions with Mussolini.
Jan. 26	Franco's forces take Barcelona.
Feb. 27	Britain and France recognize Franco's government.
Mar. 14	At Hitler's prompting, the Slovak leader Tiso proclaims a breakaway 'Slovak Free State'.
Mar. 15	German troops march into Prague and occupy Bohemia and Moravia.
Mar. 28	Hitler denounces 1934 non-aggression pact with Poland. Spanish Civil War ends with surrender of Madrid.
Mar. 31	Britain and France promise aid to Poland in the event of a threat to Polish independence.
Apr. 7	Italy invades Albania. Spain joins the Anti-Comintern Pact.
Apr. 13	Britain and France guarantee the independence of Greece and Romania.
Apr. 15	The United States requests assurances from Hitler and Mussolini that they will not attack 31 named states.
Apr. 16–18	The Soviet Union proposes a defensive alliance with Britain and France, but the offer is not accepted.
Apr. 27	Britain introduces conscription. Hitler denounces the 1935 Anglo-German naval agreement.
Apr. 28	Hitler rejects Roosevelt's peace proposals.

May 22	Hitler and Mussolini sign a 10-year political and military alliance – the 'Pact of Steel'.
Aug. 11	Anglo-French mission to the Soviet Union begins talks in Moscow.
Aug. 18	Germany and the Soviet Union sign a commercial agreement.
Aug. 23	Germany and the Soviet Union sign non-aggression pact, with secret clauses on the partition of Poland. Chamberlain warns Hitler that Britain will stand by Poland, but accepts the need for a settlement of the Danzig question. Hitler states that Germany's interest in Danzig and the Corridor must be satisfied. The Poles refuse to enter negotiations with the Germans. Hitler brings forward his preparations to invade Poland to the 26th (from 1 Sept.).
Aug. 25	Anglo-Polish mutual assistance pact signed in London. Hitler makes a 'last offer' on Poland and postpones his attack until 1 Sept.
Aug. 28–31	Britain and France urge direct negotiations between Germans and Poles, but the Poles refuse.
Aug. 31	Hitler orders attack on Poland.
Sept. 1	German forces invade Poland and annex Danzig. Britain and France demand withdrawal of German troops.
Sept. 2	Britain decides on ultimatum to Germany.
Sept. 3	Britain and France declare war on Germany.

THE SECOND WORLD WAR

1939	Sept. 1	Germany invades Poland and annexes Danzig.
	Sept. 2	Britain introduces National Service Bill calling up men aged between 18 and 41.
	Sept. 3	Britain and France declare war on Germany.
	Sept. 7	Germans overrun western Poland.
	Sept. 17	Soviet Union invades eastern Poland.
	Sept. 19	Polish government leaves Warsaw.
	Sept. 28	Fall of Warsaw.
	Sept. 30	Germany and Soviet Union settle partition of Poland. Last of British Expeditionary Force (BEF) arrives in France.
	Oct. 6	Peace moves by Hitler rejected by Britain and France; opening of Auschwitz concentration camp symbolizes systematic elimination of opponents of Nazis.
	Oct. 8	Western Poland incorporated into the Reich.
	Nov. 3	United States allows Britain and France to purchase arms in USA on a 'cash and carry' basis.
	Nov. 30	Soviet Union invades Finland.
	Dec. 13	German battleship *Graf Spee* forced to scuttle itself off Montevideo after Battle of the River Plate.
1940	Mar. 12	Finland signs peace treaty with Soviet Union ceding territory on the Karelian isthmus and in north-eastern Finland.
	Apr. 9	Germany invades Norway and Denmark.
	Apr. 14	British forces land in Norway.
	May 2	Evacuation of British forces from Norway.
	May 10	Resignation of Chamberlain as British prime minister, replaced by Winston Churchill.
	May 14	Dutch army surrenders after bombing of Rotterdam.
	May 28	Belgium capitulates.
	May 29–June 3	Over 300,000 British and Allied troops evacuated from Dunkirk.
	June–Sept.	Battle of Britain.
	June 10	Italy declares war on Britain and France.
	June 14	Germans enter Paris. French government moves to Bordeaux.
	June 16	France declines offer of union with Britain. Marshal Pétain replaces Paul Reynaud as head of French administration.
	June 17–23	Russians occupy Baltic states.
	June 22	France concludes armistice with Germany.
	June 24	France signs armistice with Italy.
	June 27	Russia invades Romania.
	July 3	Britain sinks French fleet at Oran.
	Aug. 5	Britain signs agreement with Polish government in exile in

	London and with Free French under de Gaulle (7th).
Aug. 23	Beginning of 'Blitz' on Britain.
Oct. 7	Germany seizes Romanian oilfields.
Oct. 12	Hitler cancels Operation Sealion for the invasion of Britain.
Oct. 28	Italy invades Greece. Britain offers help.
Nov. 11	Major elements of Italian fleet sunk at Taranto, Sicily.
Dec. 9–15	Italian forces defeated at Sidi Barrani in North Africa.

1941	Jan. 6	F. D. Roosevelt sends Lend-Lease Bill to Congress.
	Jan.–Feb.	Further Italian reverses in North Africa.
	Feb. 6	German troops under Rommel sent to assist Italians in North Africa.
	Mar. 11	Lend-Lease Bill passes Congress. See p. 472.
	Apr. 6	German ultimatum to Greece and Yugoslavia. Britain diverts troops from North Africa to Greece.
	Apr. 7	Rommel launches offensive in North Africa.
	Apr. 11	Blitz on Coventry.
	Apr. 13	Stalin signs neutrality pact with Japan.
	Apr. 17	Yugoslavia signs capitulation after Italian and German attack.
	Apr. 22–8	British forces evacuated from Greece.
	May 10	Rudolf Hess flies to Scotland and is imprisoned.
	May 27	*Bismarck* sunk by Royal Navy.
	May 20–31	Germans capture Crete.
	June 22	Germans launch invasion of Russia, Operation Barbarossa. Finnish forces attack on Karelian Isthmus.
	July 6	Russians abandon eastern Poland and Baltic States; systematic extermination of Jews (the Final Solution) begun by Nazis.
	July 12	Britain and Russia sign agreement for mutual assistance in Moscow.
	July 16	Germans take Smolensk.
	Aug. 11	Churchill and Roosevelt sign the Atlantic Charter.
	Sept. 8	Germans lay siege to Leningrad.
	Sept. 19	Germans take Kiev.
	Sept. 30–Oct. 2	Germans begin drive on Moscow.
	Oct. 16	Russian government leaves Moscow but Stalin stays.
	Oct. 30	German attacks reach within 60 miles of Moscow.
	Nov. 15	Renewed German offensive takes advance elements within 20 miles of Moscow.
	Nov. 20–28	German forces take Rostov but retreat.
	Dec. 5	Germans go onto defensive on Moscow front as Russians launch counter-offensive.
	Dec. 7	Japanese bomb Pearl Harbor, Hawaii and British Malaya.

Dec. 8	Britain and the USA declare war on Japan.
Dec. 11	Germany and Italy declare war on USA.
1942 Jan. 2	Britain, United States, Soviet Union and 23 other nations sign Washington Pact not to make separate peace treaties with their enemies.
Feb. 1	Pro-Nazi Quisling becomes premier of Norway.
Feb. 6	Roosevelt and Churchill appoint Combined Chiefs of Staff.
Feb. 11	German battleships make Channel 'dash' from Brest to Germany.
Feb. 15	Surrender of Singapore to Japanese.
Mar. 10	Rangoon falls to Japanese.
Mar. 28	RAF destroys much of Lübeck, first major demonstration of area bombing.
May 12–17	Russian offensive on Kharkov front defeated.
May 26	Signing of Anglo-Soviet treaty for closer co-operation.
May 29	Soviet Union and United States extend lend-lease agreement.
May 30	First British 1,000-bomber raid on Cologne.
June 6	Germans wipe out village of Lidice in Czechoslovakia in retaliation for assassination of Gestapo leader Heydrich.
June 10	German offensive in the Ukraine.
June 21	Fall of Tobruk after Rommel's advance in North Africa. Eighth Army retreats to El Alamein.
June 25	Dwight Eisenhower appointed Commander-in-Chief of US forces in Europe.
July 2	Fall of Sevastopol.
July 28	Germans take Rostov and northern Caucasus in drive to take Baku oilfields. Zhukov takes over command of southern armies.
Aug. 14	Raid on Dieppe by British and Canadians ends in failure.
Sept. 5	Germans enter Stalingrad.
Nov. 11–12	Vichy France occupied.
Nov. 19–20	Russians began counter-attack at Stalingrad, cutting off von Paulus's troops.
Nov. 27	French navy scuttled in Toulon.
Dec. 29	Final failure of effort by German forces to relieve von Paulus.
1943 Jan. 2	German withdrawal from Caucasus begins.
Jan. 14–24	Churchill and Roosevelt at Casablanca Conference, declare that they will only accept 'Unconditional Surrender'.
Jan. 31	Von Paulus surrenders at Stalingrad.
Feb. 2	Last German forces surrender at Stalingrad.
Feb. 8	Russian offensive takes Kursk.
Feb. 14	Russians capture Rostov.
Feb. 16	Russians take Kharkov.

Mar. 15	Russians forced out of Kharkov.
Apr. 20	Massacre of Jews in Warsaw ghetto.
Apr. 26	Discovery of the Katyn massacre and demand by Polish government in London for investigation by the Red Cross. Stalin breaks off diplomatic relations with Poles based in London.
May 12	Axis armies in Tunisia surrender.
May 17	RAF bombs Ruhr dams, causing widespread destruction.
June 4	French Committee of National Liberation formed under General Charles de Gaulle.
July 4	General Sikorski killed in an air crash.
July 5	Germans launch an offensive on Kursk salient, Operation Citadel.
July 10	Allied landings in Sicily.
July 12	Russian counter-offensive against Orel Salient causes Germans to halt Kursk offensive.
July 26	Mussolini forced to resign. King Victor Emmanuel asks Marshal Badoglio to form a government. Secret armistice signed with Allies.
Aug. 4	Russians take Orel.
Aug. 23	Russians take Kharkov.
Sept. 3	Allied landings in Italy; Italy surrenders unconditionally.
Sept. 25	Russians take Smolensk.
Nov. 2	Moscow declaration of Allied foreign ministers on international security.
Nov. 6	Russians take Kiev.
Nov. 28–Dec. 1	Churchill, Roosevelt and Stalin meet at Tehran.
Dec. 20	Britain and USA agree to support Tito's partisans.
Dec. 26	*Scharnhorst* sunk in Barents Sea by British ships.
1944 Jan. 22	Allied landing at Anzio in attempt to by-pass German forces blocking the road to Rome.
Jan. 27	Relief of Leningrad.
Feb. 15	Bombing of Monte Cassino by Allies fails to dislodge German defenders.
Mar. 18	Fall of Monte Cassino to Allied forces.
Apr. 2	Russians enter Romania.
June 2	Fall of Rome to Americans.
June 6	'D-Day' landings in Normandy.
June 13	V-I 'Flying Bomb', campaign opened on Britain.
July 1	Monetary and financial conference at Bretton Woods, New Hampshire, lays foundation for postwar economic settlement.
July 9	Fall of Caen to Allied troops.
July 20	Failure of 'July Plot' to assassinate Hitler.

July 26	Soviet Union recognizes the Lublin Committee of Polish Liberation in Moscow as the legitimate authority for Liberated Poland.
Aug. 1	Rising of Home Army in Warsaw. American armies begin breakout from Normandy bridgehead at Avranches.
Aug. 11	Allied landings in southern France.
Aug. 13–20	German forces destroyed in Falaise Pocket in France.
Aug. 25	De Gaulle and Allied troops enter Paris.
Aug. 30	Russians enter Bucharest.
Sept. 4	Ceasefire between Soviet Union and Finland. Armistice signed on 19th.
Sept. 5	Brussels liberated by Allied troops.
Sept. 8	V-2 rockets begin landing in Britain.
Sept. 17	Arnhem airborne landings in Allied attempt to seize vital river crossings for advance into northern Germany.
Oct. 3	Final suppression of Warsaw rising by German forces.
Oct. 14	British troops liberate Athens.
Oct. 20	Belgrade liberated by Russians and Yugoslav partisans.
Oct. 23	De Gaulle's administration recognized by the Allies as provisional government of France.
Dec. 3	Rioting in Athens and British police action sparks off communist insurrection.
Dec. 16	Germans begin Ardennes offensive, the 'Battle of the Bulge'.
Dec. 31	Regency installed in Greece by British.
1945 Jan. 3	Allied counter-attack begins in Ardennes.
Jan. 11	Truce declared in Greek Civil War.
Jan. 17	Russians take Warsaw.
Feb. 4–11	Yalta Conference. Churchill, Roosevelt and Stalin plan for Germany's unconditional surrender, the settlement of Poland, and the United Nations Conference at San Francisco.
Feb. 12	Amnesty granted to Greek Communists.
Feb. 13	Fall of Budapest to Russians.
Mar. 23	American armies cross Rhine at Remagen.
Mar. 28	End of V-Rocket offensive against Britain.
Apr. 3	Benes appoints a National Front Government in Czechoslovakia.
Apr. 20	Russians reach Berlin.
Apr. 25	Renner becomes Chancellor of provisional Austrian government.
Apr. 26	Russian and American forces link up at Torgau.
Apr. 28	Mussolini killed by partisans.
Apr. 30	Hitler commits suicide in Berlin. Dönitz is appointed successor.

May 1	German army in Italy surrenders.
May 2	Berlin surrenders to Russians.
May 3	British take Rangoon in Burma.
May 7	General Jodl makes unconditional surrender of all German forces to Eisenhower.
May 8	Victory in Europe, 'VE' day. Von Keitel surrenders to Zhukov near Berlin.
May 9	Russians take Prague.
May 14	Democratic Republic of Austria established.
June 5	Allied Control Commission assumes control in Germany, which is divided into four occupation zones.
June 22	Americans complete capture of Okinawa, campaign declared ended on 2 July.
July 12–15	Japan seeks Russian mediation to end war. 1,000-bomber raid on Tokyo; ten Japanese cities devastated by air attacks.
Aug. 6	Atomic bomb dropped on Hiroshima.
Aug. 8	USSR declares war on Japan.
Aug. 9	Atomic bomb dropped on Nagasaki; Russian troops enter northern Korea and Manchuria.
Aug. 14	Japan surrenders.

MOBILIZATION AND CASUALTIES IN THE SECOND WORLD WAR (ALL THEATRES)

	Strength of armed forces	Military killed and missing	Military wounded	Civilian dead[1]
Australia	680,000	29,395	39,803	
Austria	800,000	380,000	350,117	145,000
Britain	4,683,000	271,311[2]	277,077	95,297
Canada	780,000	39,319	53,174	
Finland	250,000	79,047	50,000	35,000
France	5,000,000 (est.)	205,000	390,000	173,000
Germany	9,200,000	3,300,000	2,893,000	800,000
Greece	150,000	16,357	49,933	155,300
Hungary	350,000	147,435	89,313	280,000
India	2,393,891	36,092	64,354	79,489
Italy	4,500,000	279,820	120,000	93,000
Japan	6,095,000	1,380,429	295,247	933,000
Netherlands	500,000	13,700	2,860	236,300
New Zealand	157,000	12,162	19,314	
Poland	1,000,000	320,000	530,000	6,028,000
Romania	600,000	300,000	219,822	465,000
South Africa	140,000	8,681	14,363	
USSR	20,000,000	13,600,000[3]	5,000,000	7,720,000
USA	16,353,659	292,131	671,278	5,662
Yugoslavia	3,741,000	305,000	425,000	1,355,000

[1] Includes Jews killed by the Nazis.
[2] 19,753 POWs died in captivity.
[3] Includes POWs who were killed or died in captivity.

THE HOLOCAUST: JEWS KILLED IN EUROPE, 1941-5

	Jewish population in 1941	Estimated number of Jews killed by country
Austria	70,000	60,000
Belgium	85,000	28,000
Bulgaria	48,000	40,000
Czechoslovakia	81,000	60,000
Denmark	6,000	100
France	300,000	65,000
Germany	250,000	180,000
Greece	67,000	60,000
Holland	140,000	104,000
Hungary	710,000	200,000
Italy	120,000	9,000
Poland	3,000,000	2,600,000
Romania	1,000,000	750,000
USSR[1]	2,740,000	924,000
Yugoslavia	70,000	58,000

[1] Includes Baltic States

THE COLD WAR AND EASTERN EUROPE SINCE 1942

1942 May 26	20-year Anglo-Soviet treaty signed, but without any territorial agreement for postwar Europe.
June–Aug.	Stalin steps up demands for opening of 'second front' to relieve pressure on Russia.
July	British suspension of convoys to Russia because of losses causes Stalin to accuse allies of lack of genuine support.
1943 Jan. 14–24	Churchill and Roosevelt agree to insist on the 'unconditional surrender' of Germany. The decision to mount an invasion of Italy, agreed by the Allied commanders, led to bitter recriminations from Stalin, who saw it as bad faith on the part of the Western powers.
Aug.	Stalin objects to not being consulted about the surrender of Italy and demands a say in the Italian settlement.
Oct.	Three-power foreign ministers' conference in Moscow agrees upon an advisory council for Italy and makes broad plans for a world security organization.
Nov. 28–Dec. 1	Meeting of 'Big Three' (Churchill, Roosevelt and Stalin) at Tehran, the first conference attended by Stalin. As well as discussing arrangements for the Allied landings in Europe and a renewed Soviet offensive against Germany, the main lines of a territorial settlement in Eastern Europe were agreed, including the Polish frontiers. No agreement was reached about the future of Germany, although there was discussion of the dismemberment of Germany.
1944 Aug. 21–Oct. 9	Dumbarton Oaks Conference draws up broad framework of the United Nations.
Sept. 11–17	Churchill and Roosevelt meet at Quebec and move towards acceptance of Morgenthau Plan for the destruction of German industry and the conversion of Germany into a pastoralized state.
Oct. 9–10	Churchill and Stalin meet in Moscow and decide on 'spheres of influence'. Romania and Bulgaria are ceded predominantly to Russian influence, Greece to Britain, and Yugoslavia and Hungary equally between Russia and Great Britain.
Dec. 3	Attempted communist insurrection in Athens.
1945 Jan. 11	Communists in Greece seek truce.
Feb. 4–11	Meeting at Yalta between Churchill, Roosevelt and Stalin decides upon 4 occupation zones in Germany and the prosecution of war criminals, and prepares Allied Control Commission to run Germany on the basis of 'complete disarmament, demilitarization and dismemberment'.

Removals of national wealth from Germany were to be permitted within two years of the end of the war and reparations were tentatively agreed. Agreement reached that the provisional government already functioning in Poland, i.e. the communist Lublin-based group, with the addition of other groups including the London Poles, be the government. A three-power commission based in Moscow would supervise the setting up of the new regime. The provisional government was pledged to hold free and unfettered elections as soon as possible. Declaration on Liberated Europe signed by the three powers to allow European states to 'create democratic conditions of their own choice'.

Feb. 12	Greek communists granted amnesty and lay down arms.
April	Members of non-communist delegation to the three-power commission in Moscow arrested. Russians conclude a treaty of alliance with the Lublin administration in Poland.
July 5	Britain and United States recognize Provisional Government of National Unity in Poland.
July 17–Aug. 1	Stalin, Truman, Churchill (after 25th, Attlee) meet at Potsdam and finalize 4-power agreement on administration of Germany and the territorial adjustments in Eastern Europe. The Oder–Neisse line is to mark the new boundary between Germany and Poland. Although Germany is to be divided into zones, it is to be treated as a single economic unit. Germans living in Poland, Hungary and Czechoslovakia are to be sent to Germany.
Oct. 28	Provisional Czech National Assembly meets, representing communist and non-communist parties.
Nov.	Tito elected President of Yugoslavia.
1946 Mar. 6	Churchill makes 'Iron Curtain' speech at Fulton, Missouri: 'From Stettin in the Baltic to Trieste in the Adriatic, an Iron Curtain has descended upon the Continent.'
May 26	At Czech elections, communists win 38% of the vote and set up a single party 'National Front' government.
May	Fighting breaks out in northern Greece, marking renewal of civil war between monarchist forces, assisted by Britain, and communist guerrillas, backed by Albania, Bulgaria and Yugoslavia.
1947 Feb. 21	The British inform the Americans that they cannot afford to keep troops in Greece because of their domestic economic difficulties and intend to withdraw them by the end of March.
Feb. 27	Dean Acheson privately expounds the 'Truman Doctrine' of

	economic and military aid to nations in danger of communist takeover.
Mar. 12	In message to Congress, President Truman outlines the Truman Doctrine 'to support free peoples who are resisting attempted subjugation by armed minorities or by outside pressures', effectively committing the United States to intervene against communist or communist-backed movements in Europe and elsewhere.
Apr. 22	Truman Doctrine passed by Congress.
Apr. 24	Council of Foreign Ministers in Moscow ends without formal peace treaties for Germany and Austria.
May 22	US Congress passes Bill for $250 million of aid for Greece and Turkey.
June 5	George Marshall, American Secretary of State, calls for a European recovery programme supported by American aid.
June 12–15	Non-communist nations of Europe set up Committee of European Economic Co-operation to draft European Recovery Programme.
Aug.	First American aid arrives in Greece, followed by military 'advisers' to assist in the Civil War against the communists.

1948 Feb. 25	Czech President Benes accepts a communist-dominated government.
Mar. 10	Czech Foreign Minister, Jan Masaryk, found dead in suspicious circumstances.
Mar. 14–31	Congress passes the Foreign Assistance Act, the Marshall Plan. $5,300 million of 'Marshall Aid' is initially allocated for European recovery.
Mar. 17	Belgium, France, Luxembourg, the Netherlands and Britain sign a treaty setting up the Brussels Treaty Organization for mutual military assistance.
Mar. 20	Russian representative walks out of Allied Control Commission, over plans for unified German currency.
Mar. 30	Russians impose restrictions on traffic between Western zones and Berlin.
April	Paris Treaty sets up Organization for European Economic Co-operation to receive Marshall Aid.
May 30	No opposition parties are allowed to stand at Czech elections and electors called on to vote for a single list of National Front candidates.
June 7	Benes resigns as President of Czechoslovakia; succeeded by Gottwald.
June 24	Russians impose a complete blockade of traffic into Berlin. Berlin airlift begins (25th).

June	Yugoslavia expelled from Comintern, effectively putting it outside direct Soviet control.
Sept. 5	Head of Polish Communist Party, Gomulka, forced to resign.
Nov. 30	Russians set up separate municipal government for East Berlin.
1949 Jan. 25	Comecon, Communist economic co-operation organization, set up.
Apr. 4	Creation of NATO. North Atlantic Treaty signed by members of Brussels Treaty Organization, with Canada, Denmark, Iceland, Italy, Norway, Portugal and the United States. It pledges mutual military assistance.
May 4	Representatives of 4 occupation powers in Germany come to an agreement for ending of Berlin blockade.
May 15	Communists take power in Hungary on the basis of a single-list election for the 'People's Front', replacing the communist-dominated coalition which had been elected in 1947.
May 12	Berlin blockade lifted.
May	Federal Republic of Germany (West Germany) comes into existence.
June	Purge of Albanian Communist Party.
Sept. 30	End of Berlin airlift.
Oct. 16	Greek communists cease fighting.
Oct.	German Democratic Republic (East Germany) comes into existence.
Nov.	Russian marshal takes command of Polish army.
Dec. 1949–Jan. 1950	Purge of Bulgarian Communist Party; 92,000 expelled.
1950 May 28	Pro-Stalinist Hoxha confirmed in power in single-list elections in Albania.
May–June	Last non-communists expelled from Hungarian government.
July	Romanian Communist Party admits to expulsion of almost 200,000 members in past two years.
Sept.	United States proposes German re-armament.
1951 Sept.	First Soviet atomic bomb exploded.
1952 Feb. 18	Greece and Turkey join NATO.
May 27	Belgium, France, Italy, Luxembourg, the Netherlands, and West Germany sign mutual defence treaty for proposed creation of a European Defence Community.
1953 Mar. 5	Death of Stalin. Khrushchev confirmed as First Secretary of the Communist Party (Sept.).
June	Risings in East Germany suppressed.
1954 May 5	Italy and West Germany enter Brussels Treaty Organization.

1955 May 9		West Germany admitted to NATO.
	May 14	Warsaw Pact formed.
1956 Feb.		At Russian 20th Party Congress Khrushchev attacks abuses of Stalin era in 'Secret Speech'.
	June	Suppression of workers' riots in Poznan, Poland; Gomulka becomes First Secretary of Polish United Workers' Party (Oct.).
	Oct.–Nov.	General strike and street demonstrations in Budapest. Russians intervene, depose Imre Nagy and crush the rising. Kadar becomes the First Secretary of the Hungarian Communist Party and Premier. Thousands of Hungarian refugees flee to the West.
1958 Feb.		Khrushchev replaces Bulganin as Prime Minister.
1961 Apr.		First manned Soviet space flight. Arrests of dissident writers.
	July	Anti-clerical legislation in Russia, restricting role of the clergy in parish councils.
	Aug.	Berlin Wall constructed to prevent flight from East to West Berlin.
	Oct.	22nd Party Congress; new Party programme and further 'de-Stalinization', including the removal of Stalin's body from Red Square mausoleum.
1962 Oct.		Cuban Missile Crisis after Soviet Union attempts to set up ballistic missile bases in Cuba. Imposition of naval 'quarantine' by the United States forces the Soviet Union to back down in the face of the threat of nuclear war. A major diplomatic triumph for the will and resolve of President John F. Kennedy.
	Nov.	Publication of Solzhenitsyn's *A Day in the Life of Ivan Denisovitch* marks first public recognition of the conditions in Soviet labour camps.
1963 Mar.		Khrushchev warns Writers' Union of 'bourgeois influences'.
	Aug. 5	Partial Test Ban Treaty signed in Moscow, banning nuclear weapon tests in the atmosphere, outer space and under water (in force from Oct.).
1964 Oct.		Brezhnev replaces Khrushchev as First Secretary.
1965 Mar.		Central Committee of the Soviet Union makes a number of agricultural reforms.
	Sept.	Central Committee approves further set of economic reforms.
1966 Feb.		Trial of leading 'dissidents', Sinyavsky and Daniel, who are sentenced to periods of imprisonment.

1967 June	Arab–Israeli 'Six Day' War leads to acute tension between United States and Soviet Union.
1968 Jan.	Soviet dissidents Ginsburg and Galanskov tried and imprisoned. Dubcek becomes First Secretary of Czechoslovak Communist Party and process of liberalization begins – 'Socialism with a human face' – including decentralization of economic planning and more open contacts with the West.
July 1	Non-proliferation treaty signed in London, Moscow and Washington.
Aug.	The Soviet Union and other Warsaw Pact forces invade Czechoslovakia and end the 'Prague Spring'. The Czech leaders are forced to agree in Moscow to the re-imposition of censorship, return to centralized planning, and the abandonment of closer links with the West. Husak takes over Party Secretaryship from Dubcek (Jan. 1969).
1969 Mar.	Dubcek demoted and sent as ambassador to Turkey; he is eventually expelled from the Party and given menial work.
Oct.	Czechoslovakia repudiates its condemnation of the Warsaw Pact invasion and consents to the stationing of Russian troops.
1970 Dec.	Widespread rioting in Poland over food prices and economic conditions; Gierek replaces Gomulka as First Secretary of Polish United Workers' Party.
1971 Feb.	Mass Jewish demonstration at Supreme Soviet building. Jewish emigration to Israel increases.
1972 Jan.	Seizure of documents and leading intellectuals in the Ukraine.
May 26	President Nixon visits Moscow. Strategic Arms Limitation Treaty (SALT 1) signed between United States and Soviet Union on limitation of anti-ballistic missile systems (in force from Oct.) and interim agreement on limitation of strategic offensive arms.
May	Disturbances in Lithuania.
1973 Apr.	Andropov and Gromyko join Politburo.
1974 Feb.	Solzhenitsyn deported from Soviet Union.
1975 Aug.	Helsinki agreement on European Security and Co-operation provides for 'Human Rights'.
Oct.	Soviet physicist and dissident Andre Sakharov awarded Nobel Peace Prize.

1976 June	Strikes and sabotage in Poland in opposition to attempted price rises which were temporarily withdrawn, although unrest is severely put down.
1977 Jan.	Dissident civil rights group 'Charter 77' formed in Prague.
June	Brezhnev replaces Podgorny as President of the Soviet Union.
1978 July	Trial of Scharansky.
1979 June	Visit of Polish Pope John Paul II to Poland helps to arouse strong national feeling.
Dec.	Soviet invasion of Afghanistan. The United States imposes a grain embargo on Russia. Large commemorative services held in Poland for those killed in the disturbances of 1970.
1980 Jan.	Sakharov sentenced to internal exile in Gorky.
Mar.–Apr.	Dissident groups in Poland advocate boycott of official Parliamentary elections on 23 Mar., and mass commemorative service for Polish officers killed at Katyn in Apr. 1940 leads to arrests.
July	Olympic Games in Moscow boycotted by the United States.
July–Sept.	Widespread strikes amongst Polish workers at Gdansk (Danzig) and elsewhere as a result of rise in meat prices. In August, Gdansk workers publish demands calling for free trade unions. Soviet Union begins jamming of Western broadcasts. Resignation of Babinch as Prime Minister (24 Aug.) and of Gierek as First Secretary of the Polish United Workers Party (6 Sept.); replaced by Pinkowski and Kania. Gierek's departure followed by the signing of the Gdansk agreement with Lech Walesa, the leader of the Gdansk 'inter-factory committee'. This recognized the new Solidarity unions, granted a wage agreement and promised a 40-hour week, permitted the broadcast of church services on Sunday, relaxed the censorship laws, promised to re-examine the new meat scales, and review the case of imprisoned dissidents. National Confederation of Independent Trade Unions, 'Solidarity', formed under leadership of Lech Walesa (8 Sept.) attracts an estimated 10 million members. 'Rural Solidarity' claims an estimated half a million farmers.
Dec.	Death of Russian Prime Minister Kosygin.
1981 Jan.	Walesa visits Pope in Rome.
Feb.	General Jaruzelski replaces Pinkowski as Prime Minister of Poland.
Dec.	After visiting Moscow, General Jaruzelski declares martial law in Poland. The leading members of Solidarity are arrested and the organization banned.

1982 Nov.	Death of Brezhnev. Andropov becomes First Secretary of the Communist Party of the Soviet Union.
1984 Feb.	Death of Andropov, Chernenko becomes First Secretary of the Communist Party of the Soviet Union.
1985 Mar.	Death of Chernenko. Gorbachev becomes First Secretary of the Communist Party of the Soviet Union. Announces programme of glasnost and perestroika.
July	Gorbachev replaces four members of politburo with his own supporters, veteran Foreign Minister, Gromyko, moved to Presidency and replaced by Gorbachev supporter Shevardnadze.
1986 Jan.	Gorbachev continues process of removing the personnel of the Brezhnev era from central and regional government.
Sept.	Solidarity announce intention of working within the existing system.
1987 June	Karoly Grosz, an economic liberal, becomes Prime Minister in Hungary.
July	Protests by Crimean Tatars in Moscow permitted to take place.
Aug.	Protests in the Baltic States demanding greater autonomy and an end to 'Russification'.
Nov.	Polish government hold referendum for programme of radical reform; Solidarity calls for boycott and the proposals are rejected. Radical Boris Yeltsin dismissed as head of Moscow Party for outspoken criticisms of conservatives.
Dec.	President Reagan and General Secretary Gorbachev sign Intermediate Nuclear Forces Treaty in Washington; a major breakthrough in East–West arms negotiations.
Dec. 17	Gustav Husak resigns party leadership in Czechoslovakia; succeeded by another conservative, Milos Jakes.
1988 Jan.	Gorbachev calls for acceleration of drive to democratization; calls special party Congress in the summer. Major reform of Soviet Constitution sets up a Supreme Soviet consisting of two chambers to meet in almost continuous session, the members selected by a Congress of People's Deputies representing national areas, social organizations and constituencies.
	Hungarian government announces end of price controls.
Feb.	Serious ethnic riots in Naborno-Karabakh region of Azerbaijan.
Mar.–Aug.	Wave of strikes and unrest in Poland; Solidarity demands talks with government.

May	Russian agreement to withdraw all troops from Afghanistan by Feb. 1989. In Hungary, Kadar relegated to post of Party President; Grosz becomes Party Secretary and Prime Minister; purge of conservatives in Central Committee and Politburo.
Dec.	Polish government accepts 'round table' talks with Solidarity. Gorbachev announces unilateral force reductions of 500,000 troops and 10,000 tanks.
1989 Jan.	Law on Association in Hungary allows political parties to be formed; new draft constitution (Mar.) drops reference to leading role for Communist Party.
Feb. 6	Solidarity and Polish government open talks on future of Poland.
Mar.–Apr.	Solidarity accepts terms for participation in elections; government agrees to admit opposition to the lower house of parliament (*sejm*); a freely elected Senate, and create office of President. Solidarity legalized.
June	First free parliamentary elections in Poland since Second World War; Solidarity obtains landslide victory in seats it is allowed to contest. Hungarian government recognizes Imre Nagy, leader of 1956 rising, and permits his reburial with full honours.
July	General Jaruzelski elected President of Poland by one-vote margin. General Kiszczak appointed Prime Minister but fails to form a government and resigns; Solidarity activist Tadeusz Mazowiecki becomes Prime Minister heading first non-communist government.
Sept.	Hungary opens border with Austria allowing flight of thousands of East Germans to the West.
Oct.	Erich Honecker replaced as President by Egon Krenz in East Germany (18th) following flight of East Germans to the West and mass demonstrations in East German cities organized by New Forum opposition group. Krenz meets opposition group (26th); travel restrictions discussed.
Nov.	East German Council of Ministers resigns en masse following huge demonstrations in East Berlin and other cities. New Forum opposition legalized and Politburo resigns (7–8th). Berlin Wall opened and travel restrictions lifted on East German citizens (9th). Reformer, Hans Modrow, President (13th). President Todor Zhivkov of Bulgaria resigns (10th). Entire Czech Politburo resigns (24th) following mass demonstrations in Prague by Civic Forum opposition group.

Dec.   Malta summit between President Bush and President Gorbachev; declare the Cold War 'at an end' (4th).

Resignation of Czech Prime Minister, Adamec, forced by further mass demonstrations and General Strike. Communist monopoly of power ended and joint interim government formed with members of Civic Forum (7th–9th).

Resignation of Egon Krenz as communist leader in East Germany (8th). Preparations for free elections begin.

Thousands reported killed in anti-Ceausescu demonstrations in Romanian city of Timisoara (19th).

Bulgaria declares it will hold free elections (19th).

Brandenburg Gate opened between East and West Berlin as symbolic act of reconciliation between the two Germanies (22nd).

Mass demonstrations in Bucharest and other Romanian cities. After initial attempts to disperse them, the army joins the crowds and Ceausescu and his wife flee (22nd). Heavy fighting between pro-Ceausescu forces and the army leaves several hundred killed and wounded in Bucharest and other Romanian cities; Ceausescu and his wife arrested and executed by Military Tribunal (25th).

Free elections announced for Apr. 1990; Ion Iliescu becomes President (26th).

Vaclav Havel, former dissident and political prisoner, unanimously elected President of Czechoslovakia (29th); Alexander Dubcek earlier elected Chairman (Speaker) of Czech Parliament (28th).

1990 Feb.   Unanimous vote of the Central Committee of the Communist Party of the Soviet Union to end the leading role of the Communist Party. Lithuanian Communist Party secedes from the CPSU to fight elections in March.

Mar.   Soviet Congress of People's Deputies votes to abolish Articles 6 and 7 of the Soviet Constitution and end the leading role of the Communist Party. Congress approves the election of Gorbachev to the new post of Executive President with sweeping powers; subsequent elections to be by popular vote.

Nationalist movements win victories in multi-party elections in Baltic Republics. Sweeping victory for Lithuanian *Sajudis* movement is followed by declaration of independence and election of non-communist Vytautas Landsbergis as the Republic's first President. Soviet government begins economic blockade of Lithuania. East German elections lead to victory (18th) of pro-unification Alliance for Germany, consisting of the Christian Democratic Union and allies, with over 48% of the vote; coalition government under CDU leader Lothar de Mazière prepares for economic unification in July and all-German elections in December. Hungarian elections result in victory for Democratic Forum with 43% of the vote; coalition government formed with Christian Democrat and Smallholder parties, seeking access to the EEC and rapid adoption of Western economic models.

Apr.   First multi-party elections in Yugoslavian Republics lead to victories for anti-communist parties in Slovenia and Croatia, increasing pressure of independence movements and the effective dissolution of the Yugoslav Communist Party.

May   Romanian elections lead to overwhelming victory of National Salvation Front under former communist minister, Ion Iliescu. The Bulgarian Socialist Party, formerly the Communist Party, obtains a clear majority in the first free elections since the overthrow of the communist regime.

June   Protests in Bucharest at domination of former communists in government lead to serious rioting; police attack demonstrators and National Salvation Front calls on miners to restore order. Czech elections lead to victory for Civic Forum/Public Against Violence with 169 of 300 seats, with backing of President Vaclav Havel.

July   East and West German economic unification on the basis of the West German currency. President Gorbachev obtains mandate from Communist Party Congress for further reform, but breakaway group declares it will form a separate party. German–Soviet agreement between Chancellor Kohl and President Gorbachev (16th) that a united Germany will have full sovereignty, including the right to join NATO; Soviet Union agrees to withdraw its 350,000 troops from East Germany within 3 to 4 years. Paris meeting (17th) of 'Two plus Four' talks, consisting of representatives from East and West Germany and the 4 former Allied powers, the United States, the United Kingdom, the Soviet Union and France, with participants from the Polish government, agrees to guarantee the existing Polish–German border along the Oder–Neisse River with a definitive treaty to be signed following German unification. Agreement to negotiate a second treaty on Polish–German relations, including reparations and protection for the rights of German minorities living in Poland. Ukraine declares its intention to become a sovereign state with its own army and foreign policy.

Aug.	Lech Walesa declares he will be a candidate for President in forthcoming elections. Growing evidence of splits within Solidarity ranks. Boris Yeltsin asserts the sovereignty of the Russian Republic and offers economic assistance to Lithuania.
Sept.	Treaty signed (12th) following 'Two plus Four' talks, agreeing to ending of special powers by the wartime Allies over Germany and for the unification with full sovereignty of East and West Germany.
Oct. 3	Reunification of Germany.
Dec.	Gorbachev granted sweeping new powers. Widespread anti-communist riots in Albania after first legal opposition party formed.
Dec. 2	First all-German elections elect conservative Kohl's CDU/CSU government: ex-communist PDS reduced to 17 seats.
Dec. 9	Lech Walesa elected President of Poland.
Dec. 20	Soviet Foreign Minister Shevardnadze resigns because of 'reactionary elements'.
1991 Jan. 13	Soviet special forces kill 14 Lithuanian demonstrators in Vilnius.
Jan. 20	Special force assault on key buildings in Latvian capital, Riga, kills 5.
Mar.	Huge majorities in Latvia and Estonia for independence. Anti-Gorbachev rally in Moscow; pro-Union majority for his referendum on maintaining the Union, but many abstentions. Albania opens diplomatic relations with West.
Apr.	Soviet Georgia declares independence. Miners' strikes in the Soviet coalfields.
May	First serious casualties in fighting between Serbs and Croats in Yugoslavia.
June 25	Croatia declares independence from Yugoslavia. Widespread fighting begins as Yugoslav army seizes Slovenian border posts. Fighting between Croatian militias and Serbian irregulars and Federal army.
Aug.	Gorbachev prepares new all-Union treaty to preserve the Soviet Union. Attempted hard-line coup in Moscow while Gorbachev on holiday in Crimea. Russian premier Boris Yeltsin defies coup and prepares to defend Russian parliament building with aid of loyal troops and populace. Coup collapses in face of popular resistance and declarations of independence by Republics. The leading plotters are arrested. Gorbachev returns to Moscow. Under pressure from Yeltsin, adopts sweeping reforms. Baltic states become

	independent states of Latvia, Estonia and Lithuania; Communist Party of Soviet Union dissolved, ending 74-year rule; Gorbachev resigns as General Secretary, retaining office of Executive President of rapidly dissolving Soviet Union. Negotiates an association with ten Republics for a looser union with a common foreign and defence policy.
Sept.	Armenia becomes 12th Soviet Republic to declare independence.
Oct.	First completely free election in Poland produces inconclusive result, proliferation of parties and turnout below 50%.
Nov. 4	Formation of independent National Guard in the Ukraine.
Nov. 18	European Community imposes sanctions on Yugoslavia.
Dec. 1	Ukraine votes overwhelmingly for independence.
Dec. 8	Leaders of Belorussia, Russian Federation and Ukraine declare that the Soviet Union is dead; in the Declaration of Minsk they proclaim new 'Commonwealth of Independent States' (CIS) with headquarters at Minsk in Belorussia.
Dec. 10	Ukrainian Parliament ratifies new Commonwealth.
Dec. 12	Russian Parliament votes 188 to 6 to approve new Commonwealth. Gorbachev declares 'My life's work is done'.
Dec. 13	Five Central Asian Republics, meeting in Ashkhabad, vote to join new Commonwealth as founding members: Gorbachev accepts existence and legitimacy of Commonwealth but does not yet resign.
Dec. 22	Leaders of 11 former Soviet Republics sign Treaty of Alma Ata, establishing new Commonwealth of Independent States. The 11 republics comprise: Armenia, Azerbaijan, Belarus (formerly Belorussia), Kazakhstan, Kyrgyzstan (formerly Kirghizia), Moldova (formerly Moldavia), the Russian Federation, Tajikistan, Turkmenistan (formerly Turkmenia), Uzbekistan and Ukraine. Only Georgia (where bitter fighting erupts in Tbilisi) does not join new CIS.
Dec. 25	Formal resignation of Mikhail Gorbachev as President of the now defunct Soviet Union; the Russian flag replaces the Hammer and Sickle above the Kremlin; key EC states (and USA) recognize independence of Russian Federation.
Dec. 30	Minsk Summit of Commonwealth of Independent States agrees future of strategic nuclear forces; no agreement on conventional forces (Ukraine, Azerbaijan and Moldova insist on separate armies) or economic policy.
1992 Jan.	EU recognizes Croatia and Slovenia.
Feb. 21	UN Security Council agrees to send a 14,000-strong force to

	Bosnia. Bosnia–Herzegovina declares independence; Bosnian Serbs proclaim separate state.
Apr. 3	The leader of Albanian Democratic Party, Sali Berisha, elected President by People's Assembly.
Apr. 6	Bosnia recognized as independent by EU and US; Serbs begin campaign of 'ethnic cleansing' in north and east Bosnia, expelling Muslim population to create a pure Serb corridor linking Serb areas of western Bosnia with Serbia. Serbian forces begin artillery bombardment of Sarajevo.
May	'Cleansing' of Muslims and Croats from Brcko begins and systematic killing at Banja Luka and elsewhere, resulting in some 3,000 dead. UN trade embargo placed on Serbia.
June	Yegor Gaidar becomes premier of Russia. Vote of no confidence in Polish government of Prime Minister Jan Olszewski. Czechoslovakian general elections held, dominated by issue of dissolution of the state. Klaus becomes Czech premier, Meciar becomes premier of Slovakia; talks on split proceed in earnest.
July	Airlift of relief supplies into Sarajevo begins. Slovak National Council approves declaration of sovereignty; resignation of Vaclav Havel as Federal President.
Aug.	Existence of Serb-run concentration camps disclosed. President Franco Tudjman and Croatian Democratic Union win victory in first Croatian elections. London Conference sets up Geneva peace talks for former Yugoslavia. Agreement reached on split of Czechoslovakia into 2 independent states on 1 Jan. 1993.
Sept.	Lithuania signs agreement with Russia for withdrawal of former Soviet troops.
Sept. 15	Federal Republic of Yugoslavia excluded from UN General Assembly.
Oct.	In Georgia, Chairman of State Council, Eduard Shevardnadze, elected parliamentary Speaker and *de facto* head of state. President Iliescu wins further four-year term in Romania.
Nov.	Lithuanian ex-communist Democratic Labour Party defeats nationalist Sajudis Party in first post-Soviet parliamentary elections. Czechoslovak Federal Parliament approves split into Czech and Slovak states. UN Security Council enforces naval blockade on Serbia and Montenegro.
Dec.	Ex-communist President Milan Kucan and ruling Liberal Democrat Party win elections in Slovenia; UN peacekeeping forces deployed in Macedonia to prevent spread of unrest. Russian Congress blocks President Yeltsin's plans for a

	referendum on the powers of the President; also removes Yegor Gaidar as premier and replaces him with Viktor Chernomyrdin (14th).
Dec. 21	Slobodan Milosević wins presidential elections in Serbia.
1993 Jan.	Formal separation of Czech and Slovak states; Havel reappointed President of Czech Republic. Geneva Peace Conference on Bosnia opens; Bosnian Serbs provisionally agree to end the war, but fighting continues.
Feb.	UN Security Council votes to create war crimes tribunal for Yugoslavia. Bosnian town of Cerska falls to Serbs.
Mar. 21	President Yeltsin announces rule by decree and plan to hold a national referendum on 25 Apr.
Mar. 28	Move to impeach the President by Congress defeated.
Apr. 1	Athens peace talks on former Yugoslavia open.
Apr. 3	Serbs reject UN peace plan; Bosnian Serbs also reject UN peace plan (25th). Former Yugoslav Republic of Macedonia admitted to UN. Russian referendum gives vote of confidence to President Yeltsin and his socio-economic policy.
May	War crimes tribunal for former Yugoslavia established at The Hague.
May 6	UN Security Council declares Sarajevo and other Muslim enclaves UN monitored safe areas.
June	Provisional agreement at Geneva on 3-way partition of Bosnia–Herzegovina into Muslim, Serb and Croat areas.
July	Guntis Alamanis of Farmers' Union elected President of Latvia.
Aug.	Last Russian troops leave Lithuania.
Sept. 21	President Yeltsin suspends parliament and calls for elections.
Oct. 3–4	Suppression of rising against President Yeltsin's suspension of parliament.
Oct. 26	Coalition government formed under Polish Peasant Party leader Waldemar Pawlak.
1994 Jan.	Reformers Gaidar and Fedorov leave Yeltsin government.
Feb. 9	Serb mortar attack on Sarajevo market, killing over 60 people, leads to UN ultimatum on removal of Serb artillery from 20 km exclusion zone.
Feb. 28	NATO fighers shoot down Serbian aircraft.
Apr.	UN safe area of Gorazde comes under Serb attack; NATO aircraft bomb Serb positions; Serbs retaliate by taking UN observers hostage.
May 29	Former communists, now Hungarian Socialist Party, come to power after 2 rounds of voting.
July	Contact Group of diplomats from Russia, USA, France,

	Britain and Germany propose division of Bosnia, but rejected by Serbs. New constitution adopted in Moldova, establishing a presidential parliamentary republic.
Aug.	Serbian government imposes sanctions on the Bosnian Serbs.
Nov.	USA announces unilateral suspension of international arms embargo following renewal of fighting in Bosnia.
Dec.	Former communists win outright majority in Bulgaria. 4-month truce agreed in Bosnia.
Dec. 1	Russia gives ultimatum to breakaway Chechen Republic to disband army and free all prisoners; failure to reach agreement leads to major military assault on Chechen Republic (27th). (See p. 330 for the Chechnya conflict.)
1995 Mar. 1	In Poland, former communist Jozef Oleksy elected Prime Minister following resignation of Waldemar Pawlak.
May	Croatian forces open fighting against Serbs. NATO planes attack Serb positions and Bosnian Serbs again take UN hostages.
June	Russia and Ukraine finally settle dispute over Black Sea fleet. Western nations send 'rapid reaction' force to Bosnia.
July	Serb forces overrun UN safe areas of Srebrenica and Zepa; by the end of the month photographic evidence of mass graves leads to the indictment of Bosnian Serb leader, Radovan Karadzic, and military chief, Ratko Mladic, for crimes against humanity.
Aug.	Further Serb mortar attacks on Sarajevo lead to NATO air strikes against Bosnian Serb military positions.
Oct. 12	New ceasefire comes into effect in Bosnia.
Nov.	Polish President Lech Walesa defeated by former communist Aleksander Kwasniewski in presidential election. Shevardnadze wins new term as President of Georgia.
Nov. 1	Yugoslav peace talks open in Dayton, Ohio; peace plan agreed (21st).
Nov. 3	President Yeltsin forced to relinquish control of four key ministries after second heart attack.
Dec. 14	Yugoslav peace agreement signed in Paris (14th).
Dec. 26	Yeltsin resumes powers.
1996 Jan.	Resignation of Polish Prime Minister Oleksy over allegations of once spying for Russia.
Jan. 5	Resignation of liberal Russian Foreign Minister Andrei Kozrev.
Feb. 15	President Yeltsin announces intention of seeking second term.
Feb. 29	Siege of Sarajevo officially ends.

Apr.	Presidents of Belarus and Russia sign a treaty providing for political, economic and military integration.
May	Ruling Albanian Democratic Party claims to have won 100 of 140 seats in general election; widespread protests by opposition.
June	Ruling Civic Democratic Party wins Czech elections.
July	Prime Minister of Ukraine survives an assassination attempt.
July 4	Yeltsin wins presidential election in second round run-off.
Sept.	First elections in Bosnia.
Nov.	Constitutional referendum in Belarus gives greater powers to President.
Dec.	Romanian general election won by reform candidate. Persistent street demonstrations in Serbia against government's refusal to accept opposition successes in municipal elections.
1997 Jan.	Serbian government concedes opposition victories after international inspection. Growing attacks on Serbian leaders in Kosovo by separatist Kosovo Liberation Army (KLA). Massive street demonstrations in Bulgaria against socialist (ex-communist) government. Serious rioting in major towns in Albania. Russian withdrawal of troops from Chechnya completed.
Mar.	Reorganization of Russian government favours reformists.
June	Internationally supervised elections held in Albania.
July	Federal Parliament elects Milosević Yugoslav President.
July 8	Hungary, Poland and the Czech Republic are invited to join NATO.
Nov.	Russian agreement with Japan aims at ending dispute over Kurile Islands and formally ends Second World War.
1998 Jan.	Havel re-elected President in Czech Republic. National Assembly in Poland ratifies Concordat with Roman Catholic Church.
Feb.–Mar.	Serbian police kill dozens of ethnic Albanians in operations against separatists. Massive anti-Serb demonstrations in Pristina, capital of Kosovo.
Mar.	Dismissal of Russian Prime Minister Chernomyrdin by Yeltsin.
Apr.	Sergei Kiriyenko confirmed as Prime Minister in Russia. Serbs vote 95% against international intervention in a referendum.
May	Shuttle diplomacy by US envoy Richard Holbrooke.
June	Viktor Orban becomes Prime Minister in Hungary.
July	Zeman becomes Prime Minister in Czech Republic.

July–Aug.	KLA expands control to 40–50% of Kosovo. Massive Serbian offensive weakens KLA. Continued heavy fighting.
Aug.	Kiriyenko dismissed; Yeltsin reappoints Chernomyrdin.
Sept.	Yevgenii Primakov approved by Duma as compromise candidate after Duma continues to reject the reappointment of Chernomyrdin. US demands ceasefire in Kosovo. UN Security Council endorses call.
Oct.	NATO allies authorize air strikes; Milosević agrees to withdraw troops (27th). Observers from Organization for Security and Co-operation in Europe (OSCE) to enter Kosovo.
Nov.	Constitutional Court confirms Yeltsin cannot stand for a further term in presidency.
Dec.	Renewed clashes of KLA with Serb border guards. Mediation attempts by US envoy Christopher Hill.

1999	Jan. 15	Discovery of 45 bodies (presumed ethnic Albanbians) in village of Racak. Expulsion of OSCE chief (18th).
	Feb. 6–23	Peace talks at Rambouillet fail to achieve breakthrough over Kosovo.
	Mar.	Czech Republic, Hungary and Poland become full members of NATO.
	Mar. 18–19	Peace deal signed by Kosovo Albanians in Paris. Rejected by Yugoslavia. Massing of Yugoslav troops around Kosovo.
	Mar. 20	Yugoslav armed units begin ethnic cleansing of Kosovo.
	Mar. 24	NATO aircraft begin air strikes against Yugoslav targets. Start of the NATO war on Yugoslavia over Kosovo (see p. 331).
	Apr.	NATO missiles hit Belgrade Ministry of Interior, Socialist Party of Serbia HQ, etc. Yeltsin warns NATO. Sacking of Serb Deputy Prime Minister Vuk Draskovic.
	May 27	Confirmation by UN War Crimes Tribunal that Milosević has been indicted as a war criminal. NATO war missions continue.
	June 10	Suspension of NATO bombing campaign after withdrawal of Serb troops from Kosovo. Subsequent stationing of NATO troops in Kosovo (KFOR) which became an international protectorate.
	Dec.	Solidarity announces its withdrawal from Polish politics to become an 'organization of employees'.
	Dec. 31	Resignation of Yeltsin in Russia.

2000	Feb.	Moldova becomes first former Soviet republic to vote Communist Party back into power.
	Mar. 26	Putin elected as President of Russian Federation.

June	Ferenc Madl elected President of Hungary. Andrej Bajuk's government takes office in Slovenia. Arrest of Russian media tycoon Vladimir Gusinsky.
Sept.	Election called for 24th (after amendment to Yugoslav constitution allows Milosević to serve two more terms). Bitterly disputed and rigged election. Federal Elections Commission calls for second round of voting. Growing discontent and protests in Serbia.
Oct.	Kwasniewski re-elected President of Poland.
Oct. 3	Milosević threatens growing number of protesters with crackdown.
Oct. 4	Protests gather momentum in southern Serbian town of Nis; despatch of thousands of riot police to fight striking miners south of Belgrade.
Oct. 5	Storming of Serbian parliament in Belgrade. Workers and sympathisers break through barriers, setting fire to parliament building.
Oct. 6	Milosević (now ousted from power) has meeting with Russian Foreign Minister.
Oct. 7	Kostunica sworn in as President.
Oct. 10	Belgrade renews diplomatic ties with UK and other NATO countries.
Dec.	Ion Illiescu re-elected President in Romania.
2001 Mar.	Arrest of Milosević (30th) after long police surveillance.
Apr. 5	Moldovan Parliament elects Communist Party leader Vladimir Voronin as President – first ex-Soviet republic to elect a communist to be head of state.
Apr. 26	Dismissal of Ukraine's pro-Western and reformist Prime Minister, Viktor Yushchenko.
June 17	National Movement for Simeon II wins Bulgarian election (with 120 seats and 43% of the vote), defeating ruling UDF (Union of Democratic Forces). Bulgaria becomes first eastern European country where a former monarch has made a political comeback.
July	Former King Simeon II (Simeon Saxe-Coburgotski) formally returns to power as Prime Minister in Bulgaria. Milosević taken to The Hague to face War Crimes Tribunal. President Kostunica appoints Dragisa Pesic (of Montenegrin Socialist People's Party) as Prime Minister (17th). Russia and China sign Treaty of Friendship, cementing the post-Soviet relations of their countries. Land Bill passes Duma (257–130), reversing nationalization of land carried out in Soviet era.
Aug.	Ohrid peace deal agreed in Macedonia (13th).

Sept.	Arms embargo on Yugoslavia (imposed in Mar. 1998) lifted by UN Security Council (marks end of last international sanctions against Belgrade). Polish general election gives electoral humiliation to Solidarity, the movement that had destroyed communism.
Nov.	Bulgarian presidential election won by former communist Georgi Parvanov (now Socialist Party leader).
2002 Feb.	Trial of Milosević at The Hague begins.
Mar.	Serbia and Montenegro announce agreement in principle to reconstitute their country as the 'Union of Serbia and Montenegro'.
Sept. 2	Slovakia returns pro-Western coalition in key elections.
Oct.	Swing to Nationalists in Bosnia and Herzegovina. Moscow theatre terrorist siege leaves 129 dead.
2003 Mar.	Putin signs decree giving extended powers to FSB (the sucessor to the KGB); referendum in Chechnya.
Oct.	Arrest in Russia of billionaire oil magnate Mikhail Khodorkovsky.
Nov.	Swing to Nationalists in Croatian elections. Massive protests in Ukraine call for resignation of the Prime Minister and rejection of cutbacks in public services. Vote rigging in Georgian elections precipitates 'Rose Revolution' to oust Shevadnardze.
Dec.	Russian parliamentary elections result in easy victory for United Russia, the pro-Putin party. Communists a distant second (7th). Ultra-nationalists (the Radical Party of Vojislav Seselj) win Serbian general election, but fail to obtain a majority.
2004 Feb.	Latvian politician Indulis Emsis nominated to become Europe's first Green Prime Minister (20th). Death of President Trajkovski of Macedonia in air crash (26th). Impeachment proceedings loom against Lithuanian President. Abrupt dismissal of Russian Prime Minister by President Putin. Replaced by Mikhail Fradkov (in March).
Apr.	Landslide presidential election victory for Putin. Lithuanian President Paksas became first European leader to face impeachment. Autocratic Slovak politician Vladimir Meciar heads presidential election race. Seven former communist countries, including the Baltic States, Bulgaria and Romania, admitted to NATO.
May	Expansion of EU embraces former communist countries (1st)

(see p. 264). Assassination of Chechen's pro-Putin President Akhmad Kadyrov (9th).

Sept.   Massacre at Beslan School in North Ossetia as troops storm terrorist hostage-takers: around 335 killed. Putin tightens his control of Russia in the aftermath.

Nov.   Political crisis in Ukraine after pro-Western opposition candidate, Viktor Yushchenko, denied victory in presidential election. Beginning of widespread street protests (the 'Orange Revolution').

Dec.   Yushchenko victorious in re-run of presidential election ordered by Supreme Court. Yushchenko finally installed as president in Jan. 2005.

WESTERN EUROPE SINCE 1945

1945 June 5	Allied Control Commission set up to administer Germany.
July	Churchill voted out as Prime Minister in Britain; Labour Party under Attlee takes power, pledges to introduce a 'welfare state'.
Dec.	De Gasperi becomes Prime Minister of Italy as head of Christian Democrat Party.
1946 Jan.	De Gaulle resigns as President of French Provisional Government after his draft constitution is rejected; he tries to rally right-wing opinion in his non-party, *Rassemblement du Peuple Français* (RPF)
Mar.	Churchill makes 'Iron Curtain' speech at Fulton, Missouri.
May	King Victor Emmanuel II of Italy abdicates; a referendum votes Italy a Republic.
July	Bread rationing introduced in Britain; more severe rationing than the war because of economic crisis.
Oct.	Fourth Republic established in France.
Dec.	Britain and USA agree economic merger of their zones in Germany.
1947 Mar.	Anglo-French Treaty of Alliance.
June	General Marshall proposes economic aid to rebuild Europe; Paris Conference (July) meets to discuss the 'Marshall Plan'.
1948 Apr.	Organization for European Economic Co-operation (OEEC) set up to receive $17,000 million of Marshall aid from the United States. Member states: Austria, Belgium, Denmark, France, West Germany, Greece, Iceland, Ireland, Italy, Luxembourg, the Netherlands, Norway, Portugal, Spain, Sweden, Switzerland, Turkey and the United Kingdom. Customs Union set up between Belgium, the Netherlands and Luxembourg – 'Benelux'.
1949 May 23	German Federal Republic comes into existence on basis of constitution drafted the previous year with Konrad Adenauer as first Federal Chancellor. Council of Europe set up for 'political co-operation', consisting of the OEEC states apart from Spain and Portugal. Strasbourg becomes headquarters for a Consultative Assembly.
Aug. 24	North Atlantic Treaty Organisation (NATO) formed including United States, Canada, United Kingdom, Norway, Denmark, Holland, Belgium, France, Italy, Greece and Turkey.

1950	Britain rejects idea of joining a European coal and steel community.
1951 Apr. 18	Paris Treaty between Benelux countries (Belgium, Netherlands and Luxembourg), France, Italy and West Germany – 'the Six' – sets up a 'Common Market' in coal and steel. A European Commission is set up as the supreme authority.
Oct.	Fall of Labour Government in Britain; Churchill returns to office. De Gaulle retires from politics.
1952 Oct.	Britain explodes an atomic bomb in Monte Bello islands, off north-west Australia.
1953	European Court of Human Rights set up in Strasbourg.
1954	Western European Union proposed by the British as a substitute for a single European army.
May	Defeat for French forces at Dien Bien Phu (see p. 462).
Aug.	Death of De Gasperi, Christian Democrat Prime Minister of Italy 1945–53.
1955 Jan.	Germany joins NATO.
Apr. 5	Resignation of Churchill as British Prime Minister. Anthony Eden takes over. Messina Conference of 'the Six' discusses a full customs union. Britain expresses preference for a larger free trade area of the OEEC countries.
1956 Oct.–Nov.	Anglo-French intervention at Suez (see p. 488).
1957 Jan. 9	Fall of Eden as a consequence of Suez crisis; Harold Macmillan takes over (10th) as Prime Minister.
Mar. 25	Rome Treaties between 'the Six' set up the European Economic Community (EEC) and Euratom.
1958 May	Rioting by French settlers in Algeria leads to French army taking over (13th); De Gaulle voted into power in France after period of chronic political instability (29th) and given power to produce a new constitution.
Oct. 9–28	Death of Pope Pius XII; election of John XXIII.
Dec. 21	De Gaulle elected President of Fifth French Republic.
1959 Nov.	European Free Trade Association (EFTA) set up as a counterweight to the EEC, comprising Austria, Denmark, Norway, Portugal, Sweden, Switzerland and the United Kingdom.
1960 Feb.	France explodes its first atomic device.

1961 Apr. 21	French army revolt begins in Algeria against De Gaulle's plans for Algerian independence.
Aug. 10	United Kingdom, Ireland and Denmark apply for membership of EEC; also Norway (1962).
Aug. 17–18	Berlin Wall erected to halt flood of refugees to West.
1962	EEC agrees Common Agricultural Policy to come into operation in 1964; a system of high guaranteed prices to be paid for out of a common fund; beginning of period of agricultural prosperity in rural Europe and huge food surpluses.
Dec.	Britain arranges with USA to adopt Polaris missile system as its nuclear deterrent.
1963 Jan.	De Gaulle vetoes British entry into EEC; Irish, Danish and Norwegian applications suspended.
June 3–21	Death of John XXIII; election of Pope Paul VI.
Aug. 5	France refuses to sign Test Ban Treaty, signalling intention to build up *force de frappe*.
Oct.	Adenauer retires as Chancellor of Germany; succeeded by Dr Ludwig Erhard.
1964 Oct.	Labour, under Harold Wilson, returns to power in Britain after 13 years of Conservative rule.
1966 Mar.	France withdraws from Military Committee of NATO. Labour government re-elected in Britain.
Nov. 30	Dr Kurt-Georg Kiesinger becomes Chancellor of Germany.
1967 Nov. 27	Further British, Irish, Danish and Norwegian application to join EEC vetoed by De Gaulle.
1968 May	Violent student unrest in Paris and mass strikes against De Gaulle's government.
Sept.	Dr Salazar of Portugal, Western Europe's longest surviving dictator, succeeded by Dr Marcello Caetano.
1969 Apr. 28	De Gaulle resigns as President after unfavourable vote in referendum on the constitution; Gaullist Georges Pompidou becomes President.
Aug.	First British troops sent to Northern Ireland (see p. 317).
Oct.	German Social Democrats take power under Willy Brandt; begins policy of *Ostpolitik*, seeking friendly relations with Eastern Europe, and encourages enlargement of EEC.
1970 Mar.	Heads of East and West Germany meet for first time.
June 18	Defeat of Labour government in Britain. Edward Heath, a committed European, leads Conservative government.

Nov. 9	Death of De Gaulle.
1971 Oct. 28	British Parliament votes in favour of application to join the Common Market.
1972 Mar. 24	Britain imposes direct rule in Northern Ireland.
Apr.	Defection from German coalition leads to early election in Nov.
Sept. 5	Arab terrorists kill Israeli athletes at Munich Olympics.
Nov.	Brandt's government returned to power with SPD as largest party in Bundestag.
1973 Jan	Britain, Denmark and Ireland join EEC; Norway does not, following unfavourable referendum vote.
May	Britain in dispute with Iceland over fishing rights – 'Cod War'.
June 22	West and East Germany join the United Nations.
Dec.	Conservative Prime Minister Heath declares state of emergency as a result of miners' strike.
1974 Feb. 28	Heath defeated in general election; Labour government in Britain under Wilson.
Apr. 2	Death of Georges Pompidou; Giscard d'Estaing becomes President (May).
Apr. 25	Military junta deposes Portuguese government, ending dictatorship and colonial wars.
May	Willy Brandt resigns following security scandal; Helmut Schmidt takes over as Chancellor.
Sept. 30	General Spinola resigns and replaced by Costa Gomes in Portugal.
Oct. 10	Labour Party in Britain obtains small majority at general election.
1975 Jan.	British government announces referendum on EEC membership
Feb. 28	German opposition leader, Peter Lorenz, kidnapped by terrorists.
Apr. 25	Portugal holds first free elections for 50 years.
June	Britain votes by two to one in referendum to remain in EEC. Greece, Spain and Portugal apply for membership.
Nov. 20	Death of Franco; King Juan Carlos I succeeds to the throne (27th).
Dec.	Terrorist attacks by Indonesian immigrants in the Netherlands.
1976 Apr. 5	James Callaghan becomes Prime Minister of Britain following resignation of Harold Wilson.

Sept. 19   Social Democratic Party in Sweden defeated for first time in 44 years.

1977 June 15   First general election in Spain for 40 years.
Señor Suarez's Democratic Centre Party wins power.

Sept. 5   German terrorists kill Dr Hans-Martin Schleyer, head of West German Employers' Federation.

1978 Mar. 16   Aldo Moro, former Prime Minister of Italy, kidnapped in Rome by Italian terrorists; found dead (9 May).

Aug. 6–26   Death of Pope Paul VI; election of John Paul I.

Sept. 28–Oct. 16   Death of Pope John Paul I; election of John Paul II, former Cardinal Karol Wojtyla, first non-Italian Pope for 400 years.

Dec. 27   First democratic government in Spain.

Dec.–Apr.   'Winter of Discontent' in Britain with widespread strikes against Labour government's wage policy.

1979 May 3   Conservatives under Margaret Thatcher take power following general election in Britain.
European Monetary System (EMS) introduced with common European Currency Unit (ECU) linking the exchange rates of the individual countries.

June   First direct elections to the European Parliament.

1980 Apr. 30–May 5   Iranian embassy in London seized by terrorists and stormed by British specialist anti-terrorist forces, the SAS.

Aug. 2   Terrorist bomb explodes at Bologna railway station killing 76 people.

Oct. 5   German coalition of SPD and Free Democrats retains power in elections.

Dec. 4   Prime Minister of Portugal, Dr da Carneiro, killed in air crash.

1981 Jan. 1   Greece becomes member of EEC.

Feb. 23   Attempted coup in Spain led by Lt-Col. Trejero Molina; leaders arrested.

Mar. 26   Social Democratic Party formed in Britain by breakaway of four senior figures from Labour Party.

May 10   François Mitterrand, leader of socialists, becomes President of France in place of Giscard d'Estaing.

May 13   Pope John Paul II shot and injured by Turkish terrorist.

July   Rioting in several inner city areas of Britain.

Nov.   Sensational by-election successes of British SDP/Liberal Alliance lead to predictions of Alliance victory if an election called.

1982 April	Britain sends Task Force to recapture Falkland Islands from Argentina (see p. 325).
May 30	Spain joins NATO.
June 15	Argentine forces on Falklands surrender.
Sept. 19	Social Democrats return to power in Sweden.
Oct.	Felipe Gonzales leads socialists to victory in Spanish elections.
	Helmut Kohl of Christian Democrats becomes Chancellor of Germany following break-up of governing coalition.

1983 Mar.	Crisis economic package in France and Cabinet reshuffle.
Mar. 6	Helmut Kohl wins a substantial electoral victory; Green Party passes 5% threshhold for seats in the Bundestag.
June 9	Margaret Thatcher returned for second term of office in Britain. Labour Party and Alliance split the opposition vote.

1984 Mar. 9	Beginning of 12-month miners' strike in Britain.
Apr. 20	Britain confirms intention to leave Hong Kong in 1997 when the lease from China expires.
July 19	French communists withdraw support from Mitterrand.
Sept. 4	Herr Honecker, East German premier, cancels trip to West Germany because of Soviet opposition.
Oct.	IRA bomb explosion at Grand Hotel, Brighton, narrowly misses killing Margaret Thatcher.

| 1985 Nov. | Anglo-Irish agreement signed between Mrs Thatcher and Dr Fitzgerald, the Irish premier, giving Irish government a consultative role in Northern Irish affairs. |
| Dec. | Single European Act agreed at Luxembourg Summit. |

1986 Jan. 1	Spain and Portugal join the Common Market.
Jan.	2 cabinet ministers resign in Britain over 'Westland Affair'.
Mar. 12	Referendum in Spain favours continued membership of NATO.
Mar.	General election in France gives socialists largest number of seats, but neo-Gaullist Jacques Chirac forms government; beginning of period of 'cohabitation' between socialist President Mitterrand and conservative Chirac.
June 22	Gonzales and socialists returned to power in Spanish elections.

| 1987 Jan. 25 | Helmut Kohl's government confirmed in office at elections. |
| June 11 | Margaret Thatcher wins an unprecedented third term as Prime Minister of Britain. |

| 1988 Apr.–May | Mitterrand defeats Chirac in French Presidential elections. |

June 5–12	Mitterrand calls elections for National Assembly but fails to achieve the expected overall majority.
Sept. 20	Margaret Thatcher's 'Bruges Speech' attacks EEC attempts to introduce socialism by the back door.

1989 June   European elections witness rise in Green votes throughout Europe. Socialist bloc increases substantially in European Parliament.

June–July   Victory of Polish Solidarity movement in elections (June) and formation of first non-communist government in Poland signals beginning of breakdown of East European Communist regimes.

Sept.   Hungary opens borders with Austria, allowing flight of thousands of East Germans to West.

Nov.   Collapse of East German regime; opening of Berlin Wall (9 Nov.); freedom of travel to West granted. Chancellor Kohl calls for united Germany. Reformer, Hans Modrow, becomes East German premier.

Dec.   First Four-Power Conference since 1971 to discuss future of Berlin and East Europe. Cold War declared ended at Malta Summit. Brandenburg Gate opened and Kohl visits East Germany to wide acclaim. Preparations for free elections in East Germany.

1990 Jan.   East German elections brought forward to March.

Feb.   East German proposal for their neutrality rejected by West Germany. West German Cabinet agrees to currency union between East and West Germany.

Mar.   Pro-unification Alliance for Germany wins East German elections and prepares for economic union in July and all-German elections in December.

July   Economic unification of East and West Germany on the basis of the West German currency. West German–Soviet agreement that a united Germany will have full sovereignty, including the right to join NATO. The Soviet Union agrees to withdraw its troops from East Germany within three to four years.

Oct. 3   Political unification of East and West Germany.

Nov.   Margaret Thatcher replaced as Conservative leader by John Major following leadership contest.

Dec.   First all-German elections since 1932 result in victory for Chancellor Kohl's conservative coalition.

1991 Jan.   Italian Communist Party changes name to 'Democratic Party of the Left' (PDS) and adopts sweeping changes in policy.

Jan.–Feb.	British and French forces participate in Gulf War against Iraq.
Mar.	British government abandons Poll Tax.
Apr.	German Chancellor Kohl suffers humiliating defeat in Rhineland–Palatinate local elections.
May	Resignation of French premier Rocard; Mme Cresson becomes France's first woman Prime Minister.
July–Oct.	European Community makes failed attempts to obtain ceasefire agreement in Yugoslavian conflict.
Oct.	Luxembourg draft plan on European Monetary Union of European Community fails to win agreement.
Dec.	Maastricht Summit on economic and political union. Britain wins opt-out clauses on monetary union and Social Charter.
1992 Apr.	Pierre Bérégovoy appointed Prime Minister in France (2nd); President Francesco Cossiga resigns in Italy. John Major leads Conservatives to fourth election victory in Britain (9th).
May	France's President Mitterrand and Germany's Chancellor Helmut Kohl announce creation of a Franco-German 'Eurocorps'.
June	Socialist Unity Party leader Giuliano Amato becomes Italian Prime Minister, leading Italy's 51st administration since the war.
Aug.	Demonstrations and acts of violence against foreign workers in Germany lead to call for restrictions on asylum provisions.
Sept.	Constitutional changes in Belgium devolve more power to regions.
Nov. 23	Neo-Nazi fire bombing in Möln kills 3 Turkish women.
1993 Jan.	Social Democrat coalition government takes office in Denmark.
Feb.	Belgium takes first steps towards a federal state.
Apr.	Italian referendum approves modification of proportional representation system for elections to Senate; Carlo Ciampi forms new government after resignation of Amato.
June	Spanish Workers' Socialist Party wins general election with reduced majority.
Aug.	Italian Senate and Chamber of Deputies approve of electoral reform for the Chamber.
Nov.	General Strike in Belgium against economic austerity package.
1994 Mar. 28	Right-wing and nationalist Freedom Alliance coalition wins overwhelming victory in elections to reformed parliament in Italy.
Apr.	Silvio Berlusconi appointed Italian Prime Minister.

June	Resignation of French Socialist Party leader, Michel Rocard, after defeat in European elections.
Aug.	Labour Party leader Wim Kok leads coalition government in the Netherlands. IRA announce a ceasefire in Northern Ireland.
Oct. 16	Chancellor Helmut Kohl's ruling Christian Democrat coalition remains in power following general election.
Nov. 16	Fall of Irish government led by Albert Reynolds.
Dec. 22	Resignation of Prime Minister Berlusconi after Northern League abandons coalition government.
1995 Jan. 13	Former Italian Treasury Minister, Lamberto Dini, appointed new Prime Minister.
Apr. 23	Lionel Jospin, the French socialist candidate, wins most votes in first round of presidential elections.
May 7	Jacques Chirac wins French presidential election.
Oct. 12	Socialist Party takes power in Portugal as minority government, ending ten years of Social Democratic rule.
Nov. 15	French Prime Minister Alain Juppé introduces reforms to cut health and social security expenditure.
1996 Jan. 8	Death of former President François Mitterrand. Resignation of Greek Prime Minister, Andreas Papandreou, due to ill-health; replaced by Costas Simitis.
Mar. 3	In Spain, conservative Popular Party, led by José Maria Aznar, defeats ruling socialists in general election.
Apr. 21	Olive Tree Alliance wins Italian general election; former Italian Prime Minister, Bettino Craxi, fined £15 million and sentenced to 8 years' imprisonment for corruption.
May	Strikes in Germany against austerity measures.
July	Following end of conscription, announced in May, France announces the disbandment of a quarter of regiments to create a purely professional army by 2002.
July 8	NATO offers membership to Hungary, Poland and the Czech Republic.
1997 Jan.	Spain refuses to recognize Gibraltar-issued passports.
Feb.	Widespread protests in France against new law to control illegal immigration.
Mar.	Kohl declares willingness to stand for re-election as Chancellor in 1998. Flood of refugees from Albania leads to declaration of state of emergency in Italy.
May–June	General election in France. Centre-right heavily defeated by socialists and communists. Resignation of Alain Juppé. Lionel Jospin becomes Prime Minister.

July	Kidnap and murder of Basque town councillor by ETA leads to 6-million-strong protests in Spain.
Sept.	Catholic Church accepts responsibility for its part in wartime deportation of Jews in France.
Oct.	Romano Prodi survives in office in Italy despite split with his communist partners.
1998 Feb.	French parliament approves reduction in working week to 35 hours by 2000.
Mar.	Advances by National Front in regional elections in France secure it the balance of power in several areas. Premier of Lower Saxony, Gerhard Schröder, selected as Social Democrat to run against Kohl.
Apr.	France ratifies treaty banning testing of nuclear weapons. French parliament votes 334 to 49 to join the single European currency.
May	Official inauguration of the single European currency in the European Union.
Sept.	Helmut Kohl ousted in general election; Social Democrats under Schröder seek coalition with Greens.
Oct.	Renewed crisis for Romano Prodi after Communists withdraw from government. Prodi defeated by one vote in confidence motion over tough budget. Massimo D'Alema constructs new coalition.
1999 Feb.	Schröder loses majority in Upper House after gains by Christian Democrats in Hessen.
Mar.	Resignation of Oskar Lafontaine as Finance Minister (succeeded by Hans Eichel). Schröder succeeds Lafontaine as party chairman. Romano Prodi nominated to succeed Jacques Santer as EU commission president.
May	Carlo Azeglio Ciampi (treasury minister) elected President of Italy.
Aug.	First hints of scandal involving Kohl and undisclosed financial donations to party.
Oct.	Further electoral defeat for Social Democrats in Berlin elections (SDP take only 22.4%, former Communists secure 18%). Guterres leads Socialist Party to major victory in Portugal.
Dec.	Election of Johannes Rau as President of Germany. Helmut Kohl faces increasing pressure over allegations that secret contributions had been made to the Christian Democrats.
2000 Jan.	Death of Italian politician Bettino Craxi. Resignation of Helmut Kohl as honorary chairman of Christian Democrats.

	Mar.	José Maria Aznar wins overall majority in Spanish general election.
	Sept.	Referendum in France approves reduction in length of presidential term from 7 to 5 years (70% majority on 30% turnout).
2001	Jan.	Jorge Sampaio re-elected as President for second term in Portugal.
	June	Collapse of 'grand coalition' in Berlin which had ruled the city for a decade.
	Dec.	Resignation of Guterres as Prime Minister in Portugal. José Manuel Durao Barroso becomes Prime Minister.
2002	Feb.	Italian Senate votes by overwhelming majority to allow return of male heirs of country's royal family, the House of Savoy.
	Mar.	Massive demonstration (2 million march in Rome) against terrorism and anti-labour laws. Left loses Portuguese general election.
	Aug.	Spanish MPs vote to ban ETA's political wing.
	Sept.	Schröder narrowly retains power in closest-fought postwar German elections (helped by strong showing of Greens). Stoiber's Christian Democrats poll strongly, but weak performance by their Free Democrat allies.
2003	July	Home rule referendum in Corsica.
	Dec.	Italy rocked by financial scandals in Parmalat company. Conviction of 15 members of 17 Nov. terrorist group in Greece. Arrest of leading ETA leaders, Gorka Palacios and Juan Luís Rubenach 'decapitates' group's leadership.
2004	Feb.	Resignation of Gerhard Schröder as chairman of SPD (he remains as German Chancellor).
	Mar.	Carnage in Madrid; 191 die and over 1,400 injured in al-Qaeda terrorist bombing of rail network. Surprise victory for Left follows in Spanish general election.
	Apr.	Largest expansion in NATO's history as 7 former communist states join (including Baltic States, Bulgaria and Romania).
	May	European Union expansion brings in Baltic States and former members of communist Eastern bloc.
	Oct.	New Treaty of Rome signed by EU states.
	Dec.	EU offers to start membership negotiations in Oct. 2005 with Turkey.

THE MIDDLE EAST

THE MIDDLE EAST SINCE 1914

1914   Outbreak of the First World War; Turkey joins the Central Powers (see p. 458).
       Egypt becomes a British Protectorate.
       British force sent to Mesopotamia to safeguard the Persian oil-fields.

1915   British advance on Baghdad, but fall back on Kut (Nov.) and besieged by Turks.

1916   Sykes–Picot agreement between Britain and France divides the Middle Eastern provinces of the Turkish Empire – Syria, Lebanon, Palestine and Iraq – between the two powers.
       Fall of Kut.

1917   Balfour Declaration on a Jewish homeland in the Middle East (for Palestine see pp. 94–8).
       General Allenby takes Jerusalem (Dec.); growing success of 'Arab Revolt' led by T. E. Lawrence and Amir Feisal.

1918   British take Amman and Damascus; French naval forces take Beirut.
       British forces free Iraq from Turkish rule (Sept.–Oct.).
       War in Middle East officially ends (31 Oct.).
       Wilson's 'Fourteen Points' propose 'self-determination'; Anglo-French agreement promises independence to peoples 'oppressed by the Turks'.
       Egyptians call for a delegation (a *Wafd*) at Versailles.

1919   Vice President of Egyptian legislative council, Saad Pasha Zaghlul, arrested and deported; Wafdist revolt by students in Cairo put down by force and over 1,000 killed (Mar.).
       Zaghlul released and attends peace conference at Versailles; President Wilson recognizes the British Protectorate (Apr.).
       Milner Commission on Egypt set up (Oct.).
       King Feisal proclaimed King of Syria (Mar.).

1920   Britain given League of Nations' mandates over Palestine, Transjordan and Iraq; France given mandates over Syria and Lebanon (Apr.).
       King Feisal expelled from Syria by French (July).
       Iraqi National Government set up, transferring government from military to civil rule (Nov.).

Breakdown of talks between Milner and Wafd leader, Zaghlul.
Soviet forces occupy northern Iran.

1921   Cairo Conference invites Feisal to become King of Iraq (Mar.);
confirmed by plebiscite (June).
Following Wafdist demonstrations, Zaghlul deported (Dec.).
Further protest strikes and demonstrations (Dec.–Mar.).
Reza Shah Pahlevi leads coup in Persia (Iran); Soviet troops leave.

1922   Egyptian protectorate ended and Egypt declared independent but with
Britain retaining its imperial communications via the Suez Canal, the
defence of Egypt and the Sudan, and the protection of foreign interests
and minorities (Feb.).
Sultan Faud becomes King of Egypt and Zaghlul released (Mar.);
Constitutional Committee set up to draft constitution (Apr.).
Anglo-Iraqi treaty signed accepting implementation of mandate.
Palestine west of River Jordan becomes part of British mandate for
Palestine; eastern area becomes part of Transjordan.

1923   Overwhelming election victory for the Wafd in general election (Sept.).
Reza Shah Pahlavi becomes Prime Minister of Iran.

1924   Zaghlul becomes Prime Minister of Egypt (Jan.).
Resigns following assassination of Sir Lee Stack, British Commander-in-
Chief (Nov.).
General Sarrail becomes High Commissioner of Syria; outbreak of
Druze rebellion.
Constituent Assembly of Iraq meets for first time (Mar.); ratifies 1922
Treaty.
British troops withdraw from Iran.
Hussein Ibn Ali, King of Hejaz, driven from his kingdom by Ibn
Saud.

1925   Wafdists gain majority in new general elections in Egypt. Zaghlul
prevented from becoming Premier by High Commissioner, Lord Lloyd.
Reza Shah Pahlavi overthrows last of the Qajar dynasty and establishes
his own as Shahs of Iran.

1926   Final suppression of Druze revolt in Syria.

1927   Death of Zaghlul; Mustafa al-Nahhas succeeds as leader of Wafd.

1930   Last Anglo-Iraqi treaty signed relinquishing British control apart from
retention of two air bases (June).

1932   Iraq joins League of Nations (Oct.).
Saudi Arabia Kingdom created by Ibn Saud.

1935   League of Nations awards Iraq control over Shatt-al-Arab waterway.

1936   Anglo-Egyptian Treaty; proposals for Franco-Syrian treaty agreed but
       not ratified.
       Discovery of oil in Saudi Arabia.

1938   Saudi Arabian oil production begins.

1939   French forces in Syria and Lebanon reinforced.
       Outbreak of Second World War (see pp. 45–50).

1940   British defeat Italian forces operating from Libya.

1941   British and Free French forces occupy Syria and Lebanon.
       German troops sent to assist Italians in North Africa (Feb.).
       Reza Shah Pahlavi deposed by British in Iran for pro-German sympathies
       and replaced by his son, Mohammed.
       British and Soviet troops occupy Iran for duration of war.

1942   German and Italian forces drive British back to El Alamein (June).
       British victory at El Alamein and pursuit of German and Italian forces
       across Libya into Tunisia (Oct.–May).

1943   Axis armies in Tunis surrender (May).
       Independent Lebanese state established.

1944   Free French concede Syrian independence.

1945   Formation of the Arab League by Egypt and five other Arab states in
       March (see p. 261).
       Fighting in Syria over delay in implementing French withdrawal.

1946   Syria becomes fully independent of the French.
       Abdullah Ibn Hussein becomes King of Jordan.

1948   State of Israel established.

1948–9   Arab–Israeli War (see pp. 302–3).
       Jordan seizes West Bank and part of Jerusalem; Egypt takes Gaza.

1949   Britain recognizes Mohammed Idris al-Senussi as Emir of Libya.

1950   Jordan annexes the West Bank of Palestine.

1951   Military government in Syria.
       Idris becomes King of Libya as an independent state.
       Iran nationalizes oilfields and refineries, including giant Abadan complex.

1952   Anti-British riots in Egypt.

1953   Overthrow of the Egyptian monarchy; Egypt becomes a Republic and
       one-party state; disbanding of the Wafd and other groupings.

1954   Civilian rule returns to Syria.

1956   Gamal Abdel Nasser elected President of Egypt; nationalization of the Suez Canal and Suez invasion by Anglo-French and Israeli forces (see p. 488).

1958   Anti-Western insurrection in Lebanon put down with assistance of US marines.
Military coup in Iraq, which is declared a Republic.

1961   Syria joins Egypt to form United Arab Republic (UAR).
Break-up of United Arab Republic.
Kuwait becomes an independent state; Iraq's claim to the territory resisted with the aid of British troops.

1963   *Coup d'état* brings radical Ba'ath Party to power in Syria as a socialist military government.

1964   Palestine Liberation Organization (PLO) founded by Yasser Arafat in Jordan.

1967   'Six Day' War between Israel and Arab states (see p. 315).

1968   Coup in Iraq led by Saddam Hussein and Ba'ath Party.

1969   King Idris of Libya overthrown by military coup; Revolutionary Command Council led by Qadhafi proclaims a Republic, institutes Qur'anic law, a welfare system, and economic development programme.
Colonel Nimeiri seizes power in the Sudan.

1970   Death of Nasser; Anwar Sadat becomes President of Egypt.
Palestine Liberation Organization moves headquarters to Beirut. General Assad seizes power in Syria.

1973   Qadhafi takes control of foreign-held oil interests in Libya. 'Yom Kippur' War (see p. 319).
Arab oil boycott against the West.

1975   Outbreak of fighting in Beirut.

1976   Syrian troops enter Lebanon.

1977   President Sadat visits Israel in major gesture of reconciliation. Short war between Egypt and Libya.

1979   Overthrow of the Shah's regime in Iran.
Ayatollah Khomeini returns from exile in France to Iran and becomes head of government.
Beginning of institution of Islamic fundamentalist regime in Iran and elimination of opponents.
Soviet Union invades Afghanistan and installs Babrak Karmal as head of new government; beginning of Mujaheddin resistance, partly influenced by Islamic fundamentalism.

Saddam Hussein becomes President of Iraq and begins purge of rivals and of Iraqi Shi'ite community.
Riots by Iranian fundamentalists in Mecca.

1980   Iran revives claim to Shatt-al-Arab waterway; Iraq bombs Iranian targets and launches land assault on Iran beginning Iran–Iraq War (see p. 324).

1981   President Sadat assassinated by Islamic fundamentalists. Islamic Commission fails to end Iran–Iraq War.

1982   Temporary ceasefire by Iraq fails to end the war (June). Israeli troops invade Lebanon (see p. 320); PLO evacuated from Lebanon.

1983   Major Iranian offensive recaptures much of territory seized by Iraq.

1984   Iran–Iraq War escalates into attacks on Iran's Kharg Island oil installations by Iraqis and Iranian attacks on foreign ships entering the Persian Gulf en route to Iraq and Kuwait.

1987   *Intifada* begins amongst Palestinians on West Bank and in Gaza (see p. 326).
United States and Britain step up naval activity in the Persian Gulf; Iranian mine-layer seized.
Iraqi warplane accidentally hits American frigate.
Rioting by Iranian pilgrims in Mecca put down.

1988   American warship in Persian Gulf mistakenly shoots down civilian Iranian airliner (July).
UN-sponsored peace accord with Afghanistan, USSR, USA and Pakistan for removal of Russian troops from May 1988 to be completed by Feb. 1989. Mujaheddin denounce ceasefire. PLO declare Palestinian independence and renounce terrorism.

1989   Final removal of Russian troops from Afghanistan completed but fighting continues between Mujaheddin and Marxist Kabul government under Najibullah.
Death of Ayatollah Khomeini; elections lead to his replacement as head of government by Hashami Rafsanjani.

1990   For the first time in Syria, independent candidates are allowed to run in the parliamentary elections, and they win 84 places in the 250-representative People's Assembly. The absolute majority (134 seats) is again gained by the Ba'ath Party (May). Northern and Southern Yemen are united as Yemen Republic (22 May).
Iraqi troops suddenly attack and invade Kuwait (2 Aug.). Saddam Hussein later claims Kuwait as the 19th province of Iraq (28 Aug.). The UN Security Council endorses sanctions against Iraq (6 Aug.). The United States decides to send troops to the area (7 Aug.). Next day,

Britain and other countries (among them several Arab states) join the USA in its decision. Resolution 678 of the UN Security Council presents an ultimatum to Iraq for it to withdraw its troops from Kuwait by 15 Jan. 1991 and – at the same time – authorizes the member states co-operating with Kuwait to use force against the aggressor if the ultimatum is not met (28 Nov.).

1991　The allied forces led by the United States begin their military action 'Desert Storm' against Iraq (17 Jan.). After the liberation of Kuwait and Iraq's total military defeat, military action ends with a ceasefire (28 Feb.). The truce concluding the war commences on 11 Apr.
At the general elections in Egypt the governing National Democratic Party wins 348 out of the 444 seats (Nov.).
In Syria, Assad is again re-elected for seven years as the President of the Republic.

1992　In Iran the moderate forces close to President Rafsanjani win the general election.
The UN Security Council orders economic sanctions against Libya since Libya has declined to hand over to the United States and Britain the two Libyan men who are charged with having bombed PanAm Flight 103 in Dec. 1988 (Apr.). In Saudi Arabia a 60-member Consultative Assembly is set up but the King still possesses absolute power.

1993　US forces launch bomb and rocket attacks on Iraq in response to Iraqi non-compliance with UN requirements (June).
Rafsanjani wins Iranian Presidential elections (June).
Palestine–Israeli agreement (Sept.).
UN Security Council restricts sanctions on Libya (Nov.).

1994　Outbreak of civil war in Yemen between northern and southern forces after failure to evolve a system of devolved government; northern forces capture Aden (July).
Israel and Jordan sign peace treaty (26 Oct.).

1995　Israel and PLO sign agreement on Palestinian self-rule in the West Bank (Sept.).
Yitzhak Rabin, Israeli Premier, shot dead by a Jewish nationalist at peace rally (4 Nov.).

1996　Iraq and United Nations agree to the sale of Iraqi oil up to $4 billion to pay for food and medicines.

1997　Libya agrees that two Libyans should be put on trial for bombing of PanAm Flight 103, but disputes location of that trial. Reformist Muhammad Khatami wins presidential election in Iran. Iran and Syria end two decades of enmity (Nov.).

1998   Renewed crisis over UN inspection teams in Iraq defused by visit of Kofi Annan (Feb.). Allies begin military build-up.
Iraq parliament votes to halt work of arms inspectors (Aug). Continued obstruction leads to US and UK air strikes (Dec.).

1999   Death of King Hussein of Jordan; succeeded by Prince Abdullah, his eldest son (Feb.).
Britain and Iran exchange ambassadors for first time since 1989 (May).
UN Resolution 1284 creates UN Monitoring, Verification and Inspection Commission (UNMOVIC). Resolution rejected by Iraq (Dec.).

2000   First visit to London by senior Iranian minister since 1979 (Jan.).
Hans Blix becomes Executive Chairman of UNMOVIC (Mar.).
Death of Hafez Assad after ruling Syria for three decades; his son, Bashar, nominated as successor (June).
Iraq rejects new weapons inspection proposals (Dec.).

2001   Growing crisis over Iraq as US and UK carry out bombing raids (Feb.).
Presidential election in Iran won by incumbent Muhammed Khatami (June). First visit by a British minister to Iran since 1979.
Terrorist attack on USA sees scenes of celebration in parts of Middle East (Sept.).

2002   President Bush includes Iran and Iraq, along with North Korea, in his 'axis of evil' speech (Jan.). Iran again rejects weapons inspection proposals (July). Growing crisis leads to passing of UN Resolution 1441 outlining an enhanced inspection regime for Iraq's disarmament to be conducted by UNMOVIC (Nov.).
A 'final chance' for Iraq to disarm. Iraq replies with 12,000-page dossier stating that there are no weapons of mass destruction in Iraq (Dec.).

2003   UN weapons inspectors end their mission and leave Iraq (19 Mar.).
Start of invasion of Iraq by US and British forces, the 'Second Gulf War' (21 Mar.) (see pp. 331–2). Control of country by Saddam Hussein ended by 9 Apr. Beginning of growing insurgency in Iraq against occupying forces. Saddam captured alive in Operation Red Dawn (Dec.).

2004   Continuing insurgency in Iraq. Heavy fighting in cities such as Kut, Karbala, Najaf and Fallujah. Transfer of sovereignty to Iraq (30 June).

2005   Elections held in Iraq (30 Jan.) against background of continuing violence. On a 58% turnout, Shi'ites largest party in 275-seat Assembly. The Kurdish leader, Jalal Talabani, chosen as President of Iraq (Apr.).

THE ATATÜRK REVOLUTION AND THE FALL OF THE OTTOMAN EMPIRE

1914   Turkey declares war on the Allies (Oct.).

1915   Dardanelles campaign.
British forces land on the peninsula (Apr.) but can make no headway.
Allied evacuation of Gallipoli begins (Dec.).

1916   Arab Revolt begins (June).

1917   Allies recognize Hussein as King of Hejaz (Jan.). Baghdad falls to the
Allies (Mar.). General Allenby sent to Palestine and captures Jerusalem
(Dec.).

1918   Damascus, Beirut and Aleppo are lost as the Turks withdraw from Syria.
Armistice agreement signed at Mudros (Oct.).

1919   Greek forces land at Izmir with Allied approval (May).
Mustafa Kemal (Atatürk) is officially dismissed from his command by the
Sultan.
Nationalist Congress meets at Erzurum under Kemal's chairmanship
(July).
Nationalist Congress at Sivas promulgates National Pact (Sept.).

1920   First Grand National Assembly under Kemal's Presidency meets in
Ankara (Apr.). Treaty of Sèvres is signed by the Sultan's government and
renounces all claims to non-Turkish territory.
Nationalists do not recognize this treaty (Aug.).

1921   Greek successes in Battle of Sakarya River threaten Ankara's security
(Aug.).

1922   Nationalists defeat the Greeks and recapture Izmir (Sept.). Armistice
agreement between the Nationalists and the Allies is signed (Oct.).
Kemal abolishes the Sultanate (Nov.).

1923   Treaty of Lausanne replaces Sèvres and guarantees Turkish independence
within its own frontiers (July). Kemal proclaims the Republic and
becomes President (29 Oct.).

1924   National Assembly abolishes the Caliphate, Ministry of Religious Affairs,
religious schools and religious courts (March/April). Constitution is
adopted (Apr.).

1925   Kurdish revolt is crushed (Apr.).

1926   Treaty of Ankara between Turkey, Britain and Iraq (June). Plot on
Kemal's life is uncovered. Ringleaders are tried and executed (June/July).

1928   Turkey is declared to be a secular state (Apr.). Latin alphabet is
introduced (Nov.).

1930   Religious riot at Menemen followed by executions (Dec.).

1932   Turkey joins the League of Nations (July).

1934   First Five-Year Plan for industrial development is announced (Jan.).
Law requiring all citizens to adopt family names is passed (June).
Kemal takes the name Atatürk (Nov.). Women are granted the vote and
made eligible to stand for election (Dec.).

1937   Autonomy of Hatay (Alexandretta) is agreed between Turkey, France and
Syria (Jan.).

1938   Atatürk dies (10 Nov.) and is succeeded by Izmet Inönü.

PALESTINE: FROM THE BALFOUR DECLARATION TO 1948

1917   Balfour Declaration is issued, supporting the establishment in Palestine of a national home for the Jewish people (2 Nov.). General Allenby captures Jerusalem (Dec.).

1919   Third migration of Zionist Jews to Palestine – *aliyah* – begins.

1920   League of Nations assigns the mandate of Palestine to Britain (April). Herbert Samuel is appointed as the first High Commissioner.

1921   Serious anti-Jewish riots by Arabs (May). First *moshav* (co-operative village), Nahalal, is founded.

1922   Britain excludes Transjordan from the 'Jewish national home' provisions of the mandate.

1924   Fourth *aliyah* begins (mainly from Poland).

1925   Hebrew University opened on Mt Scopus.

1929   First large-scale attacks by Arabs upon Jews with massacres at Hebron and Safed (Aug.).

1931   Jewish terrorist organization, Irgun Zvai Leumi, is formed.

1933   Fifth *aliyah* begins (mainly from Germany and German-held territory).

1937   Peel Commission recommends the partition of Palestine into Jewish and Arab states (July).

1937–8   Repression of the Arab Revolt in Palestine.

1939   British White Paper limits Jewish immigration and land purchase.

1946   US President, Truman, publicly endorses the demand for the immediate admission of 100,000 Jewish refugees to Palestine. British refuse (Apr.). Irgun blow up the King David Hotel, the British headquarters; 91 people are killed (July).

1947   Steamer *Exodus* turned away from Palestine with 4,500 Holocaust survivors on board (July). UN General Assembly adopts the plan to partition Palestine (Nov.).

1948   Massacre of Arab villagers at Deir Yassin by Irgun (Apr.).
        Ben-Gurion proclaims the state of Israel (14 May). Arab armies invade (15 May). UN mediator Count Bernadotte is assassinated in Jerusalem by Jewish terrorists (Sept.).

ARAB–ISRAELI CONFLICT SINCE 1948

1949   Armistice agreements are signed between Israel and Egypt, Lebanon, Jordan and Syria which set Israel's borders until 1967 (Feb.–July). Israel admitted to United Nations. Ben-Gurion elected Prime Minister.

1953   USSR breaks off relations with Israel.

1954   Israeli agents are caught and hanged in Cairo. Increasing *fedayeen* (Arab commando) attacks on Israel.

1955   Ben-Gurion again becomes Prime Minister (Nov.).

1956   Nasser announces nationalization of Suez Canal Company (July). Israel invades Egypt (Oct.). British and French attack the Canal Zone but soon withdraw under superpower pressure (Nov.). United Nations Expeditionary Forces (UNEF) take over Canal Zone.

1957   Israel withdraws from Sinai and Gaza. UNEF stationed there.

1958–9   Al-Fatah, a militant Palestinian group, founded.

1962   Adolf Eichmann, the Austrian Nazi war criminal, executed in Israel (May).

1964   Palestine Liberation Organization (PLO) formed under Nasserite auspices.

1967   Nasser closes Gulf of Aqaba to Israeli shipping (May). Six Day War gives Israel a total victory over Egypt, Syria and Jordan (5–10 June). UN Security Council Resolution 242 calls for a complete peace in Middle East.

1968–9   Reorganization of PLO with Yasser Arafat as chairman.

1969   Golda Meir becomes Prime Minister of Israel.

1970   Sadat succeeds Nasser in Egypt.

1972   Israeli athletes kidnapped at Munich Olympics by al-Fatah.

1973   Yom Kippur War (see p. 319). Egypt and Syria launch a surprise attack on Israel (6–25 Oct.).
Arab–Israeli ceasefire agreement is signed (Nov.).

1976   Menachem Begin, former leader of Irgun, forms a government.

1977   Sadat visits Jerusalem (Nov.).

1978   Israel invades southern Lebanon (Mar.). Camp David summit in USA between Carter, Begin and Sadat (Sept.). Arab summit in Baghdad denounces the Camp David Accords (Nov.).

1979 Egypt and Israel sign peace treaty which ends the state of war which had existed between the two countries since 1948 (26 Mar.). Israel agrees phased withdrawal from Sinai.

1981 Israel annexes the Golan Heights (Dec.).

1982 Israel invades southern Lebanon as far as Beirut (June). PLO evacuate Beirut (Aug.). Massacre of Palestinians in refugee camps in Chatila and Sabra, with Israeli complicity, causes outcry in Israel. Begin agrees to full and independent inquiry and sets up Kahan commission (Sept.).

1983 Kahan commission report precipitates government crisis (Feb.). Begin resigns and is succeeded by Shamir (Sept.).

1985 Israel completes the withdrawal from Lebanon. Arafat and King Hussein reach accord on common approach to negotiations, but hijackings frustrate peace process.

1986 King Hussein repudiates PLO as partner in Middle East and closes PLO offices in Jordan.

1987 Arafat unites Palestinian movement at meeting of Palestinian National Council in Algiers (Apr.).
Beginning of *intifada*, widespread unrest amongst Palestinians in occupied West Bank and Gaza Strip (Dec.).

1988 Jordan renounces role of representing Palestinians at future peace negotiations (June); PLO decares Palestinian independence (Nov.) and acceptance of Security Council Resolutions 242 and 338 recognizing Israeli independence. Arafat renounces terrorism at General Assembly of UN in Geneva.

1990 During disturbances in Jerusalem, Israeli forces shoot into crowd, killing 21 Palestinians and injuring 150 (8 Oct.).

1991 In the course of the First Gulf War (see p. 328), Iraq launches 21 Scud missiles at Israel.
Washington and Moscow announce they will act as joint chairs of Middle East peace talks in Madrid (July); Madrid peace talks inconclusive.

1992 Likud victory in Israeli elections in July suggests promise of movement over the peace talks amidst extensive bilateral negotiations between the superpowers and the principal figures concerned.

1993 Israel and the PLO sign 'Declaration of Principles' in Washington, following secret talks in Norway ('Oslo Accord').
Israel recognizes the PLO and Arafat acknowledges Israel's right to exist in peace and security. The Declaration provides for Palestinian self-rule in the Gaza Strip and part of West Bank; Israel to retain sovereignty over Jewish settlements as interim stage (13 Sept.).

1994   Israel and Jordan sign peace treaty; Israeli–Jordanian border demarcated and Jordan agrees to non-return of Palestinian refugees in return for US aid (26 Oct.).

1995   Israel and PLO sign agreement in Washington for interim Palestinian self-rule in the West Bank under the Palestinian authority; withdrawal of Israeli troops from some West Bank towns, joint control of others, but Israelis retain control of 128 Jewish settlements (28 Sept.).

1996   Suicide bombings (Feb.) kill 57 Israelis; Israel retaliates by closing the West Bank and Gaza Strip and launching raids into south Lebanon (Apr.). Election of Likud's Benjamin Netanyahu as Israeli Premier (May). Renewed violence following opening of tunnel under Mosque in Jerusalem; over 50 Palestinians and some 18 Israelis killed (Sept.). Israeli Cabinet approves further settlement (Dec.).

1997   In spite of continuing violence, Arafat and Netanyahu agree to resume talks on remaining Oslo agenda (Feb.).

1998   Tony Blair visits Israel and organizes new conference on Middle East peace in London (Apr.). Peace talks in London fail to achieve Israeli withdrawal from West Bank (May). Wye River Memorandum gives Palestinian Authority more of West Bank (Oct.).

1999   Death of King Hussein (Feb.); succeeded as King of Jordan by Abdullah. Ehud Barak (Labour) wins elections to become Prime Minister (May). Hosni Mubarrak elected to fourth term as Egyptian President (Sept.). Israel and Syria begin peace talks in Washington (Dec.).

2000   Failure of Geneva summit between President Assad and President Clinton (Mar.).
Withdrawal of Israeli army from south Lebanon (May).
Beginning of second *intifada* after visit of Ariel Sharon to Temple Mount (Sept.); widespread violence.
Resignation of Ehud Barak (Dec.); elections called.

2001   Taba Accord between Israel and Palestinians (Jan.).
Ariel Sharon elected Prime Minister of Israel (Feb.).
Israeli blockade of Ramallah (Mar.). Assassination of Israeli Minister of Tourism (Oct.); Israel retaliates, assassinating Hamas military leader.

2002   UN Security Council Resolution 1397, mentioning for first time 'two states, Israel and Palestine' (Mar.).
Israeli forces enter Jenin refugee camp (Apr.).

2003   Ariel Sharon re-elected Prime Minister (Jan.).
Release of US 'road map' for peace (Apr.) following invasion of Iraq in

March (see pp. 331–2); Palestine Prime Minister Mahmoud Abbas has increased powers.
Israel goes ahead with extension of the 'security wall' (Oct.).

2004   Death of Yasser Arafat (Dec.).

2005   Mahmoud Abbas elected President (9 Jan.) to succeed Arafat, winning 63% of vote.

AFRICA

THE MAKING OF MODERN AFRICA

1914 *East Africa*   Defeat of British forces at Tanga in East Africa by German forces; beginning of protracted guerrilla war in East Africa.

1915 *South West Africa*   Defeat of German forces in South West Africa.

1916 *East Africa*   General Smuts leads British conquest of East Africa.

1917 *East Africa*   German forces from East Africa under Lettow-Vorbeck driven into Mozambique.

1918 *Northern Rhodesia*   Lettow-Vorbeck invades Northern Rhodesia but hostilities halted by armistice.
 Africa   First Pan-African Congress convened in Paris by W. E. B. du Bois and Blaise Diagne.

1919 *Rhodesia*   Rhodesian Native National Congress formed.
 South Africa   Strikes organized in the Rand (South Africa).

1920 *West Africa*   National Congress of British West Africa formed.
 Kenya/Uganda   British East Africa divided into colony of Kenya and Uganda protectorate.

1921 *Morocco*   Abd el Krim defeats Spanish army of 11,000 men under General Silvestre in Spanish Morocco at battle of Anual, and assumes title of Emir.

1922 *Morocco*   Abd el Krim proclaims 'Rif Republic', is elected President, and sets up an elected Chamber and Council of Ministers.
 Kenya   Riots in Kenya over the expulsion of Harry Thuku, leader of the East African Association.

1923 *Africa*   Second Pan-African Congress.
 Nigeria   Nigerian National Democratic Party founded under Herbert Macaulay.
 Southern Rhodesia   Southern Rhodesia becomes a self-governing colony.

1924 *Morocco*   Spanish launch offensive against Rif Republic with army of 100,000 men and air force; Abd el Krim defeats Spanish at battle of Sidi Messaoud. General rising in Spanish Morocco. Peace talks break down when Abd el Krim demands complete

	Spanish evacuation of Morocco, complete independence and the title of Sultan.
Kenya	Kikuyu Central Association comes into being in Kenya to represent grievances of Kikuyu people.
1925 *Fr. Morocco*	Abd el Krim attacks French-protected Beni Zeroual tribe and comes into conflict with French forces defending French Morocco. French forces under Marshal Lyautey prevent Rif forces from taking Fez and Taza.
1926 *Morocco*	Franco-Spanish military agreement reached to co-ordinate suppression of Rif revolt. Franco-Spanish forces reduce Rif fortifications and take Targuist, Abd el Krim's headquarters. Abd el Krim surrenders to the French and is exiled to Réunion.
1927 *Africa*	Third Pan-African Congress.
1928 *Kenya*	Jomo Kenyatta becomes general secretary of the Kikuyu Central Association (KCA).
Senegal/Fr. Colonies	Lamine Gueye campaigns for extension of full French citizenship to all its African subjects; forms *Parti Socialiste Senegalais* at Dakar.
1933 *Kenya*	Split in Kenyan KCA when Thuku forms Kikuyu Provincial Association.
1934 *Ethiopia*	Incident at Wal Wal oasis on border between Ethiopia and Italian Somaliland heightens tension between Ethiopia (Abyssinia) and Italy.
1935 *Ethiopia*	Italy invades Ethiopia.
1936 *Ethiopia*	Italian forces occupy Addis Ababa.
1937 *Tunisia*	Rising in Tunisia against French rule.
1940 *Somaliland*	Britain evacuates Somaliland following Italian invasion.
Kenya	Leaders of Kenyan tribal associations detained.
1941 *Ethiopia*	British forces begin to occupy Italian East Africa.
1944 *Fr. Colonies*	Free French hold Brazzaville Conference to discuss future of French possessions in Africa.
Nigeria	Formation of Nigerian NCNC (Aug.); Richards proposals for a Nigerian constitution (Sept.).
1945 *Buganda*	Rioting in Buganda (later part of Uganda).
Algeria	Nationalist demonstration at Setif in Algeria leads to rioting which is suppressed by French authorities – the 'Setif massacre'.

Nigeria	Nigerian strike.
Africa	Egypt, Liberia, Ethiopia and South Africa join the United Nations as founder members. Fifth Pan-African Congress held in Manchester. Arab League founded in Cairo.

1946 *Gold Coast* Gold Coast Constitution published and becomes first British colony to have an African majority on legislative council (March); Nkrumah attends Fabian Conference at Clacton, England (Apr.).

Nigeria	Tour of Nigeria by NCNC leaders.
Algeria	*Mouvement pour le Triomphe des Libertés Democratiques* founded by Nessali Hadj in Algeria.
Fr. Colonies	French abolish forced labour in the colonies; by Loi Lamine-Gueye French citizenship extended to all inhabitants of overseas territories. *Fonds d'Investissement pour le Developpement Economique et Social* (FIDES) set up by France for development of the colonies.
Africa	*Rassemblement Democratique Africain* (RDA) founded by Bamako Congress.

1947 *Nigeria* New Constitution for Nigeria with African majority on the legislature.

Madagascar	Nationalist insurrection in Madagascar.
Gold Coast	United Gold Coast Convention founded by Dr J. B. Danquah; Kwame Nkrumah appointed Secretary.
Tanganyika	Groundnut scheme begun in Tanganyika.

1948 *Gold Coast* Boycott of European goods in Gold Coast and riots in Accra (Feb.); Watson Report (June).

Cameroon	*Union des Populations du Cameroun* (UPC) formed.
Egypt	Egyptian war with Israel begins.
South Africa	Smuts defeated by Malan in South African election. National Party begins implementation of apartheid policy.
Tunisia	Bourguiba returns to Tunis.
Senegal	*Bloc Democratique Senegalais* founded.
Zanzibar	General Strike in Zanzibar.

1949 *Gold Coast* Convention People's Party (CPP) founded in Gold Coast by Nkrumah (June); British Cabinet accepts Coussey report on Gold Coast (Oct.).

Rhodesia/Nyasaland	Victoria Falls Conference in favour of federation of Rhodesia and Nyasaland; African opposition to proposed federation.
Buganda	Riots in Buganda.
	British Cabinet accepts Coussey report on Gold Coast.

	Nigeria	Industrial disturbances and shootings at Enugu colliery and riots in southern Nigeria.
	Somalia	United Nations decide that Britain should return Somalia to Italy as a United Nations' trust territory for 10 years.
	Ivory Coast	Widespread disturbances in Ivory Coast.
1950	*Gold Coast*	'Positive Action' policy in Gold Coast.
	South Africa	Apartheid laws passed in South Africa.
	S. W. Africa	International Court rules that South West Africa should remain under United Nations' trusteeship.
	Congo	*Association des Bakongas* (Abako) formed in Belgian Congo.
	Nigeria	Action Group formed in Nigeria.
	Sierra Leone	Sierra Leone People's Party (SLPP) founded by Milton Margai.
1951	*Gold Coast*	Gold Coast constitution becomes operative (Jan.); CPP wins General Election in Gold Coast; Nkrumah becomes 'leader of government business' (Feb.).
	Nigeria	Macpherson constitution enacted in Nigeria.
	Rhodesia/Nyasaland	Victoria Falls Conference on Central African Federation; British government accepts idea of a federation of Rhodesia and Nyasaland.
	Sierra Leone	Elections in Sierra Leone; Milton Margai in office.
	Libya	Libya becomes an independent kingdom.
1952	*Gold Coast*	Kwame Nkrumah becomes Prime Minister of the Gold Coast.
	Egypt	Army coup in Egypt; committee of 'Free Officers' forces King Farouk to abdicate; General Neguib takes power.
	Ethiopia	Eritrea federated with Ethiopia.
	Kenya	Following increased violence in Kikuyuland, 'Mau Mau' Emergency proclaimed.
	South Africa	All non-whites compelled to carry passes in South Africa; non-white political organizations launch 'passive resistance' campaign against apartheid; leaders arrested.
1953	*South Africa*	Emergency powers introduced by the South African government against passive resistance; new racial laws introduced.
	Sudan	Anglo-Egyptian agreement on the Sudan.
	Egypt	Egypt becomes a republic; Party of National Liberation under Neguib becomes Egypt's sole political party.
	Kenya	Jomo Kenyatta and five others convicted of managing 'Mau Mau' in Kenya.
	Gold Coast	Nkrumah announces 'Motion of Destiny'.
	Nigeria	Nigerian Constitutional Conference held in London.

	Morocco	French deport Mohamed V from Morocco.
	Rhodesia/Nyasaland	Central African Federation of Rhodesia and Nyasaland created.
	Tanganyika	Julius Nyerere elected President of Tanganyika African Association.
	Morocco	Franco deposes the Sultan of Morocco.
1954	*Egypt*	Colonel Nasser seizes power in Egypt.
	Nigeria	Nigerian Constitutional Conference in Lagos (Jan.). Federal system of government formalized by Lyttleton Constitution (Oct.).
	Gold Coast	CPP wins elections in Gold Coast and Britain promises independence.
	Tanganyika	Tanganyika African National Union (TANU) formed with Julius Nyerere as President.
	Egypt	Anglo-Egyptian agreement on the evacuation of Suez Canal Zone.
	Algeria	Beginning of Algerian War of Independence (see p. 306).
1955	*Africa*	Bandung Conference in Indonesia (see p. 455).
	Morocco	Moroccan Army of Liberation attacks French posts in West Algeria (Aug.); King Mohamed V restored to throne by French (Nov.).
	Sudan	Beginning of armed rebellion in South Sudan.
1956	*Sudan*	Sudan becomes an independent Republic.
	Algeria	Violent settler demonstrations in Algiers.
	Fr. Colonies	Deferre introduces *loi cadre* providing for local autonomy in Black African territories.
	Morocco/Tunisia	France recognizes independence of Morocco and Tunisia.
	Egypt	Nasser nationalizes the Suez Canal (July); Egypt–Israel war and British and French landings at Suez (Nov.).
	Cameroon	Civil War in Cameroon.
	Algeria/Nigeria	Oil discovered in Algeria and Nigeria.
	Northern Rhodesia	State of emergency declared in Northern Rhodesia after miners' strike in the copper belt.
	Port Guinea and Cape Verde	African Party for the Independence of Guinea and Cape Verde (PAIGC) founded.
	Angola	Popular Movement for the Liberation of Angola (MPLA) founded.
1957	*Gold Coast/Ghana*	Gold Coast becomes independent as Ghana.
	Nigeria	Second London conference on Nigerian constitution; eastern and western regions of Nigeria become self-governing.

Fr. West Africa   Houphouet-Boigny President of Grand Council of French West Africa.

Sierra Leone   SLPP wins general election in Sierra Leone.

Tunisia   Bey of Tunis deposed; Tunisia becomes a republic.

Africa   Afro-Asian Solidarity Conference in Cairo.

1958 *Tunisia*   French military raids into Tunisia.

Togo   Togo becomes independent.

Nyasaland   Dr Hastings Banda returns to Nyasaland.

Fr. Colonies   General de Gaulle advocates a federation with internal autonomy for French overseas territories as the French Community; at Brazzaville he announces independence for French Africa.

Algeria   Algerian provisional government set up in Cairo.

Guinea   Guinea becomes independent with Sekou Touré as President; all other French African territories remain within French Community.

Sudan   Military coup led by General Abboud overthrows Sudanese government.

1959 *Nyasaland*   State of Emergency declared in Nyasaland; Dr Banda imprisoned.

Libya   Oil discovered in Libya.

Nigeria   Northern Region of Nigeria becomes self-governing.

Africa   Saniquellé meeting of Presidents Nkrumah, Tubman and Touré to plan union of free African states.

Congo   Riots in Belgian Congo.

Fr. Colonies   Senegal and Sudan demand independence and bring about the end of the French Community.

1960 *Africa*   Harold Macmillan's 'wind of change' speech in Cape Town. French atomic device exploded in the Sahara.

South Africa   Demonstration on 21 Mar. at Sharpeville fired on by South African police; 67 Africans killed.

Congo   Belgian Congo becomes independent; *Force publique* mutinies; United Nations troops sent into Congo.

Tanganyika   TANU wins election in Tanganyika and Julius Nyerere becomes Chief Minister.

Nigeria   Nigeria becomes an independent state within the Commonwealth.

Namibia   SWAPO (South West African People's Organization) founded.

1961 *Algeria*   Armed forces announce that they have taken over control of Algeria; OAS terrorism begins. Algerian peace talks begin in Evian, France.

Congo　　　　Lumumba, the Premier, murdered in Katanga.
Angola　　　　Rebellion begins in Angola against the Portuguese.
Sierra Leone　Sierra Leone becomes an independent state within the
　　　　　　　Commonwealth.
South Africa　South Africa becomes a republic and leaves the
　　　　　　　Commonwealth.
Tanganyika　Tanganyika becomes an independent state within the
　　　　　　　Commonwealth.
Rhodesia　　Rhodesia Front party formed.

1962 *Rwanda/Burundi*　Rwanda and Burundi become independent.
　　Ghana　　　　Plots against President Nkrumah's life in Ghana.
　　Uganda　　　Uganda becomes an independent state within the
　　　　　　　　Commonwealth.
　　Algeria　　　Algerian independence agreed to at end of Evian peace talks.
　　N. Rhodesia　First African government formed in Northern Rhodesia.
　　Mozambique　Frelimo headquarters set up in Dar-es-Salaam, Tanganyika.

1963 *Congo*　　　End of Katanga secession in Congo.
　　Togo　　　　President Olympio killed in Togo coup.
　　Africa　　　Organization of African Unity (OAU) formed in Addis
　　　　　　　　Ababa by 30 heads of state.
　　Rhodesia/Nyasaland　End of the Federation of Rhodesia and Nyasaland.
　　Kenya　　　Jomo Kenyatta becomes Prime Minister of Kenya.
　　Zanzibar　　Zanzibar becomes an independent state within the
　　　　　　　　Commonwealth.
　　Tunisia　　　French evacuate the naval base at Bizerta, Tunisia.
　　Kenya　　　Kenya becomes an independent state within the
　　　　　　　　Commonwealth.

1964 *Rwanda*　　Massacre of Tutsi in Rwanda.
　　Zanzibar　　Revolution in Zanzibar; Sultan overthrown and Karume
　　　　　　　　becomes President.
　　East Africa　Army mutinies in Kenya, Tanganyika and Uganda; British
　　　　　　　　troops called in to help restore order.
　　Tanganyika　Union of Tanganyika and Zanzibar as Tanzania.
　　South Africa　Rivonia trial in South Africa; Nelson Mandela, nationalist
　　　　　　　　leader, sentenced to life imprisonment.
　　Congo　　　Tshombe becomes President of Congo; revolts in Congo
　　　　　　　　provinces; Belgian parachutists land at Stanleyville and
　　　　　　　　elsewhere to rescue Europeans.
　　Malawi/Zambia　Malawi and Zambia become independent states within
　　　　　　　　the Commonwealth.
　　Mozambique　Frelimo begins armed struggle against Portuguese in
　　　　　　　　Mozambique.

1965 *Fr. Colonies* *Organisation Commune Africaine et Malagache* (OCAM) formed at conference of French-speaking heads of state at Nouakchott.

Tanzania Zhou Enlai (Chou En-lai), the Chinese Premier, visits Tanzania; one-party state adopted in Tanzania.

S. Rhodesia Rhodesia Front party wins general election in Southern Rhodesia; Ian Smith declares Rhodesia's 'unilateral declaration of independence' (UDI); UN Security Council embargo placed on Rhodesia.

Congo General Mobutu takes over complete power in Congo.

1966 *Africa* Commonwealth Conference in Lagos.

Nigeria First military coup in Nigeria led by Ibo officers; a counter-coup follows 6 months later.

Ghana President Nkrumah deposed by military and police coup in Ghana.

Uganda Milton Obote seizes the Kabaka's palace in Kampala and makes Uganda into a centralized state.

Botswana Botswana becomes an independent state within the Commonwealth.

Congo *Union Minière du Haut-Katanga* taken over by Congo government.

1967 *Tanzania* Arusha Declaration issued in Tanzania.

Sierra Leone Two army coups in Sierra Leone.

Egypt Arab–Israeli 'Six Day War'; Israelis occupy Sinai and defcat Egypt.

Congo Uprising in eastern and northern Congo ended by foreign mercenaries employed by Gen. Mobutu's central government.

E. Africa East African Community established by Kenya, Tanzania and Uganda.

Nigeria Secession of Eastern Region as independent state of Biafra; beginning of civil war in Nigeria (see p. 315).

1968 *Malawi* Malawi establishes diplomatic relations with South Africa.

Rhodesia Start of guerrilla war in Rhodesia.

Nigeria Tanzania, Ivory Coast and two other African states recognize Biafran independence.

Eq. Guinea Equatorial Guinea becomes independent of Spain.

Mali Military coup in Mali.

Swaziland Swaziland becomes an independent state within the Commonwealth.

1969 *Libya* King Idris deposed by a military coup in Libya; Colonel Qadhafi comes to power.

	Ghana	General election in Ghana returns Dr Busia as Prime Minister. Ghana expels thousands of aliens.
	Kenya	Serious political disturbances in western Kenya.
1970	*Nigeria*	End of Nigerian civil war.
	Libya	British withdrawal from military bases in Libya.
	Uganda	President Obote's 'Common Man's Charter' introduced in Uganda.
	Tanzania	Chinese offer aid to Tanzania to build railway from Dar-es-Salaam to Zambian copper belt.
	Egypt	Aswan High Dam in Egypt comes into operation.
1971	*Uganda*	General Amin leads military coup which overthrows President Obote of Uganda.
	South Africa	Central African Republic recognizes South Africa and receives economic aid from it.
	Congo/Zaïre	Congo renamed Zaïre.
	South Africa	Declaration of Mogadishu issued by eastern and central African states stating their intention to continue the armed struggle to liberate South Africa.
	S. Rhodesia	African National Council (ANC) formed in Rhodesia by Bishop Muzorewa.
1972	*Zaïre*	'African authenticity' campaign launched by President Mobutu in Zaïre.
	Ghana	Army coup in Ghana; General Acheampong overthrows Busia government.
	S. Rhodesia	Pearce Commission in Rhodesia reports an overwhelming 'no' by African population to settlement proposals.
	Uganda	President Amin begins to expel Asians from Uganda.
	Sudan	Agreement in Sudan on 'southern problem'; regional autonomy granted to the south.
	Burundi	Huto rising in Burundi suppressed with great loss of life.
	Madagascar	Military coup in Madagascar.
1973	*S. Rhodesia/Zambia*	Zambia–Rhodesia border closed by President Kaunda.
	South Africa	Serious strikes by black workers in South Africa.
	S. Rhodesia	Prime Minister Smith of Rhodesia begins talks with African nationalists in an attempt to find some form of internal settlement.
	Egypt	Israel–Egypt war; Egyptian troops retake part of Sinai.
	Africa	Oil crisis brings great increase in prices for African states.
	Ethiopia	Widespread drought in Ethiopia.
1974	*Ethiopia*	Emperor Haile Selassie overthrown by a military coup; Dergue established to rule the country.

Portuguese Colonies   Coup in Lisbon by army officers disillusioned with the African wars brings down the Caetano regime and begins the process of decolonization in the Portuguese empire in Africa.

Guinea-Bissau   Guinea-Bissau becomes independent.

1975 *Africa*   Lomé Agreement signed between EEC and 37 African states.

West Africa   Economic Community of West African States (Ecowas) Treaty signed by 15 states.

Portuguese Colonies   Portugal's withdrawal from Africa; independence for Cape Verde Islands, São Tomé and Principé. Mozambique (June) and Angola (Nov.). Civil war in Angola.

Zambia/Tanzania   Tanzam railway officially opened between Zambia and Tanzania.

S. Rhodesia   Four 'front-line' presidents at Quilemane pledge support for the Zimbabwe National Liberation Army.

Nigeria   General Murtala Mohamed, President of Nigeria, assassinated in Lagos.

Angola   South African troops invade Angola in support of UNITA forces.

1976 *South Africa*   Soweto riots and boycotts. Over 700 dead by 1977.

Spanish Morocco   Spain withdraws from Western Sahara; territory partitioned between Morocco and Mauritania. Proclamation of Sahara Arab Democratic Republic, which through its armed Polisario Front wages a guerrilla war against both occupying states.

South Africa   South Africa declares Transkei independent.

Ethiopia   'Palace coup' in Addis Ababa.

1977 *Djibouti*   Djibouti became an independent state; final withdrawal of France from African territory.

Zaïre   Invasion of Shaba province, Zaïre, by Katangese rebels.

Ethiopia   Somali-supported forces invade Ogaden; serious fighting in the region. Cuban aid to Ethiopia in the war.

Central African Rep.   Central African Empire proclaimed by Bokassa.

Ethiopia   Widespread purge in Ethiopia by the Dergue.

Nigeria   Constituent Assembly meets in Nigeria in preparation for a return to civilian government.

1978 *Tunisia*   Serious strikes in Tunisia.

S. Rhodesia   Internal agreement in Rhodesia; transitional government formed.

Ethiopia/Somalia   Somali forces defeated by Ethiopia in Ogaden war; Ethiopia steps up its attacks on Eritrean nationalist forces.

Guinea   Reconciliation of Guinea with France.

Uganda   Uganda invasion of Kagera salient in north-west Tanzania.

South Africa   'Muldergate' scandal in South Africa.

	Ghana	Gen. Acheampong deposed in Ghana.

1979 *Tanzania/Uganda*   Tanzania supports Ugandan Liberation Front in invasion of Uganda; President Amin overthrown.

Central African Rep.   Emperor Bokassa overthrown and Central African Republic re-established.

Eq. Guinea   President Macias Nguema of Equatorial Guinea overthrown.

Ghana   Junior officers coup in Ghana led by Flight-Lt Rawlings; three former heads of state executed.

Ghana/Nigeria   Elections in Ghana and Nigeria return both countries to civilian rule.

S. Rhodesia/Zimbabwe   Lancaster House talks in London on a settlement for Zimbabwe; the country reverts to British rule for transitional period.

1980 *Zimbabwe*   Elections in Zimbabwe result in an overwhelming victory for Robert Mugabe's ZANU-PF party. Mugabe becomes Prime Minister of an independent Zimbabwe.

Liberia   Military coup in Liberia by junior army officers.

Uganda   Military-backed coup in Uganda deposes President Binaisa; Dr Obote winner in first Ugandan elections for 18 years.

Tunisia/Libya   Tension between Tunisia and Libya after clashes at Gafsa.

Chad   Unrest in Chad leaves 700 dead.

1981 *Zimbabwe*   Serious clashes between ZANLA and ZIPRA guerrilla forces.

Egypt   President Sadat of Egypt assassinated in Cairo; vice-president Hosni Mubarrak becomes president.

Gambia   Coup in Gambia fails when British SAS free hostages held by rebels.

1982 *Uganda*   Further coup fails in Uganda.

South Africa Dr Treurnicht launches ultra-right-wing Conservative Party in South Africa.

Kenya   Army coup in Kenya foiled.

Lesotho   South African raid on Lesotho.

Upper Volta Army coup in Upper Volta.

1983 *Chad*   French troops sent to Chad to resist Libyan invasion.

Ethiopia   Serious drought and famine in Ethiopia, affecting between 2 and 4 million people; worldwide mobilization of aid.

1984 *Nigeria*   Major General Buhari takes power in Nigeria.

Mozambique/South Africa   Mozambique government signs peace accord with South Africa.

Nigeria   Serious religious riots in Yola, northern Nigeria.

Chad   French and Libyan forces agree to evacuate Chad.

	South Africa	P. W. Botha returned to power as President of South Africa; new tri-racial Parliament opened.
1985	*Uganda*	President Obote overthrown by army coup in Uganda. Major-General Okello sworn in as country's new leader.
	Nigeria	Further coup in Nigeria.
	South Africa	Emergency legislation in South Africa; hundreds detained and many killed following serious violence and school boycotts. Press reporting restricted. Botha promises reform but at own pace.
	Sudan	Sudanese army seizes power deposing President Nimeiri.
	South Africa/Namibia	South African troops withdraw from southern Angola; an independent government to be set up in Namibia.
1986	*Uganda*	Yoweri Museveni backed by the National Resistance Army overthrows President Okello in Uganda.
	South Africa	South African backed coup in Lesotho; South African raids into Zambia, Zimbabwe and Botswana. Widespread boycotts and violence lead to state of emergency; hundreds killed by government forces and in communal violence; over eight thousand detained. US applies trade sanctions and disinvestment by US companies begins.
	Mozambique	President Machel of Mozambique killed in plane crash; succeeded by Joachim Chissano.
	Libya	US air attack on Libya for complicity with terrorism.
1987	*Tunisia*	President Habib Bourguiba overthrown in Tunisia.
1988	*South Africa*	Nelson Mandela moved into hospital accommodation. 'Free Nelson Mandela' campaign intensifies.
1989	*Sudan*	Coup in Sudan.
	Namibia	Agreement on future independence of Namibia; UN peacekeeping force supervises departure of SWAPO guerrillas and South African forces.
	South Africa	Botha suffers stroke. De Klerk President following narrow victory in general election. Several killed during boycott and demonstrations during elections.
1990	*South Africa*	30-year ban on ANC lifted; final release from Victor Verster prison, Cape Town, of Nelson Mandela (11 Feb.). Preliminary talks on future of South Africa between de Klerk and ANC delegation (May).
	Namibia	Namibia achieves independence (20 Mar.), becoming 50th member of Commonwealth and 160th member of United Nations.
	Nigeria	Coup attempt by junior officers failed (Apr.).

Liberia	Civil war in Liberia. The rebels seize and murder President Doe (Sept.).
Tanzania	After holding the position of head of state (1985), Ali Hassan Mwinyi takes leadership of the Tanzanian Revolutionary Party over from Nyerere.
Rwanda	Tutsi guerrillas from neighbouring Uganda break into the country in order to overthrow the Hutu majority government in power (Oct.).
Chad	The rebels, led by General Idriss Deby, overthrow President Hissène Habré who has been in power since 1982 (Dec.).

1991	*Somalia*	President Mohamed Siad Barra, who came to power in Oct. 1969 with a military coup, is forced to flee from the country because of an armed uprising (Jan.). Northern Somalian separatists proclaim the Republic of Somaliland (its border identical to the former British Somalia) (May).
	Angola	The last Cuban soldier leaves the territory of the country. In Lisbon, a 'final' ceasefire agreement is signed by the leader of MPLA, José E. dos Santos, and the leader of UNITA, Jonas Savimbi (May).
	Ethiopia	President Mengistu resigns and flees from the country. The dissident armed forces seize the capital (May); Meles Zenawi, the leader of the Ethiopian People's Revolutionary Democratic Front, forms a provisional government (June). An agreement is reached between the Eritrean People's Liberation Front and the new Ethiopian government that a plebiscite will be held in two years on the issue of the independence of Eritrea (July).
	Africa	In the Nigerian town of Abuja, heads of state of the Organization of African Unity sign a treaty (June) for creating an African Economic Community by 2025.
	Zaïre	President Mobutu allows a multi-party system and, as a result of the rebellions, he appoints the leader of the opposition, Etienne Tshisekedi, as Prime Minister (Oct.).
	Zambia	At the multi-party elections held for the first time after 18 years, the opposition Movement for a Multi-party Democracy wins against the United National Independence Party, led by President Kaunda. The new President is Frederick Chiluba (Nov.).
	Nigeria	Disturbances and bloody religious clashes between Christians and Muslims (Nov.).

1992	*Algeria*	After the first round of the multi-party parliamentary elections, the fundamentalist Islamic Salvation Front achieves

a landslide victory (Dec. 1991); the election process is suspended (12 Jan.). A 5-member Supreme State Council takes over powers of head of state from the resigned President Chadli Bendjedid. The head of this state council is Mohammed Budiaf (15 Jan.). After a ban on the FIS (Mar.), civil war threatens the country. Budiaf is assassinated (29 June). The new state council chairman is Ali Khafi.

Tanzania   The Executive Committee of the Tanzanian Revolutionary Party accepts a resolution to introduce a multi-party system (Jan.).

Libya   The UN Security Council orders economic sanctions against Libya after it rejected the extradition of Libyan terrorists (Apr.).

Sierra Leone A military coup overthrows President Joseph Momoh, who has been in power since 1985. The new head of state is the President of the National Provisional Governing Council, Captain Valentine Strasser (May).

Angola   The parliamentary and presidential elections are won by the MPLA and former President dos Santos (Sept.). UNITA declares the outcome fraudulent and fighting flares up once again.

Madagascar The third unsuccessful coup attempt within 3 years takes place against the political regime of President Didier Ratsiraka (July).

Mozambique In Rome an agreement on the discontinuation of the 15-year-long civil war is signed by President Chissano and the leader of the Mozambique National Resistance Movement (RENAMO), Alfonso Dhlakama (Oct.).

Ghana   The first Presidential elections since 1979 are won by the President-in-Office, Rawlings (Nov.).

Africa   An international conference is held to provide support for starving African children (Nov.).

Somalia   Under the auspices of the UN, a large-scale humanitarian and military aid-action (Operation 'New Hope') is organized in order to revitalize the country devastated by civil war and famine (Aug.). The landing of 28,000 US troops begins (Dec.).

Kenya   The first multi-party parliamentary and presidential elections held in 26 years are won by the governing party KANU and President Daniel Arap Moi (Dec.).

1993 *Zaïre*   Military rebellion breaks out in the capital (Jan.). President Mobutu appoints Faustin Birindwa as Prime Minister (Mar.).

	Madagascar	The Presidential election is won by the opposition's candidate, Albert Zafy (Mar.).
	Niger	The first free Presidential election is won by the opposition Social Democrats' candidate, Mahamane Ousmane (Mar.).
	Eritrea	On the basis of 95% of the votes of its population (Apr.), Eritrea separates from Ethiopia and becomes an independent republic (May). Its first President is the leader of the EPLF, Isajas Afeverki.
	Somalia	Troops arrive from 20 member states of the UN, replacing the American soldiers (May). The clashes with armed gangs who control a great part of the country become more and more serious.
	Malawi	At a plebiscite, the population votes for the introduction of a multi-party system (June).
	Egypt	Mubarrak is elected as President for the third time (June). Terrorist attacks by Islamic extremists become increasingly frequent, resulting in a dramatic decrease in the tourist industry.
	Nigeria	The military leadership denounces the results of the presidential election (June), yet President Babangida still renounces power to a civilian government (Aug.). Ernest Shonekan is soon replaced by General Sani Abacha, who dissolves all the democratically elected institutions and establishes the Provisional Governing Council (Nov).
	Liberia	In Benin the representatives of the provisional government and various armed groups sign a peace treaty ordering an end to the war and announcing multi-party elections (July).
	Rwanda	A peace treaty is signed ordering the end of civil war (Aug.). In order to ensure that the treaty is observed, UN forces arrive in the country (Nov.).
	Togo	In an election boycotted by the opposition, General Eyadéma, who has been in power since 1967, is elected.
	Burundi	During an unsuccessful coup attempt by Tutsi officers, President Melchior Ndadaye, who has been in power since June as a result of the first multi-party elections in the country's history, is assassinated (21 Oct.).
	South Africa	At the CODESA negotiations an agreement is reached on the draft of an apartheid-free constitution, thus ending the rule of the white minority.
1994	*Algeria*	Failure of conference on transition to democracy (Jan.) when boycotted by all major parties leads to escalating terrorism and civil war.

Ghana	In widespread ethnic disorder, over 1,000 killed (Feb.).
Kenya	Death of Mr Odinga, leader of Kenyan opposition (Jan.); economic reforms launched to encourage foreign investment.
Zimbabwe	New opposition party formed (Jan.); exposure of corruption stemming from compulsory land purchase in 1992 by government officials (Mar.–May).
Mozambique	All-party defence force set up as part of process of reconciliation (Aug.). Multi-party elections lead to narrow victory for Frelimo under President Chissano (Oct.).
Angola	Renewed ceasefire agreement (Nov.).
Zambia	President Chiluba forced to restructure his Cabinet following accusations of corruption (Feb.); further resignations follow Western pressure (July).
Ethiopia	New constitution adopted providing for a federal government of 9 states.
1995 *Kenya*	Stock exchange opened to foreign investment (Jan.); arrest of opposition MPs (Jan.); Moi's government accused by Roman Catholic bishops of inept handling of economy (Apr.). Riots in Kibera district of Nairobi (Oct.); continuing Western pressure on Moi to reform his government and human rights record.
Ethiopia	Ethiopian People's Revolutionary Democratic Front wins overwhelming victory in May elections.
Somalia	Final UN forces leave Somalia (Mar.).
Algeria	Further attempts at reconciliation fail to halt cycle of terrorism and repression between Islamic forces and Algerian government.
Nigeria	General Abacha postpones Constitutional Conference preparing the way for civilian rule and arrests opponents (Mar.); death sentences on 14 passed (July). Deadline for new elections set for 1 Oct. 1998 but followed by execution of writer Ken Saro-Wiwa and 8 other Ogoni activists amidst worldwide protests (Nov.).
Ghana	Violent protests against economic reforms (May).
Zimbabwe	Mugabe's ZANU-PF wins elections on low turnout (May); arrest of Rev. Sithole, who is accused of plotting against Mugabe.
Mozambique	Reports of serious famine in central and southern Mozambique (Sept.); Mozambique admitted to the Commonwealth (Dec.).
Angola	Meeting of President dos Santos and UNITA leader Jonas Savimbi (May) agrees to bring Savimbi into government as one of 2 joint Vice-Presidents in return for demobilizing UNITA forces. Demobilization halted (Dec.) after fresh clashes between UNITA and government forces.

Zambia	President Chiluba continues process of dismissing corrupt ministers. Former President Kaunda arrested following his return to politics; then threatened with deportation. Closure of Lusaka University following student protests (Nov.), but President Chiluba swept to election victory after opposition boycotts election.
1996 *Zimbabwe*	President Mugabe wins presidential elections but other candidates withdraw to reduce elections to a formality (Mar.). Government proposes further land reform (June). National strike of public sector workers forces large pay increases to be phased over 3 years (Aug.).
Somalia	Factional fighting resumes (Apr.), with hundreds of casualties, including President Aidid who is shot while leading an attack (died 1 Aug.). Peace talks in November fail to prevent further fighting and over 300 casualties.
Nigeria	United Liberation Front claims responsibility for death of General Abacha's eldest son in plane crash (Jan.). New opposition organization, the United Democratic Front of Nigeria, formed (1 Apr.); Abacha purges army and air force (Mar.–May) and on 4 June gunmen kill wife of Chief Abiola, winner of quashed 1993 elections. Following demonstrations, government closes Ibadan University; Abacha government also puts down Muslim demonstrations in the north with heavy casualties (Sept.).
Ghana	President Rawlings wins sweeping victory in Presidential elections over John Kufuor of the People's National Convention Party; in the National Assembly elections Rawlings's National Democratic Congress wins 130 of the 200 seats (Dec.).
Kenya	President Moi responds to Western criticism of human rights violations by establishing a standing committee to investigate human rights violations (May).
Zaïre	Zaïre government accuses Rwanda of organizing anti-Mobutu guerrillas; fighting breaks out in eastern Zaïre forcing Hutu refugees in Zaïre to flee. As Hutu refugees stream back to Rwanda, the anti-Mobutu alliance advances deeper into Zaïre led by Laurent Kabila. President Mobutu returns to Kinshasa (17 Dec.) from France where he was undergoing surgery.
Mozambique	IMF loan of $110 million to underpin economic recovery.
Angola	Demobilization of UNITA forces proceeds, but Savimbi rejects his place in the government, forestalling attempts to set up a government of national unity (Sept.).

1997 *Zaïre*　　　President Mobutu returns to France (8 Jan.). Rebel forces enter Kinshasa and overthrow Mobutu regime (Apr.).

　　　Nigeria　　Further arrests and trials of opposition groups; 12 dissidents charged with treason (Mar.).

1998 *Kenya*　　　Daniel Moi re-elected president (Jan.).

　　　Sierra Leone Intervention force headed by Nigeria ends military junta (Jan.).

　　　Nigeria　　General Abubakar promises return to civilian rule in Nigeria in May 1999 (July).

　　　Kenya　　　Islamic militants attack US embassies in Nairobi and Dar-es-Salaam (Aug.). 250 killed.

　　　Zimbabwe　Compulsory purchase of over 800 white-owned farms planned (Nov.).

　　　Congo　　　Invasion by Rwanda and Uganda; counter-intervention by Zimbabwe, Angola and Namibia.

1999 *Sierra Leone* Rebels advance on capital (Jan.); government troops fight back (Feb.) (see p. 329).

　　　Angola　　　Renewal of violence leads to withdrawal of UN peacekeepers (Jan.).

　　　Ethiopia/Eritrea　War breaks out over disputed border region (Feb.).

　　　Congo　　　Renewal of heavy fighting in civil war (May).

　　　Nigeria　　Election of Olusegun Obasanjo as president (Feb.) (General Abubakar hands over power in June).

　　　Sierra Leone　Ceasefire in civil war (May).

　　　Morocco　　Death of King Hassan after 38-year rule.

2000 *Zimbabwe*　Voters reject President Mugabe's plans to redraft constitution (Feb.).

　　　　　　　　　Growing chaos in country.

　　　Libya　　　Trial of two Libyans accused of Lockerbie bombing (May).

　　　Ethiopia/Eritrea　Ceasefire ends 2-year war (June).

　　　Zimbabwe　Land Acquisition Act amended allowing for seizure of white farms without compensation (May). Mugabe wins general election the following month.

　　　Malawi　　Dismissal of entire cabinet amidst massive corruption scandal (Nov.).

　　　Ghana　　　Victory for John Kufuor in run-off ballot for president (Dec.).

2001 *Congo*　　　Assassination of President Kabila; his son, Joseph Kabila, becomes interim president (Jan.).

　　　Uganda　　Flawed presidential elections produce victory for Yoweri Museveni (Mar.).

　　　Africa　　　Creation of African Union as successor to the OAU (Organization of African Unity) (May).

2002	*Angola*	Death of veteran UNITA leader Jonas Savimbi while fighting government troops (Feb.).
	Zimbabwe	Mugabe re-elected President (according to official figures). Zimbabwe suspended from Commonwealth (Mar.). Mugabe dissolves Cabinet (Aug.).
	Libya	Libya offers compensation to families of victims of Lockerbie in return for lifting of sanctions (May).
	Angola	Fernando Dias dos Santos appointed Prime Minister (Nov.).
	Kenya	Landslide presidential victory for Mwai Kibaki (Dec.).
2003	*Zimbabwe*	Commonwealth extends suspension for further 9 months (Mar.). Major workers' strike in Apr.
	Congo	Joseph Kabila heads transitional government (Apr.).
	Liberia	Charles Taylor indicated for war crimes (June). Heavy fighting as rebels advance on capital.
	Rwanda	Incumbent president elected in first official presidential election since 1994 genocide (Aug.).
	Zimbabwe	Mugabe quits Commonwealth (Dec.).
2004	*Sudan*	Growing humanitarian crisis as a result of genocide in Darfur region (June–July).

TWENTIETH-CENTURY SOUTH AFRICA

1912   South African Native National Congress formed (SANNC).

1914   National Party formed under Hertzog.
Delegation visits London to protest against Natives Land Act. Afrikaner Rebellion following outbreak of war.

1915   Capture of German South West Africa.

1916   Report of Beaumont Commission on Native Lands.

1917   Industrial Workers of Africa founded.

1919   South African Native National Congress delegation (SANNC) attends Versailles Peace Conference.
Death of Botha; Smuts becomes Prime Minister; Union Parliament accepts League of Nations' mandate for South West Africa.

1920   African mineworkers strike.
Smuts forms new government.
African demonstrators killed in Port Elizabeth.

1921   Smuts increases his majority in parliamentary election.
Communist Party of South Africa formed.

1922   Strike of white miners. Black strikes organized in the Rand and passive resistance against pass laws.

1923   Native Urban Areas Act.
National Party and Labour Party form electoral pact.
SANNC renamed African National Congress (ANC).

1924   National and Labour Party win election; Hertzog Prime Minister.

1925   Afrikaans becomes official language.

1926   Mines and Works Amendment Act introduces colour bar into workplace.

1927   Nationality and Flag Acts passed; Immorality Act limiting racial mixing; Native Administration Act.

1929   National Party wins general election.

1930   Native (Urban Areas) Amendment Act. White women obtain the vote.

1931   Franchise amendments extend votes to almost all whites. Pass burning campaign in Durban area.

1932   Carnegie Commission reports on 'Poor Whites'.

1933   Hertzog and Smuts form coalition and win victory in general election.

1934   Malan forms purified National Party.
Formation of United Party.

1935   National Liberation League founded.
First meeting of All African Convention in Bloemfontein.

1936   Representation of Natives Bill removes Africans from franchise. Native Trust and Land Act.

1937   Native (Urban Areas) Amendment Act restricts black settlement in urban areas; Native Laws Amendment Act enforces influx control.
Native Representation Council begins work.

1938   United Party wins 111 seats to National Party's 27.

1939   House of Assembly votes 80–67 against neutrality in Second World War; Hertzog resigns and Smuts becomes Prime Minister. War declared.

1940   Hertzog's and Malan's supporters merge to form reunited National Party.
Xuma elected ANC President.

1941   Afrikaner Party formed.

1942   Draft Constitution for South African Republic published; coup attempt discovered and suspects interned.

1943   United Party wins general election.
ANC Youth League founded; formation of Non-European Unity Movement.

1945   Native (Urban Areas) Consolidation Act.

1946   Asiatic Land Tenure and Indian Representation Act; passive resistance by Indians begins.
African mineworkers strike.
Adjournment of the Native Representative Council.

1948   National Party under Malan and Afrikaner Party defeat Smuts.
National Party begins implementation of apartheid policy.
Apartheid introduced on surburban railways in the Cape Peninsula.

1949   Prohibition of Mixed Marriages Act.
Rioting between Zulus and Indians in Durban.
ANC adopts Programme of Action.

1950   Apartheid Laws passed including Immorality Act, Population Registration Act, Group Areas Act, Suppression of Communism Act.
Communist Party dissolves itself.
Stay-away campaign in Transvaal; 18 people killed by police.

1951   Bantu Authorities Act; Separate Representation of Voters Act removes 'Coloureds' from common voters' roll.

1952 Separate Representation of Voters Act ruled invalid. Passive resistance
      campaign against apartheid; arrest of campaign leaders and riots in
      various cities.

1953 Emergency powers introduced by South African government against
      passive resistance movement, including Criminal Law Amendment Act
      and Public Safety Act.
      Reservation of Separate Amenities Act, Bantu Education, and Native
      Labour Act introduced. Strikes by African workers illegal.
      National Party retains majority in general election.
      Liberal Party formed.

1954 Malan retires, Strijdom becomes Prime Minister.
      Federation of South African Women established.

1955 Formation of South African Congress of Trade Unions.
      Congress of the People Act. Cape Town adopts the 'Freedom Charter'.

1956 Parliament validates removal of 'coloured' voters from common roll.
      ANC accepts Freedom Charter.
      Mass women's anti-Pass Law demonstration in Pretoria.

1957 Amendments to Native Laws permit government to forbid African–
      White contacts. Stay-away protests and bus boycotts.

1958 National Party wins 103 of 163 parliamentary seats.
      Death of Strijdom; Verwoerd succeeds as Prime Minister.

1959 Apartheid introduced into higher education.
      Formation of Pan-Africanist Congress (PAC).
      Progressive Party formed when 11 United Party members resign.
      ANC decides on anti-Pass Law campaign.

1960 African representation in Parliament abolished; riots in Durban.
      Harold Macmillan makes 'Wind of Change' speech in Cape Town.
      Demonstration at Sharpeville fired on by police, 67 killed.
      Police announce suspension of Pass Laws (21 March).
      ANC announces general strike; state of emergency proclaimed;
      ANC and PAC banned; strike broken by detention of thousands of
      people; Pass Laws reimposed.
      Attempted assassination of Verwoerd.
      Majority of voters vote in favour of a Republic.

1961 South Africa becomes a Republic and leaves Commonwealth
      (31 May); renewed state of emergency leads to thousands of
      detentions.
      Verwoerd appoints Vorster Minister of Justice and Police.
      Sabotage campaign begun by National Liberation Committee.
      National Party wins general election.

1962 Sabotage Act makes sabotage a capital offence; house arrests introduced and banning powers extended.
United Nations votes for economic and diplomatic sanctions against South Africa.

1963 90-day detention without trial introduced.
Arrest of leaders of sabotage movement at Rivonia, Johannesburg.
Transkei given self-government after first elections for Transkei Legislative Assembly.

1964 Rivonia trial in South Africa; Nelson Mandela sentenced to life imprisonment. Several sabotage trials; members of African Resistance Movement gaoled.

1965 Members of underground Communist Party gaoled; period of detention without trial extended to 180 days.

1966 National Party wins general election.
Verwoerd assassinated; Vorster becomes Prime Minister.

1967 Terrorism Act provides for indefinite detention without trial. Planning Act controls influx of black population into urban areas.

1968 Progressive Party drops black members and becomes all-white party. Liberal Party dissolves itself.
'Coloured' representatives in parliament abolished.

1969 Bureau of State Security (BOSS) established.

1970 Bantu Homelands Citizenship Act offers Africans citizenship only of homelands.

1971 Declaration of Mogadishu issued by eastern and central African states stating their intention to continue the armed struggle to liberate South Africa.
President Banda of Malawi makes state visit to South Africa; Ivory Coast delegation also visits South Africa.

1972 Black People's Convention formed; Africans in 'white areas' brought under Bantu Affairs Administration Boards.

1973 Strikes in Durban.

1974 National Party wins general election.

1975 South African troops cross into Angola in support of UNITA forces; clashes with Cuban troops sent to support Angolan independence.

1976 South African troops withdraw to Namibian border following clashes with Cuban forces. Troops withdrawn into Namibia.
Uprising in Soweto black township; spreads to Cape Town.

Widespread boycotts, rioting, detentions and shootings.
Over 700 deaths.
Transkei declared 'independent' state by South Africa.

1977　Steve Biko dies while under arrest.
Mandatory arms embargo imposed on South Africa by UN Security Council.
National Party wins 145 seats to Progressive Party's 16 at General Election.
Bophuthatswana declared 'independent' by South Africa.

1978　Eventual independence for Namibia accepted.
'Muldergate' scandal erupts discrediting government;
Vorster retires as Prime Minister and is succeeded by P. W. Botha.

1979　Vorster resigns from position as State President following further 'Muldergate' revelations.
African trade unions recognized.
Talks between ANC and Chief Buthelezi, the Zulu leader, in London.

1980　Zimbabwe gains independence and elections result in overwhelming victory for Robert Mugabe's ZANU-PF party.
School boycotts in the Cape; 45 people shot in disturbances.
Sabotage destroys South Africa's major oil from coal plant.

1981　School boycott ends.
Major cross-border raids by South African forces into Angola and Mozambique.
Negotiations with Western powers over future of Namibia.

1982　Dr Treurnicht and 16 rebel members of National Party form ultra-right-wing Conservative Party.
Constitutional proposals set up 'Coloured' and Indian participation in central and local government.

1983　Referendum supports political rights for 'Coloureds' and Indians but not Africans.
Banning orders tightened on Mrs Winnie Mandela.

1984　P. W. Botha returned to power as President of South Africa; new tri-racial Parliament opened.
Peace accord with Mozambique to end cross-border raids.

1985　Government announces end to ban on mixed marriages.
Hundreds detained under emergency laws. Many deaths in rioting and school boycotts.
Botha pledges reform programme but at own pace. Severe restrictions put on press. South African troops withdraw from southern Angola in preparation for independence of Namibia.

1986   South African coup in Lesotho; South African raids into Zambia, Zimbabwe and Botswana.
Serious rioting in Alexandra township.
Bishop Desmond Tutu of Johannesburg calls for international sanctions against South Africa.
Strike by over a million black workers in Johannesburg.
Crossroads squatters' camp broken up.
Indefinite State of Emergency declared; over 8,000 black activists, trade unionists and church leaders arrested.
Commonwealth 'Eminent Persons' Group predicts 'bloodbath' if reform delayed. US votes for sanctions against South Africa and disinvestment by US companies begins.

1987   National Party wins election, gaining 123 of 166 seats, but Conservative Party with 22 displaces Liberals as official Opposition.

1988   Nelson Mandela moved into hospital accommodation; campaign to free him from custody gathers pace.

1989   P. K. Botha suffers stroke; F. W. de Klerk becomes President following elections in which both Conservatives and Liberals make gains.
Serious disturbances and mass boycotts of elections lead to several deaths.

1990   30-year ban on ANC lifted. Nelson Mandela released from Victor Verster prison, Cape Town (Feb.). Triumphant return to Soweto. First talks of de Klerk with ANC delegation on future of South Africa.
The South African Communist Party is re-established (July).
The ANC makes an agreement with the government that it will cease armed rebellion against the government in exchange for the rehabilitation of those ANC members banished for political reasons and for the dissolution of the state of emergency (Aug.).
The apartheid law which forbids the simultaneous appearance of black and white people in public places is abolished (Oct.).
Clashes between ethnic-based black political organizations competing with one another become increasingly frequent. In 1990 alone, approximately 3,000 people die in these clashes.

1991   Parliament abolishes the laws on race segregation according to place of residence, as well as the laws restricting the possession of land (June).
Parliament abolishes the law on the classification of the population according to race. With this measure, apartheid ceases to exist (June).
Mandela is elected as the President of the ANC (July). The Republic of South Africa joins as a member of the Anti-Nuclear Proliferation Treaty (July).
General amnesties are offered to those who were banished because of apartheid (Aug.). This measure involves 40,000 persons.

National round-table negotiations begin on plans for the future constitution (Conference for a Democratic South Africa, CODESA) (Dec.).

1992   The European Community withdraws the last of the sanctions against South Africa (Jan.).
At a plebiscite, 68.7% of the white population votes for the continuation of de Klerk's reforms (Mar.). 5 white members of parliament leave their own party and join the ANC (Apr.).
In Boipatong town, armed members of the Zulu tribe kill 39 black people (women among them). As a result of this massacre, various serious disturbances break out in the town (June).

1993   A Polish immigrant kills Chris Hani, the Chief Secretary of the Communist Party and the former leader of the armed wing of the ANC (13 Apr.). After the murder, bloody clashes break out in several cities across the country.
The General Assembly of the UN cancels the sanctions against South Africa (Oct.).
F. W. de Klerk and Nelson Mandela share the Nobel Peace Prize (Oct.).
At the CODESA negotiations the new anti-apartheid draft of the Constitution, which discontinues the rule of the white minority, is signed (18 Nov.). (An agreement is reached on the eradication of Bantustans (homelands); from 1 Jan. 1994 their inhabitants again receive South African citizenship.) The Constitution becomes applicable after the general election on 27 Apr. 1994. However, it is rejected by both the Zulu Inkatha Freedom Party and the white far-right Afrikaner Resistance Movement (AWB). President Clinton signs the bill abolishing American sanctions against South Africa (23 Nov.).
A provisional governing council is formed in which there are both white and black representatives (7 Dec.). The task of the council is to govern the country until the elections.
The white majority Parliament endorses the new Constitution elaborated at the CODESA negotiations, thus creating equal rights for whites and blacks for the first time in the history of the country (22 Dec.).

1994   At the parliamentary elections, the ANC almost achieves an absolute majority; the runner-up is the National Party (Apr.). The new President of the country is Nelson Mandela, and one of its new deputy Presidents is F. W. de Klerk.
Wave of strikes and continuing clashes between ANC and Inkatha supporters (July). Land Rights Act attempts redress of grievances of those who had lost land (Nov.).

1995   Death of Joe Slovo (Jan.). 'Fresh start' announced by Mandela and de Klerk following bitter disputes with ANC over indemnities from prosecution for police and government members. Murder charges laid against former Defence Minister, Gen. Malan, and 10 other officers. Draft of new Constitution presented (22 Nov.).

1996　Trial of Malan and 15 co-defendants on charges of murder and conspiracy against ANC supporters ends in acquittal (Mar.–Oct.). New Constitution approved (7 May). De Klerk announces withdrawal of National Party from government at end of June to normalize politics. Thabo Mbeki designated successor to Mandela. New Constitution signed (10 Dec.).

1997　F. W. de Klerk announces his retirement from active politics (Sept.)

1998　P. W. Botha refuses to attend hearing of Truth and Reconciliation Committee and is threatened with prosecution.
Army units suppress attempted mutiny in Lesotho (Sept.).
President Mandela receives Truth and Reconciliation Commission Report (Oct.).

1999　Trade agreement concluded with EU (Mar.).
Second non-racial election won by ANC with 66% of vote (266 of the 400 seats) (June).
Thabo Mbeki elected President. Retirement of Nelson Mandela from political life.

2000　Democratic Alliance formed as coalition to contest the forthcoming municipal elections (Jan.).
Controversy erupts over statements by President Mbeki on links between HIV and AIDS.

2001　Major fraud allegations over US arms deal (June).

2004　President Mbeki elected for second term (Apr.).

THE FAR EAST

JAPAN SINCE 1914

1914   Japan declares war on Germany; Japanese forces seize German Pacific islands and naval base in Shantung.

1918   Beginning of 'party government'. Hara Kei of the Seiyukai becomes Prime Minister, the first commoner to do so (Sept.); Japanese land with British forces at Vladivostok in Russia (Apr.).

1920   Peace concluded with Germany (Jan.); Japan given control of former German Pacific islands.

1921   Assassination of Premier Hara (Nov.). Washington Naval Conference opens (Nov.), followed by Treaty in 1922 (see p. 272).

1922   Establishment of Japanese Communist Party. Japan restores Shantung and Kiaochow (Tsingtao) to China (Nov.). Withdraws from Vladivostok.

1923   Great earthquake in Japan (Sept.).

1925   Russo-Japanese Treaty (Jan.). The Universal Manhood Suffrage Bill (increasing electorate from 3 million to 14 million) and the Peace Preservation Law are passed by the Diet.

1926   Taisho Emperor dies and is succeeded by Hirohito who assumes the title of Showa Emperor (25 Dec.).

1928   First election under universal manhood suffrage held (20 Feb.).
1929   Japan occupies Shantung peninsula in China (Apr.–May); bomb attack on Chang Tso-lin in Manchuria (4 June).

1930   Japan agrees to London Naval Treaty. Prime Minister Hamaguchi is shot dead on Tokyo station.

1931   Japanese Kwantung army occupies Manchuria (Sept.).

1932   Manchukuo Republic is proclaimed (Jan.). 'May 15th Incident' – attempted coup by junior military officers. Saito forms a non-party cabinet. Shanghai campaign (28 Mar.–3 May).

1933   Japan withdraws from the League of Nations (Mar.), following Lytton Report on Japanese action in Manchuria.

1936 'Feb. 26th Incident' – Japanese officers murder several ministers and generals. Hirohito forms a militarist cabinet. Anti-Comintern Pact signed in Berlin (Nov.).

1937 Outbreak of Sino-Japanese war after 'Marco Polo Bridge Incident' (Sept.). By the end of the year Beijing, Shanghai and Nanking are in Japanese hands.

1938 National Mobilization Bill passed (Mar.).

1939 Fighting breaks out on Manchukuo–Mongolian border with Russia (Apr.–July). Japan renounces 1911 Trade Treaty with USA (27 July).

1940 Dissolution of political parties (July–Aug.). Entrance of Japanese troops into French Indo-China (23 Sept.). Japan signs Tripartite Pact with Germany and Italy (27 Sept.).

1941 The Imperial Rule Assistance Association is established (Oct.). Soviet–Japanese neutrality pact (Apr.). Tojo becomes Premier (Oct.). Japanese attack Pearl Harbor; USA and Britain declare war on Japan on 7 Dec. (for events in the Pacific War see pp. 139–40).

1945 Atomic bombing of Hiroshima and Nagasaki. Japan accepts the terms of surrender (Aug.). Authority passes to General MacArthur as Supreme Commander of the Allied Powers (SCAP).

1946 Emperor Hirohito makes the 'Human Being Declaration' (Jan.). New Japanese constitution is promulgated (Nov.); women obtain the vote. War Crimes trials begin.

1947 Japanese women obtain rights to property and divorce.

1948 Tojo, Hirota and 5 others are executed for war crimes (Dec.).

1950 The 'Red Purge' – dismissal of suspected communist sympathizers from office – begins (Feb.). The Japanese create the National Police Reserve (Oct.).

1951 Japanese peace treaty with Allies is signed in San Francisco. Japan signs the Mutual Security Agreement with USA (Sept.).

1952 The occupation of Japan ends.

1955 Liberals and Democrats in Japan merge to form the Liberal Democratic Party.

1956 Japan is admitted to the United Nations.

1960 Demonstrations occur when the Mutual Security Agreement with USA is ratified (May). Prime Minister Ikeda announces the 'Income Doubling Plan' (Sept.).

1964　Olympic Games held in Tokyo (Oct.).

1967　Demonstrations against Japan's support for USA's involvement in the Vietnam War (Oct.).

1968　Students occupy Tokyo University Campus (June–Jan. 1969).

1970　Mutual Security Agreement with USA renewed (Jan.). Mishima Yukio attempts a coup and then commits suicide (Nov.).

1971　USA agrees to return Okinawa to Japan (June).

1975　Investigation into 'Lockheed affair' begins (Apr.).

1978　Treaty of Peace and Friendship between China and Japan signed (Aug.).

1980　Prime Minister Masayoshi Ohira dies (23 June). Zenko Suzuki forms government (July).

1982　Nakasone forms government (Nov.).

1983　Ex-Prime Minister Tanaka found guilty on charges arising from the Lockheed affair.

1986　Nakasone wins outright victory in general election after period of dependence on minority parties (July).

1987　Takeshita chosen to succeed Nakasone (Oct.).

1989　Death of Emperor Hirohito (7 Jan.); succeeded by Crown Prince Akihito. Takeshita forced to resign over 'Recruit' scandal (Apr.). Foreign Secretary, Uno, succeeds, but forced to resign over sexual allegations (July). Toshiki Kaifu became Prime Minister on 9 Aug.

1990　The LDP once more wins an absolute majority at the parliamentary elections (Feb.). At his official accession to the throne, Emperor Akihito announces the commencement of the Heisei, the 'age of peace' (Nov.).

1991　Negotiations commence on the possibility of repossessing the Kuril Islands which were seized by the Soviet Union during the last days of the Second World War (Mar.). Kiichi Miyazawa succeeds Kaifu as the leader of the LDP and the government (Nov.).

1993　The opposition's vote of no confidence overthrows the Miyazawa government (June). More than 40 MPs leave the LDP and create a new opposition group. At the unscheduled early elections, the LDP remains the strongest party but loses its majority in parliament (July). The opposition creates a 7 party coalition government (for the first time since 1955), headed by Hosokawa (Aug.). In his speech to the parliament,

Hosokawa apologizes to the peoples of Asia for Japan's deeds during the Second World War.

1994   Reform programme accepted in upper house (Jan.). Resignation of Hosokawa following corruption allegations (Apr.); short-lived Hata administration succeeded by first socialist premier, Murayama (29 June). Electoral reform package passed (Nov.) replacing multi-member constituencies with single-member constituencies. New opposition party Shinshinto (New Frontier Party) formed (Dec.).

1995   Government wins no-confidence debate amidst concern about how to deal with anniversary of end of war in Europe (June).

1996   Murayama resigns (5 Jan.); succeeded by Hashimoto, restoring LDP rule. Joint Japanese–American declaration emphasizes Japan's role in regional security (Apr.).
In Oct. elections LDP under Hashimoto take 239 out of 500 Diet seats, forming minority government.

1997   Growing financial turmoil in south-east Asia casts doubts on Japanese banking system (Nov.); £47 billion package to stabilize financial system.

1998   Asian economic crisis intensifies: yen drops to 7-year low against dollar (June). Resignation of Prime Minister Ryutoro Hashimoto after electoral setback (July). Keizo Obuchi new Prime Minister. First state visit by a Chinese head of government (Jiang Zemin) (Nov.).

2000   Yoshiro Mori takes over as Prime Minister (Apr.).

2001   Resignation of Mori; replaced by Junichiro Koizumi (Apr.).

THE MAKING OF THE CHINESE REVOLUTION, 1914–49

1917　China declares war on Germany.

1918　China makes secret military agreements with Japan.

1919　At the Versailles Conference, former German concessions in China are passed to Japan instead of back to China on the basis of 1918 agreements. This leads to the 4 May protest movement.

1921　Chinese Communist Party (CCP) is founded (July).

1923　Period of Guomindang (Kuomintang)[1] and Russian collaboration signalled by the Sun–Joffe agreement. Sun Yat-sen publishes *San Min Chu I* ('Three Principles of the People').

1925　Death of Sun Yat-sen (12 Mar.).

1926　Chiang Kai-shek comes to power. The Northern Expedition is launched (July).

1927　CCP is shattered by Chiang Kai-shek's coup in Shanghai (Apr.). The Red Army is founded. Mao Zedong's Autumn Harvest Insurrection fails (Aug.).

1928　The Northern Expedition succeeds in uniting China under the National Government of Chiang Kai-shek (Oct.).

1930　The first 'Bandit Extermination Campaign' against the CCP is launched by Chiang Kai-shek (Dec.).

1931　Japanese invade Manchuria (Sept.). The Chinese Soviet Republic is founded by Mao Zedong in Jiangxi province.

1932　Manchukuo Republic proclaimed (Jan.). Japanese invade Jehol province (Dec.).

1934　The fifth anti-CCP extermination campaign fails to break into Jiangxi. The Long March begins (Oct.). and its survivors arrive in Shanxi in Oct. 1935.

1936　Sian incident. Chiang Kai-shek captured and released (Dec.).

1937　The Marco Polo Bridge incident leads to the Sino-Japanese War. Guomindang and CCP form a 'united front'.

1938　Chiang Kai-shek withdraws to Chongqing (Chungking).

---

[1]　The romanization of Chinese characters used to be based on the Wade–Giles system, but now follows the Pinyin system, e.g. Mao Zedong not Tse-tung, Beijing not Peking. In this book we have followed the Pinyin system apart from a few other names more familiar in the older style.

1945   Japan surrenders.

1946   The Marshall mission fails. Civil war resumes between the Guomindang
        and CCP.

1948   Lin Biao begins the offensive against the remaining Nationalist
        strongholds in Manchuria (Jan.). CCP announces the creation of the
        North China People's Government (Sept.).

1949   Chiang Kai-shek resigns as President (Jan.). The People's Republic of
        China is proclaimed in Beijing by Mao Zedong (1 Oct.). Chiang Kai-shek
        and Guomindang forces withdraw to Formosa (Taiwan).

CHINA SINCE 1949

1949   Chinese People's Republic proclaimed (1 Oct.). A People's Political Consultative Conference passes Organic Laws and a Common Programme setting up a multinational, communist state with chairman of the Republic as head of state. Mao Zedong first Chairman (Oct.). Chinese Nationalist forces take refuge on Formosa (Taiwan) and garrison islands of Quemoy, Matsu and Tachen.

1950   Outbreak of Korean War (June.). Chinese troops intervene to repulse United Nations counter-offensive into North Korea (Oct.); 250,000 Chinese troops cross the Yalu River and force retreat of UN forces. Chinese invasion of Tibet (Oct.). Agrarian Law dispossesses landlords and gives land to peasants who are grouped together into collectives.

1951   UN condemns Chinese aggression in Korea (Feb.); further Chinese offensives held by UN troops (Feb.–May). Tibet signs agreement giving China control of Tibet's affairs (May); Chinese troops enter Lhasa (Sept.).

1953   Ceasefire in Korea (July). First Five Year Plan nationalizes most of industry.

1954   Permanent constitution established; guarantees dominant place of the Communist Party.

1955   US Navy evacuates 42,000 Nationalist troops and civilians from Tachen Islands following artillery bombardment.

1956   Mao encourages criticism of regime – 'a hundred flowers' to bloom.

1958   Shelling of Quemoy leads to US military build-up. Mao Zedong inaugurates Second Five Year Plan and 'Great Leap Forward' to increase industrial production by 100% and agricultural output by 35%. Collective farms to be grouped in communes and industrial production based on them.

1959   Great Leap Forward yields disappointing results following huge dislocation of production; major famine in parts of China.
Uprising in Tibet put down and Dalai Lama forced to flee to India (Mar.).

1960   Quarrel with Russia over 'revisionism' leads to withdrawal of Russian advisers and technical support.

1962   Chinese war with India in Himalayas (see p. 311).

1964   China explodes first atomic bomb.

1966   Beginning of Cultural Revolution, attempt to introduce Maoist principles in all aspects of life. Red Guards inaugurate attacks on all hierarchic and traditional features of society. Intellectuals and others forced to undergo 'self-criticism'.

1967–8   Schools and educational institutions closed by Red Guards.

1969   Chairman of Republic, Liu Shaoqi, disgraced. Border clash with Soviet Union (see p. 316).

1971   Lin Biao, deputy Prime Minister, disgraced and reportedly killed in air crash. Later reports suggest that he was executed.

1973   Deng Xiaoping, disgraced in Cultural Revolution, becomes Deputy Prime Minister.

1975   New constitution replaces single head of state with a collective, the Standing Committee of the National Peoples' Congress.

1976   Death of Mao Zedong (Sept.); Hua Guofeng becomes Chairman and Prime Minister. Begins action against 'Gang of Four' and Mao's widow, Jiang Qing.

1977   Deng Xiaoping reinstated. Jiang Qing expelled from Party and sentenced to death, but sentence commuted to life imprisonment. More pragmatic economic policy adopted.

1978   New constitution moderates constitution of 1975. China opens diplomatic relations with the United States.

1979   Chinese invasion of Vietnam (see p. 324). Demonstrations for greater freedom in Beijing. Cultural Revolution denounced as a disaster.

1980   Zhao Ziyang becomes Prime Minister, succeeding Hua Guofeng.

1981   Hu Yaobang succeeds Hua Guofeng as Chairman of Party until post abolished in 1982.

1982   New constitution approved for Communist Party abolishing posts of Chairman and Vice-Chairman. New constitution for China as a whole approved, increasing powers of Prime Minister.

1983   National People's Congress elect Li Xiannian to revived post of President; Deng Xiaoping chosen chairman of new State Military Commission. 'Rectification' campaign against corrupt officials.

1984   Modernization drive reverses emphasis on collective agriculture; relaxation of central quotas and price controls; factories given greater autonomy. Agreement reached with Britain on future of Hong Kong (Sept.).

1985   Five Year Plan announces slowdown in pace of economic reform; fewer cities open to foreign investment and party control reasserted.

1986 Campaign for greater democracy suggested by leadership; student demonstrations in Shanghai and Beijing (Dec.).

1987 Backlash against reform; Hu Yaobang forced to resign and succeeded by Zhao Ziyang. Agreement with Portugal on return in 1999 of Macao to China. 13th Party Congress (Oct.) leads to retirement of 8 senior politicians and promotion of younger technocrats. Li Peng becomes Prime Minister in place of Zhao Ziyang who is confirmed as General Secretary.

1988 Demand for greater speed in reform by Zhao Ziyang (Mar.), but inflation and industrial unrest lead to freeze on price reforms for 2 years (Sept.).

1989 Death of Hu Yaobang (Apr.) leads to student demands for his rehabilitation; sit-ins and demonstrations in several cities. 100,000 students march through Beijing (27 Apr.). Students occupy Tiananmen Square (4 May). Hunger strike amongst students (13 May); million-strong pro-democracy march through Beijing (17 May); Li Peng announces martial law (20 May). Chinese troops disperse students in Tiananmen Square causing over 1,000 deaths, and similar protests quelled in other Chinese cities (4 June). Chinese government arrests thousands of pro-democracy supporters in spite of world outrage at events of 4 June.

1990 The state of emergency is lifted (Jan.). After Deng Xiaoping's resignation, Jiang Zemin becomes President of the Central State Military Committee (Apr.).

1991 The state of war and the Cold War confrontation between Taiwan and China end (May).

1992 China joins the Anti-Nuclear Proliferation Treaty (Mar.). China and South Korea establish full diplomatic relations with one another (Aug.).

1993 At the National People's Assembly, Deng Xiaoping's political line – a mix between economic reforms and political conservatism – is dominant. The constitution is modified; one of its clauses claims that 'the Chinese state is working on creating a Socialist market economy' but the clauses referring to the leading role of the Communist Party and the dictatorship of the proletariat are not altered. Jiang Zemin is elected as the President of the country; thus the leadership of the Party, the state, and the army is concentrated in his hands (Mar.). In Beijing, a Chinese–Indian Treaty is signed (Sept.).

1994 Premier Li Peng institutes price controls on basic commodities (Mar.). Quarrel between the United States and China over human rights leads to defiant China suppressing dissidents (Apr.). None the less, US grants China 'most favoured nation' status (May). New labour law introduced guaranteeing 8-hour day and minimum wage but ending guarantee of a job for life.

1995 Jiang Zemin secures position amidst growing rumours of Deng's ill-health. Jiang Zemin welcomes talks with Taiwan (Oct.) while carrying out military manoeuvres against Taiwan.
China announces new Five Year Plan doubling national output by the year 2000 (Sept.). Further appointments made strengthening Jiang Zemin's position.

1996 China threatens missile attacks on Taiwan (Jan.), then makes missile tests in March and deploys troops opposite island of Quemoy, though later gives a private assurance (Mar.) that it will take no direct action. Deng confined to hospital (May). Meeting of Communist Party leaders in July and August confirms Jiang's position, confirmed at Party Central Committee's meeting in October.
China accuses Dalai Lama (June) of acting as a 'puppet of international forces'.

1997 Death of Deng Xiaoping (19 Feb.). Jiang Zemin assumes authority.
China assumes sovereignty over Hong Kong (July).

1998 Zhu Rongji takes over as Prime Minister (Mar.). US President Bill Clinton visits Beijing (first US Presidential visit since Tiananmen Square) (June).

1999 China reclaims sovereignty over Macao (Portugal's last remaining colony in Asia) (Dec.).

2001 China officially became a member of the World Trade Organization.

2002 Hu Jintao (Vice-President) succeeds Jiang Zemin as President (Nov.).

2003 Zeng Qinghong elected to replace Hu Jintao as Vice-President (Mar.). SARS epidemic spreads (Mar.). Massive demonstrations in Hong Kong in protest at anti-subversion laws and infringements of human rights (July).

2004 Jiang Zemin relinquishes control of armed forces (Sept.).

2005 Death of reformist former leader Zhao Ziyang (Jan.).

INDIA AND PAKISTAN, 1914–47

1917 British government announces the development of self-governing institutions in India with a view to eventual introduction of responsible government.

1919 Rowlatt Act gives power to government to imprison without trial for up to 2 years and causes unrest. Gandhi orders a general strike; widespread riots (Mar.).
Amritsar massacre when General Dyer orders troops to fire on unarmed crowd, resulting in 379 deaths (13 Apr.).
Government of India Act passed introducing the Montagu–Chelmsford reforms giving Indians a separate legislature, a share in provincial government and control over lesser ministries.

1920 Gandhi wins control of Indian National Congress and launches non-cooperation campaign (Sept.). Mohammad Ali Jinnah, president of the Indian Muslim League, leaves Congress.

1921 Disobedience campaign reaches height. Peasant attacks on landlords. Killing of Hindu landlords leads to sectarian rioting and to growing split between the largely Hindu Congress and the Muslim League.

1922 Gandhi imprisoned.

1924 Gandhi released from prison owing to his ill-health.

1927 Commission appointed under Lord Simon to study workings of Montagu–Chelmsford reforms.

1928 Gandhi becomes leader of Congress; Congress demands complete independence for India within 12 months (Dec.).

1930 Nehru as President of Congress proclaims the independence of India (26 Jan.).
Gandhi starts civil disobedience campaign against the Salt Tax; marches to the sea in protest and is arrested (May). Congress outlawed and leaders arrested.
Britain summons Round Table Conference in London, but boycotted by Congress leaders.

1931 Gandhi holds talks with Viceroy of India, Lord Irwin. Second Round Table Conference in London attended by Gandhi.

1932 Congress leaders once again arrested.

1935 Government of India Act passed (Aug.), providing for complete parliamentary self-government in the provinces and a federal government for the whole of India including the princely states. Ministers responsible to the federal legislature were to be left in charge of all subjects except defence and external affairs, which remained the responsibility of the governor-general.

1937   Elections for the provincial assemblies under the Government of India Act. Congress Party forms ministries in 7 of the eleven provinces. Projected federation delayed by failure of princely states to accede to it.

1939   Muslim League declares opposition to proposed federation because of fear of Hindu domination.

1940   Muslim League at session in Lahore demands that India be partitioned and that the Muslim areas of the north-west and north-east form separate 'independent states' i.e. 'Pakistan'.
Introduction of federation adjourned indefinitely as a result of outbreak of Second World War.

1942   Sir Stafford Cripps sent from Britain with proposals to rally Indian opinion at time of Japanese advances in south-east Asia. British promise independence at the end of the war and a new constitution. British offer Muslims and princely states the prospect of staying out of the projected India union and forming separate unions. Both Congress and Muslim League reject offer. Congress begins 'Quit India' movement and most of its leaders arrested, meanwhile Jinnah consolidates his position as head of the Muslim League.

1945   New Labour government in Britain announces that it seeks 'an early realization of self-government in India'.
In Indian elections, Muslim League strengthens its hold on Muslim areas.

1946   British offer full independence to India. Negotiations between British Cabinet Mission and Indian leaders fail to agree a plan acceptable to both Congress and Muslim League.
Muslim League declares 'direct action' to achieve Pakistan.
'Direct Action Day' (16 Aug.) provokes massive communal rioting in Calcutta leaving over 4,000 dead; spreads to Bengal, Dacca and Bihar.
Lord Wavell succeeds in drawing Congress and League representatives into an interim government but fails to bring Congress and the League into a Constituent Assembly to create a constitution for a united India.

1947   British government declares (Feb.) it will transfer power not later than June 1948 to responsible Indian hands; announces that Lord Mountbatten to replace Lord Wavell as Viceroy.
Serious communal rioting in the Punjab and elsewhere in anticipation of partition (Mar.).
Mountbatten becomes Viceroy (Mar.) and advances the date for the transfer of power from June 1948 to 15 Aug. 1947.
British government announces plan for the partition of India and the

creation of two separate dominions of India and Pakistan; the plan is accepted by Congress, the Muslim League and the Sikhs (June).
India and Pakistan become independent states (15 Aug.).
Savage communal rioting breaks out in the days before independence in eastern and western Punjab.
Mass exodus of Hindu and Sikh refugees from Pakistan and Muslims from India accompanied by massacres and rioting (Aug.–Oct.).

THE SECOND WORLD WAR IN ASIA AND THE PACIFIC, 1937–45

1937   Sino-Japanese War begins (July); Japanese take Shanghai (Nov.);
Nanking (Dec.).

1938   Japanese take Canton and Wuhan (Oct.).

1939   Japanese occupy Hainan.

1940   US fleet moved to Pearl Harbor (May). Japanese forces begin to occupy
French Indo-China (Sept.).

1941   Negotiations between US government and Japan propose neutral area in
Indo-China; US freezes Japanese assets (July).
Japanese propose withdrawal from Indo-China; America presents
counter-demands (Nov.); Japanese task force puts to sea in readiness for
attack on Pearl Harbor (26 Nov.). Tokyo tells its American ambassador
that American demands are unacceptable (28 Nov.).
Tokyo orders departure of diplomatic staff from Washington (5 Dec.).
Japanese attack Pearl Harbor (7 Dec.), destroying much of US Pacific
fleet. US declares war on Japan.
Japanese invade Thailand and Malaya; attack Hong Kong; bombard
Guam, Midway and Wake Island; attack air bases in Philippines
(8 Dec.).
Japanese invade Gilbert Islands (9 Dec.); sink *Prince of Wales* and
Repulse off Malaya and seize Guam (10 Dec.).
Japanese begin invasion of Burma (11 Dec.); make large-scale landing in
Philippines (22 Dec.); capture Hong Kong (25 Dec.).

1942   Japanese capture Manila (2 Jan.); invade Dutch East Indies (11 Jan.);
launch main invasion of Burma across Thai border (20 Jan.); seize Rabaul
and Solomon Islands (23 Jan.).
Fall of Malaya to Japanese and surrender of Singapore with capture of
130,000 Allied troops (15 Feb.).
Japanese landings in New Guinea (Mar.).
Japanese occupy Batavia (Jakarta) and rest of Java (6–9 Mar.); take
Rangoon (8 Mar.).
Japanese cut supply route to China, the Burma Road (Apr.).
Fall of Mandalay to Japanese (1 May).
Battle of the Coral Sea (4–8 May) forestalls Japanese invasion of
Australia through Port Moresby in New Guinea.
Surrender of last American and Filipino forces at Corregidor (6 May);
last British forces leave Burma (20 May). Battle of Midway (2 June);
major defeat for Japanese navy. Australian troops defeat Japanese assault
on Port Moresby (Aug.–Oct.).
Battle for Guadalcanal opens after US landing (Aug.). Allied offensive in
Arakan (Burma) begins (Oct.).

1943   Japanese withdraw from Guadalcanal (1–7 Feb.). Arakan offensive
       defeated (Mar.).
       Admiral Yamamoto killed when his aircraft shot down (Apr.).
       Mountbatten becomes Supreme Allied Commander in Burma (Aug.).
       Americans land on Makin and Tarawa in Gilbert Islands (Nov.);
       beginning of island-hopping campaign. American landing in New Britain
       (Dec.).

1944   General Stillwell's advance into northern Burma (Jan.).
       Americans land in Marshall Islands (Feb.).
       Japanese offensive into India – 'The March on Delhi' – battles of Imphal
       and Kohima defeat Japanese (Feb.–June).
       Japanese launch major offensive in South China (Apr.–Sept.).
       Americans invade Saipan, Mariana Islands (15 June).
       Battle of the Philippine Sea. Japanese carrier forces receive crippling
       defeat and retire to Okinawa (19–20 June).
       Americans retake Saipan (9 July) and Guam (26 July).
       Japanese withdraw from vital centre of Myitkyina in northern Burma
       (30 July).
       US marines take Peleliu Island in Palau Group (Sept.–Oct.)
       American forces land in Philippines (20 Oct.).
       Battle of Leyte Gulf destroys much of remaining Japanese navy
       (23–6 Oct.).

1945   Americans capture Manila (3 Feb.); marines land on Iwo Jima (19 Feb.).
       British forces cross Irrawaddy River in Burma (Feb.); American forces
       take Lashio in northern Burma, opening the 'Burma Road' to China
       (7 Mar.); Japanese evacuate Mandalay (19 Mar.).
       Large-scale incendiary raids on Tokyo begin massive air assault on
       Japanese cities (25 Feb.–Aug.).
       Americans land in Okinawa (1 Apr.).
       British take Rangoon (3 May).
       Okinawa campaign completed (2 June).
       Last Japanese forces in Burma killed or captured (4 Aug.).
       Atomic bombs dropped on Hiroshima and Nagasaki (6 and 9 Aug.).
       Russians invade Manchuria and Korea (9–12 Aug.).
       Japan surrenders (14 Aug.).

CASUALTIES IN THE PACIFIC ISLAND CAMPAIGN[1]

Dates	Island	Strength of Japanese garrison	Japanese killed	Americans killed
Aug. 1942–Feb. 1943	Guadalcanal	36,000	25,000	1,592
May 1943	Attu (N. Pacific)	2,650	2,622	549
Nov. 1943	Tarawa	4,600	4,580	1,090
June–Aug. 1944	Saipan	32,000	30,000	3,426
Sept.–Dec. 1944	Peleliu	10,500	10,000	1,500
Oct.–Dec. 1944	Leyte	70,000	65,000	3,593
Feb.–Mar. 1945	Iwo Jima	23,000	21,900	4,554
Apr.–June 1945	Okinawa	80,000	73,000	7,613

[1] Ground fighting only.
Source: C. J. Argyle, *Japan at War, 1937–45* (Arthur Barker, London, 1976), p. 139.

WARSHIPS LAUNCHED IN JAPAN AND THE UNITED STATES, 1937–45

		Battleships	*Aircraft carriers*	*Cruisers*
1937–40	Japan	2	5	4
	USA	2	2	7
1941	Japan	0	3	2
	USA	3	9	6
1942	Japan	0	6	3
	USA	3	35	10
1943	Japan	0	7	0
	USA	1	51	11
1944	Japan	0	5	1
	USA	1	44	20
1945	Japan	0	0	0
	USA	0	20	11

Source: C. J. Argyle, *Japan at War, 1937–45* (Arthur Barker, London, 1976), p. 186.

AIRCRAFT PRODUCTION IN JAPAN AND THE UNITED STATES, 1939–45

	Japan	United States
1939	4,467	2,141
1940	4,768	6,086
1941	5,088	19,433
1942	8,861	47,836
1943	16,693	85,898
1944	28,180	96,318
1945	8,263	46,001

Source: R. Goralski, *World War II Almanac, 1931–1945*
(Bonanza Books, New York, 1981), p. 438.

THE INDIAN SUBCONTINENT SINCE 1947

1947   India and Pakistan become independent states (15 Aug.); Nehru and Ali
       Khan lead their respective Cabinets. Rioting and massacres accompany
       the partition process in which up to 250,000 people die.
       Mass exodus of refugees across new borders between India and Pakistan
       in the west, smaller flow and less violence in the east between India and
       East Pakistan.
       Hindu ruler of Kashmir 'accedes' his largely Muslim state to India.
       Sikh Punjab is scene of some of most serious violence; 2 million Sikhs
       flee across border into India where they begin demand for greater
       autonomy or independence for Sikh Punjab.

1948   Assassination of Mahatma Gandhi in Delhi (30 Jan.)
       Ceylon becomes independent dominion (Feb.).
       Mohammed Ali Jinnah dies.
       UN truce line established in Kashmir leaving a third of the state in
       Pakistan hands and two-thirds in Indian.
       Pakistan demands implementation of UN sponsored plebiscite on future
       of Kashmir.
       India sets up Atomic Energy Commission.

1950   Constitution of Indian Union promulgated. India becomes a Republic
       within British Commonwealth.

1951   Liaquat Ali Khan assassinated.

1951–2   First national General Election in India confirms Congress Party
         dominance.

1954   Indo-Chinese treaty.

1955   Bulganin and Khrushchev visit India.

1956   States Reorganization Act in India.
       New constitution declares Pakistan an Islamic state.
       India begins Second Five Year Plan and builds several steel plants.

1958   Ayub Khan becomes President of Pakistan.

1959   Tibetan uprising; Dalai Lama flees to India.
       Treaty of India and Pakistan over Indus waters.

1960   Union of Kashmir with India.

1962   Indian and Chinese forces fight in the Himalayas; ceasefire agreed (see
       p. 311).

1964   Death of Nehru; Lal Bahadur Shastri Prime Minister.

1965   Indo-Pakistan War (see p. 313).

Tamil riots against Hindi language; English confirmed as official language of India.

1966   Death of Shastri; Mrs Indira Gandhi becomes Prime Minister.
        Indian government redraws boundary of the Punjab state to give it a majority of Sikhs, and attempts to appease Sikh separatist agitation.

1969   Yahya Khan President of Pakistan.

1971   Revolt in East Pakistan, which secedes from Pakistan to form state of Bangladesh (Mar.). Revolt crushed (May), but guerrilla war continues. Growing clashes with India and state of emergency in Pakistan (Nov.). War with India (Dec.) and Indian invasion of East Pakistan; Pakistan accepts ceasefire and recognizes new state of Bangladesh (see p. 318). Adjustment of border between India and Pakistan in Kashmir agreed at Simla Conference.
        Zulfikar Ali Bhutto becomes President of Pakistan.
        State of emergency declared in Ceylon following disclosure of plot to overthrow government by ultra-left JVP. Over 1,000 killed and 4,000 arrested.

1972   Pakistan leaves the Commonwealth.
        Ceylon adopts new constitution and becomes Republic of Sri Lanka.

1973   Bhutto becomes Prime Minister of Pakistan under new constitution.

1975   State of emergency declared in India because of growing strikes and unrest; opposition leaders arrested.
        Sheikh Mujibur Rahman, ruler of Bangladesh, is deposed and killed in military coup; Khandakar Mushtaque Ahmed is sworn in as President.

1977   Morarji Desai leads Janata Party to victory over Mrs Gandhi in general election – first defeat of Congress Party since independence.
        Bhutto overthrown after allegations of ballot-rigging; constitution suspended.
        Serious rioting in Tamil areas of Sri Lanka. Constitution amended to strengthen President.

1978   General Zia ul-Haq becomes President of Pakistan.

1979   Ex-prime-minister Bhutto executed.

1980   Indira Gandhi wins election victory for Congress Party and returns to power.

1981   State of emergency declared in Sri Lanka because of attacks by Tamil Liberation Tigers.

1983   General Ershad assumes Presidency of Bangladesh.

Serious violence between Sinhalese and Tamils in Sri Lanka.
Emergency rule invoked in Punjab to suppress Sikh terrorism.

1984   Indian troops storm Golden Temple in Amritsar, centre of Sikh separatists (June). Indira Gandhi assassinated by Sikh members of her bodyguard and her son, Rajiv Gandhi, becomes Prime Minister; Hindu attacks on Sikhs kill an estimated 2,000 people.
Talks between Tamils and President Jayawardene of Sri Lanka break down; conflict escalates in Tamil areas.
Fighting between Indian and Pakistan troops on the Sianchin Glacier in Kashmir.
General Zia confirmed as President by referendum.

1985   Further heavy fighting in Kashmir.
President Zia confirmed in office for five-year period.

1986   Tamils kill Sinhalese in further terror raids in Sri Lanka.
Benazir Bhutto returns to Pakistan and demands end to martial law and free elections.

1987   Emergency rule imposed in Punjab.
Rajiv Gandhi and President Jayawardene sign an accord (July) offering more autonomy to Tamil areas; Indian peace-keeping force invited into Sri Lanka to supervise. Attacks on Indian army lead to assault on Tamil strongholds in Jaffna peninsula.

1988   President Zia of Pakistan killed in air crash (Aug.); Benazir Bhutto wins largest number of seats in general election (Nov.) and becomes Prime Minister.

1989   Amid continuing violence in Sri Lanka the Indian forces agree to withdraw.
Pakistan rejoins the Commonwealth.

1990   The withdrawal of Indian forces from Sri Lanka is completed (Mar.). In Pakistan, President Khan dismisses Benazir Bhutto, who is charged with abuse of power (Sept.). The parliamentary elections are won by the Islamic Democratic Association (Oct.); Mian Nawaz Sharif becomes the new Prime Minister (Nov.).
Chandra Sekhar is the new Prime Minister of India (Nov.).

1991   The Pakistani parliament endorses laws reinforcing Islamic jurisdiction (May). Rajiv Gandhi is assassinated in a bomb attack (29 May). After the election victory of the Indian National Congress, the new President of the party, Narasimha Rao, forms a government (June).

1992   Hindu extremists destroy the Babri mosque in Ayodhya (Dec.); in the religious clashes that spread across the country some 1,200 people are killed.

1993   In Sri Lanka, fanatics of the LTTE murder President Premadasa (1 May).
His successor is the former Prime Minister, Dingiri Banda Wijetunge. In
bomb attacks in Bombay and Calcutta more than 200 people are killed
(Mar.). Concluding the year-long power struggle, President Khan and
Prime Minister Sharif – under pressure from the chief-of-staff – resign
(July). After the election victory of her party, Ms Bhutto forms a
government (Oct.); her candidate, the former minister of foreign affairs,
Faruk Ahmed Leghari, is elected as president
Indian security forces close in on the Hazratbal mosque in Srinagari
(Kashmir) (Oct.). The armed Kashmir separatists, who have seized the
building earlier, peacefully surrender in November.

1994   Strikes and demonstrations in New Delhi against India's accession to the
Uruguay Round of the General Agreement on Tariff and Trade (Apr.).
Rao government loses support in state elections (Dec.).
Benazir Bhutto acquitted of corruption charges which had caused her
downfall in Aug. 1990 (Feb.). Opposition parties withdraw from National
Assembly (Aug.).
In Sri Lanka, following elections (Aug.), Chandrika Bandaranaike
Kumaratunga is appointed Prime Minister. She wins Presidential
elections (Oct.) and appoints her mother, Mrs Sirimavo Bandaranaike,
Premier (Nov.).

1995   Rao government wins vote of censure over Kashmir (Apr.).
Chief Minister of Punjab killed by Sikh separatists (May).
Religious and factional clashes in Pakistan lead to over 1,000 deaths by
July; breakdown of negotiations between Benazir Bhutto and opposition
over political violence (Aug.). Army officers arrested for plotting Islamic
fundamentalist coup.
Breakdown of ceasefire with Tamil Tigers (Apr.) leads to continuing
clashes. President Kumaratunga offers plan for Tamil autonomy (Aug.),
but rejected. Sri Lankan government forces surround Jaffna, the Tamil
stronghold.

1996   In India, £11 million corruption scandal prompts resignation of 3
ministers and early general election (Jan.). Congress Party heavily
defeated in elections (Apr.–May) which sees rise of Hindu nationalist
Bharatiya Janata Party (BJP) and National Front–Left Front (NF–LF).
Short-lived BJP government under Atal Behari Vajpayee followed by
NF–LF administration led by H. D. Deve Gowda (June). After persistent
bribery allegations, Rao resigned leadership of Congress Party (Sept.).
Imran Khan founds new party (Apr.) in Pakistan (the Justice Movement)
amidst continuing violence. Benazir Bhutto dismissed from office by
President Leghari following murder of her brother (leader of a breakaway
faction) and renewed charges of corruption.

Sri Lankan army seals off Jaffna peninsula (Apr.) but Tamil bomb attacks continue in Colombo and elsewhere (July).

1997   Congress Party removes support from government and Gowda stands down as leader; replaced by Inder Kumer Gujral (Apr.).
        In Pakistan, the military form a 10-member security council giving armed forces a formal advisory role in government (Jan.). In elections in February the Pakistan Muslim League won a decisive victory under Nawaz Sharif over Bhutto's Pakistan People's Party (Feb.) Benazir Bhutto faced with new charges of corruption (Sept.).

1998   BJP government formed in India after inconclusive election (Mar.).
        India and Pakistan explode nuclear devices (Apr. and May).
        Economic sanctions imposed, lifted in November. State elections see big gains for Congress Party (Nov.).

1999   Indian Prime Minister Vajpayee defeated in confidence vote (Apr.).
        General election called for September. Benazir Bhutto jailed for 5 years on corruption charges (Apr.). Indian general election narrowly won by Hindu BJP (Sept./Oct.) Military coup in Pakistan led by General Musharraf ousts Nawaz Sharif (Oct.).

2000   Nawaz Sharif sentenced to life imprisonment (Apr.).

2001   General Pervez Musharraf sworn in as President (June). Bomb attack on state legislature kills 40 in Indian-controlled Kashmir (Oct.). Suicide attack by Kashmiri militants on Indian parliament in New Delhi (Dec.). India severs diplomatic links. Indian and Pakistani troops mass along their borders.

2002   Formal ceasefire agreed in Sri Lanka between government and Tamil Tiger rebels, ending 20-year conflict (Feb.). Referendum approves further 5-year term for General Pervez Musharraf in widely boycotted poll (Apr.). Renewed tension after attack on Indian army base in Kashmir (May). Both nations on brink of war. Resignation of President Badruddoza Chowdhury in Bangladesh (June). Ban on Tamil Tigers lifted ahead of peace talks which begin later in Sept.

2003   Collapse of peace talks in Sri Lanka (Apr.). Restoration of diplomatic representation and air links between India and Pakistan (May). Ceasefire announced by Pakistan in disputed Kashmir (Nov.).

2004   Meeting of Indian Prime Minister Vajpayee and President Musharraf (first such meeting since 2001) (Jan.). General election in India sees sweeping gains by Sonia Gandhi's Congress Party (Apr.). Manmohan Singh becomes Prime Minister (first Sikh to hold this office). Devastation from tsunami (26 Dec.) leaves thousands dead in India and Sri Lanka.

INDO-CHINA AND VIETNAM, 1945–75

1945   Japanese disarm French forces and an 'independent' Vietnam with Bao
        Dai as Emperor is proclaimed (Mar.).
        Japan surrenders (15 Aug.); demonstrations in Hanoi spread throughout
        the country.
        Communist-dominated Viet Minh seize power; Ho Chi Minh declares
        Vietnam independent and founds Democratic Republic of Vietnam
        (2 Sept.).
        French troops return to Vietnam and clash with communist forces;
        Chinese occupy Vietnam north of 16th Parallel (Sept.).

1946   Franco-Chinese accord allows French to reoccupy northern half of
        Vietnam (Feb.).
        France recognizes the Democratic Republic of Vietnam as a free state
        within the French Union (6 Mar.).
        Breakdown of March accord, French bombard Haiphong and Ho Chi
        Minh calls for resistance to the French; beginning of Indo-Chinese war
        with surprise attack on French bases (Dec.).

1948   French create 'State of Vietnam' with Bao Dai as head of state (June).

1949   Laos recognized as an independent state linked to France (July).
        Cambodia recognized as an independent state linked to France (Nov.).

1950   Communist China and the Soviet Union recognize the Democratic
        Republic of Vietnam led by Ho Chi Minh (Jan.).
        United States announces military and economic aid for the French in
        Vietnam, Laos and the rest of Indo-China (May).

1951   Communist offensive takes most of northern Vietnam.

1954   Battle of Dien Bien Phu (Mar.–May) ends in French defeat.
        Ngo Dinh Diem appointed Premier in South Vietnam by Bao Dai
        (July).
        Geneva Agreements on Vietnam, partitioning Vietnam along 17th
        Parallel (July).
        Peace agreement signed in Geneva providing for a referendum in 1956 to
        decide government of a united Vietnam is not signed by the United States
        or South Vietnam (Aug.).
        South-East Asia Treaty Organization (SEATO) set up in Manila to
        combat communist expansion (8 Sept.).
        Viet Minh assume formal control of North Vietnam (Oct.).

1955   United States begins direct aid to government of South Vietnam (Jan.);
        US instructors requested (May).
        Cambodia becomes an independent state (Sept.).
        Diem deposes Bao Dai and proclaims the 'Republic of Vietnam' (Oct.).

1956   Prince Sihanouk renounces SEATO protection for Cambodia (Feb.).
       Communists share power in Laos (Aug.).

1957   Communist Pathet Lao attempt to seize power in Laos (May).

1958   Communist guerrillas involved in attacks in South Vietnam.

1959   Communist Party Central Committee sanctions greater reliance on
       military activity; communist underground activity increases; Diem
       government steps up repressive measures.
       Communist Pathet Lao seek to gain control over northern Laos.

1960   Communist National Liberation Front of South Vietnam formed (Dec.).
       US advisers number 900.

1961   Pro-Western government formed in Laos; North Vietnam and Soviet
       Union send aid to communist insurgents.
       President Kennedy decides to increase military aid and advisers in South
       Vietnam (Nov.); US personnel reach over 3,000 by end of year.

1962   'Strategic hamlet' programme begun in South Vietnam (Feb.) Australian
       'Military Aid Forces' arrive in Vietnam (Aug.); American forces reach
       11,000 (Dec.).

1963   Buddhist riots in Hué against government repression; seven monks
       commit suicide by fire as part of protests; martial law introduced
       (May–Aug.)
       American-backed coup overthrows Diem (1–2 Nov.); General Duong Van
       Minh takes over (6 Nov.).
       President Kennedy assassinated; Lyndon Johnson takes over (22 Nov.).

1964   Military coup led by Major-General Nguyen Khanh replaces Minh
       government (Jan.).
       US destroyers attacked in Gulf of Tonkin (2–4 Aug.); US aircraft retaliate
       against targets in North Vietnam (4 Aug.); US Congress passes Gulf of
       Tonkin resolution authorizing use of US forces in south-east Asia 'to
       prevent further aggression' (7 Aug.).
       Number of US forces in South Vietnam reaches 23,000 by end of year.

1965   Sustained aerial bombardment of North Vietnam begins, 'Operation
       Rolling Thunder' (Mar.).
       US marines arrive at Da Nang (Mar.); US announces its troops will
       now be used routinely in combat (June).
       Period of political turmoil ends with Air Vice Marshal Nguyen Cao Ky as
       head of South Vietnamese government (June).
       US military strength reaches 181,000 by end of year; widespread anti-war
       demonstrations in the USA.

1966   Air attacks on North Vietnam resume after 37-day pause (31 Jan.).

B-52 bombers first used (Apr.).
Buddhist and student protests against the war in Hué, Da Nang and Saigon, put down by South Vietnamese troops (Mar.–June).
American strength reaches 385,000 by end of year.

1967 'Operation Cedar Falls' against communist-held 'Iron Triangle' north of Saigon (Jan.).
'Operation Junction City', biggest land offensive of the war along Cambodian border (Feb.)
General Nguyen Van Thieu elected President; Ky Vice-President (Sept.).

1968 Communist 'Tet' offensives against major cities of South Vietnam (30–1 Jan.); intense fighting in Hué and Saigon.
'My Lai Massacre' (Mar.).
President Johnson announces withdrawal from presidential race and will seek negotiations (31 Mar.).
Paris Peace Conference opens (31 May).
Bombing of North Vietnam halted (31 Oct.).
President Nixon elected and promises gradual troop withdrawal (Nov.).

1969 American troops in Vietnam reach peak of 541,500 (31 Jan.).
US raids against North Vietnam resume (5 June); Nixon announces first withdrawal of 25,000 combat troops (8 June).
Death of Ho Chi Minh (3 Sept.).
Laotian government requests US aid to resist communist pressure (Oct.).
Widespread anti-war demonstrations in the USA (Nov.–Dec.); 250,000 march in Washington (15 Nov.).

1970 US-backed Lon Nol ousts President Sihanouk in Cambodia (Mar.); Khmer Republic set up.
American and South Vietnamese forces invade Cambodia (Mar.–Apr.).
Anti-war demonstrations in American universities; six students shot at Kent State (4 May).
US ground troops withdraw from Cambodia (June).
US forces in Vietnam 335,800 (Dec.).

1971 South Vietnamese forces invade Laos to attack Ho Chi Minh trail (Feb.–Mar.).
Nixon announces withdrawal of 100,000 US troops by end of year (7 Apr.); 500,000 anti-war demonstrators march in Washington (24 Apr.).
Australia and New Zealand announce withdrawal of troops from South Vietnam (Aug.).
Nguyen Van Thieu confirmed as President in one-man 'election' (3 Oct.).

1972 Nixon announces reduction of US forces to 69,000 by 1 May (13 Jan.).
North Vietnamese forces invade South Vietnam (30 Mar.); renewed bombing of North authorized (April); mining of ports ordered (May).

Last American ground combat troops leave Vietnam (Aug.)
Peace negotiator Henry Kissinger reports substantial agreement on 9-point plan with North Vietnam (26 Oct.); US suspends talks (13 Dec.); bombing of North Vietnam resumed (18 Dec.); bombing halted after North Vietnamese agree a truce (30 Dec.).

1973   Kissinger and Le Duc Tho sign peace agreement ending the war (27 Jan.). Ceasefire in Laos concluded (21 Feb.).
Last US military personnel leave Vietnam (29 Mar.).

1974   War in South Vietnam resumes (Jan.).
Communist insurgents advance on capital of Cambodia (July).
President Nixon resigns (Aug.); US Congress puts ceiling on military aid to South Vietnam.

1975   North Vietnamese forces launch offensive; the north and central highlands fall to communists and South Vietnamese forces forced into headlong retreat (Mar.).
Cambodian capital, Phnom Penh, falls to communist insurgents (17 Apr.).
President Thieu resigns and flees to Taiwan (21 Apr.); North Vietnamese troops enter Saigon (29 Apr.) and unconditional surrender announced by President Van Minh (30 Apr.).
Pathet Lao consolidate communist takeover of Laos; Laos becomes a communist state (3 Dec.).

SOUTH-EAST ASIA SINCE 1945

1945 *Indonesia*   Unilateral declaration of independence by Republic of Indonesia (17 Aug.); Sukarno becomes President (18 Nov.).

    Vietnam   Ho Chi Minh seizes power and declares Vietnam independent.

1946 *Thailand*   King Ananda Mahidol shot dead; succeeded by Bhumibol Adulyadej (June)

    Philippines   Philippines gain independence from United States.

    Indonesia   Linggadjati agreement between Dutch and Indonesian Republic, agreeing Republic's control of Java, Madura and Sumatra as part of a federal United States of Indonesia in a Netherlands–Indonesian Union (17 Nov.).

    Vietnam   Outbreak of Indo-Chinese war between French and Viet Minh (see p. 302).

    Malaya   Malayan Union established (Apr.); Sarawak and North Borneo ceded to Britain (May–July).

1947 *Indonesia*   Formal signature of Linggadjati agreement (Mar.), but breakdown leads to 'police action' by Dutch (July).

    Philippines   United States signs 99-year lease for air and naval bases (Mar.).

1948 *Vietnam*   French create 'state of Vietnam' (June).

    Burma   Burma becomes independent (Jan.).

    Malaysia   Malayan Union becomes Federation of Malaya (Feb.); beginning of communist insurgency (May).

    Indonesia   Dutch and Indonesian truce agreement (Jan.), but communist rebellion leads to renewed fighting (Nov.–Dec.)

1949 *Laos*   Laos recognized as independent state (July).

    Cambodia   Cambodia recognized as independent state (Nov.).

    Indonesia   Peace Conference at the Hague opens (Aug.); transfer of sovereignty to United States of Indonesia agreed (Nov.) and formal independence granted (Dec.).

1954 *Vietnam*   Defeat of French forces at Dien Bien Phu (May); Vietnam partitioned (July).

1955 *Cambodia*   Cambodia becomes fully independent state (Sept.).

1957 *Malaysia*   Malay states become independent as Federation of Malaya (Aug.).

    Indonesia   Sukarno introduces authoritarian rule as 'guided democracy'.

1958 *Indonesia*   Revolt in Sumatra and Sulawesi.

1960 *Malaya*   Official end to 'emergency' (July).

1962 *Vietnam*   Major build-up of US forces in Vietnam begins.
     Burma   Military coup led by General Ne Win (Mar.); Revolutionary Council set up and publishes programme, 'Burmese Way to Socialism'. Burma Socialist Programme Party set up and all others abolished (July).

1963 *Malaysia & Indonesia*   Federation of Malaysia established (Sept.); beginning of 'confrontation' with Indonesia (see p. 311).
     Vietnam   Diem regime overthrown (Nov.).

1964 *Vietnam*   Gulf of Tonkin incident and Tonkin Resolution (Aug.).

1965 *Philippines* Ferdinand E. Marcos elected President (Nov.).
     Indonesia   Following abortive coup, Communist Party banned and thousands of members killed.
     Cambodia   Sihanouk breaks relations with United States (May).
     Singapore   Singapore becomes independent from Malaysia (Aug.).

1966 *Indonesia*   General Suharto assumes emergency powers (Mar.).
     Malaysia   Agreement signed ending 'confrontation' with Indonesia (June).

1967 *Indonesia*   President Sukarno hands over power to Suharto (Feb.).

1968 *Vietnam*   'Tet' offensive by communists (Jan.).
     Indonesia   General Suharto elected President (Mar.) and introduces 'New Order'.

1969 *Philippines* Marcos becomes first President to be re-elected.
     Vietnam   American troops in Vietnam peak at 542,000 (Jan.); gradual withdrawal begins after pledges by President Nixon.

1970 *Cambodia*   American-backed General Lon Nol ousts President Sihanouk (Mar.); American and South Vietnamese forces cross into Cambodia (Apr.).

1972 *Philippines* Marcos declares martial law and arrests Benigno Aquino along with several hundred of opposition (Sept.).
     Burma   Ne Win and 20 army commanders retire and become civilian members of government.
     Vietnam   Beginning of peace talks on Vietnam (Oct.).

1973 *Burma*   New Constitution agreed by referendum (Dec.).
     Vietnam   Americans sign peace agreement with North Vietnam (Jan.); last US military personnel leave (Mar.).
     Laos   Ceasefire in Laos (Feb.).
     Thailand   Civilian rule returns to Thailand after resignation of military rulers following death of 400 student protesters (Oct.).

1974 *Burma* Military rule formally ended and Revolutionary Council dissolved; Ne Win becomes first President of Burma as a one-party Socialist Republic (Mar.).

1975 *Cambodia* Phnom Penh falls to communist Khmer Rouge (Apr.).
Vietnam Fall of Saigon to North Vietnamese forces and end of Vietnamese War (Apr.).

1976 *Cambodia* Democratic Kampuchea established under Pol Pot, who inaugurates programme of revolutionary upheaval and terror (Jan.).
Burma Attempted coup by young officers fails (July).
Thailand Army seizes power after violent clashes between police and students (Oct.).

1979 *Cambodia* Vietnamese invasion of Cambodia deposes Pol Pot and installs Heng Samrin as head of People's Republic of Kampuchea. Khmer Rouge and Pol Pot take up guerrilla war.
Vietnam Chinese troops launch invasion of Vietnam; withdraw after bitter fighting (Feb.–Mar.).

1980 *Philippines* Opposition leader Benigno Aquino allowed to leave for United States (May).
Thailand General Prem Tinsulanonda sets up civilian–military government.

1981 *Philippines* Martial law lifted (Jan.).
Burma General San Yu becomes new President.
Thailand Unsuccessful coup attempt in Bangkok (Apr.).

1982 *Cambodia* Forces opposed to Heng Samrin regime form a coalition at Kuala Lumpur, including Khmer Rouge, Prince Sihanouk and Son Sann (June).

1983 *Philippines* Benigno Aquino assassinated at Manila airport on his return from the United States (21 Aug.).

1984 *Indonesia* Muslim riots in Jakarta suppressed by troops (Sept.).
Cambodia Vietnamese launch major offensive on guerrilla bases on Thai border; UN calls on Vietnam to withdraw from Cambodia/Kampuchea (Oct.).
Thailand Attempted coup in Thailand against Prem Tinsulandonda fails (Sept.).

1986 *Philippines* Corazon Aquino, widow of B. Aquino, elected President of Philippines; President Marcos goes into exile (Feb.); coup attempts in July and Nov. suppressed.

1987 *Philippines* New Constitution approved (Feb.); coup suppressed (Aug.).

    Cambodia Talks between Prince Sihanouk and Vietnamese Prime Minister Hun Sen in Paris on Cambodian settlement.

    Indonesia Official Golkar Party wins landslide victory in general elections (April).

1988 *Burma* Student demonstrations against Ne Win's government suppressed by the army (Mar.–July); Ne Win resigns as Party Chairman and San Yu as President (July). Brigadier-General Sein Lwin becomes President and Party Chairman and imposes martial law but resigns after riots (Aug.). General Saw Maung takes power but declares commitment to elections; BSPP becomes National Unity Party.

    Cambodia Vietnam announces it will remove all troops by Dec. 1990 (May); Jakarta talks on peace settlement (June); resumed in Beijing (Aug.) and Jakarta (Feb. 1989) fail to reach earlier date for withdrawal.

1989 *Burma* Military government announces elections will take place in May 1990 (Feb.).

    Cambodia Vietnamese forces begin withdrawal (Sept.).

1990 *Vietnam* Indicating an improvement in Chinese–Vietnamese relations, the Friendship Pass on the border of the two countries, which has been closed, is reopened (Sept.).

    Burma (Myanmar) The elections are won by the opposition National League for Democracy led by Aung San Suu Kyi, but the soldiers do not hand over power. The name of the country is changed to the Union of Myanmar (Dec.).

1991 *Thailand* A new military coup takes place (Feb.).

    Laos The new Constitution of the country reinforces the leading role of the Laotian People's Revolutionary Party and hands over power to the head of state. After Souphanouvong's resignation, Kaysone Phomvihane, the former Chief Secretary of the LPRP and former Prime Minister, is elected as the President of the People's Republic (Aug.).

    Vietnam At the Beijing Summit between the leaders of the two countries, Chinese–Vietnamese relations are normalized (Sept.).

    Myanmar The Nobel Peace Prize is awarded to the opposition politician Aung San Suu Kyi, who is being held under house arrest (Oct.).

    Cambodia In Paris, the treaty concluding the Cambodian civil war is signed. Until the general elections, the country is governed by the Supreme National Council, which comprises the representatives of 4 formerly opposing camps, and whose President is Prince Norodom Sihanouk (Oct.).

1992 *Vietnam* The endorsed new Constitution still contains reference to the leading role of the Communist Party but restricts its power; the collective governing body is replaced by a President; the Prime Minister gains greater power (Apr.).

Myanmar General Saw Maung, who has been in power since Sept. 1988, resigns (May). Several imprisoned politicians are set free.

Philippines Former Defence Minister, General Fidel Ramos, who is supported by Mrs Aquino, is elected as the President of the country (May). Since the Senate rejected the extension of the leasing contract with the United States in Sept. 1991, the last member of the US army leaves the military base in Subic Bay, thus concluding the approximately 100-year-long US military presence in the Philippines (Nov.).

Thailand After the elections resulting in the victory of the leftist opposition, Chuan Leekpai forms a coalition government (Sept.).

1993 *Indonesia* Suharto is elected as President for another 5 years (Mar.).

Cambodia After the parliamentary elections in May, won by Prince Sihanouk's party FUNCINPEC which defeated the governing Cambodian People's Party (until 1991 called the Cambodian People's Revolutionary Party), a new provisional government is formed, co-presided over by Prince Norodom Ranariddh (Sihanouk's son) and Hun Sen (June).
In accordance with the new Constitution, Cambodia becomes a constitutional monarchy; its monarch is Norodom Sihanouk (Sept.).

Vietnam As the first step in the complete cancellation of the sanctions against Vietnam, the United States significantly reduces the trade embargo against Vietnam, which has existed for 19 years (Sept.).

1994 *Vietnam* US trade embargo lifted (Feb.); agreement on Australian aid to Vietnam (Apr.).

Cambodia Meeting in North Korea between Khmer Rouge leaders and government (May), but ceasefire proposals rejected by Khmer Rouge leader, Khieu Samphan.

Myanmar House arrest of Aung San Suu Kyi extended into 1995 by the military junta on the grounds that her release would 'create unrest' (Feb.).

Indonesia Widespread industrial unrest (Feb.–Mar.). Renewed riots in East Timor (July and Nov.).

1995 *Vietnam* Announcement by President Clinton of establishment of full diplomatic relations with the United States (July). Talks with China lead to reopening of railway links, resolution of border dispute, and economic co-operation (July).

Cambodia Major Khmer Rouge offensive forces 40,000 refugees to flee (Feb.–Mar.). Khmer Rouge guerrillas forced into Thailand, provoking clashes with Thai troops.

Myanmar Government troops capture main bases of Karen separatists (Jan.–Feb.). Release of Aung San Suu Kyi from house arrest (July); appointed General Secretary of National League for Democracy. Military junta drafts new Constitution (Nov.); NLD refuses to participate.

Indonesia Further ethnic clashes in Dili, East Timor (Jan. and Sept.).

1996 *Vietnam* Government launches campaign against 'social evils' of prostitution, drug abuse, gambling and pornography (Feb.).

Cambodia King Sihanouk's half-brother found guilty in absence of plotting assassination of Hun Sen (Feb.). Major government offensive against Khmer Rouge (Jan.); China offers aid to Cambodian government (Apr.).
Major defection of 3,000 Khmer Rouge under Ieng Sary who join government forces.

Myanmar Military rulers disrupt NLD conference and arrest and imprison leaders (May–Aug.); also crackdown on weekly addresses made by Aung San Suu Kyi, arresting 500 (Sept.). Calls for trade sanctions against Myanmar by Aung San Suu Kyi, and EU withdraws special trading rights amidst widespread student protests.

Indonesia Serious rioting in Irian Jaya between immigrants and local population (Mar.). Government refuse to recognize new political party, the Indonesian United Democratic Party, and to oust the leader of the Indonesian Democratic Party, leading to serious rioting in Jakarta (July). National Commission on Human Rights condemns armed forces for human rights abuses in the July riots (Oct.).
Bishop Carlos Belo of East Timor and resistance leader José Ramos-Horta awarded Nobel Peace Prize (Oct.). Suharto government bans outdoor rallies and proceeds with trials of opposition groups (Oct.–Nov.).

1997 *Cambodia* Pol Pot taken prisoner by Khmer Rouge General Ta Mok. Show trial follows and Pol Pot sentenced to life imprisonment.

Thailand/Malaysia/Philippines Currencies slump in Asian financial crises (July).

1998 *Indonesia*   Huge fall in value of Indonesia currency caused by general collapse of confidence in 'Tiger' economies and their banking systems. Suharto re-elected President. Anti-Suharto riots sweep Indonesia following shooting of six students. Violence in Jakarta leaves 500 dead (May). Suharto resigns. Replaced by Vice-President Habibie.

    Cambodia   Death of Pol Pot, former leader of Khmer Rouge (15 Apr.).

    Myanmar   Ultimatum by Aung San Suu Kyi to junta to convene parliament (June).

    Philippines   Joseph Estrada becomes President (June).

    Malaysia   Tight controls on capital introduced as Asian economic crisis spreads (Aug.).

1999 *East Timor*   Referendum on independence promised by Indonesia (Mar.).

    Indonesia   Opposition, led by Megawati Sukarnopuri, wins general election (June).

    Indonesia   Abdurrahman Wahid becomes President, with Megawati Sukarnopuri Vice-President.

2001 *Philippines*   Following impeachment of President Estrada, Vice-President Gloria Macapagal-Arroyo becomes President (Jan).

    Indonesia   Impeachment of President Wahid; Megawati Sukarnopuri elected to succeed him (July).

    East Timor   First democratic elections won by Fretilin (the independence movement) with 55 of the 88 seats (Aug.).

2002 *East Timor*   Independence finally achieved (May).

    Indonesia   Terrorist bombing of Bali nightclub leaves 202 dead (Oct.).

2003 *Myanmar*   Arrest of Aung Sang Suu Kyi in northern Myanmar.

2004 *Indonesia*   Presidential election won by former general Susilo Bambang Yudhoyono. Defeat of incumbent Megawati Sukarnopuri.

    Indonesia/Thailand   Devastating tsunami and earthquake (26 Dec.) leave over 150,000 dead in Indonesia alone.

AUSTRALASIA

AUSTRALIA AND NEW ZEALAND[1] SINCE 1914

1914 War declared in Europe (Aug.); Australian and New Zealand forces seize German possessions in south-west Pacific.
German commerce raider *Emden* sunk by HMAS *Sydney* off Sumatra (9 Dec.).
Australian and New Zealand Army Corp (ANZAC) formed.
Labor Government formed in Australia (Sept.).

1915 Australian and New Zealand troops land at Gallipoli (25 Apr.; evacuated 18–20 Dec.).
Labor's William Hughes Prime Minister of Australia (Oct.).

1916 Referendum in Australia votes against compulsory military service overseas; Hughes leaves Labor Party.
New Zealand introduces compulsory enrolment for war service.
New Zealand Labor Party formed.

1917 Coalition National Ministry formed in Australia under Hughes; Labor Party split; second referendum defeat for compulsory military service overseas.

1919 Women become eligible for seats in New Zealand parliament.

1920 New Zealand given League of Nations mandate over former German Samoa; ANZAC Day instituted.

1921 Australia given League of Nations mandate over German New Guinea.

1926 Imperial Conference in London (Nov.) defines Dominion status. Australia and New Zealand self-governing Dominions.

1927 Seat of Australian government transferred to Canberra.

1929 Labor under James Scullin wins general election in Australia (Oct.).

1930 Statute of Westminster defines Dominion status.
Sir Isaac Isaacs first Australian Governor-General.
New Zealand introduces unemployment relief.

---

[1] Since the 1990s New Zealand has commonly been known as 'Aotearoa/New Zealand', incorporating the Maori name.

1931   Labor government defeated in Australia by newly formed United
        Australia Party led by Lyons (Dec.).

1932   Sydney Harbour Bridge opened.
        Imperial Economic Conference at Ottawa (July–Aug.) introduces limited
        imperial preferences.
        Riots against pay cuts in New Zealand (Apr.).

1933   Australia claims one-third of Antarctica.

1934   United Australia Party wins Australian elections (17 Sept.); Lyons forms
        Australian Coalition Cabinet (7 Nov.).

1935   New Zealand National government defeated and first Labour
        government under Michael Savage takes office; guaranteed butter and
        cheese prices introduced; compulsory arbitration and basic wage; railways
        nationalized; and state mortgage system.

1938   Labor election victory in New Zealand.
        Australia embarks on three-year New Defence Programme; Trade Treaty
        with Japan.

1939   Menzies becomes Prime Minister of Australia (Apr.) following death of
        Lyons.
        Australia and New Zealand declare war on Germany (3 Sept.); first
        Australian forces sent to the Middle East (Dec.).

1940   Death of New Zealand Premier Savage; succeeded by Peter Fraser.
        Australia opens direct diplomatic links with the United States with
        exchange of ministers.
        New Zealand Expeditionary Force sent to Middle East and ballot for
        military service introduced.

1941   Menzies deposed by his Cabinet (Aug.); Labor government under Curtin
        formed (Oct.).
        State Health Service introduced in New Zealand.
        Australian forces sent to Malaya; Japanese attack on Pearl Harbor
        (7 Dec.); Australia and New Zealand declare war on Japan (9).

1942   Australia requests emergency military assistance from the United States
        and Britain (Jan.); Japanese land in New Guinea (Jan.); fall of Singapore
        (15 Feb.); over 18,000 Australians killed, wounded or captured in total
        during whole Malayan campaign.
        Darwin bombed by Japanese aircraft (19 Feb.).
        General Douglas MacArthur given command of Allied forces in the
        south-west Pacific with headquarters at Melbourne (Mar.); Battle of the
        Coral Sea frustrates Japanese invasion of Australia (4–8 May).
        New Zealand introduces conscription and control of industrial
        manpower.

Lend-lease extended to Australia and New Zealand.
Japanese offensive in New Guinea held by Australians.

1943 Menzies begins reorganization of United Australia Party into Liberal
Party. Japanese air raids on Darwin and Western Australia; beginnings of
offensive in New Guinea.

1944 Australia–New Zealand Agreement (Pacific Pact) to collaborate on
matters of mutual interest (Jan.). New Guinea mainland recovered from
Japanese.

1945 Death of Australian Premier Curtin (July); Finance Minister Joseph
Chifley succeeds. Cessation of hostilities with Japan (15 Aug.);
comprehensive social security system introduced.

1946 Commonwealth government of Australia given powers in respect of
social services.

1948 Australia introduces 40 hour week; rocket range at Woomera
begun.

1949 Seven-week coal strike in Australia heightens fears of communist
influence; Labor government of Chifley defeated and Liberals under
Menzies assume office.
Snowy Mountains hydro-electric scheme commenced.
New Zealand referendum approves compulsory military training; Labor
government of Peter Fraser defeated and National government takes
office in New Zealand.

1950 Menzies introduces bill to ban Communist Party, later modified.
Australian and New Zealand forces sent to Korea.

1951 USA, Australia and New Zealand sign ANZUS treaty for mutual military
security in the Pacific.
State of emergency in New Zealand following dock strike.

1952 United Kingdom atomic bomb test at Monte Bello Islands, Western
Australia; uranium discovered.

1953 Australian Atomic Energy Commission set up.

1954 Australia and New Zealand sign Manila Pact for collective defence
against aggression in south-east Asia and south-west Pacific.

1956 Australia and United Kingdom agree on trade pact to replace Ottawa
Agreement of 1932.

1957 Preferential treatment given to New Zealand dairy produce entering
United Kingdom; New Zealand National government defeated by
Labor.

1959   Australian New Immigration Act opens way to non-English-speaking immigrants.
Australia signs Antarctic Treaty at Worthington.

1960   Social service benefits extended to Aborigines in Australia.
Labor defeated in New Zealand elections and replaced by National Government under Keith Holyoake.

1961   Menzies government returned in Australia; huge iron ore deposits discovered.

1962   Australian Aborigines given vote.
New Zealand trade pact with Japan.

1963   Huge bauxite deposits discovered in Australia; Australia adopts decimal currency. Liberal-Country Party returned; eighth Menzies government.

1966   Menzies retires from office in Australia (Jan.).
Australian troops sent to Vietnam.

1967   Australian Prime Minister Harold Holt drowned; John McEwen sworn in as acting premier (Dec.).

1968   John Gorton becomes Prime Minister of Australia (Jan.).

1972   New Zealand Labor Party under Norman Kirk wins landslide victory (25 Nov.).
Australian Labor Party wins election under Gough Whitlam.

1974   Death of Norman Kirk, New Zealand Prime Minister; succeeded by Wallace Rowling.
Whitlam returned in Australia with reduced majority.

1975   Papua New Guinea becomes independent of Australian control.
Constitutional crisis in Australia following blocking of Labor budget in Senate; Governor-General dismisses Labor Prime Minister Whitlam and caretaker Liberal government formed (11 Nov.). Malcolm Fraser leads Liberal-Country Party to election victory (Dec.).
Robert Muldoon of National Party defeats Labor in New Zealand election.

1978   Death of Robert Menzies (June).

1983   Australian Labor Party under Bob Hawke returns to power (Mar.).

1984   Labor Party under David Lange defeats Muldoon in New Zealand (July).
Hawke retains office in Australian election (Dec.).

1985   Crisis in ANZUS Pact because Lange government declares the country a nuclear-free zone, refusing port facilities to American destroyer. Hawke refuses facilities for American ships monitoring missile tests (Feb.). New

Zealand protests against French atomic tests at Muroroa Atoll. French secret service agents sink Greenpeace ship *Rainbow Warrior* in Auckland Harbour. Two French saboteurs arrested. South Pacific Forum declares South Pacific a nuclear-free zone.

1986   Australia Act makes Australia fully independent of United Kingdom (March); Queen remains sovereign.
United States announces suspension of security obligations to New Zealand (Aug.).

1987   United States withdraws concessions to New Zealand on military equipment (Feb.); Labor wins general election (Aug.).
Labor under Hawke confirmed in office in Australian general election (July).

1988   Australia celebrates Bicentenary of first settlement.

1989   David Lange resigns as New Zealand Premier (July).

1990   New Zealand celebrated 150th anniversary of Treaty of Waitangi (original treaty between the Europeans and Maoris).
Labor under Hawke wins narrow fourth election victory (Mar.). The elections in New Zealand are won by the National Party; the new Prime Minister is Jim Bolger.

1991   Owing to the deteriorating economic situation, Hawke resigns.
His successor as head of the Labor Party and the government is Paul Keating (Dec.).

1993   Labor Party led by Keating again wins the elections (Mar.).
In the elections in New Zealand, the governing National Party gains a one-person victory in the new parliament (Nov.).
The new Australian Land Law accepted by parliament recognizes the Aborigines' priority in possessing land over the rights of the white settlers (Dec.).

1994   Following the setting up of a Ministry of Maori Development in 1991, proposals for a compensation fund with a limit of NZ$1 billion are outlined (Dec.).

1995   Maori protesters over compensation fund disrupt Waitangi Day celebrations (Feb.). Queen makes formal apology to Maoris as head of state (Nov.). French atomic tests at Mururoa Atoll lead to trade boycotts by Australia and New Zealand (Sept.–Oct.).

1996   John Howard wins landslide victory in Australian general election as head of Liberal–National Coalition (Mar.). Gun controls introduced by Federal and State governments following massacre of tourists at Port Arthur, Tasmania, in April.

Jim Bolger calls election in New Zealand under new system of proportional representation, resulting in a hung parliament. Bolger remains as Prime Minister with the leader of the New Zealand First Party as Treasurer and Deputy Prime Minister (Oct.).

1997 Mrs Shipley, leader of the Labor Party, replaces Bolger as Prime Minister (Nov.) in New Zealand.

1998 Constitutional Convention meets; Australia to vote in referendum over the republic issue. Constitutional deadlock over the Wik bill.
Ruling Liberal National coalition in Australia sees its majority sharply reduced in general election (Oct.).

1999 Australians vote in referendum to retain Queen as Head of State (Nov.). New Zealand Labor Party takes 39% of the vote in general election (National Party 30.6%). Helen Clark becomes Prime Minister (Dec.).

2001 Victory for John Howard's Liberal and National coalition (81 out of 150 seats) in general election (Nov.) in Australia.

2002 Helen Clark's Labor Party re-elected at general election in New Zealand (July).
Terrorist bombing in Bhali kills nearly 100 Australians (Oct.).

2003 Commitment of 2,000 Australian troops to US-led war in Iraq (Mar.). Largest protests seen in Australia since Vietnam War.

2004 Australian general election held on 9 Oct. returns John Howard to power again for fourth term.

LATIN AMERICA AND THE CARIBBEAN

THE UNITED STATES AS REGIONAL 'GENDARME', 1912–33

1912–25   US marines occupy Nicaragua.

1914–34   US marines occupy Haiti.

1916–24   US marines occupy Dominican Republic.

1917–23   US marines occupy Cuba.

1919   US marines occupy Honduran ports.

1924   US marines land in Honduras.

1926–33   US marines occupy Nicaragua and organize the National Guard. Control of the National Guard becomes the cornerstone of political power in Nicaragua and the guarantor of the Somoza 'dynasty' for 45 years.

1932   US navy on standby during the *matanza* (peasant uprising) in El Salvador.

1933   President Franklin Roosevelt initiates the 'good neighbour' policy.

LATIN AMERICA, 1916–30

1916 *Argentina*   In first election held by secret ballot, the candidate of the Radical Party, in opposition for 30 years, is triumphantly elected. Hipolito Irigoyen, a longstanding Radical *caudillo*, assumes Presidency and initiates long-overdue reforms in labour working conditions.

1917 *Argentina*   President Irigoyen maintains Argentina's strict neutrality in the First World War despite pressure exerted by US President Woodrow Wilson.

    Brazil   The continued sinking of Brazilian shipping leads to a declaration of war on Germany. Brazil sends part of its navy to European waters and provides airmen for the Western front.

1919 *Peru*   Augusto B. Leguia, President since 1908, resorts to increasingly authoritarian methods to maintain his rule.

    Mexico   Emiliano Zapata is shot dead by troops commanded by Jesus Guajardo in Cuatutla, Morelos (Apr.). Zapata had been tricked by Guajardo's fabricated claim of mutiny against Carranza. Zapata's survival and international publicity of his activities had made him an increasing embarrassment to President Carranza.

    Brazil   Epitacio da Silva Pessoa is elected President (Apr.) and his government's high expenditure including lavish schemes for the Brazilian Centenary Exposition in 1922 leads to budget deficits and large increases in the foreign debt.

1920 *Argentina*   Leaves the League of Nations in protest at the Allies' repressive policy to defeated Germany, rejoining only in 1927.

    Mexico   General Alvaro Obrégon rebels due to Carranza's sponsorship of Ignacio Bonilla as Presidential candidate (May). Obrégon advances on Mexico City and Carranza attempts to flee to Veracruz.
Carranza's forces are defeated at Aljibes, Puebla, and he is later murdered by one of his own supporters at Tlaxcalalongo in Puebla. De la Huerta is installed interim President in Mexico City but real power lies with Obrégon.

    Chile   Arturo Alessandri of the Liberal Alliance is narrowly elected President by an electoral court following a tied election (June). Alessandri attempts to rule despite a hostile conservative opposition, particularly in the Senate.

    Mexico   General Alvaro Obrégon becomes President (Dec.) and brings stable government during his term until 1924. The charismatic Obrégon able to nominate his successor, although choice of Plutarco Elias Calles alienates the faction of De la Huerta. Obrégon ruthlessly crushes a rebellion by De la Huerta and smashes the Co-operativist Party, executing many revolutionary officers. Obrégon's agrarian and oil policies alienate US interests.

1922 Brazil
Artur Bernardes is elected President but faces considerable regional and radical opposition to his rule. A brief rebellion of the Fort Copacabana garrison in Rio de Janiero (July) led by Siquiera Campos is unsupported but constitutes a focal point to the growing *tenente* opposition to the politics of the old Republic.

Argentina
The Radical Party is returned at the general election (Oct.). Marcelo T. de Alvear is elected President but Hipolito Irigoyen remains prominent within the Radical Party.

1923 Peru
Victor Raul Haya de la Torre forms the American Popular Revolutionary Alliance (APRA) whilst in exile in Mexico. As the prototype populist reformist party in Latin America, it remains an important force in Peruvian politics to the 1980s.

Mexico
Francisco 'Pancho' Villa is assassinated (July).
In 1920 the Federal government had bought Villa a large estate to induce him to disarm and 'retire'.

1924 Brazil
A rebellion erupts in São Paulo against President Bernardes (July). Three thousand federal troops influenced by the *tenentes* hold the city for a month and then withdraw. Rebel forces led by Luís Carlos Prestes, influenced by the *tenentes* and including many of the São Paulo rebels, march through Brazil from Rio Grande to the North East states as a 'revolutionary column' harrying the military forces of President Bernardes and eventually march into exile in Bolivia in Feb. 1927.

Chile
A military junta intervenes (Sept.) as a corrupt and irresponsible Congress renders Alessandri's Presidency ineffectual.

Mexico
Plutarco Elias Calles, Industry Minister for President Carranza and Minister of the Interior under Obrégon, assumes the Presidency (Dec.). In 1926 Calles comes into conflict with the US government over agrarian and oil rights legislation and with Pope Pius X1 over the anti-clerical provisions of the 1917 Constitution.
Calles remains the pre-eminent *caudillo* in Mexican politics to 1934.

1925 *Chile*	A 'young officers' coup removes the junta of General Altamirano and Major Carlos Ibanez comes to prominence as Minister of War (Feb.). Civilian politicians back the candidacy of Emiliano Figueroa for Presidency in December but Carlos Ibanez remains the power behind President Figueroa's chaotic government.
1926 *Brazil*	Washington Luis, Minister of Justice in the previous two governments, is elected President in difficult times of conflicting regional factionalism exerting pressure upon the old Republic.
Mexico	The *Cristero* Rebellion by militant Catholics is precipitated by President Plutarco Elias Calles's rigorous enforcement of the anti-clerical provisions of the 1917 Constitution. Conservative peasant guerrillas particularly active in the western and northern states, attacking Federal government and military personnel. Federal military authorities crush the rebellion in 1929.
1927 *Chile*	An election confirms Carlos Ibanez's domination of Chilean politics and he assumes the Presidency (July), wielding dictatorial powers as the economic crisis deepens in 1929. His harsh regime survives until July 1931.
1928 *Argentina*	Hipolito Irigoyen is returned as President (Apr.) and the Radical Party appears to be in a strong position to initiate a planned policy of social reform and industrialization. However, in 1930 Irigoyen is removed in a conservative coup led by General José F. Uriburi, who installs a repressive regime.
Mexico	General Alvaro Obrégon is re-elected President but is assassinated by a religious fanatic 2 weeks later (July). Emilio Portes Gil becomes provisional President, but Plutarco Elias Calles remains the real power in Mexican politics.
1929 *Mexico*	Plutarco Elias Calles forms the National Revolutionary Party (Mar.). Under several names this party institutionalizes the Mexican revolution into a bureaucratic apparatus. By his control of the party Calles dominates Congress and Mexican politics beyond his Presidential term (1928) until 1934.
Chile/Peru	The longstanding territorial dispute between Chile and Peru is settled by treaty following US arbitration. Tacna is declared Peruvian and Arica Chilean.
1930 *Peru*	The Arequipa rebellion led by General Luís Sánchez Cerro prevents the dictator Leguia attempting to stand for a third term of office.

Colombia   Bitter factionalism within the Conservative Party, in part over corrupt use of foreign loans, paves the way for the Liberal Party to gain the Presidency for the first time in 40 years (Aug.). Moderate Liberal Olaya Herrera assumes the leadership of a government of National Concentration, which includes some Conservative ministers.

Brazil   Getulio Vargas assumes the Presidency (Oct.) in a successful revolt backed by the *tenente* movement and other elements in Brazil disillusioned by the power-broking regional cliques of the old Republic.

The support of powerful coffee-growing interests for the government of Washington Luís evaporates with the fall in foreign exchange earnings that accompanied the 1929 depression.

LATIN AMERICA, 1930–9: THE AGE OF THE DICTATORS

In Central and Latin America the Depression years saw the rise of strong men who ensured *continuismo* principally by their control of the armed forces and the ruthless suppression of opposition.

1930 *Dominican Republic* A political crisis prompted by the possible re-selection of President Vásquez gives the army commander General Rafael Leonidas Trujillo Molina opportunity to take power. Rafael Trujillo's dictatorship is ended by his assassination in 1961.

1931 *El Salvador* Arturo Arango is elected President in first free election in 20 years (Jan.). Government ousted by General Maximilio Hernandez Martinez (Dec.).
General Hernandez crushes the Salvadorean peasant movement in 1932; dictator until May 1944, when popular disgust at his brutality forces him to resign.

Guatemala General Manuel Orellana overthrows the government in a coup but unable to secure US recognition (Dec. 1930). General Jorge Ubico emerges strongman (Feb. 1931). Ubico rules by a combination of 'constitutional amendment' and intimidation until ousted in coup, 1944.

Honduras General Tiburcio Carias Andino establishes a stranglehold on Honduran politics by his control of the army. In 1932, 1937 and 1944 he crushes peasant revolts; domination of Honduras lasts until 1948.

Peru General Sánchez Cerro elected President, but internal opposition forces him to resort to emergency powers.

Argentina General Augustin Justo is elected President in a contest from which the Radical Party barred (Nov.).

1932 *Peru* Victor Raul Haya de la Torre is gaoled and his APRA reformist movement outlawed.

Chile Radical military coup removes ineffectual Liberal President and installs Carlos Davila (June). Davila flirts with a Socialist Republic. Colonel Marmaduke Grove is influential as socialist leader in this brief experiment which is ended by a second military coup (Sept.); Alessandri is compromise President.

Brazil Armed revolt in São Paulo (July), termed the 'Constitutionalist revolution', plays into hands of President Vargas who gains increasing powers in efforts to strengthen a centralized state. New constitution of 1934 codifies this change in power in favour of the Federal as against the State governments.

1932–4 *Colombia / Peru*   The territorial dispute over Leticia (and possible oil rights) results in armed conflict (1933).
League of Nations agreement in 1934 calls for Leticia to be returned to Colombia.

1932–5 *Bolivia / Paraguay*   The Chaco War fought between Bolivia and Paraguay for possession of the Chaco Boreal lowland region of the Grand Chaco (north of Argentina and west of Brazil). Bolivia desired outlet to Atlantic and believed there were oil reserves to be developed. Bitter nineteenth-century conflicts fuelled national rivalries that added to the intensity of the dispute. Bloody and exhausting conflict cost a total of 250,000 casualties (Bolivia suffering proportionately more). Paraguay in possession of the bulk of the disputed territory when truce agreed in 1935. A 1938 Peace Treaty ceded 70% of the Chaco Boreal to Paraguay and granted Bolivia a passage right through Paraguay to the sea. The political systems of both countries (particularly Bolivia) were destabilized by the strenuous war effort.

1933 *Peru*   President Sánchez Cerro is assassinated and General Oscar Benavides is appointed by Congress to finish the Presidential term.

Nicaragua   Liberal Party rebel Augusto César Sandino leads a guerrilla resistance against conservative forces and US marines until Feb. 1933, when he agrees a truce; US marines leave Nicaragua. National Guard under the control of Anastasio 'Tacho' Somoza García is the centre of political power. In 1934 Sandino is shot when leaving talks in the Presidential Palace. Somoza García does not assume the Presidency until 1937, but position always guaranteed by National Guard. In Sept. 1957 Somoza García is assassinated, but the Somoza 'dynasty's' rule continues until June 1979.

1934 *Colombia*   Reformist Liberal leader Alfonso Lopez Pumarejo assumes the Presidency after victory in an election boycotted by the Conservatives (Aug.). 'Revolution on the March' promised by Lopez delivers only moderate agrarian and labour legislation, alienates many in the conservative Liberal elite.

Mexico   Lazaro Cárdenas, Minister of the Interior since 1931, inaugurated as President (Dec.). Election a victory for the left wing of the party.
Cárdenas inevitably drawn into conflict with Plutarco Calles. Bolstered organized labour by encouraging the formation of

the Mexican Labour Confederation (CTM) in 1936, stimulated the expropriation of land for redistribution and the nationalization of oil assets.

1935 *Brazil*	The uncoordinated communist rebellion in Rio, Recife and Natal is a failure (Nov.). Most Communist Party (PCB) leaders arrested immediately, Luís Carlos Prestes captured (Mar. 1936). Rebellion used by Getulio Vargas to gain further centralized powers from Congress.
1936 *Chile*	A socialist general strike gives President Alessandri the excuse to suspend Congress and introduce martial law (Feb.).
Paraguay	Colonel Rafael Franco, leader of the *Febrerista* movement, seizes power in a coup (Feb.) and initiates a semi-corporate state until Aug. 1937, when removed by armed forces. Interim government established.
Mexico	President Lazaro Cárdenas forces Plutarco Elias Calles into exile (Apr.), resolving a power struggle within the revolutionary elite.
Peru	APRA Presidential election victory is thwarted by right-wing forces in Congress which nullify the results and grant absolute powers to General Benavides.
1937 *Argentina*	Roberto Ortiz (Radical who had worked within the Justo government) is elected President ahead of former President Alvear in a contest full of electoral irregularities (Nov.).
Brazil	President Getulio Vargas establishes the *Estado Novo*, centralized with some corporatist overtones (Nov.). Suspends payments on Brazil's foreign debt, abolishes all existing political parties (Dec.).
1938 *Colombia*	Eduardo Santos assumes the Presidency (Aug.). Election a victory for the conservative faction of the Liberal Party over the reformist wing of Alfonso Lopez. Brake on the reformism initiated by Lopez, causing the divisions within the Liberal Party to deepen.
Chile	Pedro Aguirre Cerda is inaugurated as President after a narrow victory (Dec.). The socialists initially favoured Marmaduke Grove as candidate but supported the moderate radical Cerda as 'Popular Front' candidate when Nazi activity increased and Carlos Ibanez, darling of the right, returned from exile.
1939 *Peru*	General Benavides retires and is succeeded by Manuel Prado, the first civilian President for ten years.

Paraguay   General Estigarribia, hero of the Chaco War, is elected President as unifying political figure (Apr.); negotiates reconstruction loan from the USA; develops transport links with Brazil.

Argentina   Nazi Party is dissolved by Presidential decree (May). German ambassador directs the activities of the still intact party in 1940, 1941.

LATIN AMERICA AND THE CARIBBEAN, 1940–59

1940 *Mexico* Avilo Camacho assumes Presidency (Dec.), rules until 1946. Camacho was victor in a power struggle within the Mexican Revolutionary Party (PRM); advocated an expansion of State Enterprises in the economy as outlined in the 1917 Constitution. He appeased the private sector by appointing its representatives onto some state agency boards.

1942 *Colombia* Alfonso Lopez Pumajero (the Liberal Party leader) is elected President defeating the Conservative candidate, Carlos Aranjo Velez (May). Lopez does not rule with his old confidence; scandals and factionalism combine to weaken his authority by 1945.

Argentina Ramon S. Castillo succeeds Roberto Ortiz as President (July).

1943 *Argentina* President Castillo is removed in a military coup led by Brigadier General Arturo Rawson (June). The military rule Argentina until June 1946.

1944 *El Salvador* General Maximilian Hernandez Martinez (dictator since Mar. 1931) bows to popular pressure and resigns (May) after a determined protest, 'the folded arms strike', had paralysed San Salvador.
Salvadorean politics quickly degenerates into a pattern of coup and counter-coup within a closed military caste.

Colombia Whilst inspecting military manoeuvres, President Lopez and his advisers are temporarily held by the military commander of the Pasto garrison (July).
Although the army remain loyal and Lopez is released, his authority is severely weakened.

Guatemala General Jorge Ubico (President since Feb. 1931) is ousted by a military coup encouraged by popular discontent at Ubico's increasingly rigid dictatorship (July). Juan José Arevalo, a cautious liberal reformer, is elected President and introduces legislation which allows trade union organization in the foreign plantation and railway enclaves (Dec.).

1945 *Peru* Jose Luís Bustamente, leader of the National Democratic Front, is elected President (June) but APRA emerges as the dominant force in Congress and Bustamente is forced to accept APRA cabinet members (to the chagrin of military and right-wing forces).

Colombia Lopez resigns the Presidency (July) and Alberto Lleras Camargo finishes his term of office as the party political structure cracks under intense social pressure.

Venezuela   Revolt led by elements within the military co-operating with a revamped centrist political force formed in 1941 (*Accion Democratica*) removes dictatorship of Medina Angarita (Oct.). New junta appoints Romulo Betancourt, the leader of AD, as Provisional President until Feb. 1948.

Brazil   Getulio Vargas, President since 1930, is removed in a bloodless coup which dismantles the 'Estado Novo' corporate state and installs the head of the Supreme Court as provisional President (Oct.).
Vargas remains prominent in Brazilian politics.
General Enrico Gaspar Dutra of the Social Democratic Party (PSD) defeats the candidate of the National Democratic Union (UDN) in a Presidential contest restricted to the two traditional elite parties (Dec.).

1946 *Argentina*   Juan D. Perón is elected President (Feb.). In General Election his movement gains a majority in the Legislature, defeating an alliance of political groupings termed the Democratic Union. Peron is President June 1946–Sept. 1955.

Colombia   Split Liberal Party vote between the 'official' candidate Gabriel Turbay and the 'populist' Jorge Elicier Gaitan allows the Conservative Party candidate, Mariano Ospina Pérez, to 'steal' the Presidency (May), ruling until Aug. 1950 as acrimony and bitterness penetrate the political system.

Bolivia   The government of the National Revolutionary Movement (MNR) is deposed in a rebellion (July); Victor Paz Estenssoro escapes into exile.

Chile   Gabriel Gonzalez Videla is elected President by Congress (Sept.). Chilean politics hampered by the close balance of conflicting forces throughout the postwar period.
Videla owes his election to a coalition of the Radical, Liberal and Communist parties in Congress.

Mexico   Miguel Aleman assumes the Presidency (Dec.) until 1952, a compromise candidate agreed upon by President Camacho, Lombardo Toledano and Lazaro Cárdenas. Aleman's former position of governor of the populous state of Veracruz aided his nomination, which was a defeat for the Callista faction within the Revolutionary Party.

1947 *Venezuela*   *Accion Democratica* gains a majority in Congressional elections (Dec.) and the party's Presidential candidate Romulo Gallego is victorious; assumes office in Feb. 1948.

1948 *Argentina*   The Peronist Party (PP) wins a majority in Congressional Elections, consolidating Juan Perón's government (Feb.).

Colombia	Popular Liberal politician Jorge Elecier Gaitan is assassinated in Bogota (Apr.) unleashing mass violence which devastates the capital – the *Bogotazo* – and ushers in period of bitter civil conflict known as *La Violencia* (between Conservative and Liberal party supporters) severely complicated by rural social pressures and agrarian disputes. Estimates of number of people killed (1948–57) are as high as 200,000.
Peru	President Bustamente is deposed in a coup led by Gen. Manuel A. Odria (Oct.), who rules as head of military junta until June 1950, when he seeks Presidency.
Venezuela	Army coup ousts the *Accion Democratica* government (Nov.). President Gallego and party leader Romulo Betancourt exiled; Communist Party outlawed.

1949 *Bolivia* Mamerto Urriolagoitia assumes the Presidency (May); despite MNR rebellion in Aug. 1949, rules until May 1951.

Colombia Political acrimony causes the Liberal Party candidate to withdraw and the right-wing Conservative Laureano Gomez is elected unopposed (Nov.) as the nation's political situation worsens.

1950 *Peru* General Odria assumes the Presidency in an uncontested election (July) enabling him to continue autocratic rule until July 1956.

Brazil Getulio Vargas returns to the centre of the political stage when, as the candidate of the revamped populist Brazilian Labour Party (PTB), he is elected President (Oct.) defeating Eduardo Gomez, the candidate of the traditionalist National Democratic Union (UDN). Vargas assumed the Presidency in Jan. 1951, ruling Brazil until his suicide in 1954.

Guatemala Jacabo Arbenz of *Partido Accion Revolucionario* (PAR) is elected President in a contest in which suffrage is extended to all adult males and all adult literate females (Nov.). PAR also obtains majority in Congress, raising hopes for continued reform.

1951 *Bolivia* Victor Paz Estenssoro, the MNR candidate, wins a large plurality whilst in exile (May). President Urriolagoitia hands over power to military rather than acknowledge an MNR victory. General Hugo Ballivian Rojas assumes Presidency and annuls election result.

Argentina Juan Perón is re-elected President (Nov.) and PP maintains its majority in Congress.

1952 *Bolivia* Social revolution led by the tin miners' union and labour confederation (COB) ousts the government (Apr.), installs

Hernan Siles Zuazo as MNR interim President. Victor Paz Estenssoro assumes office until 1956, when the MNR retains the Presidency. Paz Estenssoro and Siles Zuazo remain prominent politicians in Bolivia but move substantially to the right. Bolivian political system remains unstable, oscillating between ineffective civilian government and harsh military rule.

Chile
Gen. Carlos Ibanez is elected President by vote in Congress as no candidate obtained majority (Sept.).
Salvador Allende polled well for the *Frente del Pueblo*. Ibanez formed an unstable coalition cabinet, forced to reshuffle it endlessly as Chile confronted economic difficulties.

Mexico
Adolfo Ruiz Cortines emerges as the most innocuous of the three precandidates as bureaucratic control of the Revolutionary Party (PRI) assumes greater importance than any 'Callista', 'Cardenista, or left/right polemic (Dec.). Ruiz Cortines introduces female suffrage on election and rules until 1958.

Venezuela
Colonel Marcos Pérez Jimenez terminates a period of military chaos in government since the coup of 1950 by declaring himself President (Dec.). Imposes hard-line dictatorship until 1958.

1953 Colombia
General Rojas Pinilla leads a bloodless coup which removes the Conservative Party government (June).
Liberal Party boycotted elections and both national political parties involved in bitter conflict.
Rojas Pinilla attempts to legitimize regime (1953–7) electorally in 1954.

1954 Argentina
Peronism continues to dominate Argentinian politics in general election (Apr.).

Paraguay
General Alfredo Stroessner assumes Presidency (May), confirmed by July contest, in which he runs unopposed as Colorado Party candidate. Stroessner installs one of harshest and most durable dictatorships in Latin America, intact until 1989 when factionalism within the Colorado Party prompted a coup. Stroessner forced into exile in Brazil.

Guatemala
CIA-sponsored invasion of exile forces from Honduras led by Colonel Carlos Castillo Arnes ousts the mildly reformist government of Jacobo Arbenz amidst allegations of communist influence in his government (June). In 1953 the Arbenz government had introduced a land reform programme which the United Fruit Company saw as a threat to its influence in Guatemala.

Brazil 27 generals support a 'Manifesto to the Nation' demanding that the ageing President Getulio Vargas resign (Aug.). Investigation of attempted assassination of a government critic (Carlos Lacerda) had revealed a web of corruption in the Presidential entourage; Getulio Vargas committed suicide rather than resign.

1955 *Argentina* Leading sectors of army and navy combined with some air force units to oust President Perón (Sept.). 5-man junta assumes dictatorial political power, led by General Pedro Eugenio Aramburu, President until May 1958. Bitter rivalry between the military elite and the Peronist movement continues to dominate Argentinian political life.

Brazil Juscelino Kubitschek, candidate of the Social Democratic Party (PSD), is elected President (Oct.), defeating the former *tenente* Juarez Tavora who stood for the National Democratic Union (UDN). João 'Jango' Goulart, a populist figure within the Brazilian Labour Party (PTB), is elected Vice-President. Marshall Henrique Teixera Lott leads a constitutionalist coup to prevent a UDN Senate manoeuvre to block Kubitschek's inauguration as President (Nov.). Kubitschek and Goulart assume power in Jan. 1956. Kubitschek initiates 'development project' approach in his economic policy. Brasilia, the new capital, built during his Presidential term, which ended in 1961.

1956 *Chile* Left-wing parties form an electoral alliance, the *Frente de Accion Popular* (FRAP) in an attempt to remove the impasse in Presidential contests (May).

Peru Voters turn to a former President, Manuel Prado, to ease out the regime of General Odria (June).

Nicaragua Assassination of President Anastasio 'Tacho' Somoza García (Sept.) fails to remove the Somoza dictatorship; his eldest son Luís Somoza Debayle, assumes Presidency.

1957 *Colombia* General Rojas Pinilla attempts to amend the Constitutional provision of no reselection for President and is ousted by a junta led by War Minister, General Gabriel Paris (May). Plebiscite held to legitimize the 'National Front' system of bi-partisan government. Scheme did bring an end to the main phase of social conflict (*La Violencia*) but tended to reinforce the oligarchic nature of the Colombian party system. Agreement guaranteed both parties equal representation in the Legislature, whilst the Presidential terms were to be held alternately by the two parties until 1970.

Haiti	François 'Papa Doc' Duvalier is elected to the Presidency amid accusations of fraud in a hectic contest (Sept.). Bans political parties and installs his repressive dictatorship (Nov.).
1958 *Venezuela*	General strike called by a civilian political alliance against the Jimenez regime (Jan.). Spontaneous riots prompt military rebels to oust Jimenez and install a provisional government.
Argentina	Return to civilian politics; Arturo Frondizi of the Radical Civic Union (UCRI) elected President with the aid of Peronist votes (Feb.).
Chile	Jorge Alessandri Rodriguez (independent supported by Radical Party and the right) narrowly defeats both the Christian Democrat, Eduardo Frei (PDC) and Salvador Allende, the candidate of the left coalition (FRAP). Alessandri is elected by Congressional vote (Sept.).
Mexico	Performance of Adolfo Lopez Mateos as Labour Secretary to President Cortines gains him Presidential nomination and he rules until 1964.
Venezuela	Romulo Betancourt (AD) defeats Junta's candidate in Presidential Election (Dec.), ushering in era of domination of Venezuelan politics by *Accion Democratica* (until 1968). Factionalism and division within AD ranks as much as corruption scandals weakened the party's hold over national politics although AD remains an important force.
Cuba	Batista flees Cuba as Santiago and Santa Clara fall to Castro's guerrillas on 31 Dec.
1959 *Cuba*	Official anniversary of Cuban revolution, when Fidel Castro names Manuel Urrutia Lleo as President and José Miro Cardona as Prime Minister.

THE CUBAN REVOLUTION, 1917–62

1917–23	US troops occupy Cuba to guarantee US economic interests.
1925 May	General Gerardo Machado, 'the butcher', assumes Presidency.
1933 Aug.	Economic depression and Machado's dictatorial style prompt increasing protest, culminating in general strike which forces Machado into exile. The popular movement dissipates, leaving a vacuum in Cuban politics.
1935– Dec. 1940	Succession of ineffectual Presidents hold office; the Commander-in-Chief of the army, Fulgencia Batista y Zaldivar, is real ruler of Cuba.
1940– Oct. 1944	Fulgencia Batista assumes the Presidency. Cuba joins the Allies in 1944. Batista does not circumvent the election of Grau San Martin, but goes abroad until Cuba's chaotic political life offers him further opportunity to assume power.
1948 June	Carlos Prio Socarras, candidate of the 'Autentico' Cuban Revolutionary Party (PRCA), is elected President.
1952 Mar.	President Prio Socarras ousted by General Fulgencia Batista. The scheduled June 1952 election is cancelled. Congress is dissolved, political parties banned as Batista consolidates dictatorial power.
1953 July	Fidel Castro Ruiz is prominent in rebel force which unsuccessfully attacks Moncada barracks in Santiago (26th). Most rebels are killed or imprisoned. Fidel Castro makes famous 'History Will Absolve Me' speech at his trial. In subsequent imprisonment on 'Isle of Pines', a revolutionary group coalesces.
1954 Nov.	Batista is re-elected in a contest boycotted by most political groupings amid allegations of fraud and government repression.
1955 May	An amnesty bill frees some political prisoners including Fidel Castro and members of the 'July 26th Movement'.
1956 Dec.	Fidel Castro and 82 men sail from Mexico to Cuba aboard the yacht *Granma*. Only 12 men survive the initial skirmishes with Batista's forces and retreat to the Sierra Maestra, whence a growing rural guerrilla resistance to Batista unfolds.

1958 Dec.	Santiago and Santa Clara fall to Castro's guerrillas on 31st. Batista flees (1 Jan.). Castro marches on Havana.
1959 Jan.	Castro names Manuel Urrutia Lleo as President and José Miro Cardona as Prime Minister.
Feb.	Miro Cardona and Cabinet resign and Castro becomes premier.
	First Soviet–Cuban trade agreement signed in Havana, pledging the Soviet Union to import one million tons of Cuban sugar annually for 5 years.
	Soviet importance as a sugar market and as source of economic aid becomes crucial to the Cuban economy.
May	Agrarian Reform Law passed, authorizing confiscation of estates of over 1,000 acres (30 *cabellerias*). Estates were either divided amongst landless peasants and sharecroppers, or formed the basis of State Farms in the Cash Crop Sector.
July	Castro provokes Urrutia into resigning and Osvaldo Dorticos Torrado becomes President, with Castro centrally placed as Premier. This marks the end of the initial phase of the revolution when there had been a dichotomy between the nominal political leaders and the Castroite forces.
Nov.	Ernesto 'Che' Guevara is made head of the National Bank.
1960 Mar.	State Central Planning Board (JUCEPLAN) is established.
Apr.	Interests of the United Fruit Company are expropriated.
	200 Cuban troops fight with the National Revolutionary Committee in the Congo against the forces of Moise Tshombe in a gesture of solidarity.
May	Cuba re-establishes diplomatic relations with the USSR.
June–July	Oil refineries in Cuba are nationalized.
July	Law passed instigating the state takeover of US-owned economic activity in retaliation for the US abolition of Cuba's share in the sugar quota.
Aug.	CIA approach John Roselli to persuade him to organize an attempt to poison Fidel Castro.
Sept.	Local political organization and participation developed by formation of nationwide structure of 'Committees for the Defence of the Revolution'.
Oct.	Nationalization of all sugar mills and sugar-cane land. Major foreign banks nationalized.
	US embargo on all imports to Cuba.
Nov.	President Kennedy informed of CIA training of exile 'Brigade 2506' in Guatemala.

1961 Jan.	US severs diplomatic relations with Cuba.
	Fidel declares 1961 'the Year of Education' as mass literacy drive is undertaken. By Dec. 1961 the illiteracy rate had plummeted from 24% of the population to 4%. Campaign later augmented by intensive study on Worker-Farmer Improvement Courses.
Apr.	CIA-backed attempt to build an invasion beach-head in east Cuba. Cuban airfields bombed (15th) but Castro's small air force isolates the 1,500 men of 'Brigade 2506' that reached the shore, in the 'Bay of Pigs' fiasco (16–17th) (see p. 310). Castro for the first time asks the people to defend 'a socialist revolution'. In Dec. 1962 the 1,200 prisoners are allowed to travel to the USA.
July	Integrated Revolutionary Organization (ORI) is formed combining the '26 July Movement', the PSP (the old Communist Party) and student revolutionary directorate.
Nov.	The Partido Socialista Popular (PSP), the old Communist Party, is formally dissolved.
Dec.	Fidel Castro in a speech on Popular University TV declares himself a Marxist-Leninist, further disturbing the Kennedy administration in Washington.
1962 Feb.	Cuba suspended from the Inter-American System owing to US pressure.
	A national campaign of polio vaccination is initiated.
Mar.	Anibal Escalante and other 'old guard' communists purged from the government and the ORI.
	President Kennedy makes his 'We will build a wall around Cuba' speech in Costa Rica.
Apr.	CIA agent William Hunter provides poison pills and money to Cuban contacts to undertake to poison Fidel Castro. Mission not attempted.
July	US embassy property in Havana is expropriated.
July–Aug.	Raul Castro, Cuban Minister of the Armed Forces, and later Ernesto 'Che' Guevara, Minister for Industry, visit Moscow.
Sept.	Moscow statement confirms Cuba's request for arms and USSR's agreement to dispatch weapons and technical experts. Kennedy asks Congress for authority to call up 150,000 reservists.
Oct. 16–17	The Cuban Missile Crisis: US reconnaisance planes photograph Soviet intermediate-range missiles being installed in Cuba.
Oct. 22	Kennedy denounces the 'deliberately provocative and unjustified change in the status quo'.

	NATO Supreme Allied Commander in Europe alerted.
Oct 23	A Soviet broadcast denounces US blockade of Cuba. UN Security Council meets and US calls for dismantling and withdrawal of missiles.
Oct. 24	US blockade effective. U Thant (UN Secretary General) petitions both sides.
Oct. 26	Letter from Khrushchev to Kennedy offering to withdraw the missiles under UN supervision if US blockade of Cuba lifted and guarantee given that Cuba will not be invaded.
Oct. 27	Second letter from Khrushchev linking initial offer to conditional withdrawal of US missiles from Turkey. Kennedy replies on basis of first proposal.
Oct. 28	Firm undertakings given on removal of missiles under UN supervision.

LATIN AMERICA AND THE CARIBBEAN SINCE 1960

1960	*Argentina*	President Frondizi's UCRI loses majority (Mar.). Peronist Party barred from participation.
	Brazil	Janio Quadros is elected President with UDN support (Oct.) defeating the candidate of the PSD, Marshall Teixera Lott. Populist leader João 'Jango' Goulart is re-elected Vice-President. Increasing inflation and foreign debt produced by President Kubitschek's ambitious development projects hamper campaign of PSD candidate. Quadros assumed the Presidency in Jan. 1961 faced by a hostile opposition majority in Congress.
1961	*Haiti*	'Papa Doc' Duvalier is re-elected (Apr.). Consolidates his regime by dissolving legislature and installing rubber-stamp assembly.
	Dominican Rep.	Dictator Rafael Trujillo assassinated (May). Trujillo had dominated political life since 1931. Although he at times assumed the Presidency, he allowed his brother and Joaquin Balaguer to hold the highest office for 'cosmetic' reasons. The Trujillo 'dynasty' rallied briefly under his son General Rafael 'Ramfo' Trujillo, but by Dec. 1961 the family was expelled from the island.
	Brazil	President Quadros resigns in protest at Congressional opposition to his agrarian and tax reforms. Congress passes a constitutional amendment to establish a parliamentary system and much reduced powers for the Presidency (Sept.). This compromise allows João Goulart to assume the Presidency, but military opposition increases.
1962	*Argentina*	President Frondizi alienates the military hierarchy by permitting Peronist participation in Congressional elections (Mar.). Peronists win a majority but Frondizi is pressurized by the military to nullify election results in provinces where Peronism successful. The military removes President Frondizi and installs the Leader of the Senate as an interim president.
	Jamaica	The Jamaican Labour Party, headed by its founder Sir Alexander Bustamente, wins 26 of the 45 seats available in the election (Apr.), which followed Jamaica's withdrawal from the Federation of the West Indies (Sept. 1961).
	Peru	Military junta led by General Ricardo Pérez Godoy seizes power to block APRA's political ambitions, and annuls June election (in which APRA leader successful). General Godoy ousted by officers in favour of an electoral contest in Mar. 1963.

Argentina	Arturo Illia (UCRP) is elected President.
Jamaica	Becomes independent within the British Commonwealth (Aug.). Constitution guarantees opposition some representation in Upper House.
Trinidad	Trinidad and Tobago become independent within the British Commonwealth (Aug.). Eric Williams, who formed the People's National Party (PNP) in 1956, dominates both the PNP and politics in Trinidad until his death (Mar. 1981).
Chile	3 right-wing organizations form an electoral alliance, the *Frente Democratico* (FD), to counter growing left-wing organization before the 1964 Presidential Election.
Mexico	Gustavo Díaz Ordaz assumes Presidency. The organization of the Olympic Games in 1968 by the Díaz Ordaz administration provided an opportunity for protest by dissident groups, notably the student movement.
Dominican Rep.	Juan Bosch of the Democratic Revolutionary Party (PRD) is elected President and assumes office in Feb. 1963.

1963	*Brazil*	The electorate votes to restore a full Presidential System and grant President Goulart extensive executive powers (Jan.), sowing the seeds of military alienation that lead to the coup of 1964.
	Peru	In a return to civilian politics Fernando Belaunde Terry, candidate of new moderate force in Peruvian politics (*Accion Popular*), is elected (June).
	Dominican Rep.	Democratically elected government of Juan Bosch is removed by Colonel Elias Wessen y Wessen; Bosch exiled (Sept.). Military factions develop around 'constitutionalist' and 'loyalist' positions.

1964	*Brazil*	President João Goulart removed in a coup (Apr.) ushering in a long period of dictatorship. Marshall Humberto Castello Branco is approved by Congress; the first of a series of military nominees as President. Congress approves a constitutional amendment extending his term to Mar. 1967.
	Haiti	'Papa Doc' Duvalier installs himself as President for Life (Apr.).
	Chile	Eduardo Frei, the Christian Democrat candidate, is elected President (Sept.), defeating the candidate of the left-wing coalition (FRAP), Salvador Allende.

1965	*Dominican Rep.*	US supports coup leader Colonel Wessen y Wessen in the conflict between military factions following the removal of Juan Bosch's civilian government. Lyndon Johnson sends the

marines to the Dominican Republic to guarantee US interests.

Joaquin Balaguer, the trusted lieutenant of the dictator Trujillo, assumes the Presidency in 1966 and dominates the political system.

1966 *Guyana*   British Guiana gains independence within the Commonwealth as the state of Guyana (May).

Argentina   President Illia is deposed as the military re-enter politics (June). A hard-line junta led by Juan Carlos Ongania seizes power.

Brazil   Congress approves Marshall Costa e Silva as successor to Castello Branco as military President in 1967.

1967 *Nicaragua*   Major General Anastasio 'Tachito' Somoza Debayle assumes the Presidency on the death of his brother (Feb.). 'Tachito's' corrupt dictatorship provokes increasing popular opposition to the Somoza 'dynasty'.

Peru   General Juan Velasco Alvardo leads a military coup which ousts the ineffectual Belaunde administration (Oct.). General Velasco introduces nationalist measures in the export sector and attempts to tackle Peru's structural socio-economic problems, particularly the land reform issue (1968–86).

Brazil   Military President Costa e Silva suspends Congress indefinitely, initiating government by decree.

Guyana   Forbes Burnham, leader of the People's National Congress Party (PNC) wins the election that establishes his stranglehold on Guyanese politics (Dec.).

1969 *Argentina*   Military suppression of the *Cordobazo* – a mass insurrection in the city of Cordoba – prompts resignation of 5 ministers (May) and greatly weakens the Ongania regime.

Brazil   Military high command chooses General Emilio Garrastezu Medici as President following Costa e Silva's incapacity by a stroke. Medici assumes power in October.

1970 *Guyana*   Becomes a 'co-operative' republic within the British Commonwealth. In March the National Assembly elects Raymond Chang of the ruling PNC as President, replacing Queen Elizabeth II as head of state.

Argentina   Military President Juan Carlos Ongania is removed by a junta dissatisfied by his loss of political control.

The terrorist murder of a former military President, Pedro Aramburu, in May 1970, sealed Ongania's fate.

Mexico   Luis Echevarria Alvarez, candidate of the ruling Institutional Revolutionary Party (PRI), is elected President (July). PRI wins all 60 seats in the Senate and gains a majority in Congress. Luís Echevarria Alvarez had been the hard-line Minister of the Interior during the social protests of 1968.

Chile
Salvador Allende, the candidate of the Left Coalition (Popular Unity) wins a plurality in a polarized contest (Sept.). Allende assumes Presidency in Nov.

1971 Haiti
'Papa Doc' Duvalier dies and his son Jean-Claude 'Baby Doc' Duvalier succeeds him as President for Life (Apr.). The Duvaliers' repressive apparatus remains intact.

1972 El Salvador
Liberal Coalition led by José Napoleon Duarte and Guillermo Ungo win a rare free election, but are opposed by right-wing military elements which force both Duarte and Ungo into exile.

1973 Chile
The Popular Unity Government is ousted by a military coup (Sept.). Salvador Allende dies defending the Presidential palace; thousands of Popular Unity supporters are killed or imprisoned as the military junta led by General Augusto Pinochet installs a repressive dictatorship.

1976 Argentina
Chaotic Peronist government is removed by a military coup. A series of military dictatorships rules Argentina until Oct. 1983. The original junta led by General Videla dissolved Congress and used State of Siege legislation to justify mass arrests, torture and political murder. Over 15,000 people 'disappear' during military rule. General Videla succeeded briefly by Genera Viola in 1981 before General Galtieri assumes power.

Chile
Orlando Leterlier, former cabinet minister and diplomat in the Allende government is assassinated in Washington, DC, by members of the Chilean Secret Service (Sept.).

1979 Grenada
The New Jewel Movement led by Maurice Bishop ousts the repressive regime of Sir Eric Gairy (March).

Brazil
General João Baptista Figuerado assumes the Presidency, last in a line of military Presidents. His 'abertura' (opening) policy unleashes popular pressures for democratic elections.

Nicaragua
Popular resistance led by the Sandinista National Liberation Army (FSLN) forces Anastasio 'Tachito' Somoza out of power (June), ending the family's 'dynastic' control of Nicaragua politics since the 1920s. In the conflict against the Somoza regime 40,000 people died and a further 750,000 were made homeless.

El Salvador	A young officers' coup ousts the repressive regime of General Romero and forms a reformist military-civilian junta, joined by Guillermo Ungo who returns from exile.
1980 *El Salvador*	Civilian members of the junta resign, ushering in '*Romerismo sin Romero*' as the regime's emphasis moves from reform to repression. State of Siege is declared, leading to civil war. The murder of Archbishop Romero, a prominent human rights activist, symbolizes the extent of official violence.
	Subsequently over 70,000 people are killed, mainly at the hands of the security forces and the right-wing death squads.
Peru	The Maoist-influenced guerrilla group *Sendero Luminoso* ('Shining Path') begins its insurgency in the Andean province of Ayacucho. By 1989 *Sendero Luminoso* threatens Lima by isolating the capital from its hinterland.
Chile	A referendum held under State of Emergency provisions (Sept.), with all political parties banned and no use of electoral registers, adopts a new constitution which appoints Pinochet as President for a renewable 8-year term.
Jamaica	Edward Seaga's right-wing Jamaican Labour Party (JLP) wins a violent electoral campaign (Oct.) against Michael Manley's People's National Party (PNP).
1982 *Honduras*	Roberto Suoza Cordova, a conservative civilian politician, is elected to the Presidency (Jan.) but real power is still firmly held by the armed forces, who have dominated Honduran politics for over 25 years.
Honduras/Nicaragua	First in a series of joint US/Honduran military exercises began with simulated air and amphibious landings in the Cabo Gracias a Dios area, near Nicaragua (Feb.). These manoeuvres expand annually, exerting considerable pressure upon the Sandinista government.
Guatemala	General Lucas Garcia, who seized power in July 1978, becomes the most brutal of a series of military dictators since 1954. 20,000 people died at the hands of the security forces and the death squads during his rule. García ousted by a young officers' coup (Mar.). General Efrain Rios Montt, a born-again Christian, assumed the Presidency but the continued massacre of civilians by government paramilitary groups removed grounds for any guarded optimism. The suspension of US arms shipments to Guatemala is lifted.
El Salvador	Roberto D'Aubuisson's far-right ARENA party gains a majority in the Constituency Assembly, but moderate Alvaro Magana is appointed President owing to US pressure (Apr.).

Argentinian Argentinian forces invade the Falkland Islands. Britain declares a naval exclusion zone around the islands.
British navy sinks the Argentinian cruiser *Belgrano* (May) on orders from the War Cabinet. General Galtieri rejects Peruvian peace plan. British force despatched from the Ascension Islands undertakes landings at San Carlos and wins the Battle of Goose Green. British win the Battle of Port Stanley, prompting the surrender of Argentinian forces on the islands (see p. 325).

Colombia Belisario Betancur assumes the Presidency (Aug.) and attempts to draw dissident guerrilla forces into a political truce.

1983 *Guatemala* Defence Minister, General Mejia, ousts General Rios Montt from the Presidency in a near bloodless coup (Aug.), continuing Guatemalan political process of coup and counter-coup within a narrow political caste.

Argentina Leader of the Radical Party, Raul Alfonsin, is elected in return to civilian rule. President Alfonsin enjoys a 'honeymoon' period but his government's popularity worn away by failure to solve the aftermath of the 'Malvinas' (Falklands) fiasco, the undertaking of adequate judicial procedures against military personnel responsible for the 'disappearances' during military rule and Argentina's deep-rooted economic problems.

Grenada Maurice Bishop is ousted in Oct. (and later murdered) by a hard-line faction led by Deputy Prime Minister Bernard Coard and General Hudson Austin which provides an opportunity for US intervention. US naval task force (backed by a small contingent from the conservative Organisation of Eastern Caribbean States) successfully invades Grenada (Oct.) after 3 days' bitter fighting.

1984 *Nicaragua* CIA initiates the mining of Nicaraguan ports (Feb.). The Sandinista government takes its case to the World Court.

Colombia Assassination of Minister of Justice Lara Bonilla (Apr.) prompts President Betancur to attempt a clampdown on the drugs mafia.

El Salvador In a bitter run-off election, the Christian Democrat, José Napoleon Duarte is elected President. The US administration guarantees his government unprecedented levels of economic aid. President Duarte holds first exploratory talks (Oct.) with guerrilla political leaders (the FDR-FMLN).

Nicaragua The Sandinistas win 65% of the votes in national elections. Daniel Ortega is elected President (Nov.).

Chile	President Pinochet re-introduces State of Siege provisions (Nov.).
1985 *Brazil*	Tancredo Neves, the candidate of the opposition alliance dominated by Brazilian Democratic Movement (PMBD), defeats the government candidate Paulo Maluf in a contest for the Presidency (Jan.).
Nicaragua	US administration initiates a 3-year trade embargo against the Sandinista government (Apr.).
	In 1988 President Reagan attempts to tighten the economic noose around Nicaragua.
Peru	Alan García (APRA candidate) wins presidential election (Apr.). He fails to improve Peru's dire economic situation or to ease the civil conflict.
Brazil	Smooth transition to civilian rule is prevented by death of Tancredo Neves. Vice President Sarney is sworn in as President amid much confusion (Apr.).
	José Sarney is the leader of the Liberal Front (PFL), a small conservative faction of the victorious opposition alliance.
Chile	The Democratic Alliance is formed (Aug.), unifying parties across the political spectrum opposed to General Pinochet's intransigent rule. Unsuccessful assassination attempt on General Pinochet by the increasingly active Manuel Rodriguez Patriotic Front (FPMR) associated with the illegal communist party (Sept.). Pinochet regime tightens existing press censorship, arrests trade union and socialist leaders, increases mass army raids on working-class *poblaciones* in Santiago.
Guatemala	The Christian Democratic Party's candidate, Venecio Cerezo, is an easy victor in the Presidential election.
	Military leadership remains the power source in the Guatemalan political system.
1986 *Honduras*	José Azcona, dissident Liberal Party candidate, assumes the Presidency after his narrow November victory. The military leadership remains the real fulcrum of power.
Haiti	Mounting popular unrest forces 'Baby Doc' Duvalier into exile (Feb.). Popular celebrations cut short as the transitional military government, fronted by General Henri Namphy, is not over-rigorous in its dismantling of the dictatorship.
Peru	President Garcia's administration is tainted by indirect complicity with the military's massacre of over 300 *Sendero Luminoso* prisoners whilst subduing prison protests (Apr.).

El Salvador   President Duarte's government fails to halt growing economic dislocation despite massive aid from the Reagan administration. Economic austerity measures prompt greater unity of peasant and trade union groups, which organize May protests against the government.

Colombia   Virgilio Barco, the successful Liberal Party candidate, assumes the Presidency (Aug.). Efforts to open up the political system hampered by informal political power of drug interests, especially the 'Medellin Cartel'. The 6 major guerrilla groups form the Simon Bolivar Guerrilla Co-ordinating Board as a reaction to increasing right-wing death squad activity.

Brazil   The initial success of the anti-inflationary package – the Cruzado plan – benefits the government alliance electorally: the Brazilian Democratic Movement (PMBD) sweeps to power in Congressional State elections (Nov.).

Chile   Meeting between Christian Democratic and moderate conservative leaders with two junta members is first formal contact between government and opposition for 13 years.

Argentina   President Alfonsin rushes a 'final point' Bill through Congress designed to prevent further prosecution of military personnel after Feb. 1987.

1987 *Brazil*   As foreign exchange reserves fall below $4 billion, Brazil forced to suspend interest payments on its foreign debt (Feb.).

Haiti   New constitution approved by the populace (Apr.) but military rule casts shadow over forthcoming elections.

El Salvador   An FDR–FMLN peace plan is rejected by Duarte (May) and talks are suspended.

Nicaragua   Investigations into the Iran–Contra scandal prompt Congress to suspend aid to the Contras.

Panama   Colonel Roberto Diaz, a retired deputy military commander, accuses General Manuel Antonio Noriega of murder and corruption. Noriega had dominated Panamanian politics since 1983 but since July 1987 has come under increased US pressure to resign.

Central America   'Guatemalan Pact' or Arias initiative is signed by Presidents of Central American countries. Hope of progress in solving the conflicts which envelop El Salvador and Nicaragua and enmesh Honduras and Guatemala.

Argentina   The Congressional elections (Sept.) are a triumph for the Peronist movement, taking 42% of the vote as against 37% for the government.

Colombia   Jaime Pardo, the leader of *Union Patriotica* (UP) and its former Presidential candidate, is shot dead by unidentified gunmen (Oct.). Over 500 UP members are killed by right-wing death squads in 1986–7.

1988 *Argentina*   Colonel Aldo Rico, freed by a military court to house arrest, leads a second unsuccessful insurrection against President Alfonsin.

Haiti   In an electoral contest without a secret ballot or voting lists and boycotted by the four main opposition candidates, Leslie Mainigat is briefly elected President (Jan.). Following his first dispute with the military, Mainigat is removed by General Henri Namphy, who reimposes rule by military junta.

Panama   General Noriega is indicted (in absentia) in Miami on drugs offences. President Delvalle attempts to remove Noriega as defence chief but the National Assembly ousts Delvalle and installs the anti-US nationalist Manuel Solis Palma as President (Feb.).

Mexico   The lacklustre candidate of the ruling Institutional Revolutionary Party (PRI), Carlos Salinas, is belatedly declared the winner in the controversial Presidential Election, demonstrating the party's bureaucratic control of Mexican politics (July).

Chile   Opposition alliance of 16 political parties forms the basis of successful 'No' vote against the Pinochet regime (Oct.).

Brazil   The murder of 'Chico' Mendes (Dec.), prominent ecologist and peasant leader, demonstrates the intransigence of the rural elite in the north to environmental pressures for conservation of the forest resources of Amazonia.

1989 *Paraguay*   General Andres Rodriguez ousts General Stroessner's 34-year dictatorship in Paraguay. General Alfredo Stroessner is sent into exile in Brazil. General Rodriguez receives over 70% of the votes in an unreliable Presidential election termed fraudulent by the opposition (May).

Jamaica   Michael Manley's People's National Party (PNP) defeats the JLP incumbent Edward Seaga in a general election (Feb.). The PNP wins 44 of the 60 parliamentary seats.

El Salvador   The right-wing ARENA party wins both the Presidential and legislative elections. Cristiani is elected President (but hard-liner Roberto D'Aubuisson controls the party by his domination of its executive committee); as he assumes power in June the activity of death squad organizations is again on the increase.

Nicaragua   US administration claims that the Sandinista army's pursuit of Contra forces into Honduras constituted an invasion and dispatches 3,000 US troops for joint manoeuvres with Honduran forces. Contra/Sandinista talks produce the fragile Sapoa truce.

Argentina Carlos Menem, the Peronist candidate, defeats Eduardo Angeloz of the Radical Party in the Presidential election, and initiates severe programme of economic austerity in an attempt to combat inflation and the worsening foreign debt.

Chile The supporters of the military government have agreed upon Hernan Buchi as presidential candidate to face an opposition candidate, the Christian Democrat, Patricio Aylwin. Patricio Aylwin is backed by the 16-party opposition alliance and goes on to win the December election.

Colombia Murder of the leading Presidential candidate, Liberal Senator Luís Carlos Galan, by the drugs mafia steels the government of Virgilio Barco to declare war on the 'Drugs Mafia' (Aug.). The narcotics interests answer the challenge by bombing the offices of the Liberal and Conservative Parties.

Nicaragua The five Central American Presidents agree to the closure of 'Contra' bases in Honduras within three months (Aug.). US administration decreasing funds to Contras.

Panama US forces invade Panama (Dec). See p. 327.

1990 *Nicaragua* Sandinistas defeated in general election; Mrs Violetta Chamorro becomes President.

Haiti General Prosper Avril, who achieved power via a coup in Sept. 1988, resigns and leaves the country (Mar.). Until the general elections, Ertha Pascal-Trouillot, a member of the Supreme Court, becomes the provisional President of Haiti.

Colombia The Presidential elections which follow the bloody election campaign, in which, among others, three Presidential candidates were killed, and in which the M-19 guerrilla organization also participated as a political movement, are won by the candidate of the Liberal Party, César Gaviria Trujillo (May).

Peru In opposition to the world-famous writer, Mario Vargas Llosa (the candidate of the political right), an agricultural expert of Japanese origin, Alberto Fujimori, wins (June). Instead of a shock-therapy approach, Fujimori, who rejects the classical system of party rotations, promises gradual reforms and the injection of foreign capital into the Peruvian economy, which has been devastated by the enormous rate of inflation.

	Brazil	At the parliamentary elections, the right-wing political parties supporting the President's PRN gain an absolute majority in Congress (Oct.).
	Argentina	A rebellion led by Colonel Mohamed Ali Seineldin breaks out in the army. The coup attempt is suppressed in two days by forces loyal to the government (Dec.).
1991	*Chile*	The report by the Committee of Truth and Reconciliation (Rettig Committee) reveals the horrors of the Pinochet dictatorship (Mar.). The commander of the army, General Pinochet, obstructs the prosecution of those found liable.
	El Salvador	The military leader of the FMLN, Joaquín Villalobos, declares that the organization is not Marxist any longer and that its objective is to create a pluralist democracy in El Salvador.
	Haiti	General Raoul Cedras overthrows Jean-Bertrand Aristide, the first democratically elected President of the country (Sept.). Aristide has only been in office since February.
	Paraguay	At the parliamentary elections, the governing Colorado Party gains more than 60% of the votes (Dec.). The new parliament starts work on a new constitution which forbids the election of a president for two consecutive terms.
1992	*Guatemala*	After the election campaign spoiled by political murders, in the second round of voting the leader of the Solidarity Action Movement (MAS), the neo-liberal Jorge Serrano Elias, is elected as President of the country (Jan.).
	El Salvador	The civil war which has been going on for 10 years concludes with a ceasefire agreement (Jan.). The FMLN turns into a political party (May) and by the end of the year the last guerrilla surrenders his weapons. The United States cancels three-quarters of the half-billion US dollar El Salvador state debt.
	Venezuela	In February and November, unsuccessful military coups are attempted against Carlos Andrés Pérez of the Democratic Action Party (AD) who took office in 1989 (and had already been President between 1974 and 1979).
	Peru	Pointing to the consistent application of economic reform, the increasing fight against terrorism, and the corruption of the deputies, Fujimori carries out a Presidential coup with the aid of the armed forces. He suspends the constitution, dissolves the parliament, and introduces a state of emergency and censorship (Apr.). In an

195

attempt to overthrow him, unsuccessful coup attempts are launched in Nov. 1992 and May 1993.

Panama   Because of drug-smuggling and other charges, a court in Florida sentences General Noriega, the former dictator of Panama, to 40 years in prison (July).

Honduras/El Salvador   The decree of the Hague International Court finally concludes the so-called football war which broke out between the two countries in 1969 (Oct.).

Colombia   For a more efficient struggle against the guerrillas and the drug barons, a state of emergency is introduced in the whole of the country (Nov.).

Mexico   President Salinas de Gortari, with the President of the United States and the Canadian Prime Minister, signs the NAFTA Treaty in Washington (Dec.). The Senate ratifies the treaty in Nov. 1993.

Brazil   President Collor de Mello, whose liberal economic policies were initially successful but ultimately failed, is forced to resign on corruption charges. His successor is the former Vice-President, Itamar Franco (Dec.).

1993 *Jamaica*   At the parliamentary elections, the People's National Party, headed by James Percival Patterson, who took over the position of Prime Minister in Apr. 1992 from Manley who had to leave for health reasons, wins ahead of the Jamaican Labour Party (Mar.).

Paraguay   Building entrepreneur Juan Carlos Wasmosy, of the Colorado Party (founded by Stroessner), wins the first democratic Presidential elections of the country, ahead of Guillermo Caballero Vargas, the candidate of the opposition electoral union, National Collaboration (May).

Venezuela   Accused of the embezzlement of public funds and of corruption, criminal proceedings are launched against President Pérez, who is suspended (May), then finally removed from office (Sept.). The Presidential elections are won by Rafael Caldera, who held this office from 1969 to 1974, and now heads the electoral union called Convergence (Dec.). In this way the period of party rotations between the AD and the COPEI (Christian Social Party) comes to an end.

Guatemala   Pointing to the need to bring order and stability to the country, and to the need to reduce corruption and the drug trade, President Serrano dissolves the parliament and the Supreme Court, suspends constitutional rights and introduces absolute Presidential powers (May). After an initial period of support, the army turns against him and forces Serrano to resign, claiming that the events were tantamount to a coup. The parliament elects lawyer Ramiro de León Carpio, human rights activist, as the new President of the government – instead of the Vice-President who supports Serrano (June).

Bolivia The candidate of the largest opposition party, the National Revolutionary Movement (MNR), Gonzalo Sánchez de Lozada, wins the Presidential elections (Aug.).

Haiti As a consequence of the international sanctions, the Haiti leadership agrees on the return of former President Aristide to his office (July), but the agreement is never observed and terrorist activities commence again. In response, the UN orders an embargo against Haiti (Oct.).

Peru A plebiscite accepts the new constitution of the country. The new constitution allows the re-election of the President and the death penalty for terrorists (Oct.).

Curaçao As a result of a plebiscite, the population of the Caribbean island rejects independence and expresses their wish to remain a part of the Antilles (Nov.).

Colombia Pablo Escobar, the head of the Medellín drug mafia, is killed in a shoot-out with the police (2 Dec.).

Chile As a result of the economic boom, the candidate of the governing centre-left coalition, the Christian Democrat Eduardo Frei, wins the Presidential elections (Dec.). He takes office in Mar. 1994.

1994 *Argentina* President Menem's PJ party remained the largest party in the elections but lost its overall majority.
Menem launches major anti-poverty campaign, while introducing free market reforms (May). Demonstrations and general strike (July–Aug.).

Brazil Cardoso wins another 4-year term as President (Oct.).

El Salvador Presidential and legislature elections lead to victory of ARENA candidate Calderon over the left candidate Rubín Zamora. Split occurs in the former Liberation Front group.

Guatemala Agreement reached to end civil war and negotiate peace treaty by end of the year (Jan.). Elections held (Aug.), leading to coalition government, but talks collapse with the Marxist guerrilla movement in Nov.

Mexico Uprising in southern Chiapas region by armed Indian groups (Zapatistas) against the effects of North American Free Trade Agreement and demanding social reform; ceasefire agreed (Jan.). Ernesto Zedillo elected President (Aug.); forced to devalue peso after further unrest in Chiapas.

1995	*Argentina*	Following huge fall in inflation rate, President Menem wins an easy victory in the Presidential and Congressional elections (May). Serious rioting in Córdoba (June) following austerity measures. Menem calls for emergency powers to deal with the economy (Nov.).
	Brazil	Cardoso forced to set aside ambitious plans for tackling poverty as a result of general economic crisis, forcing devaluation of the *real* in March. Large-scale privatization plan introduced but faced by strikes and demonstrations.
	El Salvador	Demobilized FMLN soldiers besiege government and take hostages in protest at being betrayed over promises of jobs, housing and credit. New centre-left Democratic Party makes pact with Calderón government (Apr.).
	Guatemala	New schedule for peace talks set up (Feb.), leading to first participation in elections of left-wing candidates for 40 years. Alvaro Arzu of the Conservative Party wins largest share of vote (Nov.).
	Mexico	President Zedillo introduces austerity campaign but fails to secure foreign loans to shore up the currency (Jan.) Signs reform pact with other main parties (Feb.) and then attempts to overwhelm the Zapatistas by military force, but has to accept a stalemate and peace talks (Feb.–Mar.). Accord on future negotiations agreed (Sept.).
	Peru	President Fujimori wins a second term in office (Apr.).
1996	*Argentina*	Budget cut of $200 million forced on Menem government by IMF (Jan.); Menem takes further powers to cut government spending (Feb.). Tax rises by new Finance Minister met by strikes and protests (Aug.–Sept.).
	Brazil	Decree allows Indian land to be opened up (Jan.) – met by protests and land occupations by landless families. Further cuts in government spending launched (June).
	El Salvador	Protests against dismissals of 15,000 public service workers.
	Guatemala	President Arzu and Guatemalan Revolutionary Unity rebels (URNG) meet for peace talks in Mexico City (Feb.). Peace accord reached over a wide range of issues (May) and signed (29 Dec.), ending 36 years of civil war.
	Mexico	Peace talks between government and EXLN resumed (Jan.). Pact on electoral reform signed with other main parties (Aug.). Government mounts attack on new revolutionary group, the People's Revolutionary Army (ERP) operating in southern state of Guerrero (Aug.–Sept.).
	Peru	Arrest of leader of 'Shining Path' guerrilla movement (Jan.).

Tupac Amaru terrorists seize 430 hostages at Japanese embassy in Peru (Dec.).

1997 *Peru*   Peruvian security forces storm Japanese embassy killing all terrorists and freeing hostages.

1998 *Venezuela*   Hugo Chávez elected President (Feb.).
Brazil   Second 4-year term for Fernando Henrique Cardoso in presidential elections (Oct.).
Chile   Arrest of General Pinochet in London (Oct.).
Brazil   Economy rescued by IMF $41.5 billion package (Nov.).

1999 *Brazil*   Devaluation follows debt moratorium in one state (Jan.).
Ecuador   Currency crisis provokes declaration of State of Emergency (Mar.).
Argentina   Fernando de la Rúa victory in presidential election ends 10 years of Peronist rule (Oct.).
Venezuela   Referendum approves redrafting of constitution with increased powers for President Chávez (Dec.).

2000 *Chile*   Ricardo Escobar becomes first leftist President for 30 years (Mar.).
Peru   Re-election in dubious election of Alberto Fujimori for third term as President (May).
Mexico   Historic election victory for Vincente Fox of National Action Party in Mexican presidential elections. Ends 71 years of Institutional Revolutionary Party rule (July).
Peru   Resignation of President Alberto Fujimori as President.
Haiti   Aristide elected president again in disputed poll. Beginning of renewed turmoil in Haiti.

2001 *Argentina*   Financial crisis leads to resignation of President Fernando de la Rúa (Dec).

2002 *Venezuela*   Military coup ousts Hugo Chávez; reinstated next day after popular protests (Apr.).

2003 *Brazil*   'Lula' (Luiz Inácio Lula da Silva) sworn in as President (1 Jan.) (elected Oct. 2002).
Argentina   Nestor Kirchner elected Argentina's 6th President in 18 months (May).

2004 *Haiti*   Growing uprising in Haiti; rebels seize towns in north; flight of Aristide to Dominican Republic (Feb.).
Venezuela   Chávez wins recall referendum.
Uruguay   Tabaré Vázquez elected first left-wing President (Nov.).

NORTH AMERICA

UNITED STATES, 1914–41

1914 Aug. 4	USA makes formal proclamation of neutrality in war between European powers.
1915 Sept. 16	Haiti becomes a US protectorate.
1916 Mar. 15	US troops invade Mexico in pursuit of revolutionary leader Gen. Pancho Villa and remain until 5 Feb. 1917.
Nov. 7	Woodrow Wilson re-elected Democratic President.
Nov. 29	US marines land in Dominican Republic and remain until 1924.
Dec. 18	Wilson sends 'peace note' to all belligerents calling on them to end war and take steps to preserve future peace.
1917 Jan. 17	US pays Denmark $25 million for Virgin Islands.
Feb. 3	US breaks off diplomatic relations with Germany in protest against sinking of American shipping.
Feb. 5	Immigration Act excluding Asian labourers from US passed, despite presidential veto attempt.
Mar. 2	Zimmermann Telegram (see p. 494) suggesting German–Mexican alliance against US made public in Washington.
Mar. 2	Jones Act declares Puerto Rico a US territory and its inhabitants American citizens.
Apr. 6	USA declares war on Germany.
June 26	First of 2 million US troops land in France.
Nov. 3	US troops go into action in France for first time.
1918 Jan. 8	President Wilson announces 'Fourteen Points' to Congress as basis of peace terms and postwar settlement.
1919 Jan. 29	18th Amendment to Constitution prohibits sale, manufacture and transportation of alcoholic drink from 16 Jan. 1920 (i.e. Prohibition). Oct. 2 President Wilson disabled by stroke.
Nov. 19	Senate refuses to ratify Versailles Treaty and US membership of League of Nations by 55 votes to 39.
1919–20	Mass arrests and deportations of left-wing and trade union activists.

1920 Aug. 26	19th Amendment to Constitution gives women the vote.
Nov. 2	Republican Warren Harding defeats Democrat James Cox in Presidential election.
1921 Jan. 13	Census Bureau announces US an urban society with over half of population living in towns.
Mar. 4	Harding inaugurated as 29th President.
May 19	Immigration into US limited to 357,000 a year with quotas for nationalities.
Aug.	Wave of Ku Klux Klan (see p. 472) terrorist activity sweeps through the Southern and Mid-West states.
1922 Feb. 6	US signs Washington Treaty with Britain, France, Italy and Japan limiting size of navies.
1923 Jan. 20	US withdraws occupation forces from Germany.
Aug. 2	Harding dies. Calvin Coolidge sworn in as 30th President on 3 Aug.
Sept. 15	Oklahoma placed under martial law because of extent of Ku Klux Klan activities.
Oct. 25	Teapot Dome Scandal investigation begins into corruption in Harding's administration.
1924 Aug. 9	London Conference accepts US General Charles Dawes' plan for German war reparations payments. Germany to have $200 million international loan, 2-year moratorium on payments, and submit to financial controls.
Nov. 4	Coolidge wins Presidential election.
1926 May 10	US marines land in Nicaragua to quell insurrection and leave on 5 June.
1927 Aug. 23	Execution of anarchists Sacco and Vanzetti for murder allegedly committed in 1920 arouses worldwide protests.
1928 Aug. 27	US and France sign Kellogg–Briand Pact outlawing war; 62 other states eventually sign.
Nov. 6	Republican Herbert Hoover defeats Democrat Alfred Smith in Presidential election.
1929 Mar. 4	Hoover sworn in as 31st President.
Aug. 6–31	Hague Conference accepts US businessman Owen Young's plan for future German war reparations payments. Germany to have $300 million international loan, reparations to be reduced, financial controls imposed by 1924 Dawes Plan to be removed, and payments to be completed in 1988.
Oct. 24	'Black Thursday'. Wall Street Crash starts as 13 million shares change hands, beginning panic selling which lasts till

the end of Oct. Shares lose $30,000 million in paper value over 3 weeks. Leads to Depression which spreads from USA to Europe.

1930 Feb. 10	158 arrests in Chicago for violation of Prohibition by producing estimated 7 million gallons of whiskey worth $50 million.
Dec. 10	Congress passes legislation to provide $116 million public works scheme to alleviate unemployment.
1931 June 20	Hoover announces 'moratorium' on war debts payments to USA, effectively abandoning German war reparations.
Sept.–Oct.	Bank panic forces closure of 827 banks following run on funds by customers.
1932 Feb. 2	Reconstruction Finance Corporation set up to alleviate Depression. Lends $2 billion to banks, business and agriculture.
May 29	1,000-strong unemployed veterans 'Bonus Army' march arrives in Washington seeking relief. It is joined by supporters through the summer and rises to 17,000.
July 28	Federal troops and tanks led by Gen. Douglas MacArthur break up and disperse unemployed demonstrators in Washington.
Nov. 8	Democrat Franklin Roosevelt defeats Hoover in Presidential election.
1933 Mar. 4	Roosevelt sworn in as 32nd President.
Mar. 6	Roosevelt declares Bank Holiday until 9 Mar. to prevent run on banks. Only financially solvent banks allowed to re-open.
Mar. 9	100 days of 'New Deal' legislation to provide relief to banks, industry, agriculture and the unemployed begins. Results in over $15 billion expenditure by 1940.
Mar. 12	Roosevelt broadcasts first of Sunday radio 'fireside chats'.
Mar. 31	Reforestation Unemployment Act creates Civilian Conservation Corps to reduce unemployment through a reforestation programme.
May 12	Agricultural Adjustment Act restricts production of some crops and finances farmers for not producing.
May 12	Federal Emergency Relief Act passed.
May 18	Tennessee Valley Act passed establishing Tennessee Valley Authority to create work by extending rural electrification.
June 16	National Industrial Recovery Act creates the National Recovery Administration and the Public Works Administration.

Aug. 5	National Labor Board established under Senator Robert Wagner to arbitrate in collective bargaining disputes.
Nov. 8	Civil Works Administration established with initial $400 million funding to create 4 million jobs.
Dec. 5	Prohibition on manufacture and sale of alcohol repealed by 21st Amendment to Constitution.
1934	Agriculture devastated in Mid-Western states by drought and inadequate conservation of land.
Jan. 31	Farm Mortgage Refinancing Act passed to assist farmers with easier credit.
June 28	Federal Farm Bankruptcy Act calls a moratorium on farm mortgage foreclosures.
1935 May 27	Sections of National Recovery Act declared unconstitutional by Supreme Court.
July 5	Wagner–Connery Act establishes National Labor Relations Board with authority to encourage collective bargaining.
Aug. 14	Unemployment and old-age insurance instituted by Social Security Act.
Sept. 8	Louisiana Governor Huey Long assassinated in State Capitol building.
Nov. 9	Committee for Industrial Organization formed as eventual breakaway from American Federation of Labor. Organizes occupations of car and steel works to encourage unionization in new industrial sectors.
1936 Jan. 6	Sections of Agricultural Adjustment Act declared unconstitutional by Supreme Court.
July 30	USA signs London Naval Treaty with Britain and France to limit naval armaments.
Nov. 3	Roosevelt defeats Hoover to win Presidential re-election.
1937 July 22	Senate overturns Roosevelt's attempt to alter Supreme Court balance in his favour by appointment of liberal judges.
Oct. 5	Roosevelt calls for international sanctions against aggressive powers.
Dec. 12	Japanese aircraft bomb and sink US gunboat *Panjay* carrying Chinese refugees on Yangtse River. Japan apologizes.
1938 Jan. 28	Roosevelt calls on Congress to vote funds for expansion of Army and Navy.
May 26	House of Representatives Committee to Investigate Un-American Activities formed.

June 25	Minimum wage of 40c an hour and maximum working week of 40 hours guaranteed by 1940 under Wages & Hours Law. Child labour under 16 banned.
1939 July 1	Federal Works Agency established to co-ordinate New Deal activities.
Aug. 2	Hatch Act outlaws political activity of federal employees below policy level.
Sept. 1	Roosevelt declares in radio talk that USA will remain neutral in war.
Oct. 3	USA and 20 members of Pan-American Conference sign Declaration of Panama establishing a 300-mile neutrality zone round American continent.
Nov. 4	Neutrality Act amended at Roosevelt's insistence to allow 'cash and carry' arms sales to belligerents, effectively favouring Britain.
1940 July 30	Declaration of Havana by USA and 20 American republics bans transfer of European colonies on American continent to other European powers.
Sept. 3	US gives Britain 50 destroyers in exchange for bases in Newfoundland and the West Indies.
Sept. 16	US introduces first peacetime conscription measure to draft 900,000 recruits a year.
Nov. 5	Roosevelt wins third Presidential term by defeating Republican Alfred London.
1941 Mar. 11	Roosevelt authorized to supply war materials to Britain by Lend-Lease Act.
June 14	All German and Italian assets in USA frozen.
Aug. 9–12	Meeting between Roosevelt and Churchill off Newfoundland produces Atlantic Charter setting out postwar aims.
Aug. 18	Roosevelt abolishes limitations on size of armed forces.
Dec. 7	Japanese mount surprise attack on US naval base at Pearl Harbor, Hawaii.
Dec. 8	Congress approves Roosevelt's declaration of war against Japan.
Dec. 11	Germany and Italy declare war on USA.

For the events of the Pacific War see pp. 139–41.

UNITED STATES SINCE 1945

1945 Apr. 12	Roosevelt dies. Harry Truman sworn in as successor.
July 16	Atom bomb exploded near Alamogordo, New Mexico.
1946 Apr. 11	McMahon Act declares government monopoly over all US atomic energy activities.
July 4	US grants Philippines independence.
1947 Jun. 23	Taft–Hartley Act outlawing trade union closed shop and allowing government to impose 'cooling-off' period before strike passed by Congress despite Presidential veto.
July 26	Defense Department formed to co-ordinate military organization.
1948 Nov. 2	Truman defeats Republican candidate Thomas Dewey in Presidential election.
1949 Oct. 14	11 Communist Party leaders jailed for advocating overthrow of Government.
Oct. 26	Minimum Wage Bill raises minimum wage from 40c to 75c an hour.
1950 Jan. 21	Alger Hiss, a former State Department official, jailed for perjury after denying membership of a Communist spy organization.
Jan. 31	Truman orders work to proceed on development of hydrogen bomb.
Aug. 1	Guam becomes a United States territory.
Aug. 28	Truman takes control of railways to avert a strike. Returned to private owners 23 May 1952.
Dec. 11	Supreme Court rules that 5th Amendment to the Constitution protects an individual from being forced to incriminate himself or herself.
1951 Jan. 3	22nd Amendment to the Constitution limits Presidents to 2 terms in office.
1952 Apr. 8	Truman takes control of steel-works to avert strike; action ruled unconstitutional by Supreme Court.
July 25	Puerto Rico becomes a self-governing US commonwealth territory.
Nov. 1	First hydrogen bomb exploded at Eniwetok atoll, Marshall Islands.
Nov. 4	Republican Dwight Eisenhower defeats Democrat Adlai Stevenson in Presidential election.
1953 Jan. 20	Eisenhower inaugurated as 34th President.

Apr. 20	US Communist Party ordered to register with Justice Department as an organization controlled by the USSR.
June 19	Julius and Ethel Rosenberg executed as spies for passing atomic secrets to USSR.
1954 Apr. 22	Senate hearings into Sen. Joseph McCarthy's claims of communist subversion in army begin. They continue until 17 June.
May 17	Supreme Court outlaws racial segregation in schools.
May 24	Supreme Court declares Communist Party membership valid grounds for deportation of aliens.
Dec. 2	Senate vote of censure against McCarthy effectively ends his witch-hunt campaign.
1955 Dec. 1	Black bus boycott led by Revd Martin Luther King begins in Montgomery, Alabama, in protest against racial discrimination.
Dec. 5	American Federation of Labour and Committee for Industrial Organization merge under leadership of George Meany.
1956 Nov. 6	Eisenhower defeats Stevenson in Presidential election.
Nov. 13	Supreme Court outlaws racial segregation on buses.
1957 Sept. 24	Eisenhower despatches 1,000 paratroops to protect black high school students asserting their rights to non-segregated education in Little Rock, Arkansas.
1959 Jan. 3	Alaska becomes 49th state.
Aug. 21	Hawaii becomes 50th state.
1960 Nov. 9	Democrat John Kennedy narrowly defeats Republican Richard Nixon in Presidential election.
1961 Jan. 20	Kennedy inaugurated as 35th President.
Oct. 6	Kennedy declares that a 'prudent family' should possess a fall-out shelter to protect itself in event of nuclear war.
Dec. 5	Kennedy announces that 5 out of 7 army recruits are rejected on physical grounds and calls for public to take up exercise and become 'athletes' rather than 'spectators'.
1962 Jan. 12	State Department announces that Communist Party members will be denied passports.
Nov. 20	Kennedy signs order prohibiting racial discrimination in housing built with federal funds.
1963 June 17	Supreme Court rules religious ceremonies not essential in schools.

Aug. 28	Martin Luther King leads 200,000-strong civil rights 'freedom march' in Washington.
Nov. 22	Kennedy assassinated in Dallas, Texas, by Lee Harvey Oswald. Lyndon Johnson sworn in as 36th President.
1964 July 2	Civil Rights Act bans racial discrimination in services provision and by trade unions and businesses carrying on inter-state commerce.
Aug. 30	Johnson signs anti-poverty Economic Opportunity Policy providing almost $1 billion for community action programmes.
Sept. 27	Warren Commission appointed to investigate Kennedy assassination declares there was no conspiracy and that Oswald acted alone.
Nov. 3	Johnson defeats Republican Barry Goldwater in Presidential election.
1965 July 30	Congress passes Medicare programme providing Federal medical insurance for over-65s.
Aug. 6	Government takes powers under Voting Rights Act to compel local authorities to register black voters and to remove obstacles to their voting.
Aug. 11	Black riots begin in Watts, Los Angeles, and continue until 16 Aug. 35 die.
Oct. 17	Demonstrations throughout US against involvement in Vietnam.
Oct. 19	House Committee on Un-American Activities begins investigation into Ku Klux Klan.
Nov. 27	25,000 demonstrate in Washington against Vietnam War.
1966 July 1	Medicare comes into operation.
Nov. 8	Republican Edward Brooke becomes first black ever elected to Senate.
1967 July 23	Black riots in Detroit. Troops deployed as disturbances continue until 30 July; 40 die and over 2,000 injured.
Oct. 20	Major anti-Vietnam War demonstration in Washington.
1968 Feb. 29	National Advisory Committee on Civil Disorders (Kerner Commission) report condemns white racism in USA and calls for aid to black communities.
Mar. 31	Johnson announces he will not run for second term as President.
Apr. 4	Martin Luther King assassinated in Memphis, Tennessee. Riots in over 100 cities follow.

May 2	Black 'Poor People's March' on Washington begins. Culminates in 3,000-strong camp at 'Resurrection city'.
June 5	Sen. Robert Kennedy shot in Los Angeles while campaigning for Democratic Presidential nomination. Dies on 6 June.
Aug. 26	Anti-Vietnam War demonstrations at Democratic convention in Chicago quelled by police and troops. Disturbances continue until 30 Aug.
Nov. 8	Republican Richard Nixon defeats Democrat Hubert Humphrey in Presidential election.
1969 Jan. 20	Nixon inaugurated as 37th President.
Oct. 15	Mass demonstrations against Vietnam War throughout USA.
1970 May 4	National Guard kills four anti-war students demonstrating at Kent State University, Ohio.
1971 Apr. 20	Supreme Court upholds bussing as a means of achieving racial balance in schools.
May 2	Beginning of three-day anti-Vietnam War protest in Washington. Over 13,000 arrests.
June 3	Publication of leaked 'Pentagon Papers' disclosing hidden background to Vietnam War. Supreme Court refuses to prevent publication, 30 June.
July 5	26th Amendment to Constitution reduces voting age to 18.
Aug. 11	Law enforcing educational desegregation in 11 Southern States comes into effect.
Aug. 15	Nixon introduces anti-inflation wages and prices freeze; suspends convertibility of dollar into gold.
1972 May 15	Alabama Governor George Wallace, in the past an uncompromising segregationalist, wounded and disabled in assassination attempt.
June 17	Five men arrested burgling the Democratic National Committee offices at Watergate building, Washington. On 22 June Nixon denies White House involvement.
Nov. 7	Nixon wins landslide victory over Democrat George McGovern in Presidential election.
1973 Jan. 8–30	Watergate burglary trial. Two of the seven convicted had been 'Committee to Re-elect the President' officials, and one a White House consultant.
Feb. 7	Senate forms a committee to investigate the Watergate affair.
Feb. 27	Indians protesting against government treatment mount Siege of Wounded Knee. Two Indians die before it ends on 8 May.

Apr. 30	White House advisers H. R. Haldeman and John Ehrlichman and staff member John Dean resign over participation in Watergate cover-up.
May 11	'Pentagon Papers' case against Daniel Elsberg dismissed because government used burglary to obtain evidence.
July 16	Revelation that Nixon has taped his White House conversations since 1970, eventually showing his active involvement in Watergate cover-up.
Oct. 10	Vice-President Spiro Agnew forced to resign after disclosure of income tax evasion.
Oct. 23	Nixon ordered to surrender White House tapes to Senate Watergate investigation under threat of impeachment.
Nov. 7	Congress votes to limit Presidential powers to wage war.
Dec. 6	Gerald Ford sworn in as Vice-President.
1974 Jan. 1	3 former cabinet members and Nixon's two leading White House aides are convicted for their part in covering up Watergate events.
July 24	Supreme Court orders Nixon to release his tape-recorded conversations.
Aug. 9	Nixon resigns under threat of impeachment proceedings for involvement in Watergate. Ford sworn in as 38th President.
Sept. 8	Ford grants Nixon full pardon.
Sept. 16	Ford announces amnesty for Vietnam War draft evaders and deserters.
1976 Apr. 26	Senate Committee on Central Intelligence Agency demands stronger control over and greater accountability of intelligence services following concern over activities.
Nov. 1	Democrat Jimmy Carter defeats Ford in Presidential election.
1977 Jan. 20	Carter inaugurated as 39th President.
1978 June 6	Proposition 13 in California state referendum limits local taxes, triggering a campaign nationally to reduce federal and state taxation.
1979 Feb. 12	Carter appeals for voluntary conservation to limit effects of growing energy crisis.
Mar. 28	Serious atomic reactor accident at Three Mile Island, Pennsylvania, provokes loss of public confidence in nuclear power.
June 13	$100 million awarded to Sioux Indians as compensation for land taken from them in 1877.
Oct. 23	Congress grants Carter powers to introduce petrol rationing because of world oil crisis.

1980 Nov. 4	Republican Ronald Reagan gains landslide Presidential election victory over Carter.
1981 Jan. 20	Reagan inaugurated as 40th President.
Mar. 30	Reagan wounded in assassination attempt in Washington.
Aug. 13	Reagan's New Economic Programme projects 25% income tax reductions in 1981–4.
1986 Nov. 13	Reagan admits US arms sales to Iran, opening what becomes known as the Iran–Contra scandal.
Nov. 25	Further revelations about arms sales to Iran force resignation of National Security Adviser Adm. John Poindexter and Marine Col. Oliver North.
Dec. 2	Reagan appoints special prosecutor to investigate Iran–Contra scandal. As investigation develops details emerge of plan for proceeds of arms sales to Iran to be diverted to aiding Contra forces in Nicaragua.
1987 Mar. 3	Reagan says arms for Iran had been intended to help in release of hostages held in Middle East.
July 15	Adm. Poindexter says Reagan unaware of plan to divert Iran arms sales proceeds to aid Contras.
Aug. 12	Reagan accepts responsibility for Iran–Contra affair but denies knowledge of diversion of funds.
Oct. 19	'Black Monday': massive slump in share prices on Wall Street.
1988 Mar. 16	Poindexter and North indicted on Iran–Contra charges.
Nov. 8	George Bush defeats Democrat Michael Dukakis in Presidential election.
1989 Jan. 20	Bush sworn in as 41st President.
Nov. 18	Pennsylvania becomes first state to restrict abortions (Supreme Court gave states this right in July).
Nov. 19	Increase in minimum wage from $3.35 an hour to $4.25 by 1991.
Dec. 20	US troops invade Panama. Noriega regime overthrown; Noriega seeks asylum in Vatican nuncio's mission.
1990 Aug. 7	US forces embark for Saudi Arabia to repel Iraqis from Kuwait (Operation Desert Shield) (see p. 328).
Nov. 15	President Bush signs Bill designed to reduce federal budget deficits by $500 billion over five years. Upper personal income tax rate to rise from 28% to 31%.
1991 Jan.–Feb.	Defeat of Iraqi forces and liberation of Kuwait (Operation Desert Storm) in '100-hour war'.

July 9	President Bush cancels the sanctions set up against the Republic of South Africa in 1986.
July 10	Defense Base Closure and Realignment Commission proposals to reduce military bases accepted (start of post-Cold War run-down).
1992 Apr.–May	Rioting and arson in south-central Los Angeles following acquittal of those police accused of beating Rodney King. Death toll estimated at 52.
May	27th Amendment concerning Congressional pay rises finally becomes part of Constitution when Michigan becomes 38th state to approve.
July 15	Governor Bill Clinton of Arkansas is nominated as candidate for Presidential election (Senator Al Gore of Tennessee is nominated for Vice-President on 16 July). The populist H. Ross Perot, a Texan billionaire, temporarily withdraws from the Presidential race (17 July).
Nov. 3	Bill Clinton is elected 42nd President, defeating Bush. Independent candidate H. Ross Perot polls 19% of vote. Record number of women elected to the Senate. Carol Moseley Braun of Illinois becomes the first black woman to serve in the Senate.
Nov. 24	The last American soldier leaves the military base in Subic Bay, thus ending the US military presence (since 1898) in the Philippines.
Dec. 9	UN military force, led by US troops, arrives in Somalia.
Dec. 17	USA, Canada and Mexico sign the NAFTA Treaty.
1993 Jan. 20	Inauguration of Bill Clinton as 42nd President.
Jan. 22	Executive order of Clinton overturns restrictions on abortion imposed under Presidents Reagan and Bush.
Jan. 25	Hillary Clinton appointed to head Task Force on National Health Care Reform.
Feb. 26	Bombing of World Trade Center, New York City, kills 6 people.
Feb. 28	4 federal agents killed in botched raid on Branch Davidian site in Waco, Texas. Beginning of 51-day siege, and storming of compound.
Mar. 12	Janet Reno becomes first woman Attorney-General of the United States.
Apr. 19	FBI agents launch final assault on the Branch Davidian ranch at Waco, Texas; 80 die.
May 13	Formal abandonment of Strategic Defense Initiative ('Star Wars') programme.

June 26	US rocket attack on Iraq in retaliation for earlier attempt on the life of George Bush.
July 19	Clinton appears to remove ban on gays and lesbians serving in armed forces.
July 20	Death of Vincent Foster, Deputy White House counsellor and close friend of Bill Clinton.
July 26	Disaster areas now proclaimed in nine states after worst Mississippi floods in living memory – 'The Great Flood of 1993'.
Aug. 6	Tax-raising budget breaks election pledges.
Sept. 29	Healthcare reform package unveiled – the 1993 American Health Security Act.
Nov. 4	Democrat David Dinkins narrowly defeated as Mayor of New York.
Nov. 24	Following successful passage through the House of Representatives, the Senate also endorses the Brady Bill which creates a compulsory five-day waiting period for the purchase of firearms.
1994 Jan. 1	North American Free Trade Agreement (NAFTA) comes into force (endorsed earlier, on 18 Nov. 1993, by Congress).
Feb. 3	The 19-year old economic embargo against Vietnam is lifted.
Mar. 25	Last US troops leave Somalia.
May 30	Dan Rostenkowski, Chairman of House Ways and Means Committee, is indicted on fraud and corruption charges.
June 15	4-day tour of North Korea by ex-President Jimmy Carter. Threat of US sanctions avoided.
Aug. 18	State of emergency in Florida in anticipation of influx of Cuban refugees. President Clinton ends 30-year policy of right to asylum for Cuban refugees (19th).
July	Special counsel, Kenneth Starr, is appointed to probe Whitewater allegations.
Sept. 26	US sanctions lifted against Haiti (US troops had earlier landed in a mission to restore democracy (19th)).
Nov. 9	Sweeping Republican gains in mid-term elections. Republicans gain control of the Senate and (the first time for 40 years) the House of Representatives. Triumph of Newt Gingrich and the 'Contract with America'.
Dec. 11	Miami Summit pledges the creation of a Free Trade Area of the Americas to end trade barriers by 2005.
1995 Jan. 4	Senator Bob Dole (Kansas) becomes Majority Leader. Newt Gingrich becomes first Republican Speaker since 1954.

Mar. 2	Republican amendments to balance budget rejected by Senate.
Mar. 7	Gerry Adams, Sinn Fein leader, received at White House.
Apr. 19	Oklahoma bombing by right-wing anti-government militia leaves 168 dead. Arrest of Timothy James McVeigh.
May 2	Agreement signed with Cuba regulating immigration policies.
July 11	Establishment of full diplomatic links with Vietnam.
Aug. 17	Special prosecutor indicts business associates of Clinton over Whitewater affair.
Sept. 5	Ross Perot announces formation of the Reform Party.
Oct. 26	Senate legal affairs committee resumes investigation into the Whitewater affair.
Nov. 14	Government 'shut-down' after Budget deadlock between President and Congress.
Nov. 21	Dayton Peace Accords signed. USA commits 20,000 troops to Bosnia.
1996 Jan. 7	Longest-ever government shut-down ended by compromise Budget proposals.
Feb. 21	In primary elections, Republican Pat Buchanan wins New Hampshire, followed by victory for millionaire Steve Forbes in Arizona, 27 Feb.
Mar. 6	Senator Bob Dole wins vital primaries, effectively securing Republican Party Presidential nomination.
Mar. 20	US navy task force sent to Taiwan in stand-off with China.
July	Explosion aboard TWA flight 800 over Long Island. Over 220 dead. Bomb blast at Centennial Olympic Games at Atlanta. Two die; over 100 injured.
Aug.	Welfare Reform Bill signed by Clinton. End of the 60-year-old 'safety-net' for those in poverty.
Aug. 29	Resignation of Dick Morris, top presidential adviser, in sex scandal, overshadows Chicago Democratic Convention.
Sept. 3	Missile strike launched to punish Iraqi action over Kurds.
Oct. 14	Dow Jones passes 6,000 mark.
Nov.	Presidential election results in comfortable victory for incumbent Bill Clinton (with 49% of the vote and 379 electoral votes). Bob Dole (Republican) took 42% of the vote and 159 electoral votes. Ross Perot's Reform Party polled only 9% of the vote. Turn-out dropped to its lowest in postwar history (at 49.1%).
1998 Apr.	Second Clinton administration survives repeated allegations of sexual misconduct.
Nov.	Democrats gain in mid-term elections.

1999	Jan.	Impeachment of President Clinton begins.
	Mar./Apr.	Dow Jones average breaks 10,000 barrier.
	May	Resignation of Treasury Secretary Robert Rubin.
2000	Apr.	Beginning of slump in high-tech shares.
	Nov.	Knife-edge election between Al Gore (Democrat) and George W. Bush (Jnr). Recount in Florida amid accusations of electoral irregularities.
2001	Jan.	Inauguration of George W. Bush as 43rd President.
	May	Democrats gain control of Senate when Senator Jim Jeffords defects from Republicans to become an Independent.
	Sept. 11	Terrorist attack on America; World Trade Center devastated, Pentagon attacked and a fourth hijacked plane crashes in Pennsylvania (see p. 331 for America's military response). 'September 11' shatters America's concept of its security and invulnerability.
	Dec.	Enron (one of the world's largest energy companies) declared bankrupt. Debts exceed $13 billion.
2002	Nov.	Republicans take control of Senate in mid-term elections (51 of 100 seats). Department of Homeland Security created with Tom Ridge as secretary.
	Dec.	Dismissal of Paul O'Neill as Treasury Secretary. Replaced by John Snow.
2003	Mar.	USA and its allies invade Iraq (see p. 331).
	Nov. 25	Medicare legislation agreed by Congress.
2004	Nov.	John Kerry defeated by George W. Bush in Presidential election.
2005	Jan.	Inauguration of George W. Bush for second term as President. Confirmation of Condoleezza Rice as Secretary of State (first black woman to hold this post).

UNITED STATES AND THE WORLD FROM 1945

1945 May 8	V-E Day. End of war in Europe.
June 26	50 nations sign United Nations Charter in San Francisco.
July 17–Aug. 2	Potsdam Conference between Truman, Stalin and Churchill (later Attlee) reaches decision on division of Germany and demand for Japan's unconditional surrender.
Aug. 6	Atom bomb dropped on Hiroshima.
Aug. 9	Atom bomb dropped on Nagasaki.
Aug. 14	V-J Day. Japan acknowledges defeat.
Sept. 2	Japan formally surrenders on USS *Missouri* in Tokyo.
1946 Aug. 1	Atomic Energy Act restricts exchange of nuclear information with other nations.
Oct. 16	UN General Assembly opens in New York.
1947 Mar. 12	Truman signs Greek–Turkish Aid Bill promising the two states $400 million aid to resist Soviet aggression and internal Communist subversion. Becomes known as the 'Truman Doctrine'.
June 7	Secretary of State George Marshall proposes Marshall Plan to assist European economic recovery.
1948 Apr. 3	Marshall's European Recovery Programme enacted. By 1952 Europe receives $17,000 million in aid.
June 24	Berlin airlift begins, USA and Britain fly in 2 million tons of supplies to counter Soviet rail and road blockade. Ends following negotiations 12 May 1949.
1949 Apr. 4	USA signs North Atlantic Treaty in Washington with 11 other states to create NATO alliance.
1950 May 25	USA, UK and France conclude Tripartite Agreement to reduce Middle East tension by guaranteeing existing borders and limiting arms sales.
July 1	US troops arrive as part of United Nations force to assist South Korea, invaded by North Korea on 25 June.
Sept. 26	US troops recapture South Korean capital Seoul.
Oct. 7	US troops cross 38th Parallel into North Korea and advance by 20 Nov. to Manchurian border on Yalu River.
Nov. 29	US troops forced to retreat in Korea by heavy Chinese attack.
Dec. 19	US Gen. Dwight Eisenhower appointed Supreme Commander of NATO forces in Europe.
1951 Jan. 4	Seoul abandoned by US forces.
Mar. 14	Seoul recaptured by US troops.

Apr. 11	Gen. Douglas MacArthur dismissed by Truman from command in Korea and all military offices for defying policy by advocating attack on Communist China.
Oct. 10	Truman signs Mutual Security Act authorizing over $7 billion expenditure overseas on economic, military and technical aid.
1952 Nov. 1	USA explodes first hydrogen device at Eniwetok atoll, Marshall Islands.
1953 July 27	Armistice signed at Panmunjon ends fighting in Korea. 54,000 US servicemen died in war.
1954 Jan. 12	Secretary of State John Foster Dulles announces doctrine of 'massive retaliation' warning USSR that aggression will be met with nuclear attack.
Mar. 8	USA mutual defence agreement with Japan allows gradual re-arming of Japan.
Sept. 8	Manila Treaty creates South East Asia Treaty Organization (SEATO) of USA and seven other states for military and economic co-operation.
Dec. 2	USA signs Mutual Security Pact with Taiwan guaranteeing protection from Chinese attack. In effect until 1978.
1955 Feb. 12	Eisenhower despatches troops to South Vietnam as military advisers.
Mar. 16	Eisenhower announces that atomic weapons would be used in event of war. USA reported to have 4,000 bombs stockpiled.
July 18–23	USA attends summit meeting with Britain, France, USSR. Independence of East and West Germany recognized; Eisenhower proposes 'open skies' aerial photography plan as move towards disarmament.
Aug. 15	USA signs Austrian State Treaty with Britain, France and USSR restoring Austrian independence within 1937 borders.
1957 Jan. 5	Eisenhower Doctrine proposes military and economic aid to Middle East states threatened internally or externally by communism. Congress votes $200 million.
1958 July 15	US troops intervene in Lebanon Civil War under Eisenhower Doctrine following appeal from Lebanon President. Withdraw 25 Oct.
Aug. 23	US military preparations provoked by fears that Chinese shelling of offshore Nationalist island of Quemoy is a prelude to invasion.

1959 Sept. 15–27	Eisenhower meets Soviet Prime Minister Nikita Khrushchev at Camp David and both agree on need for 'peaceful coexistence'.
Dec. 1	USA signs Antarctica Treaty with 11 other states guaranteeing the area's neutrality.
1960 Jan. 19	USA and Japan sign mutual defence pact. Comes into effect 23 June.
May 1	American U2 spy plane shot down over USSR and pilot captured.
May 9	US announces suspension of U2 flights.
May 16	Summit conference with USSR in Paris terminated when Eisenhower refuses to apologize to Khrushchev over U2 incident.
July 11	American RB-47 reconnaissance bomber shot down over Soviet Union.
1961 Jan. 3	USA breaks off diplomatic relations with Cuba over nationalization of American property without compensation.
Mar. 1	Kennedy sets up Peace Corps as part of overseas aid programme.
Apr. 17	1,600-strong invasion of Cuba at Bay of Pigs by CIA-trained Cuban exiles with Kennedy's backing. Crushed by 20 Apr.
June 3–4	Kennedy and Khrushchev discuss German unification at unsuccessful summit conference in Vienna.
Dec. 11	USA despatches helicopters and crews to assist South Vietnam. 3,500 US troops in area.
1962 May 12	US troops deployed in Thailand to counter communist threat. They withdraw 27 July.
June 16	Defense Secretary Robert McNamara announces 'flexible response' to replace 'massive retaliation' strategy.
June 27	Kennedy promises Taiwan military assistance in event of Chinese attack.
Oct. 22–8	Cuban missile crisis. Kennedy announces aerial photography reveals Soviet missile sites in Cuba. Places Cuba under naval and air blockade to prevent delivery of missiles. Khrushchev removes missiles in return for US promise not to invade Cuba.
Dec. 18	Nassau Agreement between Kennedy and UK Prime Minister Macmillan to provide Britain with Polaris nuclear missiles for submarines.
1963 Apr. 5	Hot line connected between White House and Kremlin.
June 25	Kennedy announces on European tour that USA 'will risk its cities to defend yours'.

Aug. 5	Nuclear weapons tests in atmosphere, space and under water banned by treaty between USA, UK and USSR.
Oct. 7	White House announces aid to Vietnam will continue and that war could be won by end of 1965.
1964 Aug. 5	First US bombing of North Vietnam.
Aug. 7	Congress grants Johnson sweeping military powers under Gulf of Tonkin Resolution, following alleged North Vietnamese attacks on US destroyers, 2–4 Aug.
1965 Feb. 7	USA begins heavy sustained bombing of North Vietnam.
Feb. 18	Defense Secretary McNamara announces deterrent strategy of 'mutually assured destruction'.
Mar. 8	US combat troops land in Vietnam bringing numbers involved to 74,000.
Apr. 28	400 US Marines land in Dominican Republic to prevent left-wing takeover. The force eventually rises to 24,000.
June 15	US troops in first action against Viet Cong.
July 28	Johnson announces numbers of US troops in Vietnam will be increased from 75,000 to 125,000.
1966 Feb. 8	Declaration of Honolulu by Johnson and South Vietnam Premier Ky promises economic and social reforms in Vietnam.
Mar. 2	Defense Secretary Robert McNamara announces that US forces in Vietnam will be increased to 235,000.
June 11	US forces in Vietnam to rise to 285,000.
1967 Jan. 27	Space Treaty with UK and USSR outlaws use of nuclear weapons in space.
June 23–5	Summit meeting between Johnson and Soviet Prime Minister Kosygin in Glassboro, New Jersey.
July 22	Announcement of intention to deploy 525,000 US troops in Vietnam by end of 1968.
July 27	Puerto Rico votes against independence and to remain a US commonwealth territory.
1968 Jan. 23	North Korea seizes crew of USS *Pueblo* and accuses them of spying. They are released on 22 Dec.
Jan. 30	Viet Cong open Tet Offensive. Although a military failure for the communists, the attack has a dramatic effect on US commitment to war in Vietnam.
Mar. 16	US troops massacre 450 inhabitants in Vietnamese village of My Lai. News does not break until November. Lt William Calley given life imprisonment, 29 Mar. 1971, but sentence reduced.

Mar. 31	Johnson announces end to bombing of North Vietnam.
May 13	Preliminary Vietnam peace talks open in Paris.
July 1	USA signs Nuclear Non-Proliferation Treaty with Britain and USSR.

1969 Jan. 25	Full Vietnam peace talks begin in Paris.
Mar.	US troops in Vietnam reach their highest level at 541,000.
Nov. 3	Nixon announces intention to withdraw US forces and to 'Vietnamize' the war.
Nov. 25	USA renounces use of biological weapons.

1970 Apr. 16	Strategic Arms Limitation Talks (SALT) open between USA and USSR in Vienna.
Apr. 21	Nixon announces 150,000 US troop reduction in Vietnam over next year.
Apr. 30	US troops deployed in Cambodia.

1971 June 10	USA lifts 21-year trade embargo on China.
Oct. 25	USA signs Seabed Treaty with USSR, UK and other states banning nuclear weapons on ocean floor.

1972 Feb. 21–5	Nixon reverses US policy by visiting Communist China.
Apr. 6	USA resumes bombing of North Vietnam following communist offensive.
May 22–30	Nixon and Brezhnev agree to limit atomic weapon production at Moscow summit. Senate ratifies agreement on 3 Aug.

1973 Jan. 28	Ceasefire ends US involvement in Vietnam War. Final combat troops leave 29 Mar.
June 16–24	Nixon and Brezhnev summit meeting in US reaches agreement on co-operation to prevent nuclear war and on future arms negotiations.
July 1	Congress orders end to US bombing of Cambodia and military action in area by 15 Aug.
Oct. 17	Arab states ban oil supplies to USA in protest against support for Israel. Ends 1974.

1974 Jan. 10	Defense Secretary James Schlesinger announces 'limited strategic strike options' as new nuclear doctrine.
May 7	Ford declares Vietnam War era is over a week after Saigon falls to communists.
July 3	USA signs Threshold Test Ban Treaty with USSR, placing limits on underground nuclear testing.

1975 Aug. 1	USA signs Helsinki Treaty with USSR guaranteeing European postwar boundaries and recognizing human rights.

1977 Sept. 7	Carter signs Panama Canal Zone Treaty agreeing to evacuate Canal Zone by the year 2000.
1978 Sept. 5–17	Carter mediates at Camp David negotiations between Egyptian President Sadat and Israeli Prime Minister Begin, culminating in outline Middle East peace treaty. Treaty signed at White House, 26 Mar. 1979; effective 25 Apr. 1979.
1979 Jan. 1	USA establishes full diplomatic relations with China and severs links with Nationalist government on Taiwan.
Feb. 8	USA withdraws support from President Somoza of Nicaragua ensuring his downfall to Sandinista revolution.
Nov. 4	Iranian students occupy US Embassy in Tehran and seize 52 American hostages.
Nov. 4	USA establishes formal relations with German Democratic Republic.
1980 Apr. 24–5	8 US dead in unsuccessful helicopter attempt to rescue Tehran Embassy hostages.
Dec. 21	Iran demands $10,000 million payment for release of Embassy hostages.
1981 Jan. 20	US Embassy hostages released from Tehran as Reagan is sworn in as President.
1983 Oct. 23	241 US Marine members of peace-keeping force killed by suicide bombers in Beirut.
Oct. 25	US troops invade Grenada with forces of 6 Caribbean states to put down alleged left-wing threat. Suffer 42 dead in fighting with Grenada Army and Cuban construction workers.
1985 May 1	US bans all trade with Nicaragua.
Nov. 19–21	Reagan and Gorbachev summit in Geneva agrees on future annual meetings but fails to resolve differences over 'Star Wars' as obstacle to arms control.
1986 Jan. 7	Reagan orders US citizens to leave Libya and bans trade in retaliation for alleged Libyan involvement in international terrorism.
Feb. 18	Reagan announces $15 million military aid to anti-government guerrillas in Angola.
Mar. 20	House of Representatives rejects Reagan's $100 million aid package to anti-government Contra guerrillas in Nicaragua. Finally approves on 25 June and Reagan signs Bill on 18 Oct.

Mar. 24	US task force asserting sailing rights in Gulf of Sidra attacked by Libyan missile ships. USA sinks 2 ships and bombs coastal radar installation.
Apr. 14	American F-111 bombers strike Tripoli and Benghazi following alleged Libyan links with international terrorism.
June 18	House of Representatives votes for trade embargo on South Africa and withdrawal by US companies.
June 27	International Court rules US support of Contras in Nicaragua illegal.
July 15	US troops deployed in Bolivia to assist in operations against cocaine producers.
Sept. 26	Reagan vetoes South African sanctions proposal by House of Representatives.
Oct. 2	US Senate defies Presidential veto and imposes trade sanctions on South Africa.
Oct. 10–11	Reagan and Gorbachev meet in Reykjavik, Iceland. Blame each other for failure to achieve arms control agreement.
1987 Nov. 24	US reaches agreement with USSR on scrapping of intermediate range nuclear missiles.
Dec. 8–11	Reagan and Gorbachev summit meeting in Washington. Intermediate range missiles treaty signed; agreement on further arms reductions proposals and for a meeting in 1988.
1988 May 29	Reagan and Gorbachev meet in Moscow and agree on further intermediate range missile reductions.
July 3	USS *Vincennes* shoots down Iranian airbus over Gulf of Iran, killing 290 passengers.
Dec. 14	USA declares willingness to talk with Palestinian Liberation Organization following Yasser Arafat's 7 Dec. acceptance of Israel's right to exist. Discussions in Tunis take place 16 Dec.
1989 Jan. 4	US Navy jets shoot down two Libyan aircraft over Mediterranean.
Dec.	US forces invade Panama in operation to overthrow Noriega regime (see pp. 327–8).
1990 Aug. 7	US forces embark for Saudi Arabia to repel Iraqis from Kuwait (Operation Desert Shield).
1991 Jan.–Feb.	Defeat of Iraqi forces and liberation of Kuwait (Operation Desert Storm) (see p. 328).
July 9	Sanctions against South Africa withdrawn.

July 10	Defense Base Closure and Realignment Commission proposals to reduce military bases accepted.
1992 Nov. 24	Americans leave base in Subic Bay in the Philippines (acquired 1898).
Dec. 9	US forces deployed in Somalia.
Dec. 17	USA, Canada and Mexico sign free trade treaty.
1993 May 13	America abandons Strategic Defense Initiative ('Star Wars' programme).
June 26	US missile attack on Iraq in retaliation for earlier attempt on life of George Bush.
Oct. 3	Eighteen US soldiers killed in Somalia.
Dec.	Uruguay Round of GATT trade negotiations concluded on the basis of a 40% cut in tariffs.
1994 Jan. 1	North American Free Trade Area (NAFTA) comes into force.
Feb. 3	US economic embargo on Vietnam lifted.
Mar. 25	Last US troops leave Somalia.
June 15	Four-day tour of North Korea by ex-President Jimmy Carter.
Aug. 18	Anticipated influx of Cuban refugees; Clinton ends 30-year-old policy of right of asylum.
Sept. 26	US sanctions lifted against Haiti.
Dec. 11	United States pledges creation of free trade area of all the Americas by 2005 at Miami Summit.
1995 May 2	Agreement signed with Cuba over immigration policies.
July 11	Full diplomatic links established with Vietnam.
Nov. 21	Dayton Peace Accords commit 20,000 troops to peace-keeping in Bosnia.
1996 Sept. 3	Missile strikes launched against Iraq for assaults on Kurds.
Nov. 15	United States commits 5,000 troops to Rwanda peace-keeping force.
1997 Nov.	United States threatens military action against Iraq for violations of arms inspection agreements (crisis repeated in Mar. 1998).
1998 Aug.	Cruise missile attacks launched against Sudan and Afghanistan in retaliation for terrorist attacks on US embassies in Nairobi and Dar-es-Salaam (which had killed 223 people).
1999 July	Ban on trade with Taliban-controlled regions of Afghanistan.
Oct.	Senate refuses to ratify Comprehensive Test Ban Treaty (first ever Senate veto of nuclear treaty).

2000 May		House of Representatives grants permanent normal trade relations with China.
	July	Easing of US trade embargo on Cuba.
2001 Sept.		Terrorist attack on New York and Washington ('Sept. 11'). US responds with invasion of Afghanistan (see p. 331).
2003 Mar.		US forces invade Iraq (see pp. 331–2).
	Aug.	US troops deployed in Liberia.
	Nov.	Free Trade Agreement of the Americas reached at Miami.
2004 Aug.		President Bush outlines plans for major reduction in US forces overseas, particularly from Germany and Korea.
	Sept.	US deaths in Iraq war exceed 1,000.

CANADA SINCE 1914

1914 Canada enters the First World War (Aug.); expeditionary force raised.

1917 Coalition government formed to pursue war. Canadian troops suffer heavy losses in capture of Vimy Ridge, France (Apr.). Newfoundland obtains Dominion status. Conscription introduced (Aug.).

1918 Anti-conscription riots in Quebec; martial law imposed (Apr.).

1919 Mackenzie King takes over from Sir Wilfrid Laurier as leader of Liberal Party.

1921 Liberal Party wins general election; Mackenzie King becomes Prime Minister.

1926 King and Liberal Cabinet resign (June) as a result of a customs scandal; Liberals under Mackenzie King returned to power in elections in Sept. Canada becomes a self-governing Dominion within the Commonwealth.

1927 Richard Bennett becomes leader of Conservative Party.

1930 Conservative government under Bennett wins election victory over Liberals (July); failure to reach agreement at London Conference on tariff preferences between Canada, the other Dominions and Britain (Nov.).

1932 Bennett convenes imperial economic conference at Ottawa (July–Aug.) and gains introduction of partial imperial preference, gaining Canada access to United Kingdom markets on favourable terms.

1933 Royal Commission reports on bankruptcy of Newfoundland, recommending suspension of constitution and control by a nominated commission (Feb.).

1934 Commission appointed in Newfoundland and given British loans to assist economic recovery.

1935 Bennett announces 'New Deal'-style reforms (Jan.); Mackenzie King defeats Bennett by record majority in elections (Oct.).

1939 Canada enters war against Germany (Sept.); first Canadian troops sent to Britain (Dec.).

1942 Canadian parliament votes for conscription (July); ends relations with Vichy France (Nov.). Canadian troops suffer heavily in Dieppe Raid (19 Aug.).

1943 Mackenzie King hosts Quebec Conference between Churchill and Roosevelt.

1945 King's Liberal Party returned in general election (June).

1946   Arrests of Soviet spies allegedly involved in transfer of atomic secrets to Russia (Feb.). British Labour government authorizes the election of a Newfoundland Convention to discuss its future (June).

1948   Referendum on future of Newfoundland indecisive (June); second referendum (July) gives majority for federation with Canada. Louis St Laurent becomes Liberal leader and Prime Minister in succession to MacKenzie King (Nov.).

1949   Newfoundland becomes 10th province of Canada (Mar.); Canada signs North Atlantic Treaty (Apr.). Official Languages Act establishes English and French as dual official languages.
British North America Act gave federal parliament limited rights to amend constitution.

1950   Death of Mackenzie King (July).

1951   Old Age Security Act introduced.

1952   Collaboration on production of hydro-electric power with USA begins.

1953   Work begun on St Lawrence Seaway system of canals and locks linking the Atlantic and the Great Lakes. General election won by St Laurent for the Liberals.

1956   John Diefenbaker becomes leader of Progressive Conservative Party (Dec.).

1957   St Laurent loses general election to Diefenbaker and the Conservatives form minority government (June), ending 22 years of Liberal government.

1958   St Laurent hands over as leader of opposition to Lester Pearson; Conservatives obtain clear majority of 158 seats in new election (Mar.). Conference at Montreal institutes Commonwealth Assistance Loans.

1959   St Lawrence Seaway formally opened (June).

1963   Diefenbaker resigns (17 Apr.); Pearson forms Liberal government (22 Apr.).

1964   Canada adopts Maple Leaf emblem for national flag. Growing discontent between French- and English-speaking Canadians and growing movement for separatism in Quebec.

1967   Diefenbaker retires from politics. De Gaulle angers Canadian government by references to autonomy for French Canada on visit to Quebec (July).

1968   Pearson resigns in favour of Pierre Trudeau (Apr.): Trudeau increases Liberal majority at general election (June).

1970 *Parti québécois* gains 6 seats in Quebec National Assembly (of 110).

1972 Trudeau left as head of minority Liberal government following general election (Oct.).

1974 Trudeau regains majority in general election.

1976 *Parti québécois* gains 70 seats in Quebec National Assembly.

1977 Visit of head of *Parti québécois*, René Levesque, to France with full honours (Nov.).

1979 Trudeau defeated in general election (May); Conservative government under Joe Clark.

1980 Trudeau leads Liberals to general election victory (Feb.). Trudeau proposes 'patriation' of the Constitution, severing last constitutional links with Britain, causing violent scenes in parliament. Referendum (20 May) in Quebec votes against proposal of *Parti québécois* for negotiation for a looser political association with the rest of Canada.

1981 Canada formally asks Britain for 'patriation' of the constitution (Dec.).

1982 Canada Bill, approving patriation, passes British House of Commons. Queen Elizabeth visits Canada to formalize complete national sovereignty for Canada (Apr.). New constitution replaces Acts of 1867 and 1949, provides a bill of rights and redefines ethnic, provincial and territorial rights.

1983 Brian Mulroney takes over as leader of Conservative Party from Joe Clark (June).

1984 John Turner succeeds Trudeau as Liberal leader and Prime Minister (June). Conservatives sweep to victory in general election (Sept.), winning 211 of 282 seats.

1988 General election on issue of free trade agreement with the United States leads to further victory for Mulroney and the Progressive Conservative Party (Nov.). Free trade agreement with United States enacted.

1992 A plebiscite rejects a constitutional reform package endorsed by leaders of the 10 provinces of the country in Aug. The new Constitution would have offered a special status to French-speaking Quebec and placed greater power into the hands of the governments and legislatures of the provinces (Oct.).
Prime Minister Mulroney, with US President Bush and Mexican President de Gortari, signs the North American Free Trade Association Treaty (NAFTA) (Dec.).

1993   In accordance with the agreement signed by Prime Minister Mulroney (May), the Canadian Eskimos will receive a 2.2 million sq. km territory called Nunavut in 1999. The name means 'our land' in the language of the Inuit people.

Mrs Kim Campbell, former Minister of Defence, takes over from the retiring Mulroney as the head of the Progressive Conservative Party and the government (June). Gaining only 2 seats, the Conservatives suffer a devastating defeat at the parliamentary elections (Oct.). Jean Chrétien, the leader of the Liberals, who have won an absolute majority, forms a government (Nov.). With 54 seats, the separatist *Bloc québécois* becomes the largest opposition force.

1994   Re-election of hard-line separatist Premier Jacques Parizeau in Quebec.

1995   Federalists win narrow victory in referendum on future of Quebec (Oct.). Jacques Parizeau resigns as leader of the *Parti québécois*.

1996   Lucien Bouchard assumes leadership of *Parti québécois* (Jan.). Chrétien reshuffles his Cabinet with greater representation from British Columbia and Quebec.

1997   General election in June results in re-election of Chrétien's Liberal government with a slightly reduced majority.

2000   Comfortable Liberal general election victory; Chrétien forms third successive majority government (Nov.).

2003   Toronto badly affected by SARS outbreak (Apr.); Paul Martin becomes Prime Minister (Dec.). (having been elected to succeed Chrétien in Nov.).

2004   General election produces closest revolt in 25 years. Liberal Party largest party with 135 seats.

HEADS OF STATE AND SELECTED MINISTERS OR RULERS

AUSTRALIA

Prime Ministers

A. Fisher	1914–15
W. Hughes	1915–23
S. Bruce	1923–29
J. Scullin	1929–31
J. Lyons	1931–39
R. Menzies	1939–41
A. Fadden	1941 (Aug.)
J. Curtin	1941–45
F. Forde (acting)	1945 (July)
J. Chifley	1945–49
Sir R. Menzies	1949–66
H. Holt	1966–67
Sir J. McEwen	1967–68
J. Gorton	1968–71
W. McMahon	1971–72
E. Whitlam	1972–75
J. Fraser	1975–83
R. Hawke	1983–91
P. Keating	1991–96
J. Howard	1996–

BRAZIL

Presidents

W. Pereira Gomes	1914–18
D. da Costa Ribeiro (acting)	1918–19
E. da Silva Pessoa	1919–22
A. da Silva Bernardes	1922–26
W. Pereira de Souza	1926–30
Military junta	1930 (Oct.)
G. Dornelles Vargas	1930–45
J. Linhares	1945–46

Gen. E. Gaspar Dutra	1946–51
G. Dornelles Vargas	1951–54
J. Café Filho	1954–55
C. Coimbra da Luz (acting)	1955 (Nov.)
N. de Oliveira Ramos (acting)	1955–56
J. Kubitschek de Oliveira	1956–61
J. da Silva Quadros	1961 (Jan.–Aug.)
P. Ranieri Mazzilli	1961 (Aug.–Sept.)
J. Marques Goulart	1961–64
P. Ranieri Mazzilli (acting)	1964 (Apr.)
Marshal H. Castelo Branco	1964–67
Marshal A. da Costa e Silva	1967–69
Gen. E. Garrastazu	1969–74
Gen. E. Geisel	1974–79
Gen. J. Baptista de Fugueiredo	1979–85
J. Sarney	1985–90
F. Collor de Mello	1990–92
Itamar Franco	1992–95
F. Henrique Cardoso	1995–2002
Luíz Inácio ('Lula') da Silva	2002–

CANADA

Prime Ministers

Sir R. Borden	1911–20
A. Meighen	1920–21
W. King	1921–26
A. Meighen	1926 (June–July)
W. King	1926–30
R. Bennett	1930–35
W. King	1935–48
L. St. Laurent	1948–57
J. Diefenbaker	1957–63
L. Pearson	1963–68
P. Trudeau	1968–79
J. Clark	1979–80
P. Trudeau	1980–84
J. Turner	1984 (June–Sept.)
B. Mulroney	1984–93
K. Campbell	1993 (June–Nov.)
J. Chrétien	1993–2004
P. Martin	2004–

CHINA

Presidents

Yuan Shih-k'ai	1912–16
Gen. Li Yüan-hung	1916–17
Gen. Feng Kuo-chang	1917–18

There was a temporary restoration of the Emperor and a division between north and south in 1917.

Emperor

Hsüan-tung	1917 (July)

Northern Regime

Presidents

Hsü Shih Ch'ang	1918–22
Li Yüan-hung	1922–23
Ts'ao K'un	1923–24
Marshal Tuan Chi-jui	1924–26

De facto ruler

Chang Tso-lin	1926–28

Southern Regime

Presidents

Sun Yat-sen	1917–25
Hu Man-min	1925–27

Nanking Guomindang Regime (controlling the whole of China)

Head of Government

Chiang Kai-shek	1927–28

Republic of China (united)

Presidents

Chiang Kai-shek	1928–31

Lin Sen	1931–43
Chiang Kai-shek	1943–49
Gen. Li Tsung-jen	1949 (Jan.–Dec.)

Presidents of the Executive Yuan (Prime Minister)

T'an Yen-k'ai	1928–30
Soong Tzu-wen	1930 (Sept.–Nov.)
Chiang Kai-shek	1930–31
Sun Fo	1931–32
Chong Ming-shu (acting)	1932 (Jan.)
Wang Ching-wei	1932–35
Chiang Kai-shek	1935–38
Kung Hsiang-hsi	1938–39
Chiang Kai-shek	1939–45
Soong Tzu-wen	1945–47
Chiang Kai-shek	1947 (Mar.–Apr.)
Gen. Chang Chun	1947–48
Wong Wen-hao	1948 (May–Nov.)
Sun Fo	1948–49
Gen. Ho Ying-chin	1949 (Mar.–June)
Marshal Yen Hsi-shan	1949 (June–Dec.)

A Communist regime took power at the end of the civil war in 1949.

Chairmen of the Republic

Mao Zedong	1949–58
Marshal Zhu De	1958–59
Liu Shaoqi	1959–68
Dong Biwu	1968–75

(The office was abolished in 1975.)

Chairmen of the Communist Party

Mao Zedong	1949–76
Hua Guofeng	1976–81
Hu Yaobang	1981–82

(This office was abolished in 1982 and replaced by the post of General Secretary, which Hu Yaobang took.)

Prime Ministers

Zhou Enlai	1949–76
Hua Guofeng	1976–80

Zhao Ziyang	1980–88
Li Peng	1988–98
Zhu Rongji	1998–2003
Wen Jiabao	2003–

EGYPT

Egypt was under British occupation from 1882 and was a British Protectorate from 1914 to 1936.

Sultans

| Hussein Kemal | 1914–17 |
| Faud | 1917–22 |

Faud was proclaimed King in 1922.

Kings

Faud I	1922–36
Farouk	1936–52
Regency for Ahmad Faud II	1952–53

Presidents

Gen. M. Neguib	1953–54
Col. G. Nasser	1954–70
A. Sadat	1970–81
S. Talib (acting)	1981 (Oct.)
Lt-Gen. H. Mubarrak	1981–

FRANCE

Third Republic

Presidents

R. Poincaré	1913–20
P. Deschanel	1920 (Jan.–Sept.)
A. Millerand	1920–24
G. Doumergue	1924–31
P. Doumer	1931–32
A. Lebrun	1932–40

Marshal P. Pétain combined presidential powers with his own office of Prime Minister, July 1940, and created the post of Chief of State.

Chiefs of State

Admiral Darlan	1941–42
P. Laval	1942–45

Prime Ministers

P. Painlevé	1914–17
G. Clemenceau	1917–20
A. Millerand	1920 (Jan.–Oct.)
M. Leygues	1920–21
M. Briand	1921–22
R. Poincaré	1922–24
F. Marsal	1924 (June)
E. Herriot	1924–25
P. Painlevé	1925 (May–Nov.)
M. Briand	1925–26
R. Poincaré	1926–29
A. Briand	1929 (July–Nov.)
A. Tardieu	1929–30
M. Steeg	1930–31
P. Laval	1931–32
A. Tardieu	1932 (Feb.–June)
E. Herriot	1932 (June–Dec.)
J. Paul-Boncour	1932–33
E. Daladier	1933 (Jan.–Oct)
A. Sarraut	1933 (Oct.–Nov.)
C. Chautemps	1933–34
E. Daladier	1934 (Jan.–Feb.)
G. Doumergue	1934 (Feb.–Nov.)
P.-E. Flandin	1934–35
F. Bouisson	1935 (June)
P. Laval	1935–36
A. Sarraut	1936 (Jan.–June)
L. Blum	1936–37
C. Chautemps	1937–38
L. Blum	1938 (Mar.–Apr.)
E. Daladier	1938–40
P. Reynaud	1940 (Mar.–June)
Marshal P. Pétain	1940–42

General C. de Gaulle led a National Unity government as head of state, 1945–46. The Fourth Republic was constituted in Dec. 1946.

Fourth Republic

Presidents

V. Auriol	1947–54
R. Coty	1954–59

Prime Ministers

F. Gouin	1946 (Jan.–June)
G. Bidault	1946 (June–Dec.)
L. Blum	1946–47
P. Ramadier	1947 (Jan.–Nov.)
R. Schuman	1947–48
A. Marie	1948 (July–Sept.)
H. Queuille	1948–49
G. Bidault	1949–50
H. Queuille	1950 (July)
R. Pleven	1950–51
H. Queuille	1951 (Mar.–Aug.)
R. Pleven	1951–52
E. Fauré	1952 (Jan.–Mar.)
A. Pinay	1952–53
R. Mayer	1953 (Jan.–June)
J. Laniel	1953–54
P. Mendès-France	1954–55
E. Fauré	1955–56
G. Mollet	1956–57
F. Gaillard	1957–59

The Fifth Republic was constituted in Oct. 1958.

Fifth Republic

Presidents

Gen. C. de Gaulle	1959–69
A. Poher (interim)	1969 (Apr.–June)
G. Pompidou	1969–74
A. Poher (interim)	1974 (Apr.–May)
V. Giscard d'Estaing	1974–81
F. Mitterrand	1981–95
J. Chirac	1995–

Prime Ministers

M. Debré	1959–62
G. Pompidou	1962–68
M. Couve de Murville	1968–69
J. Chaban-Delmas	1969–72
P. Messmer	1972–74
J. Chirac	1974–76
R. Barre	1976–81
P. Mauroy	1981–84
L. Fabius	1984–86
J. Chirac	1986–88
P. Rocard	1988–91
E. Cresson	1991–92
P. Bérégovoy	1992–93
E. Balladur	1993–95
A. Joppé	1995–97
L. Jospin	1997–2002
J.-P. Raffarin	2002–

GERMANY

German Empire

Emperor

Wilhelm II	1888–1918

Chancellor

T. Bethmann-Hollweg	1909–17
G. Michaelis	1917
G. von Herling	1917–18
Prince Max of Baden	1918
F. Ebert	1918

Wilhelm II abdicated on 9 Nov. 1918 and a Republic was proclaimed.

German Republic

Presidents

F. Ebert	1919–25
P. von Hindenburg	1925–34

Reich Chancellor

P. Scheidemann	1919 (Feb.–June)
G. Bauer	1919–20
H. Müller	1920 (Mar.–June)
C. Fehrenbach	1920–21
J. Wirth	1921–22
W. Cuno	1922–23
G. Stresemann	1923 (Aug.–Nov.)
W. Marx	1923–24
H. Luther	1925–26
W. Marx	1926–28
H. Müller	1928–30
H. Brüning	1930–32
F. von Papen	1932 (May–Nov.)
K. von Schleicher	1932–33

A. Hitler was appointed Chancellor in Jan. 1933. Following the death of President Hindenburg in 1934 he took the title Chancellor and Führer.

Chancellor and Führer

A. Hitler	1934–45
Admiral C. Dönitz	1945 (Apr.–June)

Germany was occupied and divided by the Allies in 1945. The Western Zone became the Federal Republic of Germany in Sept. 1949. The Eastern Zone became the German Democratic Republic the following month.

Federal Republic of Germany

Presidents

T. Heuss	1949–59
H. Lübke	1959–69
G. Heinemann	1969–74
W. Scheel	1974–79
K. Carstens	1979–84
R. von Weizsäcker	1984–94
R. Herzog	1994–99
J. Rau	1999–2004
H. Koehler	2004–

Federal Chancellor

K. Adenauer	1949–63
L. Erhard	1963–66

K. Kiesinger	1966–69
W. Brandt	1969–74
W. Scheel (acting)	1974 (May)
H. Schmidt	1974–82
H. Kohl	1982–98
G. Schröder	1998–

German Democratic Republic

President

W. Pieck	1949–60

The office of President was abolished in 1960. Its powers were transferred to that of the Chairman of the Council of State.

Chairman of the Council of State

W. Ulbricht	1960–73
W. Stoph	1973–76
E. Honecker	1976–89

Honecker was replaced briefly as Communist Party leader by Egon Krenz. The reformist Hans Modrow became Prime Minister on 8 Nov. On 12 Apr. 1990 he was succeeded by Lothar de Maizère.

INDIA

Viceroys

Baron Hardinge	1910–16
Baron Chelmsford	1916–21
Marquess of Reading	1921–26
Baron Irwin	1926–31
Marquess of Willingdon	1931–36
Marquess of Linlithgow	1936–43
Viscount Wavell	1943–47
Earl Mountbatten	1947

Governors-General

Earl Mountbatten	1947–48
C. Rajagopalachari	1948–49

Presidents

R. Prasad	1949–62
S. Radhakrishnan	1962–67
Z. Hussain	1967–69
V. Giri	1969–74
F. Ahmed	1974–77
B. Jatti	1977 (Feb.–July)
N. Reddy	1977–82
G. Singh	1982–87
R. Venkataraman	1987–92
S. D. Sharma	1992–97
K. R. Narayanan	1997–2002
A. P. J. Abdul Kalam	2002–

Prime Ministers

J. Nehru	1949–64
G. Nanda (acting)	1964 (May–June)
L. Shastri	1964–66
G. Nanda (acting)	1966 (Jan.)
Mrs I. Gandhi	1966–77
M. Desai	1977–79
C. Singh	1979–80
Mrs I. Gandhi	1980–84
R. Gandhi	1984–89
V. P. Singh	1989–90
C. Shekhar	1990–91
P. V. Narasimha Rao	1991–96
A. B. Vajpayee	1996 (May–June)
H. D. Deve Gowda	1996–97
I. K. Gujral	1997–98
A. B. Vajpayee	1998–2004
Manmohan Singh	2004–

INDONESIA

Indonesia became officially independent from the Netherlands in Dec. 1949.

Governors-General

A. Idenburg	1909–16
J. von Limburg Stirum	1916–21
D. Fock	1921–26
A. de Graaef	1926–31

B. de Jonge	1931–36
A. van Starkenborgh Stachouwer	1936–45

Lieutenant Governor-General

H. van Mook	1942–48

Commissioners-General

W. Schermerhorn	1946–48
M. van Poll	1946–48
F. de Boer	1946–48

Presidents

M. Sukarno	1945–67
Gen. R. Suharto	1967–98
B. J. Habibie	1998–99
A. Wahid	1999–2001
M. Sukarnopuri	2001–04
S. B. Yudhoyono	2004–

Prime Ministers

M. Sukarno	1945
S. Sjahrir	1945–47
A. Sjarifuddin	1947–48
M. Hatta	1948 (Jan.–Dec.)
S. Prawiranegara	1948–49
M. Hatta	1949–50
M. Natsir	1950–51
Dr Sartono	1951 (Mar.–Apr.)
S. Wirjosandjojo	1951–52
Dr Wilopo	1952–53
A. Sastroamidjojo	1953–54
M. Hatta (acting)	1954 (July–Aug.)
B. Harahap	1954–56
A. Sastroamidjojo	1956–57
Dr Suwirjo (acting)	1957 (Mar.–Apr.)
D. Kartawidjaja	1957–63
M. Sukarno	1963–66
Gen. R. Suharto	1966–67

The office was abolished in 1967.

IRAN

Shahs

Ahmed Mirza Shah	1909–25
Reza Shah Pahlevi	1925–41
Mohammad Reza Shah Pahlevi	1941–79

Prime Ministers

A. Furanghi	1941–42
A. Solheily	1942 (Mar.–Aug.)
Q. es-Sultaneh	1942–43
A. Solheily	1943–44
M. Saed	1944 (Mar.–Nov.)
N. Bayatt	1944–45
I. Hakimi	1945 (May–June)
M. Sadr	1945 (June–Oct.)
I. Hakimi	1945–46
Q. es-Sultaneh	1946–47
S. Hekmat	1947 (Dec.)
I. Hakimi	1947–48
A. Hajir	1948 (June–Nov.)
M. Saed	1948–50
A. Mansur	1950 (Mar.–June)
Gen. A. Razmara	1950–51
H. Ala	1951 (Mar.–Apr.)
M. Mussadeq	1951–52
Q. es-Sultaneh	1952 (July)
M. Mussadeq	1952–53
Gen. F. Zaheda	1953–55
H. Ala	1955–57
M. Eghbal	1957–60
J. Emami	1960–61
A. Amini	1961–62
A. Alam	1962–64
H. Mansur	1964–65
A. Hoveida	1965–67
J. Amouzegar	1977–79

The Shah fled from Iran in Jan. 1979. Ayatollah Ruhollah Khomeini became head of a provisional government in Feb. As supreme religious leader he was acknowledged as the Islamic Republic of Iran's highest authority until his death in 1989.

Presidents

A. Bani-Sadr	1980–81
M. Raja'i	1981 (July–Aug.)
H. Khamenei	1981–89
H. Rafsanjani	1989–97
M. Khatami	1997–

IRAQ

Iraq was part of the Ottoman Empire until occupied by Britain in 1916. It was held by Britain as a League of Nations mandate until the granting of independence in 1932.

Kings

Faisal I	1921–33
Ghazi	1933–39
Faisal II	1939–58

Prime Ministers

Gen. N. Pasha es-Said	1932–33
S. Ali el Gailani	1933 (Mar.–Nov.)
J. Midfai	1933–34
A. Jaudat Bey	1934–35
J. Midfai	1935 (Mar.)
Gen. Y. Pasah el Hashimi	1935–36
S. Hikmat Sulaiman	1936–37
J. Midfai	1937–38
Gen. N. Pasha es-Said	1938–40
S. Ali el Gailani	1940–41
J. Midfai	1941 (May–Oct.)
Gen. N. Pasha es-Said	1941–44
H. el-Pachichi	1944–46
T. Suwaidi	1946 (Feb.–June)
A. el-Umari	1946 (June–Nov.)
Gen. N. Pasha es-Said	1946–47
S. Jabr	1947–48
M. el-Sadr	1948 (Jan.–June)
M. el-Pachichi	1948–49
Gen. N. Pasha es-Said	1949 (Jan.–Dec.)
S. Jawdat Ayubi	1949–50
T. el-Suweidi	1950 (Feb.–Sept.)
Gen. N. Pasha es-Said	1950–52

S. Mustafa el-Umari	1952 (July–Nov.)
Gen. N. Mohammed	1952–53
J. Midfai	1953 (Jan.–Sept.)
M. Fadil Jamali	1953–54
Gen. N. Pasha es-Said	1954–57
S. Jawdat Ayubi	1957 (June–Dec.)
A. Wahab Mirjan	1957–58
Gen. N. Pasha es-Said	1958 (Mar.–May)
A. Mukhtar Baban	1958 (May–July)

The monarchy was overthrown and a republic formed in July 1958.

Presidents

Gen. M. Najib Rubai	1958–63
Col. A. Mohammed Aref	1963–66
Maj.–Gen. A. Rahman Aref	1966–68
Maj.–Gen. A. Hassan Bakr	1968–79
S. Hussein al-Takriti	1979–2003

Saddam Hussein was overthrown by the Allied invasion of 2003 (see pp. 331–2). With the return of sovereignty to Iraq, Iyad Allawi was appointed interim Prime Minister in June 2004. In April 2005 Jalal Talabani was elected as President.

ISRAEL

Presidents

C. Weizmann (acting)	1948–49
C. Weizmann	1949–52
J. Springzak (acting)	1952 (Nov.–Dec.)
I. Ben-Zvi	1952–63
K. Luz	1963 (Apr.–May)
Z. Shazar	1963–68
E. Katzir	1968–78
Y. Navom	1978–83
C. Herzog	1983–93
E. Weizman	1993–2000
M. Katsav	2000–

Prime Ministers

D. Ben-Gurion	1948–53
M. Sharett	1953–55
D. Ben-Gurion	1955–63
L. Eshkol	1963–69

Mrs G. Meir	1969–74
Gen. Y. Rabin	1974–77
M. Begin	1977–83
Y. Shamir	1984–84
S. Peres	1984–86
Y. Shamir	1986–92
Y. Rabin	1992–95
S. Peres	1995–96
B. Netanyahu	1996–99
E. Barak	1999–2000
A. Sharon	2001–

ITALY

Kings

Victor Emmanuel III (Emperor of Ethiopia 1936; King of Albania 1939)	1900–46
Umberto	1946 (May–June)

Prime Ministers

A. Salandra	1914–16
P. Boselli	1916–17
V. Orlando	1917–19
F. Nitti	1919–20
G. Giolitti	1920–21
I. Bonomi	1921–22
L. Facta	1922 (Feb.–Oct.)
B. Mussolini	1922–43
Marshal P. Badoglio	1943–44

Italy became a Republic by referendum in June 1946.

Presidents

A. de Gasperi (acting)	1946 (June)
E. de Nicola	1946–48
L. Einaudi	1948–55
G. Gronchi	1955–62
A. Segni	1962–64
G. Saragat	1964–71
G. Leone	1971–78
A. Fanfani (acting)	1978 (June–July)
A. Pertini	1978–85

F. Cossiga	1985–92
O. Scalfaro	1992–99
C. A. Ciampi	1999–

Prime Ministers

F. Parri	1945 (June–Nov.)
A. de Gasperi	1945–53
G. Pella	1953–54
A. Fanfani	1954 (Jan.–Feb.)
M. Scelba	1954–55
A. Segni	1955–57
A. Zoli	1957–58
A. Fanfani	1958–59
A. Segni	1959–60
F. Tambroni	1960 (Mar.–July)
A. Fanfani	1960–63
G. Leone	1963 (June–Dec.)
A. Moro	1963–68
G. Leone	1968 (June–Dec.)
M. Rumor	1968–70
E. Colombo	1970–72
G. Andreotti	1972–73
M. Rumor	1973–74
A. Moro	1974–76
G. Andreotti	1976–79
F. Cossiga	1979–80
A. Forlani	1980–81
G. Spadolini	1981–82
A. Fanfani	1982–83
B. Craxi	1983–87
G. Andreotti	1987 (Feb.–June)
G. Goria	1987–88
C. De Mita	1988–89
G. Andreotti	1989–92
G. Amato	1992–93
C. A. Ciampi	1993–94
S. Berlusconi	1994 (Apr.–Dec.)
L. Dini	1995–96
R. Prodi	1996–98
M. D'Alema	1998–2000
G. Amato	2000–2001
S. Berlusconi	2001–

JAPAN

Emperors

Yoshihito	1912–26
Hirohito	1926–89
Akihito	1989–

Prime Ministers

T. Hara	1918–21
Y. Uchida	1921 (Nov.)
K. Takahashi	1921–22
T. S. Kato	1922–23
Adm. G. Yamamoto	1923–24
K. Kyoura	1924 (Jan.–June)
T. Kato	1924–25
R. Wakatsuki	1925–27
G. Tanaka	1927–29
O. Hamaguchi	1929–31
R. Wakatsuki	1931 (Apr.–Dec.)
T. Inukai	1931–32
Adm. M. Saito	1932–34
Adm. K. Okado	1934–36
F. Goto	1936 (Feb.)
Adm. K. Okado	1936 (Feb.–Mar.)
K. Hirota	1936–37
Gen. S. Hayashi	1937 (Feb.–June)
Prince F. Konoye	1937–39
K. Hiranuma	1939 (Jan.–Aug.)
Gen. N. Abe	1939–40
Adm. M. Yonai	1940 (Jan.–July)
Prince F. Konoye	1940–41
Lt-Gen. H. Tojo	1941–44
Gen. K. Koiso	1944–45
Adm. K. Suzuki	1945 (Apr.–Aug.)
N. Higashikuni	1945 (Aug.–Oct.)
K. Shidehara	1945–46
S. Yoshida	1946–47
T. Katayama	1947–48
H. Ashida	1948 (Feb.–Oct.)
S. Yoshida	1948–54
I. Hatoyama	1954–56
T. Ishibashi	1956–57
N. Kishi	1957–60

H. Ikeda	1960–64
E. Sato	1964–72
K. Tanaka	1972–74
T. Miki	1974–76
T. Fukuda	1976–78
M. Ohira	1978–80
M. Ito (acting)	1980 (June–July)
Z. Suzki	1980–82
Y. Nakasone	1982–87
N. Takeshita	1987–89
S. Uno	1989 (June–Aug.)
T. Kaifu	1989–91
K. Miyazawa	1991–93
M. Hosokawa	1993–94
T. Hata	1994 (Apr.–June)
T. Murayama	1994–96
R. Hashimoto	1996–98
K. Obuchi	1998–2000
Y. Mori	2000–2001
J. Koizumi	2001–

NIGERIA

Nigeria became independent from Britain in 1960 and a republic in 1963.

Governors

F. Lugard	1914–19
H. Clifford	1919–25
G. Thomson	1925–31
D. Cameron	1931–35
B. Bourdillon	1935–42
A. Burns	1942–43
A. Richards	1943–47
J. Macpherson	1948–54

Governors-General

J. Macpherson	1954–55
J. Robertson	1955–60
N. Azikiwe	1960–63

Presidents

(Title not used Jan. 1966–Oct. 1977, and after Dec. 1983.)

N. Azikiwe	1963–66
N. Orizu (acting)	1966 (Jan.)
Maj.-Gen. J. Aguiyi-Ironsi	1966 (Jan.–July)
Lt-Col. Y. Gowon	1966–75
Gen. M. Ramat Mohammed	1975–76
Lt-Gen. O. Obasanjo	1976–79
A. Shehu Shagari	1979–83
Maj.-Gen. M. Buhari	1983–85

Prime Minister

A. Tafawa Balewa	1957–66

Under military rule from 1966.

Heads of State and Commanders-in-Chief of Armed Forces

Maj.-Gen. J. Aguiyi-Ironsi	1966–68
Lt-Col. Y. Gowon	1968–75
Gen. M. Ramat Mohammed	1975–76
Lt-Gen. O. Obasanjo	1976–79
A. Shehu Shagari	1979–83
Maj.-Gen. M. Buhari	1983–85
Maj.-Gen. I. Babaginda	1985–93
E. Shonekan	1993 (Aug.–Nov.)
Gen. S. Abacha	1993–98
Gen. A. Abubakar	1998–99
O. Obasanjo	1999–

Shonekan was Head of Interim Government. Abacha was Chairman of the Provisional Ruling Council.

PAKISTAN

Presidents

Q. Ali Jinnah	1947–48
K. Nazimuddin	1948–51
G. Muhammed	1951–55
Maj.-Gen. I. Mirza	1956–58
Field Marshal M. Ayub Khan	1958–69
Maj.-Gen. A. Yahya Khan	1969–71
Z. Ali Bhutto	1971–73
F. Elahi Chaudri	1973–78
Gen. M. Zia ul-Haq	1978–88

I. Khan	1988–93
S. F. Leghari	1993–97
M. R. Tarar	1997–99
P. Musharraf*	1999–

*Musharraf took power in military coup.

RUSSIA

See USSR up to 1991. Leaders since the downfall of the Soviet Union have been:

Presidents

| B. Yeltsin | 1991–99 (31 Dec.) |
| V. Putin | 2000– |

Prime Ministers

B. Yeltsin	1991–92
Y. Gaidar	1992 (Jun.–Dec.)
V. Chernomyrdin	1992–98
S. Kiriyenko	1998 (Mar.–Sept.)
Y. Primakov	1998–99
V. Putin	1999–2000
M. Kasyanov	2000–2004
M. Fradkov	2004–

SAUDI ARABIA

United as a kingdom in 1932.

Kings

Abdul Aziz ibn Abdur-Rahman al-Faisal Al Sa'ud	1932–53
Saud ibn Abdul Aziz	1953–64
Faisal ibn Abdul Aziz	1964–75
Khalid ibn Abdul Aziz	1975–82
Fahd ibn Abdul Aziz	1982–

SOUTH AFRICA

Governors-General

| Viscount Gladstone | 1910–14 |
| Viscount Buxton | 1914–24 |

Earl of Athlone	1924–31
Earl of Clarendon	1931–37
Sir P. Duncan	1937–43
N. de Wet	1943–46
G. van Zyl	1946–50
E. Jansen	1951–59
L. Steyn (acting)	1959–60
C. Swart	1960–61

In 1961 South Africa became a republic and left the British Commonwealth.

Presidents

C. Swart	1961–67
J. Naudé (acting)	1967–68
J. Fouché	1968–75
N. Diederich	1975–78
M. Viljoen (acting)	1978 (Aug.–Oct.)
B. Vorster	1978–79
M. Viljoen (acting)	1979–84
P. Botha	1984–89
F. de Klerk	1989–94
N. Mandela	1994–99
T. Mbeki*	1999–

* Mbeki re-elected, 2004.

Prime Ministers

Gen. L. Botha	1910–19
Gen. J. Smuts	1919–24
Gen. J. Hertzog	1924–39
Gen. J. Smuts	1939–48
D. Malan	1948–54
J. Strijdom	1954–58
C. Swart (acting)	1958 (Aug.–Sept.)
H. Verwoerd	1958–66
B. Vorster	1966–78
P. Botha	1978–84

The post of Prime Minister was abolished in 1984 and combined with that of President.

SPAIN

King

Alfonso XIII	1886–1931

Prime Ministers

A. Maura	1917–23

Gen. M. Primo de Rivera mounted a coup in 1923 and held power until 1930.

Gen. Dánaso Berenguer	1930–31
Adm. J. Bautista Aznar (interim)	1931 (Feb.–Apr.)

Spain became a republic in Apr. 1931.

Presidents

N. Alcalá-Zamora	1931–36
M. Azaña	1936–39

Prime Ministers

Under the Republic the position of Prime Minister changed rapidly. Azaña was Prime Minister, 1931–3 and again in 1936 (Feb.–May). Largo Caballero was Prime Minister 1936–7. The last premier was Negrín.

Chief of State

Gen. F. Franco Bahamonde	1939–75

Franco designated Prince Juan Carlos as his eventual successor in 1969.

King

Juan Carlos I	1975–

UNION OF SOVIET SOCIALIST REPUBLICS

Until the 1917 Revolution, Russia was a monarchy.

Tsar

Nicholas II	1894–1917

Prime Ministers

W. Kokovtsov	1911–14
I. Goremykin	1914–16

B. Stürmer	1916 (Feb.–Nov.)
A. Trepov	1916–17
N. Golitsin	1917 (Jan.–Mar.)

Prime Ministers of the Provisional Government

G. Lvov	1917 (Mar.–July)
A. Kerensky	1917 (July–Nov.)

A Bolshevik government took power in Nov. 1917 and adopted the constitution of a Federal Republic in July 1918.

President of the Council of People's Commissars

V. Lenin	1917–22

Presidents

M. Kalinin	1922–46
N. Shvernik	1946–53
Marshal K. Voroshilov	1953–60
L. Brezhnev	1960–64
A. Mikoyan	1964–65
N. Podgorny	1965–77
L. Brezhnev	1977–82
Y. Andropov	1983–84
K. Chernenko	1984–85
A. Gromyko	1985–88
M. Gorbachev	1988–91

The dominant figure from 1917 to 1990 was the General Secretary of the Communist Party.

General Secretaries

V. Lenin	1917–22
J. Stalin	1922–53
N. Khrushchev	1953–64
L. Brezhnev	1964–82
Y. Andropov	1982–84
K. Chernenko	1984–85
M. Gorbachev	1985–91

For leaders after 1991 see **Russia**.

UNITED KINGDOM

Sovereigns

George V	1910–36
Edward VIII	1936 (abdicated, uncrowned)
George VI	1936–52
Elizabeth II	1952–

Prime Ministers

H. Asquith	1908–16
D. Lloyd George	1916–22
A. Bonar Law	1922–23
J. R. MacDonald	1924 (Jan.–Nov.)
S. Baldwin	1924–29
J. R. MacDonald	1929–35
S. Baldwin	1935–37
N. Chamberlain	1937–40
W. Churchill	1940–45
C. Attlee	1945–51
Sir W. Churchill	1951–55
Sir A. Eden	1955–57
H. Macmillan	1957–63
Sir A. Douglas-Home	1963–64
H. Wilson	1964–70
E. Heath	1970–74
H. Wilson	1974–76
J. Callaghan	1976–79
M. Thatcher	1979–90
J. Major	1990–97
A. Blair	1997–

UNITED STATES

Presidents

W. Wilson	1913–21
W. Harding	1921–23
C. Coolidge	1923–29
H. Hoover	1929–33
F. Roosevelt	1933–45
H. Truman	1945–53
D. Eisenhower	1953–61
J. Kennedy	1961–63

L. Johnson	1963–69
R. Nixon	1969–74
G. Ford	1974–77
J. Carter	1977–81
R. Reagan	1981–89
G. Bush	1989–93
W. J. Clinton	1993–2001
G. W. Bush	2001–

VATICAN

Popes

Pius X	1903–14
Benedict XV	1914–22
Pius XI	1922–39
Pius XII	1939–58
John XXIII	1958–63
Paul VI	1963–78
John Paul I	1978
John Paul II	1978–2005

VIETNAM

The central Vietnam region of Annam was a French protectorate from 1883 and part of the Indochinese Union from 1887. Between 1940 and 1945 it was controlled by Japan. French rule was restored in 1945, local autonomy within an Indochinese Federation was granted in 1946, and Vietnam became independent in 1954.

Governors-General of Indochinese Union

A. Sarraut	1911–14
J. Van Vollenhoven	1914–15
E. Roume	1915–16
J. Charles	1916–17
A. Sarraut	1917–19
M. Monguillot	1919–20
M. Long	1920–22
F. Baudouin	1922
M. Merlin	1922–25
M. Monguillot	1925
A. Varennes	1925–28
M. Monguillot	1928

P. Pasquier	1928–34
E. Robin	1934–36
J. Brévié	1936–39
G. Catroux	1939–40
J. Decoux	1940–45

High Commissioners of Indochinese Federation

G. D'Argenlieu	1945–47
E. Ballaert	1947–48
L. Pignon	1948–50
J. de Lattre de Tassigny	1950–52
J. Letourneau	1952–53

Empire of Annam

Emperors (under French protection)

Duy Tan	1906–16
Khai Dinh	1916–25
Bao Din	1925–45

Democratic Republic of Vietnam (North Vietnam)

Presidents

Ho Chi Minh	1945–69
Ton Duc Thang	1969–76

Prime Ministers

Ho Chi Minh	1945–55
Pham Van Dong	1955–76

Empire of Vietnam

Emperor

Bao Dao	1954–55

Prime Ministers

Buu Loc	1954–55
Ngo Dinh Diem	1955 (June–Oct.)

Republic of Vietnam (South Vietnam)

Presidents

Ngo Dinh Diem	1955–63
Maj.-Gen. Duong Van Minh	1963–64
Mej.-Gen. Nguyen Khanh	1964 (Jan.–Feb.)
Maj.-Gen. Duong Van Minh	1964 (Feb.–Aug.)
Maj.-Gen. Nguyen Khanh	1964 (Aug.–Sept.)
Maj.-Gen. Duong Van Minh	1964 (Sept.–Oct.)
Phan Khac Suu	1964–65
Gen. Nguyen Van Thieu	1965–75
Tran Van Huong	1975 (Apr.)
Maj.-Gen. Duong Van Minh	1975 (Apr.)

Prime Ministers

Ngo Dinh Diem	1955–63
Nguyen Ngoc Tho	1963–64
Maj.-Gen Nguyen Khanh	1964 (Feb.–Aug.)
Nguyen Xuan Oanh	1964 (Aug.–Sept.)
Gen. Nguyen Khanh	1964 (Sept.–Oct.)
Tran Van Huong	1964–65
Nguyen Xuan Oanh (acting)	1965 (Jan.–Feb.)
Phan Huy Quat	1965 (Feb.–June)
Air Vice-Marshal Nguyen Cao Ky	1965–67
Nguyen Van Loc	1967–69
Tran Van Huong	1969 (May–Aug.)
Gen. Tran Thien Khiem	1969–75
Bguyen Ba Can	1975 (Apr.)
Vu Van Mau	1975 (Apr.)

South Vietnam fell to the North in Apr. 1975 and the two states were united in 1976.

Socialist Republic of Vietnam

Presidents

Ton Duc Thang	1976–80
Nguyen Huu Tho	1980–81
Truong Chinh	1981–86
Nguyen Van Linh	1986–87
Vo Chi Cong	1987–91
Do Muoi	1991–92

| Le Duc Anh | 1992–97 |
| Tran Duc Luong | 1997– |

YUGOSLAVIA

The Serb, Croat and Slovene State formed in Dec. 1918 became known as Yugoslavia in Oct. 1929.

Kings

Peter I (originally King of Serbia)	1903–21
Alexander I	1921–34
Peter II	1934–45

Prime Ministers

S. Protić	1921 (Feb.–Dec.)
N. Pašić	1921–26
N. Uzunović	1926–28
V. Vukitčević	1928–29
Gen. P. Zivković	1929–32
V. Marinković	1932 (Apr.–July)
M. Serškie	1932–34
N. Uzonivić	1934 (Jan.–Dec.)
B. Jević	1934–35
M. Stojadinović	1935–39
D. Cvetković	1939–41

Yugoslavia was occupied by the Axis in 1941. A government-in-exile was based in London and then in Cairo.

S. Jovanovīč	1942–43
M. Trifimovīč	1943 (June–Aug.)
B. Purīč	1943–45

A republic was proclaimed in 1945.

Presidents of the Praesidium

| I. Ribar | 1945–53 |
| Marshal J. Broz Tito | 1953–80 |

After 1980 Yugoslavia had a 'Collective Presidency'. A President was selected annually from this eight-member committee.

Following the collapse of Yugoslavia, the two key Presidents of the 'rump' Yugoslavia (now officially the Union of Serbia and Montenegro) have been:

| S. Milosević | 1997–2000 (President of Serbia, 1992–97) |
| V. Kostunica | 2000– |

Following the break-up of Yugoslavia, the following independent republics have now come into existence: Bosnia–Herzegovina; Croatia; Macedonia; Serbia and Montenegro; and Slovenia. In addition, Kosovo (see p. 331) is now an international protectorate.

ZIMBABWE

Southern Rhodesia was annexed to the British Crown in 1923. A white regime declared illegal unilateral independence in 1965 and a republic in 1970. The area became independent as Zimbabwe in 1980.

Administrator

| F. Chaplin | 1914–23 |

Governors

J. Chancellor	1923–28
C. Rodwell	1928–34
H. Stanley	1934–42
E. Baring	1942–44
W. Tait	1944–46
J. Kennedy	1947–53
P. William-Powlett	1954–59
H. Gibbs	1959–65

Prime Ministers

Sir C. Coghlan	1923–27
H. Moffat	1927–33
G. Mitchell	1933 (July–Sept.)
Sir G. Huggins (later Lord Malvern)	1933–53
G. Todd	1953–58
Sir E. Whitehead	1958–62
W. Field	1962–64
I. Smith	1964–80

Between 1953 and 1963 Rhodesia was part of the Federation of Rhodesia and Nyasaland.

Prime Ministers

Sir G. Huggins	1953–56
Sir R. Welensky	1956–63

President (during period of illegal independence)

C. Dupont	1970–76
J. Wrathall	1976–80

Zimbabwe

President

C. Banana	1980–87
R. Mugabe (Executive President)	1987–

II
WARS AND
INTERNATIONAL AFFAIRS

PRINCIPAL INTERNATIONAL ORGANIZATIONS AND GROUPINGS

Arab League

Established in 1945 to promote co-operation between member states. All the Arab countries including Mauritania, Sudan and Somalia are normally members, but Egypt was suspended in 1979 after its overtures to Israel. Palestine (i.e. the PLO) also holds membership. Libya left in 2002. The League sent a peace-keeping force to Lebanon in June 1976, and tried to mediate in the civil war in the 1980s.

Secretaries-General

Abdul Azzem (Egypt)	1945–52
Abdul Hassouna (Egypt)	1952–72
Mahmoud Riad (Egypt)	1972–79
Chedli Klibi (Tunisia)	1979–90
Esmat Abdel Meguid (Egypt)	1991–2001
Amr Moussa (Egypt)	2001–

Members

Algeria (1962)	Oman (1971)
Bahrain (1971)	Palestine (PLO)
Comoros (n.a.)	Qatar (1971)
Djibouti (1977)	Saudi Arabia
Egypt (suspended 1979)	Somalia (1974)
Iraq	Sudan (1956)
Jordan	Syria
Kuwait (1961)	Tunisia (1958)
Lebanon	United Arab Emirates (1971)
Libya (1951)	Western Sahara (n.a.)
Mauritania (1973)	Yemen
Morocco (1958)	

Association of South East Asian Nations (ASEAN)

This association was formed on 8 Aug. 1967, with headquarters in Jakarta, to promote active collaboration and mutual assistance in economic, social, cultural, technical, scientific and administrative fields. The founding members were Indonesia, Thailand, the Philippines, Malaysia and Singapore. Brunei joined in 1984. Vietnam joined in 1995, Laos and Myanmar in 1997 and Cambodia in 1999. It was hoped through the association to increase the political stability of south-east Asia and to improve the rate of economic development. There is an annual meeting of Foreign Ministers, and progress has been made not only in economic co-operation but also in joint research, education, transport, etc..

Secretaries-General

Hartono Dharsono (Indonesia)	1967–78
Umarjadi Njotowijona (Indonesia)	1978 (Feb.–July)
Datuk Ali bin Abdullah (Malaysia)	1978–80
Narciso Reyes (Philippines)	1980–82
Chan Kai Yau (Singapore)	1982–84
Phan Wannamethee (Thailand)	1984–89
Rusli Noor (Indonesia)	1989–91
Roderick Yong (Brunei)	1991–98
Rodolfo C. Severino (Philippines)	1998–

Members

Brunei (1984)	Myanmar (1997)
Cambodia (1999)	Philippines (1967)
Indonesia (1967)	Singapore (1967)
Laos (1997)	Thailand (1967)
Malaysia (1967)	Vietnam (1995)

Commonwealth, the

A grouping of states, numbering 53 in 2005, which evolved from the former territories of the British Empire. The Statute of Westminster (31 Dec. 1931) defined the structure of the British Commonwealth and recognized the dominions as 'autonomous communities'. The organization works to improve economic collaboration and other forms of co-operation between member states. Not all former territories of the British Empire are members. Burma never joined; the Republic of Ireland is not a member. South Africa left in 1961, Pakistan left in 1972 and rejoined in 1989, Fiji left after the military coup in 1987, rejoining in 1997. Namibia (joined 1990), Cameroon (1995) and Mozambique (1995) are the most recent members. Zimbabwe was suspended in Mar. 2002 and left in Dec. 2003.

Secretaries General of the Commonwealth

Arnold Smith (Canada)	1965–75
Sir Shridath S. Ramphal (Guyana)	1975–89
Chief Emeka Anyaoku (Nigeria)	1989–2000
Don McKinnon (New Zealand)	2000–

Council for Mutual Economic Assistance (COMECON)

Organization established in Moscow in Jan. 1959 to improve trade between the Soviet Union and other Eastern European states. Regarded by Stalin as an instrument to enforce an economic boycott on Yugoslavia, and also used as a

Soviet response to growing Western European economic interdependence. Apart from the East European countries, Mongolia joined in 1962, Cuba in 1972 and Vietnam in 1978. Changes in Europe since 1989 left its future role uncertain and in 1991 it was formally dissolved.

Secretaries

Nikolai Faddeyev (USSR)	1949–83
Vyacheslav Sychev (USSR)	1983–91

Council of Europe

Organization established in 1949 to achieve greater European unity based on the common heritage of its member states. Matters of national defence are excluded. The original states were Belgium, Britain, Denmark, France, Ireland, Italy, the Netherlands, Norway and Sweden. They were also joined by Greece, Iceland and Turkey later in 1949, West Germany in 1951, Austria in 1956, Cyprus in 1961, Switzerland in 1963 and Malta in 1965. With the fall of communism, and the new political order in Central and Eastern Europe, membership has grown rapidly (to 44 by 2005). It is quite separate from the European Union (q.v.).

Secretaries-General

Jacques Camille-Paris (France)	1949–53
Leon Marchal (France)	1953–57
Ludovico Benvenuti (Italy)	1957–64
Peter Smithers (UK)	1964–69
Lujo Toncic-Sorinj (Austria)	1969–74
Georg Kahn-Ackermann (Federal Republic of Germany	1974–79
Franz Karasek (Austria)	1979–84
Marcelino Oreja Aguirre (Spain)	1984–89
Catherine Lalumière (France)	1989–94
Daniel Tarschys (Sweden)	1994–99
Walter Schwimmer (Austria)	1999–

European Community (EC)/European Union

Also frequently referred to as the Common Market. Came into being on 1 Jan. 1958, following the signing by the original six states (Belgium, France, Italy, Luxembourg, the Netherlands and West Germany) of the Treaty of Rome on 25 Mar. 1957. The original 6 states, who bound themselves to work together for economic and political union, were enlarged with the entry of Denmark, Ireland and the UK on 1 Jan. 1973, Greece on 1 Jan. 1981 and Spain and Portugal on 1 Jan. 1986. Under the Lomé Convention of 31 Oct. 1979, the Community made trade agreements with 58 countries in Africa, the Caribbean and the Pacific. Subsequent agreements have enlarged this number.

The 25 Members of the European Union (2005)

Austria 1995	Latvia 2004
Belgium 1957	Lithuania 2004
Cyprus 2004	Luxembourg 1957
Czech Republic 2004	Malta 2004
Denmark 1973	Netherlands 1957
Estonia 2004	Poland 2004
Finland 1995	Portugal 1986
France 1957	Slovakia 2004
Germany[1] 1957	Slovenia 2004
Greece 1981	Spain 1986
Hungary 2004	Sweden 1995
Ireland 1973	United Kingdom 1973
Italy 1957	

Presidents of the European Commission

Walter Hallstein (Federal Republic of Germany)	1958–66
Jean Rey (Belgium)	1966–70
Franco Malfatti (Italy)	1970–72
Sicco Mansholt (Netherlands)	1972–73
François-Xavier Ortoli (France)	1973–77
Roy Jenkins (UK)	1977–81
Gaston Thorn (Luxembourg)	1981–85
Jacques Delors (France)	1985–95
Jacques Santer (Luxembourg)	1995–99
Romano Prodi (Italy)	1999–2004
José Durão Barroso (Portugal)	2004–

Presidents of the European Parliament

Robert Schuman (France)	1958–60
Hans Furler (Federal Republic of Germany)	1960–62
Gaetano Martino (Italy)	1962–64
Jean Duvieusart (Belgium)	1964–65
Victor Leemans (Belgium)	1965–66
Alain Poher (France)	1966–69
Mario Scelba (Italy)	1969–71

---

[1] As the Federal Republic of Germany (i.e. West Germany).

Walter Behrendt (Federal Republic of Germany)	1971–73
Cornelius Berkhouwer (Netherlands)	1973–75
Georges Spénale (France)	1975–77
Emilio Colombo (Italy)	1977–79
Simone Veil (France)	1979–82
Pieter Dankert (Netherlands)	1982–84
Pierre Pflimlin (France)	1984–87
Lord Plumb (UK)	1987–89
Enrico Barón Crespo (Spain)	1989–91
Egon Klepsch (Germany)	1992–94
Klaus Hänsch (Germany)	1994–97
José Maria Gil-Robles (Spain)	1997–2002
Pat Cox (Ireland)	2002–

European Free Trade Association (EFTA)

Grouping of European countries whose aims are to achieve a free trade in industrial goods between members, to help achieve the creation of a general Western European market and to expand world trade in general. Three members (Denmark, Portugal and the United Kingdom) left to join the European Economic Community. In 1995 Austria, Finland and Sweden left to join the European Union, leaving only 4 members (Iceland, Liechtenstein, Norway and Switzerland).

Secretaries-General

Frank Figgures (UK)	1960–65
John Coulson (UK)	1965–72
Bengt Rabaeus (Sweden)	1972–75
Charles Muller (Switzerland)	1976–81
Magnus Vahlquist (Sweden) (Acting)	1981 (Oct.–Nov.)
Per Kleppe (Norway)	1981–88
Georg Reisch (Austria)	1988–94
Kjartan Jóhannsson (Iceland)	1994–2000
William Rossier (Switzerland)	2000–

League of Nations

International organization set up as an integral part of the Versailles Settlement in 1920 (see p. 9) to preserve the peace and settle disputes by negotiation. Although the United States refused to participate, it comprised 53 members by 1923. Based in Geneva, the League relied upon non-military means to coerce states, such as 'sanctions' (see p. 484), but found itself virtually powerless in the face of the Japanese invasion of Manchuria and the Italian invasion of Abyssinia. The League was discredited by 1939 and was dissolved in Apr. 1946 with the formation of the United Nations. (See also pp. 282–4 for a chronology of the League.)

Secretaries-General

Sir Eric Drummond (Earl of Perth) (UK)	1919–32
Joseph Avenol (France)	1933–40
Sean Lester (Ireland) (Acting)	1940–46

North Atlantic Treaty Organization (NATO)

Created by the North Atlantic Treaty of 4 Apr. 1949. The organization represented the first US commitment to European defence in peacetime. NATO came in response to Western fears about the power of the Soviet Union and the failure of the UN Security Council to operate in the face of the Soviet veto. The treaty states are obliged to take such action as they deem necessary to assist a fellow signatory subjected to aggression, although there is no obligation to fight. The treaty states are Belgium, Luxembourg, the Netherlands, Britain, the United States, Canada, Italy, Norway, Denmark, Iceland and Portugal who were original signatories plus Greece and Turkey (1952) and West Germany (1955). The reunited Germany acceded in Oct. 1990. Spain joined in 1982. With the fall of communism, the role of NATO is changing and its membership is reaching out to Central and Eastern Europe. NATO has provided support for peace-keeping operations in Bosnia. France was an original signatory, but withdrew from the organization in 1966.

Secretaries-General

Lord Ismay (UK)	1952–57
Paul-Henri Spaak (Belgium)	1957–61
Alberico Casardi (Acting)	1961 (Mar.–Apr.)
Dirk Stikker (Netherlands)	1961–64
Manlio Brosio (Italy)	1964–71
Joseph Luns (Holland)	1971–84
Lord Carrington (UK)	1984–88
Manfred Wörner	
(Federal Republic of Germany)	1988–95
Javier Solana (Spain)	1995–99
Lord Robertson (UK)	1999–2003
Jakob de Hoop Scheffer (Netherlands)	2003–

Supreme Allied Commanders, Europe

Dwight D. Eisenhower (USA)	1950–52
Matthew Ridgway (USA)	1952–53

Alfred M. Gruenther (USA)	1953–56
Lauris Norstad (USA)	1956–63
Lyman L. Lemnitzer (USA)	1963–69
Andrew J. Goodpaster (USA)	1969–74
Alexander Haig (USA)	1974–79
Bernard Rogers (USA)	1979–87
John R. Galvin (USA)	1987–92
John Shalikashvili (USA)	1992–93
George Joulvan (USA)	1993–97
Wesley Clark (USA)	1997–2000
Joseph W. Ralston (USA)	2000–02
James L. Jones (USA)	2002–

Organization for Economic Co-operation and Development (OECD)

The organization now (2005) consists of 30 countries, mostly the richer nations. Its aims are to encourage and co-ordinate the economic policies of members, to contribute to the expansion of developing countries and to promote the development of world trade on a multilateral basis. It publishes economic statistics and compiles reports on specific aspects of world economics. It is the successor to the Organization for European Economic Co-operation (OEEC).

Secretaries-General

Thorkil Kristensen (Denmark)	1961–69
Emile van Lennep (Netherlands)	1969–84
Jean-Claude Paye (France)	1984–96
Donald Johnston (Canada)	1996–

Organization of African Unity/African Union

Grouping of African states set up in 1963 after a meeting in Addis Ababa. Its formation united the rival Monrovia and Casablanca groups as well as including nearly all the independent black African states. At its first meeting the members agreed to accept inherited colonial boundaries, thus preventing many border incidents. The members also voted to boycott South Africa. It has mediated successfully in disputes amongst its members (as in 1972, in the dispute between Guinea and Senegal) and has campaigned against the vestiges of colonialism in southern Africa (as in Namibia in the 1980s). Following an initiative begun by President Qadhafi of Libya in 1999, an OAU summit in Lomé in July 2000 established the African Union as its successor. All African states belong. The first Secretary General was Amara Essy (Ivory Coast).

Secretaries-General

Diallo Telli (Guinea)	1964–72
Nzo Ekangaki (Cameroon)	1972–74
William Eteki Mbomua (Cameroon)	1974–78
Edem Kodjo (Togo)	1978–83
Peter Onu (Nigeria) (Acting)	1983–85
Ide Oumarou (Niger)	1985–89
Salim Ahmed Salim (Tanzania)	1989–2000

Organization of American States (OAS)

Regional political organization consisting of the United States and 33 other Latin American and Caribbean republics, created at the Bogota Conference in 1948. The organization has an Inter-American Conference which meets every 5 years to discuss general policies, and each member state is represented by an ambassador on its council, which oversees the implementation of OAS policy. There are provisions for *ad hoc* consultative meetings of foreign ministers and special conferences which promote co-operation in dealing with technical problems. The whole organization is served by a secretariat known as the Pan-American Union, which operates through its general headquarters in Washington.

Secretaries-General

Alberto Lleras Camargo (Colombia)	1948–54
Carlos Davila (Chile)	1954–56
José Mora Otero (Uruguay)	1956–68
Galo Plaza Lasso (Ecuador)	1968–75
Alejandro Orfila (Argentina)	1975–84
Valerie McComie (Barbados) (Acting)	1984 (Mar.–June)
João Clemente Baena Soares (Brazil)	1984–94
César Gaviria Trujillo (Colombia)	1994–

Organization of Petroleum Exporting Countries (OPEC)

This organization, whose membership is open to any country with substantial exports of crude petroleum, works to unify and co-ordinate the oil policies of its members, helps to stabilize prices in international oil markets and generally to safeguard the interests of its members. It originated in Sept. 1960 when, after a Baghdad meeting, such leading oil-producers as Saudi Arabia, Iran and Venezuela banded together to form OPEC. In 1973, OPEC precipitated a world economic crisis by agreeing price increases which eventually quadrupled the price of oil. Britain is not a member. Ecuador withdrew in 1992 and Gabon in 1995.

Secretaries-General

Faud Rouhani (Iran)	1961–64
Abdul Rahman Al-Bazzaz (Iraq)	1964–65
Ashraf Lutfi (Kuwait)	1965–66
Mohammed S. Joukhdar (Saudi Arabia)	1967
Francisco R. Parra (Venezuela)	1968
Elrich Sanger (Indonesia)	1969
Omar El-Badri (Libya)	1970
Nadim Pachachi (UAE)	1971–72
Abderrahman Khene (Algeria)	1973–74
M. O. Feyide (Nigeria)	1975–76
Ali M. Jaidah (Qatar)	1977–78
Rene G. Ortiz (Ecuador)	1979–81
Marc S. Nan Nguema (Gabon)	1981–83
Dr Subroto (Indonesia)	1983–94
Abdalla Salem El Balri (Libya)	1994 (July–Dec.)
Dr Rilwanu Lukman (Nigeria)	1995–2000
Ali Rodríguez–Araque (Venezuela)	2000–

United Nations, the

International peace-keeping organization set up in 1945 to replace the League of Nations (pp. 265–6). From the 50 states who signed the Charter of the UN in 1945, numbers had more than doubled by 1970 with the rise of independent ex-colonial states. There are now (2005) 190 members. All states have one vote in the General Assembly, and its executive, the Security Council, can call on member states to supply armed forces. UN troops have been involved in peace-keeping duties in many parts of the world since 1945, notably in the Middle East, Africa and Cyprus. (See also pp. 285–9 for a chronology of the United Nations.)

Secretaries-General

Trygve Lie (Norway)	1946–53
Dag Hammarskjöld (Sweden)	1953–61
U Thant (Burma)	1961–71
Kurt Waldheim (Austria)	1972–81
Javier Pérez de Cuellar (Peru)	1982–91
Boutros-Boutros Ghali (Egypt)	1992–96
Kofi Annan (Ghana)	1997–

Warsaw Pact

Military grouping of Russia and East European states, with a political consultative committee intended to meet twice a year with rotating venue and chairmanship. In fact it met every alternate year, with delegations led by first secretaries of the party. Committee of defence ministers met annually. Committee of foreign ministers met since 1976 annually. Military Council of national chiefs of staff met twice a year. Following the collapse of communism in Eastern Europe, by late 1990 the Warsaw Pact had effectively ceased to exist as a military alliance.

Commanders-in-Chief

Marshal I. S. Konev (USSR)	1955–60
Marshal A. A. Grechko (USSR)	1960–67
Marshal I. I. Yakubovsky (USSR)	1967–76
Marshal Viktor G. Kulikov (USSR)	1977–91

Members

Albania (ceased to participate in 1961 because of Stalinist and pro-Chinese attitudes. Withdrew in 1968)
Bulgaria
Czechoslovakia
German Democratic Republic
Hungary
Poland
Romania
USSR

MAJOR TREATIES AND INTERNATIONAL AGREEMENTS

1914   London Agreement, 15 June, between Britain and Germany concerning the Baghdad railway.
London Declaration, 5 Sept., by Britain, France and Russia not to make separate peace with the Central Powers.

1915   Treaty of London, 25 April, between Britain, France and Italy offers Italy territorial gains at expense of Austria–Hungary in return for entering War.

1916   Sykes–Picot Agreement between British and French divides between them the Middle East provinces of the Turkish Empire after Turkey's defeat, 16 May.

1917   Secret agreement of St Jean de Maurienne offers Italy part of Turkish territory after its defeat.
Secret treaty between Britain and Japan apportions German Pacific colonies between them.
Balfour Declaration supports the idea of a Jewish homeland in the Middle East, 2 Nov.

1918   Treaty of Brest-Litovsk, 3 Mar., between Russia and the Central Powers. Russia ceded territory, and made Finland and the Ukraine independent. Later invalidated.

1919   Treaty of Versailles, 28 June, between Germany and the Allies. Germany ceded territory and all its colonies to the Allies, returned Alsace-Lorraine to France, promised to pay large reparations and had its armed forces restricted. The Rhineland was demilitarized and occupied, and the League of Nations was created. Germany admitted 'war guilt'.
Treaty of Saint-Germain, 10 Sept., between Austria and the Allies, reduced Austria to a rump state following concessions to Czechoslovakia, Poland, Yugoslavia, Hungary, Italy and Romania, from the old Austria–Hungary.
Treaty of Neuilly, 27 Nov., between Bulgaria and the Allies reduced Bulgaria and provided for reparations payments.
Anglo-Afghan Treaty of Rawalpindi, 8 Aug.
Anglo-French agreement on Syria, 15 Sept.

1920   Treaty of the Trianon, 4 June, between Hungary and the Allies, reduced Hungary to a rump state and provided for reparations payments.
Treaty of Sèvres, 10 Aug., between Turkey and the Allies, reduced Turkey in size but was not accepted by the Turks.
US Senate refuses to ratify Versailles Treaty; US Congress votes to terminate war with Germany, 9 Apr.

Treaties of Tartu, 2 Feb., between Russia and Estonia, of Moscow, 12 July, between Russia and Lithuania, and of Riga, 11 Aug., between Russia and Latvia, establish Baltic States.
Treaty of Tartu, 14 Oct., between Russia and Finland creates an independent Finland.
Peace of Alexandropol, 2 Dec.: Armenia cedes half its territory to Turkey.

1921   Alliance between France and Poland, 19 Feb.; Treaty of Riga, 18 Mar., between Russia and Poland, ended war between them and defined their mutual border.
Paris Conference of Allies, 24–9 Jan., sets figure on reparations by Germany; London Ultimatum to Germany on payment accepted, 5–10 May.
Peace treaties of USA with Austria, Germany and Hungary, 25–9 May.
Four Power Pacific Treaty signed in Washington, 14 Dec.

1922   Washington Naval Agreement, 6 Feb., between Britain, France, the United States, Japan, Italy and others restricted the size of navies.
Treaty of Rapallo, 16 Apr., formed an alliance between Russia and Germany.
The 'Little Entente', 31 Aug., formed between Czechoslovakia, Yugoslavia and Romania under French auspices.
Turko-Greek armistice, 10 Oct.
US Protectionist Tariff introduced, 20 Sept.
Nine-Power Treaty secures independence of China, 6 Feb., Japan restores Shantung to China.

1923   Treaty of Lausanne, 24 July, between Turkey and the Allies replaced the Treaty of Sèvres. Confined Turkey to Asia Minor and the area around Constantinople.
Anglo-American War Debt Convention, 19 June.

1924   London Reparations Conference, 18 Aug., accepts Dawes Plan on reduced German reparations.
Geneva Protocol on Wars of Aggression, 2 Oct.

1925   Locarno Pact between Britain, France, Germany, Italy and Belgium, 1 Dec., guaranteed the current West European borders.
Geneva Protocol, 17 June, prohibited use of 'inhumane' methods of warfare.
Russo-Japanese Treaty, 20 Jan.
Russo-Turkish Treaty of Security.

1926   Reassurance Treaty between Russia and Germany, 24 Apr.
Anglo-Turkish agreement on Mosul, 5 June.
Alliance between USA and Panama, 28 July.
Treaty of Friendship between Italy and Albania, 27 Nov.

1927 Anglo-Iraqi Treaty, 14 Dec.
Alliance between Albania and Italy, 22 Nov.
Russo-Persian non-aggression Pact, 1 Oct.

1928 Briand–Kellogg Pact, 27 Aug., between Britain, France, the United
States, Germany, Italy and Japan, renounced war as a means to settle
disputes. Later adhered to by other states.
Italo-Abyssinian Treaty of Friendship, 2 Aug.; Italo-Greek Treaty of
Friendship, 23 Sept.

1929 Eastern Pact between Russia, Estonia, Latvia, Poland, Romania,
9 February; joined by Turkey, 27 Feb.
Lateran Treaties of Italy and Vatican, 11 Feb.; Young Report on
Reparations by Germany, 7 June.
Kellogg Pact came into force, 24 July.
Inter-American treaty of arbitration, 5 Jan.

1930 London Naval Agreement, 22 Apr., between Britain, France, the United
States, Japan and Italy, expanded the 1922 Washington agreements.
Young Plan came into force, 17 May.
Britain recognized independence of Iraq, 30 June.

1931 Russo-Turkish agreement on mutual naval reductions in Black Sea,
8 Mar.
Protocol on Hoover Plan, 11 Aug., to suspend German reparations for
one year.
Statute of Westminster, 31 Dec., defined structure of the British
Commonwealth and recognized the dominions as 'autonomous
communities'.

1932 Geneva Protocol on Germany's equality of rights, 11 Dec.
Anglo-French Pact of Friendship, 13 July.
Imperial Economic Conference at Ottawa signed Ottawa Agreements,
20 Aug., introducing limited preferential tariffs within British Empire.
Franco-Russian non-aggression pact, 29 Nov.
Russo-Polish non-aggression pact, 25 Jan. and 27 Nov.

1933 London Convention on definition of aggression signed by ten states,
3–5 July.
Russo-German treaties of 1926 and 1929 extended, 5 May.
Four-Power Pact signed in Rome, 15 July (Britain, France, Italy and
Germany).
Anglo-German trade pact, 27 Apr.
Non-aggression pact between Latin American countries signed in Rio,
11 Oct.

1934 Non-aggression pact between Germany and Poland, 26 Jan.
Balkan Pact, 9 Feb., with Romania, Greece, Yugoslavia and Turkey.

USA agrees independence of Philippines from 1945, 24 Mar.
Russo-Finnish non-aggression pact for ten years, 7 Apr.
Peruvian–Colombian settlement over Leticia Bay, 24 May.
Sudanese–Libyan border agreed, 20 July.
Baltic States Collaboration Treaty, 12 Sept.

1935   Franco-Italian agreement, 6 Jan., concerning colonies and Austria.
Alliance between France and Russia, 2 May, providing for mutual aid against aggression.
Anglo-German naval agreement, 18 June.
Russo-Czech Pact of mutual assistance, 16 May.
Russo-Turkish Treaty extended for ten years, 7 Nov.

1936   Peace Treaty between Bolivia and Paraguay ending Chaco War, 21 Jan.
Treaty between USA and Panama, 2 Mar.
Convention on the Straits signed at Montreux, 20 July; Turkey recovers control over Bosphorus and Dardanelles.
Anglo-Egyptian Treaty, 26 Aug., terminates military occupation.
Non-intervention agreement between Britain, France, Germany and Italy, 7 Aug., against involvement in Spanish affairs.
Germany and Japan sign Anti-Comintern Pact, 24 Nov.

1937   Anglo-Italian agreement signed, 2 Jan.
Polish-Danzig agreement, 7 Jan.
Italo-Yugoslav Pact, 26 Mar.
Non-aggression Pact between Afghanistan, Iran and Turkey, 8 July.
Anglo-Russian and Anglo-German naval agreements signed, 17 July.
Italy joins Anti-Comintern Pact, 6 Nov.

1938   Britain and Republic of Ireland signed agreement, 25 Apr.
Munich Agreement, 29 Sept., between Britain, France, Germany and Italy forces Czechoslovakia to cede territory to Germany, Hungary and Poland.
Libya declared part of Italy, 25 Oct.
Eighth Pan-American Conference in Lima issues 'Declaration of Lima' against 'all foreign intervention', 26 Dec.
Russo-Polish declaration of friendship, 28 Dec.

1939   France and Britain guarantee Polish integrity, 31 Mar.
'Pact of Steel', 22 May, between Germany and Italy formalized Rome–Berlin 'Axis'.
German–Soviet non-aggression pact, 23 Aug., for mutual aid, neutrality and spheres of influence in Eastern Europe.
Russo-Japanese armistice, 16 Sept.
Russia secures naval and air bases in Estonia, Latvia and Lithuania, 28 Sept.–10 Oct.
Anglo-French–Turkish pact of mutual assistance, 19 Oct.

1940   Treaty of Moscow, 12 Mar., established peace between Russia and
        Finland after 'Winter War', Finns cede territory.
        Tripartite Pact between Japan, Germany and Italy, 27 Sept.

1941   America signed Lend-Lease Bill for aid to Britain, 11 Mar.
        Soviet–Japanese Neutrality Pact, 13 Apr.
        German non-aggression pact with Turkey, 18 June.
        Atlantic Charter by Roosevelt and Churchill, 11 Aug.

1942   Washington Pact of 26 United Nations, 1 Jan.
        Anglo-Soviet 20-year treaty, 20 May.

1943   Casablanca conference of Allies agreed on demand for 'unconditional
        surrender' of Germany, 26 Jan.
        Marshal Badoglio of Italy signed secret armistice with Allies, 25 July.
        Quebec meeting on Allied strategy, 11–24 Aug.
        Cairo meeting of Roosevelt, Churchill and Chiang Kai-shek, 22–6 Nov.
        Tehran meeting of Roosevelt, Churchill and Stalin, 26 Nov.–2 Dec.

1944   Bretton Woods Agreement, July, to set up a World Bank and
        International Monetary Fund.
        Russia signed armistice with Finland, 4 Sept., ending Finnish
        involvement in war.
        Russia signed armistice with Romania, 12 Sept.
        Moscow conference between Churchill and Stalin, 9–19 Oct.

1945   Armistice signed with Hungary, 20 Jan.
        Yalta Agreement, 11 Feb., between Britain, Russia and the United States
        on the future of Germany, Europe and world security.
        Pact of Union of Arab States in Cairo, 22 Mar., set up Arab League.
        United Nations Charter, 26 June, established new world forum with
        Britain, Russia, France, the United States and China as leading
        powers.
        Potsdam Agreement between Britain, Russia and the United States,
        2 Aug., expanded on the Yalta Agreement.

1946   Treaty of London recognizes Transjordan as independent state, 25 May.
        Linggadjati Agreement, 15 Nov., between Dutch and Indonesians on
        creation of Indonesian Republic.
        World Bank set up, 27 Dec.

1947   Peace Treaties, 10 Feb., with Italy, Finland, Hungary, Bulgaria and
        Romania.
        Treaty of Dunkirk, 4 Mar., between Britain and France promised mutual
        aid against German aggression.
        Benelux customs union created, 14 Mar., between Belgium, Holland and
        Luxembourg.

Marshall Plan, 5 June; aid for reconstruction accepted by 16 European
countries through European Recovery Programme.
British announced Indian Independence, setting up states of India and
Pakistan, 5 July.
UN voted for partition of Palestine into Jewish and Arab states,
29 Nov.

1948   Brussels Treaty, 17 Mar., between Britain, France, Belgium, Holland and
Luxembourg, providing for mutual aid against aggression, and for
economic and social co-operation.
Organization for European Economic Co-operation (OEEC) formed by
16 West European nations, 16 Apr.
Treaty forming Organization of American States (OAS) for joint
resistance to attack, signed 30 Apr., by United States and 20 other
Central and Latin American states to come into force in 1951.

1949   Comecon (Council for Mutual Economic Assistance) set up, 25 Jan.,
by USSR and communist Eastern European states for economic
co-ordination and development.
North Atlantic Treaty, 4 Apr., between the United States, Canada, Britain,
France, Belgium, Holland, Luxembourg, Norway, Denmark, Portugal
and Iceland for mutual aid against aggression.
Statute of the Council of Europe, 5 May, by 10 West European states.
Israel signed armistice with Egypt, 24 Feb.; Jordan, 3 Apr., Syria,
20 July, establishing effective borders of new Israeli state.
The Hague conference reached agreement on independence of Indonesia,
2 Nov.

1950   US–South Korea defence agreement, 26 Jan.
Colombo Plan formed, 28 Nov., for economic development of
Commonwealth countries in Asia.

1951   Pacific Security Treaty between United States, Australia, and New
Zealand (ANZUS Pact), 1 Sept.
Japanese Peace Treaty, 8 Sept., with 48 other powers;
Japan signed Mutual Security Pact with the United States permitting
them to remain indefinitely in Japan.

1952   US–Japanese Agreement, 28 Feb., on bases in Japan.
Treaty between France, West Germany, Italy, Belgium, Holland and
Luxembourg, 27 May, created European Defence Community.
US–Israeli defence agreement, 23 July.

1953   Armistice signed in Korean War, 27 July, at Panmunjon.
Mutual defence agreement between United States and Spain, 26 Sept.,
allowing US bases.
Mutual Defence Treaty of United States with South Korea, 1 Oct.

1954 Truce signed in Indochinese War, 21 July, partitioning North and South
      Vietnam.
      Peace agreement in Geneva, 11 Aug., about future of Vietnam, not signed
      by USA or South Vietnam.
      South East Asia Collective Defence Treaty, 8 Sept., signed by US and
      7 other nations pledging joint action to protect South Vietnam and other
      nations in the area.
      London Agreement, 3 Oct., extends Brussels Pact to West Germany and
      Italy, forming the West European Union.
      Mutual Defence Treaty with Nationalist China by United States,
      2 Dec.

1955 US–Canadian agreement on operation of Early Warning System, 5 May
      (extended in 1958 to set up NORAD, North American Air Defence
      Command).
      London and Paris Agreements, 5 May, gave West Germany full
      sovereignty and brought it into North Atlantic Treaty Organization.
      Warsaw Pact formed, 13 May, between Russia and Eastern bloc powers
      for mutual assistance in the event of war.
      Austrian State Treaty, 15 May, between Britain, the United States, Russia
      and France established Austria as neutral, sovereign state.

1957 Treaty of Rome, 22 Mar., between France, West Germany, Italy, Belgium,
      Holland and Luxembourg established European Economic Community.
      UN International Atomic Energy Agency for peaceful use of atomic
      energy set up, 29 July.

1959 Ten-Power Committee on Disarmament set up, 7 Sept., representing
      Britain, Canada, France, Italy, the United States, Bulgaria,
      Czechoslovakia, Poland, Romania and the Soviet Union.
      Treaty for peaceful use of Antarctica opened for signature, 1 Dec.

1960 Japanese–US Treaty of mutual security, 19 Jan.
      Stockholm Convention, 3 May, between Britain, Denmark, Norway,
      Portugal, Austria, Sweden and Switzerland set up European Free Trade
      Association.
      Indus Waters Treaty, 19 Sept., between Pakistan and India.

1961 Organization for Economic Co-operation and Development
      (OECD), 30 Sept., replaced the OEEC and includes United States and
      Canada.

1963 Treaty of Co-operation between France and West Germany, 22 Jan.
      Partial Test-Ban Treaty, 5 Aug., between Britain, the United States and
      Russia limiting nuclear testing.
      'Hot-line' agreement reached between the United States and Soviet
      Union, 5 Apr.

1966   Malaysian–Indonesian Agreement, 1 June, ending 'confrontation'.

1967   Treaty banning nuclear weapons in space opened for signature in London, Moscow and Washington, 27 Jan.
Treaty of Tlatelolco, prohibiting nuclear weapons in Latin America, agreed for signature in Mexico City, 14 Feb.
Egypt and Jordan signed anti-Israel Pact, 30 May.
Iraq joined anti-Israel Pact, 4 June.

1968   UN Security Council called for permanent peace settlement in Middle East, 22 Nov.
Nuclear Non-Proliferation Treaty agreed and opened for signature, 1 July.

1969   Disarmament Committee renamed Conference of the Committee on Disarmament with 24 members, 26 Aug.

1970   Standstill ceasefire between Egypt and Israel in Suez Canal Zone, 7 Aug.
Treaty between West Germany and Russia, 12 Aug., renounced use of war.
Treaty between West Germany and Poland, 18 Nov., renounced use of war and confirmed existing borders.

1971   Seabed Treaty prohibiting use of seabed for nuclear weapons opened for signatures, 11 Feb.
Five-power agreement of Britain, Australia, New Zealand, Singapore and Malaysia on defence of Singapore and Malaysia, 9 Jan.

1972   SALT I anti-ballistic missile (ABM) agreement and 5-year interim agreement on limitation of strategic arms signed by USA and Soviet Union, 26 May.
Simla Peace Agreement between India and Pakistan, 3 July; 'Line of control' in Kashmir agreed, 11 Dec.

1973   Israeli–Egyptian agreement on ceasefire line following Yom Kippur War, 11 Nov.

1974   Protocol to the US–Soviet SALT ABM agreement limited deployment to a single area, 3 July; US–Soviet Threshold Test Ban Treaty signed, limiting underground nuclear tests, 3 July.
Vladivostok Accord between United States and Soviet Union, 24 Nov., established framework for future negotiations controlling strategic arms race. Israeli–Egyptian Agreement on disengagement of forces on Suez Canal, 18 Jan.
Israeli–Syrian agreement on disengagement on Golan Heights, 5 June.

1975   Act of the Helsinki Conference, 'Helsinki Agreement', 1 Aug., between 35 nations regarding European security, including a reaffirmation of human rights and proposals for economic collaboration between eastern and western 'blocs'.

Israeli–US agreement on establishment of early warning system in Sinai, 1 Sept.

Israeli–Egyptian agreement for Israeli withdrawal from Sinai and establishment of a buffer zone, 4 Sept.

1976   US–Soviet Treaty restricting nuclear explosions for peaceful purposes, 28 May.

1978   Camp David agreements between Israel and Egypt for conclusion of peace treaty and overall Middle East settlement, 17 Sept.

1979   Israel–Egyptian Peace Treaty, 26 Mar.
Salt II Agreement signed by United States and Soviet Union restricting numbers of strategic offensive weapons, 18 June; ratification withheld by the United States.
Lancaster House Agreement, London, 15 Dec., ended war in Zimbabwe and created independent state from Apr. 1980.

1981   USA, Israel and Egypt signed agreement for peace-keeping force in Sinai, 10 July.
Inhumane Weapons Convention signed in Geneva, 18 May.

1982   Israeli–Egyptian agreement on Sinai, 19 Jan., completed Israeli withdrawal.

1984   Lusaka Accord between Angola and South Africa, 16 Feb.; South Africa agreed to withdraw from Angola and SWAPO to withdraw from Namibia.
Nkomati Accord between Mozambique and South Africa, 1 Mar.; mutual non-aggression agreement and to seek end to civil war in Mozambique.
US–Soviet agreement to expand and improve 'Hot Line', 17 July.
Sino-British declaration on return of Hong Kong to China, 26 Sept.

1985   All Pacific nations sign Treaty of Raratonga, aimed at creating a nuclear-free zone in the Pacific.

1987   Ceasefire agreement reached in Iran–Iraq War, 20 Aug., policed by UN.
Arias Peace Plan signed by Presidents of Central American states to end war in Nicaragua, 1 Aug.
Intermediate Nuclear Force (INF) Treaty signed between United States and Soviet Union, 8 Dec.

1988   Geneva accord, 14 May, for withdrawal of Soviet forces from Afghanistan, beginning 15 May 1988 and to be concluded by Feb. 1989; Pakistan and Afghanistan agreed non-interference in each others' affairs.

Ceasefire agreement in Geneva, 1 Aug., reached over Namibia; timetable for withdrawal of Cuban forces from Angola reached in Nov.; UN Transition Assistance Group to supervise progress to full Namibian independence on 1 Apr. 1990.
All Cuban forces to leave Angola by July 1991.

1989   Representatives of Algeria, Libya, Morocco, Mauritania, and Tunisia sign a treaty establishing the Arab Maghreb Union, 17 Feb.

1990   Treaty on the Final Settlement with Respect to Germany signed by East Germany, West Germany, France, Britain, United States and Soviet Union, 12 Sep.
President Gorbachev and President Bush sign an agreement to destroy chemical weapons and to discontinue their production, 1 June.

1991   Leaders of the MPLA and the UNITA sign a ceasefire agreement to end the Angolan civil war, 31 May.
Heads of states of the Organization of African Unity sign a treaty to establish the African Economic Union by the year 2025, June.
START I agreement signed, 31 July, by Bush and Gorbachev.
Treaty concluding the Cambodian civil war is signed, 23 Oct., in Paris.
Heads of states of Russia, Ukraine, and Belarus decide to create a commonwealth of states, the Commonwealth of Independent States (CIS), 8 Dec., which is later joined by the other member republics of the former Soviet Union (apart from Georgia and the Baltic States), 21 Dec.

1992   Treaty ending civil war in El Salvador signed in Mexico City, 16 Jan.
In Maastricht, the Netherlands, the leaders of the countries of the European Community (after an agreement reached in Dec. 1991) sign a treaty preparing the way for their economic, financial and political unification, 7 Feb.
North American Free Trade Association (NAFTA) agreement with Canada, United States and Mexico, 17 Dec.
Open Skies Treaty signed in Helsinki, 24 Mar.
Treaty ending 15-year civil war in Mozambique signed in Rome, Oct.

1993   Presidents Bush and Yeltsin sign the START II Treaty, 3 Jan., in Moscow.
International treaty on the total abolition of chemical weapons is signed, 13 Jan., in Paris with representatives from 127 countries.
Gaza–Jericho Accord signed in Washington by Israeli Prime Minister Rabin and Palestinian leader Yasser Arafat, 13 Sept.

1994   Agreement to open US diplomatic liaison offices with Vietnam (May) following easing of economic embargo in 1992.

1995   Dayton Agreements hosted by the United States on future of Bosnia–Herzegovina.

1996   Treaty of Pelindaba signed, banning the possession and deployment of nuclear weapons on the African continent or the islands surrounding it. Comprehensive Test Ban Treaty signed by 149 states (Sept.).

1997   Founding Treaty signed between Russia and NATO, 27 May.
Russia–Chechnya Peace Agreement, 12 May.
Russo-Chinese border agreement (Nov.).
Ottawa Treaty banning landmines (Dec.).

2000   Treaty of Nice agrees enlargement of EU (Sept.).

2004   Treaty of Rome adopts constitution for EU (Oct.).

THE LEAGUE OF NATIONS

1916 President Wilson first suggests the need for a 'Peace League'.

1918 Wilson's 'Fourteen Points' includes the idea of an association of nations (Jan.); Jan Smuts publishes *The League of Nations: A Practical Suggestion* (Nov.), proposing a wide-ranging organization to deal with problems of international co-operation, disarmament, colonies, and social and labour problems.

1919 At Paris Peace Conference, 27 nations agree to Wilson's proposal for a League of Nations (Feb.). The Agreement or Covenant setting up the League is written into the Treaties of Versailles (28 June) and Saint-Germain (10 Sept.). Headquarters of League set up in Geneva. Albert Thomas, French Socialist, first director of the International Labour Organization, one of the League's committees; other committees established to deal with world health, communications, and education, not restricted to signatories of the Covenant. League begins allocation of mandates of former colonies to victorious powers and their allies.
First defiance of League's authority when Italian poet and adventurer D'Annunzio seizes part of Fiume from the League on behalf of Italy (Sept.).
Germany condemns the League of Nations as biased in favour of the Allies (June); first signs of hostility to the Covenant in the United States – Wilson goes on pro-League tour of the United States (Sept.).
United States Senate votes against amended League of Nations in 2 votes (Nov.).

1920 United States boycotts first meeting of the League (Jan.); membership of League finally rejected by Senate (Mar.).
Turks repudiate Treaty of Sèvres and defy League of Nations (see p. 10).
League fixes German war reparations of 3,000 million million marks for 30 years (Apr.).
Poland launches war against Russia in defiance of League and seizes Vilna from Lithuania.
Permanent Court of Justice set up in The Hague to advise on legal matters.
China and Austria admitted to the League (Dec.).

1921 New US President Harding rejects the League of Nations (Apr.); Baltic States join the League (Sept.). League arbitrates dispute between Sweden and Finland over Aaland islands.

1922 League arbitrates between Colombia and Venezuela.

1923 Lithuania seizes Memel from League; League eventually approves its possession (May 1924).

Italy bombards and occupies Greek island of Corfu after Italian general killed on Greek–Albanian border, in defiance of League of Nations. Paris-based Conference of Ambassadors agrees to ask for Greek apology and compensation and Italians withdraw.

1924   League accepts draft of protocol outlawing war (Sept.); presented to League Assembly (Oct.) with provision for economic sanctions to enforce judgements. 47 League members agree to compulsory arbitration of conflicts.

1925   League successfully arbitrates between Chile and Peru; induces Greeks to withdraw from Bulgaria and pay compensation (Oct.).

1926   Turkey accepts League of Nations' arbitration over Mosul. League's Disarmament Commission arranges Disarmament Conference. Disarmament Commission urges world disarmament and begins preparation of draft convention on disarmament.
Germany admitted to the League.
Brazil and Spain leave the League.

1927   League given supervisory role over German rearmament with end of Allied military control of Germany.

1928   28 League members accept Kellogg–Briand Pact.

1930   League's Disarmament Commission puts forward draft convention on disarmament but USSR and Germany vote against it.

1931   China appeals to League of Nations over Japanese aggression in Manchuria. League sends Commission under Lord Lytton.

1932   Japanese refuse to leave Manchuria and declare it to be the state of Manchukuo. Lytton Commission reports, condemning Japanese aggression and demanding their withdrawal (Oct.).
League pressure leads to Japanese withdrawal from Shanghai but not from Manchuria.

1932–34   World Disarmament Conference meets but fails to make any substantial progress; Hitler leaves the Conference (Oct. 1933).

1933   Japan leaves the League of Nations after its condemnation over Manchuria (Mar.) and extends its conquests into Jehol in northern China.

1934   USSR joins the League of Nations (Sept.).
Italy rejects League arbitration in dispute with Abyssinia (Ethiopia) (Dec.).

1935   Abyssinia's plea for League assistance (Jan.) is debated (Feb.) but no action taken.

Saar plebiscite under League supervision permits Saar to be reunited with Germany (Jan.).
League condemns German rearmament (Apr.) but with no effect.
League appoints five-power Commission on Abyssinia (May); Italy offered concessions in Abyssinia but refused by Abyssinia (Sept.).
Mussolini's invasion of Abyssinia (Oct.) condemned as aggression by League which imposes economic sanctions.
Germany leaves the League (Oct.).

1936   Italy threatened with oil embargo if it continues war against Abyssinia (Mar.).
Haile Selassie addresses League calling for assistance against Italian aggression (June).
Sanctions against Italy abandoned (July).

1937   League condemns Japanese invasion of China (Sept.) Italy leaves the League (Dec.).

1939   Spain leaves the League (May); USSR expelled for invasion of Finland (Dec.).

1944   Meeting in San Francisco of delegates of 46 states to replace the League of Nations with the United Nations Organization (April).

1946   League of Nations formally dissolved (Apr.); some of its committees, such as the ILO and World Health Organization, become agencies of the United Nations.

THE UNITED NATIONS

1941 June 12   Inter-Allied Declaration signed in London by all nations then at war with Germany to work for a 'world in which, relieved of the menace of aggression, all may enjoy economic and social security'.

    Aug. 14   Atlantic Charter issued by US President Franklin D. Roosevelt and British Prime Minister Winston Churchill detailing 8 points to 'base their hopes for a better future for the world'.

1942 Jan. 1   Declaration by United Nations signed by 26 nations in Washington approving basic points of Atlantic Charter; first official use of name 'United Nations'.

1943 Oct. 30   Moscow Declaration on General Security signed by Britain, China, Soviet Union and United States, recognizing 'the necessity of establishing at the earliest practicable date a general international organization, based on the principle of sovereign equality'.

1944 Aug. 21   Dumbarton Oaks Conference in Washington, DC, at which representatives of 39 nations discuss over three months proposals for establishing United Nations organization, agreeing on Security Council as executive branch of UN.

1945 June 26   UN Charter approved by delegates of 50 nations at international conference in San Francisco.

    Oct. 16   Food and Agriculture Organization of United Nations established to improve consumption, production and distribution of food throughout world.

    Oct. 24   UN Charter goes into effect upon ratification by majority of nations, including Britain, China, France, Soviet Union, and United States. Date celebrated annually as United Nations Day.

1946 Jan. 10   UN General Assembly begins first meeting in London with delegates of 51 nations as members.
Trygve Lie of Norway is elected first Secretary-General of UN.

    June 25   International Bank for Reconstruction and Development begins operations to assist nations by government loans.

    Nov. 4   UNESCO, United Nations Educational, Scientific and Cultural Organization, formed to promote international co-operation in solving problems such as illiteracy.

Dec. 14	Gift of $8,500,000 from US millionaire John D. Rockefeller Jr accepted by UN to buy 18 acres in New York City as site of permanent headquarters.
1947 Apr. 4	International Civil Aviation Organization established to develop international standards and regulations for civil aviation.
1948 Apr. 7	World Health Organization established to promote world health.
Sept. 17	UN peace negotiator Count Folke Bernadotte of Sweden assassinated in Jerusalem while trying to arrange truce in fighting between Arabs and Israelis.
Dec. 10	Universal Declaration of Human Rights adopted by UN General Assembly.
1949 Jan. 1	Ceasefire between India and Pakistan obtained by UN to end 2 years of fighting over control of Kashmir.
Feb.–July	Ceasefire agreements arranged between Israel and Arab states by UN negotiator Ralph J. Bunche.
Dec. 27	Netherlands grants independence to Indonesia after conference arranged by UN to settle fighting.
1950 Mar. 23	World Meteorological Organization established to promote international reporting and observation of weather.
June 27	UN Security Council calls for member nations to send troops to aid South Korea, which had been attacked by communist North Korea. Soviet Union was boycotting meetings of Security Council at this time and so could not veto measure. Troops of US and 15 other nations dispatched to aid South Korea.
1953 July 27	UN signs truce with North Korea, ending over three years of fighting.
1956 Nov. 7	UN obtains ceasefire in Suez Canal fighting between Egypt and Israeli–British–French forces; sends UN Emergency Force to supervise truce.
1957 July 29	International Atomic Energy Agency created to promote peaceful uses of atomic energy.
1961 Sept. 13	UN troops begin fighting in Congo to restore order in civil war.
Sept. 18	UN Secretary-General Dag Hammarskjöld killed in air crash in Africa while on Congo peace mission.
Nov. 3	U Thant of Burma elected as UN's third Secretary-General to succeed Dag Hammarskjöld.

1964 Mar. 4	UN peace-keeping force sent to Cyprus to prevent fighting between Turkish and Greek forces.
1966 Dec. 16	UN Security Council asks members to stop trading with Rhodesia because of its policies against black majority.
1967 June 10	UN negotiates truce in Six Day Israeli–Arab War.
1971 Oct. 25	Communist China admitted to UN and Nationalist China expelled by 76–35 vote of General Assembly.
Dec. 13	UN General Assembly votes 79 to 7 with 36 abstentions for Israel to restore to Arab countries territories acquired by force.
1972	Kurt Waldheim appointed UN Secretary-General on resignation of U Thant.
1973 Oct. 22	Ceasefire in 17-day-old Middle East War ordered by UN Security Council.
Oct. 25	UN peace-keeping force sent to Middle East to prevent further fighting between Arab nations and Israel.
1974	Special session of UN General Assembly establishes emergency relief fund for poor nations of world.
1975	International Women's Year declared by UN to promote women's equality.
1977 Nov. 4	Mandatory embargo on military supply shipments to South Africa ordered by UN; first such action against UN member.
1978	UN 6,100-strong peace-keeping force stationed in southern Lebanon, brings withdrawal of Israeli troops that invaded in March.
1982	Pérez de Cuellar becomes Secretary-General.
1987 Aug. 20	UN Secretary-General, Pérez de Cuellar, negotiates ceasefire in Iran–Iraq War. UN observer group polices the truce.
1988	UN Transition Assistance Group supervises ceasefire in Namibia and elections prior to independence.
1990	UN Security Council endorses sanctions against Iraq because of the Iraqi invasion of Kuwait (6 Aug.) To secure the compliance of its resolution, the Security Council endorses the creation of a blockade around Iraq (25 Aug.). In an ultimatum, the UN Security Council demands that Iraq withdraw its troops from Kuwait by 15 Jan. 1991. At the same time, the UN authorizes its member states to use force against

the aggressor if Iraq does not comply with the resolution. (28 Nov.).

1991	UN-brokered ceasefire agreement is signed to conclude the Angolan civil war. In order to monitor disarmament and the coming free elections, the UN sends peace-keeping forces to Angola (31 May).
July 26	UN observers arrive in El Salvador in order to monitor the disarmament process after the endorsement of an agreement concluding the civil war (Jan. 1992).
Oct. 23	Treaty bringing an end to the Cambodian civil war is signed in Paris. (In order to monitor the disarmament of the opposing sides and to organize free elections, UN peace-keeping forces are sent to Cambodia in 1992.)
Dec. 16	The UN General Assembly withdraws its resolution endorsed in 1975 which branded Zionism as racism.
1992 Jan. 1	The Egyptian Boutros-Boutros Ghali replaces Pérez de Cuellar as the Secretary-General of the UN.
Feb. 21	The UN Security Council passes a resolution to send peace-keeping forces to the former Yugoslavia.
Apr.	The UN Security Council orders economic sanctions against Libya since Libya has refused to hand over to the United States and Britain the two Libyan men who are charged with having bombed PanAm Flight 103 in Dec. 1988.
May 30	The UN Security Council orders comprehensive economic sanctions against 'rump' Yugoslavia (Serbia and Montenegro).
Sept. 23	Owing to the break-up of the country, the UN Security Council declares the dissolution of Yugoslavia and does not recognize 'rump' Yugoslavia as the legal successor of the former Yugoslavia.
Dec. 9	With the authorization of the UN Security Council, the landing of US forces in Somalia commences. (On 4 May 1993 troops from 20 countries replace the US peace-keepers.)
1993 Jan.	Approximately 80,000 UN peace-keepers are stationed at 12 locations in the world.
May 24	The UN Security Council extends the deadline of the sanctions introduced against Iraq in Aug. 1990.
May 26	The UN Security Council adopts a resolution to set up an international court for the prosecution of war criminals in the Yugoslavian war. Since the Nuremberg trials, this has been the first court of this nature. (The court is officially set up on 17 Nov. 1993.)

June 14–25   Organized by the UN, and with the participation of 166 countries, a world human rights conference is held in Vienna.

July 28   With the acceptance of Andorra into the UN, the number of member states of the United Nations is raised to 184.

Oct. 5   The UN Security Council extends the mandate of the UN peace-keeping forces stationed in the former Yugoslavia until 31 Mar. 1994.

Oct. 8   The General Assembly of the UN cancels the economic sanctions against South Africa (the arms embargo remains valid until the general elections in South Africa in Apr. 1994).

Oct. 18   The UN Security Council introduces an arms and oil embargo against Haiti and freezes Haiti's foreign assets in order to force the military leadership of the country to allow the banished President Jean-Bertrand Aristide to return to Haiti. The UN orders a naval blockade against Haiti.

Nov. 18   The UN Security Council extends the mandate of the UN peace-keeping forces stationed in Somalia until 31 May 1994.

1995   UN peace-keeping efforts in Bosnia (see pp. 328–9).

1997 Sept. 22   Kofi Annan becomes Secretary-General.
The United States agrees settlement in principle of its UN debt.
Crisis over UN inspection teams in Iraq.

1998 Feb. 23   Renewed crisis over Iraq defused by visit of Kofi Annan to Baghdad.

Mar.   Agreement reached on UN inspection of presidential sites in Iraq.

1999   East Timor peace-keeping force authorized by Security Council.

2002   UN Security Council adopts Resolution 1441 ordering Iraq to comply fully with weapons inspectors or risk serious consequences.

2005   Far-reaching reforms of UN proposed in wake of corruption scandals.

THE NEW NATIONS SINCE 1914

Some smaller states have been excluded.

Algeria	French Algeria until 1962.
Angola	Portuguese Angola until 1975.
Armenia	independent since 1991, formerly part of the Soviet Union.
Austria	rump state, created in 1918 from German-speaking part of former Austro-Hungarian Empire.
Azerbaijan	independent since 1991, formerly part of the Soviet Union.
Bangladesh	prior to 1947 part of British Indian Empire; 1947–71 known as East Pakistan.
Belarus	formerly part of Soviet Union. Independence proclaimed, 1991.
Belize	British Honduras until 1973, independent in 1981.
Benin	until 1960 part of French West Africa; then Dahomey until 1975.
Bhutan	formerly semi-autonomous kingdom linked to British Indian Empire.
Bosnia– *Herzegovina*	Formerly part of Yugoslavia. Independence declared in 1992. See pp. 328–9.
Botswana	British Bechuanaland until 1966.
Brunei	former British protectorate in British Borneo.
Burkina Faso	formerly French Upper Volta; then Upper Volta until 1984.
Burundi	formerly part of German East Africa (to 1919), thereafter part of Belgian controlled Ruanda-Urundi. Urundi became Burundi in 1962.
Cameroon	formerly French and British Cameroon. French Cameroon became independent in 1960, and in 1961 part of British Cameroon acceded to the independent, former French Cameroon to form a two-state Federal Republic, the United Republic of Cameroon in 1972 and the Republic of Cameroon in 1984.
Cape Verde	Portuguese Cape Verde until 1975.
Central African *Republic*	formerly part of French Equatorial Africa.
Chad	formerly part of French Equatorial Africa.
Congo, *Democratic* *Republic of*	formerly Belgian Congo. Known as Zaïre, 1971–97.
Congo, Republic *of*	formerly French Congo.
Croatia	independent since 1991. Formerly part of Yugoslavia.
Czechoslovakia	formerly part of Austro-Hungarian Empire (pre-1918). It was itself dissolved on 31 Dec. 1992 into the Czech Republic and Slovakia.

Czech Republic	separated from Czechoslovakia on 1 Jan. 1993 after the 'Velvet Divorce'.
Djibouti	French Somaliland until 1967, then French territory of Afars and Issas.
Egypt	British Protectorate until 1922.
Equatorial Guinea	formerly Spanish Territory of the Gulf of Guinea.
Estonia	independent after 1918. Incorporated in the Soviet Union, 1940. Regained independence, 1991.
Finland	part of Russian Empire until 1917 as autonomous Grand Duchy.
Gabon	formerly part of French Equatorial Africa.
Gambia	formerly British Gambia, then part of Confederation of Senegambia (with Senegal).
Georgia	independent since 1991. Formerly part of the Soviet Union.
German Democratic Republic	(East Germany) formerly part of the united German state, divided as a result of the Second World War, but excluding part of former German state lost to present state of Poland.
German Federal Republic	(West Germany) formerly part of the united German state divided as a result of the Second World War.
Ghana	formerly British Gold Coast, including British Togoland, formerly German Togoland (to 1922).
Greenland	formerly a province of Denmark (to 1979).
Grenada	formerly part of British Windward Islands.
Guinea	formerly French Guinea.
Guinea-Bissau	formerly Portuguese Guinea.
Guyana	formerly British Guiana.
Hungary	up to 1918 part of the dual monarchy of Austria–Hungary and the Austro-Hungarian Empire.
India	formerly part of the British Indian Empire, then including present-day Pakistan and Bangladesh.
Indonesia	formerly Dutch East Indies.
Ireland, Republic of	formerly the Irish Free State, a dominion of Great Britain (1921–48), previous to 1921 part of the United Kingdom. Also known as Eire, 1921–48.
Israel	created in 1948 out of Palestine, a British mandated territory from 1920, previously part of Turkish Empire.
Ivory Coast	formerly French Ivory Coast.
Jamaica	British colony of Jamaica until 1962.
Jordan	formerly Transjordan (from 1922), part of the united Palestine mandate of Britain (1920–2), previously part of Turkish Empire.
Kampuchea	formerly Cambodia (from 1953), previously part of French-Indochina. Now known as Cambodia again.

Kenya	formerly British colony of Kenya (to 1963), known as British East Africa to 1920.
Korea, North	formerly part of Japanese-controlled Korea (1910–45); created separate state in 1948.
Korea, South	formerly part of Japanese-controlled Korea (1910–45); created separate state in 1948.
Kuwait	protected status under Britain until independent state in 1961.
Laos	formerly part of French Indochina.
Latvia	independent after 1918. Incorporated in the Soviet Union, 1940. Regained independence, 1991.
Lebanon	French mandated territory 1920–43, previously part of Turkish empire.
Lesotho	British protectorate of Basutoland until 1966.
Libya	formerly Tripoli (as Italian colony, 1911–45).
Lithuania	independent after 1918. Incorporated in the Soviet Union, 1940. Regained independence, 1991.
Macedonia	formerly part of Yugoslavia. Independent since 1991.
Malawi	formerly part of Federation of Rhodesia and Nyasaland (1953–64), previously British protectorate of Nyasaland.
Malaysia	formerly the Federation of Malaya (to 1963), previously known as the Straits Settlements and the Federated Malay States.
Mali	formerly (with Senegal) the Federation of Mali (1959–60); previously part of French West Africa.
Mauritania	French colony of Mauritania until 1960.
Moldova	formerly part of the Soviet Union. Independent since 1991.
Mongolia	prior to 1924 Outer Mongolia.
Morocco	formerly French Morocco (to 1956) and Spanish Morocco which became part of independent Morocco in 1969.
Mozambique	Portuguese Mozambique until 1975.
Myanmar	formerly Burma until 1989. Burma was part of British India before independence.
Namibia	formerly South West Africa (to 1990), prior to 1920 German South-West Africa.
Niger	formerly part of French West Africa.
Pakistan	prior to 1947 part of British Indian Empire.
Papua New Guinea	formerly (1920–45) Australian mandated territory, thereafter Australian-governed to 1975. Prior to 1920 the area comprised German New Guinea and Australian-run Papua.
Philippines	American colony from 1898 until independence in 1946.
Poland	an ancient kingdom, but prior to 1918 Poland's territory formed part of the German, Austro-Hungarian and Russian Empires. In 1945 its boundaries were substantially altered.
Rwanda	part of German East Africa to 1919, then mandated to

	Belgium as part of Ruanda-Urundi and following the Second World War part of United Nations trust territory of Ruanda-Urundi under Belgian administration. In 1962 Ruanda became the separate state of Rwanda.
Saudi Arabia	proclaimed the kingdom of Saudi Arabia in 1932, previously comprising kingdom of Hejaz and Arabia.
Senegal	formerly part of French West Africa, in 1959 joined with French Sudan, present day Mali, in Federation of Mali, but from 1960 independent. In 1982 formed Confederation of Senegambia with Gambia.
Serbia and Montenegro	formerly part of Yugoslavia. Continued as 'rump Yugoslavia' before adopting name of Union of Serbia and Montenegro in 2003.
Sierra Leone	British Sierra Leone until 1961.
Singapore	British Crown Colony, then part of Malaysia 1963–5.
Slovakia	separated from Czechoslovakia on 1 Jan. 1993 after the 'Velvet Divorce'.
Slovenia	formerly part of Yugoslavia. Independence proclaimed, 1991.
Somalia	formerly British and Italian Somaliland, united as an independent state in 1960.
Sri Lanka	British colony of Ceylon to independence in 1948; in 1972 changed name to Sri Lanka.
Sudan	Anglo-Egyptian Sudan until independence in 1956.
Surinam	Dutch Guiana to 1954 when became an autonomous part of the Netherlands. Independent from 1975.
Syria	prior to 1918 part of Turkish Empire, then placed under French League of Nations mandate until independence in 1946.
Taiwan	ceded to Japan in 1895, the island of Formosa returned to China in 1945, but from 1949 became base for Nationalist Chinese State under Chiang Kai-shek.
Tanzania	formerly German East Africa (to 1918), then League of Nations mandated territory of Tanganyika under British control. Following independence in 1961, it joined with Zanzibar (independent in 1963) in 1964 to form Tanzania.
Thailand	known as Siam until 1939.
Togo	German Togoland until 1918 when mandated under British and French control, then United Nations Trust territory. In 1957 British Togoland joined with the Gold Coast and became part of independent Ghana. French Togoland became independent in 1960.
Trinidad and Tobago	British colony of Trinidad and Tobago until 1962.
Tunisia	French protectorate until independence in 1956.

Turkey	formerly the central part of the Ottoman Empire which included much of the Middle East and Arabia. The Turkish Republic was founded in 1923, comprising most of the modern area of Turkey.
Uganda	British protectorate until independence in 1962.
Ukraine	formerly part of the Soviet Union (after brief independence after 1918). Independence proclaimed, 1991.
Union of Soviet Socialist Republics	formerly the Russian Empire (to 1917). The USSR was dissolved with the fall of communism.
United Arab Emirates	known as the Trucial States prior to 1971.
Vietnam	part of French Indochina to 1954 when separated into North and South Vietnam, reunited as a single state in 1975.
Western Sahara	formerly known as Spanish Morocco to 1956 when divided between Mauritania and Morocco; in 1979 Mauritania relinquished its claim but it remains disputed between Morocco and an independence movement, the Polisario Front.
Yemen Arab Republic	part of the Turkish Empire until 1918, when passed to local tribal control, becoming the Yemen Arab Republic in 1962.
Yemen, Peoples' Democratic Republic	formerly under British control, including part of Aden as the protectorate of Aden; independent from 1967.
Yugoslavia	before 1918 the independent kingdom of Serbia and parts of the Austro-Hungarian Empire and Bulgaria. In 1918 Yugoslavia created as kingdom of Serbs, Croats and Slovenes.
Zaïre	formerly Belgian Congo until independence in 1959; name changed to Zaïre in 1971. It reverted to Congo in 1997.
Zambia	formerly known as Northern Rhodesia and a British protectorate; in 1953 combined with Southern Rhodesia and Nyasaland in a Federation, dissolved in 1963, becoming independent Republic of Zambia in 1964.
Zimbabwe	formerly known as British Southern Rhodesia; in 1953 combined with Northern Rhodesia and Nyasaland in a Federation, dissolved in 1963, becoming British colony of Rhodesia. It declared independence in 1965 as Rhodesia, but following the war and subsequent agreement of 1979 became Zimbabwe.

WARS AND MAJOR ARMED CONFLICTS

Mexican revolution and American interventions, 1910–17

The Mexican revolution began as peasant uprisings in the north, led by Madero in the state of Chihuahua, and in the south led by Zapata, in Moretos state. In 1911 President Díaz was forced to resign and Madero became President after an interim period. Initially disbanding his rebel armies, he used the Federal army to defeat a rising in the north and to contain the more leftward leaning forces of Zapata, who broke out into open revolution at the end of 1911 demanding radical land reform. A counter-revolution in Mexico City in 1914 led to three years of confused civil war with numerous factions led by irregular leaders, such as Francisco Villa in the north, who formed an unstable alliance with Zapata in the south. In 1914 American troops occupied Veracruz in retaliation for the arrest of American sailors, contributing to the overthrow of the counter-revolutionary regime in Mexico. In July, the moderate Carranza assumed the Presidency and was recognized by the US in 1915, but was forced to continue fighting the forces of Villa and Zapata. Villa's forces won an important battle at Torreon in 1914, but were defeated at Celaya in Apr. 1915. Crossing the American border, Villa sacked Columbus, New Mexico, in Mar. 1916 and was pursued by General Pershing into Mexico until requested to withdraw by Carranza. A Congress summoned to Mexico in 1917 established a new constitution, bringing most large-scale fighting to an end.

First World War, 1914–18

On 28 July 1914 Austria–Hungary declared war on Serbia, whom it blamed for the assassination of the Austrian heir to the throne a month earlier. Austria was supported by its ally Germany, but they were faced by the 'Entente' powers, Russia, France and Britain. In late 1914 the Germans failed to capture Paris despite the boldness of their invasion plan (the Schlieffen Plan), and the war settled into the deadlock of trench warfare on the Western Front. In the East the Germans defeated the Russian invasion of East Prussia at Tannenberg and the Masurian Lakes. In 1915 the Entente tried to break the deadlock on the Western Front by expeditions to the Dardanelles and Salonika in south-east Europe, and by inducing Italy to attack Austria, but to no avail. In 1916 both sides launched grand offensives on the Western Front, the Germans against Verdun and the Allies on the Somme, but despite enormous casualties the deadlock continued. At sea the British and Germans fought the drawn battle of Jutland. In 1917 both sides were given hope, the Germans by the Russian revolution (which eventually removed Russia from the war) and the Allies by the United States' entry into the war. The next year proved decisive. The Germans launched a last great offensive in spring 1918 but this was halted and American support tipped the scales the Allied way. Germany agreed to an armistice in Nov. Its allies, Austria and Turkey, had already given up the fight, the Austrians defeated at Vittorio Veneto in Italy and the Turks defeated by the British in Palestine and Mesopotamia. Although the major engagements were fought in Europe, British and Arab forces fought major campaigns against the Turks in Arabia and Palestine and Mesopotamia. In Africa, the German colonies of South-West Africa and Tanganyika were also the scene of fighting. In the Far East Japanese forces seized the German base of Kiaochow.

Anglo-Irish conflict, 1916–21: Irish civil war 1922–3

Rebellion broke out in Dublin on Easter Monday, 24 Apr. 1916 (the 'Easter Rising'). The rebellion was suppressed by 1 May, and Sir Roger Casement and leaders of the rising were tried and executed. Open warfare began again in 1919, and atrocities by the Irish Republican Army were matched by those committed by a special force brought in by the British, the Black and Tans. Peace was formally established by a treaty recognizing the dominion status of the Irish Free State, signed on 8 Dec. 1921. A Republican faction led by De Valera refused to acknowledge the Treaty and demanded inclusion of Ulster in the Irish state. Anti-treaty forces made raids on Ulster and arms raids in the south, but after seizing the Four Courts building in Dublin were forced to surrender and hunted down elsewhere by Free State forces. A ceasefire was accepted by Republican leaders in 1923.

Chinese civil war and 'Northern Expedition', 1916–34

An unstable government was formed in China following the revolution of 1911. The death of the first President in 1916 brought into the open conflicts already just short of outright civil war. Although a semblance of government was maintained in Beijing, much of China fell prey to rival warlords who fought one another. From 1922 the communists and nationalists in the Guomindang began to co-operate, creating an army with which to reunite China. From the nationalist base in Canton, Chiang Kai-shek emerged after the death of Sun Yat-sen (1925) to lead the nationalist troops on the 'Northern Expedition', defeating the warlords of central and eastern China; in 1927 he occupied Nanjing, which became the capital. Following the seizure of Shanghai in the same year, Chiang Kai-shek turned against the communists, killing thousands of their activists and forcing many of them to flee south. Chiang carried his campaign across the Yellow River against the northern warlords. Although meeting a reverse when he attacked the Japanese forces in Shantung, Chiang entered Beijing on 8 June 1928 when it was evacuated by the northern warlord, Marshal Chang Tso-lin. Chiang Kai-shek now turned against the communist-controlled areas of the south in Jiangxi, Hunan, Fujian, and Hebei. In a series of campaigns, initially unsuccessful, Chiang forced the communists to evacuate their last bases in Jiangxi and undertake the 'Long March' in 1934. Meanwhile nationalist control of northern China remained weak, and growing Japanese involvement in Manchuria lead to its full-scale invasion of Manchuria in 1931–2.

The Russian civil war and Russo-Polish War 1917–20

In Nov. 1917 the communists seized power in Russia but were opposed by counter-revolutionary tsarist or 'White Russian' forces. In 1918 the victorious Allied powers intervened to assist the anti-Bolshevik forces. Allied and 'White Russian' forces attacked the Bolshevik strongholds around Moscow and Petrograd from the north, based on Archangel, from the Ukraine and Caucasus in the south and from Siberia along the route of the Trans-Siberian Railway. Poland also invaded Russia in Apr. 1919. Gradually, the Red Army organized by Trotsky was able to defeat the individual 'White' armies, leading to the withdrawal of the Allied intervention forces and a Russian counter-attack on Poland. By 1920 the Bolshevik forces had defeated their rivals for power and secured control over the Soviet Union.

Third Afghan War, 1919

In May 1919 Amir Amanullah declared a holy war (*Jihad*) against Britain, crossed the border and occupied Bagh. While Jalalabad and Kabul were bombarded by the RAF, a British expedition drove the Afghans out of Bagh and forced the Khyber Pass into Afghanistan. An armistice was agreed on 31 May and the treaty of Rawalpindi was signed on 8 Aug.

The Hungarian–Romanian War, 1919

In 1919 a communist government under Bela Kun took power in Hungary. Resentful of the armistice terms proposed by the Allies after the war, the Hungarians invaded Slovakia and the Romanians, fearing that they too would be invaded, themselves attacked Hungary to forestall any further communist advances. In Aug. the Romanians captured Budapest and Bela Kun fled. The Romanians left in Nov. In 1920 Hungary's territorial losses were confirmed by the Treaty of the Trianon.

The Greek–Turkish War, 1920–3

By the Treaty of Sèvres, 1920, the Allies handed territory in Asia Minor to Greek control, but the Turks refused to accept this change, and General Mustapha Kemal resisted the Greek occupation. In 1922 he drove the Greeks from their last stronghold at Smyrna, secured control of the area around Constantinople and overthrew the Ottoman Sultan. In 1923 the Allies renegotiated the peace treaty with Turkey at Lausanne.

The Moroccan Revolt – 'the Revolt of the Rif' – 1921–6

Abd el Krim led a revolt against Spanish colonial forces, defeating Spanish armies at Das Abara and Anual, in the latter killing 10,000 Spanish troops. In 1922 Abd el Krim set up a 'Rif Republic' and in 1924 defeated another Spanish army at Sidi Messaoud. An invasion of French Morocco was halted and a Franco-Spanish army under the command of Marshal Pétain defeated the Rifs, forcing Abd el Krim to surrender in 1926, ending the Rif Republic.

Sandino revolt in Nicaragua and American intervention, 1926–34

United States Marines had occupied Nicaragua since 1912 to support a conservative regime and protect American interests. In 1926 the Marines withdrew and a peasant army organized by Augusto César Sandino took up arms in revolt. In 1927, 2,000 American troops returned but were unable to defeat the Sandino forces. Following a treaty giving some concessions to the peasants, troops were withdrawn in 1933. In 1934 Sandino was assassinated by the National Guard and two years later its commander, Somoza, became President with American support. The subsequent guerrilla movement founded in 1961, the Sandinista National Liberation Front (FSLN) was named in honour of Sandino while Somoza's son continued to rule until 1979.

Wahabi tribal unrest, 1928

Several thousand Wahabi tribesmen threatened Iraq and Kuwait, launching raids from the Arabian desert. Britain deployed armoured trains and squadrons of RAF planes to bomb and strafe the tribesmen.

Japanese invasion of Manchuria, 1931–2

From their base in Kwantung, the Japanese seized the city of Mukden, alleging Chinese sabotage of the Japanese-financed South Manchurian Railway, and went onto overrun all of Chinese Manchuria by early 1932. Chinese appeals to the League of Nations led to no decisive action against the Japanese, who created a puppet state, Manchukuo, in the conquered territory, under the deposed Manchu emperor Pu Yi. A Japanese attempt to seize the city of Shanghai, however, was frustrated by opposition from the League.

El Salvador peasant revolt, 1931–2

Asturo Araujo became President in 1931 with popular peasant support but was immediately overthrown by General Hernandez. The coup sparked off a peasant revolt in 1932, led by Farabundo Marti, which was crushed by Hernandez's troops, killing 20,000–30,000 peasants.

The Chaco War, 1932–5

Minor wars in 1928–9 and 1931–2 between Bolivia and Paraguay over control of the disputed Chaco area of Paraguay flared into major war in May 1932, following the election of the hard-liner Daniel Salamanca as President of Bolivia. Although it had a larger population and resources, Bolivia's invading forces were repulsed and eventually pursued by Paraguayan forces into Bolivia. The defeats led to the overthrow of President Salamanca in Dec. 1934, and in June 1935 Bolivia was forced to conclude a truce leaving Paraguay in possession of all the disputed area.

The Italo-Abyssinian War, 1935–6

In Oct. 1935 Mussolini invaded Abyssinia (Ethiopia) and caused an international outcry. An Anglo-French plan to partition Abyssinia between Italy and its ruler, Haile Selassie, failed, as did economic sanctions against Italy to force it to end its aggression. In May 1936 the Italian conquest was complete.

The Spanish Civil War, 1936–9

In July 1936 Spanish generals, led by Franco, rose against the Republican government and plunged Spain into civil war. Despite international declarations against foreign involvement, Italy, Germany and Portugal aided the generals, and Russia and France helped the Republicans. In addition, International Brigades were formed by volunteers from many countries to fight for the Republicans, and helped to defeat the Nationalists in the battle of Guadalajara, 1937. But by early 1939 the Nationalists held most of Spain. They finally captured Madrid on 28 Mar.

The Sino-Japanese War, 1937–45

In July 1937 the Japanese seized upon the pretext of fighting between Chinese and Japanese troops at the Marco Polo Bridge in Beijing to launch an all-out invasion of China, which the Japanese dubbed the 'China Incident'. The Japanese seized Shanghai after fierce fighting and took Nanjing and Guangzhou (Canton). The Chinese government was forced to abandon most of the Chinese coast and set up its capital in Chongqing (Chungking). Japanese forces were unable to conquer the whole of China, being resisted both by nationalist Chinese troops under Chiang Kai-shek and increasingly by the communist forces under Mao Zedong. Over half of all Japanese forces were still involved in China when war with the United States and Britain broke out in 1941. America gave assistance to the Chinese forces by airlifts from India. Communist forces waged a mainly guerrilla war in north China, while the nationalists stood on the defensive in the south-west. Clashes between the nationalist and communist forces in the run-up to Japanese surrender in Aug. 1945 prefigured the struggle for control of China which brought civil war (see pp. 301–2) and eventual communist triumph.

The Russo-Japanese conflict, 1937–9

Russia and China signed a non-aggression pact in 1937 but, when Japanese forces moved to the border of Manchuria, there was fighting with Russian forces. In 1939 there was further heavy fighting in Manchuria in which the Russians inflicted a sharp defeat on Japan. An armistice was followed by a non-aggression pact between Russia and Japan in Apr. 1941.

The Russo-Finnish War (the 'Winter War'), 1939–40, and 'Continuation War', 1941–4

War broke out on 30 Nov. 1939 over Russian claims to Karelia, but Finnish resistance under Mannerheim led to several defeats before Finland was forced to make peace and to cede territory in Karelia and the northern border area with Russia. In June 1941 the Finns joined the Germans in war against Russia, fighting mainly on the Karelian front north of Leningrad. Finland made peace with Russia in 1944, when the defeat of Germany seemed inevitable.

Second World War, 1939–45

German forces invaded Poland on 1 Sept. 1939, which led to declarations of war by Britain and France on 3 Sept. The Germans invaded the Low Countries on 10 May 1940, and France was compelled to sign an armistice on 22 June. The British army was evacuated from Dunkirk, while in the 'Battle of Britain' the German Luftwaffe failed to defeat the RAF and establish air superiority which would have made an attempted invasion of Britain possible. Italy declared war on 10 June 1940, and Britain attacked Italian forces in North Africa. For over a year Britain and its Empire stood alone against the Axis powers. In 1941, however, the war was vastly extended, Japan joining the Axis and Russia, China and America joining Britain. The Japanese rapidly overran many of the European colonies in south-east Asia, but Hitler's invasion of Russia (June 1941) eventually proved a decisive mistake. In 1942 the Germans were defeated in North Africa and Russia, in 1943 the Allies invaded Italy, and in 1944 Britain and America opened the 'Second Front' in France. The Allies linked up with the Russians on the Elbe on 28 Apr. 1945 and the Germans accepted unconditional surrender terms on 7 May. In the Far East, major Japanese forces remained committed to the indecisive war in China, but American forces in the 'island-hopping' campaign in the Pacific, and British forces via Burma, inflicted defeats on the Japanese forces. A huge bombing and submarine offensive had brought Japan near to defeat when atomic bombs were dropped on Hiroshima and Nagasaki in early Aug. 1945. Japan surrendered on 14 Aug. 1945.

The Greek civil war, 1944–9

The Greek Civil War developed out of the rivalry between communist and monarchist partisans for control of Greece as the Axis forces retreated at the end of the Second World War. British troops were sent to aid the pro-monarchist forces in 1944, while the Soviet Union took the side of the communist insurgents. After 1945, American aid enabled British troops to remain in Greece and assist the return of the monarchy. Communist resistance was seriously weakened by the break between Yugoslavia and Russia in 1948, resulting in the closure of much of Greece's northern border to infiltration and aid. The Greek communists announced an end to open conflict in Oct. 1949.

Palestine, 1945–8

Guerrilla warfare was waged by Jewish Zionists against British mandate forces and the Arab population, to achieve an independent Jewish nation. On 22 July 1945 the King David Hotel in Jerusalem, housing the British headquarters, was blown up, leaving 92 dead or missing. With the proclamation of the independence of Israel on 14 May 1948, Britain surrendered its League of Nations mandate over Palestine and withdrew its armed forces.

Indonesian War of Independence, 1945–9

The independence of the Republic of Indonesia (formerly Netherlands East Indies) was proclaimed by the nationalist leaders, Sukarno and Hatta, on 17 Aug. 1945. British, Indian and Dutch troops began to arrive on 29 Sept. 1945. British troops captured the rebel capital of Surabaya on 29 Nov. 1945. The Dutch recognized the Indonesian Republic (comprising Java, Sumatra and Madura) on 13 Nov. 1946. The withdrawal of British troops was completed on 30 Nov. 1946. A nationalist uprising on West Java on 4 May 1947 led to Dutch military action on Java on 20 July 1947. A truce arranged under UN auspices on 17 Jan. 1948 broke down, and the Dutch occupied the rebel capital, Jogjakarta, on 19 Dec. 1948. International opposition and guerrilla warfare led to the Dutch decision to withdraw, and to the independence of Indonesia on 27 Dec. 1949.

Chinese civil war, 1946–9

Civil war between the nationalist government under Chiang Kai-shek and communist forces resumed after the defeat of Japan in Aug. 1945. Through the mediation of General George C. Marshall, a truce was arranged on 14 Jan. 1946. It broke down, and American supplies to the nationalists were halted on 29 July 1946. A nationalist offensive in Shaahxi took the communist capital, Yenan, on 19 Mar. 1947, but it was retaken in Apr. 1948. As communist forces advanced,

Beijing fell on 22 Jan. 1949, Nanjing on 22 Apr. 1949 and Shanghai on 27 May 1949. Mao Zedong proclaimed the People's Republic of China on 1 Oct. 1949. The nationalists withdrew to Taiwan on 7 Dec. 1949.

Philippines, Hukbalahap insurgency, 1946–54

When the Philippines became independent on 4 July 1946, the war-time communist Anti-Japanese People's Liberation Army, or Hukbalahaps, waged a guerrilla campaign against the government of the republic. By 1950 the Hukbalahaps, with an army of 15,000 men and support of the peasantry, had established control over central Luzon. With American backing, however, a new defence secretary, Ramon Magsaysay, revitalized the Philippine armed forces. Counter-insurgency operations, together with a programme of land reform and the resettlement of dissidents, meant that by 1954 the revolt had petered out. The Hukbalahap leader, Luís Taruc, surrendered on 17 May 1954.

First Indo-China War, 1946–54

Following the surrender of Japan, Ho Chi Minh proclaimed the Democratic Republic of Vietnam at Hanoi on 2 Sept. 1945. French and British forces regained control in Saigon, and, after negotiations, French troops entered Hanoi on 16 Mar. 1946. After French naval forces shelled the Vietnamese quarter of Haiphong on 23 Nov. 1946, an abortive Viet Minh uprising took place in Hanoi on 19 Dec. 1946. Guerrilla warfare grew into full-scale conflict between the French and the Viet Minh forces under General Giap. On 20 Nov. 1953 the French established a forward base at Dien Bien Phu to lure the Viet Minh into a set-piece battle, but the garrison of 15,000 men was overwhelmed on 7 May 1954. An agreement for a ceasefire and the division of the country at latitude 17°N was signed at the Geneva Conference on 27 July 1954.

Indo-Pakistan War, 1947–9

A rebellion by the Muslim majority in Kashmir led the Hindu maharajah to accede to the Indian Union, and Indian troops were flown into Kashmir on 27 Oct. 1947. Pakistan sent aid to the Muslim Azad ('free') Kashmir irregulars, and Pakistani army units crossed into Kashmir in Mar. 1948. An undeclared state of war between India and Pakistan continued until UN mediation brought about a ceasefire on 1 Jan. 1949. India formally annexed Kashmir on 26 Jan. 1957.

Israeli War of Independence, 1948–9

Israel was invaded by the armies of its Arab neighbours on the day the British mandate ended, 15 May 1948. After initial Arab gains, Israel counter-attacked successfully, enlarging its national territory. Only the British-trained Arab Legion of Jordan offered effective opposition. Separate armistices were agreed with Egypt (23 Feb. 1949), Jordan (3 Apr. 1949) and Syria (20 July 1949).

Burmese civil war, 1948–55

In the year after gaining independence on 4 Jan. 1948, the Burmese government faced armed opposition from a wide range of dissident groups: the communists, themselves divided into the White Flag Stalinists and the Red Flag Trotskyites; a private army of war-time 'old comrades' known as the People's Volunteer Organization, who made common cause with army mutineers; ethnic minorities seeking autonomy, such as the Mons and Karens; and bands of Muslim terrorists, Mujahids, in the north of Arakan. By 12 Mar. 1949, when Mandalay fell to the Karen National Defence Organization and the communists, most of Burma was in rebel hands. But the rebels were disunited, and Mandalay was retaken by government forces on 24 Apr. 1949. The rebel capital, Toungoo, was captured on 19 Mar. 1950. The government held the initiative and was able to deal with a new threat posed by Chinese Guomindang refugees in the eastern Shan states. An offensive in Nov. 1954 reduced the Mujahid menace, and Operation 'Final Victory' was launched against the Karens on 21 Jan. 1955. Outbreaks of fighting have occurred since 1955, but never on the scale of the early years of independence.

Colombian guerrilla war after 1948

Civil war – 'La Violencia' – in 1948 allowed the military wing of the Communist Party, the Colombian Revolutionary Armed Forces (FARC), to establish itself. It was joined by other guerrilla groups from the 1960s, including the pro-Cuban ELN, the Maoist APL, the leftist M-19, and the Trotskyite ADO. Guerrilla warfare in the hinterland tied down over 57,000 troops and 50,000 paramilitary police. Attempts at a peace accord collapsed after a ceasefire in 1984–5 with all groups except the ELN. Financed by cocaine profits, the guerrilla groups have carried out kidnappings, murders and robberies, but also have fought pitched battles with Colombian troops. A National Conciliation Committee was established in Aug. 1995 to formulate peace proposals. The war has been estimated to have cost over 200,000 lives since 1948.

Karen insurgency in Burma after 1948

Since independence in 1948 the Burmese state has been faced with guerrilla insurgency from the 4-million-strong Karen population, based near the Thai border, as well as by other ethnic minorities. The Karen National Liberation Army was one of 6 groups fighting for autonomy or complete independence. Drug traffic via Thailand supplied funds for the Karen forces, who were opposed by 170,000 men of the Burmese forces. Guerrilla attacks, mainly in the Irrawaddy Delta, were countered by 'search and destroy' missions by the Burmese army. The insurgency had been contained by the 1990s.

Malayan emergency, 1948–60

The Federation of Malaya was proclaimed on 1 Feb. 1948. Communist guerrilla activity began, and on 16 June a state of emergency was declared. In Apr. 1950 General Sir Harold Briggs was appointed to co-ordinate anti-communist operations by Commonwealth forces. He inaugurated the Briggs Plan for resettling Chinese squatters in new villages to cut them off from the guerrillas. After the murder of the British high commissioner, Sir Henry Gurney, on 6 Oct. 1951, General Sir Gerald Templer was appointed high commissioner and director of military operations on 15 Jan. 1952, and on 7 Feb. a new offensive was launched. On 8 Feb. 1954 British authorities announced that the Communist Party's high command in Malaya had withdrawn to Sumatra. The emergency was officially ended on 31 July 1960.

Costa Rican civil war and rebel invasion, 1948

Civil war broke out in Mar. 1948 when President Teodoro Picado attempted to annul the elections. He allowed the communists to organize a 2,000-strong militia to support the regular army. But the forces of the National Liberation Party, led by Colonel José Figueres, gradually took control of the country and entered the capital, San José, on 24 Apr. 1948. President Picado resigned and the regular army was disbanded. On 10 Dec. 1948 Costa Rica was invaded from Nicaragua by 1,000 armed supporters of the ex-president, Calderon Guardia. The town of La Cruz fell, but the rebels had been driven out by 17 Dec. 1948.

Korean War, 1950–3

North Korean troops invaded the South on 25 June 1950. The United Nations decided to intervene following an emergency session of the Security Council, which was being boycotted by the Soviet Union. The first American troops landed at Pusan airport on 1 July 1950. General MacArthur mounted an amphibious landing at Inchon on 15 Sept. 1950, and Seoul was recaptured on 26 Sept. The advance of the UN forces into North Korea on 1 Oct. 1950 led to the entry of China into the war on 25 Nov. 1950. Seoul fell to the Chinese on 4 Jan. 1951, but was retaken by UN forces on 14 Mar. 1951. General MacArthur was relieved of his command on 11 Apr. 1951 after expressing his desire to expand the war into China. Truce talks began on 10 July 1951, and an armistice was finally signed at Panmunjon on 27 July 1953.

Chinese invasion of Tibet, 1950–9

The Chinese invaded across the eastern frontier of Tibet on 7 Oct. 1950. An agreement was signed on 23 May 1951, giving China control of Tibet's affairs, and Chinese troops entered Lhasa in Sept. 1951. The Dalai Lama remained as a figurehead ruler, but there was widespread guerrilla activity against the Chinese forces of occupation. The last serious resistance came in 1959. On 10 Mar. 1959 an uprising took place in Lhasa, but it was suppressed by Chinese tanks, and on 30 Mar. the Dalai Lama fled to asylum in India.

Indonesian civil war, 1950–62

In 1950 prolonged guerrilla campaigns began by a fanatical Muslim sect, Darul Islam, and by the South Moluccans, who proclaimed their independence on 26 Apr. 1950. In 1957 objections to Javanese domination of Indonesian affairs and suspicion of Dr Sukarno's left-wing policies led the military commanders in Borneo, Sumatra and Celebes to refuse to acknowledge the authority of the cabinet. A Revolutionary Government of the Indonesian Republic was proclaimed on 15 Feb. 1958. The authorities took military action against the right-wing rebels, capturing their headquarters at Bukittingi on 5 May 1958, and their capital, Menado, on 26 June 1958. The rebel movement finally collapsed when an amnesty was offered on 31 July 1961, and the civilian leaders surrendered. Opposition from Darul Islam was also suppressed by 1962.

Tunisian War of Independence, 1952–6

In Feb. 1952 Habib Bourguiba and other leaders of the New Constitution Party were arrested, and the ensuing disorders led to the introduction of martial law. In the countryside the Tunisian nationalists waged a guerrilla campaign, while in the towns there were terrorist outrages by nationalists and by the 'Red Hand', a secret settler organization. Preoccupied with the Algerian revolt, France granted Tunisia independence on 20 Mar. 1956.

Mau Mau Revolt, 1952–60

Violence by the Mau Mau, an African secret society in Kenya, led to a British declaration of a state of emergency on 20 Oct. 1952. Leading Kikuyu nationalists were arrested and Jomo Kenyatta was given a 7-year prison sentence in Oct. 1953. A separate East African command consisting of Kenya, Uganda and Tanganyika was set up under General Sir George Erskine. In campaigns in the first half of 1955 some 4,000 terrorists in the Mount Kenya and Aberdare regions were dispersed. Britain began to reduce its forces in Sep. 1955; the state of emergency in Kenya ended on 12 Jan. 1960.

East German workers' uprising, 1953

Demonstrations by building workers in East Berlin on 16 June 1953 spread to a number of factories the following day. More than 300 places in East Germany were affected, including major towns such as Magdeburg, Jena, Gorlitz and Brandenburg. The disorders were suppressed by security police, and curfew and martial law restrictions remained in force until 12 July 1953.

Moroccan War of Independence, 1953–6

Nationalist agitation grew when Sultan Muhammad V was forced into exile on 20 Aug. 1953 after refusing to co-operate with the French authorities. The Army of National Liberation, composed of Berber tribesmen who had seen service with the French army during the Second World War and the First Indochina War, began a large-scale guerrilla campaign in 1955. The Sultan returned on 5 Nov. 1955, and a Franco-Moroccan declaration on 2 Mar. 1956 ended the French protectorate and established the independence of Morocco.

Cuban revolution, 1953–9

An attempted uprising led by Fidel Castro in Santiago and Bayamo on 26 July 1953 was suppressed. Castro was imprisoned but granted an amnesty in May 1955. He led an unsuccessful landing in Oriente Province on 30 Nov. 1955, but commenced a successful guerrilla campaign based in the Sierra Maestro. Castro launched a final offensive in Oct. 1958, and General Batista fled the country on 1 Jan. 1959.

Algerian War of Independence, 1954–62

Algerian nationalists staged attacks on French military and civilian targets on 1 Nov. 1954. In Aug. 1956 the guerrilla groups formed the *Armée de Liberation Nationale*. The French army conducted a brutal counter-insurgency campaign, which, while effective, alienated its supporters. On 13 May 1956 criticism of army methods led the commander-in-chief in Algeria, General Massu, to refuse to recognize the government of France. General de Gaulle, returned to power on 1 June 1958, set a course for Algerian self-determination. A mutiny by the French army in Algeria, led by generals Challe and Salan, began on 22 Apr. 1961, but was suppressed. Despite terrorism by French settlers of the OAS, peace talks began at Evian-les-Bains in May 1961, and a ceasefire was agreed on 18 Mar. 1962. Algeria was declared independent on 3 July 1962.

Cyprus emergency, 1955–9

Agitation for union with Greece (Enosis) led in Apr. 1955 to the start of a campaign of terrorism and guerrilla warfare by EOKA, the militant wing of the

Enosis movement. A state of emergency was declared on 27 Nov. 1955. Archbishop Makarios of Cyprus was deported to the Seychelles on 9 Mar. 1956. A ceasefire came into effect on 13 Mar. 1959, and the state of emergency was lifted on 4 Dec. 1959. Cyprus became an independent republic on 16 Aug. 1960.

Sudanese civil wars after 1955

The conflict began in 1955 with riots in Yambio in July and mutinies by southern troops in Aug. The Anya Nya rebels, demanding secession for southern Sudan, began a guerrilla campaign in 1963. Peace talks between the insurgents and the government began in Addis Ababa in Feb. 1972. A ceasefire came into effect on 12 Mar. 1972 and the south was granted a measure of autonomy. However a mutiny of southern troops in May 1983 and opposition to President Nimeiri's imposition of Islamic law on the country in Sept. 1983 led to renewed civil war. The Sudan People's Liberation Army was formed under Colonel John Garang and President Nimeiri declared a state of emergency on 29 Apr. 1984; fighting continues. A new humanitarian crisis arose in 2004 as a revolt of conflict in Darfur province which began in Feb. 2003 between nomadic Arab tribes (the Janjawid 'men on horseback') and black African farmers.

Hungarian uprising, 1956

Student demonstrations in Budapest on 23 Oct. 1956 (following a workers' revolt in Poland in June) led to a general uprising against the government of Erno Gero. On 27 Oct. Soviet troops were withdrawn from Budapest. On 1 Nov. 1956 Imre Nagy, the new Prime Minister, announced Hungary's withdrawal from the Warsaw Pact and asked the United Nations to recognize its neutrality. Soviet reinforcements surrounded Budapest and entered the city early on 4 Nov. Resistance ended on 14 Nov. 1956.

Suez invasion, 1956

Egypt nationalized the Suez Canal on 26 July 1956. After secret talks with Britain and France, Israel invaded Sinai on 29 Oct. 1956. When Egypt rejected a ceasefire ultimatum by France and Britain, their air forces began to attack Egyptian air bases on 31 Oct. On 5 Nov. British and French forces invaded the Canal Zone. Pressure from the United Nations and world opinion forced a ceasefire at midnight on 6/7 Nov. 1956.

Lebanese civil war, 1958

Civil war broke out in Lebanon in Apr. 1958 between the pro-Western government of President Chamoun, dominated by Maronite Christians, and pro-Nasserite Muslims. Following the overthrow of the monarchy in an army coup in Iraq on 14 July 1958, President Chamoun appealed for aid, and on 15 July American troops landed in Beirut. On 23 Sep. 1958, the neutralist General Chehab took over from President Chamoun. The last American troops were withdrawn from Lebanon on 25 Oct. 1958.

Tunisian conflict with France, 1958–61

On 8 Feb. 1958 the French air force bombed the Tunisian town of Sakiet, killing 79 people, in retaliation for Tunisian assistance to the Algerian rebels. Clashes took place as Tunisia demanded the evacuation of French bases. On 17 June 1958 the French agreed to withdraw from all bases except Bizerte. On 5 July 1961 Tunisia made a formal claim to the French Bizerte base and imposed a blockade on 17 July. France sent reinforcements, who occupied the town of Bizerte in heavy fighting on 19–22 July. An agreement for the withdrawal of French troops from the town was signed on 29 Sept. 1961, and the French base was evacuated by 15 Oct. 1963.

Laotian civil war, 1959–75

The arrest of Prince Souphanouvong and other leaders of the communist Pathet Lao on 28 July 1959 marked the end of attempts at coalition government and the beginning of a 3-way conflict between neutralists under Premier Prince Souvanna Phouma, rightists under General Nosavan, and the Pathet Lao. International efforts to find a settlement led to a ceasefire on 3 May 1961 and recognition of the neutrality of Laos at a conference in Geneva on 23 July 1962. But fighting resumed in Laos, with growing involvement by North Vietnam, Thailand and the United States. The South Vietnamese army attacked Laos on 8 Feb. 1971 to disrupt the Ho Chi Minh trail. A new ceasefire agreement was reached on 21 Feb. 1973, and a coalition government formed in 1974. But communist victories in Vietnam and Cambodia in Apr. 1975 opened the door to a takeover by the Pathet Lao in Laos. The Pathet Lao declared Vientiane liberated on 23 Aug. 1975, and Laos was proclaimed the Lao People's Democratic Republic on 2 Dec. 1975, with Prince Souphanouvong as president.

Vietnam War, 1959–75

Following the division of Vietnam at the Geneva Conference in 1954, Ngo Dinh Diem became president of South Vietnam and secured American support. His government became increasingly authoritarian and repressive, and unrest grew. The communists in South Vietnam (the Viet Cong) built up their strength and launched their first attack on the South Vietnamese armed forces on 8 July 1959 near Bien Hoa, killing two American advisers. A state of emergency was proclaimed in the south on 19 Oct. 1961. After attacks on the USS *Maddox* and *Turner Joy*, the US Congress passed the Gulf of Tonkin resolution on 7 Aug.

1964, giving President Johnson wide military powers in South Vietnam. The sustained bombing of North Vietnam by US aircraft (Operation 'Rolling Thunder') began on 7 Feb. 1965. The first American combat troops landed at Da Nang on 8 Mar. 1965 and engaged the Viet Cong on 15 June. On 30 Jan. 1968, Communist forces launched their Tet offensive with heavy attacks on Saigon, Hué and 30 provincial capitals. On 31 Mar. 1968 President Johnson announced the end of the bombing of the north, and on 13 May 1968 peace discussions began in Paris. On 25 Jan. 1969 these discussions were transformed into a formal conference. American and South Vietnamese troops invaded Cambodia in 1970, and the South Vietnamese made an incursion into Laos in 1971. A new communist offensive against the south began on 30 Mar. 1972, and this led to a resumption of American bombing of the north on 6 Apr. The last American ground combat units were withdrawn on 11 Aug. 1972. American bombing was halted on 15 Jan. 1973, and a peace agreement was signed in Paris on 27 Jan. Two years later, a North Vietnamese offensive, which began on 6 Jan., overran the South, and Saigon was occupied on 30 Apr. 1975.

Congolese civil war, 1960–7

Belgium granted independence to the Congo on 30 June 1960. Widespread disorder followed. The army mutinied, and on 11 July 1960 Moise Tshombe declared the rich mining province of Katanga an independent state. The prime minister of the Congo, Patrice Lumumba, appealed to the United Nations and the establishment of a peace-keeping force was approved by the Security Council on 14 July 1960. On 14 Sept. 1960 the army Chief-of-Staff, Colonel Mobutu, seized power. Lumumba was seized by Mobutu's troops, handed over to the Katangese and murdered on 9 Feb. 1961. For the next two years, periods of armed conflict and negotiations (during which Dag Hammarskjöld, UN Secretary-General, was killed in a plane crash on 18 Sept. 1961) failed to solve the Congo's problems. Katanga's secession eventually ended when a UN offensive in Dec. 1962 forced Tshombe into exile (15 Jan. 1963). The last UN forces left the Congo on 30 June 1964. Violence continued until Nov. 1967, when a revolt by mercenaries in the eastern provinces, which had begun on 5 July, was finally suppressed.

Revolt of the Kurds in Iraq after 1961

The Kurdish minority in north-east Iraq, led by General Mustafa Barzani, rose in revolt in Mar. 1961 after the failure of negotiations on autonomy with General Kassem's regime. The Kurdish militia, the Pesh Merga ('Forward to Death'), fought a prolonged campaign, growing in strength up to 1974, thanks to support from Iran. Then on 13 June 1975 Iran and Iraq signed the Algiers Pact, by which Iran agreed to stop its supplies and close its borders to the Kurds. The revolt collapsed and, although guerrilla warfare continued, it was on a much-reduced scale. Fighting was renewed during the Iran–Iraq war (see p. 324) when Iraq was widely condemned for using chemical weapons against Kurdish insurgents, many of whom fled across the Turkish border. The Iraqi invasion of Kuwait (see Gulf War, p. 328), also brought a resurgence of fighting. The defeat of Iraq led to a Kurdish revolt in the north, which was suppressed. The Allies imposed a military exclusion zone north of the 36th Parallel, but Saddam Hussein was able to use Kurdish divisions to reassert his authority. A new era for the Kurds opened with the 2003 overthrow of Saddam Hussein.

Angolan War of Independence, 1961–75

The liberation struggle commenced in Portuguese Angola on 3 Feb. 1961, when insurgents attempted to free political prisoners in Luanda. The risings were suppressed with great bloodshed, but a guerrilla campaign developed, and by 1974 Portugal was maintaining an army in Angola of 25,000 white and 38,000 locally enlisted troops. After the coup in Portugal on 25 Apr. 1974, negotiations began, and on 15 Jan. 1975 the Portuguese agreed to Angolan independence. As rival liberation groups fought for control of the country, the independence of Angola was proclaimed on 11 Nov. 1975.

Bay of Pigs invasion (Cuba), 1961

Some 1,500 anti-Castro exiles landed in the Bay of Pigs, Cuba, on 17 Apr. 1961, in an operation sponsored by the US Central Intelligence Agency. The invasion was defeated after three days' fighting, when the expected general anti-Castro uprising failed to take place.

Guerrilla insurgency in Guatemala, 1961–96

Guerrilla warfare began soon after the revolt against the government of President Ydigoras Fuentes on 13 Nov. 1960 by junior army officers, who objected to the presence of American-sponsored training camps for Cuban exiles. The rebels were defeated, but soon launched a guerrilla campaign. In the late 1960s they allied themselves with the Guatemalan Communist Party to form the *Fuerzas Armadas Rebeldes* (Insurgent Armed Forces), a name later changed to the Guerrilla Army of the Poor. American special forces assisted in government operations against the insurgents, who were forced to switch their attacks from the countryside to the cities for a time. Retaliation by right-wing death squads resulted in thousands of deaths on both sides. In 1977 the United States halted military aid to Guatemala over human rights violations, but the embargo was lifted on 17 Jan. 1982. A state of siege was introduced on 1 July 1982. However, in Dec. 1996, after 36 years of conflict, a peace treaty was signed by the major guerrilla groups with the conservative government of President Arzu. Since the war began in Nov. 1960, an estimated 150,000 people have died and

50,000 have disappeared. Hundreds of thousands of Guatemalans, most of them indigenous, have been displaced or forced into exile.

Conflict on Irian Jaya after 1962

Following a clash between Indonesian and Dutch naval forces on 15 Jan. 1962, President Sukarno ordered military mobilization and sent armed units into West New Guinea. In a settlement negotiated through the United Nations, the Dutch agreed on 15 Aug. 1962 to hand over West New Guinea, which was incorporated into Indonesia as Irian Barat on 1 May 1963. The Free Papua Movement, opposed to Indonesian control and desiring unification with Papua New Guinea, undertook small-scale guerrilla operations. Fighting in 1984 led to the movement of over 11,000 refugees to Papua New Guinea. A 1990 peace agreement failed to end the conflict.

Indo-Chinese War ('Himalayan War'), 1962

After a series of incidents in the disputed border areas, Chinese forces attacked on 20 Oct. 1962 and drove the Indian forces back on the north-east frontier and in the Ladakh region. India declared a state of emergency on 26 Oct. 1962, and launched an unsuccessful counter-offensive on 14 Nov. 1962. On 21 Nov., the Chinese announced that they would ceasefire all along the border and withdraw 12½ miles behind the line of actual control that existed on 7 Nov. 1959.

North Yemen civil war, 1962–70

The royal government of North Yemen was overthrown in an army coup led by Colonel Sallal on 26 Sept. 1962. A civil war began, in which the republican regime was supported by up to 70,000 Egyptian troops and the royalist tribesmen were assisted by arms supplies and technicians from Saudi Arabia. Egypt's defeat in the Six-Day War in 1967 led to an agreement with Saudi Arabia for a disengagement of forces from North Yemen, signed at a meeting of Arab heads of state in Khartoum on 31 Aug. 1967. Sporadic fighting continued until Saudi Arabian mediation secured the formation of a coalition government on 23 May 1970.

'Confrontation' between Indonesia and Malaysia, 1963–6

When the Federation of Malaysia was established on 16 Sept. 1963, President Sukarno of Indonesia announced a policy of 'confrontation' on the grounds that the federation was 'neo-colonialist'. There followed a campaign of propaganda, sabotage and guerrilla raids into Sarawak and Sabah. An agreement ending 'confrontation' was signed in Bangkok on 1 June 1966 (ratified 11 Aug.).

Cypriot civil war, 1963–8

President Makarios's proposals for constitutional reform led to fighting between Greek and Turkish Cypriots on 21 Dec. 1963. There was a ceasefire on 25 Dec. A United Nations peace-keeping force was established in Cyprus on 27 Mar. 1964. On 7–9 Aug. 1964, Turkish planes attacked Greek Cypriot positions on the north-west coast in retaliation for attacks on Turkish Cypriots. There was renewed fighting between Turkish and Greek communities in 1967. A settlement was reached after mediation by the UN and the United States on 3 Dec. 1967, and the withdrawal of Greek regulars from Cyprus and the demobilization of Turkish forces held in readiness to invade was completed by 16 Jan. 1968.

Kenyan conflict with Somalia, 1963–7

The 1960 independence constitution of the Somali Democratic Republic contained a commitment to recover its 'lost territories', which included the northern frontier district of Kenya. Serious border clashes between the Kenyans and Somalis began in Mar. 1963 and diplomatic relations were broken off in Dec. Sporadic fighting continued until the two countries agreed to end the dispute by the Declaration of Arusha on 28 Oct. 1967.

Guinea-Bissau War of Independence, 1963–74

Armed resistance to Portuguese rule was launched by PAIGC in 1963. PAIGC proclaimed the independence of the republic on 24 Sept. 1973. Following the *coup d'état* in Lisbon on 25 Apr. 1974, led by General Antonio de Spinola (who had been governor and commander-in-chief in Guinea), the Portuguese recognized the independence of Guinea on 10 Sept. 1974.

Eritrean revolt, 1963–94

Eritrea was integrated into the Ethiopian Empire on 14 Nov. 1962, and a separatist movement, the Eritrean Liberation Front, took up arms the following year. Taking advantage of the instability caused by the overthrow of Haile Selassie on 12 Sept. 1974, separatist guerrillas succeeded in taking control of most of Eritrea except the capital, Asmara, by the end of 1977. The conclusion of the Ogaden War in Mar. 1978 (see p. 322) enabled the Ethiopian army, with Cuban and Soviet assistance, to launch a major counter-offensive in Eritrea on 15 May 1978. The last major town in rebel hands, Keren, fell to government troops in Nov. 1978. In 1984 the Eritrean People's Liberation Front (EPLF) launched a new offensive (and in 1987 they were joined by a guerrilla revolt in Tigré province). Faced by rising guerrilla successes, the Marxist dictator Mengistu fled Ethiopia in 1991. Asmara fell to the guerrillas. Independence was proclaimed. This was overwhelmingly confirmed in a referendum on 25 Apr. 1993.

Ethiopia, invasion by Somalia 1964

After a series of border clashes, Somali armed forces crossed into Ethiopia on 7 Feb. 1964 to assert the Somali Republic's claim to the Ogaden desert region. The Organization of African Unity called for an end to hostilities, and President Abboud of Sudan secured a ceasefire based on the original boundary on 30 Mar. 1964.

Mozambique War of Independence, 1964–74

FRELIMO launched its first attacks in Sept. 1964, and gradually took control of large areas of the countryside. By 1974 Portugal was forced to maintain an army in Mozambique of 24,000 white and 20,000 locally enlisted troops. After the coup in Portugal of 25 Apr. 1974, negotiations were opened with FRELIMO. Despite a violent revolt by white settlers in Lourenço Marques (now Maputo) on 3 Sept. 1974, a ceasefire agreement was signed on 7 Sept. 1974 and Mozambique officially became independent on 25 June 1975.

Aden, 1964–7

On 18 Jan. 1963 Aden acceded to the South Arabian Federation. British troops were involved in frontier fighting with the Yemen, and in suppressing internal disorders in Aden. A large-scale security operation was launched in Jan. 1964 in the Radfan region, north of Aden. On 26 Nov. 1967 the People's Republic of South Yemen was proclaimed, and the British military withdrawal from Aden was completed on 29 Nov. In the period 1964–7, British security forces lost 57 killed and 651 wounded in Aden.

Indo-Pakistan War, 1965

Border clashes took place in the Rann of Kutch in Apr. 1965, but a ceasefire agreement came into effect on 1 July. More serious fighting in Kashmir and the Punjab began on 5 Aug. 1965, when Muslim irregulars invaded east Kashmir. The Indian army contained these incursions, but on 1 Sept. 1965 Pakistani regular forces crossed the frontier. India launched a three-pronged attack towards Lahore on 6 Sept. As a military stalemate developed, the UN Security Council called for a ceasefire, which came into effect on 23 Sept. 1965.

Dominican civil war, 1965

Civil war broke out on 24 Apr. 1965 between the Constitutionalists, supporting former President Bosch, and the Loyalist forces of President Reid Cabral. On 28 Apr. 1965, 400 US Marines were sent in to prevent a left-wing takeover and during the next month a further 24,000 American troops were landed. A ceasefire was signed on 6 May and at the end of May an Inter-American peace-keeping force, comprising units from the United States, Honduras, Nicaragua, Costa Rica, Brazil and El Salvador, under the auspices of the Organization of American States, was formed to keep the warring factions apart.

Oman, war in the Dhofar, 1965–75

Civil war broke out in 1965 between the Sultan's armed forces and dissident tribesmen in the Dhofar, who had won control of most of the region by 1970. On 23 July 1970 Sultan Said bin Taimur was deposed by his son, Qaboos, who greatly strengthened the armed forces. With foreign assistance, including an Iranian expeditionary force of 2,000 men, the revolt was suppressed and the Sultan officially declared the war ended on 11 Dec. 1975.

Rhodesian War of Independence, 1965–79

Black nationalist guerrilla activity in Southern Rhodesia grew after the unilateral declaration of independence by Ian Smith's white minority regime on 11 Nov. 1965. Two guerrilla forces were operating: ZIPRA, the military wing of Joshua Nkomo's Zimbabwe African People's Union, based in Zambia and recruiting from the Ndebele peoples; and ZANLA, the military wing of Robert Mugabe's Zimbabwe African National Union, based in Mozambique and recruiting from the Shona peoples. These two groupings united to form the Patriotic Front on 9 Oct. 1976. A settlement for an end to the conflict based on a new constitution was reached at the conclusion of a conference at Lancaster House, London on 15 Dec. 1979. Zimbabwe became an independent republic on 18 Apr. 1980.

Chad civil war, 1965–90

The civil war in Chad originated in the mid-1960s as a conflict between the French-backed government of President Tombalbaye and a number of separatist factions in the Muslim north of the country, grouped into the *Front de Libération Nationale* and supported by Libya. By the mid-1970s FROLINAT controlled three-quarters of the country. On 6 Feb. 1978 the head of state, General Malloum, who had overthrown President Tombalbaye in 1975, announced a ceasefire with FROLINAT. Conflict then developed between two factions in FROLINAT: FAN, under Hissène Habré, and the more militant FAP, under Goukouni Oueddei, backed by Libya. Habré's army defeated FAP and captured the capital, N'Djamena, on 7 June 1982. Fighting resumed in 1983 when FAP and Libyan troops advanced and took the strategically important town of Faya-Largeau on 24 June. Habré appealed for foreign assistance and troops were sent by Zaïre on 3 July and France on 14 Aug. The Libyan advance was halted, and France and Libya signed a withdrawal agreement on 17 Sept. 1984. Libyan troops remained in the north of Chad, however, and created a *de facto* partition of the country until Goukouni Oueddei was shot and wounded in an argument with Libyan troops, and his men changed sides in 1986. A united Chadian force mounted a surprise attack and captured the Libyan air base at Ouadi Doum in Mar. 1987, forcing the Libyans to evacuate most of the territory they had occupied. In 1990, rebels of the Popular Salvation Movement, led by Idris Deby, overthrew the government of Hissène Habré and took power.

Namibian War of Independence, 1966–89

Namibia was mandated to South Africa by the League of Nations on 17 Dec. 1920. South Africa refused to recognize the South West Africa People's Organization, which was designated the 'sole authentic representative of the Namibian people' by the United Nations in 1973. SWAPO launched a guerrilla campaign in Oct. 1966 and this was stepped up in 1978 from bases in Angola and Zambia. South Africa carried out a series of attacks on SWAPO camps in Angola. SWAPO guerrilla activity in Namibia continued, despite the non-aggression pact signed by Angola and South Africa on 16 Feb. 1984. A ceasefire supervised by the UN took effect from 1989, providing for the withdrawal of Cuban and South African forces from the region to be followed by elections in Namibia and independence in 1990.

Israeli–Arab 'Six Day' War, 1967

Israel decided on a pre-emptive strike following Egypt's request for the withdrawal of the UN peace-keeping force from Sinai on 16 May, the closure of the Gulf of Aqaba to Israeli shipping on 22 May, and the signature of an Egyptian–Jordanian defence pact on 30 May. On 5 June 1967 Israel launched devastating air attacks on Egyptian air bases. Israeli forces then invaded Sinai and reached the Suez Canal on 7 June. By nightfall on 7 June Jordan had been defeated and Jerusalem and the West Bank were in Israeli hands. On 9 June Israeli troops attacked Syria and occupied the Golan Heights. A ceasefire was agreed on 10 June 1967.

Nigerian civil war, 1967–70

On 30 May 1967 the military governor of the Eastern Region of Nigeria, Colonel Ojukwu, declared the Ibo homeland an independent sovereign state under the name of the Republic of Biafra. Troops of the Nigerian federal army attacked across the northern border of Biafra on 7 July 1967. The Biafrans invaded the neighbouring Mid-West Region on 9 Aug. 1967. The federal army recaptured Biafra on 22 Sept. 1967, and Port Harcourt fell on 20 May 1968. Supply shortages and starvation finally led to the collapse of Biafran resistance after a four-pronged federal attack in Dec. 1969. The Biafran army surrendered on 15 Jan. 1970.

Philippine Communist and Muslim insurgency, 1968–96

The Hakbalahap insurgency (see p. 302) had faded by the mid-1950s, but in Dec. 1968 a congress of re-establishment was held on Luzon, which reconstituted the Communist Party. Its New People's Army (NPA) began a guerrilla campaign. The government also faced armed opposition from Muslim separatists of the Moro National Liberation Front (MNLF) on Mindanao. President Marcos declared martial law on 23 Sept. 1972. A ceasefire with the MNLF was announced on 22 Dec. 1976 after talks held in Libya, but fighting continued. President Aquino signed a 60-day truce with the NPA on 27 Nov. 1986, but fighting resumed when it expired in 1987. In Sept. 1996 a peace agreement was signed providing for the establishment of a Muslim autonomous region covering 14 provinces and 9 cities on Mindanao.

Soviet invasion of Czechoslovakia, 1968

During the night of 20/21 Aug. 1968 some 250,000 Soviet troops, accompanied by token contingents from Warsaw Pact allies Poland, Hungary and Bulgaria, crossed the Czech frontier and occupied Prague and other leading cities to reverse the liberalizing reforms of Alexander Dubcek's government, the so-called 'Prague Spring'. The Czech army was ordered to offer no resistance, but there were extensive civilian demonstrations against the occupying forces. The Soviet invasion led to the installation of a new Soviet-backed government and the end of the 'Prague Spring'.

Honduran 'Soccer' War with El Salvador, 1969

Hostilities were sparked off by the harassment of a visiting Honduran soccer team in San Salvador (in retaliation for the treatment of the Salvadorean team in Honduras) and the victory of El Salvador over Honduras in a World Cup soccer match on 15 June 1969. The underlying cause was the presence of some 300,000 Salvadorean workers living, many illegally, in Honduras. Riots led to the deaths of two Salvadoreans and the expulsion of 11,000 others. In response, the Salvadorean army crossed the border at several points on 14 July 1969. Honduras accepted an Organization of American States ceasefire call on 16 July, but El Salvador continued fighting. The OAS formally branded El Salvador as the aggressor and voted to impose sanctions on 29 July. El Salvador began to withdraw on 30 July and withdrawal was completed by 5 Aug.

Chinese border conflict with Soviet Union, 1969

Long-standing Sino-Soviet border disputes erupted into serious fighting on Damansky Island in the Ussuri river on 2 Mar. 1969. Each side blamed the other for the clash, in which 31 Soviet frontier guards were killed. The fighting spread further west to the border between Xinjiang (Sinkiang) and Kazakhstan. On 11 Sept. 1969 the Soviet Prime Minister, Alexei Kosygin, who was returning from the funeral of Ho Chi Minh in Hanoi, stopped briefly at Beijing airport for a meeting with Zhou Enlai. Talks were arranged and tension on the border subsided.

Northern Ireland civil insurgency, 1969–98

In 1968 long-standing sectarian animosity between the Catholic and Protestant communities in Northern Ireland degenerated into violent conflict, sparked by the campaign for Catholic civil rights. British troops were deployed in Londonderry on 14 Aug. 1969 and Belfast on 15 Aug. at the request of the government of Northern Ireland. The first British soldier to be killed was shot by an IRA sniper in Belfast on 6 Feb. 1971. Internment without trial was introduced on 6 Aug. 1971, and direct rule from London was imposed on 30 Mar. 1972. On 'Bloody Sunday', 30 Jan. 1972, British troops opened fire on a Catholic civil rights march, and 13 people were killed. At the peak, in Aug. 1972, there were 21,500 British soldiers in Northern Ireland, but this was reduced to 10,000 by the mid-1980s. Over 3,160 persons had died in the conflict by the end of Aug. 1994, when the IRA called a 'Complete Cessation' of Military Operations. The ceasefire was ended in Feb. 1996. It was resumed in 1997 as the political wing of the IRA, Sinn Fein, entered the peace process (which culminated in the Apr. 1998 agreement).

South Yemen conflicts with Saudi Arabia and rebel exiles, 1969–72

An unsuccessful attempt by the new left-wing government in South Yemen to assert a claim to disputed border territory led to clashes with Saudi Arabia in Nov. 1969. Saudi Arabia provided training and a base at ash-Sharawrah for South Yemeni exiles, organized into an 'Army of Deliverance', which raided into South Yemen. In 1972 fighting spread to the border between North and South Yemen. In Aug. 1972 South Yemeni exiles in the north formed a United National Front of South Yemen. Their forces, supplied by Saudi Arabia, mounted attacks on 26 Sept. 1972, which led to full-scale fighting. Arab mediation brought agreement between North and South Yemen in Cairo on 28 Oct. 1972 to meet for discussions on a merger of the two countries.

Kampuchean civil war, 1970–5

On 18 Mar. 1970, Lieutenant General Lon Nol ousted the head of state, Prince Norodom Sihanouk, who was out of the country. Sihanouk allied himself with his former enemies, the Marxist Khmer Rouge, to form the National United Front of Cambodia. Lon Nol appealed for aid on 14 Apr. 1970, and on 29 Apr. American and South Vietnamese troops mounted an incursion into Kampuchea to attack North Vietnamese Viet Cong and Khmer Rouge forces. The last American troops withdrew on 29 June 1970, The communists took control of the countryside, and in 1975 cut supply routes to the capital, Phnom Penh. Lon Nol left the country on 1 Apr. 1975 and the Khmer Rouge occupied Phnom Penh on 17 Apr.

Jordanian civil war, 1970–1

After serious clashes between Palestinian guerrillas and the Jordanian army, King Hussein declared martial law on 16 Sept. 1970. Civil war broke out in Amman on 19 Sept. as the army attacked the Palestinian refugee camps. Some 250 Syrian tanks entered Jordan in support of the Palestinians, but suffered losses in Jordanian air strikes and withdrew on 23 Sept. 1970. A ceasefire was agreed on 25 Sept. 1970. Further heavy fighting took place early in 1971 and the PLO guerrillas withdrew from Amman on 13 Apr. Their expulsion from Jordan was completed by 18 July 1971.

Indo-Pakistan War and Bangladeshi War of Independence, 1971

Elections in Dec. 1970 resulted in a landslide victory in East Pakistan for the Awami League. On 26 Mar. 1971 Sheikh Mujibur Rahman, the head of the League, proclaimed East Pakistan an independent republic under the name of Bangladesh. He was arrested, and West Pakistani troops and locally raised irregulars, *razakars*, put down large-scale resistance by 10 May 1971. Awami League fighters, the Mukti Bahini, began a guerrilla campaign, and clashes between India and Pakistan increased as millions of refugees fled into India. President Yahya Khan declared a state of emergency in Pakistan on 23 Nov. 1971. On 3 Dec. 1971 the Pakistani air force launched surprise attacks on Indian airfields. On 4 Dec. some 160,000 Indian troops invaded East Pakistan. Pakistani forces in East Pakistan surrendered on 16 Dec. 1971, and a general ceasefire came into effect the following day.

Burundi civil war, 1972–3

On 29 Apr. 1972 guerrillas from the majority Hutu tribe in Burundi attacked the ruling Tutsi minority, killing between 5,000 and 15,000 in an abortive coup. The Burundi armed forces, under Tutsi command, retaliated with assistance from Zaïre, and by the end of May 1972 the death toll amongst the Hutu had risen to an estimated 100,000. Refugees poured into neighbouring states. On 10 May 1973 Hutu rebels from Rwanda and Tanzania invaded Burundi. The Burundi army in response crossed into Tanzania on 29 June and killed 10 people. President Mobutu of Zaïre mediated an accord between the presidents of Tanzania and Burundi on 21 July 1973.

318

Uganda rebel invasion, 1972

On 17 Sept. 1972 some 1,000 armed supporters of ex-president Milton Obote, who had been overthrown by General Amin in Jan. 1971, invaded Uganda from Tanzania. The guerrillas were easily repulsed, and the Ugandan air force bombed the Tanzanian towns of Bukoba and Mwanza in reprisal. The Organization of African Unity and the Somali foreign minister mediated a peace agreement between Uganda and Tanzania, which was signed on 5 Oct 1972.

Yom Kippur War, 1973

On 6 Oct. 1973, the day of a Jewish religious holiday, Egyptian forces crossed the Suez Canal, overwhelming Israel's Bar-Lev defence line in a well-planned surprise attack. Syrian forces attacked the Golan Heights, but initial gains were surrendered by 12 Oct. In a daring counter-stroke on 15 Oct. 1973, Israeli forces crossed to the west bank of the Suez Canal and encircled the Egyptian Third Army. A ceasefire became effective on 24 Oct. 1973.

Turkish invasion of Cyprus, 1974

In July 1974 a coup in Cyprus brought to power a government favouring 'enosis' (union) with Greece, but Turkey quickly responded by invading the island to safeguard the Turkish half of the population. An armistice was agreed on 16 Aug., which left Turkish rule over one-third of the island.

Western Sahara, Polisario insurgency after 1975

The Spanish colony of Western Sahara was claimed by both Morocco and Mauritania, while there was also an independence movement, the Polisario, formed in 1973 and supported by Algeria. On 6 Nov. 1975 King Hassan of Morocco sent 350,000 unarmed Moroccans in a 'Green March' into the Western Sahara. They were recalled after three days, but agreement was reached in Madrid on 14 Nov. 1975 for a Spanish withdrawal and joint administration of the territory after 28 Feb. 1976 by Morocco and Mauritania. Their armed forces came into conflict with the Polisario, which proclaimed the Saharan Arab Democratic Republic. The Polisario concentrated on Mauritanian targets, mounting a daring raid on the capital, Nouakchott, on 7 June 1976. Morocco and Mauritania formed a joint military command on 13 May 1977, and Mauritania received support from the French air force. On 5 Aug. 1979 Mauritania came to terms with Polisario, but Morocco moved to occupy the whole of the western Sahara. Libya recognized the Polisario in Apr. 1980. In 1984 Morocco built a 1,600-mile defensive wall from the Moroccan town of Zag to Dakhla on the Atlantic coast, protecting the economically important north of the territory and creating an effective stalemate.

Lebanese civil war and invasions after 1975

Tensions between the Christian and Muslim communities in Lebanon were exacerbated by the influx of Palestinian guerrillas expelled from Jordan in 1971. A state of civil war existed after a massacre of Palestinians by Phalangist gunmen on 13 Apr. 1975. Syrian forces were drawn into the conflict on 1 June 1976. A ceasefire was agreed on 17 Oct. 1976, backed by an Arab Deterrent Force consisting mainly of Syrian troops, but fighting soon resumed. Palestinian raids into Israel led to an Israeli incursion into the Lebanon, 15 Mar.–13 June 1978. Israel launched a full-scale invasion of Lebanon on 6 June 1982 and forced a Palestinian evacuation from Beirut, beginning on 22 Aug. 1982. An agreement between Israel and the Lebanese government on 17 May 1983 proved a dead letter, but Israel withdrew its forces from the Lebanon during 1985. Fighting between the various factions continued unabated. Eventually, Syrian forces occupied West Beirut in strength on 22 Feb. 1987 to separate the warring militias, but a Christian attempt to resist Syrian domination led to renewed bitter fighting in 1989. Eventually, the warring militias were replaced by a new Government of National Reconciliation, declared in Dec. 1990. However, Israeli military operations in Lebanon continued in the 1990s in response to bombardment of northern Israel by Hizbollah guerrillas. In 1993 Israel launched an offensive against Lebanon code-named 'Operation Accountability'. On 11 Apr. 1996, Israel launched 'Operation Grapes of Wrath', a major attack on Lebanon intended to ensure the safety of Israeli citizens.

East Timor, Indonesian annexation and guerrilla war, 1975–2002

In June 1975 Portugal announced its intention of holding independence elections in its colony of East Timor. On 11 Aug. 1975 the moderate UDT, which favoured continuing links with Portugal, attempted to stage a coup, but by 20 Aug. civil war had broken out with the communist group FRETILIN. As increasing numbers of refugees fled into Indonesian West Timor, Indonesian troops entered East Timor on 7 Dec. 1975 to forestall a left-wing takeover. By 28 Dec., the Indonesians were in control, and East Timor was officially integrated into Indonesia on 17 July 1976. Guerrilla war by FRETILIN continued against Indonesian forces, with harsh reprisals leading to a death toll in excess of 100,000 by the 1990s. The guerrilla leader, Xanana Gusmao, was captured in 1993. Earlier, the massacre of civilians at the Santa Cruz Cemetery, perpetrated by Indonesian forces, had provoked international condemnation. The East Timorese vote for independence in 1999 triggered further massacres, but independence was finally achieved in 2002.

Angolan civil war, 1975–91

The three rival liberation movements signed an agreement with Portugal on 15 Jan. 1976 regarding Angolan independence, but were soon engaged in a civil war for control of the country. Major fighting between the MPLA and FNLA broke out in the capital, Luanda, on 27 Mar. 1975. During July 1975 the MPLA gained control of Luanda. In the ensuing conflict the Marxist MPLA received aid from the Soviet Union and was supported by some 15,000 Cuban troops, whilst the FNLA/UNITA alignment received supplies from the US via Zaïre, and South African military support from Oct. 1975. When independence was declared on 11 Nov. 1975, FNLA/UNITA established a rival government in Huambo. The MPLA drove FNLA forces into Zaïre and captured Huambo on 8 Feb. 1976. The US had halted its aid to FNLA/UNITA on 27 Jan. 1976. The Organization of African Unity recognized the MPLA government on 11 Feb. 1976, and South Africa announced the withdrawal of its forces on 25 Mar. 1976. UNITA continued to wage a guerrilla campaign in Angola with aid from South Africa, which sought a counter to Angola's support for the South West Africa People's Organization guerrillas fighting for the independence of Namibia. In Apr. 1989 a ceasefire was arranged, leading to the withdrawal of Cuban and South African forces and a cessation of UNITA attacks. However, the ceasefire failed to hold, but a further peace agreement was signed between UNITA and the government in May 1991. No real solution emerged and a UN peace-keeping force was despatched.

Mozambique civil war, 1976–92

From 1976 Rhodesia fostered a guerrilla campaign by anti-FRELIMO dissidents in Mozambique, which was harbouring Robert Mugabe's ZANLA fighters. After 1980, South Africa took over the support of the MNRM as part of its policy of 'destabilizing' its neighbours. The MNRM concentrated on sabotage and guerrilla raids on communications, power lines and foreign-aided development projects. Mozambique and South Africa signed a non-aggression pact, the Nkomati accord, on 16 Mar. 1984, but MNRM activity had scarcely slackened by the end of the 1980s. However, on 4 Oct. 1992 President Chissano and Afonso Dhlakama (the MNRM leader) signed a treaty in Rome ending the civil war.

Soweto uprising, 1976

Large scale rioting in the black townships of South Africa, triggered by measures to enforce learning of Afrikaans in schools, led to over 500 African deaths in the ensuing repression.

Zaïre, rebel invasions from Angola 1977–8

On 8 Mar. 1977 Zaïre's Shaba province (formerly Katanga) was invaded from Angola by some 2,000 insurgents claiming to be members of the Congolese National Liberation Front. President Mobutu accused Cuban troops of leading the invasion and appealed for African support on 2 Apr. 1977. On 10 April French transport aircraft carried 1,500 Moroccan troops to Zaïre and they helped the Zaïre army to repel the invasion. On 11 May 1978 a second invasion from Angola by some 3,000 rebels took place. French and Belgian paratroopers were sent to Kolwezi to rescue white hostages on 19 May 1978 and the invaders were dispersed. Zaïre and Angola signed a non-aggression pact on 12 Oct. 1979.

Ethiopian conflict in the Ogaden, 1977–8

The turmoil in Ethiopia after the overthrow of Emperor Haile Selassie on 12 Sept. 1974 led the Somali Republic to pursue its claim to the Ogaden by fostering a guerrilla movement in the area, the Western Somali Liberation Front. A Somali-backed offensive in 1977 gave the guerrillas control of the southern desert area, and an attack launched against Harar on 23 Nov. 1977 narrowly failed. With Cuban and Soviet support, Ethiopia launched a counter-offensive on 7 Feb. 1978 and recovered control of the Ogaden. On 9 Mar. 1978 Somalia announced the withdrawal of its forces from the Ogaden.

Sri Lanka communal strife since 1977

Tension between the Tamil minority and the Sinhalese majority in Sri Lanka led to rioting in the northern town of Jaffna, beginning on 14 Aug. 1977, in which 125 people died. The situation grew more serious in the 1980s. Acts of terrorism by the Tamil Liberation Tigers provoked violence by the army against the Tamil community. A state of emergency was declared on 4 June 1981. Two soldiers, the first military victims, were killed in an ambush in Jaffna in Oct. 1981. Talks between President Jayawardene and the Tamil United Liberation Front failed to find a political solution. In 1987 Indian troops were requested to assist the Sri Lankan government and a force of 100,000 Indian troops attacked Tamil positions in the Jaffna peninsula. Guerrilla war continued and in 1989 Indian troops began to withdraw. In the south the ultra-left JVP movement active from 1971 has conducted an increasingly bitter terror campaign after 1987. During the 1990s violence continued. President Ranasinghe Premadasa was assassinated on 1 May 1993, but a ceasefire with the Tamils was signed in Jan. 1995. It did not hold and violence continued until Norway brokered a ceasefire in 2002 (which itself collapsed in 2003).

Vietnamese invasion of Kampuchea, 1978–89

After a series of clashes on the border, Vietnamese forces and Kampuchean rebels launched an invasion of Kampuchea on 25 Dec. 1978. The capital, Phnom Penh, was occupied on 7 Jan. 1979, and a People's Republic of Kampuchea was proclaimed, with Heng Samrin as president. Guerrilla operations against the Vietnamese occupying forces were carried out by three groups: the Khmer

Rouge; guerrillas loyal to the former head of state, Prince Sihanouk; and the non-communist Khmer People's National Liberation Front. These groups formed a loose coalition in Kuala Lumpur, Malaysia on 22 June 1982. Warfare continued, especially on the Thai border, although talks aiming at a settlement began in 1987, leading to agreement on a withdrawal of Vietnamese forces in 1989.

Ugandan conflict with Tanzania, 1978–9

On 27 Oct. 1978 Uganda invaded Tanzania and occupied some 700 square miles of Tanzanian territory known as the Kagera salient. A Tanzanian counter-offensive on 12 Nov. 1978 ejected the Ugandans from the salient. In Jan. 1979, Tanzanian forces, with armed Ugandan exiles, advanced into Uganda. Kampala fell on 11 Apr. 1979 and President Amin fled the country.

Nicaraguan civil war, 1978–90

Civil war was precipitated by the murder of President Anastasio Somoza's leading opponent, newspaper editor Pedro Joaquin Chamorro, on 10 Jan. 1978. The FSLN made steady advances, and Somoza finally fled the country on 17 July 1979. Civil war continued as the Sandinista government faced two military threats: the first, the Democratic Revolutionary Front, a group of rebels led by dissident Sandinist Eden Pastora, mounted raids from its base in Costa Rica; the second, the Nicaraguan Democratic Front or 'Contras', was a force of former National Guardsmen who operated from their exile in Honduras and who received extensive American aid until the US Congress halted funding on 25 June 1984. The Sandinista regime declared a state of emergency in May 1982, but disunity among its enemies enabled it to function despite the guerrilla threat. On 8 Aug. 1987 leaders of the five Central American countries, including Nicaragua, met in Guatemala City to sign a peace accord calling for the democratization of Nicaragua and for Contra–Sandinista negotiations. A 60-day ceasefire was announced in Sapoa on 23 Mar. 1988. With the election defeat of the Sandinistas in 1990, the civil war effectively ended.

El Salvador guerrilla insurgency, 1979–92

Guerrilla activity by the left-wing Farabundo Marti National Liberation Front intensified after 1979. Conflict between the 40,000-strong Salvadorean army, backed by the United States, and 9,000 Liberation Front guerrillas reached a stalemate during the 1980s. A peace agreement was signed between the government and the FMLN in Jan. 1992 under which both sides would report their full strength of troops and weapons to ONUSAL (the UN Observer Mission in El Salvador).

Chinese invasion of Vietnam, 1979

Chinese forces launched an invasion of Vietnam on 17 Feb. 1979 in retaliation for Vietnam's intervention in Kampuchea (see pp. 322–3). Following the fall of the provincial capital, Lang Son, on 3 Mar. 1979, the Chinese government announced that it had accomplished its aims, and the withdrawal of its forces was completed by 16 Mar. 1979.

Soviet invasion of Afghanistan and subsequent civil wars

The instability of the Soviet-backed regime and growing resistance to reforms led to a full-scale Soviet invasion of Afghanistan on 27 Dec. 1979. A new government was installed under Babrak Karmal, but a considerable Soviet military presence had to be maintained in the country to combat the Mujaheddin guerrillas. Following Babrak Karmal's resignation on 4 May 1986, his successor, Major-General Najibollah, announced a six-months' ceasefire on 15 Jan. 1987, but this was rejected by the Mujaheddin. Russian troops began to withdraw in 1988 and completed withdrawal in early 1989, having lost 15,000 dead. Contrary to expectation the Kabul regime did not collapse, and attempts by the Mujaheddin forces to take Kabul and other principal cities were repulsed. Civil war continued. Renewed fighting raged in early 1993. Fighting had claimed 3,000 lives by Feb. in a struggle between the government of President Burhanuddin Rabbani and the Hezb-i-Islami of Gulbuddin Hekmatyar, and the pro-Iranian, mainly Shi'ite, Islamic Unity Party (Hezb-i-Wahdat). A new military force, the student revolutionary Taliban, entered the fray in 1994. Despite seizing Kabul in 1997, they failed to win total control of the country. The Taliban were themselves ousted by the US-led attack following 11 Sept. 2001 (see p. 331).

Iran–Iraq War, 1980–8

Hoping to exploit the instability of Iran after the fall of the Shah, Iraq abrogated the Algiers pact of 1975, by which it had been forced to accept joint control of the Shatt-al-Arab waterway, and invaded Iran on 12 Sept. 1980. Khorramshahr fell on 13 Oct. 1980, but the Iranian government did not collapse and its armed forces began to counter-attack successfully. Each side bombed the other's oil installations and attacked international shipping in the Gulf. Iran rejected Iraq's ceasefire overtures as the military stalemate deepened. On 9 Jan. 1987 Iran launched a major offensive – codenamed Karbala-5 – with the aim of capturing Basra. The Iranians advanced some distance towards their objective, while suffering heavy casualties. In 1987 and 1988 Iraq made major advances and a ceasefire was organized in Aug. 1988. The war is estimated to have cost almost a million casualties, with some of the heaviest land-fighting since the Second World War.

Somalian civil war, 1981–97

Following protracted civil war which had originally begun in 1981, law and order broke down completely. President Mohammed Siad Barre was overthrown in a coup in 1991 and an interim government appointed under Ali Mahdi Mohammed. However, by the end of the year fighting between clan-based factions developed into renewed civil war. Following widespread famine, a US-led UN force landed in Somalia in Dec. 1991 but withdrew in 1995. In Jan. 1997 leaders of the 26 factions competing for dominance in and around the capital Mogadishu agreed on the formation of a National Salvation Council to lay the ground for a government of national unity. Somalia remains lawless.

Falkland Islands (Malvinas), 1982

Argentina maintained a long-standing claim to the sovereignty of the Falkland Islands, and on 2 Apr. 1982 the Argentine dictatorship, under General Galtieri, launched a successful invasion of the islands, forcing its garrison of 18 Royal Marines to surrender. Argentine forces also seized the island of South Georgia. On 5 Apr. a British Task Force set sail to recapture the islands and on 7 Apr. an exclusion zone of 200 miles was declared around the island. On 25 Apr. South Georgia was recaptured and on 1 May air attacks began on the Argentine garrison on the Falklands. The next day the Argentine cruiser *Belgrano* was sunk by a British submarine and on 4 May HMS *Sheffield* was hit by an Exocet missile. On 21 May British troops went ashore at San Carlos. Two British frigates, the *Ardent* and *Antelope*, were sunk and others damaged by air attack, but British troops took Darwin and Goose Green by the end of May and on 11–14 June an attack on Port Stanley led to the surrender of the Argentine forces. During the conflict 255 British and 720 Argentine troops were killed. A large permanent garrison and modern airstrip have been placed on the island for its future security.

Invasion of Grenada, 1983

On 19 Oct. 1983 the army took control in Grenada after a power struggle led to the murder of Prime Minister Maurice Bishop. On 21 Oct. the Organisation of Eastern Caribbean States appealed to the United States to intervene, and on 25 Oct. US Marines and airborne troops invaded Grenada, together with token contingents from six other Caribbean countries. Resistance from the Grenadian army and 700 Cuban construction workers with paramilitary training was overcome, and order restored by 27 Oct. 1983.

Sikh separatist unrest after 1984

Separatist unrest amongst Sikhs had led to several hundred deaths in the Punjab by early 1984 and the introduction of emergency rule. Following the stockpiling of arms at the Golden Temple, Amritsar, the Sikhs' holiest shrine, the Indian army stormed the complex and in fierce fighting killed the leading Sikh militant Jarnail Sing Bhindranwale and over 700 of his followers. On 31 Oct. the Indian Prime Minister, Indira Gandhi, was assassinated by 2 Sikh bodyguards and in ensuing 'revenge' attacks over 2,000 Sikhs were killed. Terrorism by Sikh extremists and communal riots had led to several thousand deaths by 1990 and the reintroduction of emergency rule in the Punjab. The conflict remains unresolved.

Indo-Pakistan conflict in Kashmir after 1984

The UN has policed the ceasefire line established in the wake of the 1971 Indo-Pakistan war, but in the high Himalayan ranges sporadic fighting has taken place, principally around the Sianchin glacier. In May 1984 the Pakistanis launched a major infantry-artillery attack to dislodge Indian troops who had moved onto the glacier. In 1985 Pakistani planes bombed Indian positions and air combat took place. Renewed tension brought India and Pakistan to the verge of war in 1990 and again in 2003.

Burkina Faso (Upper Volta) conflict with Mali, 1985

In Dec. 1985 Burkina Faso forces invaded northern Mali over a border dispute, with each side backed respectively by Libya and Algeria. 3 days of fighting left 400 dead, but arbitration by the international court at The Hague was accepted.

Turkey, revolt of the Kurds, 1986–99

Since the mid-1980s the outlawed Kurdistan Workers' Party (PKK), a Marxist-Leninist group led by Abdullah Ocalan, has fought for an independent Kurdish state in the south-east of Turkey (where some 12 million Kurds are located). An estimated 10,000 guerrillas confronted about 200,000 Turkish soldiers. It became the bloodiest conflict in the Middle East after the Algerian Civil War. A ceasefire was signed in 1999.

Uprising or *intifada* in Arab West Bank and Gaza after 1987

In Dec. 1987, widespread unrest amongst Palestinian refugees erupted in the Israeli-occupied West Bank and Gaza strip against Israeli security forces. Rioting and terrorist incidents had led to over 600 dead by end 1989. In Apr. 1988, an Israeli special unit assassinated the PLO military commander, Abu Jihad, believing he was masterminding the violence. The *intifada* eventually led to progress towards the creation of a Palestinian authority. A second *intifada* began in 2000.

The Soviet Union, disintegration and ethnic conflict, 1988–91

During the final days of the Soviet Union, ethnic clashes were already develop-ing. Rioting between Armenians and Azerbaijanis, sparked by a dispute over control of the Nagorno-Karabakh region began on 20 Feb. 1988. In Uzbekistan, fighting between Uzbeks and Meskhetian Turks began on 4 June 1989. The armed forces also moved against nationalist movements in Georgia, Moldova, Azerbaijan and the Baltic Republics. After the collapse of the Soviet Union, serious conflicts developed in the following areas: Azerbaijan–Armenia; the Abkhazia region of Georgia; Moldova and Tajikistan. (See also Chechnya, p. 330).

Romanian revolution and civil war, 1989

On 17 Dec. 1989 security forces fired on protesters in the Romanian city of Timisoara. On 18 Dec., Romania closed its frontiers. On 20 Dec., troops sur-rendered in Timisoara. Fighting spread to Bucharest and other major cities. The army switched sides, joining the popular uprising against the Ceausescu (see p. 413) dictatorship and the hated security police (the *Securitate*). By 24 Dec. all strategic points were controlled by the revolutionary National Salvation Front. Ceausescu and his wife were executed by firing squad on 25 Dec. 1989, having been found guilty of genocide by a military court. Provisional casualty figures gave 689 dead and 1,200 injured in the revolution.

Liberian civil war, 1989–97

What began in Dec. 1989 as an invasion by the National Patriotic Front of Liberia (NPLF) against President Samuel Doe degenerated within five years to chaos as eight warlords competed for power. A breakaway Independent NPLF, which was formed in Feb. 1990, murdered President Doe in Sept. By Apr. 1991 the NPLF controlled 90% of the country, but its refusal to join an interim government of national unity thwarted attempts by the Economic Community of West African States (ECOWAS) to restore peace. A United Liberia Movement for Democracy (ULIMO) appeared on the scene in 1992. An estimated 150,000 had died and over 750,000 had been forced to flee as refugees as the factions finally agreed on an ECOWAS peace plan at the start of 1997.

US invasion of Panama, 1989

Tension between America and the corrupt Noriega dictatorship mounted during 1989, especially after the annulment of the May elections. On 20 Dec. US forces launched a ground and air invasion to overthrow the Panamanian regime and seize Noriega. Despite some resistance from the Panamanian Defence Forces and the pro-Noriega civilian militia (the 'Dignity Battalions'), US forces rapidly occupied Panama City and other key areas. Noriega fled, finding refuge in the Vatican embassy, before surrendering and being extradited to the United States.

Rwandan civil war after 1990

Despite attempts by President Juvénal Habyarimana, who had seized power in 1973, to allow the Tutsis a political role in Hutu-dominated Rwanda, a Tutsi force invaded the country from neighbouring Uganda in Sept. 1990 but was defeated within a month. In Jan. 1991 the predominantly Tutsi Rwandan Patriotic Front (FPR) guerrillas renewed the attack. Despite a ceasefire in Mar., an estimated 15,000 Tutsis were massacred by the Hutu militia between 1991 and 1993. In Feb. 1993 the FPR launched a new offensive which culminated in July 1994 – following the death of President Habyarimana in a suspicious air crash – in the capture of the capital Kigali and the formation of a government of national unity. However, following the flight of 800,000 Hutu refugees in 1994, FPR attacks on both Hutus and Tutsis continued.

The First Gulf War, 1990–1

On 2 Aug. 1990 Iraqi troops launched a surprise attack on Kuwait and invaded the country, which President Saddam Hussein then annexed on 7 Aug. and on 28 Aug. declared it to be the 19th province of Iraq. The UN Security Council condemned the invasion and demanded the immediate withdrawal of the Iraqi troops. On 10 Aug., a similar declaration was made by the Arab League (only Libya and the Palestine Liberation Organization voted against the declaration). Owing to the failure of diplomatic means, the UN voted for economic sanctions against Iraq (6 Aug.) and the United States – in alliance with other countries – started to build up their military forces in the area. On 28 Nov., the UN Security Council authorized its member states to use force against the aggressors if Iraq did not withdraw its troops from Kuwait by 15 Jan. 1991. After acquiring an absolute supremacy in the air within a matter of days, the US air force, together with its allies, bombed Iraqi positions and major cities for more than a month – carrying out a vast air offensive. In response, Saddam Hussein launched 'Scud' air missiles on Israel and Saudi Arabia, had hundreds of thousands of tons of oil poured into the Persian Gulf, and set 500 Kuwaiti oil wells on fire. On 23 Feb., a land offensive was also launched and by 26 Feb. Kuwait was fully liberated. On 28 Feb. – after Iraq's total defeat – US President Bush ordered a ceasefire.

Yugoslavian civil war (Serbo-Croat War), 1991–5

Declarations of independence by the former Yugoslav Republics of Slovenia and Croatia led to clashes on Slovenian borders from July 1991, followed by heavy fighting on Croatian territory between Croatian militia and Serbian irregulars (chetniks) backed by the Yugoslav Federal Army. Main centres of fighting were eastern and central Croatia and the Adriatic coast around Dubrovnik. Yugoslavia officially ceased to exist in Jan. 1992 and Slovenia and Croatia were recognized as independent states. On 29 Feb. 1992 Muslim leaders in Bosnia–Herzegovina declared independence. Bosnian Serbs and the Serbian leadership in Belgrade rejected this, and war began on 6 Apr. with the opening of the siege of the capital Sarajevo. Serbs were accused of 'ethnic cleansing' to secure territorial domination, and a UN trade embargo was imposed on Serbia on 31 May. Peace talks in Geneva, mediated by Lord Owen and Cyrus Vance, began on 26 Aug. On 16 Nov. a UN naval blockade was mounted against Serbia and Montenegro. Fighting continued as a further peace conference was held in Geneva on 22–3 Jan. 1993. Serbs attacked Muslim enclaves at Srebenica and Goradze. Numerous peace talks collapsed. In 1995 Croatia launched major offensives and an uneasy peace accord was signed at Dayton, Ohio. An estimated 200,000 people died in the Yugoslavian Civil War.

Sierra Leone civil war, 1991–2001

In Mar. 1991 a Revolutionary United Front (RUF) force – supported by mercenaries from Burkina Faso – advanced in 2 columns into Sierra Leone. The northern force was halted by government troops with assistance from Guinea but the southern force came close to the capital Freetown. However, by 1996 the RUF had weakened as it collapsed into competing factions. Renewed conflict came in May 1997 when the elected government of President Kabbah was overthrown by the RUF in a military coup. Kabbah was restored in Mar. 1998. The conflict continued intermittently until a peace agreement in July 2001.

Algerian civil war after 1992

An army-dominated High State Council took power in Algeria when it appeared that the fundamentalist Islamic Salvation Front (FIS) would be successful in the Jan. 1992 elections, provoking rioting and terrorism. By the end of 1993 this had developed into full-scale civil war between government troops, the FIS armed wing – the Islamic Salvation Army (AIS) – and the Armed Islamic Group (GIA). In an attempt to weaken the government's position, Islamic guerrillas attacked the oil industry and mounted attacks on foreigners. The war was also marked by a number of massacres of civilians. By the beginning of 2005, an estimated 70,000 people had been killed in the conflict.

Burundi civil war, 1994–2003

Fighting between Hutu and dominant Tutsi factions which broke out in Feb. 1994 intensified following the death in an air crash of President Cyprien Ntaryamira in Apr. The orders of his successor, interim President Sylvestre

Ntibantunganya, for both sides to disarm were ignored. Ethnic tension was increased by an influx of 200,000 Hutu refugees from neighbouring Rwanda. Government forces, allegedly co-operating with Tutsi extremists, attacked the Hutu suburbs of the capital Bujumbura, killing hundreds of civilians. By the end of 1995, an estimated 150,000 civilians had died and, as conflict heightened, refugees fled to Rwanda, Tanzania and Zaïre. Threats from extremist factions prevented the deployment of an Organization of African Unity (OAU) peace-keeping force and the overthrow of President Ntibantunganya by Pierre Buyoya in July 1996 blocked hopes that an East African force would be accepted. A ceasefire was finally agreed in 2003.

Russia–Chechnya War, 1994–6 and after 1999

Russian troops were ordered into Chechnya in Dec. 1994 to end the rebel republic's bid for independence. Fighting ensued for 21 months as Russian troops failed to subdue the population. The fighting was the worst on Russian soil since the Second World War, with Grozny, the Chechnya capital, razed to the ground. The Russian army suffered a major loss of face. On 31 Aug. 1996 Russia and Chechnya signed a peace deal, freezing the issue of independence for five years. In Jan. 1997 the withdrawal of all Russian troops from Chechnya was completed.

However, partly provoked by Chechen support for guerrillas in the adjacent Caucasus region of Dagestan, and partly because of terrorist bomb outrages in Russia itself, a renewed Russian offensive was launched against Chechnya in Sept. 1999. Massive Russian aerial bombardment was followed by a major ground offensive against Grozny launched on 25 Dec. 1999. Chechen separatists still maintain a campaign of terrorist attacks on Russian targets (including the Beslan school massacre of Sept. 2004).

Nepal civil war since 1996

Maoist-led insurgency against the Royalist government with the aim of establishing a Communist republic. By 2004 it had spread to all 75 provinces and claimed 10,000 lives. Almost two-thirds of the country was in rebel hands. Ceasefires in 2001 and 2003 failed to hold.

Zaïre civil war, 1996–97, 1998–2002

In Oct. 1996 the Alliance of Democratic Forces for the Liberation of Congo-Zaïre – led by President Mobutu Sésé Séko's long-term opponent Laurent Kabila – launched an attack on the Zaïrean army in alliance with anti-Mobutu Tutsi guerrillas and forces seeking autonomy for the Shaba and Kasai provinces. Kabila's troops were supported during the campaign by Rwanda and Uganda while Mobutu strengthened his army with white mercenaries. After a rapid advance through the country, the capital Kinshasa fell to Alliance forces in

May 1997. Kabila declared himself head of state, renaming the country the Democratic Republic of the Congo. Mobutu Sésé Séko fled to Morocco, where he died in Sept. Renewed civil war began in Aug. 1998 when rebels supported by Uganda and Rwanda rose up against the President, Laurent Kabila. Angola, Namibia and Zimbabwe came to Kabila's aid. The 5-year war cost 3.3 million lives, including Kabila's. He was assassinated in 2001, and was succeeded by his son. The leaders of Rwanda and Congo signed a peace deal in July 2002.

The Balkan War, 1999

Conflict in Kosovo, until 1989 an autonomous province in 'rump' Yugoslavia mainly inhabited by Kosovar Albanians, gradually intensified as Serbian forces embarked on a policy of ethnic cleansing. Yugoslav President Slobodan Milosević ignored a series of NATO warnings during 1998. On 24 Mar. 1999 NATO forces (including British aircraft) launched air strikes against Yugoslavia. Cruise missile attacks followed. Milosevic intensified his ethnic cleansing policy, producing a human tide of refugees into Macedonia and Albania. NATO air strikes were marked by a series of calamitous errors (including the missile attack on the Chinese embassy in Belgrade on 8 May) and a serious worsening of relations with Russia. Eventually air power (backed by a threat of a land offensive) caused Milosevic to sue for peace and a mainly NATO peace-keeping force (KFOR, with some Russian troops) was stationed in Kosovo.

Invasion of Afghanistan, 2001

After the 11 Sept. 2001 assault on America (carried out by the al-Qaeda terror group headed by Osama bin Laden), US and British forces launched attacks on Afghanistan on 7 Oct. 2001. Air attacks were launched from Pakistan and bases in central Asia, while allied forces assisted Northern Alliance rebels within Afghanistan. The Taliban regime rapidly fell: Herat was gained on 12 Nov., Kabul on 18 Nov. and Kandahar in Dec. Pockets of resistance by al-Qaeda and Taliban forces still continue to resist ISAF (the International Security Assistance Force) and the 8,000-strong US forces in Afghanistan.

Invasion of Iraq (the Second Gulf War), 2003

Following unsuccessful attempts to persuade the regime of Saddam Hussein to comply with UN resolutions on disarmament, US-led forces invaded Iraq in Mar. 2003. The attack opened on 20 Mar. with the bombing of Baghdad and central Iraq, followed by the movement of American and British troops in the far south to secure oilfields and the port of Umm Qasr. As the Americans moved north towards Baghdad, bypassing obstacles where resistance proved stronger than expected, British troops began a slow campaign to take Iraq's second city of Basra. Forecasts that the Iraqi people would rise against Saddam Hussein and that the regime's collapse would be speedy were confounded. On 3 Apr. American forces reached the airport close to the capital and on 6 Apr. Basra fell to British troops. American forces began their decisive entry into Baghdad on 7 Apr. The Saddam Hussein regime had effectively ended, but an increasingly bloody insurgency against the occupation forces developed during 2004.

CASUALTIES IN SELECTED CONFLICTS SINCE 1945

Country	Length of conflict (years)	Ended (year)	Casualties (estimates)
Afghanistan	24	2002	1,000,000
Angola	36	2002	1,500,000
Burundi	10	2003	300,000
Cambodia	30	[1]	1,850,000
Congo (Dem. Rep.)	5	[1]	2,400,000[2]
Guatemala	36	1996	200,000
Lebanon	25	1991	170,000
Liberia	14	2003	250,000
Nepal	6	[1]	10,000
Rwanda	1	1994	800,000
Sierra Leone	11	2002	200,000
Somalia	13	2003	500,000
Sri Lanka	19	2003	150,000
Sudan	35	[1]	2,000,000[3]

[1] Conflict still ongoing.
[2] Minimum estimate. Some estimates as high as 5,000,000.
[3] Excluding Darfur War, begun in Feb. 2003, which precipitated humanitarian crisis in 2004.

NUCLEAR DEVELOPMENT AND ARMS CONTROL

1902　Rutherford and Soddy investigate the radioactive transmutation of the elements.

1905　Planck and Einstein develop the idea of energy being transmitted in finite steps or 'quanta'.
Einstein proposes the special theory of relativity, predicting the mutual conversion of mass and energy.

1908　Geiger develops a counter for detecting radioactive rays.

1911　Rutherford proposes the existence of the atom; Bohr and Rutherford suggest structure of the atom.

1916　Einstein puts forward general theory of relativity.

1919　Rutherford splits the atom and demonstrates the existence of sub-atomic particles.

1925　Heisenberg and Schrödinger establish the theory of 'quantum mechanics' and the basis for atomic physics.

1932　Existence of the neutron discovered by Chadwick: particles which could split the atom.

1934　Fermi discovers that nuclei could be made to disintegrate if bombarded with neutrons themselves produced by nuclear disintegrations.

1938　Hahn and Strassmann split the uranium atom and demonstrate the release of further neutrons to produce a chain reaction.

1940　Professors Peierls and Frisch at Birmingham University in Britain produce memorandum on the design of an atomic bomb (Feb.); increased support given to research.
Soviet Union sets up committee to investigate the 'uranium problem'.
Germans set up research institute in Berlin, code-named 'The Virus House', to explore atomic developments.

1941　British Maud Committee reports favourably on possibility of atomic weapon (June).
Russian programme disrupted by German invasion and removed beyond the Urals (July).

1942　Anglo-Norwegian sabotage team wreck German 'heavy water' plant at Rjukan in Norway, crucial to German atomic research (Apr.).
Americans set up 'Manhattan Project' under US Army Corps of Engineers to administer work on the production of an atomic bomb (June). Several processes tried to achieve separation of fissile Uranium 235 from Uranium 238.

First nuclear chain reaction using plutonium takes place at the University of Chicago under direction of Fermi (Dec.).

1943   Quebec agreement between Churchill and Roosevelt agrees co-operation on atomic bomb programme (Aug.).

1944   Both uranium enrichment and plutonium reaction developed in the United States to produce atomic weapons.
Discovery of captured German documents reveals lack of progress in their atomic research.

1945   The first successful explosion of an experimental atomic device takes place at Alamogordo, New Mexico (16 July).
USAAF B29 bomber, *Enola Gay*, dropped the first atomic bomb, nicknamed 'Little Boy', on the Japanese city of Hiroshima (6 Aug.).
Second atomic bomb, nicknamed 'Fat Man', dropped on Nagasaki (9 Aug.).

1946   United Nations General Assembly passes a resolution to establish an Atomic Energy Commission (Jan.).
At the first meeting of the Atomic Energy Commission, the American delegate, Bernard M. Baruch, puts forward a plan by which the United States would surrender its atomic weapons and reveal the secrets of controlling atomic energy to an International Control Agency. The Baruch Plan rejected by the Soviet Union (June).
United States carries out the first nuclear test in peacetime at Bikini Atoll in the Marshall Islands (1 July).
President Truman signs the Atomic Energy Act, restricting exchange of information with other nations on atomic energy, thus ending co-operation between the United States and Britain in the development of nuclear weapons (6 Aug.).

1949   Soviet Union explodes an atomic bomb, ending the American monopoly of nuclear weapons (29 Aug.).

1950   Soviet Union withdraws from the Atomic Energy Commission (Jan.).

1952   Britain tests its first atomic bomb (3 Oct.).
United States explodes the first hydrogen device at Eniwetok atoll in the Marshall Islands (1 Nov.).

1953   Soviet Union tests its first hydrogen bomb in Siberia (12 Aug.).
'Atoms for Peace': President Eisenhower announces a plan at the UN General Assembly for a pool of fissile material to be available for peaceful purposes (Dec.).

1954   'Massive Retaliation': in the aftermath of the Korean War, John Foster Dulles, US Secretary of State, announces that 'Local defence must be reinforced by the further deterrent of massive retaliatory power', that is, by the threat of nuclear weapons (12 Jan.).

First atomic power station opened at Obninsk, USSR (27 June).

USS *Nautilus*, first American atomic powered submarine, commissioned (Sept.).

1955   At the Geneva Summit, President Eisenhower puts forward his 'open skies' proposal for mutual aerial photography of each other's territory by the Soviet Union and United States as a step towards disarmament (July).

1956   Britain opens first large-scale commercial nuclear power station at Calder Hall, Cumbria (23 Oct.), but mainly used for defence purposes.

1957   First British hydrogen bomb exploded near Christmas Island (15 Aug.).

UN International Atomic Energy Agency established to promote the safe use of atomic energy for peaceful purposes (July).

Soviet Union announces the successful launch of an inter-continental ballistic missile (26 Aug.).

Adam Rapacki, Foreign Minister of Poland, proposes in a speech to the UN General Assembly the creation of a nuclear-free zone in central Europe. Plan rejected by NATO on the grounds that nuclear weapons are essential to offset Soviet superiority in conventional forces (2 Oct.).

1958   First meeting of Britain's Campaign for Nuclear Disarmament (CND) held in London (17 Feb.).

Successful firing of America's first intercontinental ballistic missile, the liquid-fuelled Atlas (Nov.).

1959   Establishment of the Ten-Power Committee on Disarmament, comprising representatives from Britain, Canada, France, Italy, United States, Bulgaria, Czechoslovakia, Poland, Romania and Soviet Union (7 Sept.). Treaty for the peaceful use of Antarctica opened for signature in Washington.

1960   France explodes its first atomic device in the Sahara (13 Feb.).

First successful underwater firing of a Polaris missile from the USS *George Washington* (20 July).

First Polaris nuclear submarine, USS *George Washington*, becomes operational (15 Nov.).

United States offers 5 submarines with 80 Polaris missiles to create a NATO Multilateral Nuclear Force at the NATO ministerial meeting in Paris (Dec.).

1962   First meeting in Geneva of the Eighteen Nation Disarmament Committee, the former Ten-Power Committee with the addition of Brazil, Burma, Egypt, Ethiopia, India, Mexico, Nigeria and Sweden (14 Mar.).

US Secretary of Defence, Robert McNamara, announces in a speech at

the University of Michigan, Ann Arbor, a new strategy of 'flexible response' to replace that of 'massive retaliation' (June).
Cuban Missile Crisis: President Kennedy announces on 22 Oct. that aerial reconnaissance has established that offensive missile sites are being constructed by the Soviet Union in Cuba and that a naval and air 'quarantine' is being imposed until the sites are dismantled.
On 28 Oct. Khrushchev agrees to remove the missiles from Cuba in return for an American guarantee not to invade (Oct.).
President Kennedy meets British Prime Minister, Harold Macmillan, at Nassau in the Bahamas and agrees to make US Polaris missiles available to Britain for use with British warheads (Dec.).

1963   'Hot line' agreement between the United States and the Soviet Union (5 Apr.).
Partial Test-Ban Treaty, outlawing nuclear tests in the atmosphere and outer space and underwater (5 Aug.).

1964   First Chinese atomic explosion takes place at Lop Nor in Sinkiang province (16 Oct.).

1965   US Secretary of Defence, Robert McNamara, announces that the United States would rely on threat of 'assured destruction' to deter a Soviet attack (18 Feb.).

1966   NATO establishes the Nuclear Defence Affairs Committee (all members except France, Iceland and Luxembourg) and the Nuclear Planning Group (all members except France and Iceland) (14 Dec.).

1967   Treaty banning all nuclear weapons in outer space opened for signature in London, Moscow and Washington (28 Jan.).
Treaty of Tlatelolco, prohibiting nuclear weapons in Latin America, opened for signature in Mexico (14 Feb.).
First Chinese hydrogen bomb test carried out (17 June).

1968   Non-Proliferation Treaty opened for signature in London, Moscow and Washington (11 July).
France explodes its first hydrogen bomb (25 Aug.).

1969   President Nixon announces the decision to deploy a ballistic missile defence system, 'Safeguard', primarily to defend ICBM sites (14 Mar.).
Eight new members join the Eighteen Nation Disarmament Committee, renamed the Conference of the Committee on Disarmament (Aug.).
Five additional members join on 1 Jan. 1975.
Preparatory negotiations on Strategic Arms Limitation Talks (SALT) between the United States and the Soviet Union begin in Helsinki (17 Nov.).

1970   Strategic Arms Limitation Talks open in Vienna (16 Apr.).

First Minuteman III missiles to be equipped with multiple independently targeted re-entry vehicles (MIRVs) become operational in the United States (June).
First successful underwater launch of a Poseidon missile from USS *James Madison* (Aug.).

1971 Seabed Treaty prohibiting the emplacement of nuclear weapons on the seabed opened for signature in London, Moscow and Washington (11 Feb.).

1972 SALT I anti-ballistic missile agreement and five-year interim agreement on the limitation of strategic arms signed by the United States and the Soviet Union (26 May).

1973 Mutual and Balanced Force Reduction talks between NATO and the Warsaw Pact begin in Vienna (30 Oct.).

1974 US Secretary of Defence, James Schlesinger, announces new doctrine of 'limited strategic strike options' in the event of a nuclear war, in which a broad spectrum of deterrence would be available before the resort to large-scale strategic strikes (10 Jan.).

1974 India explodes its first atomic device at Pokharan in the Rajasthan desert (18 May).
Protocol to the US–Soviet SALT ABM agreement, limiting ABM deployment to a single area (3 July).
US–Soviet Threshhold Test Ban Treaty signed, limiting underground nuclear tests (3 July).
Vladivostok Accord between the United States and the Soviet Union, setting out the framework for future negotiations on controlling the strategic arms race (24 Nov.).

1976 US-Soviet treaty restricting nuclear explosions for peaceful purposes (28 May).

1977 United States announces that it has tested an Enhanced Radiation Weapon or 'neutron bomb' (7 July).

1978 President Carter announces the postponement of a decision on the production and deployment of the neutron bomb (7 Apr.).

1979 Major nuclear accident in the United States at Three Mile Island, Harrisburg, Pennsylvania: thousands of gallons of radioactive water and a plume of radioactive gas released (28 Mar.).
SALT II agreement signed by United States and Soviet Union, restricting numbers of strategic offensive weapons. United States withholds ratification of the treaty following the Soviet invasion of Afghanistan in Dec. 1979 (18 June).

NATO announces its intention to modernize its long-range theatre nuclear systems by the deployment of 464 ground-launched Cruise missiles and 108 Pershing II medium-range ballistic missiles in Europe (12 Dec.).

1980   Agreement to site 'Cruise missiles' in Europe (June).
President Carter signs Presidential Directive 59, emphasizing the possibility of flexible, controlled retaliation against a range of military and political targets in a prolonged nuclear war (25 July).
US Department of Defense announces its intention to build an Advanced Technology, or 'stealth', bomber with a greatly reduced radar detectability (22 Aug.).

1981   In Operation BABYLON Israeli F-16 aircraft drop 16 tons of explosives on Iraq's Osirak nuclear plant on the grounds that Iraq is manufacturing nuclear weapons (7 June).
President Reagan orders the production and stockpiling of the neutron bomb, but says that it would not be deployed in Europe without NATO's consent (6 Aug.).
President Reagan authorizes the updating of US strategic forces, including the production of 100 MX missiles and the new B1 bomber (2 Oct.).
US–Soviet negotiations on intermediate-range nuclear forces open at Geneva (30 Nov.).

1982   Strategic Arms Reduction Talks (START) between United States and Soviet Union begin at Geneva (29 June).

1983   President Reagan announces the Strategic Defense Initiative, or 'Star Wars' project, which aims to employ lasers and satellite technology to neutralize a missile attack on the United States (23 June).
Intermediate-range 'Cruise missiles' deployed in Britain, Holland and Germany (Nov.).

1986   Major nuclear accident in the Soviet Union at the Chernobyl site, north of Kiev, involving explosions, fire and release of radioactivity from No. 4 Reactor (26 Apr.).
Summit meeting on arms control between President Reagan and Mr Gorbachev at Reykjavik, Iceland, founders on the issue of the US Strategic Defense Initiative (11–12 Oct.).

1987   President Reagan announces imminent arms control deal and superpower summit with Mr Gorbachev (18 Sept.).
Deployment of Cruise missiles halted in NATO countries (Nov.).
US and USSR reach historic agreement to scrap intermediate range nuclear weapons (24 Nov.), when INF Treaty signed in Washington (8 Dec.).

1988   Moscow summit talks between Reagan and Gorbachev (29 May).

1989   Gorbachev offers unilateral cuts in short-range missiles (10 May).
Cruise missiles removed from NATO countries (June), including the
Greenham Common site in England, the scene of continuous women's
demonstrations in the 1980s. President Bush announces cuts in Strategic
Defense Initiative programme; 'stealth bomber' unveiled (July).

1990   Conference on Security and Co-operation in Europe (CSCE) signs
agreement in Paris marking formal end of the Cold War.

1991   Gorbachev and Bush agree START I Treaty after nearly 10 years of
discussions.

1993   Yeltsin and Bush sign START II Treaty (designed to halve stockpiles of
nuclear warheads held by each country). Never ratified by US Congress.

1996   Comprehensive Nuclear Test Ban Treaty agreed.
The treaty will ban any nuclear-weapon test explosion or any other
nuclear explosion. To enter into force, all 44 states that were members
of the UN Conference on Disarmament as of 18 June 1996 must deposit
their instruments of ratification.

1997   Russia–NATO Agreement concluded.

2001   Failure of talks between Putin and George Bush Jr on US National
Missile Defence (Nov.). Bush signifies intention to withdraw from 1972
ABM Treaty (Dec.).

2002   Major agreement to cut operational nuclear warheads by two-thirds over
10 years signed by Putin and Bush in Moscow (12 May).

STRATEGIC NUCLEAR WEAPONS OF THE SUPERPOWERS, 1963–85

	1963	1968	1976	1980	1985
United States					
ICBM	424	1,054	1,054	1,054	1,026
SLBM	224	656	656	656	640
LRB	630	600	373	338	241
Soviet Union					
ICBM	90	858	1,477	1,398	1,398
SLBM	107	121	845	1,028	979
LRB	190	155	135	156	170

Key: ICBM   Intercontinental ballistic missiles
      SLBM   Submarine-launched ballistic missiles
      LRB: Long-range bombers (range, over 6,000 miles)

Source: The International Institute for Strategic Studies, *The Military Balance, 1976–1977* (London, 1976), p. 75; *The Military Balance, 1985–1986* (London, 1986).

NUCLEAR WARHEAD STOCKPILES, 1945–2002

	1945	1955	1965	1975	1985	1995	2002
United States	6	3,057	31,265	26,675	22,941	14,776	12,000
USSR/Russia	0	200	6,129	19,443	39,197	27,000	22,500

Totals are estimates and include strategic (long-range) and non-strategic warheads, as well as warheads awaiting dismantling.

Source: US National Resources Defense Council.

STRATEGIC NUCLEAR ARSENALS OF OTHER STATES, 1960–86

	1960	*1976*	*1986*
United Kingdom			
Aircraft	50	50	–[1]
Land-based missiles	–	–	–
SLBM	–	64	64
France			
Aircraft	–	36	34[1]
Land-based missiles	–	18	18
SLBM	–	48	80
China			
Aircraft	–	65	110
Land-based missiles	–	50–80 (est.)	140–80 (est.)
SLBM	–	–	26

Note: SLBM: Submarine launched ballistic missiles.
  [1] Aircraft designated for strategic nuclear role only. In 1986 the United Kingdom possessed 201 land-based, short-range aircraft capable of carrying a nuclear payload plus 30 carrier-borne aircraft; France had 75 land-based, short-range aircraft, plus 36 carrier-borne.

Source: The International Institute for Strategic Studies, *The Military Balance, 1976–1977* (London, 1976), pp. 18, 21, 50; *Royal United Services Institute and Brassey's Defence Yearbook, 1967* (London, 1967), pp. 462, 465.

MAJOR ACTS OF TERRORISM AND ASSASSINATIONS

1914 June 28	Assassination of Archduke Franz Ferdinand at Sarajevo by Gavrilo Princip.
July 30	Assassination of Jean Jaurès, French socialist leader, in Paris.
1918 July 16	Execution of Tsar Nicholas and Russian royal family at Ekaterinburg.
1922 June 22	Assassination of Field-Marshal Sir Henry Wilson, Northern Irish MP, in London, by Irish Republicans.
June 24	Assassination of Walter Rathenau, German foreign minister, by anti-Semitic group.
Aug. 22	Assassination of Michael Collins, leader of pro-treaty Irish, by anti-treaty faction in County Cork.
1923 July 20	'Pancho' Villa assassinated at Parral, Mexico.
1924 June 10	Giacomo Matteotti, prominent Italian socialist, murdered by Fascists.
1927	Kevin O'Higgins, Vice-President of Irish Free State, killed by Irish Republic Army.
1928 July 17	President of Mexico, Alvaro Obrégon, assassinated.
1932 May 1	President of France, Paul Doumer, assassinated by Russian émigré.
1933 Apr. 30	President of Peru, Luís Sánchez Cevro, assassinated.
Nov. 8	King of Afghanistan, Nadir Shah, assassinated.
1934 June 30	Nazis organize murder of leaders of SA and other potential rivals (the 'Night of the Long Knives').
July 25	Chancellor of Austria, Engelbert Dollfuss, murdered by Austrian Nazis.
Oct. 9	King Alexander of Yugoslavia and Louis Barthou, French foreign minister, assassinated by a Bosnian terrorist in Marseilles.
Dec. 1	Sergei Kirov, a Bolshevik leader, assassinated, almost certainly at Stalin's behest to justify purge of opponents.
1935 Sept. 8	Senator Huey Long assassinated at Baton Rouge.
1939 Sept. 8	Leader of Romanian Iron Guard, Professor Cristescu, and Prime Minister, Armand Calinescu, assassinated.
1940 Aug. 21	Leon Trotsky assassinated in Mexico.
1941	French socialist leader, Marx Dormoy, assassinated in bombing at Montelimar, France.

1942 June 5	Yves Paringaux, French Chief-of-Staff in Vichy government, assassinated at Melum, France.
May 31	Reinhard Heydrich, German Governor of Bohemia and Moravia, assassinated by Czech partisans.
Dec. 24	Admiral Darlan, commander of French North Africa, assassinated by French right-winger in Algiers.
1944 July 20	Bomb attempt on Hitler's life at his East Prussian HQ fails.
1945 Feb. 24	Prime Minister of Egypt, Ahmed Maher Pasha, assassinated in Cairo Parliament.
Apr. 28	Benito Mussolini shot by Italian partisans.
1946 July 22	Jewish terrorist bombing of King David Hotel, British Military HQ in Jerusalem, kills 42 with 52 missing.
1948 Jan. 20	Mahatma Gandhi assassinated in Delhi by a Hindu extremist.
Sept. 17	Count Folke Bernadotte, UN mediator, killed by Jewish terrorists in Jerusalem.
Dec. 28	Prime Minister of Egypt, Nokrashi Pasha, assassinated.
1951 July 20	King Abdullah of Jordan assassinated in Jerusalem.
Oct. 6	High Commissioner of Malaya, Henry Gurney, assassinated in Malaya.
Oct. 16	Prime Minister Ali Khan of Pakistan assassinated.
1958 July 14	King Faisal II and the Prime Minister of Iraq, Nuri-es-Said, assassinated in Baghdad.
1959	Prime Minister of Ceylon (Sir Lanka), Solomon Bandaranaike, assassinated by a Buddhist monk (25 Sept, died 27 Sept.)
1960 Aug. 29	Prime Minister of Jordan, Hazza el-Majali, assassinated.
1963 Feb. 8	Prime Minister of Iraq, Abdul Karim Kassem, assassinated in Baghdad.
Nov. 1	Prime Minister of South Vietnam, Ngo Dinh Diem, killed during coup.
Nov. 22	President John F. Kennedy assassinated in Dallas, Texas.
1965 Feb. 21	Malcolm X, American Black Muslim leader, killed in New York.
1966 Sept. 6	Dr Verwoerd, Prime Minister of South Africa, assassinated in Cape Town.
1968 Apr. 4	Dr Martin Luther King, civil rights leader, assassinated in Memphis, Tennessee.

June 5	Robert Kennedy, brother of John and presidential candidate, assassinated by Sirhan Bishara.
July 23	Israeli Boeing 707 hijacked and flown to Algiers by Popular Front for the Liberation of Palestine; first major episode of air piracy.
Dec. 26	Palestinians attack Israeli 707 at Athens airport, killing one passenger.
Dec. 28	Israeli commandos take over Beirut airport and destroy 13 Arab aircraft.
1969 Aug. 22	US plane en route to Tel Aviv hijacked and forced to fly to Damascus where it is destroyed; hostages exchanged for Syrian prisoners.
1970 Feb. 10	Arab attack at Munich airport kills one Israeli and injures 11 others.
Mar. 31	German Ambassador to Guatemala kidnapped; found dead (5 Apr.).
July 31	American diplomat kidnapped and killed by Tupamaros guerrillas in Montevideo, Uruguay.
Sept. 6–12	Palestinian terrorists hijack three planes en route for New York, a fourth hijack is foiled. Two are flown to Jordan and one to Cairo. A fourth plane is hijacked and taken to Jordan; all 4 aircraft destroyed by bombs and passengers exchanged in deal for Arab terrorists in prison in Europe.
Oct. 10–18	Pierre Laporte, Quebec Labour Minister, seized by separatists in Montreal and killed.
1971 Mar. 14	Sabotage of fuel tanks in Rotterdam by pro-Palestinians.
Nov. 28	Jordanian Prime Minister, Wasif al-Tell, assassinated by Black September terrorists in Cairo.
1972 Feb. 6	Sabotage of gas-processing plants in Rotterdam by Black September.
Feb. 21–3	Hijack of Lufthansa jet from New Delhi to Athens; crew and passengers released after Palestinians paid $5 million.
Feb. 22	Provisional IRA bomb at barracks in Aldershot, Britain, kills 7 soldiers.
Mar. 21	Fiat executive Oberdan Sallustro kidnapped by Argentinian urban guerrillas; killed (10 Apr.).
May 8	Belgian airplane hijacked en route from Vienna to Tel Aviv; Israeli soldiers kill 2 hijackers.
May 30	Japanese Red Army terrorists attack aircraft passengers at Lod airport near Tel Aviv, killing 26.
July 21	Bombings in Northern Ireland kill 9 people in Belfast.

Sept. 5	Black September attack Israeli athletes at Munich Olympics; 2 athletes, 9 hostages, 5 terrorists, and one policeman die.

1973 Mar. 1	US Ambassador to Sudan and a Belgian diplomat killed when Black September seize embassy in Khartoum.
Mar. 10	Governor of Bermuda and aide assassinated.
Aug. 5	Attack on Athens airport by Palestinians kills 5.
Sept. 20	Spanish Prime Minister, Luís Carrero Blanco, assassinated by Basque terrorist bomb in Madrid.

1974 Feb. 3	IRA suitcase bomb kills 11 British soldiers on a coach in Yorkshire.
Feb. 5	Patty Hearst kidnapped by Symbionese Liberation Army.
Apr. 11	Arab terrorists kill 18 people in apartment block in Kiryat Shmona and are killed themselves.
May 17	Car bombs in Dublin and Monaghan, Ireland, kill 30.
May 28	Bomb at anti-fascist rally in Brescia, Italy, kills 7.
June 17	Bomb on Rome–Munich train by neo-Fascist Black Order kills 12.
June 17	IRA bomb at Tower of London kills one person.
Oct. 5	IRA plant bomb in Guildford, England, killing 5 and wounding 70.
Nov. 21	Birmingham, England, pubs bombed by IRA, killing 21.

1975 Mar. 25	King Feisal of Saudi Arabia assassinated.
July 4	Palestinian bomb in Jerusalem kills 14.
Dec. 2–14	South Moluccan terrorists seize train in Netherlands, killing 2 people before surrender.
Dec. 21	OPEC HQ in Vienna seized by Palestinians and Baader-Meinhof terrorists.
Dec. 29	11 killed by bomb at La Guardia airport.

1976 Jan. 4	5 Catholics assassinated in Belfast.
Jan. 5	10 Protestant workmen assassinated in Belfast.
Feb. 13	Nigerian head of state, General Mohammed, killed in attempted coup.
June 16	American Ambassador to Lebanon and aide kidnapped and killed.
June 27–July 3	Palestinian and Baader-Meinhof terrorists hijack Air France airbus en route from Tel Aviv to Paris and fly to Entebbe, Uganda. Israeli forces make surprise assault, killing 7 hijackers and 20 Ugandan troops; most hostages safely released.
July 21	British Ambassador to Ireland, Christopher Ewart-Biggs, and his secretary killed by IRA.

Aug. 11	Palestinians kill 4 people at Istanbul airport awaiting El Al flight.
1977 Apr. 7	Baader–Meinhof terrorists kill West German chief federal prosecutor and 7 others.
Apr. 10	Former Yemeni Prime Minister assassinated with Yemeni ambassador in London.
May 23	South Moluccan terrorists seize a train at Assen and a school at Bovinsmilde.
Sept. 5–Oct. 19	German industrialist, Hans-Martin Schleyer, kidnapped and murdered by terrorists.
Oct. 11	President of Yemen and brother assassinated.
Oct. 13	Lufthansa aircraft hijacked to Aden, then to Mogadishu where stormed by German commandos.
1978 Feb. 17	IRA bomb at restaurant in Belfast kills 12.
Feb. 18–19	Palestinian gunmen seize hostages in Cyprus after killing Egyptian newspaper editor, Yusuf el Sebai; Egyptian troops attempt to seize plane but 15 of them killed in gun battle.
Mar. 11	Palestinian terrorists kill 35 people on a bus travelling between Haifa and Tel Aviv.
Mar. 16	Aldo Moro, former Italian premier kidnapped and five bodyguards killed; found dead (10 May).
May 20	Arab attack on El Al flight passengers at Orly airport, Paris.
July 9	Former premier of Iraq, General al-Naif, assassinated in London.
Aug. 6	PLO office in Islamabad attacked killing 4 people.
Aug. 13	Bombing of PLO office in Beirut kills 150. Theatre bomb in Abadan, Iran, kills over 400.
Sept. 11	Bulgarian exile, Georgei Markov, assassinated in London.
1979 Jan. 29	Red Brigades assassinate public prosecutor Emilio Alessandria in Milan.
Mar. 22	British ambassador to Netherlands, Sir Richard Sykes, assassinated by the IRA in The Hague.
Mar. 30	Airey Neave, British Conservative politician, assassinated by IRA at House of Commons.
June 16	Muslim Brotherhood kill 63 Syrian cadets at Aleppo.
July 13	Palestinian attack on Egyptian embassy in Istanbul.
Aug. 27	IRA bomb kills 18 British soldiers at Warrenpoint, Northern Ireland.
Aug. 27	Lord Mountbatten and 3 others assassinated by IRA in Sligo, Ireland, by IRA bomb.
Nov. 20–Dec. 4	Grand Mosque, Mecca, seized by Muslim extremists, over 160 killed.

1980 Jan. 31	35 killed when police storm Spanish embassy in Guatemala seized by guerrillas.
Mar. 24	Archbishop of San Salvador assassinated by right-wing death-squad; 39 killed at his funeral (30 Mar.).
Apr. 30	British SAS storm Iranian embassy in London following seizure of embassy and hostages by Iranian gunmen; 2 hostages and 5 terrorists killed.
Aug. 2	Bombing of Bologna railway station by neo-fascist terror group kills 84.
Sept. 17	Assassination of Anastasio Somoza, former President of Nicaragua, in Paraguay.
Sept. 26	Bomb at Munich beer festival kills 12.
Dec. 31	Bombing of Norfolk Hotel in Nairobi, Jewish-owned, kills 16.
1981 Jan. 21	Sir Norman Strange and son assassinated by IRA in South Armagh.
Mar. 2–14	Pakistan Boeing 720 hijacked by Muslim terrorists to Kabul and Damascus; Pakistan diplomat killed.
May 13	Assassination attempt on Pope John Paul II by Turkish terrorist, Mahmet Ali Agca.
May 30	President Ziaur Rahman of Bangladesh killed by rebel army officers at Chittagong.
Aug. 30	President and Prime Minister of Iran killed by bomb.
Oct. 6	President Sadat of Egypt assassinated at military review in Cairo.
Sept. 14	President-elect of Lebanon, Bashir Gamayel, killed by bomb.
Nov. 28	Muslim Brotherhood bombing in Damascus kills 64.
1982 Mar. 30	Bomb on Paris–Toulouse train kills 6.
June 3	Israeli ambassador to London shot.
July 20	IRA bombs in Hyde Park and Regent's Park kill 10 bandsmen and soldiers.
Aug. 7	Armenian terrorists kill 11 in attack on Ankara airport, Turkey (7 Aug.).
Aug. 21	Benigno Aquino, Philippine opposition leader, killed at Manila airport.
Dec. 6	IRA pub-bombing at Ballykelly, Northern Ireland, kills 17.
1983 Apr. 18	Bomb attack on American embassy, Beirut, kills 60.
July 27	Armenian terrorists seize Turkish embassy in Lisbon; shoot-out leaves 5 terrorists dead.
Oct. 9	4 South Korean cabinet ministers and 17 others killed by bomb attack in Rangoon.
Oct. 19	Prime Minister of Grenada killed by rebels.

Nov. 4	Suicide truck-bombings of US Marine headquarters and French barracks in Beirut kill 241 Americans and 58 French. Suicide bombing of Israeli HQ in Tyre kills 60.
Dec. 17	Bombing of Harrods store in London by IRA kills 6.

1984 Oct. 12	Bombing of Grand Hotel, Brighton, by IRA kills 5, and narrowly misses killing British Prime Minister and senior ministers.
Oct. 31	Mrs Indira Gandhi, Indian Prime Minister, assassinated by members of bodyguard.
Dec. 23	Bomb on train in Florence kills 15.

1985 Apr. 12	Bombing by Muslim extremists in Madrid kills 18.
June 14–30	American jet hijacked by Lebanese Shi'ite terrorists; one American passenger killed, before hostages exchanged for Shi'ite prisoners held by Israel.
June 19	Bomb at Frankfurt airport kills 3.
July 24	Mine attack on train in Burma kills 70.
Oct. 7	Palestinians seize Italian cruise liner *Achille Lauro*, killing one passenger.
Nov. 6	M-19 guerrillas in Colombia seize Palace of Justice in Bogota; storming of building leaves all terrorists and 72 others dead.
Nov. 23–24	Egyptian airliner hijacked by PLO splinter group; one hostage and 60 others die when plane stormed by Egyptian commandos.
Dec. 27	Arab terrorist attack on Rome airport kills 14.

1986 Feb. 28	Swedish Prime Minister Olaf Palme assassinated.
Apr. 5	West Berlin discotheque bombed, one US serviceman and a woman killed.
Apr. 25	Five Civil Guards killed by Basque bomb in Madrid.
July 14	Basque separatists kill 11 Civil Guards in Madrid.
Sept. 7	President Pinochet of Chile escapes assassination attempt, but 5 bodyguards die.
Nov. 17	Action Directe terrorists kill Georges Besse, Chairman of Renault, in Paris.

1987 Apr. 17	Over 100 killed in Tamil bus ambush in Sri Lanka.
Apr. 21	Bomb in Colombo (Sri Lanka) bus station kills 150.
June 1	Lebanese Premier, Mr Rashid Karami, assassinated.
June 2	30 Buddhist monks killed by Tamil guerrillas.
June 19	Car bomb in Barcelona by Basque separatists kills 17.
July 6	36 bus passengers killed by Sikh extremists in Punjab; another 34 killed next day.
July 14	Bombing in Karachi kills 72.

Nov. 8	Bomb at Remembrance Day ceremony in Enniskillen, Northern Ireland, kills 17.
Nov. 9	Bomb in Colombo by Tamil separatists kills 32.
Nov. 29	Bomb on Korean airliner kills all 116 passengers.

1988 Mar. 6	3 IRA bombers shot by British SAS in Gibraltar.
Mar. 16	Loyalist gunman kills 3 at IRA funeral.
Apr. 14	Car bomb in Naples kills 5 US servicemen.
Apr. 22-May 5	17 killed in shoot-out with Kanak separatists in New Caledonia following seizure of hostages.
June 15	6 soldiers killed by IRA bomb at Lisburn, Northern Ireland.
Aug. 17	President Zia of Pakistan killed by bomb on aircraft.
Aug. 20	8 soldiers killed by bus bomb in Northern Ireland.
Sept. 30	60 killed by gunmen in Hyderabad, Pakistan.
Oct. 30	Petrol bomb attack by Palestinians at Jericho kills 4.
Dec. 21	Terrorist bomb kills 259 on PanAm jet which crashes in Lockerbie, Scotland, killing 11 residents.

1989 Jan. 23	Guerrilla attack on army barracks in Argentina leaves 38 dead.
Apr. 13	45 killed in Tamil bombing at Trincomalee.
Sept. 22	IRA bomb attack on barracks at Deal, England, kills 12 bandsmen.
Nov. 22	New president of Lebanon, Rene Mouawad, killed by a car bomb.
Nov. 30	Red Army Faction car bomb kills Alfred Herrhausen, chief executive of the Deutsche Bank, at Bad Homburg near Frankfurt.

1990 Jan. 2	Loyalist killed by car bomb in East Belfast.
Jan. 20	IRA bomb kills boy during Bloody Sunday anniversary march.
Feb. 4	9 dead in attack on tourist bus near Ismalia. Many wounded.
Mar. 28	Maoist guerrillas use car bombs and assassination to disrupt Peru's elections.
Apr. 3	Bomb planted by Sikh separatists kills 32 and injures 50 in Punjab.
Apr. 11	Teeside Customs in UK seizes parts of suspected 'supergun' destined for Iraq.
June	IRA bomb damages home of Lord McAlpine, ex-treasurer of the Conservative Party. Later the same month, IRA bombs Carlton Club in London's West End.
July 30	Conservative MP Ian Gow assassinated by IRA car bombs at his Sussex home.

Sept.	Sir Peter Terry, former governor of Gibraltar, shot and wounded by IRA.
1991 Feb. 7	IRA mortar bomb attack on British cabinet at 10 Downing Street.
Feb. 18	IRA bombs Paddington and Victoria railway stations, London. All London rail terminals temporarily closed.
May 21	Leader of the Congress (I) Party, Rajiv Gandhi, is assassinated near Madras.
June 15	Sikh terrorists in Punjab kill 74 in attack on 2 passenger trains.
Aug. 8	Former Iranian prime minister Shahpour Bakhtiar and his secretary assassinated in Paris.
1992 Feb 5	5 Catholics killed in Belfast betting shop. British government begins review of Protestant Ulster Defence Association (UDA) activities. UDA proscribed in August.
Feb. 16	Sheikh Abbas Mussawi (leader of pro-Iranian Hezbollah), his wife, son and bodyguards assassinated in Israeli raid on Lebanon.
Mar. 17	Israeli embassy in Buenos Aires bombed; 29 people killed and 252 wounded. The Iranian-backed Islamic *Jihad* claims responsibility.
Apr. 10	IRA bombs Baltic Exchange building in City of London; 3 dead, 80 injured.
June 29	President Mohamed Boudiaf of Algeria assassinated.
Aug. 21	Neo-Nazis launch 5 night attacks on hostels of asylum-seekers in Rostock and elsewhere.
Oct.	Death toll of 164 after Tamil rebels massacre 4 mainly Muslim villages in the northcentral district of Polonnaruwa. Worst massacre since 140 Muslims killed at Katankudy in 1990.
Nov. 14	IRA 'Bookmaker's Shop Massacre' in North Belfast. 3 killed, 12 injured. IRA bombing also devastates centre of Coleraine.
1993 Feb. 26	7 dead, 1,000 injured in car bomb explosion in World Trade Center, New York.
Mar. 12	300 dead, over 1,300 injured by co-ordinated series of bombings in heart of Bombay.
Mar. 16	80 dead in bombings in congested Bow Bazaar area of Calcutta.
Apr. 10	Leading ANC figure Chris Hani assassinated by right-wing extremist in South Africa.

Apr. 24	City of London bombed by IRA for second time (in Bishopsgate).
May 1	President Premadasa assassinated by Tamil Tiger suicide bomber.
May 27	Uffizi gallery in Florence devastated by bomb.
May 29	5 Turks killed at Solingen, Germany, after arson attacks by neo-Nazis.
July 2	40 people die in hotel in Sivas (Turkey) set ablaze by Muslim fundamentalists in protest against Salman Rushdie's novel *The Satanic Verses*. Translator of part of the book staying at the hotel.
July	Co-ordinated attacks by PKK guerrillas in 28 cities across Europe and at seaside resort of Antalya, Turkey.
July 25	12 killed when hooded gunmen attack churchgoers at St James Church, Kenilworth (a Cape Town suburb).
Sept. 8	19 dead and 22 injured in shooting at Wadeville industrial zone, east of Johannesburg.
Sept. 22	'Day of terror' as 31 die on day parliament debates formation of Transitional Council in South Africa.
Oct. 23	IRA bomb kills 10, injures 56, in attack on UDA headquarters in Shankhill Road, West Belfast.
Oct. 30	7 killed as loyalist gunmen attack Rising Sun pub, Greysteel, Northern Ireland.
1994 Apr. 6	Assassination of presidents of Rwanda and Burundi in missile attack on their plane.
Apr. 6	Suicide attack on school bus by Hamas organization in Afula (in revenge for Hebron massacre). 7 dead, 50 injured.
Apr. 13	Second revenge attack by Hamas on commuter bus at Hadera, central Israel.
Apr. 24	9 dead, 90 injured in car bomb near ANC headquarters in central Johannesburg.
July 18	Bombing of a Jewish cultural centre in Buenos Aires. 100 dead.
1995 Apr. 19	Car bomb blows up Oklahoma City federal building. 168 dead.
June	Chechen terrorists seize 1,500 people in Budennovsk, Russia (166 die).
Nov. 4	Prime Minister Yitzhak Rabin assassinated by Jewish extremist at peace rally.
1996 Mar. 4	Suicide bombing leaves 59 dead in Israel.
June 25	Truck bomb explodes at US base in Saudi Arabia. 19 dead.
July 25	Bomb explodes at Summer Olympic Games in Atlanta, USA.

1997 Sept. 4	Hamas suicide bombers claim the lives of more than 20 Israeli civilians.
Nov. 17	Islamic militants kill 62 at Luxor tourist site, Egypt.
1998 Aug. 7	US embassies in Kenya and Tanzania bombed; Islamic extremist Osama bin Laden believed to have been responsible.
Aug. 20	US cruise missiles hit suspected terrorist bases in Sudan and Afghanistan.
1999 Apr. 5	2 Libyan suspects tried in the Hague on charges of planting bomb that blew up PanAm Flight 103 over Scotland in 1988, killing 270 people.
2000 Oct. 12	The US Navy missile destroyer USS *Cole* is damaged in a terrorist attack while refueling in Aden. 17 sailors are killed; 39 are wounded.
2001 Sept. 11	Devastating attack by al-Qaeda terrorist group on New York and Washington. Hijacked planes destroy World Trade Center towers, as well as hitting the Pentagon. Around 2,996 people killed. USA responds with global war on terrorism. See p. 33
2002 Oct. 12	Bomb explodes outside nightclub in Bali, Indonesia, killing 202 people (including many Australians).
2003 May 12	Triple attacks on residential compounds in Riyadh, Saudi Arabia, kill 46 people.
2004 Mar. 11	200 people killed in terror attacks on trains in rush-hour Madrid.
Aug.	Suspected Chechen guerrillas blow up 2 Russian aircraft; 89 dead.
Sept.	Beslan school massacre in Russia after seizure by Chechen guerrillas. Around 340 hostages die. Car bombing of Australian embassy in Jakarta, Indonesia. 9 killed, 160 hurt.
2005 Feb. 14	Assassination of architect of Lebanese reconstruction, Rafik Hariri.

See p. 33

III
ECONOMIC AND
SOCIAL HISTORY

ESTIMATED WORLD POPULATION, 1900–2025

	Millions
1900	1,625
1925	1,950
1950	2,516
1975	4,076
2000	6,122
2025	8,206 (projected)

2025 projected figures are the medium variant
offered on current assessments of growth.
High and low variants are as follows:

	High	*Low*
2025	9,088	7,358

Source: United Nations, *World Population Prospects:
Estimates and Projections as Assessed in 1984*
(New York, 1986)

ANNUAL GROWTH OF WORLD POPULATION: SPECIMEN YEARS, 1950–2000

	Annual growth (millions)	*Total world population (thousand million)*
1950	38	2,555
1955	53	2,780
1960	41	3,039
1965	70	3,346
1970	78	3,708
1975	72	4,088
1980	76	4,457
1985	83	4,855
1990	83	5,284
1995	78	5,691
2000	78	6,122

Source: Various

POPULATION OF INDIVIDUAL COUNTRIES

Thousands, rounded to nearest thousand.

Afghanistan	1928	6,500 (est.)
	1950	8,420
	1960	10,016
	1970	12,457
	1980	14,607
	1988	19,340
	2002	27,756
Algeria	1936	6,000 (est.)
	1950	9,000 (est.)
	1966	11,822
	1972	15,270
	1977	17,422
	1988	23,820
	2002	31,261
Argentina	1930	10,500
	1947	15,894
	1960	20,011
	1970	23,362
	1980	27,947
	1985	31,730
	2002	36,446
Australia	1921	5,436
	1947	7,561
	1961	10,508
	1971	12,756
	1984	15,540
	2002	19,702
Bangladesh	1961	50,854 (East Pakistan)
	1974	71,479
	1981	87,120
	1988	103,630
	2002	133,377
Brazil	1930	41,100
	1950	51,976
	1960	79,967
	1970	92,342
	1980	118,675
	2002	174,619
Canada	1921	8,788[1]
	1931	10,376[1]
	1951	14,009
	1971	21,568

[1] Excludes Newfoundland

Canada—*cont.*	1981	24,343
	1985	25,660
	2002	31,244
China	1900	450,000 (est.)
	1930	485,000 (est.)
	1953	590,195
	1965	700,000 (est.)
	1975	933,000 (est.)
	1982	1,081,883
	1985	1,080,920
	2002	1,284,211
Congo, Democratic Republic	1947	10,805[1]
	1958	12,769[1]
	1970	21,637
	1983	31,944
	2002	52,557

[1] As Belgian Congo

Cuba	1950	5,858
	1960	7,029
	1970	8,572
	1985	10,038
	2002	11,267
Egypt	1947	18,967
	1957	22,997
	1966	30,076
	1976	36,626
	1988	51,320
	2002	66,341
France	1921	39,210
	1931	41,835
	1946	40,507
	1962	46,510
	1975	52,656
	1985	55,730
	2002	59,440

		West Germany	East Germany
Germany	1925	62,400	
	1939	69,500	
	1950	47,696	17,199
	1961	53,977	15,940
	1984	61,675	16,660
	2002	82,506 (united)	

Ghana	1921	2,078
	1950	4,242
	1960	6,772
	1970	8,614
	1980	11,457
	1988	14,045
	2002	20,244

India	1921	319,361 (inc. Pakistan)
	1951	356,879
	1961	435,512
	1971	548,160
	1981	685,120
	1988	789,120
	2002	1,047,671
Indonesia	1950	79,538
	1960	96,194
	1970	120,280
	1980	150,958
	1988	172,450
	2002	211,023
Iran	1928	12,000 (est.)
	1956	18,955
	1966	25,785
	1976	33,708
	1988	47,680
	2002	65,457
Iraq	1921	2,849
	1947	4,816
	1957	6,317
	1965	8,047
	1977	12,030
	1988	16,745
	2002	24,002
Israel	1921	757[1]
	1950	1,748
	1961	2,183
	1972	3,148
	1985	4,315
	2002	6,394

[1] Territory of British Palestine Mandate

Italy	1921	37,404
	1931	40,300
	1951	47,159
	1961	49,904
	1971	53,745
	1985	57,115
	2002	57,998
Japan	1900	43,763
	1930	60,000
	1950	83,200
	1960	93,419
	1970	103,720
	1980	117,060
	1988	122,400 (est.)
	2002	127,347
Korea, North	1965	11,100
	1975	16,000 (est.)

Korea, North— *cont.*	1985 2002	21,185 22,224
Korea, South	1950 1960 1970 1980 1985 2002	20,357 25,003 31,923 38,124 42,130 47,640
Malaysia	1921 1960 1970 1980 1989 2002	3,306[1] 10,992[2] 8,809[3] 14,157[3] 16,640[3] 24,370[3]

[1] Former Malay states, including Sarawak and Singapore
[2] Includes Singapore, Sarawak and Sabah
[3] Excludes Singapore which became a separate state in 1965

Mexico	1921 1950 1960 1970 1980 1988 2002	14,800 25,791 34,923 48,225 67,396 83,040 100,977
Netherlands	1920 1930 1947 1960 1971 1985 2002	6,865 7,936 9,625 11,462 13,061 14,454 16,142
Nigeria	1921 1953 1963 1975 1989 2002	18,500 (est.) 30,418 55,670 74,870 110,240 129,935
Pakistan	1951 1961 1972 1981 1989 2002	75,842[1] 93,832[1] 64,980 83,782 105,720 145,960

[1] Includes the population of East Pakistan which in 1971 became Bangladesh

Philippines	1950 1960 1970 1980 1988 2002	20,551 27,904 37,540 48,317 57,410 79,882

Poland	1921	27,200
	1931	32,107
	1946	23,900[1]
	1960	29,776
	1985	38,060
	2002	38,644

[1] The boundaries of the Polish state were substantially altered in 1945; figures for 1946 also reflect very large losses of population in the Second World War

South Africa	1921	6,928
	1946	11,416
	1960	16,003
	1970	21,488
	1980	24,886
	1989	34,335
	2002	45,172

Spain	1920	21,303
	1930	23,600
	1950	27,977
	1960	30,431
	1970	34,041
	1981	37,746
	1989	39,690
	2002	40,998

Sri Lanka	1921	4,505
	1960	10,965
	1971	12,711
	1981	14,850
	1987	16,550
	2002	18,870

Sudan	1921	5,850
	1955	10,260
	1973	12,428
	1983	20,564
	1988	24,235
	2002	37,090

Taiwan	1953	7,591
	1960	12,345
	1982	18,271
	2002	22,457

Tanzania	1921	4,122
	1948	8,000 (est.)
	1967	12,231
	1978	17,552
	1985	23,600 (est.)
	2002	34,902

Thailand	1930	11,000 (est.)
	1950	19,000 (est.)
	1967	29,700
	1979	45,221

Thailand—*cont.*	1985	50,610		
	2002	63,430		
Turkey	1927	13,648		
	1940	17,821		
	1955	24,065		
	1965	31,391		
	1975	40,348		
	1988	53,230		
	2002	69,001		
United Kingdom	1922	44,372		
	1939	47,762		
	1951	50,225		
	1961	52,709		
	1971	55,907		
	1985	56,618		
	2002	60,178		
United States of America	1920	105,710		
	1930	122,775		
	1940	131,669		
	1950	151,868		
	1960	179,979		
	1970	203,984		
	1980	227,236		
	1987	245,650		
	2002	287,602		
USSR[1]	1926	147,000		
	1939	170,500		
	1959	208,800[1]		
	1970	241,700[1]		
	1987	284,580[1]		
	2002	143,673[2]		

[1] Population includes those areas added to the Soviet Union as a result of boundary changes since 1939
[2] Russia

Vietnam	1930	16,500 (est.)[1]		
	1950	26,000[1]		
		North		*South*
	1964	17,900		15,715
	1970	23,787		21,154 (est.)
	1979	52,742[2]		
	1988	64,120[2]		
	2002	80,200[2]		

[1] As part of French Indochina
[2] North and South Vietnam were united in 1975

Yugoslavia	1921	11,985		
	1931	13,934		
	1948	15,700[1]		
	1961	18,549		
	1971	20,523		
	1981	22,428		

[1] Includes territory annexed in 1945

Zambia	1921	807
	1950	2,000
	1974	4,751
	1982	6,242
	2002	9,959
Zimbabwe	1921	807
	1931	1,130
	1951	2,320
	1974	6,100
	1982	7,532
	2002	11,377

Sources: United Nations, *Demographic Yearbook*

POPULATION DENSITY AND URBANIZATION: SELECTED COUNTRIES

For some countries figures are given for the nearest equivalent date.

	Population density (per sq. km)			Urban population (percentage)			
	1975	*1985*	*2002*	*1950*	*1970*	*1985*	*2002*
Afghanistan	30	30	43	5.8	11.0	18.5	22.0
Algeria	7	10	13	—	—	43.0	81.0
Angola	5	8	9	—	—	25.0	35.0
Argentina	9	11	13	62.5	80.7	85.0	90.0
Australia	2	2	3	68.9	85.6	86.0	85.0
Bangladesh	533	720	957	—	—	12.0	26.0
Bolivia	4	6	8	—	—	48.0	62.0
Brazil	13	17	21	36.2	55.9	73.0	80.0
Burma (Myanmar)	45	57	62	—	—	24.0	29.0
Canada	2	2	3	62.9	76.1	76.0	79.0
Chad	3	4	7	—	—	27.0	23.0
Chile	14	17	20	60.2	76.0	84.0	87.0
China	86	112	134	13.5	16.7	21.0	33.0
Colombia	18	26	36	37.1	57.2	67.4	74.0
Cuba	81	94	107	49.4	60.2	71.8	76.0
Czechoslovakia	116	126	129[1]	51.2	55.5	65.0	75.0[1]
Ecuador	24	35	48	—	—	52.0	61.0
Egypt	37	51	67	30.1	39.8	46.0	43.0
Ethiopia	23	37	60	—	—	12.0	16.0
France	96	102	109	55.9	70.0	73.0	76.0
Germany E.	156	153 }	231[2]	68.8	73.8	77.0 }	82.0[2]
Germany W.	249	245 }		71.1	—	86.0 }	
Ghana	41	59	85	14.5	29.1	39.6	37.8
Greece	69	76	83	36.8	64.7	69.7	60.1
Guatemala	57	79	110	30.5	35.7	41.4	39.4
Haiti	165	197	255	—	—	27.0	36.3

	Population density (per sq. km)			Urban population (percentage)			
	1975	*1985*	*2002*	*1950*	*1970*	*1985*	*2002*
Hong Kong	4,179	5,337	6,177	—	—	92.0	100.0
Hungary	113	114	109	36.5	45.2	54.3	63.6
India	182	246	331	17.3	19.9	26.0	28.0
Indonesia	69	90	110	12.4	17.1	26.3	43.0
Iran	20	29	40	30.1	44.0	52.0	64.7
Iraq	26	38	55	33.8	51.1	71.0	76.4
Israel	162	212	313	71.7	85.3	90.0	90.6
Italy	185	190	192	—	47.7	67.0	67.2
Japan	297	324	337	37.5	72.1	77.0	78.6
Kampuchea[3]	45	37	75	—	—	11.0	17.0
Kenya	23	39	53	—	—	20.0	34.0
Korea N.	132	176	181	—	—	64.0	62.2
Korea S.	352	428	479	21.4	40.7	65.0	83.0
Laos	14	16	24	—	—	16.0	25.0
Libya	2	2	3	—	—	65.0	87.6
Madagascar	11	18	28	—	—	22.0	30.1
Malawi	43	64	112	—	—	12.0	15.1
Malaysia	36	50	74	—	—	38.0	59.0
Mexico	30	42	51	42.6	58.7	70.0	71.3
Morocco	39	55	42	—	—	45.0	52.7
Mozambique	12	18	22	—	—	19.0	40.2
Nepal	89	122	161	—	—	8.0	13.0
Netherlands	334	351	476	54.6	78.0	88.4	90.0
New Zealand	11	12	14	—	—	84.0	86.0
Nicaragua	17	27	41	34.9	47.0	59.4	56.5
Niger	4	6	8	—	—	16.0	20.0
Nigeria	68	119	140	10.2	16.1	23.0	44.9
Pakistan	87	120	183	10.4	25.5	29.1	38.0
Peru	12	16	21	—	—	67.0	72.3
Philippines	142	191	266	27.1	33.0	39.6	60.0
Poland	109	122	123	39.8	52.3	61.0	61.8
Portugal	103	113	112	19.3	26.2	31.2	65.8
Romania	89	97	91	31.3	38.2	49.0	52.7
Russia	—	—	8	—	—	—	73.1
Saudi Arabia	3	6	11	—	20.8	72.0	86.7
Senegal	26	34	50	—	—	36.0	47.4
Sierra Leone	43	54	67	—	—	28.0	36.6
Singapore	3,872	4,274	6,158	—	—	100.0	100.0
Somalia	5	13	12	—	—	34.0	30.0
South Africa	20	31	37	42.6	47.9	56.0	57.7
Soviet Union	11	13	—	47.9	56.3	66.0	—
Spain	70	79	81	37.0	54.7	76.0	77.8
Sri Lanka	213	256	287	—	—	21.0	25.0
Sudan	6	8	15	—	—	21.0	37.1
Sweden	18	19	22	47.5	81.4	83.0	83.3
Switzerland	155	158	176	—	—	58.0	67.3
Syria	40	60	97	—	43.5	50.0	51.8
Taiwan	—	550	621	—	—	66.0	74.7
Tanzania	16	25	40	—	—	22.0	33.3

	Population density (per sq. km)			Urban population (percentage)			
	1975	1985	2002	1950	1970	1985	2002
Thailand	81	99	124	—	—	20.0	31.0
Tunisia	35	47	60	—	—	57.0	66.2
Turkey	51	68	89	28.8	34.4	46.0	66.2
Uganda	49	67	124	—	—	10.0	13.0
United Kingdom	229	236	247	80.8	78.0	92.0	88.0
United States	23	26	30	64.0	73.5	74.0	77.2
Uruguay	16	18	19	—	—	85.0	88.7
Venezuela	13	20	27	53.8	75.7	87.0	87.1
Vietnam	136	195	241	—	—	20.0	23.5
Yemen	27	50	35	—	—	20.0	25.0
Yugoslavia	83	92	—	18.5	38.6	46.0	—
Zaïre[4]	11	14	22	15.8	21.6	37.0	30.6
Zambia	6	10	13	—	—	50.0	43.9
Zimbabwe	16	22	29	—	—	25.0	36.0

[1] Czech Republic
[2] United Germany
[3] Cambodia
[4] Democratic Republic of the Congo after 1997
Sources: Various

POPULATION OF MAJOR WORLD CITIES

Numbers are given in thousands. The definition of urban areas for individual countries is often at variance with that of other countries; also, the definition of urban areas concerned has sometimes changed in the course of the past century. Figures here are for urban agglomerations unless otherwise stated.

	1921	1951	1956	1960	1966	1971	1981	1985	2002
Accra	—	136	—	338	—	564	—	860	1,551
Addis Ababa	—	—	—	—	—	1,083	—	1,408	2,113
Alexandria	—	919	1,278	—	1,081	—	2,576	—	3,328
Ankara	—	—	451	—	971	1,553	—	1,877	4,611
Athens	301	1,379	—	1,853	—	2,101	3,027	—	3,120
Auckland	164	—	—	—	—	797	—	—	371
Baghdad	—	—	656	—	1,657	2,184	—	2,200	4,958
Beijing (Peking)	—	—	4,010	—	—	7,570	—	9,452	6,634[3]
Belgrade	112	368	—	585	—	746	—	936	1,168
Berlin	3,801	3,337[1]	—	3,261[1]	3,268	—	—	3,049	3,392
Bogota	—	648	—	—	1,681	2,978	—	3,968	6,276
Bombay (Mumbai)	1,176	2,839	—	4,152	—	5,971	8,227	—	11,914
Brussels	685	956	—	1,020	1,075	—	997	982	959

	1921	1951	1956	1960	1966	1971	1981	1985	2002
Bucharest	309	—	1,237	—	1,519	—	1,979	1,995	2,027
Budapest	1,185	—	1,850	—	1,960	—	—	2,071	1,775
Buenos Aires	—	4,603	—	7,000	—	8,925	9,927	—	2,904
Cairo	—	—	2,877	—	4,220	—	5,650	—	10,345
Calcutta (Kolkata)	1,327	4,578	—	4,405	—	7,031	9,166	—	13,216
Cape Town	207	578	—	807	—	1,108	—	—	2,930
Caracas	—	694	—	—	1,764	—	2,944	—	3,177
Chicago	—	3,621	—	3,550	—	3,369	3,005	2,992	2,896
Colombo	244	—	—	—	—	—	—	—	642
Damascus	—	—	409	—	618	923	1,251	—	1,550
Delhi	304	1,384	—	2,359	—	3,647	5,714	—	12,791
Freetown	—	—	—	—	—	—	—	—	470
Guatemala City	—	284	—	439	—	707	793	—	1,167
Hamburg	986	—	1,760	—	1,851	—	—	1,600	1,702
Hanoi	—	—	—	644	—	1,400	—	—	2,155
Ho Chi Minh City[2]	—	—	—	—	—	1,825	—	—	4,549
Hong Kong	600	2,240	—	—	—	—	5,109	5,364	6,785
Houston	—	596	—	938	—	1,234	1,595	—	1,953
Istanbul	—	—	1,269	—	2,053	3,135	2,948	—	10,253
Jakarta	—	—	1,865	2,907	—	4,576	6,503	—	9,341
Johannesburg	288	884	—	1,153	—	1,441	1,534	—	2,950
Kabul	—	154	—	—	400	318	377	913	2,602
Karachi	—	1,126	—	—	2,721	3,499	5,103	—	9,269
Khartoum	—	—	—	—	—	228	—	476	924
Kiev	366	—	—	1,104	1,413	—	2,355	—	2,602
Kinshasa	—	—	290	—	508	2,008	—	2,654	4,655
Kuala Lumpur	80	—	—	—	—	452	—	938	1,298
Lagos	—	272	—	665	—	1,080	—	1,404	5,197
Lahore	282	849	—	—	1,674	2,165	2,922	—	5,063
Leningrad	722[5]	—	—	3,300	3,706	—	4,779	—	4,628[4]
Lima	—	—	—	—	—	3,318	5,259	—	7,061
Lisbon	486	790	—	817	—	762	—	807	3,447
London	7,488	8,348	—	8,172	7,914	7,281	6,754	6,851	7,074
Los Angeles	—	1,970	—	2,479	—	2,812	2,967	3,097	3,694
Madras (Chennai)	523	1,416	—	1,729	—	3,170	4,277	—	6,425
Madrid	751	—	1,775	2,260	2,559	—	3,188	3,217	2,939[3]
Managua	—	109	—	235	—	399	608	644	—
Manila	—	984	—	1,139	—	1,436	1,630	—	1,581
Melbourne	795	—	1,524	—	2,108	2,584	2,604	—	3,366
Mexico	—	2,335	—	2,698	—	7,315	—	8,831	8,591
Montreal	619	—	1,621	—	2,437	—	2,862	—	3,511
Moscow	1,050	—	—	5,032	5,507	—	8,396	8,408	8,546
New York	—	7,892	—	7,782	—	7,896	7,072	7,165	8,008
Osaka	—	—	2,547	—	3,133	—	—	2,632	2,598
Paris	2,907	2,850	4,823	2,790	—	—	8,510	—	9,644
Pusan	—	474	—	1,271	—	1,842	3,160	—	3,655
Rio de Janeiro	—	2,303	—	3,124	—	4,252	5,093	—	5,850
Riyadh	—	—	150	—	225	668	—	1,250	4,549
Rome	692	1,652	2,188	—	2,485	—	2,840	2,832	2,644
Rotterdam	511	—	712	—	1,048	—	—	1,021	989

	1921	1951	1956	1960	1966	1971	1981	1985	2002
Santiago	—	—	1,539	—	2,314	—	4,132	—	4,647
São Paulo	—	2,017	—	3,674	—	5,870	7,034	—	9,786
Seoul	—	1,446	—	2,983	—	5,433	8,364	9,646	9,854
Shanghai	—	—	6,900	—	—	10,820	—	12,048	8,937[3]
Singapore	303	—	—	—	—	2,278	—	2,529	4,204
Stockholm	419	744	—	809	1,262	1,493	—	1,562	755[3]
Sydney	906	—	1,863	—	2,445	2,874	3,022	—	3,997
Tehran	—	—	1,512	—	2,695	3,150	—	5,734	6,758
Tel Aviv	—	—	364	—	392	1,091	1,305	—	354
Tokyo	—	—	7,867	—	11,005	—	—	8,389	8,134
Toronto	521	—	1,358	—	2,158	—	3,067	—	4,881
Vancouver	117	—	665	—	892	—	1,311	—	2,079
Vienna	1,866	1,766	—	1,628	—	1,615	1,516	1,531	1,562
Warsaw	931	804	—	—	1,261	—	1,621	1,649	1,610

[1] East and West Berlin
[2] Previously known as Saigon
[3] Metropolitan area only
[4] St Petersburg
[5] The population of Leningrad was artificially depressed in 1921 as a result of the Russian revolution; its population in 1911 was 1,962,000
Sources: Various

LIFE EXPECTANCY AT BIRTH FOR WORLD AND WORLD AREAS, 1950–85

	World	Africa	Latin America	North America	East Asia	South Asia	Europe	Oceania	USSR
1950–55	46.0	37.8	51.1	69.1	42.7	39.9	65.3	60.8	64.1
1975–80	58.0	47.6	62.6	73.3	66.6	52.7	72.3	66.5	69.6
1980–85	59.5	49.3	64.2	74.4	68.4	54.9	73.1	67.9	70.9

Source: United Nations, *World Population Prospects: Estimates and Projections as Assessed in 1984* (New York, 1986)

INFANT MORTALITY RATE FOR WORLD AND WORLD AREAS, 1950–85

Deaths by age 1 year per 1,000 live births.

	World	Africa	Latin America	North America	East Asia	South Asia	Europe	Oceania	USSR
1950–55	156	191	125	29	182	180	62	67	73
1975–80	85	124	70	14	39	115	19	36	28
1980–85	78	112	62	11	36	103	15	31	25

Source: United Nations, *World Population Prospects: Estimates and Projections as Assessed in 1984* (New York, 1986)

MEDIAN AGE OF THE WORLD POPULATION BY MAJOR AREAS, 1950–85

	World	Africa	Latin America	North America	East Asia	South Asia	Europe	Oceania	USSR
1950	23.4	18.8	19.7	30.0	23.5	20.4	30.5	27.9	24.7
1975	21.9	17.5	19.1	28.6	21.5	19.0	32.3	25.7	29.1
1985	23.5	17.3	20.8	31.3	24.7	20.3	33.9	27.6	30.3

Source: United Nations, *World Population Prospects: Estimates and Projections as Assessed in 1984* (New York, 1986)

BIRTH AND DEATH RATES: SELECTED COUNTRIES, 2000

	Birth rate (per 1,000)	*Death rate (per 1,000)*
World average	22.5	9.0
Afghanistan	41.8	18.0
Albania[1]	21.2	6.5
Algeria	19.8	5.5
Angola	46.9	25.0
Argentina	18.2	7.6
Australia	12.8	7.4
Bangladesh	30.1	8.8
Belarus	9.4	13.5
Bolivia	31.9	8.6

	Birth rate (per 1,000)	Death rate (per 1,000)
Brazil	18.8	9.4
Bulgaria	9.0	14.1
Cambodia	35.2	10.6
Canada	10.8	7.5
Chad[1]	48.3	15.4
Chile	17.2	5.5
China	14.9	7.0
Colombia	22.9	5.7
Congo (Democratic Republic)	46.4	15.4
Costa Rica	19.7	4.0
Côte d'Ivoire	40.4	16.6
Cuba	12.7	7.3
Egypt	25.4	7.8
Ethiopia	45.1	17.6
France	10.8	9.1
Germany[1]	9.0	10.0
Ghana	29.0	10.3
Greece	11.7	10.5
Guatemala	35.1	6.9
Hungary	9.5	13.0
India	24.8	8.9
Indonesia	20.3	7.1
Iran	18.3	5.5
Iraq	34.6	6.2
Ireland	14.3	8.2
Israel	21.7	6.0
Italy	9.1	10.1
Japan	9.4	7.8
Kenya	28.5	14.4
Korea N.	20.4	6.9
Korea S.	11.6	5.1
Laos	36.0	12.8
Liberia	46.6	16.4
Madagascar	42.9	12.7
Malawi[1]	37.8	22.8
Malaysia	23.2	4.4
Mexico	23.2	5.0
Morocco	23.6	5.9
Mozambique	37.2	24.2
Myanmar	23.5	11.6
Nepal	34.2	10.0
Netherlands[1]	12.6	8.8
New Zealand	14.2	7.6
Nicaragua	28.3	4.9
Nigeria[1]	39.7	13.9
Pakistan	36.5	9.8
Paraguay	31.3	4.8
Peru	23.4	5.7
Poland	9.5	9.4
Romania	10.8	12.3

	Birth rate (per 1,000)	Death rate (per 1,000)
Russia	8.7	15.4
Saudi Arabia	37.5	6.0
Sierra Leone	45.6	19.6
Somalia	47.2	18.4
South Africa	19.8	15.0
Spain	10.0	9.3
Sri Lanka	17.3	6.3
Sudan[1]	37.9	10.0
Sweden[1]	10.3	10.5
Switzerland	11.0	8.7
Syria[1]	30.6	5.2
Tanzania	39.7	13.0
Thailand	14.0	6.0
Tunisia	17.1	5.0
Turkey	18.6	6.0
Uganda	48.0	22.4
Ukraine[1]	9.3	16.4
United Kingdom	11.4	10.2
United States	14.7	8.7
Uruguay	16.1	9.5
Venezuela	20.2	4.9
Vietnam	21.6	6.3
Zambia	41.9	22.1
Zimbabwe[1]	31.0	19.7

[1] 1999
Sources: Various

NATURAL INCREASE AND LIFE EXPECTANCY: SELECTED COUNTRIES, 2000

	Natural increase (per 1,000 pop.)	Life expectancy (years)	
		Male	Female
World average	13.5	—	—
Afghanistan	23.8	46.6	45.1
Albania	12.1	63.3	75.1
Algeria	14.3	68.3	71.0
Angola	21.9	37.1	39.6
Argentina	10.6	72.1	79.0
Australia	5.4	76.6	82.0
Bangladesh	21.3	60.0	61.0
Belarus	−4.1	63.4	74.7
Bolivia	23.3	61.2	66.3

	Natural increase (per 1,000 pop.)	Life expectancy (years)	
		Male	Female
Brazil	9.4	58.5	67.6
Bulgaria	−5.1	68.2	75.3
Cambodia	24.6	54.0	59.0
Canada	3.3	76.0	83.0
Chad	32.9	48.9	53.0
Chile	11.7	72.4	79.2
China	—	69.0	73.0
Colombia	17.2	66.4	74.3
Congo	31.0	47.6	50.8
Costa Rica	15.7	74.2	79.9
Côte d'Ivoire	23.8	43.6	46.3
Cuba	5.4	73.8	78.3
Egypt	17.6	61.3	65.5
Ethiopia	27.5	44.4	45.9
France	1.7	74.8	82.9
Germany	1.3	74.4	80.6
Ghana	18.7	55.9	58.7
Greece	1.2	75.9	81.2
Guatemala	4.7	63.5	69.0
Hungary	−3.5	67.1	75.6
India	15.9	61.9	63.1
Indonesia	—	65.0	69.0
Iran	12.8	68.3	71.5
Iraq	28.4	65.9	68.0
Ireland	6.1	74.1	79.7
Israel	15.7	76.6	80.4
Italy	−1.0	75.9	82.5
Japan	1.6	77.5	84.0
Kenya	14.1	46.6	48.4
Korea N.	13.5	67.8	73.9
Korea S.	6.5	72.0	79.0
Laos	23.2	52.0	55.9
Liberia	30.2	50.0	52.9
Madagascar	30.2	52.7	57.3
Malawi[1]	15.0	36.6	37.6
Malaysia	18.8	70.4	75.3
Mexico	18.2	68.5	74.7
Morocco	17.7	67.5	72.1
Mozambique	13.0	37.3	35.6
Myanmar	11.9	54.0	59.0
Nepal	24.2	60.0	59.0
Netherlands	3.8	75.8	80.7
New Zealand	6.6	75.0	81.0
Nicaragua	23.4	66.8	70.8
Nigeria	25.8	51.1	51.7
Pakistan	26.7	61.0	61.0
Paraguay	26.5	71.2	76.2
Peru	17.7	68.2	73.1

| | Natural increase (per 1,000 pop.) | Life expectancy (years) | |
		Male	Female
Poland	0.1	69.7	78.0
Romania	−1.7	66.1	74.0
Russia	−6.7	59.0	72.2
Saudi Arabia	31.5	66.1	69.5
Sierra Leone	26.0	42.4	48.2
Somalia	28.8	45.0	48.3
South Africa	4.8	50.7	51.4
Spain	0.7	75.6	82.5
Sri Lanka	11.0	70.0	76.0
Sudan	27.9	55.9	58.1
Sweden	−0.2	77.6	82.1
Switzerland	2.3	76.9	82.6
Syria[1]	25.4	67.6	70.0
Tanzania	26.7	51.0	53.0
Thailand	8.0	70.0	75.0
Tunisia	—	72.4	75.6
Turkey	12.7	68.6	73.4
Uganda	25.6	42.2	43.7
Ukraine	−7.1	60.6	72.0
United Kingdom	1.2	75.4	80.2
United States	6.0	—	—
Uruguay	4.2	70.9	78.8
Venezuela	—	70.5	76.8
Vietnam	15.3	66.8	71.9
Zambia	19.8	37.1	37.4
Zimbabwe	11.3	43.1	39.7

[1] 1999
Sources: Various

LIFE EXPECTANCY AND INFANT MORTALITY BY REGION, 2000

| Region | Life expectancy (years) | | Infant mortality (per 1,000 live births) |
	Male	Female	
World	**64.3**	**68.3**	**55.2**
Africa	**51.1**	**53.1**	**86.7**
Central Africa	47.3	50.4	107.3
East Africa	44.9	46.3	94.8
North Africa	63.2	66.7	59.0
Southern Africa	50.2	52.4	63.1
West Africa	50.3	51.5	85.6

Region	Life expectancy (years)		Infant mortality (per 1,000 live births)
	Male	Female	
Americas	**68.6**	**74.8**	**25.1**
North-America	74.3	80.0	6.8
Canada	76.0	83.0	5.1
United States	74.1	79.7	6.9
Latin America	65.2	71.6	32.4
Caribbean	67.3	72.0	43.8
Central America	67.1	72.5	34.3
Mexico	68.5	74.7	26.2
South America	63.8	70.6	32.9
Andean group	68.0	71.7	31.0
Brazil	58.5	67.6	38.0
Other South America	71.8	78.4	20.9
Asia	**65.9**	**68.9**	**53.5**
Eastern Asia	69.9	74.3	34.2
China	69.0	73.0	37.0
Japan	77.5	84.0	3.4
South Korea	72.0	79.0	7.0
Other eastern Asia	71.3	77.2	31.0
South Asia	61.4	62.3	70.4
India	61.9	63.1	64.9
Pakistan	61.0	60.0	85.0
Other South Asia	59.2	60.0	80.6
South-east Asia	**65.9**	**69.8**	**40.0**
South-west Asia	**66.4**	**71.0**	**45.2**
Central Asia	63.1	71.0	45.4
Gulf Co-operation Council	67.8	71.3	45.7
Iran	68.3	71.5	30.0
Other south-west Asia	66.4	70.6	49.3
Europe	**66.2**	**74.2**	**9.4**
Eastern Europe	63.5	73.9	15.4
Russia	59.9	72.4	15.3
Ukraine	60.6	72.0	21.7
Other Eastern Europe	68.2	76.1	13.7
Western Europe	68.6	74,3	5.0
Oceania	**71.9**	**76.8**	**26.2**
Australia	76.6	82.0	6.0
Pacific Ocean Islands	67.1	71.6	42.8

Sources: UN census data.

MAJOR POPULATION AND REFUGEE MOVEMENTS

1914   Outbreak of First World War halts massive outflow of emigrants from Europe. Thousands of Belgian refugees flee to Britain and France with German occupation of most of Belgium.

1915–20   Massacres of Armenians by Turks drive hundreds of thousands of Armenians to seek refuge in Soviet Armenia and the Near East.

1917–21   Over a million 'White Russians' flee Russia during the Revolution and Civil War, mainly to France, Britain, Turkey and the United States.

1919–22   Almost 2 million Greeks expelled from Turkey and Bulgaria to Greece and Crete; over 400,000 Turks returned from Crete and Greece to Turkey; 250,000 Bulgarians leave Greece for Bulgaria.

1933–40   Between 250,000 and 300,000 Jewish refugees flee to parts of Europe, Palestine, the United States and Latin America to escape Nazi persecution. Another 70,000 flee the Baltic States to Russia.

1939–40   130,000 *Volksdeutsche* transferred from Soviet Poland to German area of Poland.

1940   Approximately 400,000 Finns evacuate area of Karelia ceded to the USSR. 100,000 Germans from Russia and Bessarabia transferred to Poland or Germany. Several million French and Belgians flee into unoccupied southern France.

1941   Stalin deports 400,000 Volga Germans and other minorities suspected of disaffection to Siberia and Central Asia.

1944   Approximately 7 million foreign workers employed in Germany at peak of war effort.

1944–5   1.2 million Germans flee westward in face of Russian advance.

1945–50   An estimated 1 million German POWs remain in the USSR after peace. 1.4 million 'displaced persons' in Germany, mainly consisting of persons unwilling or unable to return to their home country. Continued flight from east into Allied-occupied Germany; approximately a third of West German population by 1950 consists of people not born in its territory. Repatriation of approximately 3 million Japanese from Co-Prosperity Sphere, Manchuria, Korea and China to Japanese mainland.

1947   At partition of India over 17 million Hindu and Muslim refugees flee to join co-religionists in the new independent states of India and Pakistan.

1948   Jewish population of Palestine rises to 800,000 from 84,000 in 1922 as a result of increased flow of immigrants.

1948–9   Creation of state of Israel and Arab–Israeli War lead to displacement of about a million Palestinian Arab refugees to Syria, Lebanon, Jordan and Egypt.

1948–60   Almost a million Jews, many from Eastern Europe and north Africa, emigrate to Israel.

1949   Approximately 2 million Nationalist Chinese under Chiang Kai-shek flee to Formosa (Taiwan) after communist victory in Chinese Civil War.

1950–3   Korean War displaces approximately 3 million Koreans from North to South Korea.

1956   Approximately 200,000 Hungarians flee to West following uprising.

1958   First arrivals of Commonwealth immigrants from West Indies in United Kingdom; beginnings of mass immigration to United Kingdom from West Indies and Indian subcontinent of approximately 1.5 million. By 1985 a total of 2.4 million non-whites in Britain, 40% born there.

1959   Australia alters immigration rules to facilitate non-English speaking immigrants; by 1963 there are 250,000 Italian immigrants. Dalai Lama heads flight of Tibetan refugees to India after Chinese crush revolt.

1960   Beginning of 'guest-worker' system in Germany; by 1970s approximately 2.5 million workers come from Yugoslavia and Turkey.

1971   Thousands of Bangladeshis flee into India to escape fighting in aftermath of declaration of independence.

1972   Ugandan ruler Idi Amin expels 50,000 Ugandan Asians.

1975   Communist victory in Vietnam leads to exodus of 'boat people' to other countries of south-east Asia.

1979   Soviet invasion of Afghanistan leads to an estimated 2 million Afghan refugees in camps in Pakistan.
        Thousands of refugees flee Cambodia for Thailand following Vietnamese invasion to end Pol Pot regime; Red Cross estimates 2 million people in danger inside and outside Cambodia as a result of disruption.

1980   Relief agencies report 2 million refugees in East Africa, mainly in Somalia, Ethiopia and Sudan, as a result of war and drought. Somalia estimated to have biggest refugee problem in the world and a million refugees have fled to Sudan from Ethiopia, Zaïre, Chad and Uganda.

1985   Massive drought in East Africa uproots millions of people.

1987   400,000 refugees flee from Somalia to Ethiopia to escape fighting.

1989   Opening of Hungarian part of 'iron curtain' border with Austria permits start of exodus of East Europeans to West.
        Rebellion and civil war in Liberia, not concluded until 2003, uproots an estimated 280,000 people.

1991   Break-up of former Yugoslavia leads to civil war and widespread 'ethnic cleansing' forces more than half a million people from their homes.

1991–4   Fighting in Ngorno-Karabakh region of Azerbaijan produces an estimated 325,000 refugees.

1992 Spread of fighting to Bosnia creates another wave of approximately a million refugees.

1994 An estimated 1.7 million Hutu refugees flee massacres and civil war in Rwanda.

1997 Civil war in Sierra Leone lasting until 2002 produces 130,000 refugees.

1998 Attempt by Serbian armed forces to prevent separation of Kosovo produces another wave of ethnic refugees, primarily Albanian. Following civil war and the fall of the Mobutu government, an estimated 400,000 Congolese fled abroad, while another 2 million became internal refugees.

2002 Civil war in Côte d'Ivoire displaces between 500,000 and 700,000 people. A ceasefire in Angola in Apr. 2002 still leaves an estimated 2 to 3.5 million internally displaced persons. UN estimates in mid-2002 that 1.5 million Angolans are dependent on food aid for their survival.

2003 Peace talks in Sudan, leading to an official ceasefire, still leave an estimated 4 million displaced persons.

2004 Operation of Arab militias (known as Janjawid) in western Sudan region of Darfur force a million people from their homes with 120,000 moving into neighbouring Chad.

OUTPUT OF WHEAT: SELECTED COUNTRIES, 1913–2002

Millions of metric tons

	1913	1924	1938	1950	1962	1972	1983	2002
Argentina	—	—	—	—	7.5	7.9	11.7	14.2
Australia	—	—	—	—	8.2	8.4	21.7	—
Canada	—	—	—	—	15.4	14.5	26.9	20.7
France	8.7	7.7	9.8	7.7	14.1	17.9	24.8	37.6
Germany[1]	5.1	3.1	6.3	2.6	4.6	7.1	9.0	19.8
India	—	—	—	—	11.2	26.4	42.5	74.3
Italy	5.7	4.5	8.2	7.8	9.5	9.4	8.5	—
Pakistan	—	—	—	—	4.2	6.9	12.4	21.1
Turkey	—	—	—	—	8.6	12.3	16.4	21.0
USSR	28.0	13.0	40.8	31.0	70.8	86.0	82.0	46.9[2]
USA	—	—	—	—	33.0	42.0	66.0	—

[1] West Germany only after 1945; united Germany in 2002. [2] Russia
Sources: Various

OUTPUT OF RICE: MAJOR PRODUCERS, 1962–2002

Thousand metric tons

	1962	1972	1980	1985	2002
Bangladesh	15,034	15,134	20,821	21,700	35,821
Brazil	6,123	6,761	9.776	7,760	11,168
Burma (Myanmar)	7,786	7,361	13,100	14,500	17,075
China	86,038	105,197	142,993	172,184	190,168
India	52,733	58,868	80,312	90,000	134,150
Indonesia	12,393	18,031	29,652	34,300	51,000
Japan	16,444	15,319	12,189	12,958	11,320
Korea, North	—	3,783	4,960	5,200	—
Korea, South	4,809	5,500	5,311	7,608	7,067
Pakistan	1,824	3,495	4,679	5,210	7,000
Philippines	3,957	4,898	7,836	8,150	12,415
Thailand	11,267	12,413	17,368	18,535	23,402
USA	3,084	3,875	6,629	4,523	—
Vietnam, North	4,600	4,400 ⎫	11,679	14,500	32,554
Vietnam, South	6,029	6,348 ⎭			

Sources: Various

OUTPUT OF COAL AND LIGNITE: SELECTED COUNTRIES, 1920–2001

Million metric tons

	1920	1940	1950	1960	1975	1985	2001
United States[1]	521	466	468	377	643	828	935[2]
United Kingdom	230	224	220	197	124	91	31
USSR	11	133	261	509	701	716	325[3]
Japan	29	57	49	51	20	17	4
Germany	250	267	188	240	214	207	203
(E. Germany 1950–85)			140	228	245	278	
India	20	n.a.	n.a.	n.a.	92	125	342
Australia	—	—	—	—	70	107	265[4]
China	—	—	—	—	425	715	961
South Africa	—	—	—	—	70	146	223[5]
Poland	32	47	83	114	211	117[6]	163

[1] Short tons
[2] 1998
[3] Russia
[4] 1997
[5] 1999
[6] Hard coal only
Sources: Various

OUTPUT OF STEEL: SELECTED COUNTRIES, 1910–2002

Annual production in million metric tons

	1910	1918	1930	1940	1950	1960	1975	1985	2002
United States[1]	26.5	45.2	41.4	60.8	96.4	99.3	116.6	84.6	108.6[5]
United Kingdom	6.5	9.7	7.4	13.4	16.6	24.7	20.2	15.1	18.5[5]
Germany[2]	13.7	15.0	11.5	19.0	12.1	34.1	40.4	35.7	40.8[6]
USSR	3.5	0.4[3]	5.8	18.0	27.3	65.2	141.3	154.0	106.9[7]
France	3.4	1.8	9.4	4.4	8.7	17.3	27.0	23.3	—
Japan	0.1	0.8	2.3	5.3	4.8	22.1	114.0	99.5[4]	94.2
Italy	0.7	0.3	0.5	1.0	2.4	8.2	21.8	21.7	25.8
India	—	—	—	—	—	—	4.9	10.9[4]	12.9[5]
China	—	—	—	—	—	—	25.0	29.0	105.2
Brazil	—	—	—	—	—	—	7.5	14.7	26.1[5]

[1] Figures in net tons of 2,000 lb.
[2] West Germany only after 1945; united Germany in 2002
[3] Figure reflects the disruption of the Revolution in 1917.
[4] 1982 figures.
[5] 1997 figures.
[6] 1994 figures.
[7] Russia
Sources: Various.

MOTOR VEHICLES PRODUCED: SELECTED COUNTRIES, 1921–2002

In thousands, commercial and private

	1921	1929	1938	1965	1975	1985	2002
France	55	142	227	1,616	1,694	3,148	3,176
Germany	—	96	338	3,063	3,172	3,334	4,702[4]
Italy	—	47	71	1,186	1,459	1,575	1,063
Japan	—	—	30	1,876	6,942	11,122	6,056
Spain	—	—	—	234	967	1,226	1,959
United Kingdom	95	136	445	2,180	1,647	1,313	1,641
USA	1,900	4,900	3,947[1]	9,306[2]	6,713[2]	6,739[2]	—
USSR	—	4	231	814	—	1,300	959[3]
China	—	—	—	—	—	248	1,630

[1] 1935
[2] Passenger cars only
[3] Russia
[4] West Germany 1965–85; unified Germany in 2002
Sources: Various

OUTPUT OF ELECTRICITY: SELECTED COUNTRIES, 1920–2002

In million kWh

	1920	1935	1955	1975	1985	2002
France	5.8	17.5	49.6	180.0	262.8[1]	544.0
Germany[2]	15.0	35.7	78.9	301.8	366.9	557.0
Italy	4.0	12.6	25.6	140.8	182.9[3]	278.9
Russia	0.5	26.2	170.2	1039.0	1418.0[3]	877.8
Spain	1.0	3.3	11.9	76.3	117.3[3]	212.3
Sweden	2.6	6.9	24.7	80.6	100.1[1]	145.0
United Kingdom	8.5	26.0	89.0	272.1	297.3	341.8
China	—	—	55.0	121.0	—	1421.3
India	—	—	25.5[4]	54.6	122.0[1]	509.2
United States	43.0	—	—	—	—	3778.5
Canada	—	—	—	263.3	395.4[3]	541.9
Brazil	—	—	—	56.3[5]	152.0[1]	332.3
Japan	3.8	24.7	65.2	459.0	581.1[1]	1,046.3

[1] 1982
[2] West Germany only after 1945; united Germany in 2002
[3] 1983
[4] 1964
[5] 1972
Sources: Various

OUTPUT OF CRUDE OIL: SELECTED COUNTRIES, 1950–84

Million metric tons

	1950	1960	1975	1984
Americas				
USA	285.2	384.1	411.4	487.0
Canada	3.8	27.5	70.0	82.0
Mexico	10.3	14.1	41.4	150.0
Trinidad	3.0	6.1	11.1	8.0
Venezuela	78.2	148.7	122.1	95.0
Argentina	3.5	9.2	20.2	24.0
Brazil	0.1	4.0	9.4	24.0
Middle East				
Iraq	6.7	47.5	111.0	58.5
Iran	32.3	52.1	266.7	105.0
Saudi Arabia	26.6	61.1	352.1	235.0
Kuwait	17.3	81.7	104.8	58.0
Abu Dhabi	—	—	67.3	36.0
Qatar	1.6	8.2	20.8	18.8
Egypt	2.4	3.6	11.7	36.0

	1950	*1960*	*1975*	*1984*
Africa				
Nigeria	—	1.0	88.0	68.0
Libya	—	—	72.4	52.5
Algeria	—	8.6	88.0	29.5
Angola	—	—	8.4	9.5
Gabon	—	1.0	13.1	8.0
Far East and Oceania				
China	—	5.0	77.0	110.0
Indonesia	6.5	20.6	65.5	70.5
India	—	—	8.1	28.0
Brunei	4.3	4.7	9.5	8.0
Malaysia	—	—	—	21.0
Australia	—	—	19.3	23.0
Europe				
United Kingdom	—	—	1.6	125.0
Norway	—	—	1.6	34.5
Romania	4.1	11.5	14.6	12.0
USSR	37.5	148.0	489.8	615.0

Source: J. Paxton, *The Statesman's Yearbook, 1977–78* (Macmillan, 1977), pp. xxv–xxviii; *The Statesman's Yearbook, 1985–86* (Macmillan, 1985), pp. xxii–xxiii.

OUTPUT OF CRUDE OIL: SELECTED COUNTRIES, 2000

Million barrels

Americas	
USA	2,163.0
Canada	719.7[1]
Mexico	1,099.4
Trinidad	39.3[1]
Venezuela	972.0
Argentina	277.0[1]
Brazil	468.9
Middle East	
Iraq	23.7[2]
Iran	496.0
Saudi Arabia	2,862.0
Kuwait	867.0
Abu Dhabi	—
Qatar	243.8
Egypt	30.4

Africa
Nigeria	757.5
Libya	490.3
Algeria	307.1
Angola	278.9
Gabon	110.2

Far East and Oceania
China	1,207.0
Indonesia	514.4
India	242.9
Brunei	60.0
Malaysia	247.0
Australasia	153.0

Europe
United Kingdom	884.2
Norway	1,191.0
Romania	45.1
Russia	2,323.7

[1] 1997 figure
[2] 1997 figure artificially deflated by UN sanctions
Sources: Various

FAMINES AND MAJOR NATURAL DISASTERS SINCE 1914

1914   Estimated 9 million starving on northern island of Hokkaido, Japan (Jan.); 2,500 die in Turkish earthquake (Oct.).

1915   29,000 die in earthquake in central Italy.

1918–19   Central Europe and Germany face mass starvation as a result of wartime Allied blockade and breakdown of government.

1920   Severe famine reported in China.

1921–2   Estimated 18 million suffering from starvation in Russia as a result of Civil War; estimates rise to 33 million in early 1922.

1922   1,000 die in Chilean earthquake.

1923   20,000 die in Persian earthquake (June); between 140,000 and 300,000 dead in Tokyo earthquake (Sept.) with over 2.5 million homeless.

1924   50,000 dead in floods in China.

1928–30   Widespread famine in China: estimated 2 million deaths.

1929   3,000 dead in Persian earthquake.

1930   6,000 dead in earthquake at Pegu, Burma (May); 3,000 die at Naples in earthquake (July).

1931   Over 1,000 killed at Managua, Nicaragua, in earthquake.

1931–3   Widespread famine in Russia and the Ukraine accompanying forced collectivization; several million dead.

1934   Earthquake in northern India and Nepal kills 10,000 people; typhoon in Japan kills 1,500 (Sept.).

1935   Earthquake at Quetta in Pakistan kills 20,000 people (May); 1,000 die when Oveda dam bursts in Italy (Aug.).

1937   Flooding of Ohio River, USA, makes 750,000 people homeless.

1938   Flooding of Yellow River, China, causes large casualties.

1939   Chilean earthquake kills 30,000 people (Jan.); earthquake in Turkey kills 45,000 people (Dec.).

1941–3   Siege of Leningrad causes an estimated 600,000 civilian deaths, mainly through starvation and disease.

1942–3   Famine in Bengal causes an estimated 1.5–3.5 million deaths.

1944–5   The 'Hunger Winter' in the Netherlands; approximately 15,000 die of shortages.

1945   Tidal wave in East Pakistan (Bangladesh) kills 4,000.

1948   4,000 killed in earthquake in Japan.

1949   7,000 killed in earthquakes in Ecuador.

1950   Three earthquakes in Iran kill 1,500.

1953   Over 1,200 people die in coastal floods in Low Countries and Britain (Feb.); 1,000 killed by tidal wave in Greek isles (Aug.).

1954   1,600 killed at Orleansville, Algeria, in earthquake.

1956   Typhoon in China kills over 2,000.

1957   Earthquake in northern Iran kills 2,000 people.

1958   Typhoon in Japan kills 1,300 people.

1959   Over 3,000 killed in typhoon in Madagascar.

1960   Earthquake at Agadir, Morocco, kills 12,500 (Feb.); 1,500 die in earthquake at Lars, Iran (Apr.): 3,000 die in East Pakistan floods (Oct.).

1962   Avalanche in the Peruvian Andes kills 3,000 people (Jan.); over 12,000 killed in Iranian earthquake (Sept.).

1963   10,000 die in East Pakistan hurricane (May); Skopje earthquake kills

1,000 people in southern Yugoslavia (July); dam burst in Italy kills 3,000 (Oct.); 4,000 die in Haiti hurricane (Oct.).

1964 Burst reservoir kills 1,000 people in India; typhoon kills 7,000 in Ceylon and Madras.

1965 Typhoon kills 10,000 in East Pakistan.

1966 2,000 die in Turkish earthquake.

1968 Iranian earthquake kills between 11,000 and 20,000 people.

1970 Massive floods in East Pakistan kill between 250,000 and 500,000 people (Nov.); Peruvian earthquake kills an estimated 70,000 people.

1971 5,000 killed by typhoon floods in India.

1972 Earthquake in Managua, Nicaragua, kills 10,000 people.

1973 Drought and famine in Sahel area of Mauritania, Senegal, the Gambia, Upper Volta, Mali, Niger and Chad kill an estimated 250,000 people; 100,000 die in Ethiopia.

1974 20,000 feared dead in Chinese earthquake (May); monsoon floods in Bangladesh kill 2,000 (Aug.); typhoon floods in Honduras kill 8,000 (Sept.); earthquake in Pakistan kills 4,000 (Dec.).

1975 Earthquake centred on Lice, Turkey, kills 3,000 people.

1976 Earthquake in Guatemala kills 22,000 people (Feb.); almost a 1,000 killed in Italy by earthquake (May); earthquake in Philippines kills 3,000 (Aug.); 3,700 killed at Van, Turkey, by earthquake (Nov.).

1977 Romanian earthquake kills 1,570 people.

1978 Flood of Jumna River in India kills 10,000 (Sept.); between 5,000 and 20,000 killed in Iranian earthquake (Sept.).

1978–80 Drought and famine in east Africa threaten estimated 10 million with starvation in Sudan, Ethiopia, Somalia and Djibouti.

1979 1,000 killed by hurricanes on Dominica.

1980 Algerian earthquake at El Asnam kills between 2,000 and 20,000 people (Oct.); earthquake in southern Italy kills 3,000–4,000 people (Nov.). UN relief agencies estimate 2 million facing starvation in Cambodia.

1981 Floods in Shansi province, China, kill 5,000 people.

1982 Monsoon floods in India kill several hundred and leave millions homeless (Sept.): earthquake in Yemen kills nearly 3,000 people (Dec.).

1983 2,000 killed in Turkish earthquake.

1984   10,000 killed by typhoon floods in Philippines.

1984–5   Famine in Ethiopia and neighbouring areas affects several million people prompting huge relief effort.

1985   10,000 killed in typhoon floods in Bangladesh (May); Mexican earthquake kills over 9,000 people. Volcanic eruption and subsequent mudflows at Ruiz in Colombia kill an estimated 25,000 people.

1987   Failure of Ethiopian harvest prompts fresh famine scare.

1988   Armenian earthquake kills 25,000 people.

1989   Hurricane Hugo causes massive damage (second costliest in US history) in South Carolina.

1990   Iranian earthquake in Gilan province kills 50,000 people.

1992   Hurricane Andrew causes damage as costliest in US history with over $34 billion of damage.

1993   Southern India earthquake kills between 10,000 and 30,000 people.

1995   Kobe earthquake in Japan kills 5,000 people.

1999   Turkish earthquake kills 17,000 people in cities of Izmit and Istanbul.

2001   20,000–30,000 people killed by earthquake in Gujarat state of India.

2003   Earthquake destroys centre of historic city of Bam, Iran, with 43,000 dead.

2004   Famine in Darfur region of Sudan as a consequence of civil war. Countries bordering Indian Ocean devastated by massive tsunami (the worst in modern history). Around 230,000 dead (the majority in Sumatra) but Thailand, Sri Lanka and India also badly hit.

WORLD HEALTH, DISEASE AND MEDICINE

1914–16   Widespread government campaigns against venereal diseases amongst troops in Europe, including use of drugs.

1916   First birth control clinic opened in the USA, in New York by Margaret Sanger and Ethyl Byrne.

1918–19   Influenza pandemic claims an estimated 27 million lives worldwide; first outbreaks in USA and France in spring 1918; spread rapidly to Africa, Asia and China; slackened in winter of 1918–19, but renewed outbreak in Mar. 1919.

1921   First birth control clinic opened in Britain in Walworth, London. First BCG tuberculosis vaccination carried out in France. Insulin isolated by Banting and Best in Canada, offering prospect of control of diabetes.

1922   Prohibition in the United States produces drop in alcohol-related deaths. Discovery of link between Vitamin B deficiency and rickets. Freud publishes *The Ego and the Id*.

1923   Glenny and Hopkins introduce diphtheria and tetanus immunization. League of Nations Health Organization set up in Geneva with branches in Paris, Washington, Alexandria, Sydney and Singapore to act as intelligence centre on epidemics. Scope of activities later widened to include standardization of drugs and sera. Committees set up to investigate malaria, leprosy, cancer, rural hygiene, housing and nutrition. Also action against drug traffic.

1924   Rabies baccillus isolated at Pasteur Institute, Paris. Calmette and Guerin introduce tuberculosis vaccine for general use amongst infants.

1925   Dr Henry Soutter carries out first heart-valve surgery.

1926   Pasteur Institute produces anti-tetanus serum. Doctors link smoking with mouth cancer.

1927   Vitamin C identified as ascorbic acid.

1928   Fleming makes accidental discovery of penicillin and observes its ability to kill bacteria; first patented 'sticking plasters'. First use of an 'iron lung' in Boston, USA.

1929   Butenandt and Doisy isolate the first sex hormone, oestrone. Discovery of anti-blood-clotting agent, heparin.

1930   Fluoride discovered to prevent dental caries. First intra-uterine contraceptive device.

1932   Vaccine developed against yellow fever. Vitamin C isolated.

1933   Virus responsible for influenza pandemic in 1918–19 isolated.

1935   Vitamin E isolated in United States.

1941   Successful use of first antibiotic, penicillin; becomes widely available within next three years for dealing with infections.

1944   Quinine artificially produced.

1946   US research links smoking to cancer.

1948   Antibiotic streptomycin introduced for treatment of tuberculosis. World Health Organization established, based in Geneva with offices in New York and regional offices elsewhere. WHO launches campaign against TB.

1949   Cause of sickle cell anaemia found.

1950   First kidney transplant carried out in Chicago.

1952   Artificial heart pump first used to keep patient alive in United States.

1953   Dr Salk produces successful vaccine against polio. First full chemical analysis of a protein, insulin, carried out by Dr Sanger at Cambridge. Watson and Crick discover structure of DNA. Drs Bunge and Sherman demonstrate that deep-frozen sperm remains fertile, paving way for sperm banks.

1957   Asian flu epidemic.

1958   First heart 'pacemaker' implanted in patient. The drug Thalidomide is associated with birth defects in children. Oral contraceptive – 'the pill' – becomes available.

1963   First successful kidney transplant to overcome rejection problems.

1966   WHO campaign against TB has completed 400 million tests and 180 million vaccinations.

1967   First heart transplant by Dr Christian Barnard in South Africa.

1969   Human egg fertilized in test tube for first time.

1971   First heart-lung transplant.

1975   WHO announces smallpox eradicated from Bangladesh, leaving Ethiopia only infected area.

1978   First 'test-tube baby' born with use of egg and sperm fertilized outside the womb.

1979   'Body-scanner' for diagnosis developed in Britain.

1980   WHO announces eradication of smallpox.

1981   Identification of an immune deficiency disease, AIDS, affecting homosexual groups in the United States.

1984   AIDS-causing virus discovered. World Health Organization estimates potential deaths at several million, with deaths affecting the heterosexual community also.

1985   Gorbachev launches anti-alcohol campaign in USSR.

1987   Widespread anti-AIDS campaign begun in several countries.

1989   Worldwide research on anti-AIDS drugs produces first treatments likely to slow progress of the disease. UN estimates are that 7.8 million people are HIV-positive and that over a million people have died of AIDS. Hepatitis C virus discovered.

1996   Link established between animal disease BSE (bovine spongiform encephalopathy) and human degenerative disease CJD (Creuzfeldt-Jakob disease).

1997   First cloned mammal, Dolly the sheep, created.

2002   SARS (Severe Acute Respiratory Syndrome) virus identified in southern China (Nov.) and soon affects 33 countries with thousands of people infected and over 800 deaths. WHO declared outbreak contained in July 2003. UN estimates 42 million worldwide are HIV-positive and more than half are women.

2004   Stem-cell research in Korea paves the way for cloned humans.

HIV INFECTIONS AND AIDS DEATHS WORLDWIDE, 1980–2000

Year	HIV infections (millions)	AIDS deaths (millions)
1980	0.1	0.0
1981	0.3	0.0
1982	0.7	0.0
1983	1.2	0.0
1984	1.7	0.1
1985	2.4	0.2
1986	3.4	0.3
1987	4.5	0.5
1988	5.9	0.8
1989	7.8	1.2
1990	10.0	1.7
1991	12.8	2.4
1992	16.1	3.3
1993	20.1	4.7
1994	24.5	6.2
1995	29.8	8.2
1996	35.3	10.6
1997	40.9	13.2
1998	46.6	15.9
1999	52.6	18.8
2000	57.9	21.8

Sources: UNAIDS, *AIDS Epidemic Update, Dec. 2000*, Geneva, 2000

THE ENVIRONMENT AND POLLUTION: MAJOR EVENTS SINCE 1945

1945 First atomic explosions in New Mexico and at Hiroshima and Nagasaki.

1946 First nuclear test at Bikini Atoll in the Marshall Islands.

1952–3 First hydrogen bomb tests in the Pacific Marshall Islands by the United States, and in Siberia by the USSR.

1952 London 'smog' kills an estimated 4,000 people; beginning of serious action to tackle air pollution in United Kingdom; London declared a smokeless zone (1955); Clean Air Act passed (1956). Britain explodes atomic bomb off western Australia.

1957 Major radioactive leak at Windscale nuclear plant in Cumbria, Britain.

1959 Treaty for peaceful use of Antarctica opened for signature.

1960 France begins atomic bomb testing in the Sahara.

1961 World Wildlife Fund opened.

1962 Recognition of the effects of Strontium 90.

1967 *Torrey Canyon* oil spillage off south-western Britain reveals first major concern with effects of pollution on marine environment. Treaty banning nuclear weapons from space.

1971 Seabed Treaty prohibits the emplacement of nuclear weapons on the seabed. Friends of the Earth founded.

1972 UN Conference on the Human Environment held at Stockholm.

1975 Greenpeace organization founded.

1976 Explosion at chemical plant at Seveso, Italy, releases dioxins into a large area; town evacuated and massive clean-up operation involving removal of thousands of tons of top-soil.

1977 UNESCO sets up fund to save the Acropolis, Athens, from effects of air pollution.

1979 International agreement on trans-national air pollution signed. A major nuclear accident in the United States at Three Mile Island, near Harrisburg, Pennsylvania; thousands of gallons of radioactive water and a plume of radioactive gas released. Temporary evacuation of population puts effective end to nuclear power station construction in United States.

1983 First Green deputies elected to West German parliament; first representation of specific environmental party in Western Europe.

1984 240 killed by gas explosion in Mexico (Nov.); explosion at Bhopal, India, and gas leak kills 3,000 people and injures 200,000 more (Dec.).

1986   Explosion at Chernobyl nuclear reactor in USSR spreads radioactive pollution over wide area of the Soviet Union and Western Europe. Population of Chernobyl evacuated and emergency action taken to seal the nuclear core.

1987   Widespread concern about effects of 'acid rain' on Western European forest areas and waters; agreements to reduce some emissions of sulphur dioxide by power stations.
Nimbus 7 satellite confirms hole in ozone layer over Antarctica (Oct.).

1988   Widespread deaths of seals in North Sea from viral infection claimed as a result of growing pollution.
Explosion from leak in trans-Siberian pipeline in the Urals, USSR, kills several thousand people in railway trains.
International recognition of global climatic change in depletion of 'ozone layer' and 'greenhouse effect'. First measures to reduce use of harmful CFC gases and to encourage further research.

1989   Massive spillage from oil-tanker *Exxon Valdez* off Alaska contaminates large area of coastline.
Euro-elections show continued growth of Green movement as a political force.
Crippled Iranian oil-tanker *Kharg V* creates 260 sq. km oil slick off coast of Morocco (Dec.).

1990   Explosion and fire at nuclear fuels factory in East Kazakhstan contaminates large area with beryllian metal, putting 120,000 people at risk.

1991   During Gulf War, upwards of 10 million barrels of oil released into the Persian Gulf affecting 400 miles of coast. Firing of 600 oil wells in Kuwait by Iraqi troops causes widespread air and 'Black Rain' contamination as far away as Bulgaria, Pakistan and Afghanistan.

1992   The 77,000-ton Bahamanian-flagged tanker *Prestige* sinks off the coast of Spain, creating worst recorded oil spill (Nov.).

1993   84,000-ton tanker *Braer* driven ashore on Shetland Isles, though strong winds disperse most of spill. Explosion at Tomsk-7 nuclear reprocessing plant in Russia releases radioactive cloud over 120 sq. km. of forest.

1996   128,000-ton tanker *Sea Empress* goes aground at Milford Haven, south Wales. Attempted removal of oil still leaves 72,000 tons of oil spillage (Feb.).

1997   Representatives of 160 nations sign Kyoto Protocol, an international agreement calling for gradual reduction of greenhouse-gas emissions.

Huge forest fires caused by land clearance in Indonesia and Malaysia create giant smog cloud (Aug.–Sept.).

2000   100,000 tons of contaminated sludge from a gold mine in northern Romania pollute Tisza river and Danube. Ozone 'hole' over Antarctica is largest ever, covering an area three times the size of the United States.

2001   President Bush states that USA will not participate in Kyoto Protocol until modified to US requirements.

2005   Kyoto Treaty finally ratified by Russia.

WORLD CARBON EMISSIONS FROM FOSSIL FUEL BURNING, 1950–2000

	Emissions (million tons of carbon)	Carbon dioxide concentration (parts per million)
1950	1,612	—
1955	2,013	—
1960	2,535	316.7
1965	3,087	319.9
1970	3,997	325.5
1975	4,518	331.0
1980	5,155	338.5
1985	5,271	345.7
1990	5,931	354.0
1995	6,490	362.0
2000	6,290	370.0

Sources: Various

THE CHANGED STATUS OF WOMEN: KEY EVENTS.

1893   Adoption of women's suffrage in New Zealand heightens the question of female suffrage elsewhere in the world.

1899   International Women's Congress held in London.

1900   Women participate in Olympic Games for the first time but only in restricted events.

1903   Madame Curie wins Nobel Prize. Women's Social and Political Union formed in Britain to campaign for women's rights.

1905   Union of Equal Rights for Women founded in Soviet Union. Austrian Bertha von Suttner wins Nobel Peace Prize.

1906   International agreement to ban night-shift work by women.

1907   Women in Austria obtain equal employment rights in universities and hospitals.

1908   Women taxpayers over 25 given the vote in Denmark.

1909   Women admitted to German universities. Women win vote in Australia.

1910   Women admitted to Spanish universities. International Women's Day first organized in Germany.

1911   Vote granted to women in Portugal; Norway admits women as MPs. Tan Junying founds Chinese Suffrage Society in Beijing.

1912   Californian women vote in Presidential elections for the first time. The Progressive Party adopts a suffrage clause in its programme. By 1914 ten American states have admitted women to the vote. British suffragettes turn to militant action after failure to obtain suffrage by parliamentary means. Imprisoned suffragettes go on hunger strike in prison and are force-fed.

1913   British suffragette Emily Davison kills herself by throwing herself under the King's horse at the Derby.

1914   Outbreak of First World War. Women widely mobilized for agricultural, transport, clerical, and munitions work. Women also conscripted into the auxiliary armed forces of many combatant states.

1915   Dutch socialist feminist Aletta Jacobs calls International Women's Congress for Peace.

1916   Margaret Sanger opens the first birth control clinic in the United States in Brooklyn, New York, in November. Shut down 9 days later and Sanger and her clinic nurse arrested. None the less, publishes the *Birth Control Review* from Jan. 1917.

1917   First women's suffrage movement in Japan. Provisional government in Russia grants women political rights and equalizes their employment and legal rights (July) following March demonstration by 40,000 women. Following the Bolshevik Revolution, political and civil equality for women were guaranteed and right to work enshrined in law. Lenin appoints Alexandra Kollontai as Commissioner for Social Welfare on women's issues, leading to civil marriage, easing of divorce laws, legalization of abortion, and equal custody rights by 1921. American militant suffragettes attempt to storm the White House in campaign for the vote.

1918   British women over 30 gain voting rights for the first time. Women's Rights Organization campaigns for right to vote in Argentina. British biologist Marie Stopes publishes *Married Love*, calling for sexual fulfilment in marriage. Her book *Planned Parenthood* advocating birth control arouses a storm of opposition but proves a bestseller.

1919   Weimar constitution in Germany gives women the vote for the first time. In the aftermath of the First World War, many countries extend the franchise and also introduce women's voting rights. Women's International League for Peace and Freedom founded, an international, non-violent disarmament organization, prefiguring major involvement of women in anti-war and pacifist movements. President Wilson makes women's suffrage a priority in the United States and US Congress passes the Nineteenth Amendment giving women the vote, taking effect in 1920.

1920   Women in United States vote in Presidential elections for the first time. Pope canonizes Joan of Arc.

1921   Marie Stopes opens the first birth control clinic in Europe in South London.

1922   First Congress of the International Federation of Feminine Athletes takes place in Geneva. Bertha Lutz founds Brazilian Federation for the Advancement of Women.

1923   Margaret Sanger opens first legal birth control clinic in New York after lobbying New York State legislature. Equal Rights Amendment to the US Constitution introduced into Congress, drafted by Alice Paul (not passed until 1972). First woman admitted to Académie Française.

1924   Italian government launches 'women into the home campaign' in line with Fascist emphasis on traditional role of women as mothers and homemakers.

1925   Mussolini bars women from public office. First woman State Governor in the United States in Wyoming.

1928   Genevieve Cline first woman appointed a US federal judge. Women's track and field events made part of Olympic Games.

1929   World Congress on women's work meets in Berlin.

1930   Papal encyclical *Casti Connubi* urges women to return to home and family and find true equality as wives and mothers.

1932   Amelia Earhart leaves Newfoundland to make first woman solo flight across the Atlantic. Brazilian women gain the vote. First woman elected to US Senate.

1933 Italian government offers prizes for large families.

1936 New Stalinist family law reverses direction of earlier Soviet legislation, making divorce more difficult and limiting abortion.

1939 Outbreak of the Second World War in Europe. Women are once again heavily employed in non-traditional occupations and auxiliary armed forces.

1940 Vichy regime in France bans married women from public service occupations and promotes traditional model of the family.

1941 Britain conscripts unmarried women for war work or the auxiliary armed forces. Entry of Soviet Union into the war leads to massive mobilization of women for war work and for combat duties.

1942 Entry of United States into the war leads to 7 million American women undertaking paid work for the first time.

1944 Soviet Union gives monetary rewards to large families and single persons taxed.

1946 Constitution of French Fourth Republic gives women the vote.

1948 Equal suffrage established in new constitutions of Germany, Italy and Japan. United Nations Universal Declaration of Human Rights deals with men and women equally and Article 16 includes the right to marry, forbids forced marriage, and gives women 'equal rights as to marriage, during marriage and at its dissolution'.

1949 Simone de Beauvoir publishes *The Second Sex*.

1955 Rosa Parks challenges 'whites only' segregation on a bus in Montgomery, Alabama. Soviet Union once again makes abortion legal.

1956 Greek women obtain right to vote.

1960 US Food and Drug administration announces approval of the commercial oral contraceptive – the 'pill'. It becomes widely available in North America and Europe within the next decade.

1962 US President's Commission on the status of women holds its first meeting.

1963 President Kennedy signs Equal Pay Act for women. Betty Friedan's *The Feminine Mystique* sparks debate in US on position of women.

1964 Title VII of US Civil Rights Act outlaws discrimation in employment on grounds of sex (as well as race, colour, religion or national origin).

1966   Indira Gandhi becomes Prime Minister of India. American women found National Organization for Women to ratify the Equal Rights Amendment to the constitution and defend liberalized abortion law.

1967   Britain legalizes abortion.

1968   Protests at annual 'Miss America' beauty contest by feminists. Papal Encyclical *Humanae Vitae* reaffirms Catholic doctrine of opposition to artificial birth control. Italian women demonstrate for women's rights and the legalization of abortion.

1969   Golda Meir becomes Prime Minister of Israel.

1970   Germaine Greer's *The Female Eunuch* and Kate Millett's *Sexual Politics* popularize feminist cause. Britain introduces Equal Pay Act. Italy liberalizes divorce laws.

1972   International Women's Year. US Congress passes draft Equal Rights Amendment, but lapsed through failure of sufficient states to ratify.

1973   US Supreme Court declares abortion primarily a medical decision and strikes down state laws limiting women's access to it.

1975   France legalizes abortion. Britain introduces Sex Discrimination Act.

1977   Northern Ireland women win Nobel Peace Prize.

1979   Margaret Thatcher becomes first woman Prime Minister of Britain.

1981   Norway has first woman Prime Minister.

1990   Mary Robinson becomes first woman President of Ireland.

1990–1   Collapse of Eastern European regimes removes system of guaranteed employment, childcare, and access to free healthcare.

1994   First women priests ordained in the Anglican communion.

1995   Papal encyclical *Evangelium Vitae* (Gospel of Life) re-emphasizes traditional Roman Catholic position on abortion, birth control and euthanasia.

2001   UN announces that for the first time over half of all people with HIV infections are women.

2004   Pope canonizes Gianna Beretta Molla, leader of Italian anti-abortion movement; first mother to become a modern saint.

THE TELECOMMUNICATIONS AND IT REVOLUTION

1899   Marconi transmits by wireless across the Channel. Magnetic recording of sound devised.

1900   Marconi transmits across the Atlantic.

1904   Fleming invents the electronic valve.

1907   First regular radio broadcasts begin in the United States.

1910   Experimental radio broadcasts made by Lee de Forest from Paris.

1917   Lucien Levy in France patents a tuning circuit making construction of radio sets much simpler.

1920   Marconi Wireless Telegraph Company begins broadcasting daily concerts from Chelmsford on 23 Feb. Recital by Dame Nelli Melba broadcast from Chelmsford to Europe on 15 June.

1922   British Broadcasting Corporation set up for regular daily radio broadcasts.

1926   John Logie Baird demonstrates a working television system in London.

1927   First fully electronic television system demonstrated in the United States.

1928   Baird successfully transmits TV pictures from London to New York.

1929   Colour TV demonstrated in the United States.

1931   Mechanical binary computer, the 'Z1', built by Konrad Zuse in Germany.

1933   Edwin Armstrong in the United States patents FM (Frequency Modulation) radio system, permitting much higher quality sound broadcasts. Discovery of radio emissions from stars by Karl Jansky in the United States., developing the science of radio astronomy.

1933–4   First patents applied for a radio detection and ranging (radar) system in the United States and France.

1935   A station in Berlin begins low-definition broadcasting.

1936   First practical radar system developed by Watson-Watt in Great Britain for detection of enemy aircraft. BBC establishes first high-definition public service broadcasting service from Alexandra Palace in London using both Baird and American systems; Baird system eventually dropped.

1939   Binary Calculator, the Complex Computer, using telephone relays developed in the United States. Television transmissions abandoned in Britain and Germany for duration of war.

1940   Radar system in Britain plays a major defensive role in the Battle of Britain. Germany develops system of directional radio beams to direct bombers to targets in Britain. Similar systems and counter-measures produced by both sides during the ensuing bomber offensive on Germany.

1942–3   Development of airborne and shipborne radar during Second World War.

1943   Alan Turing develops Colossus computer to break German Enigma codes, using telephone relay and 1500 valves; the world's first automatic digital computer.

1945   Whirlwind computer constructed.

1946   Television transmissions resumed in Britain. Turing presents UK's National Physical Laboratory (NPL) with design for stored-programme electronic digital computer, envisaging a plan for national computer development, but only pilot project is completed.

1947   Construction of UNIVAC computers for the US Census Bureau begins and completed in 1951, eventually producing 48 UNIVAC I computers.

1948   First transistors produced.

1948   Konrad Zuse builds 'Z3' computer using electronic relays.

1949   Colour TV system produced in the USA by RCA; first regular transmissions begin the following year.

1954   Pope opens Eurovision network in Rome.

1955   Computer firm IBM introduces magnetic disk storage for computers. Video Tape recording developed. First mass transistorized radios produced by Sony Corporation of Japan.

1959   First patent for integrated circuit in the US. First transistorized portable TVs launched by Sony Corporation.

1962   First live TV transmitted from Europe to America by Telstar satellite.

1963   Philips introduces the first compact casette. First electronic calculators introduced. First mini-computer marketed in the United States.

1964   BASIC computer language developed.

1966   Colour TV transmissions begin in Europe.

1967   Texas Instruments begin work on pocket calculator.

1969   Advanced Research Projects Agency (ARPA) at the US Department of Defence conceives concept of a diffused network of computer sites to counter nuclear strikes, creating the internet. First long-distance link established between computers in California and Utah.

1971   First microprocessor (Intel 4004) introduced. First e-mail programme written.

1973   First international computer link made, between UK and Norway.

1974   Telenet, first public e-mail server, set up.

1975   First personal computers become commercially available.

1977   Apple and Commodore bring out micro-computers.

1978   IBM develops floppy disk.

1979   Sony Corporation introduces Sony Walkman cassette player. First video recorders become available commercially.

1980   Sony and Philips introduce Compact Disk. Nintendo produces first handheld game powered by microprocessor.

1989   Nintendo Game Boy becomes worldwide success as handheld games player. Number of internet users passes 100,000.

1990   Sales of compact disks worldwide estimated to have outstripped those of vinyl records. Satellite broadcasting begins by Sky network.

1991   World Wide Web released, allowing easy access to internet and e-mail. Permission granted to private companies to offer subscriptions giving access to the Internet. Microsoft creates a simple e-mail package launching e-mail as a practical proposition.

1992   Number of internet users passes one million.

1993   First 'virtual reality' videos launched.

1995   First internet 'cafés' set up in London. First 'laptop' computers become widely available.

1998   Digital TV broadcasting begins with terrestial and satellite TV services through most of Europe.

1999   Mobile phone sales take off with increasing miniaturization of handsets. DVD (Digital Versatile Disk) sales establish foothold in recorded film and music market.

2001   An estimated 10 billion e-mails sent and received each year.

2003   'Wireless' technology permits PCs and laptops to be used without cabling.

2004   An estimated 1 billion mobile phones are owned worldwide. An estimated 20 billion e-mail messages sent each year. DVD establishes supremacy in recorded film market with c. 80 per cent of the market and more than 60 million DVD players and recorders produced worldwide.

DEVELOPMENTS IN HUMAN RIGHTS SINCE 1918

1918   Bolsheviks launch policy of 'Red Terror', following assassination attempt on Lenin. Carried out by the Cheka, it turned into an onslaught on anyone seen as a potential or real enemy of the Bolsheviks, including arbitrary arrest, deportation and execution. Tens of thousands executed or deported by 1921 aside from casualties in the civil war.

1919   Versailles Peace Conference. Covenant of the League of Nations provides for peaceful settlement of international disputes, reduction and control of armaments, and promotion of social and economic progress. League institutions set up, including International Labour Office, World Health Organization, and Mandates Commission. Nansen passports introduced for refugees. Amritsar Massacre in India causes widespread criticism of British rule.

1920   Permanent Court of International Justice set up at The Hague, Holland, able to arbitrate on international treaties and other issues, e.g. minority rights.

1921   Gandhi begins programme of civil disobedience, using non-violent methods against British rule.

1923   The Hague agreement to confine aerial bombing to military targets.

1924   In Italy, murder of socialist deputy Giacomo Matteotti by fascist thugs.

1925   In Italy, murder of Matteotti provokes crisis in Mussolini's regime and mass withdrawal of opposition deputies from the Chamber. Mussolini weathers the crisis and in the following year unleashes a further wave of violence against opponents and introduces press restrictions and bans on meetings.

1925   Geneva Protocol against the use of poison gas.

1926   Anti-Slavery Convention passed by League of Nations.

1928   Effective launch of crash collectivization plan as part of first Five Year Plan leads to mass expropriations and deportations of 'kulaks' in Russia. An estimated 2 million die in ensuing chaos and resistance by 1933, compounded by famine in the Ukraine.

1931   Gandhi begins second civil disobedience campaign; march to the sea in protest against the salt tax. Gandhi rearrested.

1933   First petition to League about Nazi discrimination against Jews. Reichstag fire (Feb.) leads Nazis to introduce dictatorship, including dissolution of political parties, trade unions and other associations. Opponents to the regime arrested and placed in concentration camps where widespread brutality practised. Nazis also begin systematic process of depriving Jews of civil rights.

1934   Hitler murders several hundred of his opponents in 'Night of the Long Knives' (June). Insurrectionary rising in Asturias region of Spain brutally suppressed by army led by General Franco. In the Soviet Union, the assassination of Kirov (Dec.) sparks off the Stalinist purges which by 1939 consume millions of old Bolsheviks, Party members, members of the armed forces and anyone deemed an opponent of the regime. Show trials and obviously forced 'confessions' gave a new dimension to twentieth-century dictatorship matched only by the racial underpinning of the later Nazi holocaust.

1936   Spanish Civil War provokes widespread atrocities on both sides with attacks on landowners and clergy by the left and arbitrary execution of opponents and prisoners by Nationalists. London agreement on rules governing submarine warfare to minimize civilian casualties.

1937   Japanese begin attack on China, widespread bombing of cities such as Shanghai. Fall of Nanking to Japanese produces orgy of rape and murder – 'the rape of Nanking' (Dec.). In Spanish Civil War, bombing of undefended Basque town of Guernica by German Condor Legion for the Nationalist forces causes international outcry.

1938   Widespread attack on Jews and Jewish property in Germany in *Kristallnacht* (Nov.).

1939   Nazi invasion of Poland puts millions of Jews in the hands of the Nazis. Soviet occupation of Poland leads to massacre of Polish officers at Katyn and occupation of Baltic States leads to mass deportations of 'kulaks', national leaders and intellectuals to the camps.

1941   Franklin Roosevelt makes 'Four Freedoms' speech on 6 Jan. 1941 in message to Congress, outlining US war aims in the event of its entry to the war: these were 'to secure freedom of speech and expression, freedom of worship, freedom from want and freedom from fear'. In August Roosevelt and Churchill draw up Atlantic Charter renouncing territorial aggression and supporting the rights of people to choose their own governments. Nazis begin *ad hoc* murder of the Jews, following the capture of large numbers of Jews in the Soviet Union. This is supplanted by the 'Final Solution', the systematic mass murder of the Jewish population of Europe, as well as gypsies and homosexuals.

1942   26 countries undertake to set up United Nations. Allies declare protection of human rights a war aim.

1943   Indiscriminate bombing of German cities arouses some protest in allied countries but to no effect.

1945   Concentration camps freed by allied troops, revealing full scale of Nazi atrocities. Allies determine to hold trials of major war criminals at Nuremberg. George Orwell's *Animal Farm* satirizes totalitarianism. Charter of United Nations signed at San Francisco.

1946   Nuremberg Judgement delivered. UN General Assembly recognizes the Judgement as international law.

1948   Universal Declaration of Human Rights adopted by UN General Assembly in Paris, recognizing the 'inherent dignity' and 'inalienable rights of all members of the human family'. In South Africa, National Party–Afrikaaner Party alliance takes office determined to impose racial segregation – apartheid.

1949   Geneva Convention on wartime treatment of prisoners-of-war and civilians.

1950   European Convention on Human Rights. South African government passes the Group Areas Act establishing the apartheid system of racial segregation.

1951   South African government introduces pass laws forcing all black South Africans to carry documents.

1954   United States Supreme Court verdict forces desegregation of elementary and secondary school system.

1955   Rosa Parks challenges bus segregation in Montgomery, Alabama, leading to the Montgomery bus boycott, lasting until Dec. 1956, giving rise to the modern civil rights movement.

1956   Khrushchev condemns Stalin and excesses of Stalinism at 20th Party Congress.

1960   Sharpeville massacre arouses worldwide protest against apartheid regime.

1961   Erection of Berlin Wall prevents further movement of people from behind the 'Iron Curtain' to the West. Amnesty International founded to campaign on behalf of political prisoners. Trial of Adolf Eichmann in Israel after his capture by Israeli agents in Latin America. One of the Nazis directly responsible for the final solution, his trial and the evidence against him did much to reawaken interest in the holocaust. Eichmann was hanged.

1963   Birmingham desegregation campaign in the United States followed by the March on Washington led by Martin Luther King to support a Civil Rights Bill sent to Congress by Kennedy.

1964   Civil Rights Act passed in the United States banning segregation in public facilities, federal programmes, schools and employment. At Rivonia trial in South Africa Nelson Mandela and other ANC activists sentenced to life imprisonment.

1965　Voting Rights Act in the United States outlaws the discriminatory registration procedures which had disenfranchised southern blacks.

1966　Trial and imprisonment of Jewish writers Yu Daniel and Abram Sinyavsky in the Soviet Union highlights plight of 'dissidents' in the Soviet Union.

1967　First UN sanctions against South Africa.

1968　Campaign by Northern Ireland Civil Rights Association for equal rights for Catholics leads to rioting.

1969　Break-up of pro-democracy march in Northern Ireland and a deteriorating security situation lead to British army being deployed and programme of reform in housing, policing and local government initiated. Convention on the Elimination of All Forms of Racial Discrimination. Police raid on gay meeting place in New York, the Stonewall Inn, leads to formation of Gay Liberation Front and Gay Activists Alliance.

1969　First Gay Pride March in New York, commemorating the Stonewall raid, becoming annual event and widely copied elsewhere.

1971　Convention on the Suppression and Punishment of the Crime of Apartheid. British government introduces internment without trial in Ulster, leading to widespread rioting in protest.

1972　UN General Assembly adopts principles for co-operation in punishment of crimes against humanity. 13 unarmed demonstrators killed by British soldiers at a demonstration in Londonderry, so-called 'Bloody Sunday'.

1973　Pinochet coup in Chile followed by widespread human rights abuses, with arbitrary arrest, murder and torture of thousands of opponents.

1974　Expulsion from the Soviet Union of writer and Nobel Prize winner Alexander Solzhenitsyn, following the publication in the West of his indictment of the Soviet labour camps, *The Gulag Archipelago*, highlights the cause of dissidents.

1975　In Helsinki Accords USSR guarantees to respect 'human rights and fundamental freedoms' following agitation about treatment of dissidents and the gulag system. Pol Pot regime assumes power in Cambodia and introduces Maoist revolutionary regime in which an estimated million people die before its overthrow in 1979.

1976　Helsinki Human Rights Group set up in USSR to monitor human rights abuses, but becomes target of persecution itself. Military junta takes power in Argentina, leading to murder of thousands of left-wingers.

1977   Human Rights Year. Charter 77 launched in Prague by human rights activists led by Vaclav Havel. UN imposes mandatory trade sanctions on South Africa and Rhodesia. Carter administration adopts human rights as an American foreign policy objective.

1981   UN Convention against all forms of discrimination against women. Leading Soviet dissident, the physicist Andrei Sakharov, is sent to internal exile in Gorky. Norway becomes first country in the world to pass a law making discrimination against homosexuals illegal. Lancaster House agreement in London paves way for end of 'whites only' rule in Zimbabwe (Southern Rhodesia).

1986   Sakharov permitted to return from internal exile as part of Gorbachev's liberalization of Soviet Union. Labour camps largely emptied and widespread 're-structuring' or perestroika.

1989   UN Convention on the Rights of the Child. Supreme Court verdict in the United States asserts rights for unborn children. Pro-democracy campaigners in Beijing crushed in Tiananmen Square massacre; major clampdown and arrests of activists, many flee abroad. Collapse of communism in Eastern Europe and demolition of Berlin Wall. Denmark is first state to give same-sex partnerships legal rights.

1990   Popularly elected Congress of People's Deputies in the Soviet Union ratifies end of the 'leading role' of the Communist Party and formation of political parties.

1991   Defeat of pro-communist coup in Soviet Union ensures survival of pro-democracy regime. Repeal of Group Areas Act in South Africa begins the dismantling of the apartheid regime. Outbreak of civil war in former Yugoslavia sees mass human rights abuses and worst massacres in Europe since the Second World War.

1993   Hague Tribunal for War Crimes in the former Yugoslavia established by UN Security Council Resolution.

1994   Rwandan genocide; Security Council establishes Rwandan Tribunal. First multi-race elections in South Africa; Mandela becomes President.

1995   Hague Tribunal indicts Bosnan Serb leadership for war crimes (May). 7,000 massacred at Srebrenica while under UN protection. Beijing Conference on Women's Rights.

1998   Japan apologizes to wartime 'comfort women'.

2003   Supreme Court in the United States invalidates state laws forbidding gay sex.

IV
BIOGRAPHIES

A

Foreign Minister, 1951–5. Negotiated German entry into NATO, EEC. Established diplomatic relations with USSR, 1955. Resigned 1963.

ABBAS, FERHAT (1900–85) Algerian nationalist. One of the leaders of the Algerian independence movement. Prime Minister of the 'provisional government' in exile in Tunisia, 1958–61. President of the National Assembly, 1962–63, after independence, but after mounting differences with Ben Bella he resigned.

ACHEAMPONG, IGNATIUS KUTU (1931–79) Ghanaian military leader who led the coup which overthrew Kofi Busia (q.v.) in 1972. He became Chairman of the National Redemption Council government with responsibility also for defence and finance. On 9 Oct. 1975 he became Chairman of the Supreme Military Council. He was deposed in the coup of July 1978.

ACHESON, DEAN (1893–1971) American statesman. As US Secretary of State from 1949 to 1955 played a key role in establishing NATO (p. 266) and in formulating American policy during the Korean War (p. 304).

ADENAUER, KONRAD (1876–1967) German statesman. Mayor of Cologne, 1917–33. Removed by Nazis. Prominent member of Catholic Centre Party in Weimar Republic. President of Prussian State Council, 1920–33. Twice imprisoned by Nazis. Founded Christian Democratic Union, 1945. Elected first Chancellor of Federal Republic, 1949; re-elected 1953, 1957. Also

ALLENDE, SALVADOR (1908–73) A founder member of the Chilean Socialist Party, he became its General Secretary in 1942. In 1945 he was elected to the Senate and served as its Vice-President and President. In 1970, as the candidate for the Popular Unity Front, he was narrowly elected as President. His policies 'to open the road to socialism' included land reforms, nationalization of industry and the mines, and opposition to American economic dominance. Following a worsening economic situation and considerable opposition to these policies, a right-wing military junta, backed by the USA, overthrew his government in Sept. 1973. Allende died whilst being overthrown in the coup.

AMIN, IDI (1925–2003) Ugandan dictator. As Uganda's army commander he overthrew the government of Milton Obote (q.v.) on 25 Jan. 1971. His period as dictator (1971–9) was marked by massacre and brutality. In 1972 he ordered the mass expulsion of Asians from Uganda. Fled to Libya in 1979 after his overthrow following a Tanzanian invasion. Lived in Saudi Arabia from 1980.

AQUINO, CORAZON (1932–) Philippine politician. Entered politics in 1985 following the 1983 assassination of her husband, opposition leader Benigno Aquino. Won 1986 Presidential election despite rigging attempt by Marcos (q.v.). Pro-Aquino demonstrations and the withdrawal of US support forced Marcos's flight. Faced 5 early attempted coups, but success in a 1987 plebiscite confirmed her as President until 1992. A further coup attempt occurred in 1989.

ARAFAT, YASSER (1929–2004) Chairman of the PLO (p. 480) 1969–2004 and head of the Executive Committee of al-Fatah (p. 451) since 1968. Founding member of al-Fatah in 1956 and worked as an engineer in Kuwait between 1957 and 1965, He steered the PLO in a moderate direction following the Oct. 1973 war, leading ultimately to the creation of a Palestinian Authority, of which he became Chairman and Minister of the Interior in May 1994 and President after 1996. Co-winner of Nobel Peace Prize in 1994, but accused by Israel of being soft on terrorism and outflanked by the militants of Hamas and Islamic *Jihad* who continued terrorist action against Israeli settlers. Election of hardliner Ariel Sharon as Premier of Israel in 2001 and an impasse in negotiations about the creation of an independent Palestinian state led to increasing violence and growing pressure upon Arafat's leadership.

ASSAD, HAFEZ ALI (1928–2000) President of Syria from 1971 to his death. Member of the Ba'ath Party (p. 454) and became Defence Minister and Commander of the Air Force in 1966. In 1970 came to power in a coup and introduced an authoritarian regime. Seeking to regain the Golan Heights lost in 1967, his attack on Israel was halted in the Yom Kippur War of 1973. His support of terrorism led to a breach with the West in the mid-1980s, but he played the role of power broker to end the civil war in Lebanon, to secure the release of Western hostages, and sided with the West in the Gulf War of 1991. Courted by the West to resolve the Middle East problem and contain Saddam Hussein

(q.v.) he showed extraordinary political longevity for a Syrian ruler and died in office. He was succeeded by his son Bashar.

ATTLEE, CLEMENT RICHARD, 1ST EARL ATTLEE (1883–1967) Elected leader of the Labour Party in 1935. In the wartime coalition government he took office as Lord Privy Seal, 1940–2, Secretary for the Dominions 1942–3 and Lord President of the Council 1943–5. He was Deputy Prime Minister 1943–5 and Prime Minister from 1945 to 1951. As Labour Prime Minister he presided over an active and able cabinet which introduced the National Health Service, comprehensive social welfare and nationalized many basic industries. He presided over the granting of independence to India, Pakistan, Ceylon (Sri Lanka) and Burma, the British withdrawal from Palestine and the onset of the Cold War.

AYUB KHAN, MOHAMMED (1907–74) Commander-in-Chief of the Pakistani army and Minister of Defence 1954–5. He became President in 1958. He was re-elected in Jan. 1965, but after widespread strikes and riots, especially in East Pakistan, he resigned in Mar. 1969.

AZAÑA, MANUEL (1881–1940) Spanish President. Founded Republican Party, 1924. Subsequently imprisoned. War Minister, 1931. First Prime Minister of Second Republic, 1931–3, and again in 1936. Imprisoned for advocacy of Catalan self-rule, 1934. President 1936–9. Fled to France, Feb. 1939.

AZIKIWE, MHAMDI (1904–96) Premier of Eastern Nigeria 1954–9, he became Nigeria's Governor-General in 1960 after independence. When Nigeria became a republic on 1 Oct. 1963 he was its first President. He was deposed in a military coup which occurred while he was in Britain in Jan. 1966.

B

BALEWA, SIR ABUBAKAR TAFAWA (1912–66) Nigerian statesman. The first federal Prime Minister of independent Nigeria, 1960–6. On 15 Jan. 1966 he was murdered in a military *coup d'état*.

BANDA, HASTINGS KAMAZU (1906–97) African nationalist. Practised as a doctor in Britain and Ghana before returning to Nyasaland, where he became President-General of the African National Congress in 1958. Riots led to the declaration of a state of emergency, and the arrest of Banda. He was released in Apr. 1960 and became leader of the Malawi Congress Party and first Prime Minister on independence. Made President for life in 1971, he was President of Malawi for almost three decades after independence until defeated in multi-party elections in 1994.

BANDARANAIKE, SIRIMAVO (1916–2000) Sri Lankan politician. Prime Minister 1960–5, the first woman Prime Minister. Prime Minister again from 1970 to 1977. Responsible for the 1972 constitution by which Ceylon became the Republic of Sri Lanka.

BATISTA, FULGENCIO (1901–73) Cuban politician. Army sergeant. Joined a coup against President Machado in 1933, took rank of colonel and attempted to develop a fascist state. Allowed formation of opposition parties, 1937; elected President, 1939. Voluntary exile in Dominican Republic, 1944. Returned as dictator after coup, 1952. Increasingly unpopular with the army and harried by guerrilla forces under Fidel Castro (q.v.) he fled from Cuba, 1958.

BEGIN, MENACHEM (1913–92) Israeli politician. Prime Minister 1977–83. Became Prime Minister of Israel when his right-wing alignment Likud won a greater number of seats than any other political party in the May 1977 elections. However, since Likud did not gain a majority, it was necessary to form a coalition with other groups represented in Parliament. Begin had commanded the Irgun, a terrorist group operating first against the British in the 1940s. After independence he led the Herut party which became part of the Likud group. He was Minister without Portfolio in the National Unity Government formed just before the Six Day War. He opposed any withdrawal from the West Bank but presided over relaxation of tension with Egypt. Joint recipient of Nobel Peace Prize with Sadat (q.v.) in 1978.

BEN BELLA, MOHAMMED AHMED (1916–) Algerian revolutionary leader. Imprisoned by French for political activities, 1950, escaped in 1952. Founded and led *Front de la Libération Nationale* (FLN) in armed struggle against France, 1954. Arrested in 1956, he was freed under terms of Evian Agreements in 1962 to become Algerian President. Overthrown in 1965 and under house arrest till 1979.

BENES, EDUARD (1884–1948) Czech statesman. Worked with Masaryk in Paris during First World War, seeking Czech independence. Principal Czech representative at Paris Peace Conference. Prime Minister, 1921–2, Foreign Minister, 1918–35. Active diplomat, chief proponent of Little Entente (Czechoslovakia, Romania and Yugoslavia, with French support). President of League of Nations Assembly, 1935. Succeeded Masaryk as President, 1935. Resigned, 1938, following Munich Agreement. President of Czech government-in-exile in London, 1941–5. Re-elected president, 1946. Resigned shortly after communist coup, 1948.

BEN-GURION, DAVID (1886–1973) Zionist leader. Chairman of the Jewish Agency, 1935–48. Proclaimed the independence of the state of Israel and subsequently became its first Prime Minister (1948–53). He was a key figure in the creation of the modern democratic state of Israel.

BERIA, LAVRENTI PAVLOVICH (1899–1953) Soviet secret police chief. Bolshevik organizer in Russian Revolution. Led secret police in Georgia, 1921–31. First Secretary of Georgian Communist Party, 1931. Appointed by Stalin (q.v.) to head Commissariat for Internal Security (NKVD), 1938–53. Deputy Prime Minister, 1941. Politburo member, 1946. Arrested and executed by rivals in Party power struggle following Stalin's death.

BERLUSCONI, SILVIO (1966–) Media tycoon and politician. Created his own party, *Forza Italia*, which gained support amidst the break-up of the postwar Italian party system in the 1990s. Formed his first government in 1994, but forced out of office in Dec. as a result of accusations of corruption. Returned as leader of a coalition government in May 2001, supported by the right-wing Northern League and *Alleanza Nazionale*, pursuing pro-enterprise and anti-immigration policies. By 2004, longest-serving postwar Italian prime minister.

BERNADOTTE, COUNT FOLKE (1895–1948) Swedish Red Cross president and United Nations mediator. Arranged exchanges of wounded Allied and German prisoners, 1943–4. Involved by Himmler in rejected peace approaches to Western Allies, Jan. 1945. Appointed UN mediator between Arabs and Jews in Palestine, May 1948. Assassinated by Jewish terrorists, Sept. 1948.

BHUTTO, BENAZIR (1953–) Pakistani politician; Prime Minister, 1988–90, 1993–6. American- and Oxford-educated daughter of Zulfikar Ali Bhutto (q.v.). Returned from exile in 1986 and became premier in Nov. 1988 following electoral victory of Pakistan People's Party (PPP). First woman leader of a predominantly Muslim nation in modern times. Dismissed for alleged corruption in Aug. 1990, but in 1993 formed a new coalition government. Renewed violence, strikes and charges of corruption overshadowed her attempts to seek rapprochement with India and ease militant Islamic tensions. Dismissed again in Nov. 1996, followed by the resounding defeat of the PPP by the Muslim League in the 1997 elections.

BHUTTO, ZULFIKAR ALI (1928–79) Pakistani politician. Appointed Prime Minister in Dec. 1971 after India's victory over Pakistan. As Foreign Minister, 1963–6, he had favoured close links with China and urged a tough line with India over the disputed state of Kashmir. After a period marked by political and social reforms he was ousted from power in 1977. Executed 1979. His daughter, Benazir Bhutto, became Prime Minister 10 years later.

BIKO, STEVE BANTU (1946–73) South African black nationalist leader. Medical student, helped found South African Students' Organization in 1968, becoming its president, and the Black People's Convention. Organized Black Community Programme to encourage black pride and opposition to apartheid. Banned by South African government, 1973. Death in police custody aroused international condemnation.

BIN LADEN, OSAMA (1957–) Saudi Arabian-born leader of al-Qaeda terrorist network. Believed to have masterminded the 1993 bombing of the New York World Trade Center and the 11 Sept. 2001 attacks on the World Trade Center and the Pentagon. Believed to have been based in

Afghanistan, he went into hiding following the American-led invasion in autumn 2001, issuing occasional video and press releases reiterating his vehement anti-American and anti-western views.

BLAIR, ANTHONY (TONY) (1953–) Prime Minister of Britain since 1997. Leader of Labour Party from 1994, pursuing modernizing agenda, and secured landslide victories in 1997 and 2001 on the basis of conservative economic and fiscal policies, with moderate social reform – the 'Third Way'. Brought about ceasefire in Northern Ireland; strong supporter of intervention in the Balkan conflict and of President Bush's 'war' on terrorism. His advocacy of war in Iraq in 2003 provoked huge opposition and continuing controversy about its justification.

BLUM, LÉON (1872–1950) French Socialist statesman. Elected to Chamber of Deputies, 1919. By 1925, established as a leader of Socialist Party. First Socialist Prime Minister, 1936, leading 'Popular Front'. Introduced important social reforms, including 40-hour working week. Formed second Popular Front, 1938. Imprisoned by Vichy regime, 1940. Accused of being responsible for French military weakness and tried, 1942. Interned in Germany during Second World War. Briefly Prime Minister of caretaker government, 1946.

BOTHA, PIETER (1916–) South African politician. Entered National Party government in 1958, held a number of posts, becoming party leader and Prime Minister in 1978. He became state President in 1984. His policy of modifying apartheid failed to satisfy black aspirations and international opinion but increasingly alienated his own right wing. Relinquished party leadership following a stroke in Jan. 1989, retaining presidency until his angry resignation, Aug. 1989. Resigned from National Party, May 1990, in protest at talks with ANC.

BOUMEDIENNE, COLONEL HOUARI (1925–78) Algerian Prime Minister and head of government, 1965–78. Ousted Ben Bella (q.v.) from power in 1965. From 1960 to 1962 he was chief-of-staff of the Algerian forces fighting for independence from France. In 1962, after independence, he became Defence Minister. From 1963 to 1965 he was Vice Premier.

BOURGUIBA, HABIB (1902–2000) President of Tunisia, 1957–88. A leading Tunisian nationalist, in 1934 he formed the Neo-Destour Party which was outlawed by France. He spent several years in prison during the struggle for independence. Bourguiba later favoured close relations with the West. In 1975 he was elected President for Life. Deposed in 1988 after he became increasingly senile.

BRANDT, WILLY (1913–92) West German Social Democratic statesman. Active in opposition to Hitler. Member of Bundestag, 1949–57. President of Bundesrat, 1955–7. Mayor of West Berlin, 1957–66. Chairman of Social Democratic Party, 1964. Joined coalition with Christian Democrats under Chancellor Kiesinger, 1966. Chancellor in SPD-Free Democrat coalition, 1969. Awarded Nobel Peace Prize, 1971. Resigned following spy scandal, 1974, remaining Chairman of SPD. Consistent advocate of improved relations with Eastern Europe (*Ostpolitik*).

BREZHNEV, LEONID ILYICH (1906–82) Soviet politician. Communist Party official in Ukraine and Moldavia. Held military posts, 1933–4. Member of Praesidium of Supreme Soviet, 1952–7. President of Praesidium, 1960–4, succeeding Marshal Voroshilov. Succeeded Khrushchev as First Secretary of Central Committee, 1964. General Secretary of Central

Committee, 1966. Chairman of Praesidium, 1977.

BUNCHE, RALPH (1904–71) United Nations official. Academic turned State Department official. Involved in establishing the United Nations; Director of Trusteeship Division, 1947; UN Under-Secretary, 1955–71. Nobel Peace Prize for work in Palestine, 1950. Led UN peace-keeping operations in Suez (1956), the Congo (1960) and Cyprus (1964).

BUSH, GEORGE HERBERT WALKER (1924–) 41st President of the United States. Republican politician. Gained lengthy experience as Vice-President, 1981–9, serving under Reagan (q.v.). The first Vice-President to be elected President since Martin van Buren in 1836. Inherited Reagan's legacy of massive budget deficit, a drugs crisis and external problems in Panama. Bush ordered the Dec. 1989 invasion of Panama to overthrow the Noriega (q.v.) regime and seize the dictator. Presided during winding down of Cold War and period of rapid change in Eastern Europe. Supported embargo on Iraq after its invasion of Kuwait in 1990 and authorized air offensive and Gulf War in 1991 to remove Iraqi forces, but stopped short of invasion of Iraq and overthrow of Saddam Hussein (q.v.). Failed to secure re-election.

BUSH, GEORGE WALKER, JNR (1946–) President of the United States from 2001. Son of former President Bush Snr. Governor of Texas, 1995–2000. Secured Presidency over Al Gore after Supreme Court ruling ended controversial series of recounts in Florida. Pursued conservative agenda of tax cuts and opposition to environmental restrictions on exploitation of natural resources. The terrorist attacks on 11 Sept. 2001 dominated his Presidency, leading to the American-led invasion of Afghanistan to topple the Taliban (p. 488) regime accused of protecting Osama bin Laden (q.v.) and

the invasion of Iraq to overthrow Saddam Hussein (q.v.). Continued unrest in Iraq and sluggish economic growth raised questions about his ability to secure re-election, but elected for second term in 2004 (Nov.).

BUSIA, KOFI ABREFA (1913–78) Nigerian politician. After the deposition of Nkrumah (q.v.) in 1966 he was made adviser to the National Liberation Council. On 1 Oct. 1969 he became Prime Minister when power was handed over to civilian government again. His government encouraged the Africanization of foreign firms. On 13 Jan. 1972 he was overthrown by the military and went into voluntary exile.

C

CAETANO, MARCELO (1906–80) Portuguese politician. Minister under Salazar (q.v.) in the 1940s and 1950s; retired to academic life in 1959. Following Salazar's retirement was Prime Minister, 1966–74. Attempted liberalization, but its limited nature and his failure to resolve colonial wars in Angola and Mozambique led to 1974 revolution and his exile.

CARTER, JAMES EARL (JIMMY) (1924–) 39th US President. Democrat Senator for Georgia, 1962–6. Elected Governor of Georgia 1971. Defeated Ford (q.v.) in Presidential election, 1976. Negotiated Panama Canal Treaty, treaty between Egypt and Israel at Camp David (see p. 457) and the unratified SALT II. Weakened by bad relations with Congress, failure to surmount world oil crisis and economic recession. Bungled rescue attempt of American Embassy hostages in Iran contributed to defeat by Reagan (q.v.) in Presidential election, 1980.

Subsequently involved in international diplomatic negotiations and overseeing elections in newly democratizing countries. Awarded Nobel Peace Prize in 2002.

CASTRO, FIDEL (1927–) Cuban revolutionary leader. Prime Minister since 1959. Formerly a lawyer, he was imprisoned in 1953 for an attack on an army barracks in Cuba. Following his release during an amnesty, he went to Mexico and organized the Cuban revolutionary movement. After attempts in 1956 and 1958, the rebels finally occupied Havana in 1959 and overthrew President Batista. He became Prime Minister and head of the armed forces on 16 Feb. 1959. A Marxist, he instituted reforms in agriculture, industry and education and broke away from American economic dominance. In 1961 he routed an invasion of US-supported exiles at the Bay of Pigs (p. 455). The following year his acceptance of Russian help and the installation of Soviet rockets led to the so-called Cuban Missile Crisis. In 1976 he became head of State and President of the Council of State.

CEAUSESCU, NICOLAE (1918–89) Romanian dictator. Member of underground Communist Party, 1936. Party Secretariat member, 1954. Deputy leader, 1957–65. General Secretary, 1965. Head of State, 1967. Combined independent foreign policy, notably criticism of the 1968 Warsaw Pact invasion of Czechoslovakia, with authoritarian regime, massive repression and personality cult. Repressed demonstrations prompted by economic crisis, 1967. Showed little sympathy for the Soviet line instituted by Gorbachev (q.v.). His corrupt regime and bankrupt economy provoked riots in 1989. Their savage repression led to the Dec. 1989 'winter revolution' (see p. 327). Executed by firing squad after secret trial, 25 Dec. 1989.

CHAMBERLAIN, NEVILLE (1869–1940) British Conservative politican. Son of Joseph Chamberlain. Lord Mayor of Birmingham, 1915–16. Director General of National Service, 1916–17. Member of parliament, 1918–40. Postmaster General, 1922–3. Paymaster General, 1923. Minister of Health, 1923, 1924–9. Chancellor of the Exchequer, 1923–4, 1931–7. Prime Minister, 1937–40. Resigned, 1940, becoming Lord President of the Council in wartime coalition, following rebellion by Conservative MPs in favour of Churchill. Much criticized for attempts to appease Germany and Italy, especially Munich Agreement, 1938. Retired from politics, 1940.

CHIANG CHING-KUO Son of Chiang Kai-shek (q.v.).

CHIANG KAI-SHEK (1887–1975) Chinese general and statesman. He took part in the 1911 Chinese revolution and became Chief-of-Staff to the revolutionary leader Sun Yat-sen. In 1928 he became commander of the Guomindang army and head of the government established at Nanking. His forces fought local war-lords, Japanese invaders and communists. He led the government during the Second World War but in 1949 was defeated by the communists and retired to Formosa (Taiwan), from where he continued to lead the Nationalist China government until his death in 1975.

CHILUBA, FREDERICK (1933–) President of Zambia, 1991–2002. He became Chairman of the Zambia Congress of Trade Unions in 1974 and was a leading opponent of the one-party rule of President Kaunda (q.v.), becoming leader of the Movement for Parliamentary Democracy (MPD) formed in July 1991. His regime became tarnished by corruption and he was replaced in Jan. 2002 by Levy Mwanawasa. Chiluba was arrested in Feb. 2003 on charges of corruption and looting the state Treasury.

CHIRAC, JACQUES (1932–) French Gaullist politician; elected to the National Assembly in 1967. Served as Prime Minister, 1974–6, 1986–8. Maintained power base as Mayor of Paris from 1977. Unsuccessful candidate in the 1981 and 1988 Presidential elections, he was elected in May 1995 to succeeed the ailing Mitterrand and again in 2002, against the far right-wing candidate Le Pen. Although he pursued France's right to conduct nuclear tests in the South Pacific in the 1990s, he showed strong pro-European sympathies, cementing his links with Germany and abandoning the franc for the euro in 1992. He opposed the US invasion of Iraq in 2003.

CHRÉTIEN, (JOSEPH JACQUES) JEAN (1934–) Canadian politician and lawyer. Prime Minister, 1993–2004. Liberal politician with extensive ministerial experience. Secretary of State for External Affairs and Deputy Prime Minister, June–Sept. 1984. First elected to Commons in 1963.

CHURCHILL, SIR WINSTON (1874–1965) British statesman. Conservative MP, 1900–4. Became a Liberal in protest at Tariff Reform policies. Liberal MP, 1906–8, 1908–22. Constitutionalist, later Conservative MP, 1924–45. Conservative MP for Woodford, 1945–64. Under-secretary at Colonial Office, 1906–8. President of the Board of Trade, 1908–10. Home Secretary, 1910–11. First Lord of the Admiralty, 1911–15. Chancellor of the Duchy of Lancaster, 1915. Minister of Munitions, 1917–19. Secretary for War and Air, 1919–21. Secretary for Air and Colonies, 1921. Colonial Secretary, 1921–2. Chancellor of the Exchequer, 1924–9. First Lord of the Admiralty, 1939–40. Prime Minister and Minister of Defence, 1940–5. Leader of the Opposition, 1945–51. Prime Minister, 1951–5. Minister of Defence, 1951–2. Knighted, 1953. Resigned 1955. Chequered

career. During First World War involved in disputes over Admiralty policy and Gallipoli campaign. Opposed Conservative policies over India and rearmament during 1930s. Advocated prevention of German expansion. Wartime leadership earned him legendary status, though not returned to power in 1945. Negotiated wartime alliance with USA and USSR. After Second World War, favoured alliance with USA against USSR.

CLINTON, WILLIAM JEFFERSON (BILL) (1946–) President of the United States, 1993–2001; defeated George Bush Snr in the 1992 Presidential elections and inaugurated in Jan. 1993. Governor of Arkansas, 1979–80 and 1983–92. Obtained approval of North American Free Trade Agreement in 1993 but Congress rejected the overhaul of the healthcare system advocated strongly by him and his wife, Hillary. He attempted to broker peace in the Middle East with historic accord between Israel and the PLO and also the Israeli–Jordan peace agreement signed in Washington in 1994. In the Dayton accords of 1995 he committed US forces to peacekeeping in Bosnia and Herzegovina. The Democrats lost control of Congress in 1994 for the first time in forty years, but Clinton was re-elected in Nov. 1996, defeating Republican Bob Dole, on the basis of a booming economy and foreign policy successes. These seemed further enhanced by his involvement in the peace process in Northern Ireland, culminating in the Good Friday Agreement of 1998, but were overshadowed by charges of personal impropriety with a White House aide, Monica Lewinsky, leading to his impeachment. Charged with perjury and obstruction of justice he was acquitted at his Senate trial in 1999. A successful economy, budget surpluses and his personal charm ensured that he retired as a highly popular President.

COOLIDGE, (JOHN) CALVIN (1872–1933) 30th US President of the United States. Massachusetts Republican State legislative member 1912–15, Lieutenant Governor 1916–18, Governor 1918. Elected as Harding's Vice-President in 1920. Succeeded to the Presidency on Harding's death, Aug. 1923, going on to win the 1924 Presidential election. Conducted *laissez-faire* policy domestically and non-intervention abroad. Declined nomination for further term, 1928. Apparent prosperity of Coolidge era exposed as illusory by the Wall Street Crash seven months after he left office.

CUELLAR, PÉREZ DE see Pérez de Cuellar

D

DAYAN, MOSHE (1915–81) Israeli politician and defence chief. Foreign Secretary under Begin, 1978–9. Defence Minister between 1967 and 1974, he was blamed for being caught unprepared when the 1973 Oct. War came. From 1953 to 1957 he was chief-of-staff of the Israeli Defence Forces. He left the army to be active in the Labour Party and he served as the Agriculture Minister from 1959 to 1964. A member of Ben-Gurion's faction, he left the Labour Party with Ben-Gurion in 1965 but rejoined the government after the 1967 Arab–Israeli war. He opposed the return of the Arab territory occupied in 1967.

DE GAULLE, CHARLES (1890–1970) French soldier and statesman. Member of French military mission to Poland, 1919–20. Lectured at Staff College. Sought to modernize Army. Published 'The Army of the Future', 1932–4. Ideas subsequently employed by German Army. Briefly a member of Reynaud's government, 1940. Fled to Britain after fall of France. Became head of Committee of National Liberation ('Free French'), 1943. Claimed status of head of government. Led unsuccessful attempt to recapture Dakar. Entered Paris, Aug. 1944. President of provisional government, 1945. Suspected of authoritarian ambitions. Resigned, 1946. Founded political group *Rassemblement du Peuple Français* (RPF), retiring from its leadership in 1953. During Algerian Crisis, 1958, invited by President Coty to form temporary government with wide executive powers. Won overwhelming victory in referendum on new Constitution. Elected first President of Fifth Republic, 1959. Granted independence to former French colonies in Africa, 1959–60. Granted Algeria independence, 1962. Developed independent nuclear deterrent. Encouraged closer ties with Federal Germany. Twice vetoed British entry to EEC, 1962–3, 1967. Re-elected on second ballot, 1965. Re-elected after May 1968 'Events', but resigned in 1969, following opposition to his plans to reform Constitution.

DENG XIAOPING (1904–97) veteran Chinese politican. Secretary-General of the Chinese Communist Party. Purged during the Cultural Revolution, but reinstated in 1973. Fell from power again, 1976. Reinstated and led attack on 'Gang of Four'. Ordered army to attack demonstrators in Tiananmen Square, June 1989. Retired from formal politics in Nov. 1989 but retained considerable backstairs influence until his death. Seen as the architect of economic transformation in China to a form of 'totalitarian capitalism'.

DESAI, MORARJI (1896–1995) Indian politician. Long-serving Congress politician. Deputy Prime Minister, 1967. Out of favour with Indira Gandhi (q.v.). Formed Janata Party, leading it to victory in Mar. 1977 general election. Became Prime Minister of India at the age of 81.

DE VALÉRA, ÉAMON (1882–1975) Irish states-man. Led group of Irish volunteers in Easter Rising, 1916. Imprisoned, released 1917. Elected MP, 1917. Leader of Sinn Fein, 1917–26. Elected president of Dail Eireann. Opposed 1921 treaty with Britain, led extreme nationalists during Civil War, 1922–3. Leader of Fianna Fail, winning 1932 elections. During 1932–8, reduced links with Britain. After 1937, Prime Minister under revised Constitution. Maintained Irish neutrality during Second World War. Lost power, 1948. Re-elected, 1951–4, 1957–9. President, 1959–73.

DIEM, NGO DINH *see* Ngo Dinh Diem.

DOLLFUSS, ENGELBERT (1892–1934) Austrian politician. Leader of Christian Social Party. Chancellor, 1932–4. Opposed by Nazis and Socialists. Used political violence as pretext for dictatorial govern-ment. Suspended parliamentary rule, 1933. Provoked and suppressed Socialist revolt. Granted authority by parliament to implement new fascist-style constitution. Murdered during attempted Nazi coup.

DRUMMOND, SIR JAMES ERIC (1876–1951) British diplomat. Joined Foreign Office, 1900. Member of British delegation to Peace Conferences, 1918–19. First Secre-tary of the League of Nations, 1919–33. British Ambassador to Rome, 1933–39. 16th Earl of Perth, 1937.

DUBCEK, ALEXANDER (1921–92) Czech politician. First secretary of the Czecho-slovak Communist Party and key figure in the 'Prague Spring' (p. 482) reform move-ment, which culminated in the Soviet invasion of Czechoslovakia in Aug. 1968; dismissed from his post, he was first President of the New Federal Assembly (Aug. 1968–Sept. 1969) then ambassador to Turkey (Dec. 1969–June 1970) before being expelled from the Communist Party. This attempt to build a national socialism with a 'human face' posed a threat to Soviet control of Eastern Europe. By 1989, however, circumstances had changed. In Dec. 1989 Dubcek was elected Chairman (Speaker) of the Czech parliament.

DULLES, JOHN FOSTER (1888–1959) American Secretary of State, 1953–9. An advocate of a hard-line against commun-ism, his foreign policy was obdurately opposed to negotiation with Russia and to American recognition of Communist China. Strongly opposed the Anglo-French invasion of Egypt in 1956 – the 'Suez Cri-sis' (p. 488). *See also* massive retaliation (p. 475).

E

EDEN, SIR (ROBERT) ANTHONY, 1st EARL OF AVON (1897–1977) Conservative politician. Eden sat as Conservative MP for Warwick and Leamington from 1925 until he retired in 1957. He acted as parliamentary private secretary to Sir Austen Chamberlain (Foreign Secretary), 1926–9, was under-secretary at the Foreign Office, 1931–3, Lord Privy Seal, 1934–5, minister without portfolio for League of Nations Affairs, 1935 and Foreign Secretary 1935–8. In 1938 he resigned in protest at the govern-ment's policy of appeasement. Wartime Foreign Secretary, 1940–5. From 1942 to 1945 he was also Leader of the Commons. He returned to the Foreign Office in 1951 and remained there until 1955. He was Prime Minister from 1955 to 1957, resign-ing in 1957 because of ill-health. Eden was an extremely experienced diplomat but he miscalculated domestic and world opinion when authorizing the ill-fated invasion of Suez in 1956.

EINSTEIN, ALBERT (1879–1955) Great scientist. Mathematical scientist famous for his theory of relativity. Awarded Nobel Prize, 1921 for his work in quantum theory. Driven from Germany by the Nazis. Warned Roosevelt in Aug. 1939 of Nazi research into uranium and alerted Roosevelt to the urgency of possible use of atomic energy in bombs.

EISENHOWER, DWIGHT DAVID (1890–1969) American statesman and military commander. After the Japanese attack on Pearl Harbor on 7 Dec. 1941 he became assistant chief-of-staff in charge of the Operations division in Washington. He was in command of the European theatre of operations in 1942, and successively Commander of the Allied forces in North Africa 1942–4, Supreme Commander of the Allied Expeditionary Force in the Western zone of Europe 1944–5, Commander of the US Occupation Zone in Germany in 1945, Chief-of-Staff of the United States Army 1945–8, and Supreme Commander of the North Atlantic Treaty Forces in Europe 1950–2. In 1952, Eisenhower won the Republican nomination for the presidency, and then the presidency itself. In Sept. 1955 he suffered a severe heart attack, and in June 1956 underwent a serious operation for intestinal disorder. He nevertheless secured re-election in Nov. 1956. He was succeeded in office by President John F. Kennedy (q.v.) in Feb. 1961.

F

FAISAL, ABDUL AZIZ SAUD, AL (1905–75) King of Saudi Arabia. After filling various government posts he became Crown Prince and Prime Minister in 1953. He competed with King Saud for power and between 1958 and 1964, when Saud was deposed, he had full control of the Saudi government.

In 1964 he was proclaimed king. A conservative monarch, he had no sympathy with radical Arab regimes and maintained close relations with the United States. It was under his rule that Saudi Arabia first claimed huge profits from oil and began to use that resource for political purposes.

FAROUK, KING (1920–65) King of Egypt, 1936–52. His attempts at land reform and economic development failed in the face of institutional corruption. Appointed increasingly anti-British governments, 1944–52. Egypt's military failure against Israel in 1948 and Farouk's personal extravagance led to his overthrow and exile, 1952.

FOCH, FERDINAND (1851–1929) French soldier, Marshal of France. Served as military instructor, 1894–9. Director of *Ecole de Guerre*, 1907–11. Wrote *Principles and Conduct of War*, 1899. Appointed Chief-of-Staff, 1917. Created Generalissimo of Allied forces from Mar. 1918; architect of Allied victory on Western Front. Field Marshal, 1919. Supervised implementation of military provisions of Treaty of Versailles.

FORD, GERALD RUDOLPH (1913–) 38th US President. Michigan Republican Congressman, 1948–73. Nixon's Vice President on resignation of Agnew, 1973. Appointed President following Nixon's resignation over the Watergate scandal, 1974. Unique in holding both offices without election. Pardoned Nixon and amnestied Vietnam War draft evaders, 1974. Defeated by Carter (q.v.) in Presidential election, 1976.

FRANCO, FRANCISCO (1892–1975) Spanish soldier and military dictator. Held command of Foreign Legion in Morocco. Chief-of-Staff, 1935. Governor of Canaries, 1936. On outbreak of Civil War, integrated Foreign Legion and Moorish troops into rebel army. Became leader of nationalist forces, 1936. Defeated Republican Government, 1939. Established corporatist, authoritarian state, acting as 'Caudillo' (Leader), and ruling Spain as absolutist leader until his death.

FUJIMORI, ALBERTO (1939–) President of Peru, 1990–2000. Of Japanese immigrant parents, he was a university rector with no political experience before becoming the independent Cambio '90 group's 1990 presidential election candidate. Instituted an austerity programme to deal with Peru's inflation and debt crisis. In Apr. 1992 he suspended the constitution and ruled with military backing. His New Majority–Cambio '90 coalition emerged as the leading party in the Nov. 1992 elections. New constitution promulgated and approved in 1993 allowing for a second Presidential term, with a third term approved by Congress in 1996. Winning a second term in 1995 Fujimori successfully combated the Shining Path (see Sendero Luminoso, p. 485) and Tupac Amaru rebel movements, including a major hostage crisis at the Japanese embassy in Dec. 1996, but was increasingly criticized for his authoritarian style and continuing economic problems.

G

GALTIERI, LT-GEN. LEOPOLDO FORTUNATO (1926–2003) Argentinian dictator, Dec. 1981 to June 1982. President of Argentina during the invasion of the Falklands (Malvinas) in May 1982. The military failure of the policy led to his removal in June 1982 and imprisonment, 1983–9.

GANDHI, INDIRA (1917–84) The daughter of Nehru, she joined the Congress Party in 1938. In 1964 she became Minister of Information and in 1966 succeeded Shastri,

becoming India's first woman Prime Minister. She survived temporary expulsion from the party leadership in 1969 and in 1971 was re-elected. In 1975 a crisis developed when the High Court declared her election as invalid. This led to the declaration of a state of emergency. Her unpopular measures resulted in an overwhelming defeat for the Congress Party in the Mar. 1977 elections and the loss of her seat. This loss of power was only temporary. Returned as Prime Minister in 1980. Assassinated by Sikh extremists, 1984. Succeeded by her son, Rajiv (q.v.).

GANDHI, MOHANDAS (MAHATMA) (1869–1948) Indian patriot, social reformer and moral teacher. He lived in South Africa 1893–1914, before returning to India to lead the independence movement. He was a dominating influence in Congress with his policies of non-violence and civil disobedience and was frequently arrested. After independence he continued his fight to rid India of the caste system and to unite Hindu and Muslim, but was assassinated in 1948 on his way to a prayer meeting.

GANDHI, RAJIV (1944–91) Indian politician. An airline pilot, he entered politics on the death in 1981 of his elder brother, Sanjay. Held a number of offices under his mother, Indira Gandhi (q.v.), before succeeding her as Prime Minister at her assassination, 1984. Despatched troops to Sri Lanka to quell militant Tamil separatists, 1987. Defeated by a relatively united opposition in Dec. 1989 elections, he was assassinated while electioneering in May 1991.

GIAP, NGUYEN VO *see* Nguyen Vo Giap.

GISCARD D'ESTAING, VALÉRY (1926–) French politician. National Assembly member, 1956–74. Led Independent Republicans. Finance Minister, 1962–74. Defeated Gaullist and left opponents in

Presidential election, 1974. Gaullist backing gave him a National Assembly majority but this weakened in the face of scandals, including one over gifts received from Central African President, Bokassa. Defeated in Presidential election by Mitterrand, 1981. Author of draft new EU Constitution debated in 2003–4.

GOEBBELS, JOSEPH (1897–1945) German Nazi propagandist. Early recruit to Nazi Party. Party chief in Berlin, 1926–30. Became Party's propaganda chief, 1929. Elected to Reichstag, 1930. Minister of Propaganda, 1933–45. Held powerful position in Nazi leadership. Made skilful use of oratory, parades, demonstrations and radio. Attracted to 'radical' aspect of Nazi ideology. Death by suicide.

GOERING, HERMANN (1893–1946) German Nazi military and political leader. First World War ace pilot. Joined Nazi Party, 1922. Given command of Storm Troopers, 1923. Elected to Reichstag, 1928. President of Reichstag, 1932–3. Entered government, 1933, as Reich Commissioner for Air, Minister President of Prussia and Prussian Minister of the Interior (hence controlled Prussian police). Created Gestapo, 1933. Head of Luftwaffe. Responsible for preparing Germany's war economy. Created General, 1933, Field Marshal, 1938 and Reich Marshal, 1940. Became Hitler's deputy during Second World War. Influence declined after Battle of Britain, 1940. Disgraced after plotting to oust Hitler, 1945. Condemned to death at Nuremberg Trials. Death by suicide.

GORBACHEV, MIKHAIL (1931–) Soviet statesman who succeeded Chernenko as general secretary of the Communist Party in 1985. His advent to power after a succession of ailing, old-guard leaders marked a major departure in the Soviet leadership. Succeeded Gromyko as President, 1988.

His reforming policies, especially perestroika and glasnost, were soon threatened by nationalism in such areas as Azerbaijan and the Baltic. His policy of non-interference was vital in the 1989 revolutions in Eastern Europe which overthrew the old communist regimes. With Reagan (q.v.) and Bush Snr (q.v.) he effectively brought the Cold War to an end, negotiating huge reductions in nuclear arsenals and conventional forces. Became Executive President, 1990 and inaugurated democratic elections, but faced growing opposition as his economic reform programme created unrest and nationalist forces grew in strength. In Aug. 1991 a communist coup against him, though defeated, completely undermined his authority and precipitated the break-up of the Soviet Union and the formation of the Commonwealth of Independent States. Overshadowed by the rise of Boris Yeltsin (q.v.), he resigned as President in Dec. 1991.

GOWON, YAKUBU (1934–) Nigerian officer and politician. Head of Federal Military Government, 1966–75. On 29 July 1966 he became Head of State of Nigeria and Commander-in-Chief of the army, following a coup which overthrew the regime of General Ironsi. He led the federal troops in the civil war (1967–70) but was overthrown in a coup on 29 July 1975.

GRIVAS, GEORGE (1898–1974) Greek army officer. Served in Second World War; supported royalists in Greek Civil War. Led EOKA guerrilla movement in Cyprus from 1953 in fight for independence from Britain and union with Greece (Enosis). Commander of post-independence Greek Cypriot National Guard. Recalled to Greece, 1967. Returned to Cyprus to wage underground struggle for Enosis which alienated Turkish Cypriot community, leading to 1975 Turkish invasion and partition of Cyprus.

GROMYKO, ANDREI ANDREEVICH (1909–89) Soviet statesman. Attached to Soviet embassy in Washington, 1939. Ambassador in Washington, 1943. Attended Tehran, Yalta and Potsdam Conferences. Elected deputy of Supreme Soviet, 1946. Became Deputy Foreign Minister, and permanent delegate to United Nations Security Council, using veto frequently. Ambassador to Britain, 1952–3. Foreign Minister, 1957–85. Signed partial nuclear test ban agreement, 1963. President of the USSR, 1985–8.

GUEVARA, ERNESTO (CHE) (1928–67) Latin American revolutionary and guerrilla fighter who became a cult figure in the 1960s. Che Guevara was born in Argentina in 1928 and trained as a doctor. He joined Castro's revolutionary army and landed in Cuba in 1956. After the overthrow of Batista in 1959, he acted as a diplomat and administrator in Cuba, and wrote a book analysing the principles and practice of guerrilla warfare. In 1966 he launched a guerrilla campaign in Bolivia, but was captured and executed by Bolivian government forces on 9 Oct. 1967. He became a symbol and martyr for radical students worldwide.

H

HAIG, ALEXANDER MEIGS (1924-) American soldier and politician. Brigade commander in Vietnam, 1966–7. President Nixon's military adviser, 1969–73, and White House Chief-of-Staff, 1973–4. Supreme Allied Commander NATO Forces Europe, 1974–8, where he survived an assassination attempt. Appointed Reagan's Secretary of State, 1981, he resigned in 1982 after increasing conflict with the administration.

HAILE SELASSIE (1892–1975) Emperor of Ethiopia 1930–74. He was exiled to Britain, 1936–41, during the Italian occupation. He was an active supporter of Pan-African unity and was a President of the Organization of African Unity (p. 267) whose headquarters were in Addis Ababa. He acted as mediator in the Sudanese and Nigerian civil wars but was himself deposed and stripped of his powers by the army in 1974.

HAMMARSKJÖLD, DAG (1905–61) Swedish statesman. Became Secretary-General of the United Nations in 1953. Killed in an air crash whilst attempting to mediate in the Congo. Posthumously awarded the 1961 Nobel Peace Prize. He previously conducted the UN through the 1956 Suez Crisis with skill and impartiality.

HARDING, WARREN GAMALIEL (1865–1923) 29th US President. Ohio Republican State Senator, 1890–1902. Lieutenant Governor, 1904–6. Elected to Senate, 1914. Won landslide presidential election victory on 'back to normalcy' platform, 1920. Facing depression, Harding reduced taxes, increased tariffs and introduced immigration controls. Called 1921–2 Washington Disarmament Conference to limit size of navies. Death in office, 1923, followed by revelations of administrative corruption (notably the Teapot Dome scandal), though the extent of Harding's awareness was unclear.

HASSAN II (1929–99) King of Morocco from 1961. Exiled with his father by the French, he returned to Morocco in 1955 and assumed command of the armed forces. He became Prime Minister in 1960. He survived attempted coups and assassinations and gradually assumed wider powers. He disputed control over the Western Sahara with Spain, Mauritania and Algeria, as well as with Polisario Front guerrillas. His death ended a reign of

38 years; he was succeeded by his son Muhammad VI.

HAVEL, VACLAV (1936–) President of Czechoslovakia, 1989–93 and of Czech Republic, 1993–2003. Former dissident and political prisoner under the communist regime. Born Prague; playwright; co-founder of Charter 77 and imprisoned for several years on trumped-up charges. Co-founder of Civic Forum, Nov. 1989, which spearheaded pro-democracy movement and mass demonstrations which toppled the Communist regime. Reluctantly accepted being drafted as presidential candidate in Dec. 1989. Presided over peaceful separation of the Czechoslovak Republic into the Czech and Slovak Republics in 1993, the Czech Republic's entry to NATO in 1999 and negotiations for entry to the European Union in 2004.

HEATH, SIR EDWARD (1916–) British Conservative politician. Entered Parliament, 1950. Party Whip, 1951–5. Chief Whip, 1955–9. Minister of Labour, 1959–60. Lord Privy Seal, 1960–3. Secretary for Trade and Industry, 1963–4. First leader of Conservative Party to be elected by ballot, 1965. Prime Minister, 1970–4. Proponent of European integration. Achieved British entry into EEC, Jan. 1973. Failed to tackle problems of inflation and industrial relations. Improved British relations with China. Following electoral defeats of 1974, replaced as leader of Party by Margaret Thatcher, 1975. He frequently attacked policies of Thatcher from backbenches.

HIMMLER, HEINRICH (1900–45) German Nazi leader and chief of Police. Early member of Nazi Party. Involved in Munich Putsch, 1923. Head of Schutzstaffel (SS), 1929. Head of Gestapo, 1934, subsequently of all police forces, 1936. Head of Reich administration, 1939. Minister of the Interior, 1943. Commander-in-Chief of Home Forces, 1944. Used elaborate system of terror, espionage, detention and murder to reinforce totalitarian state. Bore major responsibility for racial extermination policies. Made attempts to negotiate unconditional surrender before end of war. Tried at Nuremberg. Death by suicide.

HIROHITO (1901–89) Emperor of Japan. Regent, 1921; survived assassination attempt, 1924; succeeded to throne, 1926. Backed Tojo's urging of war against Britain and US, 1941. Threw weight behind those arguing for peace in 1945, accepting Allied unconditional surrender demand in August. Avoided trial as war criminal because General Douglas MacArthur saw him as crucial factor in post-1945 Japanese political stability. Discarded traditional divine status, 1946. Official visits abroad in the 1970s marked recognition of Japan's growing economic status. His culpability in Japan's road to war is still disputed by historians.

HITLER, ADOLF (1889–1945) Dictator of Germany. Born in Austria. Served in Bavarian Army during First World War, becoming lance corporal, twice decorated with Iron Cross. Joined German Workers' Party in Munich, 1919, transforming it into National Socialist German Workers' Party (NSDAP/Nazi Party), based on extreme nationalism and anti-Semitism. Attempted putsch in Munich, 1923, which proved abortive, though making him a national figure. While in prison wrote his political testament, *Mein Kampf*. Began to re-organize Nazi Party, 1925. Established unrivalled position as leader of Party. Created efficient propaganda machine and organized elite guard, Schutzstaffel (SS). Helped to power by Great Depression. Nazi Party won 107 seats in 1930 Reichstag elections, becoming second largest party. In elections, July 1932, won 230 seats (highest they ever achieved). Appointed Chancellor by Hindenburg, Jan. 1933, though Nazis still a minority in Reichstag. Following

Reichstag fire and Enabling Act, assumed dictatorial powers. Other political parties dissolved. Nazi Party purged of rivals by 1934. On death of Hindenburg, 1934, became President, uniting position with that of Chancellor as Führer ('Leader'). Internal opposition ruthlessly suppressed. Rearmament programme expanded in 1935, aiding economic recovery. Occupied Rhineland, 1936. Rome–Berlin 'Axis' negotiated, 1936. Annexed Austria, 1938 (*Anschluss*). Gained Sudetenland after Munich Agreement, 1938. Seized remainder of Czechoslovakia, 1939. After non-aggression Pact with USSR (Molotov–Ribbentrop Pact, Aug. 1939), invaded Poland, 1 Sept. 1939, precipitating Second World War. Achieved swift military successes through 'Blitzkrieg' campaigns, but fatal error was in attacking Russia, June 1941. Ordered 'final solution' (i.e. mass genocide), of the Jewish people in such camps as Auschwitz and Treblinka where millions died. Faced combined opposition of USSR, USA and Britain. Survived assassination attempt, July 1944. Committed suicide during closing stage of war.

HO CHI MINH (1890–1969) Vietnamese nationalist and revolutionary. Leader of the Vietnam revolutionary nationalist party of Indo-China, which struggled for independence from France during and after the Second World War. In 1945 the independent republic of Vietnam was formed with Ho Chi Minh as president. In 1954 the decisive victory over the French at Dien Bien Phu (p. 462) led to the Indo-China armistice and the Geneva Agreements. Holding power until his death in 1969, he succeeded in welding together the elements of nationalism and communism in North Vietnam. Troops were sent against South Vietnam and, largely through his efforts, a unified socialist Vietnam was brought about in 1975.

HOOVER, HERBERT CLARK (1874–1964) 31st US President. Businessman and organizer of relief operations following First World War, appointed Secretary of Commerce by President Harding, 1921. Elected Republican President in 1928, his attempts to combat the Depression through a Reconstruction Finance Corporation and the relief of state debts failed. Defeated by Roosevelt in 1932 presidential election. Appointed co-ordinator of food supplies to war-ravaged countries, 1946. Headed Hoover Commission to reorganize federal government structure, 1947–49, 1953–55.

HOOVER, (JOHN) EDGAR (1895–1972) Head of US Federal Bureau of Investigation. Lawyer in Department of Justice, 1917. Special assistant to Attorney General, 1919. FBI Assistant Director, 1921; Director, 1924–72, serving under eight Presidents. Reorganized the Bureau, concentrating on gangsters in the 1930s, enemy spies in the 1940s and communist subversion after 1945. His role became increasingly controversial in the 1960s, when the FBI was accused of harassing anti-Vietnam-War and black civil rights activists.

HOXHA, ENVER (1908–85) Albanian politician. Joint founder and General Secretary of the Albanian Communist Party (now the Albanian Labour Party) from 1941 to 1985. His significance in the international communist movement was his firm support of China in the Sino-Soviet dispute. He broke diplomatic relations with the USSR in 1961, officially withdrew Albania from the Warsaw Pact in 1968. He kept Albania in isolation under a rigid Stalinist regime.

HU JINTAO (1942–) General Secretary of Chinese Communist Party 2002–3, President from Mar. 2003. Trained as an engineer and opposed to the Cultural Revolution; rose as protégé of Deng Xiaoping, becoming youngest party secretary in Guizhou province and then in

Tibet, where he declared martial law in 1989. Appointed General Secretary in Nov. 2002 he made modest moves towards liberalization, such as the reporting of Politburo meetings and a strengthened constitution. A technocrat, he continued economic development.

HUA KUOFENG (1922–) Chinese communist leader. Rapid rise to power from the obscurity of party secretary in a part of Hunan in 1955 to membership of the Central Committee in 1969 and the Ministry of Public Security. In 1973 he moved up to the politburo. Following Chou's death in Jan. 1976 he was a surprise appointment as acting Prime Minister. This post was confirmed in Apr. After the death of Mao in Oct. 1976 he became Chairman of the Central Committee of the Chinese Communist Party, resigning in 1981.

HUSSEIN, KING IBN TALAL (1935–99) King of Jordan 1952–99. Succeeded to the throne upon the abdication of his father. His crown was supported by the tribes and the army, as well as subsidies from the United States. Lost the West Bank and east Jerusalem in the Six Day War (see p. 315). His pro-Western sympathies were often at odds with his neighbours and the militants of the PLO (p. 480), who were expelled after fighting between them and the government in 1970–1. He renounced all claims to the West Bank in favour of the PLO in 1988 and signed a peace treaty with Israel in Washington in 1994. He was succeeded by his son, King Abdullah II, who continued his father's policy of seeking a settlement of the Israeli–Palestinian conflict and maintaining relationships with his other Middle Eastern neighbours.

HUSSEIN, SADDAM (1937–) Iraqi dictator. Born in Tikrit, north of Baghdad. Joined the Ba'ath Party (p. 454). Involved in Oct. 1959 assassination attempt against Brigadier Qassem. Fled to Egypt, before returning to Syria and entering (by marriage) the Syrian Ba'athist leadership. Became President of Iraq, July 1979. Ran Iraq through a clique of Tikriti family relations and by ruthless use of terror. Seen initially as less of a threat than the militant Islamic fundamentalism in Iran and elsewhere, he was supported by the West after he launched an enormously bloody and ultimately unsuccessful war against Iran (see p. 324). However, disquiet with his attempts to develop biological, chemical and nuclear weapon grew and he provoked a major international crisis by his invasion of Kuwait in Aug. 1990. Forced out of Kuwait in the first Gulf War of 1991, he suppressed revolts by the Kurds in the north and in the south with ferocity, including the use of poison gas. Flouting UN monitoring of his weapons' programmes and subject to UN sanctions, his regime was toppled by an invasion of US-led coalition forces in Apr. 2003. Forced into hiding he was captured in Dec. 2003 and put on trial in 2005.

J

JAGAN, DR CHEDDI (1918–97) Independent nationalist. The first Prime Minister of independent Guyana, President, 1992–7.

JARUZELSKI, GENERAL WOJCIECH (1923–) Polish soldier and politician. Long and distinguished army career. Became Chief of General Staff, 1965, Minister of Defence, 1968, and member of Politburo, 1971. Became Prime Minister after resignation of Pinkowski, 1981. Declared martial law in effort to tackle economic crisis and to counter growth of Solidarity movement. Solidarity banned and its leaders detained and tried. Lifted martial law, July 1983, but retained emergency powers. Elected

President, 1989, but resigned following the breakdown of communist rule and the first multi-party elections.

JIANG ZEMIN (1926–) Chinese communist leader. President, 1993–2003. As the party leader in Shanghai he was appointed Party Secretary by Deng Xiaoping (q.v.) following the ousting of Zhao Ziyang after the Tiananmen Square massacre. Following Deng's death in 1997 as State President and General Secretary of the Communist Party he presided over the rapid economic modernization of China while maintaining political authority in the hands of the Party and the army. At the 16th Party Congress in 2002 Hu Jintao was elected to succeed him. Jiang retained the post of Chairman of the Party's Central Military Affairs Commission until Sept. 2004.

JINNAH, MOHAMMED ALI (1876–1948) Pakistani statesman. One of the makers of modern Pakistan. President of the Muslim League. First Governor-General of independent Pakistan.

JOHN PAUL II, POPE (1920–2005) Born Karol Wojtyla. Student and actor, 1938. Quarryworker in German-occupied Poland. Ordained as priest, 1946. Appointed bishop, 1958, Archbishop of Cracow, 1964, Cardinal, 1967. In Oct. 1978 elected as first non-Italian Pope since 1552. Doctrinally conservative, an extensive world traveller, his popular appeal much in evidence at mass rallies. Survived assassination attempts in May 1981, when he suffered gunshot wounds, and in 1982. Visits to Poland offered protection to Solidarity leaders during period of martial law; maintained extensive schedule of travel in spite of growing frailty and an unyielding defence of conservative positions on doctrinal and sexual issues.

JOHNSON, LYNDON BAINES (1908–73) 36th President of the United States, 1963–8. Elected to the House of Representatives in 1938 and to the Senate in 1948. Became Democratic leader in the Senate in 1953. Despite suffering a severe heart attack in 1955, he held the post until he became Vice President of the United States in Jan. 1961. After completing the presidential term to which the assassinated President Kennedy had been elected, he was nominated to run as Democratic candidate for the presidency in 1964, an election which he won by a large majority. Because of disenchantment within the Democratic Party over his administration's policies towards Vietnam, he did not run for re-election in 1968. He was succeeded by Richard M. Nixon (q.v.).

K

KASAVUBU, JOSEPH ILEO (1910–69) Zaïrean politician who favoured a federal state. He became President in 1960 with Lumumba (q.v.) as Prime Minister after a post-independence election gave neither a majority. He was deposed by the army in Nov. 1965 in a military coup led by Mobutu (q.v.).

KAUNDA, KENNETH DAVID (1924–) Zambian politician. President of Zambia, 1964–91. As leader of the Zambia National Congress, he was imprisoned for 9 months, but was released in 1960 and became leader of the United National Independence Party. As President of Zambia from 1964, was the creator of the political philosophy of humanism and as one of the front-line presidents played an important part in the independence negotiations in Rhodesia and Mozambique. He assumed autocratic powers in 1972 to prevent tribal break-up but, after a new constitution in 1973, his presidency was confirmed. Defeated in 1991 election following economic decline and illiberalism.

KEMAL ATATÜRK (MUSTAFA KEMAL) (1881–1938) Creator of modern Turkish nation. Joined Young Turk reform movement. Entered army, winning quick promotion. Fought Italians in Tripoli, 1911, and in Balkan Wars. Involved in Gallipoli campaign during First World War. Led national resistance after Greek invasion following Turkey's defeat. Renounced loyalty to Sultan and formed provisional government in Ankara, 1920. Led Turks in War of Independence until 1922, expelling Greeks, deposing Sultan and establishing republic. Became first President of Republic, 1923–38. Architect of modern secularized state. Emancipated women. Sought to build strong nation from homelands of Anatolia and residue of European Turkey. Did not attempt to regain former Arab possessions. Territorial settlement with Greece achieved at Treaty of Lausanne, 1923.

KENNEDY, JOHN FITZGERALD (1917–63) American statesman and 35th President. Born May 1917 in Boston, Massachusetts. The son of Joseph Kennedy, a successful businessman and ambassador to the United Kingdom, and a Roman Catholic. He graduated from Harvard University in 1940 and served in the US Navy. Elected to the House of Representatives in 1946. He defeated Henry Cabot Lodge for one of the Massachusetts Senate seats in 1952, and in Nov. 1960 defeated Richard Nixon (q.v.) in the presidential election by a narrow margin. On 22 Nov. 1963 he was assassinated in Dallas, Texas. A commission under the Chief Justice of the United States Supreme Court, Earl Warren, concluded that he had been killed by one Lee Harvey Oswald, acting alone. He was succeeded by the Vice President, Lyndon Baines Johnson, on the afternoon of his death. His short period as President witnessed the Cuban Missile Crisis. His style and charisma made him one of the most admired and popular presidents of modern times.

KENNEDY, ROBERT FRANCIS (1925–68) American politician. Presidential campaign manager for his brother, John F. Kennedy, 1960. US Attorney General, emphasizing civil rights and investigating institutionalized crime, 1961–4. Democratic Senator for New York, 1965–8. Assassinated in Los Angeles, June 1968, while campaigning for Democratic presidential nomination on black rights and anti-Vietnam War platform.

KENYATTA, MZEE JOMO (1893–1978) Kenyan national leader. President of Kenya, 1964–78. In 1952 he was arrested on suspicion of leading the Mau Mau rebellion (p. 305) and sentenced to 7 years' imprisonment followed by detention. He was released in 1961 and as President of the Kenya African National Union became Prime Minister in 1963 and President in Dec. 1964.

KEYNES, JOHN MAYNARD, 1ST BARON KEYNES (1883–1946) British economist. Worked at Treasury during First World War. Chief representative at negotiations prior to Treaty of Versailles. Criticized reparations plans in *The Economic Consequences of the Peace*, 1919. Made radical proposals for dealing with unemployment by provision of public works. Ideas influenced Liberal Party's election manifesto, 1929. Full proposals on economic controls in interests of maintaining full employment appeared in *The General Theory of Employment, Interest and Money*, 1936. Inspired 'Keynesian Revolution' during and after Second World War. Rejected classical belief in self-regulating economy. Argued need for government expenditure to be adjusted to control level of public demand. Advised Chancellor of the Exchequer during Second World War. Chief British delegate at Bretton Woods Conference, 1944. Involved in discussions leading to creation of International Monetary Fund and World Bank.

KHAMA, SIR SERETSE (1921–80) Botswana national leader. A lawyer exiled from Botswana 1950–6, he founded the Botswana Democratic Party in 1962 and in 1966 became the first President of Botswana at independence. As a front-line president (p. 466) he played a leading role in Rhodesian independence negotiations and in discussions of the subsequent problems of Southern Africa.

KHOMEINI, AYATOLLAH (1900–89) Iranian religious leader of Shi'ite Muslims. His denunciation of the Shah's Westernizing reforms and female emancipation led to arrest and exile in France. Urged Iranian army to overthrow Shah and institute Islamic republic. Returned to Tehran when the Shah fled, 1979, and remained the dominant figure until his death, severing relations with the West, enforcing religious fundamentalism, and waging 1980–8 Gulf War with Iraq. Issued death threat against Salman Rushdie, author of novel *The Satanic Verses*.

KHRUSHCHEV, NIKITA SERGEYEVICH (1894–1971) Soviet politician. Joined Communist Party, 1918. Fought in Civil War. Member of Central Committee of Party, 1934. Full member of Politburo and of Praesidium of Supreme Soviet, 1939. Organized guerrilla warfare against Germans during Second World War. Premier of Ukraine, 1944–7. Undertook major restructuring of agriculture, 1949. Became First Secretary of All Union Party on death of Stalin, 1953. Sensational denunciation of Stalinism, 1956. Relegated Molotov, Kaganovich and Malenkov (potential rivals), 1957. Succeeded Bulganin as prime minister, 1958–64. Official visits to USA, 1959, India and China, 1960. Deposed, 1964, after criticism of his reforms, especially in agriculture.

KIM IL-SUNG (1912–94) Korean communist. Communist leader of the Democratic Republic of Korea since 1948. He took the title of President in 1972 and became the centre of an ever-growing personality cult. With Soviet backing he instigated the Korean War (p. 304) in 1950 and presided over a stern, communist autocracy until his death, marked by his personality cult and growing economic problems. Succeeded by his son, Kim Jong-il.

KING, MARTIN LUTHER (1929–68) American black civil rights leader. Ordained as Baptist minister, 1947. Began non-violent civil rights campaign in Montgomery, Alabama, leading boycott of racially segregated buses, 1955–6. Founded Southern Christian Leadership Conference, 1957. An effective orator, notably in his Washington 'I have a dream' speech, 1963. Awarded Nobel Peace Prize, 1964. His assassination in Memphis, Tennessee, Apr. 1968, provoked widespread black riots throughout America.

KISSINGER, HENRY (1923–) American academic and politician. German-born; US citizen, 1943. Professor of Government, Harvard, 1958–71. Adviser in Nixon's (q.v.) Presidential campaign, 1968. White House National Security Adviser, 1969–73, playing a greater foreign policy role than the Secretary of State. Conducted diplomatic missions in Middle East, southern Africa and Vietnam. Joint Nobel Peace Prize winner with Vietnamese negotiator Le Duc Tho for extricating US from Vietnam. Secretary of State under Nixon and Ford (q.v.), 1973–7.

KLERK, FREDERIK WILLEM DE (1936–) South African politician. He was a representative of the National Party from 1972, then Minister of Home Affairs, 1982–6 and Minister of Education and Planning, 1986–9. Appointed leader of the National Party from Feb. 1989 and President of the Republic, Aug. 1989 to 1994. As President, he played a crucial role in the ending of the apartheid system. Together with Nelson Mandela (q.v.) he was awarded the Nobel Peace Prize. After the election victory of the African National Congress in May 1994, he became a Vice-President of South Africa. Announced his retirement from active politics in 1997.

KOSYGIN, ALEXEI (1904–80) Soviet politician. Communist Party Central Committee member, 1939. Minister for Economic Planning, 1956–7. State economic planning commission chairman and first Deputy Prime Minister, 1960. Succeeded Khrushchev as Chairman of the Council of Ministers (Prime Minister), 1964. Increasingly overshadowed by Brezhnev (q.v.), his moves towards industrial and agricultural decentralization and consumer goods production largely failed. Resigned on health grounds, 1980.

L

LAVAL, PIERRE (1883–1945) French politician. Member of Chamber of Deputies, 1914–19, and from 1924 onwards. Originally a socialist, became independent after 1927, on elevation to Senate. Minister of Public Works, 1925. Minister of Justice, 1926. Prime Minister, 1931–2, 1935–6. Foreign minister, 1934–6. Negotiated Hoare–Laval Pact with Britain, 1935. Proponent of closer ties with Germany and Italy. After fall of France, 1940, played major role in creation of Pétain's Vichy regime. Prime Minister, 1942–4. Collaborated with Germany, e.g. in supply of forced labour. Fled to Germany, then Spain, after liberation of France. Repatriated, tried and executed for treason.

LAWRENCE, THOMAS EDWARD (1888–1935) 'Lawrence of Arabia'. British archaeologist

sent to persuade Arabs to intensify anti-Turkish campaign, 1916. Skilled guerrilla tactician. Entered Damascus with British troops at head of Arab army, Oct. 1918. Felt Arab interests were betrayed by post-war treaties. Because of this, and other more complex personal motives, sought anonymity by joining the Army and the Air Force under assumed names. Killed in a motorcycle accident.

LE DUC THO, (1911–90) Vietnamese nationalist. A founder member of the Viet Minh (p. 492), he led the North Vietnamese delegation at the Paris peace talks.

LEE KUAN YEW (1923–) Singapore elder statesman. He was one of the founders of the Singapore Socialist People's Action Party in 1954 and was the long-serving Prime Minister, 1959–90. Under his leadership, Singapore has seen remarkable economic development, but political opposition has often been stifled.

LENIN, VLADIMIR ILYICH (V. I. ULYANOV) (1870–1924) Russian revolutionary leader and architect of Soviet state. After expulsion from Kazan University for political activity, absorbed writings of Marx. In St Petersburg organized League for the Liberation of the Working Class. Exiled to Siberia, 1897. In London, 1903, when Russian Social Democratic Labour Party divided into Mensheviks and Bolsheviks. Led Bolshevik wing and published newspaper, *Iskra* ('The Spark'). Involved in abortive Russian Revolution, 1905. Controlled revolutionary movement from exile in Switzerland. Smuggled into Russia by Germans, 1917. Overthrew Kerensky's provisional government and became head of Council of People's Commissars. Ended war with Germany and concluded treaty of Brest-Litovsk, Mar. 1918. Civil war with 'White' armies continued until 1921. As Chairman of Communist Party, established virtual dictatorship and dissolved

Constituent Assembly. Created Communist International.

LIAQUAT, ALI KHAN (1896–1951) Pakistan politician. Prominent member of Muslim League before the Second World War. First Prime Minister of independent Pakistan, 1947–51, and, after death of Jinnah (q.v.) in 1948, the nation's dominant figure. His refusal to declare Pakistan an Islamic state and attempts at friendlier relations with India aroused extremist anger, and he was assassinated in 1951.

LIE, TRYGVE (1896–1968) Norwegian social democratic politician. First Secretary-General of the United Nations, 1946–53. Advocated admission of Communist China to UN. Helped secure UN aid for South Korea to fight aggression by North Korea.

LIN BIAO (1908–71) Chinese communist military leader. Party member, 1927. Led an army on the Long March and against the Japanese. Waged successful campaign against Guomindang forces, 1948. Led Chinese armies in Korean War, 1950–2. Appointed Marshal, 1955, and Minister of Defence, 1959. Co-operated with Mao in Cultural Revolution and nominated at 1969 Party Congress as his eventual successor. Reportedly died in a plane crash in Mongolia, after attempting a coup in Beijing, Sept. 1971.

LIU SHAO-CHI (1898–1974) Chinese communist leader. Elected to Party Central Committee, 1927. Party principal vice-chairman on establishment of People's Republic, 1949. Chairman of People's Republic, 1959. His position weakened in the Cultural Revolution when he faced criticism for viewing workers as the main revolutionary force rather than, as Mao argued, the peasantry. Stripped of all political posts, Oct. 1968.

LLOYD GEORGE, DAVID, 1ST EARL LLOYD GEORGE OF DWYFOR (1863–1945) British Liberal statesman. Member of Parliament, 1890–1945. President of the Board of Trade, 1905–8. Chancellor of the Exchequer, 1908–15. Introduced controversial People's Budget, 1909, proposing increased taxation to fund social reform and naval rearmament. Budget rejected by House of Lords, causing constitutional crisis leading to Parliament Act, 1911. Minister of Munitions, 1915–16. Secretary for War, 1916. Prime Minister, 1916–22. Leader of the Liberal Party, 1926–31. Created Earl Lloyd George, 1945. Dynamic and efficient war-time leader. Attended Paris Peace Conference, 1919. Opposed calls for draconian penalties on Germany. Faced economic problems at home in postwar period. Continuing violence in Ireland led to creation of Irish Free State, 1921, weakening Lloyd George's position, as did revelations of his sale of honours. Forced to resign, 1922, when Conservatives left coalition. Never held office again.

LON NOL, GENERAL (1913–85) Former Prime Minister and Minister of Defence in Cambodia. Leader of the coup which overthrew Prince Sihanouk (q.v.) in Mar. 1970. He headed the Republican forces in the civil war, as well as holding the office of President, but was exiled following their defeat by the Khmer Rouge (p. 472) in 1975.

LUMUMBA, PATRICE (1925–61) Zaïrean politician who favoured central government as opposed to a federation. He became Prime Minister and Minister of Defence in 1960, with Kasavubu (q.v.) as President, after a post-independence election gave neither side a majority. He was dismissed by Kasavubu in Sept. 1960, and captured and reportedly shot by Katangan rebels.

LUTHULI, ALBERT (1899–1967) African Nationalist. Former Zulu chief who became a leading figure in the ranks of the African non-violent resistance leadership. Awarded Nobel Prize for Peace in 1960.

LUXEMBURG, ROSA (1870–1919) Polish-born German revolutionary leader. Major theoretician of Marxism. Imprisoned for opposition to First World War, 1915–18. Founded German Communist Party in 1918 with Karl Liebknecht, based on earlier Spartacist group. Opposed the nationalism of existing socialist groups, as shown by their participation in war. Critical of German Social Democrats in government. Sought to restrain more violent colleagues, but unable to prevent Spartacist uprising, Jan. 1919. Brutally murdered by counter-revolutionary troops.

M

MACARTHUR, DOUGLAS (1880–1964) US General. Army Chief-of-Staff, 1930–35. Supreme Allied Commander, South West Pacific, Second World War. Received Japanese surrender, 1945. Led occupation forces in Japan, 1945–51, playing a decisive role in preserving Japanese stability. Commander-in-Chief UN forces in Korean War, 1950–1. Dismissed by Truman (q.v.) for urging spread of war into China, contrary to official policy. Failed to win nomination as candidate in 1952 Presidential election.

MCCARTHY, JOSEPH (1908–57) American politician. Republican Senator for Wisconsin. McCarthy alleged in 1950 that over 200 Government employees were either Communist Party members or sympathizers,

though he provided no evidence. Chairman of the Senate Sub-committee on Investigations, 1953, where he accused numerous Democrats and Liberals of communist sympathies. His attacks on the Army aroused President Eisenhower's antagonism, leading to a Senate motion of censure against McCarthy in 1954 which ended his career.

MACHEL, SAMORA (1933–86) Mozambique nationalist leader. First President of Mozambique, 1975–86. President of Frelimo (p. 466) from 1970, Machel became President of the transitional government in Mozambique in 1974 and President on independence in 1975. As one of the front-line presidents (p. 466), he was involved in Rhodesian independence negotiations. Killed in plane crash, 1986.

MACMILLAN, (MAURICE) HAROLD, EARL OF STOCKTON (1894–1987) Conservative politician. Macmillan was Conservative MP for Stockton-on-Tees 1924–9, 1931–45, and for Bromley 1945–64. Served as minister resident at Allied HQ in NW Africa, 1942–5, Secretary for Air, 1945, Minister for Housing and Local Government, 1951–4, Minister of Defence, 1954–5, Foreign Secretary, 1955, Chancellor of the Exchequer, 1955–7 and Prime Minister, 1957–63. As early as the 1930s Macmillan revealed himself as an advocate of the Tory paternalist tradition in the Conservative Party, a stance which suited the mood of the 1950s and facilitated his rise to the premiership. His term in Downing Street was seen as something of a high point of postwar prosperity. But by the time of his resignation in 1963, it appeared to many people that Macmillan's style of leadership was dated and out of touch with the new decade. He retired owing to ill-health. Famous also for his 'Wind of Change' recognizing the need for decolonization in Africa.

MAHATHIR, DR MOHAMAD DATUK SERI (1925–) Prime Minister of Malaysia, 1981–2003. Trained as a doctor; joined the United Malays National Organisation (UMNO) in 1946 and elected to parliament in 1964. Expelled from UMNO and lost parliamentary seat after accusing the then Prime Minister of neglecting the Malay community. Seen as champion of Malays against the influential but minority Chinese population. Elected Prime Minister in 1981 he pursued a policy of positive discrimination in favour of Muslim Malays, but resisted the fundamentalist goals of the leading Muslim opposition party. He presided over Malaysia's emergence as an Asian 'tiger' economy and a tripling of national income per head in his premiership. He was criticized for using dubious legal charges against his opponents and ignoring environmental concerns about the exploitation of forest resources.

MAKARIOS, ARCHBISHOP (1913–77) President of Cyprus from 1960 to his death, except for a short interval in 1974. Also, head of the Greek Orthodox Church in Cyprus. Originally a supporter of Enosis, or union with Greece, he conducted negotiations with the British in the mid-1950s and was deported by them in 1956. He was released in 1957 but did not return to Cyprus until 1959. He was elected President in 1960 and during his time in office supported Cypriot independence. Forced into 5-month exile after attack on Presidential palace in 1974. He returned to a divided island, and was unable to reassert Greek supremacy over the Turkish Cypriot minority.

MALAN, DANIEL (1874–1959) South African politician. Dutch Reformed Church preacher, 1905–15. Elected as Nationalist MP, 1918. Intense Afrikaaner nationalist, opposed South African involvement in Second World War. Prime Minister, 1948–54. Instituted apartheid, dividing South Africa on racial lines between black, coloured and white.

MANDELA, NELSON ROLIHLAHLA (1918–) South African nationalist leader and President since 1994. A lawyer, member of the African National Congress (ANC) executive, 1952; advocated multi-racial democracy. Went underground on banning of ANC, 1961; organized *Umkonto we Sizwe* ('Spear of the Nation') for non-terrorist violent action. Arrested and imprisoned for five years, 1962. Sentenced to life imprisonment at trial for sabotage under Suppression of Communism Act, 1963. Remained a symbol of resistance to apartheid, with his (then) wife Winnie playing an active role both within South Africa and internationally. Finally released in Feb. 1990, and assumed role of primary negotiator in the dismantling of apartheid with De Klerk (q.v.). Swept to victory in 1994 elections as leader of the ANC and first black President of South Africa. Successfully managed post-apartheid regime and reconciliation process though there were criticisms of the failure to combat poverty, crime and the AIDS crisis. Retired as President in 1999 as a still widely respected figure within and outside South Africa.

MAO TSE-TUNG *see* Mao Zedong.

MAO ZEDONG (1893–1976) Chinese communist leader. Full-time revolutionary, 1923. Saw the peasantry as the main revolutionary force rather than, as in classical Marxism, the urban working class. Chairman of Kiangsi Soviet Republic, 1931. Driven out by Guomindang forces, led the Long March to north-west China. Allied with Guomindang against Japanese, 1937. Rejected Stalin's postwar urging to continue alliance with Guomindang, and won a civil war, becoming People's Republic chairman, 1949. Initially followed Soviet model of agricultural collectivization and industrial development. 'Let a hundred flowers bloom' policy, 1956, sought intellectual support by encouraging ultimately unwelcome criticism of Party. The 1958 'Great Leap Forward' was a turn to small-scale labour intensive programmes and was followed by a bitter ideological split with the Soviet Union. The 1966–9 'Great Proletarian Cultural Revolution' attempted to accelerate radicalism by rallying the masses and students against the Party bureaucracy. The ensuing chaos and its consequent brake on Chinese development remained unresolved at Mao's death.

MARCOS, FERDINAND EDRALIN (1917–89) Philippine politician. President of the Philippines, 1965–86; also Prime Minister, 1973–86. His regime was marked by massive corruption. Ousted from power in a peaceful coup by Corazon Aquino (q.v.) after rigged elections in Feb. 1986. Given exile haven in Hawaii by the USA, where he died in 1989. His wife, Imelda, was subsequently pursued to recover money looted from the state by the Marcos regime.

MARIAM, LT-COL. MENGISTU HAILE (1937–) Ethiopian leader. Came to power in the 1971 revolution which overthrew Emperor Haile Selassie. Mengistu became first President of Ethiopia in 1987 after a plebiscite approved the country's new constitution.

MEIR, GOLDA (1898–1978) Israeli Prime Minister from 1969 to 1974. After independence, she was very active in the Labour Party and was appointed Minister to the Soviet Union in 1948. In 1949 she became the Minister of Labour, a post she held until she was appointed Minister for Foreign Affairs in 1956. She resigned as Minister in 1965 and served as Secretary of the Labour Party until 1968. Elected Prime Minister, 1969. Secured victory in Yom Kippur War (q.v.). Resigned unexpectedly, 1974.

MENZIES, ROBERT GORDON (1894–1978) Australian politician. Member of Victoria Legislative Assembly, 1928–34. United Australia Party MP, 1934. Appointed Attorney General, 1935. Resigned, becoming party leader and Prime Minister, 1939. His concentration on the war lost him his party's leadership in 1941. Transformed the UAP into the conservative Liberal Party, 1943–5. Prime Minister, 1949–66, encouraging industrial development and an active foreign policy. Succeeded Churchill as Lord Warden of the Cinque Ports, 1965.

MITTERRAND, FRANÇOIS MAURICE (1916–96) French politician. Socialist deputy, 1946. Held ministerial office in 11 governments under the 4th Republic. Unsuccessful Left candidate against De Gaulle (q.v.) in presidential election, 1965. Socialist Party secretary, 1971. Defeated in presidential election, 1974. Elected President, defeating Giscard d'Estaing (q.v.), 1981. Backed by a National Assembly Socialist majority, attempted radical economic policy, 1981–3. After 1986 Assembly elections, shared power with Gaullist majority led by Chirac (q.v.) and moderated policy. Re-elected President, 1988, defeating Chirac. Helped draft the Maastricht Treaty of 1992, strengthening the EU, but his Presidency was dogged by economic problems, charges of corruption and his ill-health. Chirac succeeded him as President in 1995.

MOBUTU, SÉSÉ SÉKO (1930–97) Congolese politician. President of Zaïre 1965–97. At the independence of the Congo he was colonel and Chief-of-Staff of the army. Following the dismissal of Lumumba (q.v.) by Kasavubu (q.v.) he set up a caretaker government, and in 1961 he restored Kasavubu and led attacks on Katanga. In 1965 he deposed Kasavubu and became President and in 1966 Prime Minister and Minister of Defence. He was deposed in

1997 after presiding over one of the most corrupt regimes of modern Africa. Congo was known as Zaïre during his long dictatorship.

MOI, DANIEL ARAP (1924–) Kenyan politician, President of Kenya 1978–2002. Member of Legislative Council, from 1957; Chairman, Kenya African Democratic Union, 1960–1. Minister for Education, 1961–2; Local Government, 1962–4; Home Affairs, 1964–8. Vice President, 1967–78; became President following death of Kenyatta (q.v.) in 1978. Instituted one-party state and survived coup attempt in 1982. As increased power shifted to the Presidency, faced growing international criticism for corruption and abuses of human rights. Multi-party elections were permitted in 1992, the first in three decades. Moi won a fifth term as President in 1998, but was not permitted to seek re-election in 2002, when the National Rainbow Coalition's candidate, Mwai Kibaki won a landslide victory.

MOLOTOV, VYACHESLAV MIKHAILOVICH (1890–1986) Soviet politician. Emerged as prominent Bolshevik during November Revolution, 1917. Loyal colleague of Stalin, 1921 onwards. Member of Politburo, 1926–57. Helped implement Five Year Plan, 1928. Premier, 1930–41. Foreign Minister, 1939–49. Negotiated Pact with Ribbentrop, Aug. 1939. Deputy premier, 1941–57. Negotiated treaties with Eastern bloc countries, 1945–9. Became member of ruling triumvirate following death of Stalin, 1953. Negotiated Austrian State Treaty, 1955. Minister of State Control, 1956–7. Became Foreign Minister again, 1957. Influence declined with rise of Khrushchev. Ambassador to Mongolia, 1957–60. Retired, 1961–2.

MONNET, JEAN (1888–1979) French politician, economist and diplomat. Member of Inter-Allied Maritime Commission,

1915–17. First deputy secretary-general of League of Nations, 1919–23. Chairman, Franco-British Economic Co-ordination Committee, 1939–40. Became Minister of Commerce, 1944. Fostered establishment of National Planning Council, becoming head of Council, 1945–7. Architect of European Community. Chairman, Action Committee for United States of Europe, 1955–75. Instrumental in foundation of European Coal and Steel Community. President of ECSC, 1952–5.

MOUNTBATTEN (OF BURMA), LOUIS MOUNTBATTEN, 1ST EARL (1900–79) Naval commander. At the outbreak of the Second World War Mountbatten was commanding the Fifth Destroyer Flotilla. In 1941 his ship, HMS *Kelly*, was sunk in the Mediterranean and he was nearly drowned. He was then appointed adviser on combined operations. His largest operation was the Dieppe Raid in Aug. 1942, which though a failure, taught valuable lessons. Mountbatten was then appointed supreme commander in southeast Asia, arriving in India in Oct. 1943 to find a diversity of problems. After the war he was Viceroy of India, and presided over the partition of the subcontinent and the independence of India and Pakistan. He later returned to a naval career. In 1955 he was First Sea Lord and in 1959 Chief of the Defence Staff. He was assassinated by Irish extremists in 1979.

MUBARRAK, HOSNI (1928–) Egyptian politician. President since 1981. Air Force Chief-of-Staff, 1969–72 and Commander-in-Chief, 1972–5. Vice President, 1975–81. Vice Chairman of National Democratic Party (NDP), 1976–81; NDP Secretary General, 1981–2. President following assassination of Sadat (q.v.), 1981 by Muslim extremists. Continued dialogue with Israel, including return of Sinai to Egyptian control in 1982. Faced rioting over economic problems in 1986 and continuing opposition from Islamic fundamentalists, forcing the maintenance of emergency powers, though his Presidency has been renewed by six-yearly referendums and the NDP has an overwhelming majority in the People's Assembly. He sided with the West in the Gulf War of 1991.

MUGABE, ROBERT GABRIEL (1924–) Zimbabwean politician. Entered politics, 1960. Deputy Secretary General of Zimbabwe African People's Union (ZAPU), 1961. Arrested, 1962; fled to Tanzania, formed Zimbabwe African National Union (ZANU), 1963. Detained in Rhodesia, 1964–74. Joint leader with Nkomo (q.v.) of Mozambique-based Patriotic Front guerrilla campaign, 1976–9. Attended Lancaster House independence conference, 1979. First Prime Minister of Zimbabwe following election victory over Nkomo and Muzorewa (q.v.), 1980. Moved towards one-party state. Merged ZANU and ZAPU, 1987. Executive President since 1987. His authoritarian rule, the expropriation of white farmers to resettle 'war veterans', and consequent economic dislocation within Zimbabwe attracted growing criticism.

MUJIBUR RAHMAN, SHEIKH (1920–75) Bangladesh politician who led the Awami League (q.v.) to victory in the 1970 general election. In Mar. 1971 he proclaimed the independence of Bangladesh and was arrested and convicted of treason. After the intervention of India in the civil war he was released and became Prime Minister and later President of the new nation. In Aug. 1975 he and his family were assassinated.

MUSSADEQ, MOHAMMED (1880–1967) Iranian politician. Foreign Minister, 1922–4. Withdrew from politics but returned to Parliament, 1942. Violently nationalist speeches against Anglo-Iranian Oil Company carried him into office as Prime Minister, 1951. Falling output following nationalization of company and loss of Western expert advisers prevented promised social reforms. Overthrown in coup encouraged by Shah, with CIA support, and arrested, 1953.

MUSSOLINI, BENITO (1883–1945) Dictator of Italy. Originally a socialist. Imprisoned for political activities, 1908. Editor of socialist national newspaper, *Avanti*, 1912–13. Resigned from party having been criticized for supporting war with Austria. Founded newspaper, *Il Popolo d'Italia*, Milan, 1914. Organized groups (*fasci*) of workers to campaign for social improvements. Amalgamated into Fascist Party, 1919. Elected to Chamber of Deputies, 1921. During period of civil unrest, led 'March on Rome', 1922. Appointed Prime Minister by King Victor Emmanuel III, 1922. Headed fascist/nationalist coalition, as Duce, 1922. Dictatorship established, 1925. Single party, corporatist state instituted, 1928–9. Large-scale public works introduced. Lateran Treaty settled church state relations, 1929. Expansionist foreign policy: Corfu incident, 1924; invasion of Abyssinia, 1935; intervention in Spain, 1936. Created 'Axis' with Hitler, 1936. Left League of Nations, 1937. Annexed Albania, 1939. Declared war on France and Britain, 1940. Invaded Greece, 1940. Military setbacks in East Africa and Libya. Heavily dependent on Germany by 1941. Forced to resign following coup by Victor Emmanuel III and Marshal Badoglio, 1943. Detained, but freed by Germans. Established republican fascist government in German-controlled north Italy. Captured and executed by Italian partisans, Apr. 1945.

MUZOREWA, BISHOP ABEL (1925–) Zimbabwean bishop of the United Methodist Church and nationalist leader. Led the ANC (p. 451) opposition to the

Smith–Home proposals in 1971. In 1975 he led the ANC delegation at the Victoria Falls talks and in 1976 represented them at Geneva. Formerly in exile in Lusaka, he returned to Rhodesia to lead the internal group of the ANC after the split in 1977, and in Mar. 1978 was one of the nationalist leaders to sign the internal Rhodesian settlement. Member, transitional government, Zimbabwe–Rhodesia, 1978–80. Heavily defeated by Mugabe (q.v.) in 1980 elections.

N

NAGY, IMRE (1896–1958) Hungarian politician. Lived in USSR, 1930–44. Reforming Agriculture Minister in Hungarian Provisional Government, 1945–6. Prime Minister, 1953–5. Attempted liberalization led to loss of office and expulsion from Communist Party. Reappointed in Oct. 1956 Hungarian Rising; overthrown by Soviet intervention, Nov. 1956. Arrested and secretly executed, 1958. Officially rehabilitated, 1988.

NASSER, GAMAL ABDEL (1918–70) Leading Arab nationalist. President of Egypt, 1954–70. Educated at the Royal Military Academy, he fought in the 1948 Arab–Israeli war and, like all officers, was disgusted with King Farouk's provision of faulty arms to his troops. Founded the Free Officers group which overthrew the monarchy in 1952. For the first two years, Nasser hid behind the figurehead of Neguib (q.v.). But as Neguib was building a popular following and demanding more power, Nasser ousted him in 1954. Nasser then became Prime Minister and Chairman of the Revolutionary Command Council, Egypt's governing body. After decades of unstable governments, Nasser

did bring political stability to Egypt although this was done at the cost of increasing government control. The economy, under constant strain from the Arab–Israeli conflict and a rapidly increasing population, was quite another matter. Nasser committed Egypt to a course of socialism and nationalized first foreign firms and then Egyptian. His policies contributed to the 1956 Suez crisis (p. 488). State planning controlled most of the economy. Nasser had an active Middle Eastern policy and sought to foster Arab unity and lead the Arabs. This often caused bad relations with the more conservative Arab states, and involved him in a misbegotten unity with Syria and in the Yemen misadventure. Despite this, he was a widely respected figure in the Arab world for the pride he had brought to its people. He tried to resign after the June 1967 defeat, but his people refused to permit it.

NEGUIB, MOHAMMED (1901–84) Egyptian general and politician. As member of Free Officers Movement overthrew King Farouk (q.v.), 1952. President of Egypt, 1952–4. Forced to resign and placed under temporary house arrest by young officers led by Nasser (q.v.), 1954.

NEHRU, PANDIT JAWAHARLAL (1889–1964) Indian national leader and statesman. First Prime Minister and Minister of Foreign Affairs when India became independent in 1947. A leading member of the Congress Party, he had been frequently imprisoned for political activity. Under his leadership India progressed, and in world affairs his influence was for peace and non-alignment.

NETO, AGOSTINO (1922–79) Angolan politician. Imprisoned four times between 1952 and 1960 and from 1960 to 1962 for nationalist activities. Led guerrilla war against Portugal as President of People's Movement for the Liberation of Angola (MPLA), 1962–74. President of Angola since 1975. Defeated South African backed rivals with Cuban assistance, 1976.

NE WIN U (1911–90) Burmese political leader. Member of anti-British 'We Burmans Association' in 1930s. Chief-of-Staff of collaborationist army in Japanese-occupied Burma, 1942–4. Led guerrilla force supporting Allies against Japan, 1944. General and second-in-command of army on Burmese independence, 1948. Caretaker Prime Minister, 1958–60. Seized power in coup, 1962, leading the Burmese Socialist Programme Party (BSSP) to create a one-party state. President, 1974–81. Faced increasing resistance from communist and minority groups. Resigned as BSSP chairman following violently suppressed anti-government demonstrations, 1988.

NGO DINH DIEM (1901–63) First President of South Vietnam. Provincial governor 1929–32, but became increasingly anti-French. Founded anti-colonialist and anti-communist National Union Front, 1947. Banned and exiled by French. Following 1954 Geneva Agreements, he returned to become Prime Minister of an anti-communist government. President of South Vietnam following a rigged election in 1955, his authoritarian regime was increasingly unpopular. Victim of a CIA-engineered coup, he was assassinated, 1963.

NGUYEN VAN THIEU (1923–) President of South Vietnam, 1967–75. Previously he had pursued an army career, becoming Chief-of-Staff in 1963. His period in office saw the fall of Saigon and the final communist takeover of South Vietnam.

NGUYEN VO GIAP (1912–86) Vietnamese general who defeated the French at Dien Bien Phu (pp. 462–3). Withstood American intervention in the Vietnam war which followed. Deputy Prime Minister and Commander-in-Chief, North Vietnam.

NIMEREIRI, GAAFAR MOHAMED, AL- (1930–) President of the Sudan, 1969–85. Educated in the Military Academy, he served in the army and became its Commander-in-Chief. In 1969 he mounted a *coup d'état* and became Prime Minister and President of the Revolutionary Command Council. He survived several attempts to oust him from power until his overthrow in a military coup in Apr. 1985.

NIXON, RICHARD MILHOUSE (1913–94) 37th US President. Elected as Republican to House of Representatives, 1946; Senate, 1950. Vice President under Eisenhower (q.v.), 1953–61. Narrowly defeated by Kennedy (q.v.) in presidential election, 1960. Won presidential election, 1968. Ended American involvement in Vietnam, eased US–Soviet relations and opened diplomatic links with Communist China. Re-elected President, 1972. Controversial second term saw resignation of Vice President Agnew, 1973, and Nixon's own resignation, 1974, under threat of impeachment for involvement in Watergate conspiracy.

NKOMO, JOSHUA (1917–99) Zimbabwean politician. President, African National Congress, 1957–9. In exile, 1959–60. President, National Democratic Party, 1960. Helped found and became President of Zimbabwe African People's Union, 1962. Imprisoned, 1964–74. Joint leader with Mugabe (q.v.) of Patriotic Front guerrilla movement, 1976–9. ZAPU defeated by Mugabe's Zimbabwe African National Union (ZANU) in post-independence elections, 1980. Minister of Home Affairs in coalition government, 1980–1. Co-operation with Mugabe ended by violent tribal differences, 1982. Party vice-president on merger of ZANU and ZAPU, 1987.

NKRUMAH, KWAME (1909–72) African Nationalist. President of Ghana, 1960–6.

He became Prime Minister of Gold Coast in 1951 and was Prime Minister at independence in 1957. On 1 July 1960 he became first President of the Republic of Ghana and was a leading advocate of Pan-Africanism. His government, hit by economic depression and an increasingly dictatorial nature, was overthrown by a military coup in Feb. 1966. He took refuge in Guinea until his death.

NORIEGA, GENERAL MANUEL ANTONIO (1938–) Panamanian dictator. Military background. Became chief of G-2, the Panama intelligence agency in 1969. After President Torrijos was killed in an air crash in 1981, took over control of armed forces, becoming in 1983 *de facto* ruler of Panama. Subverted 1984 presidential election. Indicted by US juries of drug trafficking and racketeering, 1988. Survived coup attempt, Oct. 1989. Fled US invasion force seeking to capture him, Dec. 1989, taking refuge in Vatican embassy, Surrendered to US forces, 3 Jan. 1990. Flown to Florida to face drug trafficking charges.

NYERERE, JULIUS KAMBARAGE (1922–99) President of Tanzania, 1964–85. He was a founder member of the Tanganyika African National Union, Prime Minister at independence and in 1964 became President of Tanzania. Internationally known as a political philosopher, putting forward many of his views on the theory and practice of socialism in the Arusha declaration (q.v.). One of the most respected African nationalists and Commonwealth statesmen until his retirement in 1985.

O

OBASANJO, OLUSEGUN (1937–) Nigerian politician. Became Nigerian Head of State

in Feb. 1976 after an unsuccessful coup in which President Mohammed was killed.

OBOTE, OPOLO MILTON (1924–) Ugandan politician. President of Uganda, 1966–71 and from 1980–5. Led the opposition party in Uganda before becoming Prime Minister in 1962. He was President from 1966 to 1971 when he was deposed by Idi Amin (q.v.) whilst attending the Commonwealth Conference in Singapore. He was exiled to Tanzania. Following the invasion by Ugandan dissidents in 1979, aided by the Tanzanian army, he was elected President in 1980. Deposed, 1985.

OJUKWU, CHUKWENMEKA ODUMEGWU (1933–) President of Biafra, 1967–70. As military governor of the eastern states of Nigeria he announced their secession as Biafra. In Jan. 1970, as the rebellion collapsed, he escaped to the Ivory Coast, leaving Colonel Effiong to surrender.

ORTEGA SAAVEDRA, DANIEL (1945–) Nicaraguan politician. Underground activist against Somoza (q.v.) regime, 1959. Member, National Directorate of Sandinista Liberation Front (FSLN), 1966–7. Imprisoned, 1967–74. Resumed anti-Somoza activity, fighting successful guerrilla campaign, 1977–9. Member of the Junta of National Reconstruction, 1979. President, 1981–90.

P

PAHLEVI, MUHAMMED REZA SHAH (1919–80) Shah of Iran; ruled after his father's abdication in 1941, until 1979. His coronation was not until 1967. His position during the early years of his reign was precarious, and in 1953 he was forced to flee Iran for a short time. He later became an absolute ruler. In 1962, to gain popular support, he decreed the White Revolution, an extensive reform programme which included such items as land reform, a literacy campaign and the emancipation of women. He maintained close relations with the USA and built up a formidable defence capacity with its help. However, his dictatorial rule, and the excesses of the Savak (the secret police) helped fuel the fundamentalist Islamic movement led by Ayatollah Khomeini (q.v.), which overthrew him in a mass popular uprising in 1979.

PARK CHUNG HEE (1917–79) South Korean general. Led the military coup in South Korea in 1961. He was at first acting President but was subsequently elected to office in 1963 and was re-elected in 1967 and 1971.

PERES, SHIMON (1923–) Israeli Defence Minister from 1974 to 1977 and Labour Party candidate for Prime Minister in the May 1977 elections. During the 1948 war, Peres commanded the Israeli navy, and afterwards became an arms purchaser for the new state. He remained a member of Ben-Gurion's faction, and, when Ben-Gurion left the ruling Labour Party in 1965, Peres followed. He helped the faction return to power after the 1967 Arab–Israeli war. In 1974 and 1977 he narrowly lost the nomination for Prime Minister to Rabin, but, with Rabin's resignation as leader of the party in Apr. 1977, Peres achieved the nomination. Considered moderate on the Arab–Israeli conflict, following Labour's victory in the 1992 election he was appointed Foreign Minister and involved in the talks with the Palestine Liberation Organization (PLO) in Norway in 1993 and a prime mover in the Israeli–PLO accord of Sept. 1993 and the Jordanian–Israeli peace treaty of 1994. Shared the Nobel Peace Prize in 1994.

PÉREZ DE CUELLAR, JAVIER (1920–) Peruvian diplomat. Peru's United Nations representative, 1971–5, presiding over the UN Security Council in 1974. From 1979 to 1981 he was UN Under-Secretary General for special political affairs and became Secretary General in 1982. Successfully negotiated ceasefire between Iran and Iraq in their 8-year Gulf War, Aug. 1988.

PERÓN, JUAN DOMINGO (1895–1974) Argentine general and President. Influenced by fascism, participated in a military coup, 1943, becoming Minister of Labour and Social Security. Elected President, 1946 and 1951. Attempted to rally urban working class against traditional landed interests with anti-American nationalism and welfare policies. Eva Duarte de Perón (1919–52), his politically astute wife, played a central role. Her death, and growing confrontation with the Church, weakened his popularity. Ousted by the military and exiled, 1955. A *peronista* revival encouraged his return to victory in the 1973 Presidential election.

PÉTAIN, HENRI PHILIPPE (1856–1951) French soldier and politician. Entered army, 1876. Lectured at Ecole de Guerre, 1906 onwards. Became colonel, 1912. Commanded an army corps, 1914. National renown followed defence of Verdun, 1916. Commander-in-chief of French armies in the field, 1917. Created Marshal of France, 1918. Vice-president, Higher Council of War, 1920–30. Led joint French–Spanish campaign against insurgents in Morocco, 1925–6. Inspector-general of army, 1929. Became Minister of War, 1934. Ambassador to Spain, 1939. Became Prime Minister, June 1940. Secured armistice with Germany. Given powers by National Assembly to rule by authoritarian means, July 1940. Became head of state in unoccupied ('Vichy') France, 1942. Obliged to flee France with retreating Germans, 1944. Sentenced to death for treason, 1945, but sentence commuted to life imprisonment by De Gaulle.

PILSUDSKI, JOSEF (1867–1935) Polish soldier and statesman. Exiled to Siberia for political activities, 1887–92. Founded Polish Socialist Party, 1892. Became editor of Polish underground socialist newspaper, *Robotnik*. Increasingly nationalist in outlook. Sought Japanese support for Polish rising during Russo-Japanese War, 1904. Recruited by Austria to lead Polish legion against Russia, 1914. Interned by Germans, 1917. On release, became commander of all Polish armies. Elected Chief of State, 1918. Remained dictator until Constitution established, 1922. Led Polish campaign against Bolsheviks, 1919–20. Created field marshal, 1920. Commanded army unit until retirement, 1923. Carried off military coup in 1926. Served as Prime Minister, 1926–8, 1930. Retained dictatorial powers until his death in 1935. Unable to convince France of threat from Nazi Germany, he concluded Non-Aggression Pact with Germany, 1934.

PINOCHET, AUGUSTO (1915–) Chilean general. Led right-wing military coup against socialist President Allende, 1973. Outlawed political parties and repressed Left and liberals. Commander-in-chief of armed forces, 1973–80. President of Government Council, 1973–74. President of Chile, 1974–89. An Oct. 1988 referendum calling for elections represented a personal rejection of Pinochet. Stood down as President but initially retained control over the armed forces. Later arraigned on human rights charges, though his fitness to plead through ill-health was in dispute.

POL POT, SALOTH SAR (1928–98) Kampuchean political leader. Joined underground Communist Party, 1946. Student in Paris, 1950–3. Became Kampuchean Communist Party secretary in 1963, and

organized Khmer Rouge guerrillas who captured capital Phnom Penh in Apr. 1975. His programme to destroy Western influence and return to agricultural society led to 3–4 million deaths. Prime Minister, 1976–9. Overthrown by invading Vietnamese army, sentenced to death in absence. Reformed guerrilla army with Chinese support, but believed to have given up leadership in 1985. His supporters active after Vietnam's withdrawal from Kampuchea in 1989. His death, in hiding, was confirmed in 1998.

POMPIDOU, GEORGES (1911–74) French politician. Member of resistance during Second World War. Aide to General de Gaulle, 1944–6. Member of Council of State, 1946–54. Deputy director-general of tourism, 1946–9. Director-general of Rothschild's (banking house), 1954–8. Chief of De Gaulle's personal staff, 1958–9. Involved in drafting of Constitution of Fifth Republic. Negotiated ceasefire agreement with Algerian nationalists, 1961. Prime Minister, 1962–8. President, 1969–74. Pursued policies similar to those of De Gaulle (q.v.).

PUTIN, VLADIMIR (1952–) Russian President since Jan. 2000. Former KGB officer, entered politics with the collapse of the Soviet Union and became head of the Federal Security Service in 1998 and secretary to the presidential Security Council in 1999. Appointed premier by President Yeltsin in Aug. 1999. On Yeltsin's resignation, succeeded him and was then confirmed as President in the Mar. 2000 elections. Made suppressing the Chechnya conflict his prime objective, securing an uneasy peace by force. Signed a major nuclear arms reduction treaty with President Bush in May 2002 and re-elected President in 2004, but amidst concern about growing anti-democratic tendencies and continuing spectacular attacks by Chechnyan terrorists.

Q

R

QADHAFI, COLONEL MUAMMAR, AL- (1941–)
Libyan leader. Entered the Libyan army in 1965 and overthrew the monarchy in a coup in 1969 and has headed the Libyan government since then. Has sought to remould Libyan society in accordance with socialist Islamic beliefs and has pusued abortive attempts to unite with neighbouring countries. Supported the Palestinian cause and funded terrorist movements abroad, including the IRA. Clashes with US naval and air forces culminated in the US bombing of Qadhafi's headquarters in the capital in 1987. Complicit in bombing of PanAm Flight 103 over Lockerbie in Scotland in 1988. A US trade embargo in 1986 was followed by UN sanctions in 1992. In 1999 Libya handed over for trial two of its intelligence officers allegedly responsible for the Lockerbie bombing. Secured resumption of diplomatic relations with all but the USA by 2002 and in aftermath of US 'war on terror' and capture of Saddam Hussein (q.v.) Qadhafi opened his secret weapons' programmes up to international inspection and sought normalization of relations.

QUISLING, VIDKUN (1887–1945) Norwegian soldier, politician and traitor. Military attaché in Petrograd, 1918–19, Helsinki, 1919–21. Minister of War, 1931–3. Expanded right-wing National Unity Party. Visited Germany, 1939. Advised Hitler on creation of sympathetic regime in Norway. Headed puppet regime following German occupation, 1940. Tried and executed, 1945. His name is synonymous with treachery.

RABIN, YITZHAK (1922–95) Israeli politician. Prime Minister from 1974 to 1977. He resigned in Apr. 1977 as head of the Labour Party and its candidate for Prime Minister over his wife's illegal bank account in the United States. Two weeks earlier he had defeated Shimon Peres (q.v.) for the Labour nomination. Rabin had a long career in the army and served as its Chief-of-Staff between 1960 and 1964. He was ambassador to the United States from 1968 to 1973. Returned as Minister of Defence, 1984; then as Prime Minister, 1992. Took a leading part in the peace accords in the Middle East in 1993–4, but was criticized for being 'soft' on the PLO. He was assassinated on 4 Nov. 1995 by a right-wing Jewish extremist.

RAHMAN, TUNKU ABDUL (1903–90) First Prime Minister and Minister of External Affairs in the Federation of Malaya. He became first Prime Minister of Malaysia in 1963. Following rioting and the declaration of a state of emergency, he resigned in 1970. The 'founding father' of independent Malaysia.

REAGAN, RONALD (1911–2004) US President, 1980–8. Former film actor; Republican Governor of California, 1967–74. Defeated Carter (q.v.) in 1980 Presidential election; re-elected, 1984. First term marked by 'Reaganomics': tax-cutting, reductions in public spending which hit the poor, and maintenance of high military expenditure. Expressed intense anti-Soviet rhetoric. Military intervention in Grenada, 1983. In second term developed warmer relations with Soviet Union under Gorbachev (q.v.), with summit meetings at Geneva and Reykjavik. Reagan's hitherto impregnable personal popularity was undermined from 1986 by controversy over covert arms sales to Iran and support for Contra forces in Nicaragua.

RIBBENTROP, JOACHIM VON (1893–1946) German Nazi diplomat. Involved in negotiations between Hitler and German government. Helped organize Nazi government, 1933. Ambassador at large, 1935. Concluded Anglo-German Naval Treaty, 1935, and Anti-Comintern Pact, 1936. Ambassador in London, 1936–8. Foreign Minister, 1938–45. Responsible for giving German foreign policy a distinctly 'Nazi' character. Negotiated Molotov–Ribbentrop Pact, 1939, and Pact with Italy and Japan, 1940. Tried as war criminal at Nuremberg. Hanged, 1946.

ROMMEL, ERWIN (1891–1944) German soldier. Served on Romanian and Italian fronts during First World War. Lectured at War Academy. Joined Nazi Party, 1933. Commanded 7th Panzer Division, penetrated Ardennes, May 1940. Became commander of 'Afrika Corps', 1941, earning nickname 'The Desert Fox'. Defeated by campaigns of Alexander and Montgomery, 1942–3. Given task of strengthening defences in France, 1944. Active in resistance to Allied landings in Normandy, June 1944. Implicated in plot to assassinate Hitler. Apparently forced to commit suicide, Oct. 1944.

ROOSEVELT, FRANKLIN DELANO (1882–1945) 32nd US President. Democrat State Senator, New York, 1911–12. Assistant Secretary to the Navy, 1913–20. Disabled by polio, 1921. Governor of New York, 1928. Defeated Hoover in Presidential election, 1932. Instituted 'New Deal' to counter Depression, with 'Hundred Days' of legislation, 1933. Devalued dollar and extended federal government role through public works, agricultural support, labour legislation and business protection. Re-elected 1936, 1940, 1944. Attacked for rad-

icalism, some legislation was declared unconstitutional by the Supreme Court, 1937. Maintained wartime neutrality, 1930–41, but supported Britain materially through Lend-Lease. Declared war on Axis powers, Dec 1941. Attended wartime conferences with Stalin and Churchill, notably Yalta, which delineated East–West postwar spheres of European influence. Died in office at moment of victory over Germany.

S

SADAT, ANWAR AL- (1919–81) President of Egypt, 1970 to 1981. Joined the Free Officers (p. 466) in 1950 and participated in the 1952 coup which overthrew the constitutional monarchy. Sadat held various important positions in the government, and was Vice President at the time of Nasser's death. He was one of the very few of the Free Officers left in power at this point, probably because he had never sought to build a following of his own and so constituted no threat to Nasser. He became provisional President at Nasser's death and later was elected to the post. His dramatic peace initiative, including a historic visit to Jerusalem, altered the diplomatic status quo in the Middle East, and led to the Camp David peace treaty of 1978. Sadat was assassinated in 1981.

SAKHAROV, ANDREI DIMITRIEVICH (1921–89) Russian nuclear physicist. Achieved international fame as a human rights campaigner and dissident. Awarded Nobel Prize, 1975. Rehabilitated by Gorbachev, 1988.

SALAZAR, ANTONIO DE OLIVEIRA (1889–1970) Portuguese dictator. Professor of economics at Coimbra University, 1916. Minister of Finance, 1926, 1928–32. Prime

Minister, 1932–68. Also Minister of War, 1936–44, Foreign Minister, 1936–7. Principal architect of authoritarian constitution introduced in 1933. Implemented fascist-type government on virtually dictatorial lines, stifling political opposition. Restored public finances and modernized transport system. Organized public works schemes. Maintained Portuguese neutrality during Second World War and maintained Portuguese empire in Angola and Mozambique.

SHAMIR, YITZHAK (1914–) Israeli politician. Served as Prime Minister after Begin's resignation in 1983. In 1984, entered into a coalition with the Labour Party, sharing the position of Prime Minister with Peres on a rotating basis. Foreign Minister, 1984 to 1986, then Prime Minister again according to the agreement. Adopted hard-line repressive policies against the *intifada*, the uprising of the Arabs in the occupied territories.

SHARON, ARIEL (1928–) Israeli Prime Minister since 2001. Identified with hard-line policies over the West Bank and a definitive peace treaty with the newly constituted Palestinian Authority. Instituted controversial security wall in attempt to restrict wave of suicide bombings.

SHASTRI, SHRI LAL BAHADUR (1904–66) Indian politician. Succeeded Nehru (q.v.) as Prime Minister in 1964. Died of a heart attack after the Soviet-backed Tashkent talks aimed at bringing about peace between India and Pakistan.

SIHANOUK, PRINCE NORODOM (1922–) Cambodian leader. Elected head of state in Cambodia following the death of his father in 1960. He was deposed in 1970 and set up the Royal Government of National Union for Cambodia (GRUNC) in exile in Beijing. He returned to power in Apr. 1975, following the defeat of the Republican forces, but resigned on 5 Apr. 1976.

SINGH, VISHWANATH PRATAP (1931–) Prime Minister of India from 1989 to 1990. Former Congress (I) politician. Various posts, including Defence Minister, under Indira Gandhi. Broke with Congress, 1987. President, Janata Dal coalition which ousted Rajiv Gandhi from power in 1989 election.

SITHOLE, REVD NDABANINGI (1920–) Zimbabwean churchman and nationalist. A Congregational minister, he was originally the Chairman of ZAPU. When it split in Aug. 1963, he became leader of ZANU. He spent ten years in gaol and after his release in the 1974 amnesty, went into exile in Zambia with a section of the ANC led by Muzorewa (q.v.). In 1976 he withdrew a section of ZANU from the ANC and attended the Geneva Conference, contesting with Mugabe the claim to be leader of ZANU. He returned to Rhodesia in July 1977 and allied himself with Muzorewa again. In Mar. 1978 he became a party to the internal Rhodesian agreement.

SMITH, IAN DOUGLAS (1919–) Leader of White Rhodesia. After posts as Deputy Prime Minister, Minister of Treasury, Defence and External Affairs he became leader of the ruling Rhodesia Front and Prime Minister in 1964. After winning an overwhelming majority in the general election in May 1965 he made a Universal Declaration of Independence (UDI) on 11 Nov. 1965. In June 1969 his decision to declare a Republic and introduce an apartheid-type constitution was endorsed by a referendum. Forced to negotiate an internal settlement with Bishop Muzorewa (q.v.) in 1978. Smith became Minister without Portfolio in the Zimbabwe–Rhodesia government of Muzorewa. Came to London in 1979 for the talks which settled the Rhodesia crisis.

SMUTS, JAN CHRISTIAN (1870–1950) South African statesman and soldier. Fought on behalf of the Boers in the Boer War (1899–1902). Prime Minister of the Union of South Africa, 1919–24 and again 1939–48. Worked to heal differences within South Africa and maintain membership of the Commonwealth. Seen as too pro-British by Afrikaaners. Defeated in 1948 by the National Party under Malan (q.v.).

SOLZHENITSYN, ALEXANDER ISAYEVICH (1918–) Russian novelist and leading dissident. Author of *One Day in the Life of Ivan Denisovich*, a damning indictment of life in one of Stalin's prison camps (where Solzhenitsyn himself was imprisoned). Expelled from Soviet Writer's Union, 1969. Nobel Prize for Literature, 1970. Expelled from Russia in 1974, he lived in the USA before returning to Russia in 1994.

SOMOZA, ANASTASIO (1925–80) Nicaraguan general and politician. Member of family ruling Nicaragua from 1936 to 1979. President 1967–73, 1974–9. Imposed martial law, 1972. Lost US support through human rights violations. Overthrown by Sandinista Liberation Front guerrilla forces, 1979. Assassinated in Paraguay, 1980.

SOUPHANOUVONG, PRINCE (1902–95) Laotian leader. Fought with independence troops against the French in Laos and later led the Pathet Lao (p. 479) in their struggle against the government of Souvanna Phouma. In the 1974 coalition government he led the Joint National Political Council and became President of the Lao People's Democratic Republic from 1975 to 1986.

STALIN, JOSEF VISARIONOVITCH (J. V. DJUGASHVILI) (1879–1953) Soviet leader. Expelled from seminary for political activities, 1899. Exiled to Siberia twice. Attended conferences of Russian Social Democrats in Stockholm, 1906, and London, 1907. Expert on racial minorities in Bolshevik Central Committee, 1912. Became editor of *Pravda*, 1917. Worked with Lenin in Petrograd during Revolution, 1917. Member of Revolutionary Military Council, 1920–3. People's Commissar for Nationalities, 1921–3. General Secretary of Central Committee of Communist Party, 1922–53. During Civil War, supervised defence of Petrograd. Co-operated with Kamenev and Zinoviev to exclude Trotsky from office, 1923. (Secured Trotsky's exile, 1929.) Gained control of Party at 15th Congress, 1927. Embarked on policy of 'Socialism in One Country' through Five Year Plans, 1928. Achieved rapid economic development. Eliminated political opponents in series of 'show trials', 1936–8. Massive machinery of repression created. Chairman of Council of Ministers, 1941–53. During Second World War, as Commissar of Defence and Marshal of the Soviet Union, took over direction of war effort. Present at Tehran, Yalta and Potsdam conferences. Established firm control of Eastern European Communist 'satellites', with exception of Yugoslavia, during postwar period. 'Personality cult' of Stalin officially condemned by Khrushchev at Party Congress, 1956.

STEVENS, SIAKA PROBYN (1905–88) Sierra Leone politician. Elected Prime Minister of Sierra Leone on 21 Mar. 1967, but was overthrown and exiled without taking office. He was restored to power on 26 Apr. 1968, and became President when Sierra Leone became a republic in 1971. Established one-party state until retirement in 1985.

STEVENSON, ADLAI EWING (1900–65) American politician. Democrat Governor of Illinois, 1949–53. Unsuccessful Democrat candidate against Eisenhower in presidential elections, 1952 and 1956. US Ambassador to the United Nations, 1960–5.

STRESEMANN, GUSTAV (1878–1929) German statesman. Elected to Reichstag, 1907–12, 1914–29. Leader of National Liberals, 1917. Took nationalistic position during First World War, supported High Command. Became more moderate after war. Founded People's Party (DVP), 1919. Advocated meeting Germany's commitments under Treaty of Versailles, thereby gaining confidence of Allies. Became Chancellor during crisis year, 1923. Foreign Minister, 1923–9. Restored Germany's diplomatic position. Concluded Locarno Pact, 1925. Achieved German entry into League of Nations, 1926. Secured reduction of reparations demands. Negotiated terms for Allied evacuation of Rhineland. Supported Dawes Plan, 1924, and Young Plan, 1929. Awarded Nobel Peace Prize, 1926.

STRIJDOM, JOHANNES (1893–1958) South African politician. Elected Nationalist MP, 1929; acknowledged by 1934 as an ultra-Afrikaner leader. Prime Minister following the death of Malan (q.v.), 1954–8. Extreme advocate of apartheid, responsible for legislation removing voting rights from Cape Coloureds, for undermining liberal multi-racial universities, and for the 1956–8 Treason Trial.

SUHARTO, GENERAL (1921–) Indonesian general and politician. Leader of the army who took over control in Indonesia in Mar. 1966. Power was handed over to him by Sukarno (q.v.) in Feb. 1967. He was acting President until Mar. 1968, when he was elected to office by the People's Consultative Assembly. He was re-elected in Mar. 1973 and also became Prime Minister and Minister of Defence. His increasingly authoritarian rule and the Asian financial collapse of 1997 led to rioting in 1997 and to him being deposed in 1998.

SUKARNO, AHMED (1901–70) Indonesian nationalist leader. First President of Indo-nesia. After an abortive communist coup in 1965 in which he was implicated, the army took over in Mar. 1966. He nominally held power until Feb. 1967, when he handed over to General Suharto (q.v.).

SUN YAT-SEN (1867–1925) Chinese revolutionary and nationalist. Lived abroad after failure of attempted rising in 1895. After further unsuccessful risings, he succeeded in 1911 in overthrowing the ruling Manchu dynasty. Became first President of Republican China. He shortly afterwards resigned in favour of Yuan Shih-kai.

SYNGMAN RHEE (1875–1965) South Korean politician. Elected President of the Republic of Korea (South Korea) in 1948 and held office until Apr. 1960 when he was forced to resign and leave the country. His regime was corrupt and authoritarian.

T

THANT, U (1909–74) Burmese diplomat. Secretary-General of the United Nations, 1962–72.

THATCHER, MARGARET HILDA (née ROBERTS) (1925–) British Conservative politician. Mrs Thatcher was Conservative MP for Finchley from 1959 to 1992. She was parliamentary secretary to the Ministry of Pensions and National Insurance 1961–4, and secretary of state for education and science 1970–4. In 1975 she was elected leader of the Conservative Party. Between 1975 and 1979 she led the party away from the centrist policies of Heath (q.v.) and adopted a monetarist stance on economic problems and a tough line on law and order, defence and immigration. In May 1979 she became Britain's first woman Prime Minister, following her election victory. In spite of considerable unpopularity and very high unemployment, Mrs Thatcher's conduct of the Falklands War and Labour's disarray led to a landslide victory at the polls in 1983. Her second term was marked by growing emphasis on liberalizing the economy, especially the rapid privatization of major public concerns. In 1987 she achieved a record third term of office with a majority of over 100 in Parliament but rapidly encountered mounting political and economic difficulties. Her 'Iron Lady' stance earned her a place alongside Reagan (q.v.) in the ending of the Cold War. Suspicious of European centralization, she none the less signed the Single European Act of 1986 and attempted to resolve the Northern Ireland conflict. Following the resignation of senior ministers and the loss of crucial by-elections she was forced from office in 1990. Out of office she continued to mount attacks on the European Union but was widely revered in former communist-controlled Europe and America. Created Baroness Thatcher of Kesteven in 1992.

TITO, JOSIP BROZ (1892–1980) Yugoslav statesman. Member of Yugoslav Communist Party since early 1920s, becoming its Secretary-General, 1937. Led Yugoslav partisan forces during Second World War. Become marshal, 1943. After war, pursued independence from USSR, 1948. First President of Yugoslav Republic, 1953–80. Pursued independent foreign policy, encouraging co-operation among non-aligned nations.

TODD, REGINALD STEPHEN GARFIELD (1908–92) Prime Minister of Southern Rhodesia in 1953 at the formation of the Federation with Northern Rhodesia and Nyasaland. In 1958 his liberal policies led to his rejection by his party, the United Federal Party. Between 1965 and 1966 and between 1972 and 1976 he was under government restriction orders. At the

Geneva talks in 1976 he was adviser to Joshua Nkomo (q.v.).

TOJO, HIDEKI (1884–1948) Japanese general and politician. Chief of State in Manchuria, 1938–40. Minister of War, 1940–1. Prime Minister 1941–4. Identified with militant expansionist war party from 1931; created military dictatorship; authorized Pearl Harbor attack, bringing USA into Second World War, 1941. Resigned as Japan suffered military reverses, 1944. Attempted suicide on Japan's defeat, 1945. Tried and executed as war criminal, 1948.

TOURÉ, SEKOU (1922–84) Guinean politician and trade unionist. Became Head of State in Guinea in Oct. 1958 on independence. He was awarded the Lenin Peace Prize in 1960.

TROTSKY, LEV DAVIDOVICH (L. D. BRONSTEIN) (1879–1940) Russian revolutionary of Ukrainian-Jewish descent. Exiled to Siberia, 1898. Joined Lenin in London, 1902. Became an independent socialist, 1902. Hoped to achieve reconciliation between Bolsheviks and Mensheviks. Returned to Russia, 1905, and organized first Soviet in St Petersburg. Exiled to Siberia again. Returned to St Petersburg from New York, May 1917. Chairman of Petrograd Soviet, Nov. 1917. First Commissar for Foreign Affairs. Delayed conclusion of Treaty of Brest-Litovsk, 1918. Commissar for War during Civil War, creating Red Army. After death of Lenin, and disagreements with Stalin, excluded from office. Theory of 'Permanent Revolution' condemned by Communist Party. Lost influence over Party policy, 1925. Expelled from Communist Party, 1927. Deported, 1929. Wrote *History of the Russian Revolution* while in France (1931–3). Murdered by Stalinist agent in Mexico, 1940.

TRUDEAU, PIERRE (1919–2000) Canadian politician. Elected as Liberal member of the Federal Parliament, 1965. Minister of Justice and Attorney General, 1967. Succeeded Lester Pearson as Prime Minister, 1968. Strong opponent of separatism for French-speaking Quebec. Defeated in 1979 election. Returned to office as Prime Minister, 1980–4.

TRUMAN, HARRY S. (1884–1972) 33rd US President. Served US Army in France, 1918. Democratic Senator, Missouri, 1935–44. Elected as Roosevelt's Vice President 1944, succeeded him on death in Apr. 1945. Authorized dropping of atomic bombs on Japan, Aug. 1945. Surprise victor in 1948 Presidential election on 'Fair Deal' civil rights and social reform platform, but unable to push legislation through conservative Congress. Vigorous anti-communist foreign policy: Truman Doctrine; Marshall Plan for European recovery; Berlin airlift; creation of NATO, and US participation in UN forces in Korea.

TSHOMBE, MOISE KAPENDA (1919–69) Congolese Prime Minister and President, 1964–5. He announced the secession of Katanga from Zaïre in July 1960 and led the Katanga forces until 1963, when UN forces took control and he went into exile. In 1964 he was recalled to lead the central government, but was dismissed in 1965 and again went into exile. Having been sentenced to death by the Kinshasa High Court, his plane was hijacked to Algiers where he was placed under house arrest until his death.

V

VERWOERD, HENDRIK FRENSCH (1901–66) South African Prime Minister, 1958–66. In 1950 he became Minister of Native Affairs in South Africa, where he was responsible for putting apartheid (p. 452) into practice. He then became leader of the Nationalist Party and on 2 Sept. 1958 became Prime Minister. He was assassinated on 6 Sept. 1966. Strong advocate of a South African Republic outside the Commonwealth (which South Africa left in 1961).

VORSTER, BALTHAZAR JOHANNES (1915–83) South African Prime Minister, 1966–78. Formerly Minister of Justice, he became South African Prime Minister in 1966 following the assassination of Verwoerd (q.v.). As Prime Minister he tried to make diplomatic contacts with black African states and attempted to help solve both the Rhodesian and Namibian problems. He maintained strict apartheid, winning a landslide victory from the white electorate in 1977. Forced to resign by the Muldergate scandal (p. 475).

W

WALDHEIM, KURT (1918–) Austrian diplomat and politician. Diplomat, 1945–64, mainly at United Nations. Foreign Minister, 1968–70. Failed to win presidential election, 1971. UN Secretary-General, 1971–82. Largely unsuccessful term because of East–West mutual mistrust. President of Austria, 1986. During election campaign reputation was undermined by questions about his wartime activities and the extent of his awareness of Nazi atrocities.

WALESA, LECH (1943–) Polish trade unionist. Former Gdansk shipyard worker. Emerged as leader of independent 'Solidarity' trade union. Solidarity comprised some 40 per cent of Polish workers by late

1980. Mounted outspoken opposition to economic and social policies of government. Detained following imposition of martial law, Dec. 1981. Released months later. During his detention, Solidarity was banned. Continued to hold prominent position. Granted audience with Pope John Paul II, 1983. Awarded Nobel Peace Prize, 1983. Guided Solidarity throughout 1980s, but declined to hold office when, in Sept. 1989, Solidarity became part of Poland's first non-communist government for 40 years. Took position of President of Poland in 1990 until his defeat in the 1995 presidential election.

WEIZMANN, CHAIM (1874–1952) Zionist leader. Headed British Zionist movement before First World War. Advised Foreign Office during planning of Balfour Declaration, 1917. Head of World Zionist Movement after 1920. Became head of Jewish Agency for Palestine, 1929. Elected first President of Israel, 1948.

WELENSKY, ROLAND (ROY) (1907–91) Deputy Prime Minister and Minister of Transport of the Central African Federation from 1953 to 1956 when he became Prime Minister and Minister of External Affairs. He remained Prime Minister until the break-up of the Federation in 1963.

WILSON, THOMAS WOODROW (1856–1924) 28th US President. Lawyer and academic. Democratic Governor, New Jersey, 1910. Inaugurated President, 1913. Liberal domestic policy. 'Big Stick' policy in Latin America. Determined on neutrality in First World War. Re-elected to Presidency, 1916; declared war on Germany, 1917. Announced 'Fourteen Points' for reshaping of postwar world on basis of national self-determination and the creation of an international forum, Jan. 1918. Congress refused to ratify Wilson's signing of Versailles Treaty, particularly objecting to participation in League of Nations.

Awarded Nobel Peace Prize, 1919. Suffered incapacitating stroke, 1919.

YELTSIN, BORIS NIKOLAYEVICH (1931–) Russian politician. Former Communist Party leader in Sverdlovsk, 1975. Promoted by Gorbachev (q.v.) to be Party leader in Moscow, 1985, and initially seen as Gorbachev's chief radical ally in reforming the Soviet state; after disagreements with him, forced to resign in 1987. In 1989 elected to Moscow constituency with overwhelming support, becoming President of the Russian Federation in May 1990. Popular for his support for reform, his defence of democracy during the Aug. 1991 coup attempt made him the undisputed leader of the Russian Federation. Created the Commonwealth of Independent States thereby breaking up the Soviet Union in 1991. Became President of Russia in direct elections in Dec. 1991. Although he successfully overcame the 1993 communist rising in Moscow, he faced grave economic problems and a war in Chechnya (see p. 330). Re-elected in 1996 in spite of serious health problems. His increasingly erratic policies witnessed the appointment of 5 premiers in 17 months. In Aug. 1999 he appointed Putin (q.v.), who succeeded him when Yeltsin finally resigned at the end of 1999.

ZHOU ENLAI (1898–1976) Chinese communist leader. He organized the revolt in Shanghai in 1927, established a partnership with Mao in 1931 and took part in the Long March of 1934–5. After talks with Chiang Kai-shek (q.v.) to establish a coalition failed, he became Prime Minister and Foreign Minister of the new China in 1949. During the Cultural Revolution he used his influence to restrain extremists. He died in office in Jan. 1976.

V
GLOSSARY OF TERMS

A

AFRICAN NATIONAL CONGRESS (ANC)
Black South African pressure group,
formed in 1912 at Bloemfontein to promote the welfare of blacks in South Africa.
Its origins date from the formation in Cape
Colony in 1882 of the Native Education
Association. Banned from South Africa
in 1961. Its leader, Nelson Mandela (q.v.),
the symbol of black African hopes, was
convicted of sabotage in 1964 and sentenced to life imprisonment. Mandela was
released in 1990 and the ANC ban lifted.
After the first multi-racial elections in
1991, the ANC became the governing party
in South Africa.

AFRICAN NATIONAL COUNCIL (ANC) Black
Rhodesian pressure group, initially set up
in 1971 to oppose the Smith–Home settlement proposals for Rhodesia (p. 314). In
1975, with the backing of the Organization
of African Unity (p. 267), Muzorewa (q.v.)
led an ANC delegation to the Victoria
Falls conference representing all the
nationalist groups. This unity did not last
and, by 1977, after groupings and regroup-
ings, the ANC was divided into two main
wings, led respectively by Muzorewa and
Nkomo.

AL-FATAH The Syrian branch of the
Palestinian liberation movement. It
became the most powerful force in the
Palestine Liberation Organization (q.v.)
after the Arab–Israeli war of 1967.

AL-QAEDA Terrorist group established by
Osama bin Laden in the early 1990s as a
Sunni Muslim force in Afghanistan to
combat non-Islamic Arab governments,
and establish a world Islamic state. In
1998 al-Qaeda declared it a religious duty
to kill Americans and their allies. It is
thought to have up to several thousand
members internationally in loosely
organized cells. As well as being suspected
of planning and undertaking the Sept.
2001 attacks on the New York World Trade
Center and the Pentagon, al-Qaeda is said
to have been responsible for killing US
troops in Somalia in 1993, bombing US
embassies in Kenya and Tanzania in
1998 and a US warship in Yemen in 2000.
The US government claimed in Dec. 2001
to have destroyed its central core in
Afghanistan.

ALIYA Jewish term meaning the 'going-up'
or return of Jews from the diaspora to
what they consider their homeland, first
to Palestine and later to Israel, during the
twentieth century.

ALLIANCE FOR PROGRESS Conceived and
implemented during the Kennedy administration (1961–3). An attempt to promote
economic development in Latin America
through extensive and varied United
States' assistance. The Alliance for Progress began in Aug. 1961 with the signature
of a charter by representatives of 20
American states at Punta del Este in
Uruguay. Action began in Mar. 1962,
with the declared aim of increasing living
standards in these countries by 2½% per
annum.

ANC *see* African National Congress, African National Council.

ANSCHLUSS The idea of union between Austria and Germany, current after the collapse of the Habsburg Monarchy in 1918 and given further impetus after Hitler became German Chancellor in 1933. The deliberate destabilization of the Austrian government by the Nazis in 1938 led to the resignation of Chancellor Schuschnigg and his replacement by Arthur Seyss-Inquart, a Nazi nominee who invited the Germans to occupy Austria. The union of Austria with Germany was proclaimed on 13 Mar. 1938.

ANTI-CLERICALISM Term applied to the opposition to organized religion, largely directed against the power of the Roman Catholic Church. Anti-clericalism was prevalent during the revolutionary period in France and throughout the nineteenth century. Also apparent in Spain, especially during the Second Republic, 1931–9, in Germany as a result of the *Kulturkampf* and sporadically in Italy.

ANTI-COMINTERN PACT The agreement between Germany and Japan signed on 25 Nov. 1936 which stated both countries' hostility to international communism, also signed by Italy in 1937. In addition to its commitment to oppose the Soviet Union, the pact also recognized the Japanese regime which had ruled Manchuria since 1931.

ANTI-SEMITISM Term used to describe animosity towards the Jews, on either a religious or a racial basis. Originally coined by racial theorists of the later nineteenth century, anti-Semitism can take a number of different political, economic or racial forms. A number of political parties in Germany and Austria were based on anti-Semitism, and it also appeared in France via the *Action Française*. Economic and political anti-Semitism was also a feature of Tsarist Russia with frequent pogroms (q.v.) against Jewish communities, a form of activity which recurred in the Soviet Union in 1958–9 and 1962–3. Outbreaks of anti-Semitism continue to occur (e.g. in France in the 1990s).

ANZAC Acronym for Australian and New Zealand Army Corps. It became famous in the Gallipoli Campaign of 1915.

ANZUS PACT Name given to the Pacific Security Treaty signed by Australia, New Zealand and the United States on 1 Sept. 1951. It is of indefinite duration, and marked a reorientation and new independence in defence policy by Australia and New Zealand towards the United States and away from the United Kingdom. New Zealand later withdrew from the Pact as part of its anti-nuclear policy.

APARTHEID The South African doctrine of racial segregation, put forward by the National Party under Dr Malan in 1948, and subsequently practised under successive governments of Strijdom, Verwoerd, Vorster and Botha. Although virtually universally condemned by the world outside, the South African defence of apartheid was that it allowed for the separate development of the Bantu population along their own lines, ultimately leading to self-governing African states (Bantustans, q.v.) in South Africa. In practice, under apartheid the Black African population was long the subject of a continuing stream of discriminatory legislation, including the 1949 Prohibition of Mixed Marriages Act, the 1950 Suppression of Communism Act, the 1950 Group Areas Act, and the much-criticized 1963 'Ninety-Day Law' under which the police had powers of arbitrary confinement without recourse to the courts. The result was the suppression of all internal opposition to White supremacy. The Africans were consigned to a role as a disenfranchised and politically powerless labour force. With the release of Nelson Mandela and the coming of black majority rule, all the pillars of apartheid have been dismantled.

ARMS RACE The Cold War rivalry between the USSR and the Western powers, particularly the USA, to establish supremacy in arms production.

ARUSHA DECLARATION Socialist theory of development put forward by President Nyerere (q.v.) of Tanzania in Feb. 1967. He was sceptical about the motives of countries offering aid in Africa and felt that a developing country should control its own resources and encourage self-reliance. His theories were then put into practice in Tanzania through nationalization of banks and insurance companies, Africanization of foreign assets and nationalization of many European-owned firms, as well as the setting up of 'Ujamaa' villages which concentrate people into co-operative settlements.

ARYAN The name given to a 'superior' European race, whose existence was promulgated by the Nazis. Their racial theory is, of course, nonsense.

ASEAN or Association of South-East Asian Nations: *see* pp. 261–2.

ATLANTIC CHARTER A statement of principles agreed by Churchill and Roosevelt on behalf of Britain and the United States in Aug. 1941, on the conduct of international policy in the postwar world. These included no territorial or other expansion; no wish for territorial changes other than those agreed by the peoples concerned; respect for the rights of all peoples to choose their form of government; desire for general economic development and collaboration; the need to disarm aggressor nations, and the wish to construct a general system of international security. Although mainly a propaganda exercise, the US refused to acknowledge any future international obligations in spite of British pressure. The Charter was endorsed by the Soviet Union and fourteen other states at war with the Axis powers in Sept. 1941.

AUTARKY The policy of economic self-sufficiency, as witnessed in Nazi Germany prior to the Second World War, aiming at total home production to the exclusion of all imported items.

AWAMI LEAGUE A political party proposing independence for East Pakistan, which won 167 seats out of 300 in the Pakistan general election held in Dec. 1970. The Pakistan authorities refused to open the new National Assembly and civil war broke out. The leader of the Awami League, Sheikh Mujibur Rahman, became Prime Minister of the new nation of Bangladesh but in Jan. 1975 abolished all political parties and replaced them by a single party.

AXIS A term first used by Mussolini on 1 Nov. 1936 to describe fascist Italy's relationship with Nazi Germany, established by the October protocols of 1936. He referred to the Rome–Berlin Axis, which was reinforced by a formal treaty in May 1939, the Pact of Steel. In Sept. 1940, Germany, Italy and Japan signed a tripartite agreement which led to the term 'Axis Powers' being used to describe all three, as well as their Eastern European allies.

AYATOLLAH Islamic title, given to the most learned teachers and scholars in Shi'ite Iran. The title came into prominence to refer to Ayatollah Khomeini (q.v.), the leader of the 1979 Islamic revolution in Iran.

AZANIA Term used by black nationalists to denote South Africa.

AZAPO Azanian People's Organization. Black consciousness movement formed in South Africa in 1977.

B

BAADER–MEINHOF GROUP An anarchist terrorist group active in West Germany in the 1970s. It was led by Andrea Baader (1943–77) and Ulrike Meinhof (1934–76) with funds channelled via East Germany. Both were captured, and died in high-security prisons.

BA'ATH PARTY Syrian political party founded in 1941, whose name means 'renaissance' in Arabic; its goals are Arab unity, socialism and freedom. It has branches in several Arab countries but has seen its greatest power in Iraq and Syria. Its support has come mainly from the military, intellectuals and the middle class.

BAGHDAD PACT *see* Central Treaty Organisation, p. 458.

BALANCE OF POWER A theory of international relations which aimed to secure peace by preventing any one state or group of states from attaining political or military strength sufficient to threaten the independence and liberty of others. It was based on the maintenance of a counter-force equal to that of the potential adversaries, and was the central theme of British policy in Europe against the French and, from 1904 to 1914, the Germans. This was epitomized by the creation of the Entente Cordiale of 1904 with France to counter the threat from Germany, and later the Triple Entente of 1907 of Britain, France and Russia to balance the Triple Alliance of 1882 of Germany, Austria-Hungary and Italy. In the interwar period, Britain again attempted to create a balance against French power by encouraging the rapid recovery of Germany. The policy was abandoned in the 1930s as Germany and Japan began to pursue more aggressive foreign policies, which could not be countered by the League of Nations' security system, nor by further alliances.

BALFOUR DECLARATION A crucial document fundamental to an understanding of Jewish claims to Palestine. In a letter of 2 Nov. 1917 to the British Zionist leader Lord Rothschild, Arthur Balfour, the Foreign Secretary, stated Britain's support for the establishment of a Jewish national home in Palestine. It included the provision that nothing should be done to prejudice the civil and religious rights of the non-Jewish communities in the area. The letter's terms were incorporated into Britain's League of Nations' mandate for Palestine. The real commitment in the Balfour Declaration has been hotly contested ever since.

BALTIC STATES Term used for Estonia, Latvia and Lithuania, part of the Soviet Union from 1940 to 1991. Having gained their independence following the First World War, the Baltic States were seized by the Soviet Union in 1940 as part of the 1939 Nazi–Soviet Pact. Growing agitation for independence in the late 1980s came to a head with the abortive 19 Aug. 1991 coup in Moscow. Declarations of independence resulted in diplomatic recognition from Scandinavia, the European Community and, most important, the United States (on 2 Sept.). All three countries have now become UN members and (in 2004) members of the EU.

BAMBOO CURTAIN Term used to describe the isolation of communist China from 1948 to 1971 when, with the admission of China to the United Nations and the visit of Nixon (q.v.) to Beijing, the 'bamboo curtain' was lifted. The term is analogous to 'Iron Curtain' (q.v.) used to denote Russia and Eastern Europe.

BANDUNG CONFERENCE Conference in 1955 largely organized at the initiative of the Colombo Powers and China, to herald a new era of Afro-Asian solidarity. Its guiding principles were the 'Five Principles' of Peaceful Co-existence which had emerged from the settlement of the Sino-Indian conflict over Tibet (29 Apr. 1954). These were: mutual respect for territorial integrity and sovereignty; non-aggression; non-interference in each other's internal affairs; equality and mutual benefit; peaceful co-existence and economic co-operation. Despite general agreement, not all countries accepted the neutralist position in world affairs advocated by China. Division and dissent marked the Second Bandung Conference in 1965.

BANNING ORDER An order used in South Africa during the apartheid era to prohibit a person engaging in, say, political activity, being interviewed or quoted by the media.

BANTUSTAN The supposedly independent tribal homelands in South Africa (e.g. Transkei) during the apartheid era. None received international recognition.

BARBAROSSA, OPERATION Code name for German invasion of Russia, June 1941.

BATTLE OF BRITAIN *see* p. 300.

BAY OF PIGS (Cochinos Bay) A coastal area in southern Cuba. On 17 Apr. 1961, Cuban exiles trained and assisted by the US Central Intelligence Agency (CIA) landed at the Bay of Pigs in an attempt to overthrow the communist regime of Fidel Castro. The operation was planned during the later stages of the Eisenhower adminis-

tration, but inherited and implemented by the Kennedy administration. The failure of the insurgents was due to many factors: the unfavourable terrain surrounding the Bay of Pigs; lack of support from local inhabitants, and the absence of sufficient military support for those who landed on the island. The result of the attempt was disastrous for the Cuban exiles, of whom more than 80 were killed and over 1,000 captured; it also represented the first, and most serious, diplomatic failure of the Kennedy administration. The claims of the United States of non-involvement in the affair were scarcely credible, and the Castro regime was made to appear stronger and less vulnerable.

BIAFRA The name given to the eastern region of Nigeria on its attempted secession in 1967.

'BIG FIVE' Permanent members of the UN Security Council: the USA, USSR (then Russia), Britain, China and France.

'BIG FOUR' Representatives of the major victorious powers of the First World War at the Paris Peace Conference of 1919. They were Lloyd George, Woodrow Wilson, George Clemenceau and the Italian Prime Minister, Vittorio Orlando.

'BIG THREE' Leaders of the major Allied powers during the Second World War: Churchill, Stalin and Roosevelt.

BLACK MONDAY Term applied to the collapse of the New York Stock Exchange on 19 Oct. 1987, when the Dow Jones Industrial Average fell by 22.6%, bringing major falls in other markets around the world. It was the worst fall since 1929. See Black Thursday.

BLACK MUSLIMS American Black movement whose twin pillars of belief are Black superiority and racial separation. Its best known leader was perhaps Malcolm X, who was assassinated in Feb. 1965.

BLACK PANTHER PARTY Name derived from the symbol used by Black Power candidates in 1966 when fighting elections in Alabama. See below.

BLACK POWER Radical black movement which emerged in the United States, partly reflecting dissatisfaction with the lack of progress of the civil rights movement. It was at its most aggressive in the late 1960s, and there were fears in the USA that inter-racial strife of civil war dimensions might erupt in the cities. However, the 1970s saw some improvement in the position of American blacks and that, together with the deaths of Black Power leaders such as George Jackson and Malcolm X, weakened the movement.

BLACK SEPTEMBER Extremist Palestinian terrorist group founded in 1971 and named after the Black September of 1970, during which King Hussein (q.v.) virtually eliminated the guerrilla presence in Jordan. The commando group has piled up a long series of outrages, among them the assassination of the Jordanian Prime Minister, Wasif al-Tell, and the attempted assassinations of the Jordanian ambassadors to Switzerland and the United Kingdom, 1971; the murder of a number of Israeli athletes at the Munich Olympics, 1972; and the murder of the American ambassador and two other foreign diplomats in Khartoum, 1973.

BLACK THURSDAY 24 Oct. 1929, the day the Wall Street crash began, when the first major fall in confidence in the US stock market occurred. The 'Crash of 29' led to the slump of the 1930s.

BLITZKRIEG (Ger.: lightning war) A theory of warfare which involved a rapid attack on a very narrow front to create penetra-tion in depth. The technique involved prior aerial bombing to reduce enemy resistance and then the deployment of highly mobile armoured columns. Used extensively by the German army in the Second World War, and especially by General Guderian in the campaign against France in 1940. Also abbreviated to 'Blitz' in English to describe the heavy bombing and night attacks on British cities by the German air force during the Second World War.

BOAT PEOPLE Term used to describe those persons, both Chinese and non-communist Vietnamese, seeking to escape from Vietnam after 1975 when South Vietnam fell to communist North Vietnam. Many escaped, in overladen small boats, to Malaysia, Hong Kong, etc. Many fell prey to pirates. The problem became acute again in the 1980s as economic hardship in Vietnam provoked further waves of refugees into Hong Kong. Against an international outcry, Britain began repatriation to Vietnam in Dec. 1989.

BOLSHEVIK (Russ.: member of the majority). A term applied to the radical faction of the Russian Social Democratic Party, which split in 1903. Lenin led the Bolsheviks in opposition to the more moderate Mensheviks. The Bolsheviks came to power in Russia after the October Revolution of 1917, and the name was retained by the Soviet Communist Party until 1952.

BOSS Bureau of State Security, the South African Secret police force accused of many illegal actions both inside and outside South Africa during the era of apartheid.

BRAINS TRUST Originally the nickname of the group of advisers, mainly economists and businessmen, who helped Roosevelt (q.v.) formulate his New Deal policies. Now the term is more generally applied to any such small advisory group.

BRAINWASHING Term originating from the mental and frequently physical torture used by the communists in the Korean War (see p. 304) to persuade their captured prisoners to alter their view of society.

BRETTON WOODS The scene of an international conference held in July 1944 to consider British, Canadian and American proposals for a postwar international monetary system. The final agreement was largely based on American plans and proposed the convertibility of currencies and stable exchange rates in order to encourage multilateral trade. One of the results of Bretton Woods was the setting up of the International Monetary Fund (q.v.) and World Bank.

BREZHNEV DOCTRINE The doctrine was developed by Leonid Brezhnev, First Secretary of the Communist Party of the Soviet Union, as a justification for the invasion of Czechoslovakia by 5 Warsaw Pact countries in 1968; it maintained that the Socialist community of nations may intervene in the affairs of one of its members, if it sees it as necessary and for the public good. Under Gorbachev, the doctrine was abandoned and there was no intervention in 1989 as Eastern Europe reshaped its political system.

BRINKMANSHIP Term used to describe the policy of going to the brink (i.e. of nuclear war) to force another power to climb down or seek a negotiated settlement. An example is the policy of Kennedy during the Cuban Missile Crisis (q.v.). The term originated with John Foster Dulles, American Secretary of State, 1953–9.

BROEDERBOND White secret society formed after the Boer War to maintain Afrikaaner dominance in South African cultural, economic and political life, and which influenced National Party policy.

BUFFER STATE A small state established or maintained between 2 larger states to prevent clashes between them or to prevent either taking control of strategic territory.

BUNDESTAG The German federal parliament first established in May 1949 for West Germany, elected for a 4-year term by universal suffrage.

BUSHIDO The Samurai code of honour dating from the twelfth century which is a continuing influence in Japanese life. Similar to medieval European chivalry, it promotes a concept of personal honour based on courage, honesty, justice and simplicity.

BUSSING American practice of moving children by bus to schools in different areas, to prevent educational facilities in the 1970s becoming entirely black or white. The intention was to encourage racial harmony, but many white parents complained that the practice infringed the right to choose where their children were educated.

C

CAMP DAVID The US Presidential retreat in Maryland. On 5–17 Sept. 1978 President Carter chaired talks at Camp David between President Sadat of Egypt and Prime Minister Begin of Israel and agreement was reached on a treaty finally signed on 26 Mar. 1979. Israel pledged to withdraw from Sinai; to stop settlement on the West Bank and the Gaza Strip; to end Israeli military government of the West Bank within 5 years, after which the Palestinian inhabitants of the area would elect a government. Syria and the PLO rejected the agreement.

CANAL ZONE An area 5 miles each side of the 40-mile-long Panama Canal in Central America, granted to the United States in 1903. The zone was administered by a United States governor and controlled by the US army. Following increasing agitation for return of the zone, President Carter and Panamanian General Torrijos signed a treaty on 7 Sept. 1977 promising its return by 1 Jan. 2000. It has now been returned.

CAP *see* Common Agricultural Policy.

CASABLANCA POWERS A loose association of more radical African states consisting of Ghana, Guinea, Mali, Morocco, UAR and Algeria, set up in 1961. They combined with the Monrovia states to form the Organization of African Unity (p. 267).

CAUDILLISMO Term used in Spanish and Latin American politics denoting the almost absolute power of the head of state and the personal loyalty of his supporters. Examples are Franco in Spain (see below), and Perón in Argentina.

CAUDILLO, EL (Sp.: the leader) Title assumed by Francisco Franco in 1937 as head of the insurgent nationalist forces in the Spanish Civil War, and of the so-called Burgos government. His authority was reinforced in July 1947 with the declaration that he should remain 'Caudillo' or head of state for life pending the restoration of the monarchy.

CENTO *see* Central Treaty Organization.

CENTRAL INTELLIGENCE AGENCY (CIA) An American agency, headed by a director appointed by the President with Senate approval, that works under the National Security Council to co-ordinate intelligence activities in the interest of national security. The CIA evaluates intelligence information supplied by the Army, Navy, Air Force, State Department and other intelligence-gathering civilian and military agencies. This information is disseminated among various units of the national government to aid the formulation of foreign and defence policy. The CIA also engages in worldwide intelligence-gathering activities. The Congressional Charter establishing the CIA specifically prohibits the use of its resources for internal surveillance. As a result of alleged breaches of the charter, Congress has created a 'watchdog' select committee to oversee CIA operations.

CENTRAL POWERS Initially members of the Triple Alliance created by Bismarck in 1882, namely Germany, Austria–Hungary and Italy. As Italy remained neutral in the First World War, the term was applied to Germany, Austria–Hungary, their ally Turkey and later also Bulgaria.

CENTRAL TREATY ORGANIZATION (CENTO) The Baghdad Pact was signed by Turkey and Iraq on 24 Feb. 1955. The Pact was joined by the United Kingdom on 4 Apr. 1955, by Pakistan on 23 Sept. 1955 and by Iran on 3 Nov. 1955. Iraq withdrew on 24 Mar. 1959, and the name was changed to the Central Treaty Organization on 21 Aug. 1959. The United States signed bilateral defence agreements with Iran, Turkey and Pakistan on 5 Mar. 1959. The Treaty provided for mutual co-operation for security and defence. The Islamic Revolution in Iran dealt a major blow to the organization.

CHARTER 77 Group of civil rights activists formed in Czechoslovakia in 1977 in the wake of the Helsinki Agreement to monitor abuses by the authorities. They were themselves subject to imprisonment and harassment.

CHEKA Extraordinary commission, or secret political police force, established by the Bolsheviks (q.v.) in post-revolutionary

Russia to defend the regime against internal enemies.

CHETNIKS Originally Serbian guerrillas seeking liberation from the Ottoman Empire. Active against German supply lines in occupied Balkan states during the First World War. They also opposed German occupation in the Second World War and were aided by the British until 1944. Some commanders collaborated with the Germans and Italians against Tito's partisans.

CHRISTIAN DEMOCRACY Anti-communist, moderate political movement formed in many European countries with the development of a mass electorate in the late nineteenth and twentieth centuries. Amongst the largest was the Italian Christian Democrat Party founded in 1919, and the major representative of Catholic, moderate opinion. The German National People's Party, formed in 1918, and the German Centre Party, formed in 1870, also represent this tradition, latterly taken up by Adenauer's Christian-Democratic Union, formed in 1945. Many other European countries have political parties with this or similar labels.

CIA *see* Central Intelligence Agency.

CIVIL DISOBEDIENCE The policy of non-violent, non-co-operation with the British in India during the struggle for independence. The policy was propagated by Gandhi with great success.

CIVIL RIGHTS MOVEMENT Movement to secure access for American blacks to voting and citizenship rights guaranteed by the 14th and 15th Amendments to the US Constitution in 1868 and 1870. A National Association for the Advancement of Colored People was formed in 1909, but little progress was made for 50 years. In 1957 Federal troops were used in Little

Rock, Arkansas, to enforce a 1954 Supreme Court ruling banning segregated education. A black campaign of sit-ins, boycotts and demonstrations in which Dr Martin Luther King (1929–68) emerged as a leader prompted civil rights legislation by the 1960s Kennedy and Johnson administrations. Riots in Harlem (1964) and Watts (1965) revealed dissatisfaction with the pace of achievement and encouraged the growth of black militancy. In the 1970s and 1980s many blacks felt their progress towards full equality, particularly in education and employment, was weakened by what they saw as unsympathetic Republican administrations.

COD WAR Popular term for the fishing dispute between Iceland and Great Britain between 1972 and 1976.

COLD WAR Protracted state of tension between countries, falling short of actual war. The term was first used in a US Congress debate on 12 Mar. 1947 on the doctrine expounded by Harry S. Truman (1894–1972) promising aid to 'free peoples who are resisting attempted subjugation by armed minorities or by outside pressures'. A direct product of the civil war in Greece (1946–9), the doctrine bore the wider implication that the USA would actively respond anywhere in the world to what it saw as direct encroachment by the USSR. The practical division of Europe occurred as a result of the Eastern European states' rejection of US Marshall Aid (q.v.), often under pressure from the Soviet Union, and their subsequent membership of Comecon (p. 262). This division into two hostile camps was completed by the creation of NATO in 1949–50 (p. 266) and the Warsaw Pact in 1955 (p. 269). The Cold War between the Soviet Union and the USA continued into the 1970s before being superseded by a period of detente. The main crises within the Cold War period were the Russian invasion of Hungary in

1956; of Czechoslovakia in 1968; the Berlin Blockade of 1948, and the Cuban Missile Crisis of 1962. Western outrage at these supposed manifestations of Soviet expansion was tempered by the British and French involvement in Suez in 1956, and the US involvement in Vietnam during the 1960s and early 1970s. The advent of Gorbachev in Russia and the events of 1989 in Eastern Europe are regarded as marking the end of the Cold War.

COLLABORATION Support by the population (or part of it) for an enemy occupier of a country. The term was much used in the Second World War in such countries as France and Norway.

COLLECTIVE SECURITY The policy of guaranteeing the security of one country jointly by several others. Originated in the 1924 Geneva Conference.

COLLECTIVISM Political concept which demands that the state plays a more interventionist role in the society to promote the development of the society along collectivist lines. Rights and obligations in collectivist theory are socially derived and are based upon the conception that a notion of common good pervades, or ought to pervade, the society.

COLLECTIVIZATION The process of transferring land from private to state or collective ownership. Extensively operated in the Soviet Union during the early 1930s, when peasants' individual holdings were combined to form agricultural collectives (*Kolkhoz*) or in some cases state-owned farms (*Sovkhoz*), run by state employees.

COLOMBO PLAN Coming into force on 1 July 1951, the plan was a co-operative attempt by both developed and developing countries to further the economies and raise living standards in south and southeast Asia. It was originally intended to last

until 1957, but has been successively extended.

COLONELS, GREEK Term applied to the Greek right-wing military junta led by two colonels which seized power in Apr. 1967. The authoritarian regime collapsed in 1974, after the failure of its intervention in Cyprus.

COLOUR BAR The separation of people along racial divisions. Usually manifested, as in South Africa during the apartheid era, by prohibiting black people from entering white-only areas. *See* apartheid.

COMINTERN Abbreviated title of the Third International established in Mar. 1919 to promote revolutionary Marxism. By 1928 it had become a vehicle for Stalin's ideas. Finally dissolved in May 1943 as a goodwill gesture to the Soviet Union's Western allies. Though its stated purpose was the promotion of world revolution, the Comintern functioned chiefly as an organ of Soviet control over the communist movement.

COMMON AGRICULTURAL POLICY (CAP) The controversial policy of the European Community which subsidizes farmers from a Common Agricultural Fund contributed to by member states.

COMMON MARKET *see* pp. 263–5.

COMMONWEALTH *see* p. 262.

CONCENTRATION CAMP Camp for the detention of political and other opponents. Such camps as Belsen and Auschwitz claimed millions of victims – Jews, gypsies and ethnic minorities – in Nazi-controlled Europe. The first camps in Nazi Germany were established in 1933 in Dachau and Oranienburg. The name was originally coined to describe the camps used to intern the rural civilian population by the British during the Boer War (1899–1902) in South Africa.

CONDUCATOR (leader, Führer) Title used by the Romanian communist dictator Nicolae Ceausescu (q.v.).

CONFRONTATION Term applied to the armed conflict between Indonesia and Malaysia in the 1960s. *See* p. 311.

CONGRESS (1) the two chambers of the US legislature – i.e. the more powerful Senate, and the 405 member House of Representatives. (2) Common abbreviation for the Indian National Congress, formed in 1885 and the main vehicle of Indian nationalism. *See* p. 469.

CONTAINMENT US policy aimed at preventing the extension of communist influence. George Kennan argued in 1947 that the USSR should be faced with a 'patient but firm and vigilant containment of Russian expansive tendencies.' Examples in practice have been economic aid to Europe under the Marshall Plan, and military engagement in Korea and Vietnam.

CONTRAS Exiles from Nicaragua after the 1979 victory of the Sandinista revolution, who continued to support former right-wing dictator Anastasio Somoza Debayle from neighbouring Honduras and mounted armed attacks in north-west Nicaragua. After Somoza's death in 1980 the Contras continued their anti-Sandinista campaign with American backing, but the electoral defeat of the Sandinistas in 1990 effectively ended their activities.

CO-PROSPERITY SPHERE The term used by Japan between the wars to describe the area of Asia which it hoped to control and develop, stretching from the USSR's Pacific coast to Timor in the south, and east from Burma to New Guinea. Japan

succeeded in occupying a large part of the area in the Second World War.

CUBAN MISSILE CRISIS On 22 Oct. 1962 President Kennedy (q.v.) announced on television that United States surveillance had established the presence of Soviet missile sites in Cuba, and that he was imposing a quarantine on Cuba to prevent the shipment of further offensive weapons. With the threat of nuclear war imminent, tense negotiations took place. On 28 Oct. Khrushchev agreed to remove the missiles, and in return Kennedy lifted the blockade and agreed not to invade Cuba.

CULTURAL REVOLUTION The term used to describe the convulsions in Chinese society caused in 1965 by Mao Zedong's movement to purge the country of his opponents and to bring about a revolution in popular ideology.

D

DALAI LAMA The spiritual and also temporal leader of the Tibetan people. After Chinese troops occupied Tibet in 1951, a major rebellion took place in 1959. The Dalai Lama subsequently fled to India. Awarded Nobel Peace Prize, 1989.

DAWES PLAN Proposals drawn up by American banker Charles G. Dawes (1865–1951) in 1924 for the settlement of German war reparations by an annual payment of 2,000 million marks.

D-DAY Code name for 6 June 1944, the first day of Operation Overlord, the allied landings in Normandy. Three British and Canadian divisions landed on 'Gold', 'Juno' and 'Sword' beaches and two American divisions landed on 'Omaha' and 'Utah' beaches. By the evening a beach-head 24 miles long and 4 miles deep was established, at the cost of 10,000 casualties.

DECOLONIZATION The European withdrawal from overseas possessions after the Second World War. Britain withdrew from India and Pakistan in 1947, and the majority of its African colonies gained independence by the 1960s. France freed Indo-China, Algeria and Tunisia after liberation wars in the 1950s. Belgium, the Netherlands and Portugal had relinquished most of their colonies by the 1970s. The final acts of decolonization were the return of Hong Kong to China by Britain in 1997 and the return of Macao to China by Portugal in 1999.

DEMILITARIZED ZONE An area following approximately the 38th Parallel which divides North and South Korea. Following cessation of hostilities in the 1950–3 Korean War, it was agreed that no military forces should enter the area. A similar zone divided Vietnam along the 17th Parallel.

DENGISM Chinese economic modernization programme introduced by Deng Xiaoping in 1984. China turned to decentralized management in industry, the encouragement of market forces, individual enterprise and foreign investment. By the late 1980s there were fears of inflation and unemployment and complaints of corruption. Harshly suppressed demands for political liberalization in 1989 appeared to force a step back in the programme but the programme soon resumed.

DESTALINIZATION The overturning of the 'cult of personality' that had surrounded Soviet dictator Stalin (q.v.) who died in 1953. At the 20th Party Congress in Russia, the attack on Stalin and his purges was led by Khrushchev (q.v.). The process included renaming Stalingrad (which became Volgograd in 1961). Under Gorbachev's glasnost, there were soon further revelations of the evils of the Stalin era.

DETENTE A French diplomatic term meaning a reduction in tension between two adversary states, widely used to describe Soviet–American and Sino-American relations since 1968. The policy of detente has been characterized by a large number of personal summit meetings between US and Soviet and US and Chinese leaders, which have resulted in agreements on trade, cultural exchanges and limited arms control. The Helsinki Agreement of 1975 represented the existence of a more general detente between the western and communist nations. With the advent of Gorbachev in Russia, detente and co-operation had effectively ended the Cold War (q.v.) by the end of the 1980s.

DETERRENCE Strategy by which one country deters an adversary from launching a nuclear attack by the threat of instant nuclear retaliation. A so-called 'balance of terror' exists between two countries when both have a high level of assured destruction capability – that is, when neither can expect by a first strike against the enemy's nuclear force to do sufficient damage to prevent a retaliatory second strike causing unacceptable destruction to its own cities. The United States and the Soviet Union operated a range of retaliatory systems to ensure that they maintained this assured destruction capability.

DIEN BIEN PHU, BATTLE OF The crucial battle which lost the French Empire in Indo-China. In Nov. 1953, the French commander in Indo-China, General Navarre, fortified Dien Bien Phu, a valley 200 miles west of Hanoi, with 15,000 men to cut the supply routes of the Viet Minh guerrillas (q.v.) into Laos and to draw them into a pitched battle. But the French had underestimated the capability of General Giap (q.v.), the Viet Minh commander, to concentrate men and heavy artillery on the hills overlooking Dien Bien Phu. The vital airfield was rendered unusable, and the French garrison was overwhelmed on 7 May 1954. The defeat ended French power in Indo-China, and this was confirmed at the conference taking place in Geneva. See also p. 302.

DIRTY WAR Term applied to the vicious Argentine military campaign used against such left-wing guerrilla groups as the Monteneros from 1976 to 1978.

DISSIDENTS Term used particularly in the context of Russia, Eastern Europe and China to refer to those who refused to conform to the politics and beliefs of the communist society in which they lived. They were frequently imprisoned and persecuted. Among the most famous was Alexander Solzhenitsyn, the Nobel Prize-winning novelist, expelled from Russia in 1974.

DOLLAR DIPLOMACY Term used first by Latin Americans, later more generally, to refer disapprovingly to the use of economic influence by the United States in promoting its overseas interests.

DOMINO THEORY Refers to the existence of relations of political dependence between several states. Should any one power fall under communist control, the theory argued that others would also fall, like a row of dominoes. The first explicit formulation of the theory appeared in 1954 in support of arguments for American military assistance to certain non-communist regimes in Indo-China. Both South Vietnam and Laos were seen as 'first dominoes', and their alleged strategic relationship to the rest of south-east Asia was the explanation of the importance

attached by successive US administrations to preventing the forcible overthrow of their regimes by communist-supported insurgents.

DRANG NACH OSTEN (Ger.: push to the east) The German desire for territorial gains in Eastern Europe.

DUCE Title assumed by Benito Mussolini (q.v.). The title means, literally, leader.

DUMA Russian parliament established by the Tsar in 1905 in response to demands which emanated from the abortive revolution of 1905. Free elections to the first two Dumas led to radical demands and rapid dissolution by the government. The Third Duma, elected with much greater government interference, did produce some limited administrative and land reform instigated by premier Stolypin. In spite of government disapproval, the Duma remained a platform for protest and in Nov. 1916 warned the government of impending revolution. As a result of its criticisms of the government, the Duma was suspended for much of the war period. Since the fall of the Soviet Union, the lower house of the Russian parliament has again been known as the Duma.

E

EASTERN BLOC Term which referred to the communist states of Eastern Europe, including the Balkan states of Yugoslavia and Albania. With the fall of communism, and the accession of many of these states to the European Union in 2004, the term is no longer used.

EASTERN FRONT Term used in both World Wars to describe the battle-front between Germany and Russia.

ENOSIS From the Greek word meaning 'to unite', the term used to describe the aims of the Greek Cypriot movement for the political union of Cyprus and Greece. The Turkish minority (c. 20% of the population) has consistently feared and opposed such a union. The coup by EOKA supporters (q.v.) in July 1974 prompted a Turkish invasion of Cyprus, and the island is now divided, with the 40% of the island in Turkish control proclaimed as a Turkish federated state.

ENTEBBE RAID Daring Israeli commando operation to rescue hostages. On 27 June 1976 an Air France Airbus from Tel Aviv to Paris with 12 crew and 247 passengers was hijacked by members of the Popular Front for the Liberation of Palestine (p. 481) and forced to fly to Entebbe in Uganda. Negotiations began over the hijackers' demands, and non-Israeli hostages were released. During the night of 3–4 July, 3 Israeli Hercules C-130 transport aircraft landed at Entebbe airport, rescued the hostages and flew them back to Israel, refuelling en route at Nairobi, Kenya.

EOKA The anti-British, Greek-Cypriot terrorist movement, founded and led by Colonel Grivas to force a British withdrawal from Cyprus. It was most active from 1955 to 1959, with Cyprus becoming an independent country within the Commonwealth in 1960. *See also* Enosis (above) and Makarios (p. 430).

ESCALATION Term for increasing the intensity or area of a conflict. It was particularly associated with the increases in the scope of the American effort in the Vietnam War. Significant stages in the process of escalation were the first bombing of North Vietnam in Aug. 1964, after incidents in the Gulf of Tonkin, followed by the decision to begin regular bombing of the North in Feb. 1965 and to commit ever-increasing numbers of combat troops.

ETA Initials of the militant Basque terrorist group in Spain seeking to re-create in northern Spain the short-lived republic of Euzkadi (Oct. 1936–June 1937). It has been responsible for numerous acts of violence. *See also* pp. 343–55.

EUROCOMMUNISM The policy of individual communist parties in Western European countries to seek and pursue their own political paths, not dominated by or taking orders from Russia – as had happened under the domination of the Comintern (q.v.) in the interwar period.

EUROPEAN COMMUNITY *see* pp. 263–5.

F

FAIR DEAL The political programme advocated by US President Truman (q.v.) in 1948, when running for his second term as President. It was a progressive set of policies which, although denying the need for a planned economy, advocated housing, health and education policies all aimed at extending social justice at home, as well as economic and military aid programmes abroad.

FALANGE The only political party permitted in Franco's Spain. Founded by José Antonio Primo de Rivera in 1933 as a right-wing movement opposed to the Republic. Primo de Rivera was assassinated in Nov. 1936, in the early months of the Spanish Civil War. The movement survived his death to be used by Franco when the Grand Council of the Falange replaced the Cortes as the legislative body in Spain between June 1939 and July 1942.

FASCISM An Italian nationalist, authoritarian, anti-communist movement developed by Mussolini after 1919, which became the only authorized political party in Italy after the March on Rome in 1922. The movement derived its name from the *fasces* (bundle of sticks), the symbol of state power in ancient Rome. More generally applied to authoritarian and National Socialist movements in Europe and elsewhere (e.g. Nazi).

FEBRUARY REVOLUTION The revolution in Russia on 8 Mar. 1917 (February in the Julian Calendar). Demonstrators protesting in St Petersburg at food shortages and against the war were joined by troops, and the Duma appointed a provisional government under Prince Lvov. Tsar Nicholas II abdicated on 15 Mar. and Russia attempted to move towards constitutional democracy under the liberal intelligentsia, until the October Revolution.

FEDAYEEN Palestinian guerrillas who raided Israel under the leadership of the Grand Mufti, following their expulsion from Palestine by the Israelis in 1948–9. The word derives from the Arabic for those who risk their lives for a cause. The fedayeen eventually came under the leadership of the PLO.

FELLOW TRAVELLER Term, most often used in connection with the Communist Party, describing an individual who sympathizes with the position of a political group but is not a member.

FIFTH COLUMN Expression used by Gen. Mola during the Spanish Civil War (1936–9). He claimed that his four columns advancing on Madrid would be aided by a 'fifth column' of sympathizers in the city itself. The term was used widely in the Second World War to describe secret enemy sympathisers.

FINAL SOLUTION Translation of the German *Endlösung*, used to describe the destruction of European Jewry carried out by Nazi Germany in occupied countries between 1941 and 1945.

FIVE YEAR PLAN System of economic planning first adopted in the Soviet Union between 1928 and 1933. The plan laid down short-term aims and targets for the development of heavy industry and the collectivization of agriculture. The second plan, 1933–7, aimed at increased production of consumer goods but the third, 1938–42, returned to the primacy of heavy industry, largely directed towards rearmament. The 5-year plan has since been adopted as a planning method by other socialist countries.

FOOD FOR PEACE An important part of America's foreign aid programme. Congress established 'Food for Peace' in 1954 in order to reduce American farm surpluses, to increase foreign consumption of American produce and to strengthen America's position with the developing nations. Vast quantities of wheat were then sold to nations for their local currencies which were usually returned to preserve economic stability. By 1973, Congress had authorized a 4-year programme involving an annual sum of $2.5 million. One of the major recipients of such American assistance has been India, a state which had not always associated itself diplomatically with the United States.

FOUR FREEDOMS Freedoms enumerated as basic human rights by President Franklin D. Roosevelt (1882–1945) in his annual message to the US Congress in Jan. 1941. They are the freedoms (1) of speech and expression, (2) of religion, (3) from want and (4) from fear.

FOURTEEN POINTS A peace programme put forward by President Woodrow Wilson to the US Congress on 8 Jan. 1918 and accepted as the basis for an armistice by

Germany and Austria–Hungary. Later it was alleged that the Allied powers had violated the principles embodied in the 'Fourteen Points', especially in relation to the prohibition of *Anschluss* (q.v.), the union of Germany with Austria. The original points were: the renunciation of secret diplomacy; freedom of the seas; the removal of economic barriers between states; arms reductions; impartial settlement of colonial disputes; evacuation of Russia by Germany and its allies; restoration of Belgium; German withdrawal from France and the return of Alsace-Lorraine; readjustment of the Italian frontiers; autonomous development of nationalities in Austria–Hungary; evacuation of Romania, Serbia and Montenegro and guarantees of Serbian access to the sea; free passage through the Dardanelles and the self-determination of minorities in the Ottoman Empire; creation of an independent Poland with access to the sea; and the creation of a general association of states.

FREE FRENCH The *Forces Françaises Libres* made up of French troops and naval units who continued the fight against Nazi Germany after the fall of France in the summer of 1940. In opposition to the Vichy regime in France, General de Gaulle established a 'Council for the Defence of the Empire', and later the *Comité National Français*. The Free French were active against Vichy forces in Syria and Miquelon and St Pierre in 1941. On 19 July 1942 the Free French were renamed the *Forces Françaises Combatantes* (French Fighting Forces). The FFC represented de Gaulle's main claim as the true representative of French liberation. As the Allied forces liberated France in the summer of 1944, the FFC were able to provide the first Allied troops to enter Paris, after an uprising organized by the *Forces Françaises de l'Intérieur*.

FREE OFFICERS Radical Egyptian nationalist and republican movement of young army officers, nominally led by Mohammed Neguib but Gamal Abdel Nasser (1918–70) was its most influential figure. Egypt's military failure against Israel in 1948 encouraged growing support and the movement mounted a bloodless coup against King Farouk on 23 July 1952. Neguib became President but was deposed by Nasser in Nov. 1954.

FREE WORLD Term used in the West to describe non-communist countries, particularly during the Cold War era.

FRENTE DE LIBERTAÇÃO DE MOÇAMBIQUE (FRELIMO) The nationalist guerrilla movement in Mozambique which, in 1964, launched an armed struggle for independence. By the early 1970s they claimed control over much of the north. The leader of FRELIMO became President of the provisional government in 1974 and President on independence in 1975.

FRENTE NACIONAL DE LIBERTAÇÃO DE ANGOLA (FNLA) This anti-Marxist Angolan group was in control of the north of Angola at independence. Joint FNLA/UNITA troops were virtually defeated by the MPLA (q.v.) by Feb. 1976, but sporadic fighting continued. *See* p. 320.

FRONT-LINE PRESIDENTS The term used to designate the black African Presidents who were actively involved in attempts to bring about a peace settlement in South Africa: Presidents Neto of Angola, Khama of Botswana, Chissano of Mozambique, Nyerere of Tanzania, Kaunda of Zambia and Mugabe of Zimbabwe.

FÜHRER (Ger.: leader) Title first coined in 1921 to describe Hitler as head of the Nazi Party. After his appointment as Chancellor in 1933, the term was used more widely to describe him as 'Führer' of Germany.

G

GANG OF FOUR Radical Chinese communist leaders – Wang Hongwen, Zhang Chungqiao, Yao Wenyuan and Jiang Qing – denounced by party moderates who gained power in 1976 after the death of Mao Zedong. The Gang, which argued for continuing revolutionary purity rather than economic pragmatism, was arrested and accused at a show trial of plotting to take control of the army. Jiang Qing – Mao's widow – was given a suspended death sentence in 1981.

GATT *See* General Agreement on Tariffs and Trade.

GAULLIST A follower of General de Gaulle (q.v.), usually associated with authoritarianism and nationalist sentiment.

GAZA STRIP Disputed territory under Israeli occupation. Swollen with refugees and taken by Egyptian troops in the 1948 war, Gaza was under harsh Egyptian rule 1948–67. Israel occupied Gaza briefly in 1956–7, and had hoped to prevent its being used to mount guerrilla attacks on Israel, but was forced to return it to Egypt. Israel conquered the area in June 1967 and put it under military administration. At first the Arab population was extremely restive and difficult to control, but the situation quietened after a time. Gazans were permitted to enter Israel to work, and were a useful source of skilled and unskilled labour. The Israeli government has established Jewish settlements in Gaza. Like the West Bank (q.v.), the Strip has been the scene of many demonstrations and riots in recent years. In 1994 it was granted limited self-rule. There are currently proposals for an Israeli withdrawal.

GENERAL AGREEMENT ON TARIFFS AND TRADE (GATT) An international agreement which came into force in 1948. The countries belonging to GATT account for over 80% of world trade, and are pledged to encourage free trade. There were a series of negotiating conferences on the reduction of tariffs and the abolition of import restrictions. By 1993 over 108 countries were contracting parties and 29 others were applying GATT rules. It inaugurated the Kennedy Round (1964–7) the Tokyo Round (1973–9) and the Uruguay Round (1986–93). Negotiations were eventually concluded in 1993 and over 120 nations signed the GATT accord in Apr. 1994. GATT has been superseded by the World Trade Organization.

GESTAPO The Secret State Police (*Geheime Staatspolizei*) established by Goering in Prussia in Apr. 1933 to arrest and murder Nazi opponents. In Apr. 1934 the Gestapo was enlarged under Himmler, and eventually became part of the SS.

GLASNOST The liberalizing 'openness' of the Soviet intellectual atmosphere encouraged by Mikhail Gorbachev, following his appointment as Communist Party secretary in Mar. 1985.

GLOBALIZATION The alleged deleterious spread of capitalism and consumerism world-wide attacked by left-wing and environmental critics for increasing third world poverty and damaging the environment.

GOLD STANDARD A country on the gold standard is in the position where its central bank will exchange gold for its currency on demand. The UK came off the gold standard in 1914, returning briefly 1925–31. The gold standard provided a convenient method of fixing exchange rates, but has now been generally abandoned.

GOLKAR The political party ruling Indonesia under President Suharto.

GOOD NEIGHBOUR POLICY Foreign affairs position taken by US President Franklin D. Roosevelt (1882–1945) in an effort to move from isolationism towards closer relations with other states, particularly in South America.

GREAT CRASH The Wall Street stock market collapse, beginning on 24 Oct. 1929 when 132 million shares were sold in panic trading following a 2 year speculative boom. The crash forced an American business slump, which affected European financial stability and led to the 1930s Depression.

GREAT LEAP FORWARD The Chinese Communist attempt in 1958–61 to make a rapid move towards communism. Large-scale agricultural collectivization was instituted and private consumption reduced. Bad harvests and the ending of technical assistance from the USSR following ideological disputes undermined the attempt.

'GREAT SOCIETY' Expression used by US President Lyndon Johnson (1908–73) to describe what he hoped would emerge from his administration's 1963–8 progressive civil rights and welfare legislation.

GREEN REVOLUTION The expansion of agricultural production in developing countries since 1945 by the increasing use of chemical fertilizers, pesticides and high-yield crop seeds. These techniques have been increasingly criticized for their environmental effects.

GREENS The West German ecology party which made a dramatic advance in state elections in 1979 and which, despite internal divisions, remains an influential force. From the late 1980s Green parties in other European countries began gaining significant support in elections and, while winning few seats, have forced an acknow-ledgement of environmental issues on other political parties.

GUIDED DEMOCRACY The ideology of President Sukarno's regime in Indonesia from 1959 to 1965. Sukarno attempted to unite national, religious and communist forces under a strong executive government, but was overthrown by the army in Oct. 1965.

GULAG ARCHIPELAGO The title of Alexander Solzhenitsyn's denunciation of the Russian communist system, based on his and other victims' experience of the Soviet labour camps. Gulag is an acronym for the Russian name of the State Administration of Correctional Labour Camps.

GUOMINDANG *see* Kuomintang

HAGANAH Secret force formed in 1936 by the Jews in Palestine to defend themselves against Arab attacks. Haganah fought in Apr. and May 1948 to prevent Arabs severing links between Tel Aviv and Jerusalem, and the force became the basis of the army when Israel was created.

HAWKS Term used to describe Americans who argued that intensification and escalation of US involvement in the 1965–72 Vietnam War provided the best guarantee of its most effective conclusion.

HERRENVOLK (Ger.: master race) A doctrine expounded by the Nazis who used the supposed superiority of the 'Aryan' race as a justification for German territorial expansion and the enslavement of 'inferior races'.

HEZBOLLAH Militant Iranian backed terrorist group active in Lebanon since the 1980s. Its name means 'Party of God'.

HOLOCAUST, THE Name given to the death of around 6 million Jews at the hands of the Nazis during the Second World War. Also known by the Jewish term 'Shoah'. (*See* table, p. 52.)

HOT LINE A direct telecommunications link between the White House and the Kremlin, which was set up by a memorandum of understanding signed by the United States and the Soviet Union in Geneva on 20 June 1963. The need for such a direct channel of communication for negotiations in times of crisis had been demonstrated by the Cuban Missile Crisis of Oct. 1962. It was used, for example, during the Middle East War in June 1967.

HUK Originally the Philippine 'People's Army against Japan' formed among communist-led peasants in Mar. 1942, which came increasingly under Chinese communist influence. Outlawed in 1948 and 1957 for its campaign against landlords and the government, the Huk was reorganized as the 'New People's Army' in the early 1970s. The movement continued its campaign despite the fall of President Marcos in 1986.

HUNDRED FLOWERS Chinese communist government attempt to win intellectual support in 1956–7, based on Mao Zedong's declaration, 'Let a hundred flowers bloom and a hundred schools of criticism compete'. The policy was abandoned when it became clear how extensive the resulting criticism would be.

I

ILO *see* International Labour Organization

INDIA, PARTITION OF The division of British India on independence into India, Pakistan (and now Bangladesh), Burma (Myanmar) and Ceylon (Sri Lanka).

INDIAN NATIONAL CONGRESS Party formed as an educational association in 1885 to encourage Indian political development and which grew into an opponent of British rule. Mohandas Karamchand Gandhi (1869–1948) became its leader in 1915, and Congress conducted a non-violent civil disobedience campaign through the 1920s and 1930s. Its leaders were interned by Britain between 1942 and 1945. On independence in 1947 Congress president Jawaharlal Nehru (1889–1964) became India's first Prime Minister, with a policy of industrialization and non-alignment in foreign affairs. The Congress Party, apart from a period in opposition from 1977–80, formed every government since independence to the defeat of Rajiv Gandhi in 1989.

INDO-CHINA French south-east Asian colonies in Annam, Cambodia, Cochin-China, Laos and Tonkin. They were held by France from the 1860s until July 1954, when the Geneva Agreements recognized Cambodia, Laos and Vietnam as independent states.

INTERNATIONAL BRIGADES Volunteer brigades formed to support the Republican cause in Spain during the Spanish Civil War. Composed mainly of left-wing and communist sympathisers from all parts of Europe and the United States, the volunteers saw the fight against Franco's nationalist insurgents as part of the wider struggle against European fascism.

INTERNATIONAL LABOUR ORGANIZATION (ILO) Originally established in 1919 as an independent body which would act in association with the League of Nations (q.v.) to improve working conditions, wage levels, industrial healthcare, etc. It is now a specialist agency of the United Nations.

INTERNATIONAL MONETARY FUND (IMF) Organization set up at the Bretton Woods conference in 1944 which came into operation in 1947. Members contribute a quota to the fund and can negotiate a loan if they are in debt. The intention was that the IMF would help to stabilize exchange rates, but since floating exchange rates have developed, countries tended to allow their currencies to lose value rather than borrow from the IMF.

INTIFADA Name given to the Arab uprising which began in 1988 in the Israeli-occupied Gaza Strip (q.v.) and West Bank (q.v.). A second *intifada* began in 2000.

IRAN–CONTRA AFFAIR Term used for scandal under Reagan administration involving diversion of funds to Contras in Nicaragua. *See* p. 323.

IRON CURTAIN A symbol of the frontier between the 'communist' and the 'free' world. The term was used by Winston Churchill with reference to Eastern Europe, when he said at Fulton, Missouri, in Mar. 1946: 'From Stettin in the Baltic to Trieste in the Adriatic an iron curtain has descended across the Continent.' The term was much in use during the Cold War. However, the advent of Gorbachev to power and the revolutionary changes in Eastern Europe in 1989, including the rapid dismantling of the Berlin Wall and the symbolic opening of the Brandenburg Gate crossing, have made the term redundant.

ISLAMIC REVOLUTION An outgrowth of the reassertion of Islamic values in the late 1970s, initially in Saudi Arabia, encouraged by the confidence flowing from wealth based on oil. In Mar. 1979 Iran was declared an Islamic Republic following the overthrow of the Shah and his replacement by a Shi'ite-dominated Revolutionary Council under Ayatollah Khomeini. The regime rejected Western influence and values and enforced Islamic law. Gen. Mohammed Zia ul-Haq's military government in Pakistan similarly based itself on Islamic law ('Shariah') whilst a more extreme example can be found in the Taliban (q.v.) regime in Afghanistan.

ISOLATIONISM Policy of avoiding alliances and having minimal involvement in international affairs. The USA remained isolationist until the early twentieth century and returned to the policy in the 1920s and 1930s following its involvement in the First World War. After 1945, America's role as leader of the West forced an abandonment of isolationism but a return to the policy has been a recurring demand of some conservative Republicans, first in the early 1960s and again after the 1965–72 Vietnam War.

J

JAMAHIRAYA Libyan expression meaning 'the state of the masses'. In Mar. 1977 Col. Muammar Qadhafi proclaimed his country to be the Socialist People's Libyan Arab Jamahiraya.

JANATA Alliance of opposition groups formed against the Indian Congress Party in 1977. Morarji Desai led Janata to victory against Mrs Gandhi in the July 1979 election but the alliance succumbed to internal divisions and went down to electoral defeat in 1980.

JULY CONSPIRACY Otherwise known as the Hitler Bomb Plot, this was an attempt by disaffected sections of the German officer corps to assassinate Hitler and end Nazi rule in order that negotiations could take place with the Western Allies. The plot involved a bomb placed in Hitler's East Prussian headquarters by Col. von Stauffenberg on 20 July 1944 and was assumed to have succeeded by accomplices in Berlin, who thus committed themselves to a new government. Hitler's almost miraculous survival signalled the failure of the plotters, and the attempt was used as an excuse by Hitler to purge the army and execute other high-ranking officials known to oppose the regime.

K

KADETS The 'Constitutional Democrats', a Russian liberal party which emerged after the 1905 Revolution. Strongly represented in the pre-1917 Duma, the Kadets argued for a democratic republic between the Feb. and Oct. 1917 Revolutions, but were banned by the Bolsheviks in Jan. 1918.

KAISER Emperor of Germany after German unification in Dec. 1870. The title derived from 'Caesar' and was held by successive kings of Prussia until William II's abdication in Nov. 1918.

KAMIKAZE Bomb-laden Japanese aircraft which made suicidal attacks on Allied warships in the Second World War. The word, which also described the pilots, derived from the Japanese 'divine wind'.

KANU Kenya African National Union. Led by Jomo Kenyatta (1897–1978) from 1947 onwards, the party's base was in the Kikuyu tribe and it soon became the only legal party following Kenyan independence in 1963.

KELLOGG–BRIAND PACT The General Pact for the Renunciation of War formulated by US Secretary of State Frank B. Kellogg and French Foreign Secretary Aristide Briand. Nine powers signed and formally renounced war in Aug. 1928. They were eventually joined by 56 other states.

KEMALISM Ideology of Kemal Atatürk, who as President, 1923–38, attempted to modernize and secularize Turkey by encouraging industrial development, imposing Western dress and lifestyles, outlawing polygamy and replacing the Arabic with the Latin script.

KEYNESIANISM Theory and practice derived from the economist Maynard Keynes, particularly his General Theory (1936). It encouraged state intervention to secure economic growth through the management of overall demand by fiscal means, and laid the basis for post-1945 welfare capitalism.

KHALISTAN The name of the independent homeland in the Indian subcontinent sought by militant Sikh activists.

KHALSA The Sikh Commonwealth in the Punjab, India, known as the 'brotherhood of the pure'. Derived from the Arabic for pure, sincere, free.

KHEDIVE Title granted by the Ottoman Empire to the hereditary pasha of Egypt between 1867 and 1914. It was replaced by the title Sultan when Britain occupied Egypt.

KHMER ROUGE The communist guerrilla troops who defeated the republican forces in the Cambodian civil war (p. 317).

KNESSET The 120-member single-chamber Israeli legislature. Members are elected for four years by universal suffrage under proportional representation.

KREMLIN (Russ.: citadel) Refers to the citadel in Moscow occupied by the former Imperial Palace. The administrative headquarters of, and synonymous with, the government of the former USSR.

KU KLUX KLAN A white supremacist secret society formed in the US Southern States following their defeat in the American Civil War in 1865. The Klan's terrorist violence forced the imposition of martial law in some areas and it was suppressed by the 1880s. It revived in 1915 and extended its terror campaign to Catholics, Jews and the left. A further resurgence came in response to 1960s civil rights legislation.

KULAKS (Russ.: tight-fisted person) Term used to describe Russian peasants who were able to become landowners as a result of the agrarian reforms of 1906 and were encouraged by Lenin's NEP.

KUOMINTANG Nationalist Chinese democratic republican party founded in 1891 by Sun Yat-sen, led from 1925 by Chiang Kai-shek. The party governed China from 1928 and led the resistance to Japanese occupation from 1937 to 1945. Under Chiang the Kuomintang degenerated into a military oligarchy, and he was overthrown by the communists in 1949. Chiang and his followers retreated to Taiwan, with American support.

L

LATERAN TREATIES Agreement signed between Mussolini and Pope Pius XI on 11 Feb. 1929 establishing a Concordat between fascist Italy and the Catholic Church, recognizing the Vatican City State's sovereignty and compensating the Papacy for possessions confiscated in 1870.

LEAGUE OF NATIONS *see* p. 265.

LEBENSRAUM (Ger.: living space) Slogan adopted by German nationalists and especially the Nazi Party in the 1920s and 1930s to justify the need for Germany to expand territorially in the east. The theory was based on the alleged overpopulation of Germany and the need for more territory to ensure food supplies. Interpreted by some Germans as the desire for a return to the frontiers of 1914, the attack on the Soviet Union suggests that Hitler's interpretation of the concept was much wider.

LEND-LEASE Act passed by the US Congress on 11 Mar. 1941, authorizing President Roosevelt to lend or lease arms and equipment to states 'whose defence the President deems vital to the defence of the United States', despite America's neutrality. Aid went to Britain, China and the USSR.

LIBERATION THEOLOGY The attempt by some Central and South American Roman Catholic priests to work with a 'bias to the poor' by reconciling in practice Christian theology with Marxist economic and social analysis.

LIKUD An alliance of Israeli right-wing parties which won the May 1977 general election under Menachem Begin's leadership, replacing Mapai and the Labour Party for the first time. Likud went on to further success in the 1988 elections.

LITTLE BOY The name given to the first atomic bomb, dropped on Hiroshima by the US aircraft *Enola Gay* on 6 Aug. 1945.

LITTLE ENTENTE Complex of alliances between Yugoslavia and Czechoslovakia (1920), Czechoslovakia and Romania (1921), and Yugoslavia and Romania (1921), consolidated in the May 1929 Treaty of Belgrade, to deter Austria and Hungary from retrieving territory lost in 1918. The term was used disparagingly and the Entente collapsed under the pressure of events in the 1930s.

LOMÉ CONVENTIONS, First signed on 28 Feb. 1975 between the European Community and 46 African, Caribbean and Pacific countries, of which 22 were members of the Commonwealth, 18 were formerly associated with the Six (q.v.) under the Yaoundé Convention, and 6 had no previous links with members of the European Community. The Convention included provisions to allow duty-free entry into the Community of all imports from the ACP States except about 4% of imports of agricultural products. It also set up the Stabex Scheme and the European Development Fund and concerned general industrial, technical and financial co-operation. The original Lomé Convention has been much expanded by subsequent agreements. Lomé IV, concluded in 1989, was signed by 70 countries.

LONG MARCH The 8,000-mile retreat of communist forces from Oct. 1934 to Oct. 1935 under Guomindang attack. The march, led by Mao Zedong, Zhu De and Lin Biao, was from the beleaguered Jiangxi Soviet to the more defensible Yenan region in north-west China. Of the 100,000 who set out only 30,000 survived, but the march

was seen as an inspiring epic of the Chinese Revolution.

LUFTWAFFE The German air force, illegal by the Treaty of Versailles, but openly developed by the Nazis from 1935 onwards under Marshal Hermann Goering. Initially impressive in the *Blitzkrieg* of 1939–40, it was eventually overwhelmed by superior Allied air power.

M

MCCARTHYISM Unsubstantiated accusations of disloyalty and abuse of legislative investigatory power that engender fear of real or imagined threats to national security. The term derives from the behaviour of Senator Joseph R. McCarthy (1909–57) of Wisconsin who, in the early 1950s, made repeated unsubstantiated accusations of treachery against public officials (particularly in the State Department) under the protection of his Senatorial immunity.

MAGINOT LINE French defensive fortifications stretching from Longwy to the Swiss border. Named after French minister of Defence André Maginot, the line was constructed between 1929 and 1934 as a means of countering a German attack. Owing to the Belgians' refusal to extend the line along their frontier with Germany, and French reluctance to appear to 'abandon' Belgium and build the line along the Franco-Belgian border to the sea, the defensive strategy relied on the Germans' inability to penetrate the Ardennes forest. This hope was seen as misguided when the Germans were able to turn the French flank by an advance through Belgium, and the Maginot Line was still virtually intact when France surrendered on 22 July 1940.

MAHATMA Title (from the Sanskrit 'great soul') bestowed on Indian national leader Mohandas Karamchand Gandhi (1869–1948) by his Hindu followers, in recognition of his asceticism, simplicity and what they saw as saintly qualities.

MALVINAS The Argentinian name for the Falklands Islands in the South Atlantic, which both Britain and the Argentine claim. The islands were occupied by Argentina on 2 Apr. 1982 and retaken by Britain on 14 June.

MANCHUKUO The name given to the Chinese province of Manchuria by the Japanese when they occupied it in 1931. They installed a puppet regime under the last Chinese Manchu emperor, Henry Pu Yi, which was overthrown by Chinese communists and the USSR in 1945.

MANDATES Rights granted to certain states at the end of the First World War by the League of Nations to administer the colonies and dependencies of Germany and the Ottoman Empire. The mandates came in three forms. Some territories were under only a limited-term mandate while they prepared for independence; the British control over Iraq, Palestine and Transjordan, and the French control of Lebanon and Syria came into this category. Others were to be administered indefinitely because of their lack of development. This included all the German colonies in Africa, except for South West Africa. The third category were also to be administered indefinitely but could be treated as part of the mandate powers' territory. South West Africa, New Guinea and Samoa were included in these.

MANHATTAN PROJECT Code name for the development from Aug. 1942 of the atomic bomb at Oak Ridge, Tennessee, by a team of British, German and US scientists. The first experimental explosion was made in the New Mexico desert on 17 June 1945.

MAOISM Revision of Marxism to suit Chinese conditions undertaken by Mao Zedong (1893–1976). Mao argued that in non-industrialized countries the peasantry rather than the urban proletariat was the main force for revolutionary change. The peasantry would ally with the working class to overthrow the feudal classes, and advance to socialism without an intervening capitalist stage. Revolution had in Mao's view to be permanently renewed, as the 1966–9 Cultural Revolution demonstrated. His ideas brought China into conflict with the USSR, which claimed that it was the fount of Marxist ideology. Following Mao's death China increasingly and swiftly adopted economic modernization and moves towards a market economy under his successors.

MAPAI The Israeli Workers' Party (Miphlegeth Poalei Israel), formed in Palestine in 1930. Dominated by David Ben-Gurion (1886–1973) from 1930 to 1965, the party served in every coalition government from 1948 to 1977. Mapai combined with two small socialist parties in 1968 to form the Israeli Labour Party.

MAQUIS Guerrilla resistance fighters, who liberated Corsica in 1943. Maquis groups in mainland France increased greatly in 1943 and 1944, and those in Brittany were particularly effective in hampering German movements prior to D-Day on 6 June 1944.

MARSHALL PLAN United States plan for the economic reconstruction of Europe, named after Secretary of State General George C. Marshall. The Organization for European Economic Co-operation was established to administer the aid in Apr. 1948, but the Soviet rejection of the Plan meant that most of the monetary aid went to Western Europe. Between 1948 and 1952 the US provided some $17,000 million which was a crucial element in European postwar recovery.

MARXISM The ideological basis of state socialism and of communism formulated by Karl Marx (1818–83) and Friedrich Engels (1820–95), since subject to much revision and development. Marx claimed to have discovered that history moved dialectically towards socialism through a developing thesis, antithesis and synthesis. This dialectic showed itself in class struggle. The basis of any society lay in its means of production and the ownership of those means. The culture, politics and morality of any society were a superstructure built upon the economic base and reflected the interests of the ruling class. Revolution came when developing productive methods came into irreconcilable conflict with the system of ownership. Industrialism had emerged out of agricultural feudalism and the bourgeoisie had overthrown the nobility to enable itself to carry capitalist development forward. Capitalism, which faced its own contradictions, would in turn be overthrown by the industrial working class which would create socialism. Whatever the weaknesses of Marx's claim to have discovered a scientific truth, his analysis did provide many socialists with a strong ideological self-confidence.

MARXISM-LENINISM An interpretation of Marxism made by Lenin (1870–1924), whose leadership of the Bolshevik seizure of power in Russia in 1917 gave his ideas great influence. Lenin's analysis of imperialism sought to explain capitalism's continuing survival. Imperialism enabled capitalist states to find new markets and sources of raw materials, and to wean a domestic 'labour aristocracy' from revolution with a share in the fruits of colonial exploitation. He saw the working class as incapable of realizing the need for socialism unaided, and developed the concept of the Party, a professional elite which would lead the struggle against capitalism and exercise a post-revolutionary dictatorship of the proletariat.

MASSIVE RETALIATION Name given to a defence doctrine announced by John Foster Dulles (q.v.) in Jan. 1954, which laid down that the correct way for the United States to meet local communist aggression was by responding 'vigorously at places and with means of our own choosing'. The implied threat was that the United States would no longer observe the self-imposed restraints of the Korean War (p. 304) but might use its full nuclear capability against the Soviet Union in response to acts of communist aggression anywhere in the world. The advantage of the policy was that it meant a saving on conventional forces, but there was a problem of credibility, as it would be extremely difficult to convince the Russians that the United States would really initiate nuclear war to counter all minor acts of aggression.

MAU MAU The Mau Mau was a militant African secret society active in Kenya between 1952 and 1960. A state of emergency was declared and some 10,000 British troops sent to Kenya. About 13,500 people were killed during the troubles, and the Mau Mau emergency was a vital factor persuading Britain to decolonize.

MAY EVENTS Paris student demonstrations on 2 May 1968 over educational issues developed into broader political protests. After violent riots on 10–11 May, 10 million workers mounted a general strike and workplace occupations, threatening the Republic's stability. Concessions to workers and students ended *les événements*, but the position of President Charles de Gaulle was undermined.

MULDERGATE South African political scandal in 1978 over alleged misuse of state funds by Information Minister Connie Mulder, which led ultimately to the resignation of President Vorster in June 1979. The name was a reference to the Nixon Watergate scandal.

MULTILATERALISTS Term most often used with reference to nuclear weapons, describing the position taken by those arguing that a state possessing nuclear arms should not relinquish them alone – the argument of unilateralists – but should negotiate mutual disarmament with other states.

MULTILATERAL NUCLEAR FORCE (MNF) An abortive American proposal of the early 1960s for the creation of a mixed-manned NATO force of 25 surface vessels. They would be armed with Polaris nuclear missiles, but there would be an American veto on their use. Despite French and British rejection of the plan, the United States and West Germany decided to go ahead in June 1964, but this decision was later reversed. An alternative British scheme, the Atlantic Nuclear Force, was also dropped.

MUSLIM BRETHREN Founded in 1928 in Egypt by Hassan al-Banna as as Islamic revival movement. By 1939 the Brethren played a considerable role in the nationalist movement and were a powerful organization with mass support. The society often clashed with the government and was dissolved in 1948 because of its use of violence and assassination as political weapons. Following the 1948 assassination of the Prime Minister by one of the Brethren, al-Banna was himself assassinated. By 1951 the organization was permitted to reconstitute itself. Initially the society enjoyed good relations with the officers who led the 1952 revolution, but these soon deteriorated. The Brethren saw their political role evaporating and tried to undermine the government. In 1954 they made an unsuccessful attempt to assassinate Nasser. Hundreds of arrests followed. The society went underground, but was further decimated by more arrests in 1965–6. Branches were established in Syria in 1937. The Brethren there also sided with the nationalists but they never formed a paramilitary movement. In 1952 the government dissolved the society, but permitted it to reform again in 1954. Its activity was also curbed during Syria's union with Egypt.

MY LAI A Vietnamese village where US troops massacred 450 inhabitants on 16 Mar. 1968 during an operation against the Viet Cong. The incident became public in Nov. 1969, further undermining the already unpopular US position in Vietnam. On 29 Mar. 1971 Lt William Calley was sentenced to life imprisonment for his part in the crime, but his sentence was later reduced.

N

NAFTA The North American Free Trade Agreement, established by executive agreement between the United States and Canada in 1987 and subsequently ratified by them. Also joined by Mexico. The agreement provided for the abolition of all tariffs between them by 1999.

NASSAU AGREEMENT An agreement concluded on 18 Dec. 1962 between President Kennedy and Harold Macmillan, under which America provided Britain with Polaris nuclear missiles. This 'favoured nation' treatment proved a major factor in De Gaulle's decision to veto Britain's Common Market application shortly afterwards.

NATO *see* p. 266. *see* p. 266.

NAZI Popular contraction of 'National Socialist' and used to describe both the German NSDAP as a party and its individual members. The party was ideologically attached to right-wing authoritarianism (c.f. Italian fascism q.v.) but also included strong anti-Semitism and a belief in the racial supremacy of the 'Aryan' race. The party was led by Adolf Hitler from 1921 until his death in 1945. It was initially based in Munich and suffered a setback in its involvement in the Beer Hall Putsch of Nov. 1923. Nevertheless, the party under Hitler's guidance underwent a resurgence in the late 1920s and achieved a major electoral breakthrough when it captured 107 seats in the Reichstag. Their electoral success continued into 1932 and, in an attempt to provide some form of consensus government, Hitler was offered the Chancellorship in 1933. After the 'seizure of power', Nazi party organizations such as the SS and DAF came to dominate many facets of life in Germany. The party organization collapsed at the end of the Second World War and was made illegal after the German surrender.

NEO-COLONIALISM Term coined by Kwame Nkrumah (1909–72), President of Ghana, 1960–6, to describe the ability of the Western capitalist powers to retain economic and political control over the former European colonies, despite their nominal independence.

NEO-FASCISM Expression used to describe the fascist movements that emerged in Europe following the defeat of the German and Italian varieties in the Second World War but which attempt to preserve a democratic image. Among the most significant are the *Front National* in France and the *Movimento Sociale Italiano* in Italy. In Britain, the National Front and the British National Party have remained marginal but the collapse of communist control in Eastern Europe saw a growth of neo-fascist groupings in the 1990s.

NEW DEAL The economic and social programme of US President Franklin D. Roosevelt to combat the Depression in his first 2 terms (1932–40). The first phase involved devaluing the dollar, expanding business credit, aiding small farmers and creating employment through public works. From this emerged the Civilian Conservation Corps, the Civil Works Administration and the Tennessee Valley Authority. The second phase introduced social insurance through a Social Security Act and strengthened union rights with a National Labor Relations Act. Always controversial and arousing accusations of 'socialism', sections of the programme were declared unconstitutional by the Supreme Court, but the New Deal helped reduce unemployment from 17 to 10 million.

NEW ECONOMIC POLICY (NEP) Introduced in Russia by Lenin at the 10th Party Congress in Mar. 1921. Disturbances and food shortages had made it impossible to impose communism and some amelioration was introduced. Private commerce was permitted and some banks reintroduced. The incentives this provided helped to improve food production and created a more contented peasantry. The NEP was finally abandoned in Jan. 1929 in favour of the Five Year Plan and the collectivization of agriculture.

NEW ORDER The economic and political integration of Europe under German domination which, according to Nazi propaganda, would have benefited the whole continent rather than simply provide Germany with economic resources to exploit.

NIGHT OF THE LONG KNIVES The night of 29–30 June 1934, when the SS murdered Capt. Ernst Röhm and 150 SA leaders on Hitler's orders, together with a large number of other potential opponents of the regime. The SA was alleged to be planning a coup, and on this basis the massacre was retrospectively legalized.

NINE, THE Belgium, Denmark, France, Italy, Ireland, Luxembourg, the Netherlands, the United Kingdom and West Germany, that is, the nine members of the European Community (see p. 263) after its enlargement in Jan. 1973. Norway, which had signed the Treaty of Accession, failed to ratify it and did not join. In 1982 the Nine became Ten when Greece joined the Community, and Twelve when Spain and Portugal joined. By mid-2004 the Nine had expanded to 25.

NIXON DOCTRINE Policy of distributing the burden of collective defence more equitably as between the United States and its allies. The doctrine was first enunciated on the island of Guam in 1969, when President Nixon expressed the willingness of the United States to provide military supplies and economic assistance to friendly nations, but seemed to rule out the likelihood of providing American ground troops for local conflicts in south-east Asia. The doctrine required allies to assume 'primary responsibility' for their own defence, and was at first thought to apply exclusively to south-east Asia. Later, the concept of 'limited assistance' was developed in a series of statements and actions by members of the Nixon administration into a general principle which would guide the relations between the United States and her allies.

NON-INTERVENTIONIST The policy of avoiding involvement in the wars or internal conflicts of other states. Britain and France played a rigidly non-interventionist role in the 1936–9 Spanish Civil War, virtually ensuring the collapse of the Republic. Germany and Italy supported the nationalist insurgents and the USSR, to a lesser extent, aided the Republic, while all declared a nominal non-intervention.

NON-PROLIFERATION TREATY Treaty intended to prevent the proliferation of nuclear weapons signed in Washington, London and Moscow on 1 July 1968. It came into force on 5 Mar. 1970.

NUREMBERG RALLIES Mass rallies orchestrated by Propaganda Minister Joseph Goebbels at Nazi Party Congresses in Nuremberg from 1933 to 1938, intended to rouse participants and impress observers with oratory and militaristic display.

OAS (1) Organization of American States see p. 268. (2) Organisation de l'Armée Secrète, a right-wing French terrorist organization led by Gen. Raoul Salan, which threatened the 5th Republic in 1961–2. Most members were ex-Algerian colonists who opposed President Charles de Gaulle's attempts to extricate France from Algeria, and they attempted to assassinate him several times.

OAU *see* pp. 267–80.

ODER–NEISSE LINE This is the boundary line of the River Oder and its tributary, the Western Neisse, which was established as a frontier between Poland and Germany after the Second World War. It was accepted by the UK, the USA and the USSR at the Potsdam Conference, on the understanding that a final delimitation would take place later. An agreement made between the German Democratic Republic and Poland in 1950 described the line as a permanent frontier, and in 1955 the East German and Polish governments made a declaration to this effect. It was not accepted by the German Federal Republic, the UK and the USA. In pursuit of improved relations with Eastern Europe the Chancellor of the German Federal Government, Willy Brandt, signed a treaty with Poland in Dec. 1970 in which both countries accepted the existing frontiers.

OECD *see* p. 267.

OGPU Soviet security police agency, established in 1922 as the GPU and retitled OGPU after the formation of the USSR in 1923. Founded to suppress counter-revolution and enemies of the system, it was used by the leadership to uncover political dissidents and, after 1928, in enforcing the collectivization of agriculture. After 1930 it monopolized police activities in the Soviet Union before being absorbed by the NKVD in 1934.

OIL EMBARGO In response to the Oct. 1973 Arab–Israeli war, 7 Arab states imposed an embargo on oil shipments to the United States to persuade the latter to press Israel to withdraw from territory occupied in the 1967 war. The embargo on the United States was lifted in Jan. 1974.

ORGANIZATION FOR ECONOMIC COOPERATION AND DEVELOPMENT (OECD) *see* p. 267.

ORGANIZATION OF AFRICAN UNITY (OAU) *see* pp. 267–8.

ORGANIZATION OF AMERICAN STATES (OAS) *see* p. 268.

OSTPOLITIK Eastern policy developed in the German Federal Republic by Kurt Kiesinger to normalize relations with communist countries other than the Soviet Union who recognized the German Democratic Republic. It led to the conclusion of peace treaties with the USSR and Poland (1972), and border agreements over traffic and communications between East and West Berlin.

OVERLORD Code name for the Allied landings in Normandy to liberate German-occupied France in June 1944. The name emerged from a conference in Quebec between Churchill and Roosevelt in Aug. 1943.

P

PACT OF STEEL The military alliance concluded between fascist Italy and Nazi Germany in May 1939, despite which Italy remained a 'non-belligerent' for the first 9 months of the Second World War.

PALESTINE LIBERATION ORGANIZATION *see* PLO.

PARTISANS Originally referring to Russians who harried Napoleon's supply lines during his advance on Moscow in 1812, the term is now generally used to describe guerrilla bands fighting behind enemy lines. In the Second World War partisan forces were often communist-led, notably in German-occupied Russia and in Yugoslavia under Tito.

PASS LAWS The requirement during the apartheid era that black South Africans should carry pass-books to be produced on demand, a humiliating procedure intended to restrict their movements. The laws were increasingly the source of black anger.

PATHET LAO A Laotian rebel movement led by Prince Souphanouvong (q.v.) and established in 1949. It collaborated with the Viet Minh (q.v.) in the invasion of Laos in 1953. During the civil war it fought against the Royal Lao government troops and took part in the coalition government set up in 1974. In early 1975 it effectively took over control of the country and in December its leader Prince Souphanouvong became President of the Lao People's Democratic Republic.

PATRIOTIC FRONT The unexpected grouping of Zimbabwean nationalists Mugabe (q.v.) and Nkomo (q.v.) in Geneva in 1976 led to the formation of the Patriotic Front which had the support of the OAU (p. 267). Smith refused to negotiate with them. Their military forces were divided into 2 separate groups: ZANU led by Mugabe from Mozambique and ZAPU led by Nkomo from Zambia.

PEACE CORPS A US agency that administered the foreign aid programme adopted in 1961, under which American volunteers were sent to developing countries to teach skills and generally to assist in raising living standards. Most developing countries took advantage of the availability of this service, but others were highly critical and refused to allow the volunteers into their countries.

PEARCE COMMISSION A Commission led by Lord Pearce and set up in Rhodesia following the Smith–Home agreement of Nov. 1971. The report disclosing the result of the 'test of acceptability' was published on 23 May 1972 and showed that the people as a whole did not regard the proposals as an acceptable basis for independence.

PEARL HARBOR The US naval base in Hawaii attacked by Japanese carrier-borne aircraft on 7 Dec. 1941, destroying five US battleships, 14 smaller vessels and 120 aircraft and killing over 2,000. America declared war on Japan the following day.

PENTAGON The 5-sided US Department of Defense building in Virginia on the outskirts of Washington, DC. Often used as a synonym for American military interests.

PERESTROIKA From the Russian 'restructuring', an attempt led by Mikhail Gorbachev (Communist Party Secretary, 1985, President, 1988) to regenerate the stagnant Soviet economy by encouraging market forces, decentralizing industrial management, and democratizing the Party and government machinery. The policy was overtaken by the collapse of the Soviet Union.

PETRODOLLAR Following the massive increases in oil prices in 1975, OPEC members had huge balance of payment surpluses in dollars which they wished to invest. This money, known as petrodollars, was partly lent to developing countries for purchase of machinery, but much was invested in US government securities and in the money markets of London and New York.

PHONEY WAR The phase of military inactivity on the Western Front between the fall of Poland in Sept. 1939 and the German attack on Norway and Denmark in Apr. 1940. The period was also known by Britain as the 'Bore War', by the French as *la drôle de guerre*, and as the 'Sitzkrieg', a pun on the German *blitzkrieg*.

PLO Palestine Liberation Organization formed in May 1964 in Jordan to unite Palestinian Arabs against Israel. It was led by Yasser Arafat. The PLO mounted guerrilla attacks on Israel and Israeli-occupied territory and was involved in international terrorism. Israel refused to recognize the PLO, but the PLO did take part in the peace process and an embryonic Palestine state began to emerge only to see more bloodshed with the second *intifada* (q.v.).

PLURALISM A pluralistic society is one in which a plurality of interests are represented by the institutions which constitute the society. Pluralism demands that independent organizations should be able to operate in the same social or political system.

POGROM Attacks on Jews encouraged by the Tsarist authorities in 1881. The word comes from the Russian for 'destruction', and pogroms extended into Eastern Europe, forcing many Jews to emigrate. Hitler ordered such an attack on Jews in Nov. 1938 during which synagogues, businesses, homes and hospitals were damaged or destroyed.

POLARIS The United States Navy's contribution to the United States strategic offensive forces consisted of 41 nuclear-powered submarines, each initially equipped with 16 Polaris intermediate-range ballistic missiles, which first became operational in 1961 and could be fired while the submarine is submerged.

POLISH CORRIDOR The Treaty of Versailles decided that the new Polish state should have direct access to the sea. In order to provide this, a large area of West Prussia and Posen, where many Germans lived, was assigned to Poland. The 'Corridor' also had the effect of cutting East Prussia off from the rest of Germany. Danzig (Gdansk), standing at the mouth of the Vistula and the natural artery of Polish trade, but a German city and formerly part of Germany, was placed under League of Nations control, Poland remaining responsible for its foreign relations. The creation of the 'Corridor' was bitterly resented by German nationalists, and Hitler's demands for the return of Danzig and parts of the 'Corridor' formed part of the crisis which brought about war in Sept. 1939.

POLITBURO The Political Bureau of the Communist Party, the party's executive committee and the centre of power in communist-controlled states.

POPULAR DEMOCRATIC FRONT FOR THE LIBERATION OF PALESTINE (PDFLP) Marxist resistance movement which was formed under the leadership of Nayef Hawatmah in 1969 as a splinter group from the PFLP (q.v.). Originally it was Syrian-backed. The PDFLP, along with al-Fatah (q.v.) took a more moderate stance on the Palestinian problem since the 1973 Oct. War. It supported participation in negotiations at Geneva and indicated a willingness to form a national authority on whatever territory could be liberated from Israel. However it has not recognized Israel's right to exist. Its members fought on the side of the Leftists in the Lebanese civil war and in Nov. 1976 clashed with the Syrian-backed Palestinian guerrilla organization.

POPULAR FRONT Name used to describe the alliance of communists, socialists and liberal democrats which was designed to combat fascism in Europe between 1935 and 1939. Alliances under this name gained power in Spain, and in France under Léon Blum.

POPULAR FRONT FOR THE LIBERATION OF PALESTINE (PFLP) Founded in 1967 when several smaller resistance groups merged. The organization was led by George Habash. Of Marxist-Leninist orientation, the PFLP has seen its role as that of midwife to revolutionary change in the Arab world. It has believed that only with that change could the unity necessary for a successful confrontation with Israel be achieved. It did not join the PLO (q.v.) until 1970, and since the 1973 Oct. War formed part of the rejectionist front – supported by Iraq and Libya – which asserts the need to continue the armed struggle with Israel and opposes a negotiated settlement. The PFLP withdrew from the PLO in Sept. 1974 and also cut its ties with the Palestine Central Council, but remained a member of the Palestine

National Council. The intervention of Syria in the Lebanese civil war brought about a limited rapprochement between the rejectionist front and the PLO, but it was short-lived. The PFLP left the PLO in 1993, opposing peace negotiations with Israel. It has since concentrated on attacking Israelis and moderate Palestinians. It claimed responsibility for the assassination of an Israeli minister in Oct. 2001.

POTSDAM CONFERENCE The last inter-allied conference of the Second World War, held at Potsdam outside Berlin (11 July–2 Aug. 1945). The meeting between Winston Churchill (until 26 July when a general election brought Attlee and the Labour Party into power), President Truman and Marshal Stalin (with Bevin, Eden, Byrnes and Molotov attending) was to formulate future Allied policies, to lay the basis for definitive peace settlements and to reach agreed policies on the treatment of Germany. The idea of partitioning Germany into a number of states was dropped and principles governing the treatment of the whole of Germany leading to disarmament, de-Nazification and demilitarization were agreed upon. The differing views of the Russians and the Western powers on reparations were amongst the most intractable problems of the conference. It was agreed that the city of Königsberg (now Kaliningrad) was to be transferred to the USSR and that the Polish–German frontier should be on the Oder–Neisse line (q.v.). The western interpretation of the Yalta Declaration on Liberated Europe could not be realized and the question of the Turkish Straits remained unsettled.

'PRAGUE SPRING' Name given to the period of attempted liberalization in Czechoslovakia under Dubcek, who was Secretary of the Communist Party in spring 1968. The attempt was brought to an end by the intervention of Warsaw Pact troops in Aug. 1968 and Dubcek's replacement by Husak.

PRAVDA Soviet newspaper. Organ of the Central Committee of the Communist Party of the Soviet Union. First Marxist daily with a mass circulation; founded in 1912.

PUPPET GOVERNMENT A government allowed to retain a façade of independence but which is controlled by an external power. An example was Manchukuo, Japanese-occupied Manchuria from 1932 to 1945.

QUAI D'ORSAY The Seine embankment in Paris on which the French Foreign Office is situated: by extension, a term for the Foreign Office itself.

QUISLING Eponym for leader of an enemy-sponsored regime, deriving from Vidkun Quisling (1887–1945) (q.v.).

RABAT CONFERENCE The 1974 Arab summit meeting which confirmed the PLO in its role as the only legitimate representative of the Palestinians. For the first time King Hussein of Jordan agreed that the Palestinians had a right to sovereignty in all of liberated Palestine, under PLO leadership.

RAPACKI PLAN Proposal in Feb. 1958 by Polish Foreign Minister Adam Rapacki (1909–70) to create a nuclear-free zone by banning the manufacture and stationing of nuclear weapons in Czechoslovakia, Poland, East and West Germany. Rejected by Britain and the USA because the USSR would retain conventional military superiority in the area.

RAPPROCHEMENT Diplomatic expression deriving from the French, signifying the re-establishment of friendly relations between hitherto hostile states.

RED BRIGADES Italian left-wing urban guerrilla group which emerged in the early 1970s. As well as carrying out numerous terrorist actions, the Brigades kidnapped and murdered former prime minister Aldo Moro in 1978, intending to destabilize the Italian state.

RED CHINA The People's Republic of China, set up in Beijing on 1 Oct. 1949 following communist victory over nationalist forces in the civil war.

RED GUARDS Youths in the Chinese People's Liberation Army given authority to agitate through the country spreading radicalism. They became prominent for their enthusiasm as Mao Zedong's shock-troops in the 1966–9 Cultural Revolution, denouncing 'revisionism' and 'bourgeois decay'.

REICH The term used to describe the German Empire. The First Reich was considered to have been the Holy Roman Empire and thus the unified Germany after 1870 was known as the Second or *Kaiserreich*. This enabled Hitler's ideas of an enlarged Germany to be known as the Third Reich, although this name was officially dropped in the 1930s.

REICHSTAG The German parliament (building) in Berlin created by the Constitution of 1871. Representatives were elected by universal suffrage and repre-

sented a concession to democracy, although the Reichstag could not initiate legislation and could only block certain measures. Moreover, government ministers were not appointed by, nor responsible to, the Reichstag. Nevertheless, it became the focal point of politics (if not decision making) in the 1890s during the reign of Wilhelm II. The building was destroyed by fire on 28 Feb. 1933; its destruction was used by the Nazis for propaganda purposes against the left and to pass a number of restrictive decrees. Following the reunification of Germany, the seat of government returned to Berlin and the Reichstag building has been restored to its original use.

REPARATIONS Payments imposed on powers defeated in war to recompense the costs to the victors. Most commonly associated with the payments inflicted on Germany at the end of the First World War, although the actual amount was not fixed until Apr. 1921, when the sum was set at £6,600 million plus interest. The Dawes and Young Plans later reduced the repayments until the effects of the Depression caused reparations payments to be abandoned after the Lausanne agreement in 1932. Apart from their international ramifications, reparations payments played an important part in the domestic politics of the Weimar Republic.

RESISTANCE The popular term for the opposition to the Nazi regime, both inside Germany and in the occupied countries, 1940–5. From Jan. 1942, the Free French began to organize resistance groups and in May 1943, the Maquis (q.v.) liberated Corsica. By 1945 resistance groups were active throughout Europe but were often divided amongst themselves on ideological grounds, providing the basis for postwar political conflicts.

REVISIONIST Term applied by orthodox Marxists to one who attempts to reassess the basic tenets of revolutionary socialism. Originating in Germany in the 1890s and 1900s, its chief exponents were Edouard Bernstein and Karl Kautsky. Regarded as heresy in the Soviet Union, the Cuban, Chinese and Albanian Communists have since used the same term to describe the Moscow line.

RHODESIAN FRONT White Rhodesian party led by Ian Smith (q.v.). In the 1977 elections the Rhodesian Front held all 50 white seats in the Rhodesian parliament.

S

SA Abbreviation of the German *Sturmabteilung* or Storm Battalion, sometimes known as 'Brownshirts' from their uniform. Groups of ex-soldiers organized in quasi-military formations from 1923 to support the Nazis. Under their leader, Röhm, the force grew rapidly to an estimated four and a half million men by June 1934, when both Hitler's and the army's fear of its power prompted Hitler's murder of Röhm and the leaders of the SA in the 'Night of the Long Knives' (q.v.). Although it remained in existence, the power of the SA as a political force was broken.

SADAT INITIATIVE Proposal by Egyptian President Anwar Sadat (1919–81), prompted by Egypt's inability to maintain high military expenditure, that he should visit Israel to explain the Arab position on the Middle East before the Knesset. The offer was accepted by Israeli Prime Minister Menachem Begin (1913–92) and a visit took place on 19–21 Nov. 1977. Sadat's tacit recognition of Israel was condemned by the PLO and a number of Arab states and led to his assassination in 1981.

SALT *see* Strategic Arms Limitation Talks

SANCTIONS Term usually applied to economic boycott of one country by another. Sanctions were the chief weapon of the League of Nations (q.v.) against countries who were thought not to be fulfilling their international obligations. An economic boycott was imposed on Italy in Oct. 1935, following the invasion of Abyssinia, but its terms were limited and largely ineffective. These were finally lifted in July 1936. Similar sanctions were imposed on Rhodesia in 1965 by Britain and the UN, but proved ineffective. More recently sanctions have been imposed on such states an Libya and Iraq.

SANDINISTAS The Sandinista Liberation Front which waged a guerrilla war against Nicaraguan dictator Gen. Anastasio Somoza, driving him from power in July 1979. The Sandinistas won the sympathy of the Church, the unions and the middle classes and ruled post-revolutionary Nicaragua until their surprise election defeat in 1990.

SAVAK Iranian Secret Police under the Shah.

SCHLIEFFEN PLAN The plan devised in 1905 by Gen. Count Alfred von Schlieffen (1833–1913), Chief of the German General Staff, to attack France through Belgium. Though modified, it laid the basis for the German army's advance in Aug. 1914, the violation of Belgian neutrality bringing Britain into the war.

SDI Strategic Defense Initiative, also known as 'Star Wars', a plan announced by President Reagan in Mar. 1983 to protect the United States from nuclear attack by destroying missiles with satellites outside the atmosphere. Reagan offered to share the technology to demonstrate its peaceful intent. The plan was abandoned in 1993.

SEABED TREATY Treaty banning the installation of weapons of mass destruction on the seabed and ocean floor or in the subsoil thereof beyond a 12-mile coastal zone. Signed in Washington, London and Moscow on 11 Feb. 1971. It came into force on 18 May 1972.

SECOND FRONT The invasion of Normandy agreed upon at the Quebec Conference in Aug. 1943 and mounted in June 1944. Stalin had appealed to the Western Allies to launch a Second Front in the West to ease German pressure on Russia since 1941.

SECURITATE The Romanian secret police under the Ceausescu (q.v.) dictatorship. Their brutal suppression of disturbances in Timisoara in Dec. 1989 sparked the Romanian revolution. Their loyalty and fanaticism caused hundreds of deaths in the civil war. Disbanded by the provisional government. Many were summarily executed.

SEGREGATION The separation of white and black races in public and private facilities. Laws requiring the segregation of the races have been on the statute books of several American states. In 1896, the Supreme Court ruled that such laws were valid under the separate but equal doctrine under which blacks could be segregated if they were provided with equal facilities. As a result of this doctrine, segregation spread to schools, public transport, recreation and housing. By the 1940s the Supreme Court began to weaken the doctrine of 'separate but equal' by insisting on facilities being, indeed, equal. Finally, in 1954, the Court reversed the separate but equal formula, ruling that segregation based on race or colour was, in fact, incompatible with equality. Since this judgement, court-order desegregation coupled with legislation on civil rights in 1957, 1960, 1964, 1965 and 1968, has removed the edifice of govern-

ment-sanctioned segregation. *See also* apartheid.

SENDERO LUMINOSO The Communist Party of Peru, a Marxist guerrilla movement founded in 1970. The title, which means 'Shining Path', is derived from the Peruvian Marxist José Carlos Mariátegui's declaration that 'Marxism-Leninism will open the shining path to revolution'.

SHARIAH *see* Islamic revolution.

SHARPEVILLE In Mar. 1960 South African security forces fired on Africans demonstrating against pass laws outside a police station: 67 were killed and many injured. A state of emergency was declared, African leaders arrested and the two leading African political parties, the ANC and PAC were banned under the Suppression of Communism Act.

SHI'ITES Members of the Iranian Muslim sect Shiah, which believes that Muhammad's son-in-law Ali was his true successor, unlike the orthodox Sunni, who acknowledge the succession of Omar. The divergence between the two branches of Islam is now doctrinal. In Iraq, the Shi'ites were persecuted by Saddam Hussein. Shi'ite radicals led the 2004 uprising in their holy city of Najaf.

SHOAH *see* Holocaust.

SHUTTLE DIPLOMACY After the 1973 Arab–Israeli War, American Secretary of State, Henry Kissinger, began a series of visits to facilitate negotiations between the countries involved in the conflict. These made clear the American preference for a piecemeal approach to the conflict rather than a reconvening of the Geneva Conference. Although three disengagement agreements involving small Israeli withdrawals from Syrian and Egyptian territory were achieved, this method left unresolved the central question of the Palestinians. Nothing further was accomplished after 1975 for many years.

SINN FEIN Gaelic for 'Ourselves alone'. Irish Nationalist party founded in 1902 by Arthur Griffiths (1872–1922) and formed into the Sinn Fein League in 1907–8 when it absorbed other nationalist groups. The group rose to prominence in the 1913–14 Home Rule crisis, when many Sinn Feiners joined the Irish Volunteers and many Dublin workers joined the organization. Sinn Fein members were involved in the Easter Rising in 1916. It is still the name of the political wing of the IRA (the Irish Republican Army).

SIX, THE The original six countries, Belgium, France, Italy, Luxembourg, the Netherlands and West Germany, who together created the European Coal and Steel Community in 1952, and the European Economic Community and Euratom in 1958.

SIX DAY WAR The 5–10 June 1967 war between Israel and the Arab states, provoked by an Egyptian blockade of the Gulf of Aqaba. Israel bombed Egypt, Iraq, Jordan and Syria on 5 June; destroyed Egyptian armoured forces, reached the Suez Canal, and captured the West Bank of the Jordan on 7 June; then captured the strategic Syrian Golan Heights. These territories were then occupied by Israel.

SMITHSONIAN AGREEMENT In Dec. 1971, agreement was reached by the finance ministers of the Group of Ten in an attempt to restore stability to the world monetary system. The USA dropped its 10% surcharge on imports and devalued the dollar by 85% and some European currencies were revalued. This did not, in fact, lead to a return to fixed exchange rates, but does provide a landmark for currency value charges.

SOCIAL DEMOCRACY Non-doctrinaire, socialist or socialist-inclined political movement of the nineteenth and twentieth centuries, combining concern for greater equality with acceptance of a mixed economy and representing a non-communist left-wing tradition, often drawing support from organized labour. Notable examples include the Social Democratic Party of Germany, founded in 1875, and the Swedish Social Democratic Labour Party, formed in 1880.

SOCIAL FASCIST Term of abuse used by communists against Social Democratic and Labour Parties from 1928–34, in line with the Comintern view that rivals for working-class support were 'the left wing of fascism'.

SOCIALISM IN ONE COUNTRY Doctrine expounded by Stalin in Russia after it became clear that the Revolution of 1917 was not going to affect the other states of Europe. The main task was to create a socialist society without help from outside, either political or economic.

SOLIDARITY Polish trade union and reform movement formed in the 1970s in the shipyards of Gdansk to demand liberalization of the Polish communist regime and the formation of free trade unions. Under its leader, Lech Walesa, the movement won important concessions from the government before the threat of Soviet invasion and the assumption of power by the Polish army led to the banning of the organization and the imprisonment of its leaders. It survived as a clandestine organization. Solidarity continued throughout the 1980s, representing the voice of the mass of the workers in Poland. In 1989, it joined in forming the first non-communist government in Poland since 1948. It declined rapidly in post-communist Poland and is no longer a political force.

SOUTH-WEST AFRICA PEOPLE'S ORGANI-ZATION (SWAPO) An independence movement founded in 1959, which in 1966 began guerrilla activity against South African forces. It was banned from Namibia and operated over the border. In 1989 its leader, Sam Numoja, returned to Namibia in anticipation of independence in 1990.

SOVIET Workers' councils which emerged spontaneously in the 1905 Russian Revolution and re-appeared in 1917. Intended to encourage and reflect direct working-class participation in political activity, they were effectively dominated by the Bolsheviks (later the communists) after 1917, and became national administrative organs.

SOWETO Riots occurred here in 1976 following widespread strikes and general unrest in the South African townships. The immediate cause of trouble was opposition to the compulsory use of Afrikaans for instruction in schools.

SPARTACISTS German Socialist Party (SPD) radicals led by Rosa Luxemburg and Karl Liebknecht, who went on to form the German Communist Party (KPD) in 1918 and led a bloodily suppressed revolutionary rising in Jan. 1919. The name came from Spartacus, the leader of a slave rebellion in Rome in 73 BC.

SPECIAL RELATIONSHIP The relationship between Britain and the United States, one allegedly based on historical links of culture and kinship running deeper than diplomatic expediency.

SS Abbreviation of German *Schutzstaffel* or Guard Detachment. Hitler's personal bodyguard of dedicated Nazis founded in 1923 as a rival to Röhm's SA (q.v.). Placed under the command of Heinrich Himmler in 1929, the SS carried out the liquidation of the SA leadership in June 1934 and in July became an independent organization with its own armed units. *SS-Verfugunstruppe* (Special Task Troops), organized as regular soldiers, were formed from 1935 and as the *Waffen-SS* comprised a group of elite regiments, separate from army control. Other sections of the SS provided concentration-camp guards – the *SS-Totenkopfverbände* – and police squads in occupied territory.

STALINISM The arbitrary bureaucratic rule, personality cult and political purges underpinning Stalin's attempt to create 'socialism in one country' through enforced agricultural collectivization and a rapid build-up of heavy industry. More recently the term was used as a synonym for the Soviet and East European communist regimes.

STATE CAPITALISM Lenin's expression for the compromise with financial interests which, combined with increased central economic control, was an attempt to preserve Bolshevik power in 1918. Latterly, a pejorative left-wing description of Soviet society, in which a privileged bureaucratic elite allegedly exploits the working class through its own monopoly of economic and political power.

STRATEGIC ARMS LIMITATION TALKS (SALT) The United States and the Soviet Union embarked on SALT with the object of limiting the level of competition between them and reducing the size of their strategic nuclear armaments. Preliminary negotiations took place in Helsinki in Nov. and Dec. 1969, and an agreement on anti-ballistic missile systems and an interim agreement on strategic offensive arms were concluded by President Nixon (q.v.) in Moscow on 26 May 1972. The second phase of the negotiations, SALT II, opened in Geneva on 21 Nov. 1972. In talks between President Ford (q.v.) and Chairman Brezhnev (q.v.) at Vladivostok in Nov. 1974, an agreement was reached setting down guidelines for a pact to control the strategic arms race for the period 1977–85. However, the technical and political problems involved in framing such a pact meant that no definitive treaty could be signed.

SUCCESSION STATES The states formed after the First World War from the territory of the former Austro-Hungarian Empire, or incorporating parts of it. These included Poland, Czechoslovakia, Yugoslavia, Romania, Hungary and Austria.

SUDETENLAND German-speaking area of northern Bohemia assigned to Czechoslovakia in 1919. Claimed by Hitler for the Reich, the Sudetenland became the centre of an international crisis in 1938 over Germany's attempt to revise the Versailles Treaty by force. The threat of general European war was temporarily averted by the Munich Agreement, in which Czechoslovakia was forced to cede the Sudetenland to Germany.

SUEZ CRISIS Major diplomatic crisis in 1956. Following Egyptian nationalization of the Suez Canal on 26 July 1956, Israel invaded Sinai on 29 Oct. When Egypt rejected a ceasefire ultimatum by France and Britain, their air forces began to attack Egyptian air bases on 31 Oct. On 5 Nov. Franco-British forces invaded the Canal Zone and captured Port Said. Hostilities ended at midnight on 6–7 Nov. following a ceasefire by the UN, and the Franco-British forces were evacuated.

SUMMIT CONFERENCE Meeting between the leaders of great powers to discuss issues of major long-term interest or to resolve specific areas of tension. The expression was used by Winston Churchill (1874–1965) when he called for a 'parley at the summit'.

SWASTIKA Ancient religious symbol in the shape of a hooked cross. In European mythology it became linked (in its right-handed form) with the revival of Germanic legends at the end of the nineteenth century. Adopted by a number of extreme right-wing groups in Germany after the First World War, including the Erhardt Brigade, a *Freikorps* unit active in the Kapp Putsch. It was also adopted by Hitler as the symbol of National Socialism and in Sept. 1935 became Nazi Germany's national emblem.

SYNDICALISM Theory which advocates the ownership and organization of industry by workers and their organizations, usually trade unions. This is in contrast to the socialist theory of ownership by the state. Syndicalism is also associated with the belief in the power of trade unionism and the use of the general strike as a weapon to bring about major social and political change. Although often associated with anarchists, many of the syndicalists in the 1920s joined the communist or fascist parties.

T

TALIBAN A faction of Islamic fundamentalist students who seized power in Kabul, the capital of Afghanistan, in Sept. 1996, imposing harsh fundamentalist laws, including stoning for adultery and severing hands for theft. Women were required to cover themselves in public from head to toe. The Taliban's scorched-earth tactics and human rights abuses isolated it from the international community. Although the Taliban controlled about 90% of the country by 1998, only three governments – Pakistan, Saudi Arabia and the UAE – recognized the Taliban as Afghanistan's legitimate government. The Taliban regime was overthrown by the American invasion after 11 Sept. 2001 (see p. 331).

TANKER WAR Attacks made on oil tankers in the Persian Gulf in the 1980–8 Iran–Iraq War. Iraq attacked shipping trading with Iran in 1984: Iran replied with attacks on tankers using the ports of Iraq's Arab supporters.

TASHKENT AGREEMENT A declaration of truce took place between India and Pakistan after a conference convened at Tashkent in the USSR (3–10 Jan. 1966). Alexei Kosygin, Chairman of the Council of Ministers of the USSR, acted as mediator between Lal Bahadur Shastri (q.v.), Prime Minister of India and Ayub Khan (q.v.), President of Pakistan, in a settlement which ended the war on the Kashmir border and restored India–Pakistan relations.

TEHRAN CONFERENCE Wartime meeting in Tehran, Persia (28 Nov.–1 Dec. 1943) between Winston Churchill, President Franklin D. Roosevelt and Marshal Stalin (with the combined Chiefs-of-Staff, Anthony Eden and Harry Hopkins attending) to plan military strategy in Europe and the Far East. It was agreed that 'Overlord', the Anglo-American invasion of northern France, would take place on 1 May 1944. Stalin promised that Russia would join in the war against Japan in the Far East after victory over Germany had been achieved. The future of Poland and Germany was also discussed.

TERRORISM A tactic intended to achieve political ends or gain publicity for a cause by creating a climate of fear through assassination, bombing, kidnapping and the seizure of aircraft. Most non-communist countries have suffered terrorism since the 1960s. For an extended chronology see pp. 343–53.

TEST-BAN TREATY Treaty signed by the USA, USSR and Britain after five years' negotiation on 5 Aug. 1963, agreeing not to test nuclear weapons in outer space, the atmosphere or under the ocean. In the following 2 years over 90 other states signed, though France and China refused and have carried out atmospheric nuclear tests.

TET Communist Viet Cong and North Vietnamese attack on Saigon (now Ho Chi Minh City) and 140 other towns and villages during the Tet lunar new year festival. The 'Tet Offensive' ran from 20 Jan. to 25 Feb. 1968. The communists gained nothing materially, casualties on both sides were heavy, but the South Vietnamese government was undermined and America's commitment to the Vietnam War significantly weakened.

THIRD INTERNATIONAL Otherwise known as the Communist International or the Comintern. Founded by Lenin in Mar. 1919 to unite revolutionary socialists. Finally disbanded by Stalin in May 1943 as a concession to his Western allies.

THIRD REICH Term used to describe the Nazi dictatorship in Germany, 1933–45. Originally coined by the Nazis to describe the expanded Germany of their theories, the term was dropped from official usage in the 1930s.

THIRD REPUBLIC The term used to describe the government of France from the Franco-Prussian War in 1871 to the fall of France in 1940 and the establishment of the Vichy Regime (q.v.).

THIRD WORLD Underdeveloped and poor nations in Africa, Asia and Latin America which are neither part of the capitalist industrialized West nor of the communist Eastern bloc.

THIRTY-EIGHTH PARALLEL The line of latitude 38° north dividing South Korea from communist North Korea, established at the 1945 Yalta Conference. The intention that the two states should ultimately unite was ended by the 1950–3 Korean War.

'THOUSAND DAYS' The period in office of US President John F. Kennedy (1917–63) from his inauguration in Jan. 1961 to his assassination in Nov. 1963. Kennedy initiated civil rights legislation and moves towards a nuclear test ban, authorized the Bay of Pigs invasion, outmanoeuvred the USSR in the Cuban Missile Crisis and drew the USA more deeply into the Vietnam War.

TIANANMEN SQUARE Massacre of pro-democracy demonstrators (mainly students) in the main square of Beijing by hard-line Chinese government forces, 4 June 1989.

TLATELOLCO, TREATY OF Treaty prohibiting nuclear weapons in Latin America signed in Mexico City on 14 Feb. 1967 by 14 countries.

TONKIN RESOLUTION Following alleged North Vietnamese attacks on American shipping in the Gulf of Tonkin, both Houses of the US Congress gave US President Lyndon Johnson (1963–9) sweeping powers to use force in the area on 7 Aug. 1964. Immediate escalation of US involvement in the Vietnam War followed.

TOTAL WAR The mobilization of a nation's entire economic, ideological and military resources in wartime to achieve victory, as with Britain, Germany and the Soviet Union in the Second World War.

TROTSKYIST Follower of León Trotsky (1870–1940), the Soviet revolutionary leader who lost the power struggle with Stalin in 1924 and was assassinated in Mexico in 1940. Trotsky condemned Stalin's excessive Russian nationalism and the increasingly bureaucratic and dictatorial nature of his socialism. Trotskyism found support among disillusioned Western communists following the 1956 Soviet invasion of Hungary, and among student activists in the 1960s and 1970s.

TUPAMAROS Marxist urban guerrilla movement in Uruguay named after Tupac Amarus who led an eighteenth-century Peruvian Indian revolt against Spain. Initially effective, the 1,000-strong movement was weakened by a police and right-wing paramilitary offensive in 1972.

TWENTY-ONE DEMANDS Demands made upon China by Japan on 18 Jan. 1915 with a threat of military action if they were not met. They were an attempt to make China a Japanese protectorate by forcing the appointment of advisers. Japan was restrained by Britain, but gained control over Manchuria and Shantung, a 50% interest in China's leading iron and steel company, and a limitation on foreign influence in China's coastal regions.

U-BOATS German submarines (*untersee*) which operated widely in both World Wars, particularly in the North Atlantic, sinking merchant shipping carrying supplies to Britain.

UDI The illegal and widely condemned Unilateral Declaration of Independence made by Ian Smith's white Rhodesian Front government on 11 Nov. 1965 in an attempt to avoid moving towards black majority-rule in Southern Rhodesia.

UNEQUAL TREATIES Term used by the Chinese to describe conditions imposed upon them by imperialist states, particularly the agreement on an Open Door policy in China reached by Belgium, Britain, France, Italy, Japan, the Netherlands, Portugal and the United States at the 1921 Washington Conference.

UNIÃO NACIONAL PARA A INDEPENDEN-CIA TOTAL DE ANGOLA (UNITA) Angolan nationalist group which was in control of the south of Angola at independence. Joint UNITA and FNLA troops were defeated by the MPLA by Feb. 1976, but UNITA continued a guerrilla struggle from its strongholds in the south of Angola.

UNITED FRONT The Communist Party tactic of forming alliances with socialist and working-class parties to face what is seen to be a common enemy, for example fascism, usually during a period of communist weakness.

UNITED NATIONS *see* p. 269.

U-2 INCIDENT On 1 May 1960 an American U-2 high-altitude reconnaissance aircraft was brought down over the Soviet Union near Sverdlovsk while on a photographic mission. As a result, the Russians cancelled the summit meeting with President Eisenhower in West Berlin on 16 May 1960. The pilot, Francis Gary Powers, was sentenced to ten years' imprisonment, but was exchanged for the Soviet spy Colonel Abel on 10 Feb. 1962.

URBAN GUERRILLAS Groups using military methods and terrorist tactics in cities to achieve political ends. The most notable were the Red Brigades in Italy and the Red Army Faction in Germany in the 1970s, and the Provisional IRA in Northern Ireland from the early 1970s onwards.

VELVET DIVORCE The division on 1 Jan. 1993 of Czechoslovakia into the separate states of the Czech Republic and Slovakia. So called because of the apparent amicable nature of the separation, but also an ironic reference to the 1989 Velvet Revolution that overthrew communist rule.

VELVET REVOLUTION Popular, non-violent uprisings in Prague and other Czech cities in 1989, which overthrew the communist regime.

VERSAILLES, TREATY OF Treaty ending the First World War signed by Germany and the victorious powers in 1919. Germany lost its colonies; ceded territory to Belgium, Lithuania and Poland; returned Alsace-Lorraine to France; had its army reduced to 100,000 with limitations on weapons and a ban on submarines and an air force; acknowledged war guilt and promised to pay reparations. The treaty also established the League of Nations. Germany complained of the Treaty's harshness and it remained a source of bitterness, used by the Nazis in their rise to power.

VICHY French provincial spa town where the interim autocratic French government was established between July 1940 and July 1944. The Vichy regime was anti-republican, and collaborated extensively with the Germans who occupied the areas it controlled in Nov. 1942. After the liberation of France in 1944, Pétain and the Vichy ministers established a headquarters in Germany.

VIET CONG Communist guerrilla troops who fought in South Vietnam on behalf of the National Liberation Front.

VIET MINH A communist political group in North Vietnam founded by Ho Chi Minh (q.v.) in 1941 to work for independence. In 1945 its forces entered Hanoi and formed a provisional government under Ho Chi Minh. From 1951 it worked as part of the Deng Lao Dong Vietnam (Vietnam Workers' Party).

W

WAFD The leading Egyptian nationalist party between the wars, forming a government under Nahas Pasha in 1936. He was dismissed by King Farouk in 1938 and his restoration to office by Britain in 1941 (on the grounds that he favoured the Allies) weakened Wafd's nationalist standing. Returned to power in the 1950 elections, the Wafd faced civil disorder, was sacked by Farouk in 1952 and dissolved in 1953.

WAFFEN SS An elite military force, part of the Nazi SS (*Schutzstaffeln*), made up of Germans and anti-communist volunteers from most European states. 40 divisions were deployed in the Second World War.

WAR COMMUNISM The Bolshevik attempt begun in 1918 to overcome economic collapse by nationalizing larger enterprises, partially militarizing labour, requisitioning agricultural produce by force and introducing a state monopoly of exchange. Its unpopularity and ultimate ineffectiveness led to the New Economic Policy of 1921.

WAR CRIMINAL A concept which emerged at the end of the First World War in a 'Hang the Kaiser' campaign. At the Nuremberg Trials after the Second World War, 177 Nazis were accused by the Allies of planning to wage an aggressive war and of genocide, and were sentenced to death.

WARLORDS Generals who dominated provinces in a politically fragmented China between 1916 and 1928, waging war on one another with private armies.

WARSAW PACT *see* pp. 269–70.

WATERGATE General term given to a variety of illegal acts perpetrated by officials in the Nixon (q.v.) administration (1969–74), and subsequent efforts to 'cover up' their responsibility for these acts, which led eventually to the resignation of President R. M. Nixon and the succession to the Presidency of Vice-President Gerald R. Ford (q.v.). Specifically, 'Watergate' refers to a burglary, by a group of 7 men acting under the orders of the White House, of the Democratic national party headquarters located in the Watergate building in Washington DC. Other illegal acts included within the general term 'Watergate' were: bribery, illegal use of the CIA, FBI and other government agencies for political and partisan purposes, income tax fraud, the establishment and use by the White House of an unofficial 'plumbers' group designed to discover the source of leaks to the press, the use of 'dirty tricks' during the 1972 election campaign, and illegal campaign contributions. As a result of these Watergate crimes many cabinet officers, presidential assistants and other administration officials were convicted of various crimes. It produced a spate of new laws concerning secrecy in government and regulation of campaign practices. It also produced a Supreme Court decision which, for the first time, limited the doctrine of 'executive privilege' by holding that the privilege cannot be used to prohibit disclosure of criminal misconduct.

WEIMAR Town where the German National Constituent Assembly met in Feb. 1919. It gave its name to the German Republic of 1918–33. The town was chosen to allay fears of the Allied powers and the other German states about Prussian domination in Berlin, and also to escape from the associations attached to the former capital city. The economic problems which beset the Weimar Republic and the concomitant unemployment facilitated the rise of Hitler, and in Mar. 1933 he suspended the Weimar Constitution of July 1919 to make way for the Third Reich (q.v.).

WEST BANK The West Bank of the Jordan River was annexed by King Abdullah of Jordan after the 1948 war. It was taken by Israel in 1967 and placed under military administration. East Jerusalem was not only annexed but its boundaries were extended, in defiance of international law. To establish a firm hold on the city, Israel had evicted Arab families and replaced them with Jews. In 1970 a government plan to double the Jewish population of the city by 1980 was published. The United Nations was to condemn Israel several times for its actions in East Jerusalem. Archaeological excavations have also called forth UN protest. The Israeli government insists on maintaining secure borders in any settlement but there is conflict over how much territory this involves. Groups of religious extremists, such as Gush Emunim, opposed the return of any territory and insist on the right to settle in all of Biblical Israel. They have gone so far as to set up illegal settlements which the government has been loath to dislodge. The government itself set up extensive Jewish settlements on the West Bank. These, in turn, undermined its claim to be willing to return Arab territory and are an obstacle to peace. In the past years Arabs on the West Bank have grown increasingly restive. Riots and demonstrations have culminated in the uprising known as the '*intifada*' (q.v.). There is also considerable division within Israel over policy towards the West Bank.

WESTERN FRONT The zone of British, French and German military operations in the First World War. It extended, largely in lines of trenches, from Nieuport on the Belgian coast, through northern France to the area around Verdun.

WHITE RUSSIANS Term for Russians living on western border of Soviet Union, but used generally to describe counter-revolutionary forces in the aftermath of the Bolshevik Revolution of 1917.

WINTER WAR The war from 30 Nov. 1939 to 12 Mar. 1940 which followed the Soviet invasion of Finland. Finland surrendered, ceding territory to the USSR and promising not to join an alliance against her.

Y

YALTA CONFERENCE The most crucial 'Big Three' meeting of the war held at Yalta in the Crimea (4–11 Feb. 1945). Agreements reached between Winston Churchill, President Franklin D. Roosevelt and Marshal Stalin (with the chiefs of staff, Molotov, Stettinus, Anthony Eden and Harry Hopkins attending) virtually determined the reconstruction of the postwar world. France was admitted as an equal partner of the Allied Control Commission for Germany but the practical details of Allied control were not worked out in Protocols III, IV, V and VI. The future of Poland, one of the most contentious issues of the conference, was referred to in the ambiguously worded Declaration on Poland in Protocol VII, where no agreement was made as to the reconstruction of the Polish government. Being anxious to secure a firm Russian undertaking to join in the war against Japan, Roosevelt acceded to

Stalin's condition that Russia should resume its old rights in China, lost as a result of the Russo-Japanese war of 1904–5, and a secret tripartite agreement was signed to this effect on 11 Feb. 1945. Protocol I set out the agreement reached on the creation of a World Organization of the United Nations and the voting formula for the Security Council. It was agreed to call a conference in San Francisco in Apr. 1945, to draw up a charter for the United Nations.

YEZHOVSCHINA A word used to describe the Stalinist purges of the 1920s and 1930s. The name derives from the head of the Soviet secret police, N. I. Yezhov.

YOM KIPPUR The Jewish day of atonement, a period of religious observance. During this period Egyptian and Syrian forces moved against Israel on 6 Oct. 1973. Israel counter-attacked on 8 Oct. threatening Cairo and Damascus. The 'Yom Kippur War' ended with a ceasefire arranged by the United Nations on 24 Oct.

YOUNG PLAN The proposal made on 7 June 1929 by US businessman Owen D. Young (1874–1962) for a settlement of German war reparations. Payments were to be reduced by 75% and made annually until 1988. Germany accepted the plan, but Hitler refused to make further payments after 1933.

Z

ZIMMERMANN TELEGRAM Coded message of 19 Jan. 1917 from the German foreign minister, Arthur Zimmermann, to the German minister in Mexico, urging the conclusion of a German–Mexican alliance in the event of a declaration of war on Germany by America when Germany resumed unrestricted submarine warfare against shipping on 1 Feb. Mexico would be offered the recapture of its 'lost territories' in New Mexico, Arizona and Texas. Intercepted by British Naval Intelligence, the telegram was released to the American press on 1 Mar., greatly inflaming feeling against Germany, and helping to precipitate the American Declaration of War against Germany on 6 Apr. 1917.

ZIONISM The belief that the Jews should create a homeland in Palestine, suggested by Theodor Herzl (1860–1904), who felt the Jews were threatened by East European pogroms. Until then Palestine had been generally seen by Jews as a spiritual rather than physical homeland. An initial reluctance among many Jews who felt assimilated in Europe was overcome by the experience of the Nazi Holocaust. The state of Israel was set up in 1948.

VI
TOPIC BIBLIOGRAPHY

This bibliography is arranged in broadly geographical terms to allow concentration on particular aspects of world history and the sub-themes within it. Some topics such as imperial expansion and decolonization are of worldwide scope, and contain works relating to more than one geographical area.

INTRODUCTORY WORKS

The later sections of J. M. Roberts, *A History of the World* (1976) and W. H. McNeill, *A World History* (new edn, 1979) are excellent introductions to the modern world. Exclusively twentieth-century in focus are J. A. S. Grenville, *The Collins History of the World in the Twentieth Century* (1998) and his earlier *A World History of the Twentieth Century, 1900–84* (2 vols, 1980–5), E. J. Hobsbawm, *The Age of Extremes: the short twentieth century, 1914–1991* (1994) and N. Lowe, *Mastering Modern World History* (3rd edn, 1997). More thematic in treatment are J. Black, *The World in the Twentieth Century* (2002) and A. Iriye and B. Mazlish, *The Global History Reader* (2004), while P. Calvocoressi, *World Politics since 1945* (8th edn, 2001) and P. M. H. Bell, *The World since 1945: an international history* (2001) cover the period since the Second World War. G. Barraclough, *An Introduction to Contemporary History* (1967) raises some major themes, as do J. Major, *The Contemporary World: a historical introduction* (1970) and the more recent A. Best, J. M. Hanhimaki, J. Maiolo, and K. E. Schulze, *International History of the Twentieth Century* (2003). The development of the world beyond Europe and North America is examined in P. Worsley, *The Third World* (1967) and C. E. Black, *The Dynamics of Modernization: a study in comparative history* (1967). Important interpretations of the development of the modern world are J. Roberts, *The Triumph of the West* (1985), I. Wallerstein, *The Modern World System* (1974) and J. A. Hall, *Powers and Liberties: the causes and consequences of the rise of the West* (1985). For international relations see W. R. Keylor, *The Twentieth Century: an international history* (4th edn, 2001), and *A World of Nations: the international order since 1945* (2003), J. P. D. Dunbabin, *The Cold War: the Great Powers and their Allies. International relations since 1945* (2 vols, 1994), G. Lundestad, *East, West, North, South: major developments in international politics, 1945–1991* (1991) and S. J. Ball, *The Cold War: an international history* (1997). For treaties see J. A. S. Grenville and B. Wasserstein (eds), *The Major International Treaties of the Twentieth Century: a history and guide with texts* (2001).

The economic history of the twentieth century is considered in W. Ashworth, *A Short History of the International Economy since 1850* (4th edn, 1987) and A. G. Kenwood, *The Growth of the International Economy, 1820–2000: an introductory text* (4th edn, 1999). The Penguin series on the history of the world economy should also be consulted: G. Hardach, *The First World War, 1914–1918* (1977); D. H. Aldcroft, *From Versailles to Wall Street, 1919–1929* (1977); C. P. Kindleberger, *The World in Depression, 1929–1939* (1977); and A. S. Milward, *War, Economy and Society, 1939–1945* (1977).

For the world monetary system as a whole see D. Calleo, *The Imperious Economy* (1982); on America's role and more generally, L. Tson Kalis (ed.), *The Political Economy of International Money* (1985); C. P. Kindleberger, *Power and Money: the economics of international politics and the politics of international economics* (1970); S. E. Rolfe and J. L. Burkle, *The Great Wheel: the world monetary system: a reinterpretation* (1974). The specific role of the multi-national companies is discussed in L. Turner, *Invisible Empires: multinational companies and the modern world* (1970) and *Multinational Companies and the Third World* (1973), E. T. Penrose, *The Large International Firm in Developing Countries: the international petroleum industry* (1968), and M. Wilkins, *The Maturing of Multinational Enterprise: American business abroad from 1914 to 1970* (1974). P. Bairoch, *The Economic Development of the Third World since 1900* (1975), H. Myint, *The Economics of Developing Countries* (4th edn, 1973) and G. Myrdal, *The Challenge of World Poverty: a world anti-poverty programme in outline* (1970) specifically examine the world beyond the major industrial powers. The role of aid as part of the nexus linking the developed and less developed world is considered from various points of view in J. A. White, *The Politics of Foreign Aid* (1974), T. Hayter, *Aid as Imperialism* (1971), L. D. Black, *The Strategy of Foreign Aid* (1968) and M. I. Goldman, *Soviet Foreign Aid* (1967). On globalization see J. Bhagwati, *In Defense of Globalization* (2005) and M. Wolf, *Why Globalization Works* (2005).

The energy question is considered in G. Foley and C. Nassim, *The Energy Question* (1976), P. R. Odell, *Oil and World Power* (4th edn, 1974) and G. C. Tugendhat and A. Hamilton, *Oil the Biggest Business* (rev. edn, 1975). The rise of OPEC is examined in M. S. Al-Otalba, *OPEC and the Petroleum Industry* (1975) and Z. Mikdashi, *The Community of Oil Exporting Countries: a study in governmental co-operation* (1972). More recent concerns, such as the rise of Third World debt, are considered in H. Lever and C. Huhne, *Debt and Danger: the world financial crisis* (1985).

For population developments there is an excellent survey of world population from earliest times in C. McEvedy and T. Jones (eds), *Atlas of World Population History* (1978) and for more contemporary preoccupations see K. and A. F. K. Organski, *Population and World Power* (1961), T. McKeown, *The Modern Rise of Population* (1976), W. D. Barrie, *The Growth and Control of World Population* (1970) and R. Symonds and M. Carter, *The United Nations and the Population Question, 1945–70* (1973). For particular areas see S. Chandrasekhar (ed.), *Asia's Population Problems: with a discussion of population and immigration in Australia* (1967), D. Chaplin (ed.), *Population Policies and Growth in Latin America* (1971), W. A. Hance, *Population, Migration, and Urbanization in Africa* (1970) and J. I. Clarke and W. B. Fisher, *Populations of the Middle East and North Africa* (1971).

Urban development is considered generally in J. H. Lowry, *World City Growth* (1975), K. Davis, *World Urbanization, 1950–1970* (2 vols, 1969–72), P. M. Houser and L. F. Schnore (eds), *The Study of Urbanization* (1965), T. H. Elkins, *The Urban Explosion* (1973), W. D. C. Wright and P. H. Steward, *The Exploding City* (1972) and P. Hall, *The World Cities* (2nd edn, 1977). Urban change in Europe and North America is considered in the last section of L. Mumford, *The City in History: its origins, its transformation, and its prospects* (1961) and his *The Urban Prospect* (1968), P. Hall (ed.), *Europe 2000* (1977), J. Gottman (ed.), *Megalopolis:*

the urbanized northeastern seaboard of the United States (1962) and A. Sutcliffe (ed.), *Metropolis, 1890–1940* (1984) which includes an essay on the Tokyo area. Third World studies include D. J. Dwyer, *The City in the Third World* (1968) and *The City as a Centre of Change in Asia* (1972), T. G. McGee, *The Urbanization Process in the Third World: explorations in search of a theory* (1971), G. W. Breese, *Urbanisation in Newly-Developing Countries* (1966), W. A. Hance, *Population, Migration and Urbanization in Africa* (1970) and G. K. Payne, *Urban Housing in the Third World* (1977). P. Lloyd, *Slums of Hope? Shanty towns of the Third World* (1979) digests an enormous amount of literature on the processes and effects of urban migration and has an excellent bibliography. Also on the social effects of urbanization see W. Mangin (ed.), *Peasants in Cities: readings in the anthropology of urbanization* (1970), R. E. Pahl, *Patterns of Urban Life* (1970), A. Southall (ed.), *Urban Anthropology: cross-cultural studies of urbanization* (1973), and B. J. L. Berry, *The Human Consequences of Urbanization: divergent paths in the urban experience of the twentieth century* (1973).

Amongst the ideologies affecting twentieth-century development, on nationalism see B. Anderson, *Imagined Communities* (1991); A. D. Smith, *Theories of Nationalism* (1971) looks at various approaches; see also his edited collection, *Nationalist Movements* (1976). E. Kedourie, *Nationalism* (1960) is an introduction to the ideology; see also H. Seton-Watson, *Nations and States: an enquiry into the origins of nations and the politics of nationalism* (1977) and E. Gellner, *Nations and Nationalism* (1983). Also valuable are B. Akzin, *States and Nations* (1964), K. W. Deutsch, *Nationalism and Social Communication: an inquiry into the foundations of nationality* (2nd edn, 1966) and the older F. O Hertz, *Nationality in History and Politics* (1944). Nationalism as a phenomenon of particular regions can be studied in A. Cobban, *The Nation State and National Self-Determination* (1969) and R. Pearson, *National Minorities in Eastern Europe, 1848–1944* (1983), E. Kedourie (ed.), *Nationalism in Asia and Africa* (1971), F. R. Von der Mehden, *Religion and Nationalism in Southeast Asia: Burma, Indonesia, the Philippines* (1963), G. Antonius, *The Arab Awakening: the story of the Arab national movement* (1938), S. Haim (ed.), *Arab Nationalism: an anthology* (1962), T. Hodgkin, *Nationalism in Colonial Africa* (1956), D. A. Rustow, *A World of Nations: the problems of political modernization* (1967), A. P. Whitaker and D. C. Jordan, *Nationalism in Contemporary Latin America* (1966) and R. Emerson, *From Empire to Nation: the rise to self-assertion of Asian and African peoples* (1970).

Of the other powerful ideologies, socialism and communism, there are introductory texts in D. McLellan, *Marx* (1975) and *Engels* (1975), G. Lichtheim, *Marxism, an Historical and Critical Study* (1961) and *A Short History of Socialism* (1969), R. N. C. Hunt, *The Theory and Practice of Communism* (1963), and F. Claudin, *The Communist Movement: from Comintern to Cominform* (1975). The anarchist tradition is discussed in G. Woodcock, *Anarchism* (1963) and J. Joll, *The Anarchists* (1969).

Liberalism is less well served, although it had an important legacy from the nineteenth century, but see H. J. Laski, *The Rise of European Liberalism* (2nd edn, 1947) and A. Arblaster, *The Rise and Decline of Western Liberalism* (1984). The important force of social democracy can be examined in R. J. Harrison, *Pluralism and Corporation: the political evolution of modern democracies* (1980), J. Haywood, *Trade Unions and Politics in Western Europe* (1980), M. Kolinsky and W. Paterson (eds), *Social and Political Movements in Western Europe* (1976), R. Miliband, *Parliamentary Socialism* (1961), I. Campbell and W. Paterson, *Social Democracy in Post-War Europe* (1974) and W. Paterson and A. Thomas, *Social Democratic Parties in Western Europe* (1977).

Two general works which deal with the nature of regimes are Barrington Moore, *Social Origins of Dictatorship and Democracy* (1966) and R. Aron, *Democracy and Totalitarianism* (1968). See also P. Wiles, *Economic Institutions Compared* (1977) and A. Ellis and K. Kumar (eds), *Dilemmas of Liberal Democracies* (1983), T. Skocpol, *States and Social Revolutions* (1979), M. Olson, *The Rise and Decline of Nations* (1982) and J. H. Goldthorpe (ed.), *Order and Conflict in Contemporary Capitalism* (1984).

The role of revolution in the modern world is discussed in J. Dunn, *Modern Revolutions: an introduction to the analysis of a political phenomenon* (2nd edn, 1989), Chalmers Johnson, *Revolution and the Social System* (1964) and *Revolutionary Change* (1968), P. Calvert, *Revolution* (1970) and *A Study of Revolution* (1970). Third world revolutions are specifically examined in F. J. Carrier, *The Third World Revolutions* (1976), G. Chaliand, *Revolution in the Third World: myths and prospects* (1977), J. S. Migdal, *Peasants, Politics and Revolution: pressures towards political and social change in the third world* (1975) and E. R. Wolf, *Peasant Wars of the Twentieth Century* (1969).

Almost inseparable from the idea of revolution in the less developed world is guerrilla warfare and terrorism. For the former, Che Guevara, *Guerrilla Warfare* (1969) and G. Fairbairn, *Revolutionary Warfare: the countryside version* (1974) are particularly relevant. For terrorism see G. Wardlaw, *Political Terrorism* (2nd edn, 1989), W. Laqueur, *Terrorism* (1977), P. Wilkinson, *Political Terrorism* (1974) and S. Segaller, *Invisible Armies: terrorism into the 1990s* (2nd edn, 1987). The specific phenomenon of urban guerrilla warfare is considered in R. Moss, *Urban Guerrillas* (1972), A. Burton, *Urban Terrorism* (1975), and R. Clutterbuck, *Protest and the Urban Guerrilla* (1973), while the implications for societies are discussed in P. Wilkinson, *Terrorism and the Liberal State* (1977) and R. Clutterbuck, *Living with Terrorism* (1975).

The political role of the military is discussed in S. E. Finer, *The Man on Horseback: the role of the military in politics* (2nd edn, 1976) and M. E. Howard (ed.), *Soldiers and Governments: nine studies in civil–military relations* (1957); specifically on the role of the military in the third world see M. Janowitz, *Military Institutions and Coercion in the Developing Nations* (1977). S. Andreski, *Military Organisation and Society* (2nd edn, 1968) is a classic exposition of the role of warfare in society, but see also A. Marwick, *War and Social Change in the Twentieth Century* (1974), M. R. D. Foot (ed.), *War and Society* (1973), B. Brodie, *War and Politics* (1973) and A. Buchan, *War in Modern Society* (1968).

Much of recent discussion has been focused on the issue of 'total war', for which see Marwick (above) and N. F. Dreisziger (ed.), *Mobilisation for Total War: the Canadian, American and British experience, 1914–1918, 1939–1945* (1981).

The influence of nuclear weapons upon the world scene is considered in J. Newhouse, *The Nuclear Age: a history of the arms race from Hiroshima to Star Wars* (1989), B. Brodie (ed.), *The Absolute Weapon: atomic power and world order* (1972), G. H. Quester, *Nuclear Diplomacy: the first twenty-five years* (1970), and L. Freedman, *The Evolution of Nuclear Strategy* (1981).

For the evolution of warfare see J. F. C. Fuller, *The Conduct of War, 1789–1961: a study of the impact of the French, Industrial and Russian Revolutions on war and its conduct* (1961). C. McInnes and G. D. Sheffield (eds), *Warfare in the Twentieth Century: theory and practice* (1988) is a more recent collection of studies, while C. Cook and J. Stevenson, *The Atlas of Modern Warfare* (1978) provides an account and analysis of military history since 1945. There are excellent maps in T. Hartman (with J. Mitchell), *A World Atlas of Military History* (1984) and see also L. W. Martin, *Arms and Strategy: an international survey of modern defence* (1973). The geopolitics of military power is discussed over a long period in P. Kennedy, *The Rise and Fall of the Great Powers: economic change and military conflict, 1500–2000* (1988).

There are now regular updates of worldwide armed conflicts in J. Laffin (ed.), *War Annual* (1986–) and in the Royal United Services and Brassey's *Defence Yearbook*. The definitive assessment of size of the world's armed forces and their composition, including nuclear armouries, can be found in the International Institute for Strategic Studies, *The Military Balance*, published annually. L. A. Sobel (ed.), *Political Terrorism* (1975) contains a narrative of terrorist activity from 1968 to 1974.

A good atlas is essential to the understanding of twentieth-century world affairs. G. Barraclough (ed.), *The Times Atlas of World History* (1978) and R. I. Moore (ed.), *The Newnes Historical Atlas* (1981) are two excellent examples though neither is concerned solely with the twentieth century. M. Gilbert, *Recent History Atlas: 1870 to the present day* (1966) is a useful supplement concentrating on the modern era. For reference purposes there is a wealth of statistical material in B. R. Mitchell, *European Historical Statistics, 1750–1975* (2nd edn, 1980) and *International Historical Statistics: Africa and Asia* (1986). There is a wide range of data in *The Statesman's Yearbook*, published annually since 1864, while the United Nations *Statistical Yearbooks* (1945–) provide valuable additional material, and for the earlier period see the League of Nations *Statistical Yearbooks* (1920–). For demographic data see the United Nations, *Demographic Yearbooks* (1945–). For chronological outlines of events see S. H. Steinberg, *Historical Tables, 58BC–AD1978* (10th edn, 1979) and D. Mercer (ed.), *Chronicle of the 20th Century* (1988).

EUROPEAN HISTORY

There are several general histories which include the twentieth century as part of their broad coverage of European history as a whole, notably N. Davies, *Europe a History* (1996), J. M. Roberts, *A History of Europe* (1996) and J. Stevenson, *The History of Europe* (2002). For the twentieth century see J. Joll, *Europe since 1870: an international history* (1973), J. M. Roberts, *Europe, 1880–1945* (2nd edn, 1989), H. James, *Europe Reborn: a history, 1914–2000* (2003) and T. Buchanan, *Europe's Troubled Peace, 1945–2000* (2005). Europe's role as part of the larger world history of the twentieth century is discussed in P. Calvocoressi, *World Politics since 1945* (new edn, 2001), P. M. H. Bell, *The World since 1945: an international history* (2001), E. Hobsbawm, *The Age of Extremes: the short twentieth century, 1914–1991* (1994), and G. Lundestad, *East, West, North, South: major developments in international politics, 1945–1990* (1991).

International relations are considered in E. H. Carr, *The Twenty Years' Crisis, 1919–1939: an introduction to the study of international relations* (1961), G. Ross, *The Great Powers and the Decline of the European States System, 1914–1945* (1983) and J. P. Dunbabin, *International Relations since 1945* (1994). Other themes are considered in C. and R. Tilly, *The Rebellious Century, 1830–1930* (1978), on protest movements, P. Flora and A. J. Heidenheimer (eds), *Development of Welfare States in America and Europe* (1981), G. Luebert, *Liberalism, Fascism or Social Democracy: social classes and the political origins of regimes in interwar Europe* (1991) and S. Salter and J. Stevenson (eds), *The Working Class and Politics in Europe and America, 1929–1945* (1989).

For general reference on European affairs see J. Stevenson, *Macmillan Dictionary of British and European History since 1914* (1991) and on specific parts of Europe, A. Webb, *The Longman Companion to Central and Eastern Europe since 1919* (2002), M. McCauley, *The Longman Companion to Russia since 1914* (1998), A. Blair, *The Longman Companion to the European Union since 1945* (2000), and R. and B. Crampton, *Atlas of Eastern Europe in the Twentieth Century* (1996). For statistical information see B. R. Mitchell, *European Historical Statistics, 1750–1950* (1975) and for the later period the annual edition of *The Statesman's Yearbook*.

European diplomacy, 1871–1914

A. J. P. Taylor, *The Struggle for Mastery in Europe, 1848–1918* (1954) remains a remarkably thorough analysis of the diplomatic struggles, while R. Albrecht-Carrié, *A Diplomatic History of Europe from the Congress of Vienna* (1961) provides the wider background. Another well-established but essential account is W. L. Langer, *European Alliances and Alignments, 1871–90* (1951), which he followed with *The Diplomacy of Imperialism, 1890–1902* (1956). See also F. R. Bridge and R. Bullen, *The Great Powers and the European States System* (1980). On individual countries see C. Andrew, *Théophile Delcassé and the*

Making of the Entente Cordiale (1968) and P. V. Rolo, *Entente Cordiale* (1969).

The origins of the First World War have attracted a vast literature. J. Joll, *The Origins of the First World War* (1985) is a recent modern overview. The decision by individual countries to go to war is examined in K. Wilson (ed.), *Decisions for War, 1914* (1995) and R. J. W. Evans and H. Pogge von Strandmann (eds), *The Coming of the First World War* (1988). H. Strachan, *The First World War, Volume 1: to arms* (2001) is a massive new treatment; parts one and two represent a fresh appraisal of the war's origins and the relationship of the European war to the worldwide rivalries of the great powers. See too A. Mombauer, *The Origins of the First World War: controversies and consensus* (2002) which sets out to examine the current historiography concerning the war's origins. B. Schmitt, *The Outbreak of War in 1914* (Historical Association pamphlet, 1964) analyses the role of the Alliance systems in the outbreak of war, which is more fully related in his study, *The Coming of the War* (2 vols, 1930). The great classic of the 'diplomatic' school of thinking is L. Albertini, *The Origins of the War of 1914* (3 vols, 1952–7). Shorter and more recent accounts are L. C. F. Turner, *The Origins of the First World War* (1970) and H. W. Koch, *The Origins of the First World War* (1984 edn). Also useful is the short account of the break-up of the nineteenth-century international system, R. Langhorne, *The Collapse of the Concert of Europe, 1890–1914* (1981), while M. S. Anderson, *The Eastern Question, 1774–1923* (1966) provides a wider perspective on that particular problem. Among the most important later interpretations has been F. Fischer, *Germany's War Aims in the First World War* (1967) which sees the war as a result of Germany's prewar expansionism. See also his *War of Illusion* (1972) and *From Kaiserreich to Third Reich* (1986). On Germany see V. Berghahn, *Germany and the Approach of War in 1914* (1973), I. Geiss, *German Foreign Policy, 1871–1914* (1976), and G. Ritter, *The Schlieffen Plan* (1958). J. C. G. Rohl (ed.), *1914: Delusion or Design? The testimony of two German diplomats* (1973) has important material on attitudes in German ruling circles. Austria–Hungary's role is considered in R. Bridge, *From Sadowa to Sarajevo* (1972) and A. S. Williamson, *Austria–Hungary and the Origins of the First World War* (1991); France in J. Keiger, *France and the Origins of the First World War* (1983); Russia in D. Lieven, *Russia and the Origins of the First World War* (1983); and Britain in Z. S. Steiner, *Britain and the Origins of the First World War* (1977). The specific rivalry of Britain and Germany is considered in the classic E. L. Woodward, *Great Britain and the German Navy* (1935), but is now updated on the naval side by A. J. Marder, *From the Dreadnought to Scapa Flow, vol. I: the road to war, 1904–14* (1961) and on the political side by P. Kennedy, *The Rise of the Anglo-German Antagonism, 1860–1914* (1980). The arms build-up in general is considered in D. Stevenson, *Armaments and the Coming of War in Europe, 1904–1914* (1996). M. Howard discusses the 'climate' of 1914 in Evans and Pogge von Strandmann (eds), *The Coming of the First World War* (above), and Europe's readiness for war is considered in his 'Reflections on the Great War' in his *Studies in War and Peace* (1970). The commercially published course units of the Open University course on War, Peace and Social Change: Europe, 1900–1955, have in A. Marwick, B. Waites, C. Emsley and I. Donnachie, *Book I: Europe on the Eve of War* (1990), Unit 6, a useful step-by-step guide to the debates.

The First World War, 1914–18

There are numerous general histories of the war but among the most approachable are A. J. P. Taylor, *The First World War: an illustrated history* (1966), I. F. W. Beckett, *The Great War, 1914–1918* (2001), C. Falls, *The First World War* (1966) and B. H. Liddell-Hart, *History of the First World War* (1970). M. Ferro, *The Great War* (1963) is another short, readable introduction. See also J. Terraine, *The Western Front, 1914–18* (1964). For works which place the military aspects of the war in a broader context see K. Robbins, *The First World War* (Oxford, 1984), B. Bond, *War and Society in Europe, 1870–1970* (1984) and G. Hardach, *The First World War* (1977).

Of more recent accounts see D. Stevenson, *The First World War* (2004), J. Keegan, *The First World War* (1998) and H. Strachan's *Oxford Illustrated History of the First World War* (1998). N. Ferguson, *The Pity of War* (1998) offers a stimulating set of fresh perspectives. H. Herwig, *The First World War: Germany and Austria-Hungary* (1997), although concerned with only two of the combatants, is vitally concerned with the war's conduct and conclusion.

The nature of the new warfare is discussed in J. Ellis, *Eye-Deep in Hell* (1976) and A. E. Ashworth, *The Trench Warfare* (1980), while A. Horne, *The Price of Glory: Verdun, 1916* (1964), L. Macdonald, *They Called it Passchendaele* (1983) and M. Middlebrook, *The First Day on the Somme* (1971) and *The Kaiser's Battle* (1983) (on Germany's 1918 offensive) give full treatment of individual battles.

The effect of the war on individual societies can be traced in J. Kocka, *Facing Total War: German society, 1914–1918* (1985), A. Rosenberg, *Imperial Germany: the birth of the German Republic* (1931), A. Marwick, *The Deluge: British society and the First World War* (1965), A. J. May, *The Passing of the Habsburg Monarchy* (2 vols, 1966), L. Kochan, *Russia in Revolution, 1890–1918* (1966), J. J. Becker, *The Great War and the French People* (1983), and N. Stone, *The Eastern Front* (1978). General coverage of such issues is provided by A. Marwick, *War and Social Change in the Twentieth Century* (1974) and J. M. Winter and R. M. Wall (eds), *The Upheaval of War: family, work, and welfare in Europe, 1914–1918* (1981). The wider cultural impact of the war is discussed in P. Fussell, *The Great War and Modern Memory* (1975), J. M. Winter, *The Experience of World War I* (1988), M. Ceadel, *Pacifism in Britain, 1914–1945* (1980), S. Ward (ed.), *The War Generation* (1975), F. Field, *Three Frenchwriters and the Great War* (1970) and H. Klein (ed.), *The First World War in Fiction* (1976).

The revolutionary effects of the war are discussed in C. L. Bertrand (ed.), *Revolutionary Situations in Europe, 1917–1922* (1977) and F. L. Carsten, *Revolution in Central Europe, 1918–1919* (1972). For Germany, see A. J. Ryder, *The German Revolution* (1966) and D. Geary, 'Radicalism and the worker: metalworkers and revolution, 1914–1923', in R. J. Evans (ed.), *Society and Politics in Wilhelmine Germany* (1978).

War aims and the failure of early peace attempts are discussed in F. Fischer, *Germany's War Aims in the First World War* (1987), V. Rothwell, *British War Aims and Peace Diplomacy* (1971), C. Andrew and A. Kanya-Forstner, *France Overseas* (1981), as well as A. J. P. Taylor, *The Struggle for Mastery in Europe, 1848–1918* (1954). See also M. Kitchen, *The Silent Dictatorship* (1976) on the growing role of the German General Staff.

The Russian Revolution and Lenin, 1917–24

M. McCauley (ed.), *The Russian Revolution and the Soviet State, 1917–21* (1980) provides a full set of documents, while L. Trotsky, *The History of the Russian Revolution* (1977) is an account by a leading revolutionary. H. Shukman (ed.), *The Blackwell Encyclopedia of the Russian Revolution* (1988) is a mine of information with a good, short introduction on the historiography of the Revolution. There are memoirs by N. Sukhanov, *The Russian Revolution, 1917* (1955), J. Reed, *Ten Days that Shook the World* (1961) (the latter an American observer of the October Revolution) and A. Kerensky, *The Kerensky Memoirs* (1966). For this and the later period of Soviet history see M. McCauley, *The Longman Companion to Russia since 1914* (2000).

The basic account of the events of 1917–24 can be traced in the excellent general histories by R. Service, *A History of Twentieth-Century Russia* (1997) and by G. Hosking, *A History of the Soviet Union* (1990); see also McCauley (as above).

There are good starting points in R. Pipes, *The Russian Revolution, 1899–1919* (1990), O. Figes, *A People's Tragedy: the Russian Revolution, 1891–1924* (1996), J. D. White, *The Russian Revolution, 1917–1921* (1994), and E. Acton, *Rethinking the Russian Revolution* (1990). Among the national histories which deal with the breakdown of the regime see H. Seton-Watson, *The Russian Empire, 1801–1917* (1967), J. N. Westwood, *Endurance and Endeavour: Russian history, 1812–1971* (1973) and L. Kochan and P. Abraham, *The Making of Modern Russia* (1983). R. B. McKean, *The Russian Constitutional Monarchy, 1907–1917* (Historical Association pamphlet, 1977) synthesizes much earlier research. There are also useful essays in R. Pipes (ed.), *Revolutionary Russia* (1968) and a useful, short interpretative essay in J. Dunn, *Modern Revolutions* (1972), ch. 1.

E. H. Carr, *A History of Soviet Russia: the Bolshevik Revolution* (3 vols, 1966) provides the standard account of these years, although his *The Russian Revolution from Lenin to Stalin* (1980) is shorter. Other accounts on aspects of this period are provided by G. Katkov, *Russia, 1917: the February Revolution* (1967),

R. Pipes, *The Formation of the Soviet Union* (1954) and M. Ferro, *October 1917: A social history of the Russian Revolution* (1980).

Several works approach the period from a biographical viewpoint, including B. Wolfe, *Three Who Made a Revolution* (1966), on Lenin, Trotsky and Stalin, D. Shub, *Lenin* (1966), R. Service, *Lenin: a biography* (2002), A. B. Ulam, *Lenin and the Bolsheviks* (1965), I. Deutscher, *Stalin* (1966), and I. Deutscher, *The Prophet Armed: Trotsky, 1879–1921* (1963). On the Marxist background to Bolshevik thinking see E. Wilson, *To the Finland Station* (1947).

The civil war period and allied intervention are discussed in G. Swain, *The Origins of the Russian Civil War* (1995), J. Bradley, *Allied Intervention in Russia* (1968), R. Ullman, *Intervention and the War: Anglo-Soviet Relations, 1917–21* (1961), while R. Service, *The Bolshevik Party in Revolution, 1917–23* (1979) and T. Rigby, *Lenin's Government* (1979) look at Soviet institutions in this period.

A work looking beyond 1924, towards Stalinism, is S. Fitzpatrick, *The Russian Revolution, 1917–32* (1982). The long-term development of foreign policy is considered in A. B. Ulam, *Expansion and Coexistence, Soviet foreign policy, 1917–27* (1968).

Italy from unification to Mussolini, 1871–1943

For general background to Italian history see D. Mack Smith, *Italy: a modern history* (1959) and M. Clark, *Modern Italy, 1871–1982* (1984). Helpful short introductions to the fascist era are M. Blinkhorn, *Mussolini and Fascist Italy* (1984) and J. Whittam, *Fascist Italy* (1996).

On the pre-fascist period, C. Seton-Watson, *Italy from Liberalism to Fascism* (1967) is the standard work. Relations between Church and State are examined in A. Jemolo, *Church and State in Italy, 1850–1950* (1960) and R. A. Webster, *The Cross and the Fasces: Christian democracy in Italy, 1860–1960* (1960). Popular disorder is considered in J. A. Davis, *Conflict and Control: law and order in nineteenth century Italy* (1988). For the continuation of unrest up to the Fascist era see F. M. Snowden, *Violence and the Great Estates in the South of Italy: Apulia, 1900–1922* (1986), and on the role of the army J. Gooch, *Army, State and Society in Italy, 1870–1915* (1989). R. Bosworth, *Italy and the Approach of the First World War* (1983) covers foreign policy. See also C. Tilly, L. Tilly, and R. Tilly, *The Rebellious Century, 1830–1930* (1975), ch. 3. For postwar events see P. Spriano, *The Occupation of the Factories* (trans. edn 1975), M. Clark, *Antonio Gramsci and the Revolution that Failed* (1977), and G. Williams, *Proletarian Order* (1975). The best overall study of the fascist takeover is A. Lyttleton, *The Seizure of Power, 1919–29* (1973), while the local dimension is considered in P. Corner, *Fascism in Ferrara* (1975) and F. Snowden, *The Fascist Revolution in Tuscany, 1919–1922* (1989). The position of the monarchy, crucial in 1922 and thereafter, has received admirable treatment in D. Mack Smith, *Italy and its Monarchy* (1990). General treatments of the period include A. Cassels, *Fascist Italy* (1985) and A. De Grand, *Italian Fascism, its Origins and Development* (1989); see also

P. Morgan, *Italian Fascism, 1915–1945* (new edn, 2003). Intellectual aspects of fascism are considered in A. Lyttleton, *Italian Fascism from Pareto to Gentile* (1973), J. Pollard, *The Fascist Experience in Italy* (1998), and, comparatively, in A. J. De Grand, *Fascist Italy and Nazi Germany: the 'fascist' style of rule* (1995) and R. Griffin, *The Nature of Fascism* (1993). Particular aspects of fascist policy are considered in C. Duggan, *Fascism and the Mafia* (1989), V. de Grazia, *The Culture of Consent: mass organisation of leisure in Fascist Italy* (1981) and R. Sarti, *Fascism and Industrial Leadership in Italy, 1919–1940* (1971). The general effects of the fascist regime on society can be traced in J. Dunnage, *Twentieth Century Italy: a social history* (2003), ch. 3. For working-class responses see P. Corner on 'Italy', in S. Salter and J. Stevenson (eds), *The Working Class and Politics in Europe and America, 1929–1945* (1990) and for women under fascism see M. Durham, *Women and Fascism* (1998).

For biographies of Mussolini see D. Mack Smith, *Mussolini* (1982), R. Bosworth, *Mussolini* (2002), and the older L. Fermi, *Mussolini* (1961). On foreign policy see R. Mallett, *Mussolini and the Origins of the Second World War, 1933–1940* (2003) and D. Mack Smith, *Mussolini's Roman Empire* (1977); also E. M. Robertson, *Mussolini as Empire Builder* (1977), mainly on 1932–6. E. Wiskemann, *The Rome–Berlin Axis* (1949) and F. W. Deakin, *The Brutal Friendship* (1966) concentrate on the German alliance.

The Weimar Republic, 1919–33

Introductions include D. Bookbinder, *Weimar Germany* (1996), C. Fischer, *The Rise of the Nazis* (2nd edn, 2002), J. Hiden, *The Weimar Republic* (2nd edn, 1996), and *Republican and Fascist Germany: themes and variations in the history of the Third Reich, 1918–1945* (1996). More substantial works are H. Heiber, *The Weimar Republic: Germany, 1918–1933* (1993) and E. Kolb, *The Weimar Republic* (1988). E. Eyck, *History of the Weimar Republic* (2 vols, 1962, 1963) is a full and useful study of the period. A. J. Nicholls, *Weimar and the Rise of Hitler* (4th edn, 2000) is shorter and more analytical. A more recent reinterpretation is A. McElligot, *Rethinking the Weimar Republic: problems and perspectives* (2004) and there is an important group of essays in R. J. Bessel and E. J. Feuchtwanger (eds), *Social Change and Political Development in the Weimar Republic* (1981). A series of essays which amount to a general history of the period can be found in M. Fulbrook, *Twentieth Century Germany: politics, culture and society, 1918–1990* (2001), pt I, chs 1–4.

The revolution of 1918–19 and the birth of Weimar has received quite full treatment. A. Rosenberg, *Imperial Germany: the birth of the German republic* (1931) remains a useful, if old, account; A. J. Ryder, *The German Revolution* (1967) concentrates on the Socialists (see also the shorter account in his Historical Association pamphlet of the same title, published in 1959). F. L. Carsten, *Revolution in Central Europe, 1918–19* (1971) is excellent on the 'grass roots' establishment of workers' and soldiers' councils, and J. P. Nettl, *Rosa Luxemburg* (1969) provides a biography of a leading revolutionary. R. Cooper, *Failure of a Revolution: Germany in 1918–19* (1955) criticizes the Social Democrats, for whom see also R. N. Hunt, *German Social Democracy, 1918–1933* (1970) and W. L. Guttsman, *The German Social Democratic Party, 1875–1933* (1981).

Two important studies of inflation of the early 1920s and its impact are G. D. Feldman, *The Great Disorder: politics, economics and society in the German inflation, 1914–24* (1996) and N. Ferguson, *Paper and Iron: Hamburg business and German politics in the era of inflation, 1897–1927* (1995). Two of the leading politicians of the Weimar era are examined in H. A. Turner, *Stresemann and the Politics of the Weimar Republic* (1963), H. W. Gatzke, *Stresemann and the Rearmament of Germany* (1954) and A. Dorpalen, *Hindenburg and the Weimar Republic* (1964).

J. W. Wheeler-Bennett, *The Nemesis of Power: the German army in politics, 1918–45* (1980 edn) is critical of the military under Weimar. The same theme is covered by F. L. Carsten, *The Reichswehr and German Politics, 1918–33* (1966) and the older and more general, G. Craig, *The Politics of the Prussian Army, 1640–1945* (1955). The political rise of the Nazis at 'grass roots' level can be traced in M. Kater, *The Nazi Party, 1919–45* (1984), W. S. Allen, *The Nazi Seizure of Power* (1966), and J. Noakes, *The Nazi Party in Lower Saxony* (1971). There is a useful set of essays in E. Matthias and A. J. Nicholls (eds), *German Democracy and the Triumph of Hitler* (1971) and P. D. Stachura (ed.), *The Nazi Machtergreifung* (1983). On Nazi support see also T. Childers, *The Nazi Voter, the social foundations of Fascism in Germany 1919–1933* (1983). The effects of the Depression are recorded in K. Harclach, *The Political Economy of Germany in the Twentieth Century* (1980); also D. Geary, 'Unemployment and Working Class Solidarity, 1929–33', in R. J. Evans and D. Geary (eds), *The German Unemployed* (1987) and P. D. Stachura (ed.), *Unemployment and the Great Depression in Weimar Germany* (1986).

For the impact of the Nazis on Weimar see C. Fischer, *The Rise of the Nazis* (2nd edn 2002), R. J. Evans, *The Coming of the Third Reich* (2003), F. McDonough, *Hitler and the Rise of the Nazi Party* (2003), and Nicholls, above. On Hitler himself the fullest treatment is now I. Kershaw, *Hitler, 1889–1936: hubris* (1998), but see also his shorter *Hitler* (2000), the older A. Bullock, *Hitler, a study in tyranny* (1964), W. A. Carr, *Hitler: a study in personality and politics* (1978). The 'failure' of Weimar and the rise of the Nazis is considered in I. Kershaw (ed.), *Weimar: why did German democracy fail?* (1990).

Nazi Germany, 1933–45

There is an enormous amount of work on Hitler and the Nazis. H. R. Trevor-Roper's introduction to *The Last Days of Hitler* (1978 edn) remains impressively perceptive. Of the biographies of Hitler, the standard work is now I. Kershaw's two-volume study, *Hitler, 1889–1936: hubris* (1998) and *Hitler, 1937–1945:*

nemesis (2001). Among a number of other studies, A. Bullock, *Hitler* (1964) remains a readable but full account, J. C. Fest, *Hitler* (1974) and J. Toland, *Adolf Hitler* (1976) are long and detailed, while N. Stone, *Hitler* (1980) is short but stimulating. J. C. Fest, *The Face of the Third Reich* (1970) looks at Hitler's deputies, one of whom receives full coverage in E. K. Bramsted, *Goebbels and National Socialist Propaganda* (1965). Two interesting attempts at 'psycho-history' can be found in W. Langer, *The Mind of Adolf Hitler* (1972) and W. Carr, *Hitler: a study in personality and politics* (1978).

Up-to-date and succinct accounts of the rise of the Nazis can be found in C. Fischer, *The Rise of the Nazis* (2nd edn, 2002), R. J. Evans, *The Coming of the Third Reich* (2003), F. McDonough, *Hitler and the Rise of the Nazi Party* (2003), S. J. Lee, *Hitler and Nazi Germany* (1998), D. Geary, *Hitler and Nazism* (2000), J. Stephenson in M. Fulbrook (ed.), *Twentieth Century Germany: politics, culture and society, 1918–1990* (2001), which also contains excellent short accounts of the main features of the Nazi state, by I. Kershaw (the Nazi dictatorship), O. Bartov (on the Germans at war) and N. Stargardt (on the 'final solution').

The best single account is I. Kershaw, *The Nazi Dictatorship* (3rd edn, 1993), but see also M. Brozat, *The Hitler State* (1981), N. Frei, *National Socialist Rule in Germany: the Führer state* (1993), J. Dulffer, *Nazi Germany, 1933–1945* (1995), K. Bracher, *The German Dictatorship* (1973) and K. Hildebrand, *The Third Reich* (1984). D. Orlow, *A History of the Nazi Party, 1933–45* (1973), D. Welch, *The Third Reich: politics and propaganda* (1994), G. C. Browder, *Hitler's Enforcers: the Gestapo and the SS security service in the Nazi revolution* (1996), D. F. Crew, *Nazism and German Society, 1933–1945* (1994), R. Gruenberger, *A Social History of the Third Reich* (1974) and J. P. Stern, *The Führer and the People* (1975) cover various aspects of the Third Reich, while J. Hiden and J. Farquharson, *Explaining Hitler's Germany* (1983) looks at historical views of the Nazi regime. J. Noakes (ed.), *Government, Party and People in Nazi Germany* (1980) has several good essays and a detailed bibliography. On other aspects of German society see A. Schweitzer, *Big Business in the Third Reich* (1964), D. Guerin, *Fascism and Big Business* (1979), R. J. O'Neill, *The German Army and the Nazi Party, 1933–1939* (1966), Z. A. B. Zeman, *Nazi Propaganda* (1964), E. K. Bramsted, *Goebbels and National Socialist Propaganda 1925–1945* (1965), J. S. Conway, *The Nazi Persecution of the Churches* (1968), and G. Lewy, *The Catholic Church and Nazi Germany* (1964). On women see J. Stephenson, *Women in Nazi Germany* (2001) and J. Stibbe, *Women in the Third Reich* (2003). On the performance of the economy see H. James, *The German Slump* (1988).

Hitler's opponents are considered in H. Graml (ed.), *The German Resistance to Hitler* (1970) and I. Kershaw, *Popular Opinion and Political Dissent in the Third Reich: Bavaria, 1933–1945* (1986). On the position of the working class see S. Salter, 'Germany', in S. Salter and J. Stevenson (eds), *The Working Class and Politics in Europe and America, 1929–1945* (1989); also useful is D. J. K. Peukert, *Inside Nazi Germany: conformity, opposition and racism in everyday life* (1987). Hitler's anti-Semitism is considered in Kershaw, *Nazi Dictatorship*, ch. 5

(see above) and H. Krausnick, 'The Persecution of the Jews', in H. Krausnick and M. Brozat, *Anatomy of the SS State* (1968), but see also L. Dawidowicz, *The War against the Jews, 1933–45* (1975), D. J. Goldhagen, *Hitler's Willing Executioners* (1996) and K. Schleunes, *The Twisted Road to Auschwitz* (1970). More recent treatments include M. Burleigh and W. Wippermann, *The Racial State: Germany, 1933–45* (1991), J. Burrin, *Hitler and the Jews* (1994) and on the euthanasia programme M. Burleigh, *Death and Deliverance: euthanasia in Germany, c. 1900–1945* (1994).

Foreign policy is considered in G. I. Weinberg, *The Foreign Policy of Hitler's Germany: diplomatic revolution in Europe, 1933–1936* (1970) and *The Foreign Policy of Hitler's Germany: starting World War II* (1980). K. Hildebrand, *The Foreign Policy of the Third Reich* (1973) stresses Hitler's pragmatism, while W. Carr, *Arms, Autarky and Aggression: a study in German foreign policy, 1933–1939* (1972) relates economic policy to foreign policy. Two important recent studies of the outbreak of war in 1939 are D. Cameron Watt, *How War Came* (1989) and R. Overy and A. Wheatcroft, *The Road to War* (1989); see also P. M. Bell, *The Origins of the Second World War in Europe* (2nd edn 1997), R. J. Overy, *The Origins of the Second World War* (2nd edn, 1998), and C. Leitz on Germany in R. Boyce and J. A. Maiolo (eds), *The Origins of World War Two* (2003).

On Hitler's economic policies see W. Carr, *Arms, Autarky and Aggression*, B. A. Caroll, *Design for Total War: arms and economics in the Third Reich* (1968), and B. H. Klein, *Germany's Economic Preparations for War* (1959). T. Mason, 'The Primacy of Politics: Politics and Economics in National Socialist Germany', in S. J. Woolf (ed.), *The Nature of Fascism* (1968) discusses the Nazi attitude to economics, a view taken up by A. Milward in W. Laqueur (ed.), *Fascism: a readers' guide* (1979). For the German economy at war see A. Milward, *The German Economy at War* (1965) and his wider *War, Economy and Society 1939–1945* (1977).

Stalin's Russia, 1923–53

For introductions see R. Service, *A History of Twentieth Century Russia* (1997), M. Maudsley, *Stalin and Stalinism* (1990) and G. Hosking, *A History of the Soviet Union* (1985). Stalin's place as legatee of the Revolution, whether fulfilling or betraying it, is raised in A. B. Ulam, *The New Face of Soviet Totalitarianism* (1963) and S. Fitzpatrick, *The Russian Revolution* (1982); the classic 'betrayal' view is L. Trotsky, *The Revolution Betrayed* (1937). There are several good biographies, notably R. Service, *Stalin* (2004), I. Deutscher, *Stalin* (1966), A. B. Ulam, *Stalin* (1973), and R. H. McNeal, *Stalin: man and ruler* (1988). Recent general treatments include G. Ward, *Stalin's Russia* (1993), M. McCauley, *Stalin and Stalinism* (2nd edn, 1995), and C. Gill, *The Origins of the Stalinist Political System* (1990). Also helpful are R. Tucker, *Stalin in Power: the revolution from above, 1928–1941* (1990), M. Lewin and I. Kershaw (eds), *Stalinism and Nazism:*

dictatorships in comparison (1997), S. Fitzpatrick, *Stalinism: new directions* (1999) and P. Boobbyer, *The Stalin Era* (2000).

For the background to collectivization and industrialization see Hosking, *History of the Soviet Union* (above) and A. Nove, *An Economic History of the U.S.S.R.* (1972). For collectivization see R. W. Davies, *The Socialist Offensive* (1976) and on industrialization his *The Industrialisation of the Soviet Union* (1980). The political dimension of modernization is considered by H. Kuromiya, *Stalin's Industrial Revolution: politics and workers, 1928–1932* (1988) and his essay on the USSR in S. Salter and J. Stevenson (eds), *The Working Class and Politics in Europe and North America, 1929–45* (1989). Soviet claims to have avoided the world depression are examined in R. W. Davies, 'The Ending of Mass Unemployment in the USSR', in D. Lane (ed.), *Labour and Employment in the U.S.S.R.* (1986). Factors assisting support for the Stalinist regime are considered in S. Fitzpatrick, *Education and Social Mobility in the U.S.S.R., 1921–1934* (1979). On the Terror see R. Conquest, *The Great Terror* (1968; rev. edn, 1990) and J. Arch Getty, *Origins of the Great Purges: the Soviet Communist Party reconsidered, 1933–1938* (1985). R. Medvedev, *Let History Judge: the origins and consequences of Stalinism* (2nd edn, 1989) is a view from a leading Soviet historian, reflecting the post-Gorbachev openness about the Stalinist past. For the development of recent ideas about the Terror see B. McLoughlin and K. McDermott, *Stalin's Terror: high politics and mass repression in the Soviet Union* (2002). Two important 'inside' accounts of Stalin's circle and the mentality behind the Terror are D. Rayfield, *Stalin and his Hangmen* (2004) and S. Sebag-Montefiore, *Stalin: the court of the red tsar* (2003).

For the Communist Party see L Shapiro, *The Communist Party of the Soviet Uniion* (1970) and the early sections of his *The Government and Politics of the Soviet Union* (rev. edn, 1967). The new working-class 'vanguard' is considered in L. Viola, *The Sons of the Fatherland* (1987), while the military are examined in J. Erickson, *The Soviet High Command: a military-political history, 1918–1941* (1962) and R. R. Reese, *The Soviet Military Experience* (1999). The position of the peasantry is put in long-term perspective in J. Channon, *The Russian and Soviet Peasantry, 1880–1991* (1997), but see also S. Fitzpatrick, *Stalin's Peasants: resistance and survival in the Russian village after collectivisation* (1996) and L. Viola, *Peasant Rebels under Stalin* (1996).

For Russia at war see A. Werth, *Russia at War* (1965), A. Dallin, *German Rule in Russia, 1941–5* (1957), J. Barber and M. Harrison (eds), *The Soviet Home Front, 1941–1945* (1991), and S. J. Main, *The USSR and the Defeat of Nazi Germany, 1941–45* (1997). Two detailed accounts of major episodes in the war are A. Beevor, *Stalingrad* (2002) and J. Barber and A. Dzeniskevich (eds), *Life and Death in Besieged Leningrad, 1941–1944* (2004), while G. Uehling, *Beyond Memory: the 1944 deportation of the Crimean Tatars* (2004) deals with the fate of one minority victimized in the war.

The development of Soviet foreign policy is discussed in G. F. Kennan, *Russia and the West under Lenin and Stalin* (1961), A. B. Ulam, *Expansion and*

Co-existence (1967), J. Haslam, *Soviet Foreign Policy, 1930–33* (1983) and *The Soviet Union and the Struggle for Collective Security* (1984), R. C. Raack, *Stalin's Drive to the West, 1938–1945* (1995), G. Mastny, *Soviet Insecurity and the Cold War* (1994) and S. Goncharov, J. Lewis and X. Litai, *Uncertain Partners: Stalin, Mao, and the Korean War* (1995).

Eastern Europe and the Balkans between the wars

An introduction to the Balkans can be found in D. P. Hupchick, *The Balkans: from Constantinople to Communism* (2002). An up-to-date and more closely focused study of Eastern Europe can be found in R. J. Crampton, *Eastern Europe in the Twentieth Century – and After* (1997), but see also R. Okey, *Eastern Europe, 1740–1985* (2nd edn, 1986), H. Seton-Watson, *The 'Sick-heart' of Modern Europe: the problem of the Danubian lands* (1975) and his older general work on the whole region, *Eastern Europe between the Wars* (1962) and J. Rothschild, *East Central Europe between the Two World Wars* (1974), while a wider perspective is given in A. Palmer, *The Lands Between: a history of East Central Europe since the Congress of Vienna* (1970). C. A. Macartney and A. Palmer, *Independent Eastern Europe* (1962) and H. and C. Seton-Watson, *The Making of New Europe* (1981) are also helpful.

A. Polonsky, *The Little Dictators* (1975) covers each East European state after 1918 in turn, and there are various individual works on East European states, such as A. J. Prazmowska, *A History of Poland* (2004), L. Kontler, *A History of Hungary* (2002), H. Hoensch, *A History of Modern Hungary* (1988), R. Clogg, *A Short History of Modern Greece* (1979), L. Benson, *Yugoslavia: a concise history* (rev. edn, 2003), M. Macdermott, *A History of Bulgaria* (1962), S. Pollo and A. Puto, *The History of Albania* (1981), S. Fischer-Galati, *Twentieth Century Rumania* (1970).

With regard to German expansionism in the 1930s and the countries from which it sought territory or even annexation see A. Polonsky, *Politics in Independent Poland, 1921–39* (1972), on Austria's position, J. Gehl, *Austria, Germany and the Anschluss, 1931–9* (1963) and G. Brook-Shepherd, *Anschluss* (1963).

On the more complex Czechoslovakian issue see I. Lukes, *Czechoslovakia between Stalin and Hitler* (1996), J. W. Bruegel, *Czechoslovakia before Munich* (1973), E. M. Smelser, *The Sudeten Problem 1933–8* (1975), and, for background, J. Korbel, *Twentieth Century Czechoslovakia* (1977).

The Spanish Civil War, 1936–9

R. Carr, *Spain, 1808–1939* (1966; rev. edn, *Spain, 1808–1975*, 1982) is an essential starting point, rooting the Civil War in Spanish development, as does his *The Spanish Tragedy* (1977). G. Brenan, *The Spanish Labyrinth* (1943) is widely recognized as a modern classic for its deep understanding of the Spanish context.

P. Preston (ed.), *Revolution and War in Spain, 1931–1939* (1984) has an extremely useful historiographical essay by the editor. See also F. R. de Meneses, *Franco and the Spanish Civil War* (2001).

H. Thomas, *The Spanish Civil War* (rev. edn, 1977) remains a well-balanced narrative, but see also G. Jackson, *The Spanish Republic and the Civil War* (1965). For the experience of the Spanish Republic as a whole during the war, the most comprehensive treatment is now H. Graham, *The Spanish Republic at War* (2002). On the origins of the war, P. Preston, *The Coming of the Spanish Civil War* (2nd edn, 1994) gives emphasis to the land question, as does E. E. Malefakis, *Agrarian Reform and Peasant Revolution* (1970). R. Carr (ed.), *The Republic and the Civil War in Spain* (1971) is another useful collection of essays, as is M. Blinkhorn (ed.), *Spain in Conflict 1931–1939: democracy and its enemies* (1986).

On the right-wing forces see P. Preston, *The Politics of Revenge: fascism and the military in 20th century Spain* (1995), F. Lannon, *Privilege, Persecution and Prophecy: the Catholic Church in Spain, 1875–1975* (1987), M. Vincent, 'Spain', in T. Buchanan and M. Conway (eds), *Political Catholicism in Europe, 1918–1965* (1996), R. Robinson, *The Origins of Franco's Spain* (1970), S. Payne, *Falange* (1961), and the biographies of Franco by P. Preston, *Franco* (1993), B. Crozier, *Franco* (1967), and J. Trythall, *Franco* (1970). On the left see S. Payne, *The Spanish Revolution* (1970) and P. Broué and E. Témine, *The Revolution and the Civil War in Spain* (1972), the latter critical of the communists' role. Two books sympathetic to the anarchists are V. Richards, *Lessons of the Spanish Revolution* (1957) and M. Bookchin, *The Spanish Anarchists* (1977). The role of the communists is also considered in D. T. Cattell, *Communism and the Spanish Civil War* (1955) and B. Balloten, *The Grand Camouflage* (1961), reissued as *The Spanish Revolution: the left and the struggle for power during the Civil War* (1979). A fascinating case study of a group which exemplifies the complexities of Spanish politics is M. Blinkhorn, *Carlism and Crisis in Spain 1931–1939* (1975); see also M. Blinkhorn, 'Spain', in S. Salter and J. Stevenson (eds), *The Working Class and Politics in Europe and North America, 1929–1945* (1990).

The international dimension has received reassessment recently in M. Alpert, *A New International History of the Spanish Civil War* (2nd edn, 2004) but see the older D. Puzzo, *Spain and the Great Powers, 1936–41* (1962). Individual themes are considered in V. Brome, *The International Brigades* (1965), J. F. Coverdale, *Italian Intervention in the Spanish Civil War* (1977), J. Edwards, *Britain and the Spanish Civil War* (1979), and E. H. Carr, *The Comintern and the Spanish Civil War* (1984). G. Weintraub, *The Last Great Cause* (1976) is an exposé of the war of propaganda carried out by both sides to enlist support. On the most famous episode – the bombing of Guernica – see G. Thomas and M. Witts, *Guernica* (1975) and H. R. Southworth, *Guernica! Guernica! a study of journalism, diplomacy, propaganda and history* (1977).

France, 1918–44

Several general texts can be consulted, including J. F. McMillan, *Dreyfus to de Gaulle: politics and society in France, 1898–1969* (1985) and his *Twentieth Century France: politics and society in France, 1898–2003* (2004), M. Larkin, *France since the Popular Front: government and people, 1936–1986* (1988), R. Vinen, *France, 1934–70* (1996) and M. Agulthon, *The French Republic, 1879–1992* (1993), but more narrowly see also P. Bernard and H. Dubieff, *The Decline of the Third Republic, 1914–38* (1985) and W. Fortescue, *The Third Republic in France, 1870–1940* (2000).

The important Popular Front era is discussed in J. Jackson, *The Popular Front in France: defending democracy, 1934–1938* (1988) and its leading figure in J. Coulton, *Léon Blum* (1974). The most important party of the interwar years is examined in P. Larmour, *The French Radical Party in the 1930s* (1964), while there is a useful survey of the right in R. Austin, 'The Conservative Right and the Far Right in France: the Search for Power, 1934–44', in M. Blinkhorn (ed.), *Fascists and Conservatives* (1990); see also W. D. Irvine, *French Conservatism in Crisis* (1979) and C. A. Micaval, *The French Right and Nazi Germany, 1933–9* (1972). For the left see the survey essay by R. McGraw, 'France', in S. Salter and J. Stevenson (eds), *The Working Class and Politics in Europe and North America, 1929–45* (1990), R. Tiersky, *The French Communist Party, 1920–1970* (1974), and E. Mortimer, *The Rise of the French Communist Party, 1920–1947* (1984). The role of the army is considered in A. Horne, *The French Army in Politics* (1984). On the important question of social reform see P. V. Dutton, *Origins of the French Welfare State: the struggle for social reform in France, 1914–1947* (2002).

On the approach to war see A. Adamthwaite, *France and the Coming of the Second World War* (1977) and also his *Grandeur and Misery: France's bid for power in Europe, 1918–1939* (1992). The military fall of France is discussed in A. Horne, *To Lose a Battle: France, 1940* (1979) and R. Collier, *1940: the world in flames* (1980). J. Jackson's studies, *The Fall of France* (2003) and *France: the dark years, 1940–44* (2001), link the collapse of France with the complex politics of occupation and Vichy. The politicians involved in the collapse are considered in H. R. Lottman, *Pétain: hero or traitor?* (1985), R. Griffiths, *Marshal Pétain* (1970), S. Hoffman, 'The Vichy Circle of French Conservatives' in his *Decline or Renewal? France since the 1930s* (1974), and G. Warner, *Pierre Laval and the Eclipse of France* (1968), and J. Lacouture, *De Gaulle: the rebel: 1890–1944* (trans. edn, 1990). The Vichy regime is examined in R. Aron, *The Vichy Régime, 1940–4* (1958), R. Paxton, *Vichy France* (1972), and R. Kedward, *Occupied France: collaboration and resistance, 1940–44* (1985). R. Cobb, *French and Germans, Germans and French* (1983) and R. Kedward and R. Austin (eds), *Vichy France and the Resistance: ideology and culture* (1985) examine aspects of the interaction. The resistance is the subject of P. Burrin, *Occupied France: collaboration and resistance, 1940–44* (1996), R. Kedward, *Resistance in Vichy France*

(1978), M. Dank, *The French against the French* (1978), and M. R. D. Foot, *Resistance* (1976). The specific issue of anti-Semitism is set out in P. Kingston, *Anti-Semitism in France during the 1930s* (1983) and R. Paxton and M. Marrus, *Vichy France and the Jews* (1981). On the Liberation see H. Footit, *War and Liberation in France: living with the liberators* (2004).

Interwar diplomacy

Of the overall accounts of the interwar period, E. H. Carr, *The Twenty Years Crisis* (new edn, 1981) remains a challenging work but see also H. Gatzke, *European Diplomacy between the Two World Wars* (1972), and R. A. C. Parker, *Europe, 1919–45* (1969). The impact of the Paris Peace Conferences and their immediate aftermath are discussed in A. J. Mayer, *The Policy and Diplomacy of Peacemaking: containment and counter-revolution at Versailles, 1918–19* (1968) and G. Schulz, *Revolution and Peace Treaties* (1972), while F. P. Walters, *A History of the League of Nations* (1960) remains the most thorough account of that body. The longer term effects of Versailles are discussed in R. Henig, *Versailles and After, 1919–1933* (1995) and S. Marks, *The Illusion of Peace: international relations in Europe, 1918–1933* (2nd edn, 2003); M. Kitchen, *Europe Between the Wars* (1999) and R. Overy, *The Inter-War Crisis, 1919–1939* (1994) take the story through to the Second World War, the latter with some documents.

On the origins of the Second World War there are a number of introductions: see P. M. H. Bell, *The Origins of the Second World War in Europe* (2nd edn, 1997), R. Overy, *The Origins of the Second World War* (2nd edn, 1998), E. M. Robertson, *The Origins of the Second World War* (1976) and A. Adamthwaite, *The Making of the Second World War* (3rd edn, 1992). A. J. P. Taylor, *The Origins of the Second World War* (1961) is still exciting and very readable, though its arguments have been undermined. The definitive account of the European crisis in Sept. 1939 is now D. Cameron Watt, *How War Came: the immediate origins of the Second World War, 1938–9* (1989); also valuable are R. Overy and A. Wheatcroft, *The Road to War* (1989) and V. Rothwell, *The Origins of the Second World War* (1995). A very useful collection of essays is G. Martel, *Origins of the Second World War* (2nd edn, 1999). A study which embraces the outbreak of war in both Europe and Asia is M. Lamb and N. Tarling, *From Versailles to Pearl Harbour: the origins of the War in Europe and Asia* (2001).

On specific events and issues, N. Rostow, *Anglo-French Relations, 1934–6* (1984) analyses Western policies at a key period, while K. Robbins, *Munich* (1968) and T. Taylor, *Munich* (1979) look at the most criticized episode in 1930s diplomacy. S. Newman, *March, 1939* (1976) concentrates on the British guarantee to Poland, which was so vital in the outbreak of war. On French policy see especially A. Adamthwaite, *France and the Coming of the Second World War* (1977), and on Germany, G. L. Weinberg, *The Foreign Policy of Hitler's Germany* (1970) and W. Carr, *Arms, Autarky and Aggression* (1972). On British appeasement in general see especially M. Gilbert, *The Roots of Appeasement* (1966),

K. Middlemas, *Diplomacy of Illusion* (1972), and W. R. Rock, *British Appeasement in the 1930s* (1976). See also the essays by N. Medlicott and M. Howard in D. Dilks (ed.), *Retreat from Power: Studies of Britain's Foreign Policy of the Twentieth Century: Vol. One, 1906–1939* (1981).

The Second World War, 1939–45

For general introductions see A. W. Purdue, *The Second World War* (1999) and R. A. C. Parker, *Struggle for Survival: the history of the Second World War* (1990), both more balanced than the older but still valuable studies by B. Liddell Hart, *The Second World War* (1990) and A. J. P. Taylor, *The Second World War: an illustrated history* (1976). G. Weinberg, *A World at Arms: a global history of World War II* (1994) and P. Calvocoressi and G. Wint, *Total War* (1974) put the European conflict in the wider context. On the key issue of outcome, see R. Overy, *Why the Allies Won* (1996). For the impact of the war on the combatants, A. Marwick, *War and Social Change in the Twentieth Century* (1974) concentrates on the social effects. D. Irving, *Hitler's War* (1983) gives an account of the war from the German perspective, for which see also O. Bartov, 'From Blitzkrieg to Total War' in M. Fulbrook (ed.), *Twentieth Century Germany* (2001). On Russia, see A. Werth, *Russia at War* (1965), J. D. Barber and M. Harrison, *The Soviet Home Front, 1941–1945: a social and economic history of the USSR in World War II* (1991) and S. Bialer (ed.), *Stalin and his Generals* (1971). For Britain see A. Calder, *The People's War* (1969). On the economic conduct of the war see A. S. Milward, *War, Economy and Society, 1939–1945* (1977), also his *The German Economy at War* (1965) and R. Overy, *War and Economy in the Third Reich* (1995).

The opening phase of the war is covered by B. Collier, *1940: the world in flames* (1980) and *1941: Armageddon* (1982). The controversy over the effectiveness and morality of the bombing offensive against Germany is considered in N. Frankland, *The Bombing Offensive against Germany* (1965) and M. Hastings, *Bomber Command* (1979). For the German side of the air war see D. Irving, *The Rise and Fall of the Luftwaffe* (1973). For the war at sea see D. Macintyre, *The Battle of the Atlantic* (1961), J. Costello and T. Hughes, *The Battle of the Atlantic* (1977) and W. Frank, *The Sea Wolves* (1955). The decisive struggle on the Eastern Front is considered in A. Clark, *Barbarossa* (1965) and J. Erickson, *The Road to Stalingrad: Stalin's war with Germany* (1975) and *The Road to Berlin* (1983).

For the final phase of the war see E. Belfield and H. Essame, *The Battle for Normandy* (1965), C. Duffy, *Red Storm on the Reich: the Soviet March on Germany, 1945* (2000), C. Ryan, *The Last Battle* (Berlin) (1974), and A. Beevor, *Berlin: the downfall, 1945* (2002). Specifically on the new forms of mobile warfare pioneered in 'Blitzkrieg' see H. Guderian, *Panzer Leader* (1952) and F. W. von Mellenthin, *Panzer Battles* (1955). Technical developments affecting the conduct of the war are discussed in R. V. Jones, *Most Secret War* (1978) and B. Johnson,

The Secret War (1978). Increasing attention has been given to the conduct of the war and its effects upon those engaged in it. O. Bartov, *The Eastern Front, 1941–45: German troops and the barbarisation of warfare* (1986) and *Hitler's Army; soldiers, Nazis and war in the Third Reich* (1991) is a brilliant analysis of the conduct of the war in the east, but see also C. Browning, *Ordinary Men: Reserve Police Battalion 101 and the Final Solution in Poland* (1992), T. Schulte, *The German Army and Nazi Policies in Occupied Russia* (1989) and, more generally, P. Addison and A. Calder (eds), *Time to Kill* (1995) on servicemen.

The fate of areas conquered by the Germans is considered in W. Warmbrunn, *The Dutch under German Occupation* (1963), G. Hirschfield, *Nazi Rule and Dutch Collaboration* (1988), A. K. Hoidal, *Quisling: a study in treason* (1989), A. Dallin, *German Rule in Russia, 1941–5* (1957), and on France see especially P. Burrin, *Occupied France: collaboration and resistance* (1996), H. R. Kedward and R. Austin (eds), *Vichy France and Resistance* (1985), J. Sweets, *Choices in Vichy France: the French under German occupation* (1986), H. R. Kedward and N. Wood (eds), *The Liberation of France* (1995) and R. O. Paxton, *Vichy France* (1973), while the synthesis by N. Atkin, *The French at War, 1934–1944* (2001) links interwar conflicts with wartime ones. Other important countries are considered in A. Pramowska, *Civil War in Poland, 1942–1948* (2004), R. Clogg, *Greece, 1940–1949: occupation, resistance, civil war* (2002), containing annotated documents, and O. Vehvilainen, *Finland in the Second World War: between Germany and Russia* (2002). The various resistance movements are analysed in H. Michel, *The Shadow War: resistance in Europe, 1939–45* (1972), S. Hayes and R. White (eds), *Resistance in Europe, 1939–1945* (1975), and M. R. D. Foot, *Resistance* (1976). On the fate of the Jews see M. Marrus, *The Holocaust in History* (1989), L. S. Dawidowicz, *The War against the Jews* (1975), and G. Fleming, *Hitler and the Final Solution* (1984).

On diplomacy during the war see H. Feis, *Churchill, Roosevelt, Stalin* (1957), W. H. McNeill, *America, Britain and Russia* (1953) and G. Kolko, *The Politics of War* (1968). D. Carlton, *Churchill and Stalin* (1999), examines a key 'big power' relationship and the Soviet view is discussed in V. Mastny, *Russia's Road to the Cold War* (1979) and R. C. Raack, *Stalin's Drive to the West, 1938–1945: the origins of the Cold War* (1995). For the origins of the Cold War see J. Young, *The Cold War in Europe, 1945–91* (2nd edn 1996).

The Holocaust

Hitler's *Mein Kampf* (1925–6) is available edited by D. C. Watt (1969) and there is considerable factual material in M. Freeman, *Atlas of Nazi Germany* (new edn, 1995) and W. Laqueur (ed.), *The Holocaust Encyclopedia* (2001). Participant accounts include O. Frank, *The Diary of Anne Frank* (1947), Primo Levi, *If This is Man* (1979), O. Lengyel, *Five Chimneys* (1959), E. Kogon, *The Theory and Practice of Hell* (1950), H. Kruk, *The Last Days of the Jerusalem of Lithuania: chronicles from the Vilna ghetto and the camps, 1939–1944* (ed. B. Harshav, 2002), and H. Fried, *The Road to Auschwitz: fragments of a life* (ed. M. Meyer, 1990). Recently available in English is V. Klemperer, *I Shall Bear Witness: diaries, 1933–41* and *Till the Bitter End, 1942–45* (1998–9).

For general perspectives see M. Marrus, *The Holocaust in History* (1989), Y. Bauer, *Rethinking the Holocaust* (2002), C. Browning, *The Path to Genocide* (1992), P. Burrin, *Hitler and the Jews: the genesis of the Holocaust* (1994), and R. Hilberg, *The Destruction of the European Jews* (3 vols, 1985). Older accounts include L. S. Davidowicz, *The War against the Jews* (1975), K. Schleunes, *The Twisted Road to Auschwitz* (1970), and G. Fleming, *Hitler and the Final Solution* (1984). The latter tend to follow the view that the Holocaust was the outcome of long-term policy, the so-called 'intentionalist' view, which is usefully discussed in I. Kershaw, *The Nazi Dictatorship* (1989), especially ch. 5; see also N. Stargardt, 'The Holocaust' in M. Fulbrook, *Twentieth Century Germany* (2001). Recent collections of essays which examine aspects of the debate over Nazi policy are O. Bartov (ed.), *The Holocaust: origins, implementation, aftermath* (2000), D. Cesarani (ed.), *The Final Solution: origins and implementation* (1994), G. Hirschfield (ed.), *The Policies of Genocide: Jews and Soviet prisoners of war in Nazi Germany* (1986) and W. Pehle (ed.), *Nov. 1938: from Reichkristallnacht to genocide* (1991).

On non-Jewish victims see Hirschfield (above), G. Grau (ed.), *Hidden Holocaust? Gay and lesbian persecution in Germany, 1933–1945* (1995), D. Kenrick and G. Puxon, *The Destiny of European Gypsies* (1972) and M. Burleigh, *Death and Deliverance: 'euthanasia' in Germany, c. 1900–1945* (1994), B. Muller-Hill, *Murderous Science: elimination by scientific selection of Jews, Gypsies and others, Germany, 1933–1945* (1988), and U. Herbert, *A History of Foreign Labour in Germany, 1880–1980* (1990).

On the complicity or conformity of Germans with the Holocaust see the controversial view of D. Goldhagen, *Hitler's Willing Executioners: ordinary Germans and the Holocaust* (1996), but see also C. Browning, *Ordinary Men: Reserve Police Battalion 101 and the Final Solution in Poland* (1992) and his *Nazi Policy, Jewish Workers, German Killers* (2000), S. Friedlander, *Nazi Germany and the Jews: the years of persecution, 1933–1939* (1997), M. Burleigh and W. Wippermann, *The Racial State: Germany, 1933–1945* (1991), T. Schulte, *The German Army and Nazi Policies in Occupied Russia* (1989), O. Bartov, *Hitler's Army: soldiers, Nazis, and war in the Third Reich* (1991) and D. Peukert, *Inside Nazi Germany: conformity, opposition and racism in everyday life* (1993). See also D. Bankier, *The Germans and the Final Solution: public opinion under Nazism* (1992) and U. Herbert, *Forced Foreign Labour in the Third Reich* (1997). The 'denial' of one leading Nazi is considered in G. Sereny, *Albert Speer: his struggle with truth* (1995).

The complicity of other states is considered in M. Marrus and R. Paxton, *Vichy France and the Jews* (1981) and G. Hirschfield and P. Marsh (eds), *Collaboration in France: politics and culture during the occupation, 1940–44* (1989), P. F. Sugar (ed.), *Native Fascism in the Successor States, 1918–45* (1971),

E. Mendelsohn, *The Jews of East Central Europe between the World Wars* (1987), M. Michaelis, *Mussolini and the Jews* (1978), J. Steinberg, *All or Nothing: the Axis and the Holocaust* (1990) and M. Dean, *Collaboration in the Holocaust: crimes of the local police in Belorussia and Ukraine, 1941–44* (2000). On the failure of the Allies to assist the Jews more decisively see L. D. Rubinstein, *The Myth of Rescue* (1999).

Reactions to the Holocaust by its victims are considered in E. Cohen, *Human Behaviour in the Concentration Camp* (1998) and P. Levi, *The Drowned and the Saved* (1980). The wider question of how the Holocaust is perceived and commemorated is examined in J. E. Young, *Holocaust Remembrance: the shapes of memory* (1994) and his *The Texture of Memory: Holocaust memorials and meaning* (1993). See also Z. Amishai-Maisels, *Depiction and Interpretation: the influence of the Holocaust on the visual arts* (1993), T. Cole, *Images of the Holocaust: the myth of the Shoah business* (1999) and Y. Eliach, 'Documenting the Landscape of Death: the Politics of Commemoration and Holocaust Studies', in Y. Bauer (ed.), *Remembering the Future*, vol. III (1989).

Moral dilemmas raised by the Holocaust and the development of the idea of genocide are considered in J. Glover, *Humanity: a moral history of the twentieth century* (1999) and W. D. Rubinstein, *Genocide* (2003).

The Cold War

Good introductions to the present state of knowledge can be found in J. L. Gaddis, *We Now Know: rethinking Cold War history* (1997) and J. Young, *The Cold War in Europe, 1945–91* (new edn, 1996). J. Isaacs and T. Downing, *Cold War* (1998) is a good popular account with documents and illustrations to accompany a television series. Other introductory accounts are D. Painter, *The Cold War: an international history* (1999), B. Lightbody, *The Cold War* (1996), D. Reynolds, *The Origins of the Cold War in Europe* (1994), W. Loth, *The Division of the World, 1941–55* (1988), T. G. Paterson, *Meeting the Communist Threat: Truman to Reagan* (1988) and D. Painter and M. Leffler, *The Origins of the Cold War: an international history* (1994). Soviet policy is now better understood through the partial opening of the Soviet archives; see especially R. C. Raack, *Stalin's Drive to the West, 1938–1945: the origins of the Cold War* (1995) and V. Mastny, *The Cold War and Soviet Insecurity: the Stalin years* (1996). The older studies by A. B. Ulam, *Expansion and Coexistence* (1968) and T. W. Wolfe, *Soviet Power and Europe, 1945–70* (1970) have to be seen in the light of more recent work. There are other general works, most being American: J. W. Spanier, *American Foreign Policy since the Second World War* (1980) is pro-American, S. E. Ambrose, *Rise to Globalism* (1983) and W. Lafeber, *America, Russia and the Cold War* (1982) are more questioning of US policy, while L. J. Halle, *The Cold War as History* (1967) is still a useful, balanced account on part of the period.

The early years of the Cold War have received most coverage. Again there are conservative accounts, such as G. F. Hudson, *The Hard and Bitter Peace* (1966) and H. L. Feis, *From Trust to Terror* (1970), criticisms of America in G. and J. Kolko, *The Limits of Power* (1972) and D. Yergin, *Shattered Peace* (1977). J. L. Gaddis, *The United States and the Origins of the Cold War* (1973) is good, and on the British see V. Rothwell, *Britain and the Cold War, 1941–7* (1983) and A. Deighton (ed.), *Britain and the First Cold War* (1989). Coverage of the continental states is slight, but on France see G. de Carmoy, *The Foreign Policies of France* (1970) and, on the early years, E. Furniss, *France, Troubled Ally* (1960).

Western European democracy since 1945

For general coverage see T. Buchanan, *Europe's Troubled Peace, 1945–2000* (2005), D. Urwin, *A Political History of Western Europe since 1945* (1997), the latter sections of H. James, *Europe Reborn: a history, 1914–2000* (2003) and J. R. Wegs, *Europe since 1945* (5th edn, 2004). Europe's place in the world order is considered in P. Calvocoressi, *World Politics since 1945* (1982). Other general studies of the immediate postwar era include W. Laqueur, *Europe since Hitler* (1970), M. Crouzet, *The European Renaissance since 1945* (1970) and R. Morgan, *West European Politics since 1945* (1972). Rather narrower is F. R. Willis, *France, Germany and the New Europe, 1945–67* (1969), while F. Fry and G. Raymond, *The Other Western Europe* (1980) looks at the smaller democracies. On economic reconstruction, see A. S. Milward, *The Reconstruction of Western Europe 1945–51* (1984), and M. J. Hogan, *The Marshall Plan* (1988).

On France in this period see R. Gildea, *France since 1945* (1996), R. Vinen, *Bourgeois Politics in France, 1945–1951* (1995), and on the Fourth and Fifth Republics, see P. M. Williams, *Crisis and Compromise: Politics in the Fourth Republic* (1964 edn), P. M. Williams and M. Harrison, *Politics and Compromise: politics and society in de Gaulle's republic* (1971). P. Thody, *The Fifth French Republic: presidents, politics and personalities* (1998) and N. Atkin, *The Fifth French Republic* (2004) are more recent studies. See also J. Ardagh, *The New France* (1978) and M. Anderson, *Conservative Politics in France* (1974). See also the studies of de Gaulle by D. Cook, *Charles de Gaulle* (1984), S. Berstein, *The Republic of de Gaulle, 1958–69* (1993), H. Gough and J. Hone, *De Gaulle and 20th Century France* (1994). For Germany see as introduction M. Fulbrook (ed.), *Twentieth Century Germany: politics, culture, and society, 1918–1990* (2001), Pt II, which has synoptic essays on both west and east Germany, and on unification, L. Kattenacker, *Germany since 1945* (1997), I. Derbyshire, *Politics in Germany from Division to Unification* (1991), D. Childs, *The Fall of the GDR: Germany's road to unity* (2001), C. Ross, *The East German Dictatorship: problems and perspectives of the GDR* (2002) and K. H. Jarausch, *The Rush to German Unity* (1994). More generally see P. O'Dochartaigh, *Germany since 1945* (2003), A. J. Nicholls, *The Bonn Republic: West German democracy, 1945–91* (1997), P. Pulzer, *German Politics, 1945–1995* (1995), D. L. Bark and D. R. Gress, *A*

History of West Germany, 1945–90 (2nd edn, 1993) and K. Larres and P. Panayi (eds), *The Federal Republic of Germany since 1949* (1996). On personalities see T. Prittie, *The Velvet Chancellors* (1979) and his *Adenauer* (1971); see also R. Irving, *Adenauer* (2002).

On Italy see M. Clark, *Modern Italy, 1871–1982* (1984), P. Ginsborg, *A History of Contemporary Italy: society and politics, 1943–1988* (1990), and also his *Italy and its Discontents: family, civil society, state, 1980–2001* (2001). S. Tarrow, *Democracy and Disorder: protest and politics in Italy, 1965–75* (1989), and in the short Oxford History series see P. McCarthy, *Italy since 1945* (2000) with a current bibliography. See also J. Dunnage, *Twentieth Century Italy: a social history* (2003) and the latter sections of N. Carter, *Modern Italy in Historical Perspective* (2004).

Among other countries, Spain provides an interesting barometer of the spread of democracy in Western Europe: see R. Carr, *A History of Spain, 1808–1980* (rev. edn, 1980), R. Carr and J. P. Fusi, *Spain: dictatorship to democracy* (1979), D. Gilmour, *The Transformation of Spain* (1985) and P. Preston, *The Triumph of Democracy in Spain* (1986). For Greece see D. H. Close, *Greece since 1945: politics, economy and society* (2002).

Decolonization

See M. E. Chamberlain, *Decolonisation* (2nd edn, 1990), R. Holland, *European Decolonization, 1918–1981: an introductory survey* (1985), H. Grimal, *Decolonisation: the British, French, Dutch and Belgian empires, 1919–1963* (1980), and W. Mommsen and J. Osterhammel, *Imperialism and After: continuities and discontinuities* (1986). For Africa see J. D. Hargreaves, *Decolonisation in Africa:* (1988), P. Gifford and W. R. Louis (eds), *The Transfer of Power in Africa: decolonisation, 1940–1960* (1982), and on the French experience in Africa A. Horne, *A Savage War of Peace: Algeria, 1954–1962* (1977) and D. S. White, *Black Africa and de Gaulle: from the French empire to independence* (1979). Asian independence is considered in H. Gelber, *Nations out of Empires: European nationalism and the transformation of Asia* (2001) and R. Jeffrey, *Asia: the winning of independence* (1981). For south-east Asia see J. Stockwell and N. Tarling (eds), *The Cambridge History of South East Asia, vol. 2* (1992), B. W. and L. Andaya, *A History of Malaysia* (2nd edn, 2001), A. Short, *The Communist Insurrection in Malaya, 1948–1960* (1975), H. Tinker, *Burma: the struggle for independence, 1944–48* (1983–4), A. Reid, *The Indonesian National Revolution, 1945–1950* (1974), A. Short, *The Origins of the Vietnam War* (1990), M. Shipway, *The Road to War: France and Vietnam, 1944–7* (1996), F. Logevall, *The Origins of the Vietnam War* (2001) and S. Karnow, *Vietnam: a history* (1994).

Specifically on Britain see J. Darwin, *The End of the British Empire* (1991) and *Britain and Decolonisation* (1988); also N. White, *Decolonisation: the British experience since 1945* (1999) and D. Kennedy, *Britain and Empire, 1880–1945* (2002). For the French experience of decolonisation see R. F. Betts, *France and*

Decolonisation, 1900–1960 (1991) and A. Clayton, *The Wars of French Decolonisation* (1994). F. Feredi, *Colonial Wars and the Politics of Third World Nationalism* (1994) and J. P. D. Dunbabin, *International Relations since 1945, Vol. II: the post-imperial age* (1994) put decolonization in international perspective. The domestic impact is considered in M. Kahler, *Decolonisation in Britain and France: the domestic consequences of international relations* (1984).

The movement for European unity

There are general introductions in D. W. Urwin, *The Community of Europe: a history of European integration since 1945* (1994), A. Blair, *The European Union since 1945* (2004), P. Thody, *An Historical Introduction to the European Union* (1997), M. Dedman, *The Origin and Development of the European Union, 1945–1995* (1996) and S. Henig, *The Uniting of Europe: from discord to concord* (1997). Also useful on the movement towards unity are M. Anderson, *States and Nationalism in Europe since 1945* (2000) and A. Milward, *The European Rescue of the Nation State* (1999).

The fullest account of the early years of the unity movement can be found in W. Lipgens, *A History of European Integration, 1945–7* (1982), though this is very detailed. J. W. Young, *Britain, France and the Unity of Europe, 1945–51* (1984) is shorter and more analytical, while on the early 1950s see E. Fursdon, *The European Defence Community* (1981), on the vain bid to create a 'European Army'. On the Common Market itself see R. Pryce, *The Politics of the European Community* (1973) and A. M. Williams, *The European Community* (1994).

American relations with the European unity movement are discussed by M. Beloff, *The United States and the Unity of Europe* (1963) and R. Manderson-Jones, *Special Relationship* (1972), while British relations are discussed in M. Camps, *Britain and the European Community, 1955–63* (1964) and U. Kitzinger, *Diplomacy and Persuasion* (1974).

For the development of the European Community in the 1970s see W. Feld, *The European Community in World Affairs* (1976), J. Fitzmaurice, *The European Parliament* (1978), and V. Herman and J. Lodge, *The European Parliament and the European Community* (1978).

Eastern Europe since 1945

There are introductions to Eastern European affairs in R. J. Crampton, *Eastern Europe in the Twentieth Century – and after* (1997), M. Pittaway, *Brief Histories: Eastern Europe, 1939–2000* (2002), G. Swain, *Eastern Europe since 1945* (3rd edn, 2003) and R. Bideleux and I. Jeffries, *A History of Eastern Europe: crisis and change* (1987). For the Balkans see R. J. Crampton, *The Balkans since the Second World War* (2002). The essential background can be found in J. L. H. Keep, *Last of the Empires: a history of the Soviet Union, 1945–1991* (1996) and P. G. Lewis, *Central Europe since 1945* (1994); also F. Fejto, *A History of the People's*

Democracies (1971), R. Okey, *Eastern Europe, 1740–1985* (2nd edn, 1986), and H. Seton-Watson, *The East European Revolution* (1985). On the early background to postwar Eastern Europe see M. McCauley (ed.), *Communist Power in Europe, 1944–49* (1977), and on the general decay of Soviet influence see G. Ionescu, *The Break-up of the Soviet Empire in Eastern Europe* (1965), Z. Brezezinski, *The Soviet Bloc* (1974), L. Labedz (ed.), *Revisionism* (1962) and H. Seton-Watson, *Nationalism and Communism, Essays, 1946–63* (1964): the impact of Gorbachev is considered in K. Dawisha, *Eastern Europe, Gorbachev and Reform: the great challenge* (1988).

For individual countries see M. Fulbrook, *Anatomy of a Dictatorship: inside the GDR, 1949–1989* (1995), M. McCauley, *The German Democratic Republic* (1983), M. Fulbrook's collection *Twentieth Century Germany: politics, culture, and society, 1918–1990* (2001), Pt II, which has synoptic essays on both East Germany and unification, L. Kattenacker, *Germany since 1945* (1997), I. Derbyshire, *Politics in Germany from Division to Unification* (1991), D. Childs, *The Fall of the GDR: Germany's road to unity* (2001) and K. H. Jarausch, *The Rush to German Unity* (1994).

C. Ross, *The East German Dictatorship: problems and perspectives of the GDR* (2002), J. Madarasz, *Conflict and Compromise in East Germany, 1971–1989* (2003) and P. O'Dochartaigh, *Germany since 1945* (2003) are further recent treatments. There are also valuable studies available in D. Childs (ed.), *Honecker's Germany* (1985), and *The GDR, Moscow's German Ally* (1983), J. P. Nettl, *The Eastern Zone and Soviet Policy in Germany, 1945–50* (1951), and J. Stele, *Socialism with a German Face* (1977). On Yugoslavia see D. Rusinow, *Yugoslav Experiment, 1948–1974* (1977), P. Auty, *Tito* (1974) and, more generally, F. Singleton, *Twentieth Century Yugoslavia* (1976). On Hungary see G. Litvan, *The Hungarian Revolution of 1956* (1996), F. Vali, *Rift and Revolt in Hungary* (1961), and M. Molnar, *Budapest 1956: a history of the Hungarian Revolution* (1971). On Czechoslovakia see V. V. Kusin, *Intellectual Origins of the Prague Spring* (1971), G. Golan, *Reform Rule in Czechoslovakia* (1973) and H. G. Skilling, *Czechoslovakia: the interrupted revolution* (1976). For Poland see generally R. F. Leslie (ed.), *A History of Poland since 1863* (1983), N. Bethell, *Gomulka* (1969), N. Ascherson, *The Polish August* (1981), and T. Garton Ash, *Polish Revolution: Solidarity 1980–82* (1983). A. Prazmowska, *A History of Poland* (2004) brings the picture up to date.

The collapse of communism is discussed in R. Okey, *The Demise of Communist Eastern Europe: 1989 in Context* (2004), while on Yugoslavia see V. Meier, *Yugoslavia: a history of its demise* (1999); see also G. Stokes, *The Walls Came Tumbling Down* (1993), A. Heller and F. Feher, *From Yalta to Glasnost: the dismantling of Stalin's empire* (1990), and D. Selbourne, *Death of the Dark Hero: Eastern Europe, 1987–9* (1990). G. Prins (ed.), *Spring in Winter: the 1989 revolutions* (1990), M. Frankland, *The Patriot's Revolution: how Eastern Europe won its freedom* (1990) and M. Glenny, *The Rebirth of History* (1990) are all freshly drawn views of the momentous events of 1989. An analysis of Russian developments can be found in H. Smith, *The New Russians* (1990), M. Galeotti, *The Age of Anxiety: society and politics in Soviet and post-Soviet Russia* (1995), and G. Smith (ed.), *Nationalities of the Former Soviet Union* (1995). See also P. Desai, *Perestroika in Perspective: the design and dilemmas of Soviet reform* (1989), S. Kull, *Burying Lenin: the revolution in Soviet ideology and foreign policy* (1992) and R. Sakwa, *Gorbachev and his Reforms, 1985–1990* (1991).

First-hand information is available now in M. Gorbachev, *Memoirs* (1997) and slightly greater distance from the events has sustained more considered accounts, such as R. K. Daniels, *Russia's Transformation: snapshots of a crumbling system* (1998), M. Galeotti, *Gorbachev and his Revolution* (1997) and M. McCauley, *Gorbachev* (1998). G. W. Breslauer, *Gorbachev and Yeltsin as Leaders* (2002), D. Marples, *The Collapse of the Soviet Union* (2004) and J. Smith, *The Fall of Soviet Communism, 1986–1991* (2004) span the transition from Soviet rule to break-up. The longer-term factors affecting the collapse of the Soviet regime are considered in G. Roberts, *The Soviet Union in World Politics* (1998), R. Sakwa, *Soviet Politics in Perspective* (1998), P. Hanson, *The Rise and Fall of the Soviet Economy, 1945–1991* (2002) and M. Beissinger, *National Mobilisation and the Collapse of the Soviet State* (2002).

THE MIDDLE EAST

For introductory reading on the Middle East see R. Ovendale, *The Longman Companion to the Middle East* (2nd edn, 1998), B. Lewis, *The Shaping of the Modern Middle East* (1994), M. E. Yapp, *The Near East since the First World War* (2nd edn, 1996), I. Asad and R. Owen, *The Middle East* (1983), A. Hourani, *The Emergence of the Modern Middle East* (1980), S. N. Fisher, *The Middle East: a history* (1979), G. Lenczowski, *The Middle East in World Affairs* (4th edn, 1980), N. Bethell, *The Palestine Triangle* (1979), A. Goldschmidt, *A Concise History of the Middle East* (1979), P. Mansfield, *The Arabs* (1976) and W. R. Polk, *The Arab World* (1980). The broad sweep of Middle Eastern history is considered in the latter part of G. E. Perry, *The Middle East, Fourteen Islamic Centuries* (1983). Particular themes can be explored through M. Halpern, *The Politics of Social Change in the Middle East* (1963) and P. Mansfield, *The Middle East: a political and economic survey* (4th edn, 1973); B. Schwodran, *The Middle East, Oil and the Great Powers* (1973) and Y. Porath, *In Search of Arab Unity, 1930–1945* (1986). T. G. Fraser, *The Middle East, 1914–1979* (1980) is a helpful collection of documents. On other themes see Y. Sayigh and A. Shlaim (eds), *The Cold War and the Middle East* (1997), F. Venn, *The Oil Crisis* (2002). B. Milton-Edwards, *Islamic Fundamentalism Since 1945* (2004) and Z. M. Badawi, *Jihad: from Qu'ran to Bin Laden* (2004).

The Turkish revolution

S. J. and E. K. Shaw, *History of the Ottoman Empire and Modern Turkey, vol. II* (1977), W. Yale, *The Near East: a modern history* (1958) and B. Lewis, *The Emergence of Modern Turkey* (1973) are good starting points. For Kemal Atatürk see Lord Kinross, *Ataturk – the rebirth of a nation* (1964), while contemporary accounts of relations between Greece and Turkey can be found in A. Toynbee, *The Western Question in Greece and Turkey* (1922) and H. Edils, *The Turkish Ordeal* (1928).

The mandates in Iraq, Syria and Lebanon

Initially see J. C. Hurewitz, *The Middle East and North Africa in World Politics: Vol. II* (1979). E. Munroe, *Britain's Moment in the Middle East, 1914–1971* (2nd edn, 1980) is a classic account of British involvement; see also P. Mansfield, *The Ottoman Empire and its Successors* (1973). On Iraq see T. A. J. Abdullah, *A Short History of Modern Iraq* (2003), Sir A. T. Wilson, *Mesopotamia 1917–20, a clash of loyalties* (1931), S. H. Longrigg, *Iraq, 1900 to 1950* (1953) and P. Marr, *The Modern History of Iraq* (1985). For Syria and Lebanon see A. H. Hourani, *Syria and Lebanon* (1946), S. H. Longrigg, *Syria and Lebanon under French Mandate* (1958), N. A. Ziadeh, *Syria and Lebanon* (1957).

Egypt

General accounts can be found in P. J. Vatikiotis, *The History of Egypt from Muhammad Ali to Sadat* (2nd edn, 1980), J. Berque, *Egypt: imperialism and revolution* (1972), A. Sattin, *Lifting the Veil: the British in Egypt, 1800–1956* (1988) and J. C. B. Richmond, *Egypt, 1798–1952* (1977). For the early period see Monroe, *Britain's Moment*, Lord Lloyd, *Egypt Since Cromer* (1933–4), J. Darwin, *Britain, Egypt and the Middle East: imperial policy in the aftermath of war, 1918–22* (1980), Mahmud Zayid, *Egypt's Struggle for Independence* (1965), and A. Hourani, *Arabic Thought in the Liberal Age, 1789–1939* (1962). For the post-1945 period see S. K. Aburish, *Nasser* (2005), R. Stephens, *Nasser: a political biography* (1971), R. Ovendale, *The Origins of the Arab–Israeli Wars* (1984), R. Mabro, *The Egyptian Economy: 1952–1972* (1974) and I. Beeson, *Sadat* (1981). On the Suez crisis see W. Roger Louis and R. Owen (eds), *Suez 1956: the crisis and its consequences* (1989). An important view of social change is contained in J. Neinin and Z. Lockman, *Workers on the Nile: nationalism, communism, Islam and the Egyptian working class, 1881–1954* (1988).

The creation of Israel and the Arab–Israeli conflict

A helpful introduction is T. G. Fraser, *The Arab–Israeli Conflict* (2nd edn, 2004), as is C. D. Smith, *Palestine and the Arab – Israeli Conflicts: a history with documents* (2004). J. C. Hurewitz, *The Middle East and North Africa in World Politics: Vol. II* (1979), Monroe, *Britain's Moment*, W. R. Louis, *The British Empire in the Middle East, 1945–1951* (1984) (see above) and N. Bethell, *The Palestine Triangle* (1979) are essential works. Some useful first-hand evidence can be found in R. Storrs, *Orientations* (1937), R. H. S. Crossman, *Palestine Mission: a personal record* (1947) and M. Begin, *The Revolt* (1951). The history of the Zionist movement is covered in the three volumes by D. Vital, *The Origins of Zionism* (1980), *Zionism: the formative years* (1982) and *Zionism: the crucial phase* (1987). On the origins see L. Stein, *The Balfour Declaration* (1961) while H. W. Sachar, *History of Israel: from the rise of Zionism to our time* (1985) and *From the Aftermath of the Yom Kippur War* (1989) is a comprehensive history of Israel. M. J. Cohen, *Palestine: retreat from the mandate: the making of British policy, 1936–45* (1989) and *Palestine and the Great Powers, 1945–1948* (1982) deal in detail with the British period. G. Antonius, *The Arab Awakening* (1938) and R. Ovendale, *The Origins of the Arab Israeli Wars* (1984) examine the growth of conflict; see also E. W. Said, *The Question of Palestine* (1980). A. Shlaim, *Collusion Across the Jordan: King Abdullah, the Zionist movement and the partition of Palestine* (1988) and I. Pappe, *Britain and the Arab–Israeli Conflict, 1948–51* (1988) discuss the early years, while the American involvement is considered in Z. Ganin, *Truman, American Jewry and Israel, 1945–1948* (1979). Cohen's work (see above) has received a fresh format as M. J. Cohen's *Palestine to Israel: from mandate to Independence* (1988). On the later years of the Israeli state see A. Sella and

Y. Yishai (eds), *Israel: the peaceful belligerent, 1967–79* (1986). On the Palestinians see Y. Sayigh, *Armed Struggle and the Search for State: the Palestinian National Movement, 1949–1993* (1997).

Arab nationalism and the Islamic revolution

Y. Porath, *In Search of Arab Unity, 1930–1945* (1986) discusses the attempt to weld the Arab world into a larger whole. The important non-Arab power of great influence since the 1960s is considered in H. Amirsedeglu and R. W. Ferrier, *Twentieth Century Iran* (1977) and N. R. Keddie, *Roots of Revolution: an interpretative history of modern Iran* (1981), while the Islamic dimension is examined in S. A. Arjomand, *The Turban for the Crown: the Islamic revolution in Iran* (1988). P. Marr, *The Modern History of Iraq* (1985), D. Hopwood, *Syria, 1945–1986: politics and society* (1988), and U. Dann, *King Hussein and the Challenge of Arab Radicalism: Jordan, 1955–1967* (1989) examine other states since 1945. M. Shemesh, *The Palestinian Entity, 1959–1974* (1988) and H. Cobban, *The Making of Modern Lebanon* (1985) examine two major sources of conflict. R. B. Betts, *The Druze* (1988) examines one of the major factions in the Lebanese conflict. On the Iraq–Iran war see D. Hiro, *The Longest War: the Iran–Iraq conflict* (1989) and the modern respective histories of Iraq and Iran, T. A. J. Abdullah, *A Short History of Modern Iraq* (2003) and A. Ansari, *Modern – Iran since 1921: the Pahlevis and after* (2003). On Islamic funamentalism see B. Milton-Edwards, *Islamic Fundamentalism since 1945* (2004) and Z.M. Badawi, *Jihad: from Qu'ran to Bin Laden* (2004). The Palestinian dimension is discussed in Z. Schiff and E. Ya'ari, *Intifada* (1990) and Y. Sayigh, *Armed Struggle and the Search for a State: the Palestinian National Movement, 1949–1993* (1997).

AFRICA

There are useful introductions in P. Curtin, S. Feierman, L. Thompson and J. Vansina, *African History* (2nd edn, 1995), J. D. Fage, *A History of Africa* (1995), F. Cooper, *Africa since 1940: the past of the present* (2002), P. Nugent, *Africa since Independence: a comparative history* (2004), M. Crowder and R. A. Oliver, *The Cambridge Encyclopedia of Africa* (1990), M. Crowder (ed.), *The Cambridge History of Africa, Vol. viii: 1940–75* (1984), J. Iliffe, *Africans: the history of a continent* (1995), P. J. M. McEwan and R. B. Sutcliffe (eds), *The Study of Africa* (1965), B. Freund, *The Making of Contemporary Africa* (1984), J. Hatch, *Africa Today and Tomorrow* (1965) and *Africa Emergent: Africa's problems since independence* (1974), B. Davidson, *Africa in Modern History* (1978), H. S. Wilson, *The Imperial Experience in Sub-Saharan Africa since 1870* (1977) and M. Crowder, *Historical Atlas of Africa* (1985).

For the colonial period and decolonization see J. D. Hargreaves, *Decolonization in Africa, 1945–64* (1988), L. H. Gann and P. Duignan (eds), *The History and Politics of Colonialism, 1870–1960* (4 vols, 1969–75), P. Gifford and W. R. Louis, *The Transfer of Power in Africa: decolonization, 1940–1960* (1982), P. Gifford and W. R. Louis, (eds), *Decolonization and African Independence* (1988), and W. H. Morris-Jones and G. Fischer, *Decolonization and After: the British and French experience* (1980). The post-colonial period is considered broadly in D. Fieldhouse, *Black Africa, 1945–1980* (1986), J. Jackson and C. Rosberg, *Political Rule in Black Africa* (1982), S. Decalo, *Coups and Army Rule in Africa* (1976), W. F. Gutteridge, *Military Regimes in Africa* (1975), G. Hunter, *The New Societies of Tropical Africa: a selective study* (1962), R. I. Rotberg and A. A. Mazrui (eds), *Protest and Power in Black Africa* (1970), P. C. Lloyd, *Africa in Social Change* (1971), A. A. Mazrui, *Political Values and the Educated Class in Africa* (1977), C. Rosberg and T. M. Callaghy, *Socialism in Sub-Saharan Africa* (1977), T. M. Shaw and K. A. Heard, *The Politics of Africa: dependence and development* (1979) and W. Tordoff, *Government and Politics in Africa* (1984).

External influences on Africa, other than from the colonial powers, are discussed in K. Somerville, *Foreign Military Intervention in Africa* (1990), J. Darwin, 'Africa in World Politics', in N. Woods (ed.), *Explaining International Relations since 1945* (1996), P. Duignan and L. H. Gann, *The United States and Africa: a history* (1984) and R. D. Mahoney, *JFK: ordeal in Africa* (1984). The issue of Pan-Africanism and African Nationalism is discussed in C. Legum, *Pan-Africanism* (1962) and I. Geiss, *Pan-Africanism* (1974); see also G. Padmore (ed.), *Colonial and Coloured Unity: history of the Pan-African Congress* (2nd edn, 1963) and T. L. Hodgkin, *Nationalism in Colonial Africa* (1956). Two important sets of documents are J. A. Langley, *Ideologies of Liberation in Black Africa, 1956–1970: documents on modern African political thought from colonial times to the present* (1979) and J. Minogue and J. Molloy, *African Aims and Attitudes: selected documents* (1974). Some reference data can be found in W. M. Hailey, *An African Survey* (rev. edn, 1956) and B. R. Mitchell, *International Historical Statistics: Africa and Asia* (1982).

Colonial policy

The phasing of African developments can be traced in M. E. Page (ed.), *Africa and the First World War* (1987), R. D. Pearce, *The Turning Point in Africa: British colonial policy, 1938–1948* (1982), A. Cohen, *British Policy in Changing Africa* (1959), L. H. Gann and P. Duignan, *African Proconsuls* (1978), J. M. Lee and M. Petter, *The Colonial Office, War and Development Policy* (1982) and S. Constantine, *The Making of British Colonial Development Policy, 1914–40* (1984). The effects of the Second World War are discussed in D. Killingray and R. Rathbone (eds), *Africa and the Second World War* (1986) and for the postwar period see Y. Baugura, *Britain and Commonwealth Africa* (1983), D. Fieldhouse, 'The Labour Governments and the Empire-Commonwealth', in R. Ovendale (ed.) *The Foreign Policy of the British Labour Governments, 1945–51* (1984), E. Mortimer, *France and the Africans, 1944–60* (1969), and G. Clarence-Smith, *The Third Portuguese Empire, 1825–1975* (1985).

North Africa

See J. Berque, *French North Africa: the Maghrib between two world wars* (1967), M. Bennoune, *The Making of Contemporary Algeria, 1830–1987* (1988), D. C. Gordon, *The Passing of French Algeria* (1966), P. Bourdieu, *The Algerians* (1962), E. O'Balance, *The Algerian Insurrection, 1954–62* (1967) and A. Horne, *A Savage War of Peace* (rev. edn, 1988). The essay in J. Dunn, *Modern Revolutions* (2nd edn, 1989) has an excellent analysis of the Algerian revolution, while F. Fanon, *Studies in a Dying Colonialism* (1955) and *The Wretched of the Earth* (1965) are two important studies of the causes of the Algerian revolt. For the post-revolutionary situation see S. Amin, *The Maghreb in the Modern World* (1970). On other parts of North Africa see W. D. Swearington, *Moroccan Mirages: agrarian dreams and deceptions, 1912–1986* (1988). A valuable recent study of North and West Africa is D. B. C. O'Brien and C. Coulou (eds) *Charisma and Brotherhood in African Islam* (1988).

West Africa

See J. F. Ajayi and M. Crowder, *A History of West Africa* (2nd edn, 1987), M. Crowder, *A History of West Africa: A.D. 1000 to Present* (1985) and his *West Africa under Colonial Rule* (1968), J. D. Hargreaves, *The End of Colonial Rule in West Africa: essays in contemporary history* (1979) and *West Africa Partitioned: Volume 2: the elephants and the grass* (1985), C. Harrison, *French Policy Towards Islam in West Africa, 1860–1960* (1988), S. Dunn, *West African States* (1978), and R. Schachter-Morgenthau, *Political Parties in French-Speaking West Africa* (1964); see also J. Suret-Canale, below.

Particular countries are discussed in M. Crowder, *Senegal: a study in French assimilation policy* (rev. edn, 1967), D. Austin, *Politics in Ghana, 1946–60* (1964), and C. L. R. James, *Nkrumah and the Ghana Revolution* (1977), J. Coleman, *Nigeria: Background to Nationalism* (1958), K. Ezera, *Constitutional Developments in Nigeria* (1960), K. W. J. Post and G. D. Jenkins, *The Price of Liberty: personality and politics in colonial Nigeria* (1973), B. Dudley, *An Introduction to Nigerian Government and Politics* (1982) and S. Egite Oyovbaire, *Federation in Nigeria: a study in the development of the Nigerian state* (1983). See also M. Crowder, *Nigeria: an introduction to its history* (1979) and *The Story of Nigeria* (4th edn, 1978).

Tropical and Equatorial Africa

See J. Suret-Canale, *French Colonialism in Tropical Africa, 1900–1945* (1971), C. Young, *Politics in the Congo, Decolonization and Independence* (1965), H. F. Weiss, *Political Protest in the Congo* (1967), R. Slade, *The Belgian Congo* (1960), R. Anstey, *King Leopold's Legacy: the Congo under Belgian rule, 1908–60* (1966), J. Gerard-Libois, *Katanga Secession* (1966) and R. Lemarchand, *Political Awakening in the Congo* (1964). M. Njeuma (ed.), *Introduction to the History of Cameroon* (1989), R. A. Joseph, *Radical Nationalism in Cameroon* (1977) and D. A. Low, *Buganda in Modern History* (1971) examine other states. J. Pottier, *Re-Imagining Rwanda: conflict, survival, and disinformation in the late 20th century* (2002) discusses the post-genocide regime.

East and Central Africa

For introduction see V. Harlow, E. M. Chilver and A. Smith (eds), *History of East Africa, Vol. II* (1965) and D. A. Low and A. Smith (eds), *Vol. III* (1976), J. Saul, *State and Revolution in East Africa* (1979) and K. Ingham, *A History of East Africa* (3rd edn, 1975). E. A. Brett, *Colonialism and Underdevelopment in East Africa* (1973) and P. H. Gulliver (ed.), *Tradition and Transition in East Africa* (2004) raise general issues. On Sudan see R. O. Collins and F. M. Deng (eds), *The British in the Sudan, 1898–1956*, (1984) and D. F. Gordon, *Decolonization and the State in Kenya* (1986); on Kenya. Kenya's Mau Mau movement is discussed in C. G. Rosberg and J. Nottingham, *The Myth of Mau Mau* (1966) and in W. R. Ochieng and K. K. Janmohamed (eds), *Some Perspectives on the Mau Mau Movement* (special edition of the *Kenya Historical Review*, Nairobi, 1977); see also on Kenya G. Wasserman, *Politics of Decolonization: Kenya Europeans and the land issue, 1960–1965* (1976), C. J. Gertzel, *The Politics of Independent Kenya, 1963–69* (1970) and D. Goldsworthy, *Tom Mboya* (1982). J. lliffe, *A Modern History of Tanganyika* (1979), C. Pratt, *The Critical Phase in Tanzania, 1945–1968: Nyerere and the emergence of a socialist strategy* (1976) and G. Hyden, *Beyond Ujaama in Tanzania* (1980) cover one of the other major East African states, while Uganda is examined in J. J. Jorgensen, *Uganda: a modern history* (1981) and G. A. Ginyera-Pincwa, *Apolo Milton Obote and His Times* (1977). A combined economic history of Kenya and Uganda is R. M. A. Van Zwanenberg and A. King, *An Economic History of Kenya and Uganda, 1800–1970* (1975). The Central African Federation is discussed in R. Gray, *The Two Nations* (1960) and P. Mason, *Year of Decision* (1960); see also A. J. Wills, *An Introduction to the History of Central Africa* (3rd edn, 1973), while the rise of opposition to white rule in the region is considered in R. Rotberg, *The Rise of Nationalism in Central Africa* (1965). R. Blake, *A History of Rhodesia* (1977) is a broad survey, but T. O. Ranger, *Peasant Consciousness and Guerrilla War in Zimbabwe* (1985), R. Hodder-Williams, *White Farmers in Rhodesia, 1890–1965* (1984) and R. Palmer, *Land and Racial Domination in Rhodesia* (1977) examine the rural situation, while the general economic background is discussed in I. Phimister, *An Economic and Social History of Zimbabwe, 1890–1948* (1988). For the white declaration of UDI and the subsequent war see M. Loney, *White Racism and Imperial Response* (1974) and D. Martin and P. Johnson, *The Struggle for Zimbabwe* (1981). Two useful groups of studies are C. Stoneman (ed.), *Zimbabwe's Inheritance* (1982) and G. Peele and T. O. Ranger (eds), *Past and Present in Zimbabwe* (1983). For Zambia see A. Roberts, *A History of Zambia* (1976), E. L. Bergen, *Labour, Race and Colonial Rule: the copperbelt from 1924 to independence* (1974), C. J. Gertzel *et al.*, *The Dynamics of the One-party State in Zambia* (1984), and W. Tordoff (ed.), *Administration in Zambia* (1980).

Southern Africa

For Angola see J. Marcum, *The Angolan Revolution, Vol. 1, 1950–62* (1969), B. Davidson, *In the Eye of the Storm: Angola's people* (1974) and G. J. Bender, *Angola under the Portuguese: the myth and the reality* (1978). The other Portuguese colony, Mozambique, is discussed in A. and B. Issacman, *Mozambique: from colonialism to revolution* (1983), E. Mondlane, *The Struggle for Mozambique* (1969), and T. W. Henriksen, *Revolution and Counter-Revolution: Mozambique's war of independence, 1964–74* (1983). For South Africa see M. Wilson and L. Thompson (eds), *The Oxford History of South Africa, Vol. II. 1870–1966* (1971) and T. R. H. Davenport, *South Africa: a modern history* (3rd edn, 1987). S. Dubow, *Racial Segregation and the Origins of Apartheid in South Africa, 1919–36* (1988) deals with the development of the character of the South African regime, while B. Davidson, J. Slovo and A. R. Wilkinson, *Southern Africa: the new politics of revolution* (1976) examines the movements and responses in the whole of southern Africa. T. G. Karis and G. Carter (eds), *From Protest to Challenge: a documentary history of African politics in South Africa, 1882–1964* (4 vols, 1972–7) provides source material. L. Marquand, *The Peoples and Policies of South Africa* (4th edn, 1969), G. Carter, *The Politics of Inequality: South Africa since 1948* (1958), J. Hoagland, *South Africa, Civilisations in Conflict* (1973) and T. D. Moodie, *The Rise of Afrikanerdom: power, apartheid and the Afrikaner civil religion* (1975) are all useful studies. The opposition to the dominant apartheid policy is considered in J. Robertson, *Liberalism in South Africa, 1948–1963* (1971), P. Walshe, *The Rise of African Nationalism in South Africa: the African National Congress, 1912–1952* (1970), H. Adam and H. Giliomee, *Ethnic Power Mobilized* (1979), T. Lodge, *Black Power in South Africa since 1945* (1983), and R. Harvey, *The Fall of Apartheid: the inside story from Smuts to Mbeki* (2nd edn, 2003). See also the overall appreciation of A. Guelke, *Rethinking Apartheid: South Africa in the twentieth century* (2004).

ASIA

The Indian subcontinent

The historiography is dominated by the theme of empire and decolonization, in spite of more than fifty years of independent politics for the new states of India, Pakistan and Sri Lanka. For imperial policy in general and decolonization see earlier (pp. 523–4), but specifically on India see G. M. Brown, *Modern India: the origins of an Asian democracy* (2nd edn, 1993), D. A. Low, *Eclipse of Empire* (1991), I. Copland, *India, 1885–1947: the unmaking of an empire* (2001), H. Kulke and D. Rothermund, *A History of India* (4th edn, 2004), P. Robb, *A History of India* (2002), A. Jalal and S. Bose, *Modern South Asia* (2nd edn, 2003), S. Wolpert, *A New History of India* (1977), P. Heehs, *India's Freedom Struggle, 1857–1947: a short history* (1988), W. T. De Bary, *The Sources of Indian Tradition* (1958), S. Sarkar, *Modern India, 1885–1947* (1988), R. J. Moore, *The Crisis of Indian Unity, 1917–1940* (1974), B. R. Tomlinson, *The Political Economy of the Raj, 1914–1947* (1979) and D. A. Low, *Congress and the Raj: facets of the Indian struggle* (1977). The role of Gandhi has received short introductory treatment in A. Copley, *Gandhi* (1987), but much more substantially in J. M. Brown, *Gandhi: prisoner of hope* (1989), while M. K. Gandhi, *Autobiography* (1966) is an important source. P. Moon, *Gandhi and the Making of Modern India* (1968) and D. Arnold, *Gandhi* (2001) are also available.

The early phase in the movement for independence is considered in P. G. Robb, *The Government of India and Reform: policies towards politics and constitution, 1916–1921* (1976), S. R. Mehrotra, *India and the Commonwealth, 1885–1929* (1965) and Gandhi's role in J. M. Brown, *Gandhi's Rise to Power: Indian politics, 1915–1922* (1972) and J. M. Brown, *Gandhi and Civil Disobedience: the Mahatma in Indian politics, 1928–1934* (1977). The growing power of the Congress in the localities is considered in C. A. Bayly, *The Local Roots of Indian Politics: Allahabad, 1880–1920* (1975), C. J. Baker, *The Politics of South India, 1920–1937* (1974), while specifically Muslim nationalism is considered in P. Hardy, *The Muslims of British India* (1972), whose leader, Jinnah, is examined in S. Wolpert, *Jinnah of Pakistan* (1984) and A. Jalal, *The Sole Spokesman: Jinnah, the Muslim League and the demand for Pakistan* (1985); see also I. Talbot, *Provincial Politics and the Pakistan Movement, 1937–47* (1989). The run-up to Partition is in F. G. Hutchins, *India's Revolution: Gandhi and the Quit India Movement* (1973), B. N. Pandey, *The Break-Up of British India* (1969), R. J. Moore, *Churchill, Cripps and India, 1939–1945* (1979) and *Escape from Empire: the Attlee government and the Indian problem* (1983), H. V. Hodson, *The Great Divide: Britain–India–Pakistan* (1969) and C. H. Philips and D. Wainwright, *Partition of India: politics and perspectives, 1935–1947* (1970). Mountbatten's role is discussed in P. Ziegler, *Mountbatten* (1987). Post-partition India is discussed in B. Zachariah, *Nehru* (2004), S. Gopal, *Jawaharlal Nehru* (1970), M. Brecher, *Nehru: a political biography* (1959) and M. Edwardes, *Nehru: a political biography* (1971). See

P. J. Nehru's *Glimpses of World History* (1989) and, on the earlier phase of the independence movement, his *An Autobiography* (1942). Indira Gandhi has been the subject of a recent biography, I. Malhotra, *Indira Gandhi: a personal and political biography* (1989). India's relations with other states after 1947 are considered in C. Heimsath and S. Mansingh, *A Diplomatic History of Modern India* (1971), W. J. Barnds, *India, Pakistan and the Great Powers* (1972) and A. Stein, *India and the Soviet Union: the Nehru era* (1969). India's agricultural development is considered in B. M. Bhatia, *Famine in India, 1860–1965* (2nd edn, 1967) and F. R. Frankel, *India's Green Revolution: economic gains and costs* (1971).

On the background to the emergence of Pakistan see the works cited above on Jinnah; see also the essay on Jinnah in H. Tinker, *Men who Overturned Empires: fighters, dreamers and schemers* (1987) and K. B. Sayeed, *Pakistan: the formative phase, 1857–1948* (rev. edn, 1968). Pakistan's development is considered in L. Binder, *Religion and Politics in Pakistan* (1963) and E. I. Rosenthal, *Islam in the Modern National State* (1965); see also the essay by Halliday in F. Halliday and H. Alavi (eds), *State and Ideology in the Middle East and Pakistan* (1988). The break-up of Pakistan and the emergence of Bangladesh is considered in K. Siddiqui, *Conflict, Crisis and War in Pakistan* (1972), R. Jahan, *Pakistan: failure in national integration* (1972) and W. Wilcox, *The Emergence of Bangladesh* (1973). Pakistan's foreign policy is examined in S. M. Burke, *Pakistan's Foreign Policy: an historical analysis* (1973). The Bhutto years are considered in S. J. Burki, *Pakistan under Bhutto, 1971–1977* (2nd edn, 1988). On Sri Lanka see S. Arasaratnam, *Ceylon* (1964) and A. J. Wilson, *Politics in Sri Lanka, 1947–1979* (2nd edn, 1979).

South-east Asia

N. Tarling (ed.), *The Cambridge History of South-East Asia, Vol. 2* (1992), D. G. Hall, *A History of South-East Asia* (4th edn, 1981), J. F. Cady, *The History of Post-War Southeast Asia* (1974) are useful introductions; see also D. J. Steinberg, *In Search of South-East Asia: a modern history* (1971), J. M. Phivier, *South-East Asia from Colonialism to Independence* (1974).

The histories of individual south-east Asian countries are considered in S. Karnow, *Vietnam: a history* (1994), J. F. Cady, *A History of Modern Burma* (1968) and D. E. Smith, *Religion and Politics in Burma* (1965), see also F. R. Von der Mehden, *Religion and Nationalism in Southeast Asia: Burma, Indonesia, the Philippines* (1963) and D. K. Wyatt, *The Politics of Reform in Thailand: education in the reign of King Chulalongkorn* (1969).

The Indonesian nationalist movement is considered in G. M. Kahin, *Nationalism and Revolution in Indonesia* (1953), B. Dahm, *History of Indonesia in the Twentieth Century* (1971) and *Sukarno and the Struggle for Indonesian Independence* (1969); see also J. D. Legge, *Indonesia* (1964). H. J. Benda, *The Crescent and the Rising Sun: Indonesian Islam under the Japanese occupation, 1942–1945* (1958), L. H. Palmier, *Indonesia and the Dutch* (1962) and M. Ricklefs, *A History of Modern Indonesia* (1981) are helpful studies. The role of Sukarno is considered in the essay in H. Tinker, *Men who Overturned Empires: fighters, dreamers and schemers* (1987) and J. D. Legge, *Sukarno: a political biography* (1972). The communist role in Indonesia is discussed in L. Palmier, *Communists in Indonesia: power pursued in vain* (1973), A. Brackman, *Indonesian Communism* (1963), and R. T. McVey (ed.), *Indonesia* (1963). The army's role is considered in H. Crouch, *The Army and Politics in Indonesia* (1978). R. E. Elson, *Suharto: a political biography* (2002) deals with the strong man who followed Sukarno.

On Malaya see A. Milner, *The Invention of Politics in Colonial Malaya* (2001), J. G. Butcher, *The British in Malaya, 1880–1941* (1979), T. N. Harper, *The End of Empire and the Making of Malaya* (2001) and M. Jones, *Conflict and Confrontation in South East Asia, 1961–1965: Britain, the United States, Indonesia, and the creation of Malaysia* (2001). Malayan independence receives some attention in R. Jeffrey, *Asia: the winning of independence* (1981), but see B. W. Andaya and L. Y. Andaya, *A History of Malaysia* (2nd edn, 2001) for a more substantial account. The communist attempt at a seizure of power is considered in A. Short, *The Communist Insurrection in Malaya, 1948–1960* (1975); see also J. M. Gullick, *Malaysia* (1969), W. R. Roff, *The Origins of Malay Nationalism* (1967), M. E. Osborne, *Region of Revolt: focus on Southeast Asia* (1971) and A. C. Brackman, *South-East Asia's Second Front: the power struggle in the Malay archipelago* (1966).

For the Philippines see T. A. Agoncillo, *A Short History of the Philippines* (1969), O. D. Corpuz, *The Philippines* (1965) and the essays in F. R. Von der Mehden, *Religion and Nationalism in Southeast Asia: Burma, Indonesia, the Philippines* (1963) and M. E. Osborne, *Region of Revolt: focus on Southeast Asia* (1971). See also A. Jorgenson-Dahl, *Regional Organisation and Order in South-East Asia* (1982).

Indochina, and especially Vietnam, has attracted huge attention. For the earlier part of its history see D. G. Marr, *Vietnamese Anti-Colonialism, 1885–1925* (1971), M. E. Osborne, *The French Presence in Cochin China and Cambodia* (1969), W. J. Duiker *The Rise of Nationalism in Vietnam, 1900–1941* (1976) and E. J. Hammer, *The Struggle for Indochina, 1940–55* (1966). J. Buttinger, *Vietnam: a dragon embattled: Vol. I, From Colonialism to the Vietminh; Vol. II, Vietnam at War* (1967) is a major narrative history, while R. B. Smith, *An International History of the Vietnam War: Vol. I, Revolution versus Containment; Vol. II, The Struggle for South East Asia, 1961–65* (1983–5) are the first two volumes of four placing the war in an international context; for a crucial episode, see J. Cable, *The Geneva Conference of 1954 on Indochina* (1986). A. Short, *The Origins of the Vietnam War* (1989) is a useful modern summary. See also the chapter in J. Dunn, *Modern Revolutions* (2nd edn, 1988). F. Logevall, *The Origins of the Vietnam War* (2001) and M. Hall, *The Vietnam War* (1999) are two short complementary studies with documents; see also K. Ruane, *War and Revolution in Vietnam* (1998), D. L. Anderson, *The Vietnam War* (2004) and G. Kolko, *Vietnam: anatomy of a peace* (1997). S. C. Tucker, *Vietnam* (1991) and M. J. Gilbert, *Why the North Won the Vietnam War* (2002) predominantly examine the military aspects, while G. J. De Groot, *A Noble Cause? America and the Vietnam War* (1999) examines the war from the American perspective. The dynamics of the communist insurrection are discussed in R. Smith, *Vietnam and the West* (1968), P. J. Honey, *Genesis of Tragedy: the historical background to the Vietnam War* (1968), J. M. McAlister, *Vietnam: the origins of revolution* (1969), and D. J. Duncanson, *Government and Revolution in Vietnam* (1968). The peasant origins of the war against the colonial powers is exemplified in J. Race, *War Comes to Long An: revolutionary conflict in a Vietnamese province* (1972). For Ho Chi-minh see J. Lacouture, *Ho Chi-minh: a political biography* (1968) and H. Tinker, *Men who Overturned Empires: Fighters, Dreamers and Schemers* (1987). North Vietnam's relations with other powers are considered in P. J. Honey, *Communism in North Vietnam: its role in the Sino-Soviet Dispute* (1963) and I. V. Gaiduck, *The Soviet Union and the Vietnam War* (1996). On Cambodia see M. Leifer, *Cambodia: the search for security* (1967), W. G. Burchett, *The China–Cambodia–Vietnam Triangle* (1981) and B. Kiernan, *The Pol Pot Regime: race, power and genocide in Cambodia under the Khmer Rouge* (1996).

Central Asia

M. McCauley, *Afghanistan and Central Asia* (2002) deals both with the history of Afghanistan and the former Soviet Central Asian Republics before and after the break-up of the Soviet Union. M. Ewans, *Afghanistan – a new history* (2nd edn, 2002) concentrates on the recent history of the country, as do W. Maley, *The Afghanistan Wars* (2002) and N. Nojumi, *The Rise of the Taliban in Afghanistan* (2002).

China

A general background exists in B. Elleman and S. Paine, *Modern China, 1644–2000* (2004) and on the twentieth century E. Moise, *Modern China, a History* (2nd edn, 1994). For the substantial multi-volume history of the modern era see J. K. Fairbank and A. Feuerwerker (eds), *The Cambridge History of China, Vols 12 and 13: Republican China* (1983, 1986) with an abridged edition by L. Eastman, *The Nationalist Era in China, 1927–49* (1991), and on the Communist era, vols 14 and 15 (below). A more general treatment can be found in J. K. Fairbank, *China: a new history* (1998) and his *The Great Chinese Revolution, 1800–1985* (1988). See also A. Lawrence, *China under Communism* (1998) and L. Benson, *China since 1949* (2002) for introductions to the communist era. For more detailed studies, L. Bianco, *Origins of the Chinese Revolution, 1915–49* (1972), C. P. Fitzgerald, *The Birth of Communist China* (1964), J. E. Shendan, *China in Disintegration: the republic era in Chinese history, 1912–1949* (1976) and J. Chesnaux, C. Barbier and M. C. Bergere, *China from the 1911 Revolution to Liberation* (1978) deal with the pre-communist regime. J. Chesnaux, *Peasant*

Revolts in China, 1840–1949 (1973) and C. A. Johnson, *Peasant Nationalism and Communist Power: the emergence of revolutionary China, 1937–1945* (1962) look at the dynamics of peasant protests; see also R. H. Myers, *The Chinese Peasant Economy: agricultural development in Hopei and Shantung, 1890–1949* (1970). Chow Tse-tung, *The May Fourth Movement: intellectual revolution in modern China* (1960) looks at the earlier reform movement, and H. Z. Schiffrin, *Sun Yat-sen and the Origins of the Chinese Revolution* (1970) and C. M. Wilbur, *Sun Yat-sen: frustrated patriot* (1976) discuss its most famous leader. See also on the origins of the communists J. Chesnaux, *The Chinese Labor Movement, 1919–27* (1968) and A. Dirlik, *The Origins of the Communist Party of China* (1989). The ideologies contending for power in China are considered in J. B. Grieder, *Hu Shih and the Chinese Renaissance: liberalism in the Chinese Revolution, 1917–37* (1970) and M. Meisner, *Li Ta-chao and the Origins of Chinese Marxism* (1967). The standard works on communist China are R. MacFarquar and J. K. Fairbank (eds), *The Cambridge History of China, Vol. 14: The People's Republic: the emergence of Revolutionary China, 1949–65* (1987); *Vol. 15: Revolutions within the Chinese Revolution, 1966–82* (1991; abridged and ed. R. MacFarquar as *The Politics of China: the eras of Mao and Deng*, 2nd edn, 1997) and J. Guillermaz, *The Chinese Communist Party in Power* (1976). For Mao see S. R. Schram, *Mao Tse-tung* (1966) and *The Political Thought of Mao Tse-tung* (1969), B. J. Schwartz, *Chinese Communism and the Rise of Mao* (1967), H. H. Salisbury, *The Long March* (1985), P. Carter, *Mao* (1976), S. Uhalley, *Mao Tse-tung: a critical biography* (1975), H. Suyin, *Wind in the Tower: Mao Tse-tung and Chinese revolution, 1949–1975* (1976), and L. W. Pye, *Mao Tse-tung: the man in the leader* (1976). W. Hinton, *Fanshen: a documentary of revolution in a Chinese village* (2nd edn, 1972), J. Chen, *A Year in Upper Felicity: life in a Chinese village during the Cultural Revolution* (1973) and Ch'ing K'un Yang, *A Chinese Village in early Communist Transition* (1959) are good studies 'on the ground' of village life at different phases after the revolution. A. Eckstein, *China's Economic Revolution* (1977), N. R. Chen and W. Galenson, *The Chinese Economy under Communism* (1969) and D. H. Perkins (ed.), *China's Economy in Historical Perspective* (1975) examine the economy, while the workings of the regime are considered in D. J. Waller, *The Government and Politics of Communist China* (1973) and J. Domes, *The Internal Politics of China, 1949–72* (1973). The People's Army is considered in J. Gittings, *The Role of the Chinese Army* (1967), while J. W. Lewis, *Party leadership and Revolutionary Power in China* (1970) and J. M. H. Lindbeck (ed.), *China: management of a revolutionary society* (1971) give some insight into the dynamics of party leadership. J. Myrdal and G. Kessle, *China: the revolution continued* (1971) give some insight into the cultural revolution. For China's foreign relations see M. B. Jansen, *Japan and China: from war to peace, 1894–1972* (1975), W. Gungwu, *China and the World since 1949* (1977), and J. Gittings, *The World and China, 1922–1972* (1974). Russia's relationship with China is examined in O. E. Clubb, *China and Russia: the 'Great Game'* (1971), W. E. Griffith, *The Sino-Soviet Rift* (1964), D. Zagoria, *The Sino-Soviet Conflict,*

1956–61 (1961) and D. Floyd, *Mao against Khrushchev: a short history of the Sino-Soviet conflict* (1964). For relations with the United States see J. K. Fairbank, *The United States and China* (1971). The impact of the Korean involvement is discussed in A. L. George, *The Chinese Communist Army in Action: the Korean War and its aftermath* (1967) and see also P. Van Ness, *Revolution and Chinese Foreign Policy: Peking's support for wars of national liberation* (1970). On Chinese involvement with its southern neighbours see W. G. Burchett, *The China–Cambodia–Vietnam Triangle* (1981).

Japan

There is a good modern survey in J. E. Hunter, *The Emergence of Modern Japan: an introductory history since 1853* (1989), but see also K. Pyle, *The Making of Modern Japan* (2nd edn, 1996), A. Waswo, *Modern Japanese Society, 1868–1994* (1996), E. Bruce Reynolds (ed.), *Japan in the Fascist Era* (2004), M. Schaller, *The American Occupation of Japan* (1985), D. Gary Allinson, *Japan's Postwar History* (1997), G. A. Gordon (ed.), *Postwar Japan as History* (1993) and P. Duus (ed.), *The Cambridge History of Japan, Vol. 6* (1988). On the economic history of modern Japan see G. C. Allen, *A Short Economic History of Japan, 1867–1937; with a supplementary chapter on economic recovery and expansion, 1945–1970* (3rd edn, 1972), W. W. Lockwood, (ed.), *The State and Economic Enterprise in Modern Japan* (1965) and on the earlier history *The Economic Development of Japan: growth and structural change, 1868–1938* (1954), B. K. Marshall, *Capitalism and Nationalism in Prewar Japan: the ideology of the business elite, 1868–1941* (1967) and J. W. Morley (cd.), *Dilemmas of Growth in Prewar Japan* (1971). A critical view of Japanese economic impact in Asia is contained in J. Halliday and G. McCormack, *Japanese Imperialism Today: 'Co-prosperity in Greater East Asia'* (1973). C. Nakane, *Japanese Society* (1970) has some useful themes; see also S. Watanabe, *The Peasant Soul of Japan* (1988), P. Lehmann, *The Roots of Modern Japan* (1982), and on the particular forms Japanese society took in the first half of this period see R. J. Smethurst, *A Social Basis for Prewar Japanese Militarism: the army and the rural community* (1974), T. C. Smith, *The Agrarian Origins of Modern Japan* (1959), T. R. H. Havens, *Farm and Nation in Modern Japan: agrarian nationalism, 1870–1940* (1974) and R. Storry *The Double Patriots: a study of Japanese Nationalism* (2nd edn, 1973). R. A. Scalapino, *Democracy and the Party Movement in Japan: the failure of the first attempt* (1953) examines political development. See also R. A. Scalapino and J. Masumi, *Parties and Politics in Contemporary Japan* (1962). Two recent studies examine the life of the emperor: E. Behr, *Hirohito* (1989) and E. P. Hoyt, *Hirohito* (1989).

Japanese foreign relations are examined in I. Nish, *Japanese Foreign Policy, 1860–1942* (1977) and M. B. Jansen, *Japan and China: from war to peace, 1894–1972* (1975). A. Iriye, *After Imperialism: the search for a new order in the Far East, 1921–1931* (1955) and *Across the Pacific: an inner history of American–East Asian Relations* (1967) and J. B. Crowley, *Japan's Quest for Autonomy, 1930–1938*

(1966) examine the interwar years. Japan's search for a secure area of economic control and its disastrous consequences are examined in F. C. Jones, *Japan's New Order in East Asia: its rise and fall, 1937–1945* (1954). D. Borg and S. Okamoto (eds), *Pearl Harbour as History: Japanese–American relations, 1931–41* (1973) examines the background to the pivotal event. The study by A. Iriye, *The Origins of the Second World War in Asia and the Pacific* (1987) now provides a good overview of the origins of the war. M. E. Weinstein, *Japan's Post-War Defence Policy, 1947–1968* (1971) examines the peaceful role of Japan in the postwar world, while E. O. Reischauer, *The United States and Japan* (3rd edn, 1965) and A. Iriye and W. I. Cohen (eds), *The United States and Japan in the Post-War World* (1989) deal with the postwar character of Japanese–American relations. K. Van Wolferen, *The Enigma of Japanese Power* (1989) poses some questions about Japan's role as an economic superpower with little military power.

Recent politics in Japan are discussed in G. Curtis, *The Japanese Way of Politics* (1988), J. A. A. Stockwin, *Japan: divided politics in a growth economy* (rev. edn, 1998), B. Eccleston, *State and Society in Postwar Japan* (1989) and K. Yamamura and Y. Yasuba (eds), *The Political Economy of Japan, Vol. 1: the domestic transformation* (1987). A discussion of the late twentieth-century Japanese economy can be found in T. Nakamura, *The Postwar Japanese Economy* (2nd edn, 1995).

AUSTRALASIA

C. Hartley Grattan, *The South-West Pacific since 1900* (1963) offers a comprehensive history of the region in the first half of the century which can be complemented by R. C. Thompson, *The Pacific Basin since 1945: an international history* (2001) which weaves the history of Australasia into Pacific history. On the Pacific islands see S. Roger Fischer, *A History of the Pacific Islands* (2002), W. P. Morrell, *The Great Powers in the Pacific* (1965) and M. R. Peattie, *Nanyo: the rise and fall of the Japanese in Micronesia, 1883–1945* (1988). For Australia itself see F. K. Crowley (ed.), *A New History of Australia* (1974), F. K. Crowley, *Modern Australia in Documents, 1901–1970* (2 vols, 1973) and R. Ward, *The History of Australia: The Twentieth Century, 1901–1975* (1978). Though somewhat older, G. Greenwood (ed.), *Australia: a social and political history* (1955) is still helpful, as on the early twentieth century are W. K. Hancock, *Australia* (1930) and W. F. Whyte, *William Morris Hughes: his life and times* (1956). R. Ward, *Australia* (1965) and D. Pike, *Australia: the quiet continent* (1962) are also helpful one-volume studies.

On interwar Australia see J. Mackinolty (ed.), *The Wasted Years: Australia's great depression* (1982), while the impact of the Second World War is discussed in P. Hasluck, *The Government and the People, 1942–1945* (1970). Postwar developments are considered in G. Bolton, *The Oxford History of Australia, Volume 5: 1942–1995: The Middle Way* (1996), D. Horner, *The Lucky Country: Australia in the sixties* (2nd edn, 1966) and J. D. B. Miller, *Australia* (1966). Australia's involvement in the region is considered in D. M. Horner, *High Command: Australia and Allied strategy, 1939–1945* (1983) and P. King (ed.), *Australia's Vietnam: Australia in the second Indo-China War* (1983).

For New Zealand see K. Sinclair, *A History of New Zealand* (rev. edn, 2000) and *A Destiny Apart: New Zealand's search for national identity* (1986), M. King, *The Penguin History of New Zealand* (2004) and J. Rowe and M. Rowe, *New Zealand* (1967). Also useful are W. H. Oliver, *The Story of New Zealand* (1960), W. P. Morrell and D. O. W. Hall, *A History of New Zealand Life* (1957) and H. G. Miller, *New Zealand* (1950). Particular aspects of New Zealand's history are considered in P. Baker, *King and Country Call: New Zealanders, Conscription and the Great War* (1989), J. B. Condliffe, *New Zealand in the Making* (2nd edn, 1959), mainly dealing with economic and social history, and his *The Welfare State in New Zealand* (1959). On the Second World War see F. L. W. Wood, *The New Zealand People at War* (1958).

THE AMERICAS

There are numerous histories of the United States, but amongst the most helpful introductions are H. Brogan, *The Penguin History of the United States* (2nd edn, 2001), J. Spiller, T. Clancey, S. Young and S. Mosley, *The United States, 1763–2001* (2004), P. Jenkins, *A History of the United States* (2nd edn, 2002), H. Zinn, *A People's History of the United States* (3rd edn, 2003), and M. A. Jones, *The Limits of Liberty: American history, 1607–1980* (1983). See also A. Nevins and H. S. Commager, *America: the story of a free people* (1976), S. E. Morrison, H. S. Commager and W. Leuchtenburg, *A Concise History of the American Republic* (1969) and Carl Degler, *Out of the Past* (3rd edn, 1984). For the twentieth century, R. Hofstadter, *The Age of Reform: Bryan to F. D. R.* (1955) covers the period from the end of the nineteenth century to the Second World War, while on the interwar years see W. E. Leuchtenburg, *The Perils of Prosperity* (1958) and *Franklin Roosevelt and the New Deal* (1963). For the period after the Second World War see A. L. Hamby, *The Imperial Years: the United States since 1939* (1976) and *Liberalism and its Challenges: F.D.R. to Bush* (2nd edn, 1992), W. H. Chafe, *The Unfinished Journey: America since World War II* (3rd edn, 1995), J. Patterson, *Great Expectations: the United States, 1945–1974* (1996), D. W. Grantham, *Recent America: the United States since 1945* (1987), W. Leuchtenburg, *In the Shadow of FDR: from Harry Truman to Ronald Reagan* (1983), R. V. Damms, *The Eisenhower Presidency, 1953–1961* (2002) and W. H. Chafe and R. Sitkoff (eds), *A History of Our Time* (1987).

On particular topics in North American history see C. Degler, *At Odds: women and the family in America from the revolution to the present* (1980), A. J. Badger, *The New Deal: the depression years, 1933–40* (1989) and A. L. Hamby, *The New Deal: analysis and interpretation* (2nd edn, 1981), K. Verney, *Black Civil Rights in America* (2000), B. Dierenfield, *The Civil Rights Movement* (2004), W. T. Martin, *The Civil Rights Movement: struggle and resistance* (2nd edn, 2003), C. Vann Woodward, *The Strange Career of Jim Crow* (3rd edn, 1974) on the history of racial segregation, and on the growth of the cities C. N. Glaab and A. T. Brown, *A History of Urban America* (1976); M. A. Jones, *American Immigration* (1960) deals with one of the major themes of the early years of twentieth-century America. H. Pelling, *American Labour* (1960) examines the organized working class, while for American social history in general see W. Issel, *Social Change in the United States, 1945–1983* (1985). The broad sweep of America's foreign relations is discussed in R. D. Schulzinger, *American Diplomacy in the Twentieth Century* (1984), S. Ambrose, *Rise to Globalism: American Foreign Policy, 1938–80* (2nd edn, 1981) and L. C. Gardner, *Covenant with Power: America and the world order from Wilson to Reagan* (1984). T. G. Fraser, *America and the World since 1945* (2002), M. McCauley, *Russia, America and the Cold War, 1949–1991* (3rd edn, 2004), J. P. Dunbabin, *The Cold War: the great powers and their allies* (1994) and G. J. De Groot, *A Noble Cause? America and the Vietnam War* (1999) deal with the postwar period.

For the West Indies and Caribbean region see S. Randall and G. Mount, *The Caribbean Basin: an international history* (1998), M. Chamberlain (ed.), *Caribbean Migration: globalized identities* (1998), J. H. Parry and P. M. Sherlock, *A Short History of the West Indies* (3rd edn, 1960) and J. R. Ward, *Poverty and Progress in the Caribbean, 1800–1960* (1985). On Latin America see T. H. Donghi, *The Contemporary History of Latin America* (1993), L. Bethell (ed.), *The Cambridge History of Latin America, Vols IV–VIII* (1984–6), E. Williamson, *The Penguin History of Latin America* (1992), T. Skidmore and P. Smith, *Modern Latin America* (2nd edn, 1989), J. Ward, *Latin America: development and conflict since 1945* (1997) and V. Bulmer-Thomas, *The Economic History of Latin America since Independence* (1994). Studies of some of the themes dominating Latin American history are P. Calvert, *Latin America: internal conflict and international peace* (1969), S. and B. Stein, *The Colonial Heritage of Latin America: essays on economic dependence in perspective* (1970) and C. Furtado, *Economic Development of Latin America: historical background and contemporary problems* (2nd end, 1976). The useful collection by E. P. Archetti, P. Cammack and B. Roberts (eds), *Latin America* (1987) surveys some major common elements in the history of the continent. Also useful are J. Cockcroft *et al.*, *Dependence and Underdevelopment: Latin America's political economy* (1972), I. L. Horowitz, *Radicalism in Latin America* (1969) and J. J. Johnson, *Latin America in Caricature* (1980).

Specific issues are considered in J. J. Johnson, *The Military and Society in Latin America* (1964) and A. Stepan, *The Military in Politics* (1971), W. S. Stokes, *Latin American Politics* (1959), J. L. Mecham, *Church and State in Latin America: a history of politico-ecclesiastical relations* (rev. edn, 1966), H. A. Landsberger (ed.) *The Church and Social Change in Latin America* (1970), F. C. Turner, *Catholicism and Political Development in Latin America* (1971), H. A. Landsberger (ed.), *Latin American Peasant Movements* (1969), A. Pearce, *The Latin American Peasant* (1975), L. E. Aguilar (ed.), *Marxism in Latin America* (1969) and J. Kohl and J. Litt, *Urban Guerrilla Warfare in Latin America* (1973). The relations of Latin America with its northern neighbour are the subject of S. P. Bemis, *The Latin American Policy of the United States: an historical interpretation* (1943), G. Connell-Smith, *The Inter-American System* (1966) and C. Blasier, *The Hovering Giant* (1976).

Among the most relevant histories of individual countries are J. Smith, *The History of Brazil* (2002) and R. M. Levine, *The History of Brazil* (2003), D. K. Lewis, *The History of Argentina* (2003) and D. Rock, *Argentina, 1516–1987* (1986), N. Hamilton, *The Limits of State Autonomy: postrevolutionary Mexico* (1982) and L. Bethell (ed.), *Mexico since Independence* (1991) and J. Dominguez, *Cuba: order and Revolution* (1978).

The Mexican revolution

For background see L. Bethell (ed.), *The Cambridge History of Latin America, Vol. VII* (1986) and *Mexico since Independence* (1991). The standard history is now A. Knight, *The Mexican Revolution* (1987). On the social and economic background see F. Chevalier, *Land and Society in Colonial Mexico: the great hacienda* (2nd edn, 1970) and P. Friedrich, *Agrarian Revolt in a Mexican Village* (2nd edn, 1970). J. Womack Jr, *Zapata and the Mexican Revolution* (1969). James D. Cockcroft, *Intellectual Precursors of the Mexican Revolution, 1900–13* (1968) and E. R. Wolf, *Peasant Wars of the Twentieth Century* (1969) provide context. The other personalities involved are examined in S. R. Ross, *F. I. Madero, Apostle of Mexican Democracy* (1955), C. Beals, *Porfirio Diaz: dictator of Mexico* (1932), and C. C. Cumberland, *Mexican Revolution: genesis under Madero* (1974). The effects of the Revolution are discussed in C. W. Reynolds, *The Mexican Economy: twentieth century structure and growth* (1970), F. Tannenbaum, *Peace by Revolution: Mexico after 1910* (2nd edn, 1966), H. F. Cline, *Mexico: revolution to evolution, 1940–1960* (1962), S. R. Ross, *Is the Mexican Revolution Dead?* (2nd edn, 1966), P. G. Casanova, *Democracy in Mexico* (2nd edn, 1970), F. Chevalier, 'The *Ejido* and Political Stability in Mexico', in Claudio Veliz (ed.), *The Politics of Conformity in Latin America* (1967), R. Carr, 'Mexican Agrarian Reform, 1910–60', in E. L. Jones and S. J. Woolf (eds), *Agrarian Change and Economic Development: the historical problems* (1969) and R. Vernon, *The Dilemma of Mexico's Development* (1963).

The United States and the First World War

See for introduction L. C. Gardner, *Imperial America: United States foreign policy since 1898* (1984) and F. R. Dulles, *America's Rise to World Power* (1955). A. S. Link, *Woodrow Wilson and the Progressive Era* (1954) is a multi-volume work, but a shorter treatment can be found in J. A. Thompson, *Woodrow Wilson* (2002) or R. H. Farrell, *Woodrow Wilson and World War I, 1917–1921* (1985). A. S. Link, *Wilson the Diplomatist: a look at his major foreign policies* (1957) summarizes his views and has been revised recently as *Woodrow Wilson: revolution, war and peace* (1979). Also available is A. S. Link, *Woodrow Wilson: a brief biography* (1963) and A. S. Link (ed.), *Woodrow Wilson and a Revolutionary World: 1913–1921* (1982). T. A. Bailey, *Wilson and the Lost Peace* (1944) is critical, while P. Birdsall, *Versailles Twenty Years After* (1941) is more sympathetic to the problems of peace-making. On the crucial rejection of the League by the Senate see also R. J. Bartlett, *The League to Enforce Peace* (1944) and T. A. Bailey, *Woodrow Wilson and the Great Betrayal* (1945). The effect of the war on American society is considered in D. M. Kennedy, *Over Here: the First World War and American society* (1980) and J. D. Keene, *The United States and the First World War* (2000) which also has some documents.

The Republican era

See A Brinkley, 'Prosperity, Depression and War, 1920–1945', in E. Foner (ed.), *The New American History* (1997), B. Noggle, *Into the Twenties: the United States from armistice to normalcy* (1974), J. D. Hicks, *Republican Ascendency: 1921–1933* (1960), F. Allen, *Only Yesterday: an informal history of the 1920s* (1931), A. M. Schlesinger, *The Crisis of the Old Order* (1957) and D. H. Burner, *The Politics of Provincialism: the Democrats in transition, 1918–1932* (1968). See also W. E. Leuchtenburg, *The Perils of Prosperity: 1914–32* (1958) and D. M. Smith, *The Great Departure: the United States and the search for a modern order: a history of the American people and their institutions, 1917–1933* (1979). The overall drift of foreign policy is considered in J. B. Duroselle, *From Wilson to Roosevelt: foreign policy of the United States* (1963).

Important social issues are considered in A. Sinclair, *Prohibition* (1962) and K. Allsopp, *The Bootleggers* (1967). The black migration from the south is considered in J. Hope Franklin, *From Slavery to Freedom: the history of American Negroes* (5th edn, 1980) and on particular cities see G. Osofsky, *Harlem: the making of ghetto* (1966) and A. Spear, *Black Chicago* (1967); see also G. Myrdal, *An American Dilemma* (1962), H. Cayton and St Clair Drake, *Black Metropolis* (1962), and N. I. Huggins, M. Kilson and A. Fox, *Key Issues in the Afro-American Experience, Vol. 2* (1971). The reaction is considered in D. Chalmers, *Flooded Americanism* (1965) and K. T. Jackson, *The Ku Klux Klan in the City, 1915–1925* (1967). Organized labour is considered in H. Pelling, *American Labour* (1960), J. G. Rayback, *History of American Labour* (1966), J. Wienstein, *The Decline of Socialism in America* (1967), P. Taft, *Organized Labour in American History* (1964), *The AF of L in the Time of Gompers* (1959) and *The AF of L from the Death of Gompers Till the Merger* (1959).

For the politics of the era up to the Great Crash see W. A. White, *A Puritan in Babylon* (1938), on Coolidge and on Hoover the essay in R. Hofstadter, *The American Political Tradition* (1967) and M. L. Fausold *The Presidency of Herbert C. Hoover* (1985). On the Crash itself see J. K. Galbraith, *The Great Crash, 1929* (1955), but on the economy in general see J. Potter, *The American Economy between the World Wars* (rev. edn, 1985), M. A. Berstein, *The Great Depression: delayed recovery and economic change in America, 1929–1939* (1987) and K. Brunner (ed.), *The Great Depression Revisited* (1981).

Roosevelt and the New Deal

A. J. Badger, *The New Deal* (1987), A. L. Hamby, *The New Deal: Analysis and interpretation* (2nd edn, 1981), C. Gordon, *New Deals* (1994), and M. Heale, *Franklin D. Roosevelt: the New Deal and War* (1999) are good introductions to the period, and see M. Simpson, *Franklin D. Roosevelt* (1989) and P. Renshaw, *Franklin D. Roosevelt* (2004) on the President. Important studies are H. Sitkoff (ed.), *The New Deal* (1985), K. S. Davis, *FDR: the New Deal years, 1933–1937: a history* (1986), J. Braemer (ed.), *The New Deal: Vols I and II* (1975), and L. Cohen, *Making a New Deal* (1990); see also W. E. Leuchtenburg, *Franklin Roosevelt and the New Deal* (1963) and A. M. Schlesinger, *The Age of Roosevelt* (1956–60). Other political figures of the New Deal era are considered in T. H. Williams, *Huey Long* (1969) and D. H. Bennet, *Demagogues in the Depression* (1969). Important sources are R. Moley, *After Seven Years* (1939), an auto-biography by one of Roosevelt's advisers, G. Rexford Tugwell, *The Battle for Democracy* (1935), from another aide, and F. Perking, *The Roosevelt I Knew* (1947). The atmosphere of the era is captured brilliantly in the oral history volume of Studs Terkel, *Hard Times* (1970) and J. Steinbeck's *The Grapes of Wrath* (1939). For the institutions and effects of the New Deal see R. Jackson, *The Struggle for Judicial Supremacy* (1938), H. Ickes, *Back to Work: the story of the PWA* (1935) and D. Lilienthal, *TVA: democracy on the march* (1944). Organized labour is considered in the essay on the United States by P. Renshaw in S. Salter and J. Stevenson (eds), *The Working Class and Politics in Europe and America, 1929–1945* (1990). See also M. Derber and E. Young (eds), *Labor and the New Deal* (1961), W. Galenson, *The CIO Challenge to the AFL* (1960), and W. R. Brock, *Welfare, Democracy and the New Deal* (1989). Amongst collections there is a useful essay on FDR in R. Hofstadter, *The American Political Tradition* (1967) and E. C. Rozwene, *The New Deal: revolution or evolution* (1959) and A. H. Cope and F. Krinsky (eds), *Franklin Roosevelt and the Supreme Court* (1964).

On foreign policy see H. Feis, *The Road to Pearl Harbour* (1953), the relevant chapter in L. C. Gardner, *Imperial America* (1973), R. Dallek, *Franklin D. Roosevelt and American Foreign Policy, 1932–1945* (1972), R. A. Divine, *The Reluctant Belligerent: American entry into World War II* (1968), S. Adler, *The Uncertain Giant, American foreign policy, 1921–41* (1965), D. Borg and S. Okameto, *Pearl Harbour as History: Japanese–American relations, 1931–1941* (1973) and A. Iriye, *The Origins of the Second World War in Asia and the Pacific* (1987).

The Second World War and the Cold War

For the general literature on the origins of the Cold War see pp. 521–2, but especially the recent studies which have resulted from the partial opening of former Soviet archives, such as J. L. Gaddis, *We Now Know: rethinking Cold War history* (1997), M. McCauley, *The Origins of the Cold War, 1941–1949* (3rd edn, 2003) and *Russia, America and the Cold War, 1949–1991* (3rd edn, 2004), and R. Crockatt, *The Fifty Years War: the United States and the Soviet Union in world politics, 1941–1991* (1996). Specifically on American responses see R. Dallek, *FDR and American Foreign Policy, 1932–45* (1979) and D. Yergin, *Shattered Peace: the origins of the Cold War and the national security state* (1990).

S. E. Ambrose, *Rise to Globalism: American foreign policy, 1938–1980* (rev. edn, 1980) takes the story through from the prewar phase, while H. Feis,

Churchill, Roosevelt and Stalin (1967) examines the Grand Alliance. D. B. Rees, *The Age of Containment: the Cold War, 1945–1965* (1967), H. Feis, *From Trust to Terror, the onset of the Cold War, 1945–1950* (1970), M. Sherwin, *A World Destroyed: the atomic bomb and the Grand Alliance* (1975), G. Alperoritz, *Atomic Diplomacy: Hiroshima and Potsdam* (2nd edn, 1985) and L. B. Davis, *The Cold War Begins: Soviet–American conflict in East Europe* (1974) deal with the early phases of the dispute between the Alliance partners. W. LaFeber, *America in the Cold War: twenty years of revolutions and response, 1947–1967* (1969) and *America, Russia and the Cold War, 1945–1971* (3rd edn, 1976), D. Horowitz, *From Yalta to Vietnam: American foreign policy in the Cold War* (rev. edn, 1969) and R. Douglas, *From War to Cold War, 1942–48* (1981) are all useful. J. Smith, *The Cold War, 1945–65* (1989) and M. McCauley (above) are guides to the increasingly complex debate, now highlighted in D. Carlton and H. M. Levine, *The Cold War Debated* (1988). The impact of anti-communism in America is discussed in D. Caute, *The Great Fear: the anti-communist purge under Truman and Eisenhower* (1978) and R. Divine, *Eisenhower and the Cold War* (1981). America's policy towards Europe is considered in J. Gimble, *The Origins of the Marshall Plan* (1976), M. J. Hogan, *The Marshall Plan: America, Britain and the reconstruction of Western Europe, 1947–1952* (1988), A. Grosser, *The Western Alliance: European–American relations since 1945* (1980), R. Morgan, *The United States and West Germany* (1974), R. Osgood, *NATO: the entangling alliance* (1962), and H. Jones, *A New Kind of War: America's global strategy and the Truman Doctrine in Greece* (1989). The later phase of the Cold War is considered in L. Freedman, *The Evolution of Nuclear Strategy* (1981), F. Halliday, *The Making of the New Cold War* (1983), and II. M. Levine and D. Carlton, *The Nuclear Arms Race Debated* (1986).

Particular areas are considered in E. J. Hammer, *The Struggle for Indo-China, 1940–1955* (1966), D. F. Fleming, *America's Role in Asia* (1969), S. Klebanoft, *Middle East Oil and US Foreign Policy: with special reference to the US energy crisis* (1974), G. Lenczowski, *Russia and the West in Iran, 1918–1948: a study in big power rivalry* (1968), W. R. Polk, *The United States and the Arab World* (rev. edn, 1969), J. Cotler and R. Fagan, *Latin America and the United States; the changing political realities* (1974), F. Parkinson, *Latin America, the Cold War and the World Powers, 1945–1973: a study in diplomatic history* (1974), R. Emerson, *Africa and United States Policy* (1967), J. Mayall, *Africa: the Cold War and After* (1971), E. O. Reischauer, *The United States and Japan* (3rd edn, 1965) and N. Safran, *The United States and Israel* (1963).

On particular crises see on Korea S. Hugh Lee, *The Korean War* (2001), S. Sadler, *The Korean War: an interpretative history* (1999), C. A. MacDonald, *Korea: the war before Vietnam* (1986), D. Rees, *Korea: the limited war* (1970) and P. Lowe, *The Origins of the Korean War* (1986). The American relationship with Cuba is considered in L. D. Langley, *Cuban Policy of the United States: a brief history* (1968), R. F. Smith, *The United States and Cuba: business and diplomacy, 1917–1960* (1961), H. M. Pachter, *Collision Course: the Cuban Missile Crisis and coexistence* (1963), E. Abel, *The Missiles of October: the story of the Cuban Missile Crisis* (1966), and G. Allison, *Essence of Decision: explaining the Cuban Missile Crisis* (1971). For a recent overview of the Cuban–US relationship, see M. H. Morley, *Imperial State and Revolution: the United States and Cuba, 1952–1986* (1987).

America and the Vietnam War

R. B. Smith, *An International History of the Vietnam War, vol. I, 1955–61, vol. II, 1961–5* (1983–5) is a major treatment of the war in global context. See also A. Short, *The Origins of the Vietnam War* (1989). A. Buhite, *The Dynamics of World Power: a documentary history of US foreign policy, 1945–73, vol. 4* (1973) has documents; see also D. Ellsberg, *The Pentagon Papers* (1972) and M. E. Gettleman (ed.), *Vietnam and America: a documentary history* (1985). The best detailed treatments are G. C. Herring, *America's Longest War* (1986), W. J. Duiker, *US Containment Policy and Conflict in Indo-China, 1961–75* (1994), G. J. De Groot, *A Noble Cause? America and the Vietnam War* (1999), R. J. Walton, *Cold War and Counterrevolution: the foreign policy of John F. Kennedy* (1972), L. Berman, *Lyndon Johnson's War: the road to stalemate in Vietnam* (1989), B. Van Den Mark, *Into the Quagmire: Lyndon Johnson and the escalation of the Vietnam War* (1991), S. Ambrose, *Nixon* (1987–91) and S. Karnow, *Vietnam: a history* (1984). The history of American involvement is also viewed in Ambrose, *Rise to Globalism* (see above), J. W. Spanier, *American Foreign Policy since World War II* (10th rev. edn, 1985) and M. Berkowitz *et al.*, *The US Foreign Policy Process and Context; from the Marshall Plan to Vietnam* (1985), and A. F. Krepinevich, *The Army and Vietnam* (1986). F. Fitzgerald, *Fire in the Lake, the Vietnamese and the Americans in Vietnam* (1972) discusses the American role in Vietnam. G. Kahin and J. W. Lewis, *The United States in Vietnam* (2nd edn, 1975) and J. L. Horowitz, *Ideology and Utopia in the United States, 1956–76* (1977) discuss the implications of the war for America, as does A. Schlesinger, *The Bitter Heritage; Vietnam and American democracy* (1966) and G. Kolko, *Anatomy of a War: Vietnam, the US and modern historical experience* (1986). The most prominent casualty of the war is discussed in H. Y. Schandler, *The Unmaking of a President: Lyndon Johnson and Vietnam* (1977), while the repercussions on the campuses are considered in James A. Michener, *Kent State: what happened and why* (1971), J. Axelrod *et al.*, *Search for Relevance: the campus in crisis* (1969), J. and S. Erlich (eds), *Student Power, Participation and Revolution* (1970), and J. Foster and D. Long (eds), *Protest! Student Activism in America* (1970).

American domestic politics since 1945

Some of the broad themes are considered in M. Marable, *Race, Reform and Rebellion: the second reconstruction in Black America, 1945–1982* (1984),

R. Gatlin, *American Women since 1945* (1987), W. Issel, *Social Change in the United States, 1945–1983* (1985), and K. Fox, *Metropolitan America: urban life and urban policy in the United States, 1940–80* (1985). On general politics see J. Patterson, *Grand Expectations: the United States, 1945–1974* (1996), D. W. Grantham, *Recent America: the United States since 1945* (1987), W. Leuchtenburg, *In the Shadow of FDR: from Harry Truman to Ronald Reagan* (1983), H. Parmet, *The Democrats: the years after FDR* (1976), D. Reinhard, *The Republican Right since 1945* (1983), E. Ladd and C. Hadley, *Transformations in the American Party System: political coalitions from the New Deal to the 1970's* (1975) and F. Greenstein, *Leadership in the Modern Presidency* (1988).

The Truman era has attracted considerable attention. For a short recent introduction see M. Byrnes, *The Truman Years, 1945–1953* (2000), then A. L. Hamby, *Man of the People: a life of Harry S. Truman* (2nd edn, 1998), R. Donovan, *Conflict and Crisis: the presidency of Harry S. Truman, 1945–1948* (1977) and *Tumultuous Years: the presidency of Harry S. Truman, 1949–1953* (1982), M. J. Lacey (ed.), *The Truman Presidency* (1989), B. Bernstein (ed.), *Politics and Policies of the Truman Administration* (1970), D. R. McCloy, *The Presidency of Harry S. Truman* (1986) and on McCarthyism D. Caute, *The Great Fear: the anti-communist purge under Truman and Eisenhower* (1978); R. M. Freeland, *The Truman Doctrine and the Origins of McCarthyism* (2nd edn, 1985) and R. M. Freid, *Men Against McCarthy* (1976). On the Senator himself see R. Rovere, *Senator Joe McCarthy* (1959). The Truman and Eisenhower years are considered together in W. O'Neill, *American High: the years of confidence, 1945–60* (1987).

On Eisenhower see S. Ambrose, *Eisenhower: Soldier and President* (1990), R. V. Damms, *The Eisenhower Presidency, 1953–1961* (2002), P. Lyons, *Eisenhower: portrait of the hero* (1974), C. C. Alexander, *Holding the Line: the Eisenhower era* (1975), G. Reichard, *The Reaffirmation of Republicanism: Eisenhower and the Eighty-Third Congress* (1975), R. A. Divine, *Eisenhower and the Cold War* (1981), E. Richardson, *The Presidency of Dwight Eisenhower* (1979) and R. F. Burk, *Dwight D. Eisenhower: hero and politician* (1987). On civil rights see T. Branch, *Parting the Waters* (1989) and D. Garrow, *Bearing the Cross: Martin Luther King and the Southern Christian Leadership Conference* (1986) which concentrate on the King years. Wider in focus are Marable (above), R. Cook, *Sweet Land of Liberty: the African American struggle for civil rights in the twentieth century* (1997), R. Weisbrot, *Freedom Bound: the history of America's civil rights movement* (1990), D. King, *Separate and Unequal* (1996), H. Sitkoff, *The Struggle for Black Equality in America* (1981) and A. Meier and E. Rudwick, *CORE: a study in the civil rights movement, 1942–1968* (1973). A. Badger and B. Ward (eds), *The Making of Martin Luther King and the Civil Rights Movement* (1995), A. Morris, *The Origins of the Civil Rights Movement: black communities organising for change* (1984) and L. Dittmer, *Local People: the struggle for civil rights in Mississippi* (1994) offer more detailed studies, while H. D. Graham, *The Civil Rights Era: origins and development of national policy, 1960–1972* (1990), S. Lawson, *In Pursuit of Power: southern blacks and electoral politics, 1965–1982* (1985), and A. Hacker, *Two Nations: black and white, separate, hostile, unequal* (1992) look at the outcomes.

The Kennedy era is discussed in H. Brogan, *Kennedy* (1996), J. N. Giglio, *The Presidency of John F. Kennedy* (1991), H. Parmet, *JFK: the presidency of John F. Kennedy* (1983), R. Reeves, *President Kennedy* (1993), B. Miroff, *Pragmatic Illusions: the presidential politics of John F. Kennedy* (1976), T. C. Sorensen, *The Kennedy Legacy* (1969) and J. Schlesinger, *Robert Kennedy and His Times* (1978). On specific aspects see A. D. Donald (ed.), *John F. Kennedy and the New Frontier* (1967), C. M. Brauer, *John F. Kennedy and the Second Reconstruction* (1977), D. Knapp and K. Polk, *Scouting the War on Poverty: social reform politics in the Kennedy administration* (1971) and R. J. Walton, *Cold War and Counter-revolution: the foreign policy of John F. Kennedy* (1972). Spanning the Kennedy–Johnson era are J. Heath, *Decade of Disillusionment: the Kennedy–Johnson Years* (1975) and J. Sundquist, *Politics and Policy: the Eisenhower, Kennedy and Johnson years* (1968). On the Johnson era see L. Berstein, *Promises Kept* (1991) and *Guns or Butter? The presidency of Lyndon Johnson* (1995), V. D. Bornet, *The Presidency of Lyndon B. Johnson* (1983), J. Patterson, *America's Struggle Against Poverty* (1995), R. A. Divine, *The Johnson Years* (1987), and P. K. Conkin, *Big Daddy from the Pedernales, Lyndon Baines Johnson* (1987). On the Vietnam War see above, especially Berman and Van Den Mark, also H. Y. Schandler, *The Unmaking of a President* (1977).

The Ford and Nixon administrations are discussed in A. J. Reichley, *Conservatives in an Age of Change: the Nixon and Ford administrations* (1981), S. Ambrose *Nixon* (1987–91), R. Morris, *Richard Milhouse Nixon: the rise of an American politician* (1990), H. Parmet, *Richard Nixon and his America* (1990), L. Friedman and W. F. Levantrosser (eds), *Richard M. Nixon: politician, president, administrator* (1991), and more generally G. Peele, *Revival and Reaction: the right in contemporary America* (1984).

Canada

K. McNaught, *The Penguin History of Canada* (rev. edn, 1988) is an introduction, but see also P. S. Li, *The Making of Post-War Canada* (1997). G. S. Graham, *A Concise History of Canada* (1968) and J. M. Bliss (ed.), *Canadian History in Documents, 1763–1966* are also useful. J. M. S. Careless and R. Craig-Brown (eds), *The Canadians, 1867–1967* (1967) is a collaborative work dealing with Canadian history decade by decade and with a series of thematic chapters to conclude. The development of the once separate province of Newfoundland is considered in R. A. Mackay (ed.), *Newfoundland: economic, diplomatic and strategic studies* (1946) and St J. Chadwick, *Newfoundland: island into Province* (1967). M. Wade, *The French Canadians, 1760–1967* (rev. edn, 1968) examines the background to the tension between French Canada and the rest of the country. See also M. Rioux and Y. Martin (eds), *French Canadian Society* (1964), R. Cook, *Canada and the French–Canadian Question* (1966), E. M. Corbett,

Quebec confronts Canada (1967), R. Jonas, *Community in Crisis: French Canadian nationalism in perspective* (1967), T. Sloan, *Quebec: the not-so-quiet revolution* (1965), and P. E. Trudeau, *Federalism and the French Canadians* (1968).

On the economy see R. E. Caves and R. M. Holton, *The Canadian Economy: prospect and retrospect* (1959), H. G. Johnson, *The Canadian Quandary: economic problems and policies* (1963), and H. G. J. Artken, *American Capital and Canadian Resources* (1961). The relationship of Canada with the United States and its place in world affairs is considered in J. S. Dickey (ed.), *The United States and Canada* (1964), J. K. Gordon (ed.), *Canada's Role as a Middle Power* (1966), W. L. Gordon, *A Choice for Canada: independence or colonial status* (1966), P. V. Lyon, *The Policy Question: a critical appraisal of Canada's role in world affairs* (1963) and L. T. Marchant, *Neighbours taken for granted: Canada and the United States* (1966).

The Cuban revolution

There is a good introduction in H. Thomas, *Cuba, or the Pursuit of Freedom* (1971). For the American involvement with Cuba see L. D. Langley, *Cuban Policy of the United States: a brief history* (1968) and R. F. Smith, *The United States and Cuba: business and diplomacy, 1917–60* (1960) and M. H. Morley, *Imperial State and Revolution: the United States and Cuba, 1952–1986* (1987). On the background to the revolution see R. F. Smith (ed.), *Background to Revolution: the development of modern Cuba* (2nd edn, 1966), R. E. Ruiz, *Cuba: the making of a revolution* (1968) and W. MacGaffey and C. R. Barnett, *Cuba: its people, its society, its culture* (1962). On the character of the Castro revolution see A. Suarez, *Cuba: Castroism and communism, 1959–66* (1967), K. S. Karol, *Guerrillas in Power: the course of the Cuban revolution* (1970), and H. L. Matthews, *Castro: a political biography* (1969). Also important are J. Dominguez, *Cuba: order and revolution* (1978), S. Farber, *Revolution and Reaction in Cuba, 1933–1960* (1976), A. MacEwan, *Revolution and Economic Development in Cuba* (1981), and C. Brundenius, *Economic Growth, Basic Needs and Income Distribution in Revolutionary Cuba* (1981). Earlier studies of the effects of the revolution are C. Mesa-Lago (ed.), *Revolutionary Change in Cuba: polity, economy, society* (1972), R. Fagen, *The Transformation of the Political Culture in Cuba* (1969), D. Seers (ed.), *Cuba: the economic and social revolution* (1964) and M. Zeitlin, *Cuban Working Class* (1967).

For the Cuban Missile Crisis see M. White, *The Cuban Missile Crisis* (1996), M. Beschloss, *Kennedy and Khrushchev: the crisis years* (1991), J. A. Nathan, *The Cuban Missile Crisis Revisited* (1992) and R. J. Walton, *Cold War and Counterrevolution: the Foreign Policy of John F. Kennedy* (1972). On Cuba's effects more widely, see B. Levine (ed.), *The New Cuban Presence in the Caribbean* (1983) and C. Blasier and C. Mesa-Lago (eds), *Cuba in the World* (1979).

The Caribbean, Central and Latin America

On these areas see the general works cited on pp. 543–4. On the Caribbean J. H. Parry and P. M. Sherlock, *A Short History of the West Indies* (3rd edn, 1960), J. R. Ward, *Poverty and Progress in the Caribbean, 1800–1960* (1985) and M. Cross and G. Henman (eds), *Labour in the Caribbean: from emancipation to independence* (1988) are all useful. For individual countries see, on Brazil, F. Bradford Burns, *A History of Brazil* (2nd edn, 1980) and on the early part of the century, G. Freyre, *Order and Progress: Brazil from Monarchy to Republic* (1970). Its economic development is considered in W. Baer, *The Brazilian Economy: growth and development* (2nd edn, 1983), W. Dean, *The Industrialisation of São Paulo, 1880–1945* (1969), and C. Furtado, *The Economic Growth of Brazil* (1963). The general political history is considered in R. M. Levine, *The Vargas Regime: the critical years, 1934–1938* (1970), J. D. Wirth, *The Politics of Brazilian Development, 1930–1954* (1970) and T. E. Skidmore, *Politics in Brazil, 1930–44: an experiment in democracy* (1967). The role of the military is considered in A. Stepan, *The Military in Politics: changing patterns in Brazil* (1971) and in P. Flynn, *Brazil: a political analysis* (1978). The role of labour is examined in K. P. Erickson, *The Brazilian Corporative State and Working-Class Politics* (1977) and J. Humphrey, *Capitalist Control and Worker's Struggle in the Brazilian Auto Industry* (1982), while racial issues are discussed in C. N. Degler, *Neither Black Nor White: slavery and race relations in Brazil and the United States* (1971). See also J. H. Rodrigues, *Brazil and Africa* (1965), T. E. Skidmore, *Black into White: race and nationality in Brazilian thought* (1974) and D. T. Heberly, *Three Sad Races: racial identity and national consciousness in Brazilian literature* (1983). Some general interpretations are A. Stepan (ed.). *Authoritarian Brazil: origins, policies and future* (1973), T. C. Bruneau and P. Fancher (eds), *Authoritarian Capitalism: Brazil's contemporary economic and political development* (1981), S. A. Hewlett, *The Cruel Dilemmas of Development: twentieth century Brazil* (1980) and P. Evans, *Dependent Development: the alliance of multinational, state and local capital in Brazil* (1979). On foreign policy see S. E. Hitton, *Brazil and the Great Powers, 1930–1939: the politics of trade rivalry* (1975) and F. McCann, *The Brazilian American Alliance, 1937–1945* (1973).

For Argentina see in general, Y. F. Rennie, *The Argentine Republic* (1945), J. R. Scobie, *Argentina, a City and a Nation* (2nd edn, 1971), D. Rock, *Argentina, 1516–1982* (1986) and *Argentina in the Twentieth Century* (1975), G. Pendle, *Argentina* (3rd edn, 1963) and H. S. Ferns, *Argentina* (1969). The early history of the country in this period is dealt with in D. Rock, *Politics in Argentina, 1890–1930: the rise and fall of radicalism* (1975), P. H. Smith, *Politics and Beef in Argentina: patterns of conflict and change* (1969), while the role of the military is considered in R. A. Potash, *The Army and Politics in Argentina, 1928–1945* (1969), continued in *The Army and Politics in Argentina, 1945–1962* (1980); see also P. H. Smith, *Argentina and the Failure of Democracy, 1904–55* (1974). The economic background is examined in C. F. Díaz Alejandro, *Essays on the*

Economic History of the Argentina Republic (1970), while the experience of Argentina's economy in the depression is considered in M. Falcoff and R. H. Dolkart, *Prologue to Peron: Argentina in depression and war, 1930–1943* (1975). The link with the rise of Peronism is also considered in J. R. Barager (ed.), *Why Peron Came to Power: the background to Peronism in Argentina* (1968). The Peronist phenomenon is examined in F. C. Turner and J. E. Miguens, *Juan Peron and the Reshaping of Argentina* (1983) and there is a good biography by J. A. Page, *Peron: a biography* (1983), while on Eva see N. Fraser and M. Navarro, *Eva Peron* (1980) and J. M Taylor, *Evita Peron: the myths of a woman* (1979). The labour policies pursued by Peron are the subject of S. L. Bailey, *Labour, Nationalism and Politics in Argentina* (1967). For the postwar history see R. A. Potash, *The Army and Politics, 1945–1962* (above) and P. H. Smith, *Argentina and the Failure of Democracy* (above); see also G. W. Wynia, *Argentina in the Postwar era: politics and economic policy-making in a divided society* (1978) and C. H. Waisman, *Reversal of Development in Argentina: postwar counterrevolutionary policies and their structural consequences* (1987).

For a general history of Chile see B. Loveman, *Chile: the legacy of hispanic capitalism* (1979). Also useful are A. J. Bauer, *Chilean Rural Society: from the Spanish Conquest to 1930* (1975), M. J. Mamalakis, *The Growth and Structure of the Chilean Economy: from independence to Allende* (1976), and B. Loveman, *Struggle in the Countryside: politics and rural labour in Chile, 1919–1973* (1976). The armed forces are considered for the early period in F. M. Nunn, *Chilean Politics, 1920–1931: the honourable mission of the armed forces* (1970) and later in *The Military in Chilean History: essays on civil-military relations, 1810–1973* (1976). The labour movement is examined in A. Angell, *Politics and the Labour Movement in Chile* (1972) and see P. W. Drake, *Socialism and Populism in Chile, 1932–52* (1978). The controversial events leading to the overthrow of Allende are the subject of P. Sigmund, *The Overthrow of Allende and the Politics of Chile, 1964–1976* (1977), B. Stallings, *Class Conflict and Economic Development in Chile, 1958–1973* (1978), A. Valenzuela, *The Breakdown of Democratic Regimes: Chile* (1978) and F. C. Gill, R. Lagos and H. A. Lansberger (eds), *Chile at the Turning Point: lessons of the socialist years, 1970–1973* (1979). Big business is discussed in T. H. Moran, *Multinational Corporations and the Politics of Dependence: copper in Chile* (1974) and on the Church see B. A. Smith, *The Church and Politics in Chile: Challenges to modern Catholicism* (1982).

There is a single volume history of Uruguay in R. H. FitzGibbon, *Uruguay: Portrait of a Democracy* (1986) and on Paraguay see G. Pendle, *Paraguay: a riverside nation* (1967) and P. H. Lewis, *Paraguay under Stroessner* (1980).

The Andean states are discussed in J. M. Malloy, *Bolivia, the Uncompleted Revolution* (1970) and H. S. Klein, *Parties and Political Change in Bolivia, 1880–1952* (1969) while for Peru see F. Pike, *The Modern History of Peru* (1967), V. Alba, *Peru* (1977) and R. Thorp and G. Bertram, *Peru, 1890–1977: growth and policy in an open economy* (1978); the agrarian unrest in Peru is considered in F. E. Mallon, *The Defense of Community in Peru's Central Highlands: peasant struggle and capitalist transition, 1860–1940* (1983), P. F. Klaren, *Modernization, Dislocation and Aprismo: origins of the Peruvian Aprista Party, 1870–1932* (1973) and S. Stein, *Populism in Peru: the emergence of the masses and politics of social control* (1980). The role of military rule is examined in G. D. E. Philip, *The Rise and Fall of the Peruvian Military Radicals, 1968–1976* (1978), F. Lowenthal, *The Peruvian Experiment: continuity and change under military rule* (1975), D. Booth and B. Sorj (eds), *Military Reformism and Social Classes: the Peruvian experience, 1968–80* (1983), F. Bourricand, *Power and Society in Contemporary Peru* (1970), and F. Lowenthal and C. McClintock (eds), *The Peruvian Experiment Reconsidered* (1983); see also E. V. K. Fitzgerald, *The State of Economic Development: Peru since 1968* (1976). The continuing social upheaval on the land and in the slums is examined in H. Handelman, *Struggle in the Andes: peasant mobilization in Peru* (1975), C. McClintock, *Peasant Cooperatives and Political Change in Peru* (1981), and D. Collier, *Squatters and Oligarchs: authoritarian rule and policy change in Peru* (1976); see also H. Blanco, *Land or Death: the peasant struggle in Peru* (1972). For Venezuela see E. Lieuwen, *Venezuela* (1965) and J. Ewell, *Venezuela: a century of change* (1984) and, for Surinam, H. E. Chin and H. Buddingh, *Surinam: politics, economics and society* (1987).

The history of the Amazon region is considered in J. Hemming, *Amazon Frontier: the defeat of the Brazilian Indians* (1988) and *Red Gold: the Conquest of the Brazilian Indians* (1988).

For Central America see R. Lee Woodward, *Central America: a nation divided* (1976), D. E. Schulz and D. H. Graham, *Revolution and Counter Revolution in Central America and the Caribbean* (1984), and T. L. Karnes, *The Failure of Union: Central America, 1824–1960* (1961). On individual countries see R. N. Adams, *Crucifixion by Power: essays on the Guatemalan national social structure, 1944–1966* (1970), W. J. Griffith, *Empires in the Wilderness: foreign colonization and development in Guatemala, 1834–1944* (1965), S. Kinzer, *Bitter Fruit: the untold story of the American coup in Guatemala* (1981), and R. H. Immerman, *The CIA in Guatemala: the foreign policy of intervention* (1982). Nicaragua is discussed in R. Millett, *Guardians of the Dynasty* (1977), T. W. Walker, *Nicaragua: the land of Sandino* (1981), and for the post-1979 period, H. Weber, *Nicaragua: the Sandinista Revolution* (trans. edn, 1981). On El Salvador see T. P. Anderson, *Matanza: El Salvador's communist revolt of 1932* (1971), E. Layoyra, *El Salvador in Transition* (1982), S. Webre, *José Napoleon Duarte and the Christian Democrat Party in Salvadorian Politics: 1960–1974* (1975); and on the civil war M. E. Gettleman *et al.*, *El Salvador: Central America in the New Cold War* (1981).

MAPS

NORWAY

SWEDEN

FINLAND

Helsinki

Oslo

Leningrad

Stockholm

Baltic Sea

ESTONIA

North Sea

LATVIA

Riga

USSR

DENMARK

Memel

LITHUANIA

Copenhagen

Danzig Free City

Kiel

Vilna

Minsk

EAST
PRUSSIA

HOLLAND

GERMANY

Berlin

Warsaw

POLAND

BELGIUM

Weimar

SAXONY

Aachen
Bonn

Breslau

Coblenz

Prague

Cracow

Lvov
(Lemberg)

LUX.

Mainz

SAAR

CZECHOSLOVAKIA

ALSACE-
LORRAINE

BAVARIA

Munich

Vienna

Budapest

BESSARABIA

AUSTRIA

TRANSYLVANIA

SWITZERLAND

Graz

HUNGARY

Cluj

ROMANIA

Trent

Trieste

SLOVENIA

YUGOSLAVIA

Belgrade

Bucharest

CROATIA

SERBIA

Sarejevo

ITALY

BOSNIA

Adriatic Sea

MONTENEGRO

BULGARIA

Sofia

MACEDONIA

TURKEY

ALBANIA

GREECE

Lost by Germany 1919

Saar: League of Nations control 1919–35

Demilitarised Rhineland 1919–36

Austria-Hungary until 1918

Plebiscite areas

Former territory of Imperial Russia

Map 1 Central European frontiers, 1919–37

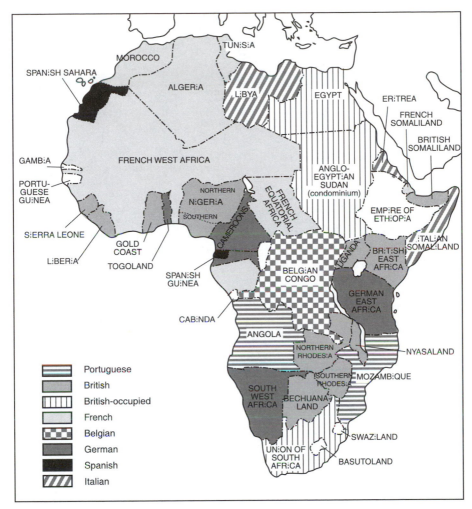

Legend:

- Portuguese
- British
- British-occupied
- French
- Belgian
- German
- Spanish
- Italian

Map labels:

MOROCCO
SPANISH SAHARA
ALGERIA
TUNISIA
LIBYA
EGYPT
ERITREA
FRENCH SOMALILAND
BRITISH SOMALILAND
GAMBIA
FRENCH WEST AFRICA
ANGLO-EGYPTIAN SUDAN (condominium)
PORTUGUESE GUINEA
NORTHERN
NIGERIA
SOUTHERN
FRENCH EQUATORIAL AFRICA
EMPIRE OF ETHIOPIA
SIERRA LEONE
GOLD COAST
LIBERIA
TOGOLAND
CAMEROONS
SPANISH GUINEA
ITALIAN SOMALILAND
UGANDA
BRITISH EAST AFRICA
BELGIAN CONGO
GERMAN EAST AFRICA
CABINDA
ANGOLA
NORTHERN RHODESIA
NYASALAND
SOUTHERN RHODESIA
MOZAMBIQUE
SOUTH WEST AFRICA
BECHUANALAND
SWAZILAND
UNION OF SOUTH AFRICA
BASUTOLAND

Map 2 Africa in 1914

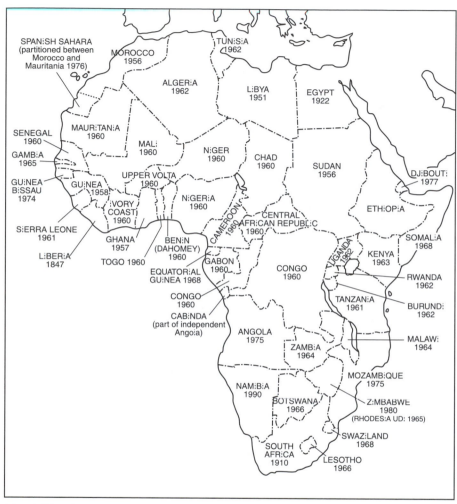

Map 3 The chronology of African independence

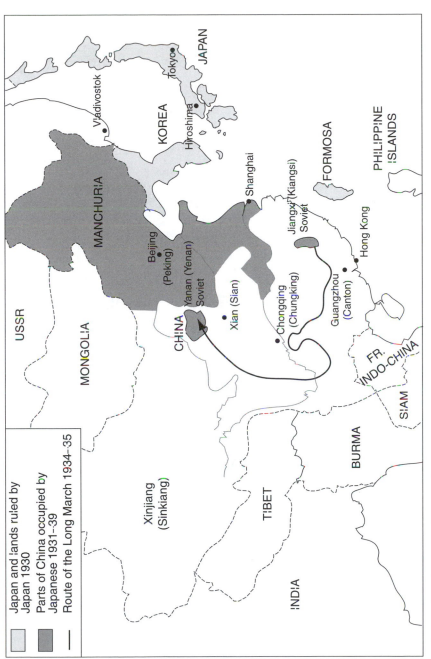

Map 4 China and the Chinese revolution

Legend:

- Japan and lands ruled by Japan 1930
- Parts of China occupied by Japanese 1931–39
- Route of the Long March 1934–35

USSR

MONGOLIA

Xinjiang (Sinkiang)

TIBET

INDIA

MANCHURIA

Vladivostok

KOREA

Hiroshima

Tokyo

JAPAN

Beijing (Peking)

Yanan (Yenan) Soviet

CHINA

Xian (Sian)

Shanghai

Chongqing (Chungking)

Jiangxi (Kiangsi) Soviet

FORMOSA

PHILIPPINE ISLANDS

Guangzhou (Canton)

Hong Kong

FR. INDO-CHINA

SIAM

BURMA

Map 5 Japanese expansion, 1931–45

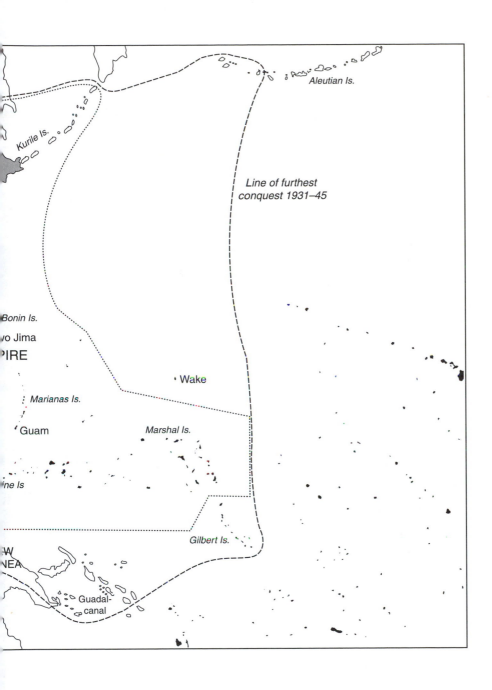

Aleutian Is.

Kurile Is.

Line of furthest
conquest 1931–45

Bonin Is.

vo Jima

PIRE

• Wake

Marianas Is.

Guam

Marshal Is.

ne Is

Gilbert Is.

W
NEA

Guadal-
canal

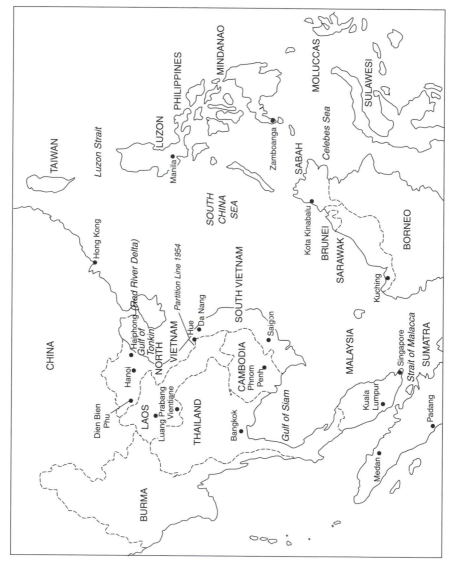

Map 6 South-east Asia in the 1960s

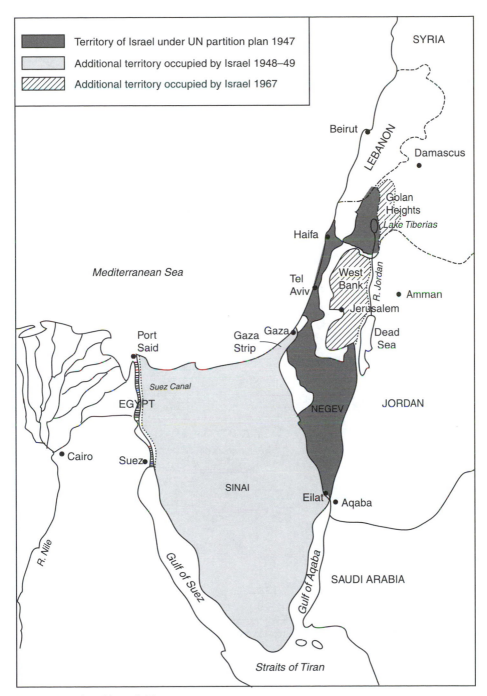

Legend:
- Territory of Israel under UN partition plan 1947
- Additional territory occupied by Israel 1948–49
- Additional territory occupied by Israel 1967

SYRIA

Beirut

Damascus

LEBANON

Golan
Heights

Lake Tiberias

Haifa

Mediterranean Sea

Tel
Aviv

West
Bank

R. Jordan

Amman

Jerusalem

Dead
Sea

Port
Said

Gaza
Strip

Gaza

JORDAN

Suez Canal

EGYPT

NEGEV

Cairo

Suez

SINAI

Eilat

Aqaba

R. Nile

Gulf of Suez

Gulf of Aqaba

SAUDI ARABIA

Straits of Tiran

Map 7 Israel and its neighbours

Map 8 The Caribbean and Central America

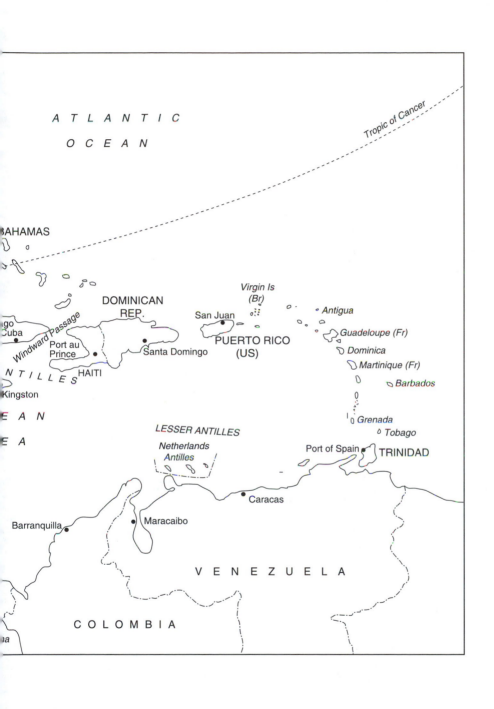

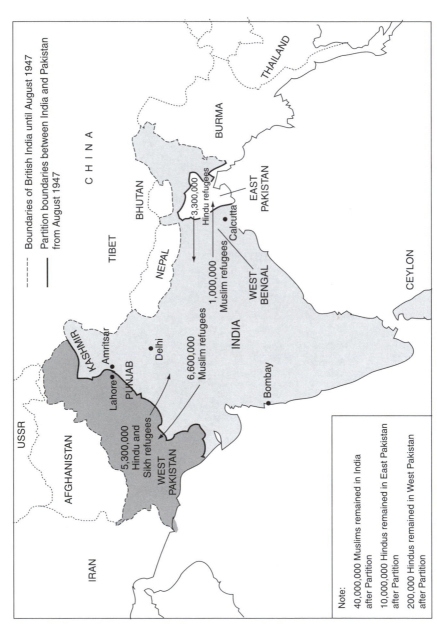

Map 9 India and Pakistan after Partition, 1947

Boundaries of British India until August 1947

Partition boundaries between India and Pakistan from August 1947

C H I N A

USSR

IRAN

AFGHANISTAN

KASHMIR

Lahore

Amritsar

PUNJAB

Delhi

WEST PAKISTAN

5,300,000 Hindu and Sikh refugees

6,600,000 Muslim refugees

Bombay

INDIA

NEPAL

BHUTAN

TIBET

1,000,000 Muslim refugees

3,300,000 Hindu refugees

Calcutta

WEST BENGAL

EAST PAKISTAN

BURMA

THAILAND

CEYLON

Note:

40,000,000 Muslims remained in India after Partition

10,000,000 Hindus remained in East Pakistan after Partition

200,000 Hindus remained in West Pakistan after Partition

Map 10 The Soviet Union in Eastern Europe

INDEX